For Pat, an entr
from A[signature]
30/ix/01

Michael Young

Also by Asa Briggs

A HISTORY OF BROADCASTING IN THE UNITED KINGDOM (*five volumes*)
A SOCIAL HISTORY OF ENGLAND
A STUDY OF THE WORK OF SEEBOHM ROWNTREE
TOYNBEE HALL (*with Anne Macartney*)
CHARTIST STUDIES (*editor*)
ESSAYS IN LABOUR HISTORY (*two volumes, editor with John Saville*)
THE AGE OF IMPROVEMENT
THE NINETEENTH CENTURY (*editor*)
VICTORIAN CITIES
VICTORIAN PEOPLE
VICTORIAN THINGS
FINS DE SIÈCLE (*editor with Daniel Snowman*)
GO TO IT: Working for Victory on the Home Front, 1939–45

Michael Young
Social Entrepreneur

Asa Briggs

© Asa Briggs 2001

All rights reserved. No reproduction, copy or transmission of this publication may be made without written permission.

No paragraph of this publication may be reproduced, copied or transmitted save with written permission or in accordance with the provisions of the Copyright, Designs and Patents Act 1988, or under the terms of any licence permitting limited copying issued by the Copyright Licensing Agency, 90 Tottenham Court Road, London W1P 0LP.

Any person who does any unauthorised act in relation to this publication may be liable to criminal prosecution and civil claims for damages.

The author has asserted his right to be identified as the author of this work in accordance with the Copyright, Designs and Patents Act 1988.

First published 2001 by
PALGRAVE
Houndmills, Basingstoke, Hampshire RG21 6XS and
175 Fifth Avenue, New York, N. Y. 10010
Companies and representatives throughout the world

PALGRAVE is the new global academic imprint of
St. Martin's Press LLC Scholarly and Reference Division and
Palgrave Publishers Ltd (formerly Macmillan Press Ltd).

ISBN 0–333–75023–3

This book is printed on paper suitable for recycling and made from fully managed and sustained forest sources.

A catalogue record for this book is available from the British Library.

Library of Congress Cataloging-in-Publication Data
Briggs, Asa, 1921–
    Michael Young : social entrepreneur / Asa Briggs.
      p. cm.
    Includes bibliographical references and index.
    ISBN 0–333–75023–3 (cloth)
     1. Young, Michael Dunlop, 1915– 2. Sociologists–
–Great Britain—Biography. 3. Social change.
HM479.Y68 B75 2000
301'.092—dc21
[B]
                                                                                         00–053097

10 9 8 7 6 5 4 3 2 1
10 09 08 07 06 05 04 03 02 01

Printed and bound in Great Britain by
Antony Rowe Ltd, Chippenham, Wiltshire

Contents

List of Plates	vii
Acknowledgements	viii
Abbreviations	ix
Foreword: Who? Which? Where? Why?	x
1. In Lieu of an Autobiography	1
2. Michael When Young	25
3. Party Politics	66
4. Two Places; One Purpose	110
5. Merit and/or Solidarity	155
6. Education for Change	183
7. Necessary Research	220
8. A World Agenda	258
9. Mutual Aid	280
10. Unfinished Business	310
Afterword: *The Last Victorian?*	329
Notes	332
Main Writings of Michael Young	393
The Young Family Tree	400
Index	401

List of Plates

1. Entrance to the courtyard, Dartington Hall, 1925. The little girl is Christine Gilpin. (© Dartington Hall Trust)
2. Michael's oil painting of High Cross House on the Dartington Hall Estate, 1931. (© Dartington Hall Trust)
3. Michael's wartime work pass, 1941.
4. The Institute of Community Studies, Victorian Park Square, Bethnal Green
5. A street of Bethnal Green, interviews, 1950s (from an Oxford House booklet).
6. Sophie, Sasha and Michael. (© Catherine Shakespeare Lane)
7. Michael Young and his daughter Gaia, October 1998.
8. Michael with students, study week, School for Social Entrepreneurs, June 1999 (© Charles Armstrong: Circus Foundation)
9. Michael Young, June 2000 (© Charles Armstrong: Circus Foundation)

Acknowledgements

I am grateful to Howard Newby for suggesting this book when he was Chairman of the Economic and Social Research Council and for the assistance of the Council in making it possible and providing me with access to relevant archives. I owe a further particular debt to Wyn Tucker and Sue Chisholm at the Institute of Community Studies, to Geoff Dench, Tony Flower, James Cornford and to all Michael's colleagues there. I have interviewed or corresponded with Michael's relatives, including his relatives in Australia. Among the people who have provided me with sometimes unique information are Peter Willmott, Peter Laslett, Peter Townsend, Paul Barker, Naomi McIntosh and Lord McIntosh, Lord Runciman, Susan Crosland, Hilary Perraton, and Paul Cumo of the Gulbenkian Foundation. David Blumer provided family information. The Dartington Trustees have been helpful at many points and have provided me with the first and second of my illustrations. The portrait of Michael, Sasha and Sophie (Plate 6) is the copyright of Catherine Shakespeare Lane, its photographer. Plates 8 and 9 are the copyright of Charles Armstrong: Circus Foundation.

Kate Gavron kindly read through the text of this book in its final stage and made helpful comments. As in the preparation of all my books I have been given indispensable support by Pat Spencer and Susan Hard. I am solely responsible, however, for the approach followed and for the content.

ASA BRIGGS

Abbreviations

ANC	African National Congress
BJS	*British Journal of Sociology*
CAC	Central Advisory Council for Education
CR	*Contemporary Record*
DES	Department of Education and Science
EcHR	*Economic History Review*
EPA	Educational Priority Area
ESRC	Economic and Social Research Council
GP	Gabriel Productions
ICS	Institute of Community Studies
LPRD	Labour Party Research Department
LSE	London School of Economics
NIESR	National Institute of Economic and Social Research
NLSC	National Life Story Collection
NS	*New Society*
PEP	Political and Economic Planning
PPE	Philosophy, Politics, Economics Degree
PSI	Political and Social Institute
SACHED	South African Committee of Higher Education
SDP	Social Democratic Party
SSRC	Social Sciences Research Council
TUC	Trade Union Congress
UNESCO	United Nations Educational Social and Cultural Organisation
WEA	Workers Educational Association

Foreword: Who? Which? Where? Why?

This is a book that covers a large part of the twentieth century and moves into the new millennium. It examines and assesses some of the most important features, trends and attitudes of the period – the increase in material wealth and its unequal distribution; the lengthening of the human age span; the changing shape of the family and of family relationships; great emphasis on education at all levels, what it achieves, fails to achieve and should achieve.

The book explores the period through the life and work of one man, Michael Young, Lord Young of Dartington, a fascinating life not just because of its span and its variety, but because of Michael's extraordinary capacity both to generate ideas and to create organisations. Many of his ideas are far better known than he is: some of the organisations have become institutions. They include the Consumers' Association – hence the word *Which?*, the title of its magazine, in the title of this Foreword; the National Extension College and the International Extension College – hence the word *Where?*, the periodical of the Advisory Centre for Education, ACE, which announced their creation; the Open University, in the conception of which Michael played a unique role; and the University of the Third Age which in the new millennium looked back and honoured him and its other founders.

The words 'Which?' and 'Where?' have broader connotations than this. Among Michael's other 'firsts' he was the first Chairman and Executive Director from 1965 to 1968 of the Social Sciences Research Council. What it set out to do and did under his direction is a revealing story in itself, and there are many such stories in this book, big and small, which concern health and housing as well as education, transport. Scarcely any facet of social policy has not been examined or influenced by him. He has always treated research as essential to action as well as understanding. When an interviewer asked him in 1994 what were the common themes running through his work, thought and action he replied: 'Everything derives from research, and to be any good as a researcher, you have to be prepared to change your mind. The most valuable people in any enterprise are its severest critics. So it is all very empirical.'

The word 'all' in the last sentence, however, is misleading. Research is not all empirical, and since Michael is highly intuitive, the ideas that he generates are related both to research and to action, in complex, not simple, ways. They have infuriated as well as inspired. There has been no one like him, although he has had many fellow workers and several co-authors, some, like Peter Willmott, for more than one book. For me the word that stands out in his 1994 interview is 'enterprise'. How ideas are implemented involves more than committed effort. There are risks to take, as many or even more in social enterprise than in profit-making business.

When Noel Annan included Michael in his book *Our Age: Portrait of a Generation* (1990) – he had got to know him in Cambridge – he took full account of the range of Michael's initiatives, describing him memorably, Chinese fashion, as 'sowing' not seed but 'dragon's teeth'.

> Whatever field he tilled, he sowed dragon's teeth, and armed men seemed to spring from the soil to form an organisation and correct the abuses or stimulate the virtues he had discovered.
>
> Were consumers conned by manufacturers? Let them form an association to test the products and apprise their worth. ... Did studies of kinship and family reveal that few in East London would ever enter higher education? Let an Open University, teaching through correspondence and television, be set up.

In *Our Age* Annan was identifying individuals who not only represented their age but who helped to fashion it. Michael's contribution is too little known, even among historians or politicians. That is a special reason for writing this book. It draws attention, too, to those individuals who thought and felt in diametrically opposite ways. One of them was Margaret Thatcher. Their polarity began with their attitudes towards the word 'society' and widened to cover almost all aspects of 'policy'.

In his evaluation, Annan went on to note that the fields of social enterprise within which Michael moved included education, health, mutual aid, the arts, and social development in the Third World. He was right to end his impressive list of Michael's responsibilities with the Third World. His interest in it and commitment to it are intense, and recently he has spent much of his year in post-apartheid South Africa, devoting his attention to education, the essential ingredient in its future.

When, why and, not least, how Michael has achieved his various purposes – and how they were identified by him – are questions which have to be answered, and I begin and end my book with the most recent of the many organisations which Michael has created, a School for Social Entrepreneurs. When he welcomed the first people to join it on 5 January 1998, he told them that the Institute of Community Studies in Bethnal Green, the place of their meeting, had provided 'a revolving door for many new enterprises' since its foundation by him 45 years earlier. Many of them were established. Some had moved or disappeared.

In this address it was the word 'new' that Michael was stressing when he linked it with enterprise. It is a word that had been debased in the last years of two centuries, nineteenth- and twentieth-century *fins de siècle*. Another of the key words in his vocabulary had always been the word 'innovation'. It figured in the title of a volume of his miscellaneous writings, published in the United States in 1983, *Social Scientist as Innovator*. The foreword to it was written by an American interpreter of his and our age, very different from Annan – the American sociologist Daniel Bell, working in the other Cambridge across the Atlantic. Drawn to Michael through his lectures, articles, pamphlets and books, Bell described him as 'a social designer, an architect, in the metaphorical sense of the term, [a man] whose passions lie in the social use of social knowledge, a devotion to empirical research and the application of that research to social practice'. Bell concluded by stressing Michael's 'sophisticated awareness of the political process through which social policy and new social institutions have been guided'. The last point was crucial.

Michael himself frankly recognises that there has often been more than a touch of opportunism as he has turned from ideas to action; and for this reason it is not enough in considering the timing of his actions to examine the content of his lectures, articles, books and (even) pamphlets. It is essential to consider context too. Not all the many people who have interviewed him have appreciated this. Others have even without an interview. Thus, in 1991 Frank Field, writing anonymously in the *Sunday Times*, included Michael in a list of the 1,000 people who had influenced the century most, noting how he bridged the gap between the non-party PEP's approaches to the welfare state and those of the Labour Party. Six years later in a survey of the ideas that had shaped post-war Britain by David Marquand and Antony Seldon Michael was placed in a chapter that was called 'Ideas are not enough', a title of which he himself would approve: it puts both ideas and 'intellectuals' in their place. Michael has always been as much of a doer as a thinker.

Among the other names given to Michael besides 'innovator' and 'architect' are 'mover and shaker' and 'campaigner', and in trying to answer 'Why?' questions there is good reason for choosing either of them and for comparing him with other movers and shakers and other campaigners. Yet to focus entirely on these aspects of his life may lead to too hasty a judgement on the quality of his ideas, not just their plenitude but their range and the manner in which they were advanced. They have to be weighed. Returning to Annan's metaphor, some of the ideas were scattered everywhere, 'broadcast' in its original sense: some failed to grow when the dragon's teeth were carefully sown. Many of them, settled or planted, took root. Some were big idea; some were small. Some grew; some never reached above the ground.

Michael himself has had as much to say about ideas as about organisation. One of his most memorable comments about them comes from one of his lesser known and now most dated books, *Revolution from Within*, which he wrote with Marianne Rigge in 1983. 'Ideas can never be buried like people. Dust to dust will not return. But ideas, however dead they seem and however deeply buried, are liable to work their way out when their time comes again and gain a kind of immortality above ground as though they had never been put away below it.' For this reason Michael himself often used the adjective 'inert' rather than 'dead' in talking of them. Another word, familiar to gardeners, was 'sleeping'.

Within this context, time, which deeply interests Michael, involves more than timing. It is quite inadequate to think of Michael's ideas in terms of chronological sequences. They move around in circular fashion, so that the various books which have been written by him at very different times, as they have been, like the various organisations which have been created in very different circumstances and with different purposes in mind, echo and re-echo the same ideas and images. The ideas have influenced people very different from himself, and the organisations have sometimes taken on a shape very different from that which he envisaged. Yet they form part of a twentieth-century pattern that recurs even when Michael is not involved. When the first Chairman of the renamed Economic and Social Research Council, Sir Douglas Hague, chosen by Thatcher and from a very different background from Michael's, discussed the future strategy of the Council in 1983, his theme might have been chosen by Michael, with whom he had little in common and who was chosen by Thatcher from the world of the Business Schools – 'Change, its context, its management, and adaptation to it'. 'The change theme,' Hague wrote, 'is concerned with understanding what is wrong, what needs to be done and in what order, and then facilitating adaptation in a country where traditions and instincts are settled to the point of inertia.'

My own book does not follow a strict chronological sequence. Nor has it been written in strict chronological order: I have been more concerned with themes than with episodes. Indeed, the title of my last chapter, 'Unfinished Business', is the only chapter title about which I never had any doubt. Michael goes on thinking, researching and acting as energetically as ever. The next century is always in view. He would have agreed with Dean Inge, a man with his roots in the last century and very different from himself, renowned for his gloom, not, as Michael is, for his mischief, that 'we are always sowing our future; we are always reaping our past'.

My own book has taken several years to complete, and once in the course of writing it Michael, who likes faster tracks than I do, told me in a letter written in 1994 that I must feel 'like a portrait painter whose subject won't stand still'. He is certainly no more prepared to stand still now than he has ever been. 'The best is yet to come', he told his 1994 interviewer – with a characteristic laugh, accompanied by an equally characteristic shrug of the shoulders – and there certainly was far more to come, including a book of essays about him, *Young at Eighty*, which was presented to him on his eightieth birthday at an Institute of Community Studies party in Bethnal Green. At another ICS party there in 2000 he looked attentive and alert. He retains as always a keen physical presence.

The book covered most of the different aspects of his work as seen by the contributors, his friends, with most of whom I have talked either before 1994 or subsequently. His eightieth birthday was a convenient vantage point in time for them as for him, just as a millennium is for me. It was not a conventional *Festschrift* party, however, nor indeed a conventional eightieth birthday party, for to the surprise of most people present, including me, he chose the occasion to announce his third marriage to Dorit Uhlemann. The arrival of a new child, his sixth, a daughter Gaia (a name with echoes), followed soon afterwards. 'A Bit of a Do' was the title of a gossipy article by Rebecca Hardy in the *Daily Mail* describing the event in November 1995. Michael was now in a new state of being, a very different way of describing it, but none of his threads with the past were broken. He himself was surprised at his party when his friend Robert (now Lord) Gavron announced that the School for Social Entrepreneurs was a *fait accompli*. It was not then.

As must already be clear, in writing this book, I have always had to be prepared for surprises. It is no more a conventional biography than *Young at Eighty* was a conventional *Festschrift*. Michael wanted me to write it not as a close friend but as a social historian, and I have considered it my chief task to evaluate the contribution, distinctive and significant, that he has made – and is still making – to thought and life in the century to which he (and I) unmistakably belongs. I have tried to leave the way open for other evaluations, providing the necessary evidence. I am sure that they will be forthcoming – in reviews as well as in books.

Michael has had to cope with change in his own life, and he has chosen to make it central in his thought. It is never enough for him, however, to take change as a *fait accompli*. Making a difference to society is what counts. 'Entrepreneurs' in any walk of life, he wrote in 1998 for the brochure of the second year of the School for Social Entrepreneurs, are people who 'organise change'.

> They know a good idea when they see one, whether it's their own or someone else's, and they know now to make it work. They are the midwives of invention. Just as the original theatrical entrepreneurs knew how to put on a show [and we are back to one of his own metaphors], so today's social entrepreneurs know how to get a show on the road. … Social entrepreneurs do exactly the same thing. They spot gaps in our social fabric. … Their aim is to enrich society, to bridge the gap between the powerful and the powerless, and to create a commonwealth of opportunity.

Michael was not looking for clones. Nor does he want to create them. He knows that the twenty-first century will have a different shape from the twentieth. 'There will be a different generation to contend with by then.' These words appeared not in 1998 but in a letter which he wrote to the *Guardian* in October 1971, a newspaper that has played an important part in his life, after he had heard that the Labour Party was planning to abandon innovatory research projects in that section of its central office which he himself had headed from 1945 to 1951. Research, he argued, was more necessary than ever.

He reiterated this message in his address to the School of Social Entrepreneurs in January 1998 when he turned to the future of 'the voluntary sector' to which they would belong and expressed the hope that what they thought and did would help the sector to raise its sights. The School should be 'a kind of think tank' with a research unit attached that might straddle the School and the Institute. And he ended with a disarming sentence that acquires its full significance only in the light of the pages that follow. 'In encouraging research the School should at least in one respect be like an orthodox university.'

Here begins the study of a thoroughly unorthodox person. There can be a wryness about him along with a stubbornness, and it can be disconcerting. He hopes that he is 'a romantic'. Yet he also describes himself as lacking in confidence. A certain 'elusiveness' can keep him at a distance even from those whom he knows best. There is shyness too, rare in a mover and shaker. There is perseverance, one of his strongest qualities, but there is also obstinacy. Although he professes distaste for publicity, he is shrewd in employing it. While he is sometimes reluctant to stand back from his own experiences, he is seldom averse to making self-judgements. Thus, he says that he loves opposition and 'likes riding and reaching something which isn't a general opinion'. This in his own words 'is a kind of vanity which goes with a sort of perseverance and bloody-mindedness'. He believes in 'community', but he is very much his own man. He has always liked parties, perhaps his eightieth less than most, but he carries on business there with a glass in his hand. Long after giving up smoking (see below, p. 65) he 'allowed' cheroots to be smoked at parties (not least by himself).

He gets bored with routines and likes surprises: one television interviewer was amazed to hear him make a spirited defence of 'meritocracy', a system of society which he always attacked: the interviewer was then at a total loss to know what questions to ask. His distaste for any 'orthodox university' has not prevented him from dealing with them, often in entangled fashion, at different periods of his and their life. In terms of sickness and health, which have caused him many problems, again at different ages, he has been a survivor, the simplest of description. Many of his ideas will survive far longer than he will. Some of them, indeed, are more topical than they were when he first launched them. He is still on the attack, seldom noisy, always alert.

1
In Lieu of an Autobiography

The title of this first chapter needs explanation. Some people are far too busy to write their autobiographies. Others lack the impulse to do so. There are some who even do not want biographies and specify so in their wills.[1] In Michael Young (hereafter referred to as Michael) the strength of the autobiographical impulse is clearly evident in memorable passages from many of his books and even more from his lectures. He likes recalling and recording past experiences, and he has more than one story to tell. He enjoys listening to the stories of other people too. *Family and Kinship in East London* (1957), co-authored with Peter Willmott, is packed with stories, all of people who otherwise would have been forgotten. One of his later books, which includes sections on ideas, old and new, consists largely of success stories, some of them Smilesian in character, of individuals involved in cooperative activities in industry.[2]

Why no autobiography? First, because having written many words, Michael has preferred both his impulses and his ideas ultimately (sometimes speedily) to be expressed in social enterprises rather than in words – 'thought, word, deed': and, second, because while he has retired from the executive direction of many of them, he remains so actively involved in their fortunes that he had no time to spend time writing an autobiography. One of his later books, co-authored with Tom Schuller in 1991, is called *Life after Work*.[3] Michael himself has never gone through such a phase: 'I would like to try those things I haven't done,' he told an interviewer in 1990 – and he has revealed much about himself, far more than most people, in interviews – 'but unfortunately just as I'm getting ready for that I get a new idea which sort of keeps me on my rail, on the old rail.'[4]

How old this rail, 'my rail', is requires examination in relation to both ideas and organisation. The railway metaphor seems wrong as a metaphor applied to Michael as does the metaphor used in the title of the first chapter of *The Symmetrical Family* (1973), again written with Willmott, which deals with people moving together, 'The Slow March'. Michael is too restless to be content with railway travel. He moves far faster. One unforgettable anecdote about him depicts him crouched over the wheel of a 'souped up' Austin Mini, travelling at 90 miles an hour on two journeys to meet a prisoner who had told him that he had read *Family and Kinship in East London* and wanted to talk to him about it. As he drove, Michael, not brought up to be a philosopher, but always wishing to be one, was discussing with a friend 'the solipsistic principles of metaphysics'.[5]

When Michael was President of Birkbeck College in 1989, a non-executive post – and he rarely took up such posts – he decided to study for a degree in philosophy and make up for what he had missed. (Since then he has often quoted David Hume.) He was interested not only in what his tutors told him – and he established a good working relationship with David Wiggins and Geoffrey Thomas – but in his fellow students, who played and replayed the lectures they heard and listened to when on their London journeys. One was a taxi driver, who listened as he drove around London in his cab. Another was a man in the rag trade who did the same as he drove between the East End and Bloomsbury. At the lectures there were some students 'with plastic bags and motor cycle helmets'.[6] Cars, motor cycles and taxis often figure in this book, including an old taxi in the history of the Institute of Community Studies.[7]

In Michael's life (almost) everything has been in motion, for he has conceived of a wide range of new organisations as well as coined new words, the most famous of them, 'meritocracy'. The words themselves live. Thus, in a *Dictionary of Modern Thought* under the entry 'Young', the reader is referred immediately without comment to the entry 'meritocracy': there is no other reference to him.[8] Used in the title of the second of his best-known books *The Rise of the Meritocracy* (1958), it is a word that has passed into the language.[9] Like the adjective 'meritocratic', it is now commonly used in relation to societies, past, present and future, societies which are often completely different from those which Michael studied or dreamed about.[10]

In *The Symmetrical Family* (1973), the most systematic of his books, also co-authored with Willmott, readers are told in its first pages that 'old words do not have to be demolished before new ones are made.

Language is more nearly in perpetual motion than a city', which in the case of London is considered 'the cradle of what will be'. Yet London for Young, as for Willmott, was a historical as well as a social product. (Almost) everything, they realised, including words, people and cities, has roots. When Michael envisages the future he explores the past. 'If the present embodies the past in all cities, here [in London] it does so with special vividness. The one is there alongside the other in almost every street.'[11]

The organisations that Michael has created have a life of their own, like words, and many of them have roots in the past. Two of the best known of them are the Consumers' Association and the Open University. The former is familiar to thousands of people through the magazine *Which?*: its first number appeared in 1957. The latter took in its first students in 1971 and more quickly than any other British university in history graduated its 100,000th student. From the start these two organisations struck diverse social chords, and people other than Michael, some very different from him, were to shape their evolution. Only Michael, however, knows the full story of their beginnings: he enjoys 'being in at the beginning', and there have been many 'firsts' in his life. Two among them were the National Extension College and the International Extension College. There has always been an international dimension to Michael's thought and work.[12]

The timing of the many beginnings was always crucial, but it was not always he who determined this, as he himself would stress. There were coincidences and conjunctions which dominate the chronology, as in the case of the four bodies mentioned or, just as striking, the newly-founded Social Science Research Council in 1965. These must be identified. So, too, must what Michael called in *The Rise of the Meritocracy* 'the social forces which have shaped our time'.[13] None the less, the biographical element in this book must be strong. While no one else in the twentieth century made as much of the word 'society' as Michael did, just as no one else was more suspicious of it than Margaret Thatcher, this does not mean that Michael did not attach supreme importance to every individual's life and to the talents – and chances – that shape it. His own life history has been unique.

Born during the First World War, on 9 August 1915, he was physically unfit to take part in the Second, but his direction of PEP (Political and Economic Planning) was of immediate and long-term intellectual and social importance, and when he moved to the Labour Party as Head of its Research Department in 1945 he was largely responsible for the draft of its election manifesto, *Let Us Face the Future*. Since then he has always been facing the future positively, determined to shape it.

The story of the last body that Michael brought into existence, his School for Social Entrepreneurs (1998), is for him *the* story of stories, still unfinished. It gives unity and continuity to a life of imagination and of endeavour. Yet he has other new bodies in mind. Having often been described, long before 1998, as 'Britain's premier social entrepreneur', even 'probably the most successful "entrepreneur" of social enterprises in the world', at the beginning of a new millennium he is looking for other social entrepreneurs from different parts of the country who will take us into a better future. Like himself, they will be required to translate their own diverse ideas into action.

The School is driven by Michael's confident belief that those people attracted by it and who join it – of other future Schools to be associated with it, perhaps locally more than nationally – will 'initiate new innovatory projects'. His own project is not without risks but now has access to financial as well as human resources. In Britain, although not in the United States, the not-for-profit sector of the economy is not usually identified with entrepreneurship.[14] Some people in Britain hate that word. Michael himself prefers to use the word 'enterprise' which in his mind – and in his will – goes together with 'innovation'.[15] Research, which figures prominently in every chapter in this book, is the necessary hyphen that links them together.

Michael, in character, told the founder members of his new School on 5 January 1998 that it was 'neither a university with ancient rules, hallowed by tradition' nor 'a modern university tied up into the routines of government finance'. It was not to be tied to place either, although its inaugural meeting took place in Bethnal Green in the Institute of Community Studies building, beautifully brightened up for the occasion, and on a day when the meeting was followed characteristically by a party. 'Introducing an innovation is also an exercise of entrepreneurship,' he told the members (they were not in any ordinary sense pupils), 'and for me entrepreneurship is best thought of as a concentrated and targeted kind of learning ... The idea [behind it] has to be subject to continuous examination, a continuous trial of and error, even when it is only an idea.'[16] Success could never be taken for granted, however strong motivation might be.

Peter Drucker, an admirer of the Open University, who shares many of Michael's insights, has called one of his impressive sequence of books on management *Innovation and Entrepreneurship* (1989). It deals less with the psychology and character traits of entrepreneurs than with their actions, assured, as Michael is, that innovation and entrepreneurship are purposeful tasks that can be organised. His approach, like Michael's, is practical. For Drucker, as for Michael, 'innovation is change that creates a new dimension of performance'.[17]

All Michael's activities, however labelled, have been concerned with purposive 'change'. This is a more tricky word than 'enterprise' or even 'innovation', used as it is in many different ways, as are many of the key words that Michael employs. He singles out 'fraternity' as well as 'liberty' and 'equality' among the values in the French revolutionary trinity, and he always associates 'enterprise' and 'fairness'. These values, different from Victorian values, are all related to change, a fact of life which the Victorians themselves had to confront.[18] 'Industry' and 'communications' were among *their* key words, and changes associated with these have often been compared with late twentieth-century changes in what is now thought of as a 'post-industrial society' in the process of a long-term 'communications revolution'.

For some twentieth-century people, as Queen Elizabeth put it in the late 1990s, the world was changing 'almost too fast for us older ones'.[19] And as in Queen Victoria's age – and earlier – there was resistance to change and to the technology which often went with it. Michael, older than Queen Elizabeth – he wrote an article in 1953 about her Coronation[20] – has always believed in charting unplanned change, seeking to anticipate it, as well as in planned change, not all of which is initiated by the State. Indeed, he has always regarded personal involvement in change as his major enterprise, encouraging others to be equally involved, collectively as well as individually, thereby turning purposive change into social enterprise.

The relationship between individual and collective involvement is one of the main themes in this book. As long ago as 1963 Michael anticipated the rise of 'a new individualist philosophy which will be expressed not only in beliefs but in action',[21] but he never lost faith in 'mutual aid'. 'The best form of economic and social organisation is one that involves small groups of freely cooperating individuals in pursuit of common ends, whether those groups are called family businesses, or small companies or cooperatives or clubs.'[22] The term 'public service' figures relatively rarely in Michael's vocabulary, although he appreciates the historic role of such service in a hierarchical society, and in his *The Rise of the Meritocracy* he imagined that 'domestic service' would be restored 'in a very large way' in a meritocratic future.

One of his key words is 'community', an old word which can carry with it emotive power, not least for himself, as in the name of the Institute of Community Studies in Bethnal Green. Michael uses the word, which is difficult to define, but which unlike almost all other terms relating to social organisation seems never to be used unfavourably,[23] more often than the word 'society', which pivots on 'social structure'.[24] The ICS, started in 1953, is the one institution created by Michael that pulls all the rest together, and after using the word 'community' in its title he came to stress community action more than community structure.[25] No. 18 Victoria Park Square, where it was located, was designated a 'Mutual Aid Centre' in 1977, by which time it had already spawned more than 20 community initiatives.[26] For a few of the first people who worked with Michael there was a certain incompatibility between the research and 'mutual aid' concepts. Michael himself saw none. Nor did his closest associates.

Many of the community initiatives were concerned with education and health, two of Michael's major preoccupations, but there were others that reflected his ingenuity and enterprise in identifying social openings. Thus, 'Commuter Study Clubs', popularly known as 'the Brain Train', was founded in 1980 to provide classes in commuter trains in and out of London – that really was travelling by rail – and as a social enterprise survived the end of nationalisation. Ten years later, he opened 'Language Line' as a telephone interpreting service for Bengalis, Somalis, Vietnamese and Chinese in Tower Hamlets within which Bethnal Green is incorporated. They were a new presence in a place where there had been earlier waves of immigration, some of them bringing with them innovation, some the habits and prejudices of the past. Language Line went on to offer a service outside Tower Hamlets in 140 languages with a turnover of over £4 million. Its clients included the Police and Health Authorities.

Michael's intention – or aspiration – to direct change as well as to interpret it figures prominently in all the chapters in this book. I myself like to probe beginnings, but I am concerned too, as he is, with impacts and outcomes. How frank would he have been in giving his own explanations had he written an autobiography? Why have some of his ideas been more easily implemented than others? What have been his relationships with the people who have worked with him? Many have been good; some have not. Some with whom they were not good have been very helpful to me. How are his books related to his activities? There is much in them, not the least interesting parts, that is speculative. This is the philosopher side of Michael. The political side has always been important too. In what ways did he approach and become involved in party political activity?

During the 1930s, down to the Stalin/Hitler Pact, he had flirted with the Communist Party and had visited the Soviet Union (with Anthony Blunt also in the group) in 1936. Thereafter, however, the Labour Party, which he joined at the age of 16, was the party of his primary allegiance, 'old' and 'new', and unlike some of the leaders of his Party, Michael expected it to win the 1945 general election, and for the next six years he was deeply involved in policy-making, working, in his own words, 'for the most radical democratic government of the century'. Already, however, he was changing his perspectives before the general election of 1950, and 'was beginning to think that [a] great opportunity had been missed'. The country was losing the 'dynamic push that we had been given during the war and what happened immediately after it'. It was threatening 'to dry up and gradually go into the sand. Unless, unless.' As he told a knowledgeable political interviewer nearly half a century later, 'it was the "unless" that I specially became interested in'.[27]

By 1960 he was contemplating a new Consumers' Party, which, according to a Gallup Poll, would have appealed to a quarter of the electorate,[28] and 21 years later he joined but very quickly left the newly founded Social Democratic Party. For Michael there are limits and limitations to party-dominated politics, and he has regarded them as being in some ways like the limits and limitations of action by the State. He has always looked for 'grass-root' reactions, and in his own social enterprises he has sought support wherever he can find it, outside as well as inside party offices, often attracting it in unlikely quarters. With others, this has now become a fashionable stance.

So, too, has a sociological approach to the issues involved in policy-making. In Michael's long entry in *Who's Who*, which must be one of the most frequently consulted of its entries, there is no reference to sociology, the subject with which Michael is invariably and inevitably associated, and which for him must also be associated with grass roots. (There is a reference to sociology in the *International Who's Who*.) In Britain sociology has often been considered as socialism, and Michael, fresh from the Labour Party's Central Office, was not alone in identifying the two. Nor was the French sociologist Raymond Aron alone in thinking that this was one of the troubles of British sociology: in his view, it was largely 'an attempt to make intellectual sense of the political problems of the Labour Party'.[29]

If Michael had decided to use the Labour Research Department as a base from which to enter the House of Commons, as, for example, did

Denis (later Lord) Healey, a colleague there, he would have had a very different kind of public career ahead of him, that of a minister, from that which was to follow.[30] This was a second 'if' in his life: he trained as a barrister after he left school at Dartington in 1935 and became one but never practised. There was a third 'if' to come. Years later, if he had decided to stay in Cambridge, where he was made a Fellow of Churchill College in 1959, he would have had a very different third kind of career, that of a don. Somewhat donnish in appearance, he might be taken to be one, but being a don did not suit him in Cambridge or in other quite different university settings, among them Ahmadu Bello University in Nigeria (1974) or the Center for Advanced Study in Behavioral Studies, Palo Alto in California (1956).[31]

Birkbeck in London was different. It was always congenial because it was dealing with adults, as were the Open University and the National Extension College.[32] The one continuous institutional attachment in Michael's life, however, was neither a college nor a university, but the ICS: in a letter of 1992 he described his work there since 1953 as his 'main job'.[33] He was its founder, and it comes second in his *Who's Who* entry before his three marriages. Nevertheless, any study of Michael, biographical or analytical, must begin still earlier at Dartington in Devonshire, the place which, as was required by the College of Heralds, he chose to have associated with his peerage – Lord Young of Dartington – offered him by James (later Lord) Callaghan in 1978.

Dartington estate and school had been founded as part of an 'experiment' by Leonard and Dorothy Elmhirst, with a strong American input, four years before Michael arrived there as a boy there in 1929, learning for four years how to carry out practical tasks as well as to pursue classroom studies, but above all learning about himself. Dartington, which Michael was to serve as a Trustee from 1945 to 1995, was far more than a school for him, just as the ICS was to be far more than a university.[34] They were both 'communities', the products of 'enterprise'. That for Michael was the right pattern: they were contiguous in his mind, if not for the people who worked in either of them.

Michael's autobiographical statements about contiguities and continuities in his own development take precise, even factual, form in the link passages in the volume of his miscellaneous writings which is preceded by Daniel Bell's foreword.[35] Take, for example, lines from his Epilogue to the volume which begins with the sentence, 'This book reflects a lifetime's interest in the future, that is changing anticipations at different points in the century. It also expresses two dominant moods ... the first, radical, restless and optimistic ... the second less aerated, less optimistic, more concerned with the prevention of further decline than with the achievement of further progress.'[36]

My own book incorporates an anthology of such self-judgements, including Michael's somewhat curious assertion that the reason why quite a few of the ideas that he has had have worked in practice is because he has distrusted them: 'I have never had an idea that I was sure about.'[37] He has not made a list. 'Because of distrusting them,' he has added, 'I have never been set back much by failures because I've almost *expected* them to fail.' If he did go ahead and 'have a go', the element of distrust was strong enough to allow 'the idea to be changed and sharpened and take its own course'.

Such comments must be related to other published and unpublished evidence, and in writing about Michael I have drawn on my own memories too. My experience of the twentieth century sometimes converged with his, but just as often contrasted with it, as, indeed, do my temperament and my views on religion as well as on politics. I am six years younger than he is, and come from a quite different social background: there was no Dartington in my life nor East End; I had a very different kind of education from him (elementary school; grammar school; Cambridge); and after code-breaking as a soldier in the Enigma team at Bletchley I made what looked like a conventional return to 'academic life' in an 'orthodox' university – Oxford, not Cambridge. Industrial Leeds, still Victorian Leeds, figured next: it is not on his map. Then, briefly, and at this point we have shared the same map, Australia (1960–1), before I was the first academic to be appointed to the first of Britain's seven new universities, Sussex, of which I later became Vice-Chancellor.

I have subsequently been directly involved in some of the same enterprises as he has, notably the Open University, which I helped to plan and of which I was Chancellor for 16 years. Not surprisingly, I know well many of the people who move through these pages and have written on some of the themes which Michael has explored, including education and health, sometimes in depth. I have also from time to time reviewed his books as they have appeared. In a sense, therefore, this book is in lieu of my own autobiography as well as of his.

Because Michael is fully aware of the complexities and ambiguities of twentieth-century experience, which carries with it ironies and contradictions, this was doubtless one of the reasons why he (and not the Economic and Social Science Research Council) chose a historian to write this book. While uneasy with dates, he has always been deeply interested in history, not least in the kind of history that his friend

Raphael Samuel fostered in participatory history workshops at Ruskin College, Oxford. It is relevant that Samuel, who lived in London's East End, was involved in the early years of the ICS.[38] The kind of history that Samuel wrote tapped the roots. It fed on memory and revelled in detail.

Michael himself, who sometimes wrote along these lines, has never been afraid of historical generalisations or of speculations about the nature of history.[39] Indeed, there are so many references to history in his writings, both general and specific, that he might well have been a historian himself. He has coined many memorable phrases as well as new words, like 'the soil grows castes, the machine makes classes' or 'an institution is the way that a habit perpetuates itself'.[40] 'Habits are not usually chosen with deliberation: they just grow, wild flowers rather than cultivated ones.'[41]

The Rise of the Meritocracy, where the first of these phrases occurs, takes the form of an essay set in the future, purporting to be a doctoral thesis by a future Michael Young, a historical sociologist, on the 'historical causes' of 'May risings' in 2034, which culminated in a new Peterloo. He was wise enough to conclude: 'Too severe a sociological analysis may suggest that history has slid to its present conclusion as inevitably as the morning rocket arrives on the moon. There is nothing mechanical about history. Stupidity has not been routed by sociology.'[42] He also states that 'in holding a mirror to the past, even the historian can seldom escape the image of his own inquiring face'.

In *The Symmetrical Family*, Michael, along with Willmott, turned to pre-industrial social history with curiosity and with diligence as well as with curiosity. 'The most vexed question in the protracted debate on the effects of industrialisation in England has been about the balance of losses and gains to different sections of the population, especially in the period up to 1850 ... What would have happened had there been no industry?'[43] Within this perspective the word 'pre-industrial' means as much to Michael as it does to Peter Laslett, a Cambridge friend of his and mine, who in 1965 published a landmark study, *The World We Have Lost*. Indeed, it means more to Michael than Daniel Bell's adjective 'post-industrial', which quickly took off during the 1960s, to be followed by the vaguest of words, 'postmodern'. For another American sociologist, Lee Rainwater, who wrote the foreword to the American edition of *The Symmetrical Family,* 'the methodological mix' in it of survey and historical analysis made its conclusions 'much more powerful than either method [by itself] could have done'.[44]

The family is at the core of all Michael's thinking, feeling and writing, but taken by itself his own family history, which must incorporate that of the Elmhirsts too, is absorbing. There was, in fact, little symmetry in Michael's own absorbing family history, stretching back through several generations. Part of the story was set outside England. Although he was born at Hale, not far from Manchester, he arrived in Australia in 1917 and lived there until 1925. (The word 'Australia' does not figure in the index of Y*oung at Eighty* or in the 'biographical outline' of his life presented there.)

The only reason that his parents went to Australia in 1917, when he was a baby, their only child, was to try to save their marriage. With fair hair, blue eyes and a winning smile, his mother, Edith, an Irish romantic, whose own mother called her 'a child of love', had fallen in love herself, when young but already married, with a Russian, who might have been a Communist agent. She herself believed passionately in the Russian Revolution – for her the Revolution was 'all mixed up with Ireland' – and in the 1930s she was to join the Communist Party, before Michael became attached to it.

The family's fares to Australia were paid by Michael's Australian grandfather out of the sale of war bonds, information which angered his mother as much as her not being told that they were going there until after the tickets had been bought. Parents and baby travelled to Australia by a circuitous route, stopping to see New York, the Niagara Falls and the Rockies on the way. This was the first of Michael's many visits to North America, which he was to learn most about through the Elmhirsts, a very different pair from his own parents, while still a teenager: in 1933 he was able through them to stay at the White House and meet and talk to President Roosevelt, dine with most of his Cabinet, and even give the President unsolicited advice on Cuba. Roosevelt listened. On another journey across the Atlantic on the *Bremen*, the great German ocean liner, he was able to listen to Leonard Elmhirst questioning Henry Ford.

All this was unpredictable in the early 1920s when neither travel nor a new environment in Australia could sustain the Youngs' marriage, and in 1922 Gibson Young, Michael's father, returned to England leaving Michael and his mother behind. There she became fully aware of her own talents for the first time, becoming a friend of the author of *The Legend of the Nineties* (1954), Vance Palmer, a writer who in his time did more than any other Australian writer to identify the 'Australian-ness' of what even to many Australians was an unknown continent.[45] When she and Michael followed Gibson back to England a year later the marriage was in effect dead, and it was clear that it could never be revived.

Michael's father died at the age of 47, having returned to Australia in 1937. His mother lived to be 95. She was a presence, therefore, in the most creative period of Michael's life while his father was a memory. Their lives interacted, although Michael was no more capable of staying with her for long than Gibson had been. Late in life she lived at Totnes, the nearest town to Dartington, where Michael had moved briefly from London after Cambridge, and she remained there after he returned. She outlasted Dorothy Elmhirst, who herself lived to the age of 81 and died in 1968.

It was London, however, which had shaped Edith's world during the 1930s and 1940s, when she moved in literary and artistic circles and welcomed to her home oppressed foreigners and disturbed fellow citizens. She could inspire love and devotion. One writer who was very close to her was the Indian Mulk Raj Anand. She was genuinely interested in painting, and could paint well herself. So could her brother, who was a Royal Academician. So, too, could – and did and does – Michael, who always notes paintings as the first things to observe when he goes into a house. 'They always tell one quite a bit about people, but are also interesting as expressions of what people think are beautiful. The way beauty comes into the lives of everyone, most ordinary people, is one of the wonders of the world.'[46]

Any attribution of Michael's views on family to his parents' broken marriage must be examined carefully in the light of the whole of Michael's life, including his own experiences as a husband and a father. His attitudes to his parents were mixed, and he blamed his mother, not his father, for the partings that separated them. He knew more about her love affairs, some of them lasting relationships, than he knew about his father's, and he knew about them sooner. As a result he was introduced to Bohemia long before being introduced to Bethnal Green, sooner, indeed, than he was introduced to Dartington. He was fond of his father, who as a child in Australia had shown enough talent as a musician to persuade his own father to send him to the Manchester School of Music where he studied the violin with Josef Brodsky, founder of the Brodsky Quartet.

Short in height as an adult, Gibson Young looked like King Alfonso of Spain, with whom he was happy to be compared. When he returned to England from Australia in 1922 he could not make a living as a violinist and took up singing instead, giving recitals around the country, and later, successfully, became a conductor of choral music. He organised a weekly choir at St. Martin in the Fields, and acquired wider fame when he led crowds in community singing. He also worked for Lord

Beaverbrook in his Empire Crusade campaign, travelling around England's holiday resorts complete with loudspeaker van. Despite crippling asthma, which was to be inherited by Michael, he was a brilliant showman.

In politics he was a Liberal during the 1920s, and in 1929, the year when Michael went to Dartington, already beginning to be interested in politics himself, he was Liberal Party agent in Cirencester at the time of the general election. This was a circumstance which doubtless encouraged Michael to stand as a Liberal candidate at a school election. Neither was successful. Michael, who was glad to receive a letter from his father bearing the stamp 'Election Communication', secured only two votes.

During the 1930s, according to Michael, his father became a socialist. More important for Gibson himself, however, was the fact that he became music critic to the *Daily Express*, a role that he had long wished to fill; and after further crippling attacks of asthma he returned to Australia, where he became Musical Director of the Australian Broadcasting Commission before dying of pleurisy in 1938 (before the death of his own father).[47] When he died Michael was so shocked, according to his mother, that he would not speak of him for over a year.[48]

One of Michael's interviewers had asked him as his first question – before turning to his parents – who his grandparents were, and this was, in fact, very much to the point. He might even have asked about his great-grandparents had he been looking for stories of adventure and romance. On his father's side of the family, Michael's great-grandfather, George, was a gold rush pioneer who luckily found a great gold nugget which he wisely cashed at once, using the proceeds to start a printing firm which published the first local newspaper, the *Bendigo Advertiser*. Michael's great grandmother, Miriam, was born on board ship, between Melbourne and Samoa, and Michael just remembers seeing her in Melbourne, 'dressed in black in a darkened room full of Victorian furniture'. She was the daughter of an English missionary to the South Seas, Joseph King, 'a very practical missionary, always cheerful and optimistic',[49] a Congregationalist associated with the London Missionary Society.[50]

On his mother's side one great-grandparent was equally interesting, Alexander Dunlop, a Quaker architect, who insisted on daily Bible reading. His son, Michael's grandfather, Daniel Dunlop, handsome and debonair, was born in Kilmarnock but brought up on the Isle of Arran by Alexander's father and mother-in-law, the father a Gaelic-speaking fisherman. An early Theosophist, Daniel became a follower of Rudolf Steiner, founder of the Anthroposophical Society in 1913, and he was interesting and important enough as an Anthroposophist to inspire a long, unconventional biography.[51]

Before and after becoming Chairman of the British Anthroposophical Association Dunlop cast a spell over many people, particularly women. Just as important in relation to family history was that he believed in research, 'skill in action', and in the importance of adult education, as Michael was to do: Rudolf Steiner House in north London owes a great debt to him. He also created two organisations – one national, the British Electrical and Allied Manufacturers' Association, and one international, the World Power Conference (later renamed the World Energy Conference), first held in 1924. (The thirteenth, at Cannes in 1986, was to be opened by President Mitterrand.) As a disciple of Steiner, Dunlop combined willpower with clairvoyance.[52] He was a successful businessman, too, who had a private table at the Royal Court Hotel in Chelsea. He crossed the Atlantic frequently, and lived for a time in the United States. That was another of Michael's American connections.

When Michael was a baby, his father was working as Public Relations Manager for the American-based Westinghouse Company, which had its main factory in Trafford Park, Manchester, and Dunlop had been responsible for finding Michael's father a Westinghouse job. That is why Michael was born nearby in Hale. Dunlop had married an Irish girl, Louisa Fitzpatrick of Dublin, and spending several years in Ireland he got to know W.B. Yeats, who shared his interest in the occult.[53] He was mentioned too, *en passant*, by James Joyce in *Ulysses*. Curiously, although the young Michael did not know it, Dunlop believed in the mid-1920s that the world was passing under the influence ('rulership') of Michael, one of the Masters who watched over mankind and guarded worldly fortunes. His own special contribution to Anthroposophy was to spread a so-called 'Michael prophecy', grounded in the medieval past.[54]

Michael, whose second name is Dunlop, is incurious about such fascinating details concerning his mother's side of the family. He was curious enough, however, to get details of his family tree on his father's side from David Blumer in Australia. His Australian grandfather, whom he remembered well, J.B. Young, who died in 1938, had two daughters as well as one son, Gibson, Michael's father; and one of the daughters, Florence, to whom his grandfather was particularly attached, played a big part in the first stages of Michael's life. It was she who chose Dartington for him as a place to be educated after a tour of English progressive schools, and it was his grandfather who paid his first year's fees there before Michael won a scholarship.[55] Florence also had an African as well as an Australian or British connection, for she later married the Reverend R.C. Blumer, Principal of Prince of Wales College, Achimota, in what was then the Gold Coast. It was one of the main educational institutions in West Africa before the University of Ghana was created after independence.

This was a remarkable family background, with diverse genes but curiously interwoven experiences. Because so much is interwoven it makes it far too simple in dealing with Michael's intense sense of family to explain everything, as a psychoanalyst might do (and Michael is very familiar with psychoanalysis), in terms of his experiences as the only son of a split marriage. His parents' families were extended families both in time, a subject that has fascinated Michael, the writer, and in place. They were never tied to one place, and in that respect were completely unlike the extended families of Bethnal Green, who were to win Michael's affection. The 'head' of one of the latter told him in a working-class oral autobiography, a literary and social genre of its own, 'I was bred and born in Bethnal Green, and my parents and their parents before me. I wouldn't leave Bethnal Green. I wouldn't take a threepenny bus ride outside Bethnal Green.'[56]

Michael's most influential book, *Family and Kinship in East London*, written in co-partnership with Willmott, evokes a strong sense of place.[57] Yet, significantly, it begins with time. 'This book is about the effect of one of the newest upon one of the oldest of our social institutions.' The new institution was a 'housing estate', 'hundreds of which have been built since the war': the old institution was 'the family'. The setting, London's East End, was 'the scene of great social changes' in Michael's own lifetime, the greatest of them after 1958. The same working-class inhabitant of Bethnal Green, whom he quoted, recalled that for him 'local history [did] not have to be learnt from books: it [was] passed on by word of mouth from parents to children'.

For Michael there are rhythms in time as well as contrasts, and, as has been noted, cycles as well as sequences;[58] and a generation after writing *Family and Kinship*, long after housing estates had given way to high-rise tower blocks and they in their turn had become unfashionable, Michael in a review was to describe interest in time as 'becoming popular, so much so that authors are finding themselves hard put to find new ways of playing with the word'.[59] Among the persons who had already passed beyond use of the word 'time' to the study of time processes, including the right time to sow and to plant seeds, was Rudolf Steiner, who explored trends in history and links in time across the centuries.[60]

In the forefront of Michael's own personal history the Elmhirsts, who gave him love while at Dartington and afterwards, were more important than his real parents. 'With my own parents,' he told them in 1958, 'it was always (or usually) one or the other. Hence the terrors of choice.'[61] 'Clearly what I must do is to behave in my life as you do in yours,' he had written to them twelve years earlier.[62]

Barbara (Lady) Wootton, who knew Michael well, noted that in *The Elmhirsts of Dartington* he laid no claim to 'detachment',[63] a revealing statement in itself, since there is an implicit, if not explicit, denial of detachment in all of Michael's thought and work. The personal and the organisational are always entangled, the imaginative and the practical. Many of Michael's autobiographical statements about love and intuition, scattered through his writings, echo Dorothy, just as his statements about the need to be practical echo Leonard, who among his other gifts was 'a spotter of blocked drainpipes'.[64] Michael's years at Dartington were the happiest years of his life, complete in themselves, as the Elmhirsts believed years of childhood should be. In 1925 they had stated as one of the objects of their experiment 'to release the imagination, to give it wings, to open wide the doors of the mind'. This was 'perhaps the most vital service that one being can render another'.[65]

Dartington released them for Michael. But it rendered an even greater gift, which would inadequately be described as a 'service'. The school and the community to which he always felt that he 'belonged' would never have meant so much to him had there not been love behind it and had not the Elmhirsts in effect adopted him as a child of their own. In his own life he insists that he is 'delighted' when he finds 'people to work with' who have 'some spark of originality and some capacity to love'. 'The capacity to love is the greatest gift of mankind.'[66]

There was wealth as well as love at Dartington when Michael arrived there. It could never have started as a 'social educational experiment' in 1925 unless wealth had been behind it, and in this case the wealth was inherited and American, Dorothy's share in a substantial Whitney fortune. Michael had inherited no wealth, but the Elmhirsts were unstintingly generous to him on many occasions when he was in difficult family circumstances. Moreover, at the critical point in his public life, when he set up the ICS in 1953, Elmhirst money, not substantial, was indispensable.[67] Receiving gifts taught him a lot about giving. He was to go on to develop an almost uncanny art of raising money, sometimes from the most unlikely benefactors. Recognising, as he did, the value of money, he always regarded it as instrumental.

Michael's mother recognised how much Michael owed to the Elmhirsts when she wrote in her revealing but somewhat steamy autobiography (she found time and motivation to produce one, along with several novels) that during his last years at Dartington Michael was 'growing rapidly closer to Dorothy Elmhirst than he was to me; her family was becoming his family; she as his good bountiful mother, had taken the place of his own wayward, erring mother. I tried not to resent it.'[68]

Michael's experiences with the families that he himself created echoed those of his parents, he once said, rather than those of the Elmhirsts. Yet he had difficulties of his own that they never experienced. Nor were his attitudes the same as theirs. His marriage in 1945 to his first wife, Joan Lawson, an art student, ended 15 years later in divorce, but she did not disappear from his life. There had been three children by that marriage, two sons and a daughter, Emma. Michael himself was an only child and he has only one grandson, Griffin, son of his second son, David, a guitar player and recording studio manager. The first child, Christopher Ivan, born in July 1946 at Mile End hospital, was autistic – he had suffered brain damage at birth – and how best to deal with him caused considerable parental strain. From the age of two to the age of nearly 30 he was in the care of Dr. D.W. Winnicott, 'kindness personified', whom Michael describes as a 'really wonderful man', a magical doctor'. Chris spent some years in Steiner schools, one in Aberdeen: he was in Littlemore Hospital in Oxford for eight years, moving later to a Home not far from Dartington where Michael continued to see him regularly.

Michael's second marriage, to Sasha Moorsom, novelist, ceramic sculptor and broadcaster, by whom he had another son, Toby, and daughter, Sophie, meant everything to him. Two years after her death from cancer at the age of 62 he still found it difficult to write about it as 'her death'. 'It wasn't a death: Sasha died.'[69] Above her obituary, the *Guardian* printed a remarkable and deeply moving photograph by Catherine Shakespeare Lane of her taken the day after she died with Michael and Sophie by her side. Sophie, born in 1961, had become a Buddhist, living in a Theravada monastery for 11 years before leaving it to look after her mother in the last weeks of her illness, and Michael felt that the controversial publication of the photograph was in the Buddhist tradition. There was complete openness about death.[70] At a funeral service held on 22 June 1993 at St Bartholomew the Great Church, West Smithfield, everyone present was asked to bring one flower to place on the open coffin.

It was on holiday in Provence in a place that Michael and Sasha both loved – Sasha wrote her first novel about it, *A Lavender Trip*, in 1976 – when she learned that she had cancer. Michael, troubled throughout his life with ill health, had recently had an operation for a secondary cancer in the liver. Now it was she, not he, who was to die first. A few weeks before her death she had organised a concert in St Bartholomew's Church of the music of a distant relative, Anthony Scott, which she attended, 'looking joyful' in a wheelchair. She had written the words of one song, 'Always in My Mind', which she hoped would be – and was – sung by Cleo Laine. Such experiences influenced Michael's approach to suffering and death, the subject of his last book.[71]

Music, the key to his father's life, but not to his, had begun a new life at Dartington with the arrival there of Imogen Holst in 1943 (she had first visited it in 1938), and its Music Summer School, still lively and strong, has attracted people to Dartington who would never otherwise have gone there. It was while he was at school there that Michael developed his intuitive sense, which went with a love of the arts. He took part in plays (he has tried once since to write one), and learned pottery from Bernard Leach. He had taken up painting even before he went there. The BBC and Sasha taught him for the first time to appreciate poetry fully.[72]

Michael wrote poems too, as did Sasha, and their daughter Sophie, who had for a time been a pupil at Dartington, introduced a published edition of a collection of their poems which appeared just after Sasha's death. She found pattern there, as I have found it in the whole of Michael's work.[73] Rather than arrange the poems in chronological order she looked for themes and echoes, listening quietly and recognising that 'other readers may pick up different tunes'. One poem by Michael is called 'The Metronomic Moon'. In it he wrote:

> When the time is ripe (soon now)
> The metronomic moon on cue will let slip
> The north wind to bite the branches bare and
> Lay out the bony tree against the back-lit tomb-grey sky.
> In other years I would say, how lucky we are,
> The people inside our house,
> But the luck has not brought us mercy.

'Luck' and 'mercy' would have been related to each other in Christian terms by Michael's great-grandmother; Michael's mother, like her father, would have related them both to 'karma'. Michael, however, was galvanised into characteristic activity by disaster. He attacked the Tomlinson Report which threatened the closure of St. Bartholomew's Hospital, where Sasha was operated on, and later he wrote to the Prime Minister, then John Major, objecting to the contemplated closure of the Royal Marsden Hospital. He had a sympathetic reply in Major's own handwriting beginning 'Dear David' – Major had confused Michael with Lord Young of Graffham, raised to the peerage five years after Michael. The Marsden was reprieved, although this correspondence doubtless did not determine the judgement.

There was irony there, however, as there often has been in Michael's life. He had been interested in hospices and in funeral rituals before Sasha's suffering and death, just as he was interested in marriage rituals for those who did not want a church service or in 'covenants' for those partners who did not marry at all. All this suggests, in other words, that his own family experiences in youth and in age were not solely responsible for his ways of thinking and feeling. There were other sources which counted. His relationship with his son Toby, Sophie's younger brother, who had rejected the idea of going to Dartington and had gone instead to Totnes Comprehensive School, then to Brasenose College, Oxford, where he got a First in PPE, to Harvard (as a Fulbright Scholar), and to Cambridge, where he began a PhD, raised general questions concerning the family that Toby, a journalist and founder of the *Modern Review*, discussed frankly in a BBC radio programme about sons with famous fathers. In the unlikely pages of *The Sun*, articles by Michael and Toby had appeared on the same page in an article called *The Page 6 Debate*.[74] Michael favoured the legalisation of cannabis, Toby opposed it. 'I just can't adjust to the shock of my father arguing in favour of legalising a practice I've spent a large part of my life feeling guilty about, largely because I thought he disapproved of it. I am currently in the throes of trying to give it up, along with all other drugs, because I recognise what a destructive force they have been.'

It is always necessary in any study of Michael's ideas and activities to turn from genes to themes, from family history to intellectual history. Intellectual pedigrees matter as much as family trees. The term 'mutual aid', covering a wide variety of his activities, was Prince Kropotkin's, who before 1914 attacked the 'stultifying' role of the State.[75] But the idea was older. Michael looked back to the Rochdale Pioneers and to Robert Owen, and he was interested in the Cooperative Movement as well as in the cooperative ideal. His book of quotations concerning cooperation took him back to the Middle Ages. Modern authors might have included, alongside Owen, the French socialist Pierre Josèphe Proudhon, although Michael never read him.[76] Tawney, whose life overlapped Michael's, always figured in Michael's list of references, and H. G. Wells was often 'thrown in for spice'.[77]

Tawney was a mentor, offering not spice but substance, a master indeed. Cole, who was never entirely at ease with Tawney, did not fulfil the same role for Michael, although their lives overlapped too, and much of Michael's writing, while very different in style, echoes his.[78] Michael owed little to Marx. Despite or because of his brief spell in the Communist Party, he never felt the appeal of Marxist ideology for the rest of his life. Nor did he find himself at home with Emile Durkheim or Max Weber, both of whom were on a recommended reading list when Michael was being introduced to sociology at LSE. Weber had had little direct influence on Tawney, although he might have had. The same applied to Durkheim and Michael.[79]

It is a still more difficult task to consider the relationships, usually creative, sometimes fraught, between Michael and his contemporaries than it is to trace back lines in time to 'the dead' whom Michael prefers to think of as real contemporaries.[80] Some contemporaries still living, a few of them still as active as he is, have collaborated with him in his books, others in his social enterprises, some in both. Independent-minded though he is, he could never have done without them – at more than one level – and they figure prominently in this book. His closest colleagues at the beginning of the Institute of Community Studies were three Peters, Willmott, co-author and for a time co-director of the Institute, Marris, who in 1976 became Professor of Social Policy Planning at the University of California, Los Angeles and Berkeley, and Townsend, whose influential studies of poverty moved far beyond those of Booth and Rowntree.

It is most to the point, perhaps, in dealing with Michael's thinking, to continue with a highly selective list, headed by Richard Titmuss, who supervised his LSE doctoral thesis, and Ed Shils, who died while this book was in its last stages and whose obituary in the *Guardian* was written by Michael: he had a greater influence on Michael than Titmuss. Others on the list were François Lafitte, journalist and later professor, illegitimate son of Havelock Ellis, whom Michael met in the 1930s and who shared many of his beliefs; Charles Madge, poet as well as co-founder of Mass Observation, and later a Professor of Sociology and President of the British Sociological Association, who, like Titmuss and Michael, had never read for a degree in the subject;[81] Peter Laslett, Fellow of Trinity College,

Cambridge, who, combining deep knowledge and deep feeling, cooperated with Michael in advancing 'open learning' and who has written as much as Michael has done about the family as an institution;[82] and Anthony Crosland, Michael's closest friend in high politics, 'the sort of leader open to new ideas who keeps people like me in and with the Labour Party'.[83]

Tony Flower is now a trustee of ICS, and directly connected with it are Geoff Dench, who is also a Professor of Sociology at Middlesex University and was co-editor, along with Kate Gavron and Tony Flower, of *Young at Eighty*. Paul Barker, assistant editor of the pioneering periodical *New Society* from 1965 to 1968 and editor from 1968 to 1986, who has been involved in many of Michael's social enterprises, is now its Chairman.[84] Other people close to Michael are Roger Warren-Evans, indispensable, reform-minded lawyer on the Trust; W. G. (later Lord) Runciman, sociologist and businessman, who was Treasurer of the Child Poverty Action Group from 1972 to 1997 and a member of the Social Science Research Council from 1974 to 1979;[85] Eric Midwinter, historian, educated at Cambridge and co-founder with Michael, Laslett and Dianne Norton, of the University of the Third Age;[86] A. H. (Chelly) Halsey, sociologist and 'ethical socialist';[87] Peter Hall, geographer and planner, knighted in 1998, who has written many books, culminating in *Cities in Civilization* (1998);[88] and Tony Dodds, Executive Director of the International Extension College, which he worked for from its start in 1971 and who along with Hilary Perraton has kept Michael involved in the Third World.

All these people figure prominently in the pages that follow, often in more than one connection. The first of Michael's collaborators – on a now forgotten wartime study, *Will the War Make Us Poorer?* (1943) – had been a man much older than himself, am experienced public servant, Sir Henry Bunbury, an accountant, born in 1876, and a founder member of the Directorate of PEP. There should be an equally long list of the women on whom Michael has depended, particularly Wyn Tucker, brought in by Ann Cartwright, who worked with him for 39 years, and Sue Chisholm, who has been his personal secretary since 1971. They are the keepers of the word – and the work.

Naomi Sargant, Lady McIntosh of Haringey, is a keeper of memories. She took a London University degree in sociology and worked from 1955 to 1967 with Gallup and served as Pro-Vice-Chancellor (Student Affairs) of the Open University from 1974 to 1978 before becoming from 1981 to 1989 Senior Commissioning Officer for Educational Programmes at Channel 4 – and much else. Along with her husband,

Andrew MacIntosh, whom she met when working with Gallup, she vividly recalls the first years of the ICS. McIntosh has recalled vividly Michael's first speech in the House of Lords in 1978, when he flouted the convention that maiden speeches should be short (ten minutes) and unprovocative.[89] He spoke for 18 minutes on what he called 'mundane matters', but at the same time stressed that 'because something is mundane' it does not by any means mean it is uncontroversial'.[90] He touched, therefore, on many of the themes that had most concerned him earlier in his life and how he had approached them. There was a practical twist to his observations, however, for example his 'mundane suggestion' to British Rail, later implemented after British Rail had ceased to be, that 'if high speed inter-city trains are late beyond a certain point, [there is] no reason why there should not be a partial refund to the passengers'.

Ann Cartwright had drawn Michael into the field of health, as Prudence Smith had done into the BBC, while Marianne Rigge, co-author and co-director in many of Michael's projects, was involved both in ideas and organisations. Kate Gavron, publisher and researcher, a Trustee of the Institute, has been extremely helpful to me in reading the text of this book. I could not have written it at all without the cooperation and care of Wyn Tucker and Sue Chisholm. They have been as willing to cope with my awkward timetable as they always have been with Michael's.

The sources for a life of Michael are more widely scattered than those that Michael found at Dartington when he wrote his book on the Elmhirsts which he considered writing 20 years before it appeared. One of the advantages of living in a large house, he wrote then, was that there was room to store archives: 'people who live in large houses do not have to throw things away.'[91] Some of Michael's papers, particularly early letters, are stored there now in well-kept archives. The SSRC papers (in formidable bulk) are kept at Swindon. Most of his papers, however, along with his books, including lecture notes – and these have survived in surprisingly large quantities – are now stored in cardboard filing boxes in the Institute at Bethnal Green. The Institute is crammed with papers, just as it is crammed with people working on the Institute's many community ventures. Among the papers, Michael's letters applying to Foundations for funding support are particularly revealing: they discuss both projects and methods, not to speak of finance. So, too, are the reports which he sent to them. Eventually these papers and those in Michael's own possession will make their way to the library of Churchill College, Cambridge. Others are still with PEP and the Labour Party, and the SDP files and those of the Tawney Society are at Essex University.

Michael's influence, defying time, will doubtless survive not only through paper but through people on whom the future of his community ventures will depend. He has often caught time on the wing, and in writing about him I have tried to catch it too. Commenting on the collection of Michael's essays in *Social Scientist as Inventor* (1983), Martin Bulmer, historian of sociological research in Britain, observed that no such collection could convey Michael's 'manifold achievements, particularly in bridging the worlds of public life and social science' and that only a 'full biography' could do this.[92] I have no doubt that my own book will not be the last to place him in time.

Having called this first introductory chapter 'In Lieu of an Autobiography', I knew that I must end it with a description of Michael's birth from the only existing autobiography that could cover it adequately, his mother's. This, indeed, is where my book has to begin, beyond the access of Michael's memory. The birth was recalled at length by his mother in language totally different from his:

> The evening before the pains began, believing my time was near, I took my cumbersome body upstairs to the bedroom and, lighting a candle in the gathering darkness, lowered my weight carefully on to the bed. Presently I closed my eyes as though in prayer that all might be well, and I felt a hand slip gently to the nape of my neck, just under my hair, and clasp it tenderly, protectively, as though to give me courage to face my ordeal. Believing Gibson had returned earlier than usual, I turned round expecting to find him standing behind me. Nobody was there. It was uncanny to feel the handclasp and yet to be alone in the shadowy room! A great sense of well-being welled up within me. All fear of my coming ordeal vanished in the presence of what I am credulous enough to believe was the spirit of my unborn child. Oddly enough, my son, both in his boyhood and as a man, has a habit of clasping my neck tenderly to console me should I be distressed. That evening I knew, with a certainty my husband called wish fulfilment, that I was to have a son whom I felt would be a clearer, strong, more loving character than myself. I decided, there and then, to call him Michael.
>
> The sole connection between my angelic visitor and the sleeping infant, wrapped in a shawl, whom the gnome-like midwife placed in my arms after I woke from a drugged sleep was the name. I thought his flushed cheeks and downy head perfect.

Edith thought also that his face resembled her father's. 'Tracing a likeness to my father in his mouth and chin it was as though my father had returned in the shape of a son.'[93]

2
Michael When Young

It seems right that London's fascinating Museum of Childhood, formerly the Geffrye Museum, is situated not far from the home of the Institute of Community Studies on the edge of Victoria Park Square in Bethnal Green. As Chelly Halsey wrote in *Young at Eighty*, 'Now that he is aged 80 it has become more clear than ever that Michael looks for redemption in childhood. He seeks, that is, the foundations of high civility, creativity and fellow feeling in the way in which human beings are reared.'[1] Interest in child 'rearing', stimulated by problems in his own family, had led Michael into psychology in the late 1940s, and it had gone on to shape his approach to sociology – and to education.

Among Michael's papers is a copy of the opening address delivered by him in August 1974 at the centenary of the University of Adelaide. It bore the arresting title 'The Shortening of Childhood and the Lengthening of Education'.[2] The content of the address – a plea for more democracy in schools, less bureaucracy, more informality and more *à la carte* and less *table d'hôte* fare in the curriculum – was less interesting than the title or the idea behind it. In the light of Michael's other writings there was nothing new in what he had to say. None the less, in discussing 'earning and learning' in Adelaide, a city and a university that he was to revisit in 1999 and the home of an old Australian friend Hugh Stretton, Michael must have arrested his audience by demanding the removal of legal prohibitions against children working. He had raised this issue before, and he was to raise it again.[3] What he said was controversial since it ran counter to most Labour Party thinking, including the thinking of one of his mentors, Tawney, and one of his ex-colleagues, Townsend.[4]

Child labour had a long history, as the Museum of Childhood itself demonstrates, but Michael himself never felt exploited at Dartington, the school which he attended from 1929 to 1933 during the depression years when large numbers of adults were 'out of work'. At the age of fourteen he was engaged, along with his fellow pupils, in three different businesses at once: he was not only labouring in the fields but learning something about business organisation, including double-entry bookkeeping. He also held one share (through Dartington School Bank) in an outside enterprise, United Molasses.

One of the three businesses, launched with a loan of £100, was a poultry farm, Darfowls Ltd., which supplied both the school and the market in nearby Totnes with eggs from a mixed flock of 200 White Leghorns and Rhode Island Reds. (The prices charged to the school were those prevailing in Totnes market, the first of the many markets that Michael was to encounter.) Getting up early and scraping droppings out of the hen houses was a regular task, almost as important to the business as marketing. There was one operation, however, that Michael found difficult to carry out – that of wringing the chickens' necks. This did not impede his business progress. At the end of a year's working, his poultry cooperative (the first of many cooperatives with which Michael was to become involved) paid a dividend of 4 shillings.[5] There is a file marked 'Poultry' in the Dartington archives, although it deals not with prices or with dividends, but with the hens themselves, including 'pre-potent cockerels', acquired from a farm in Massachusetts.

Michael was not as successful in the other two businesses, forestry and fruit farming, although he preferred the first to the second, a preference which would not have encouraged his Australian grandfather, who paid his first year's fees: he had done so because he had reflected that if Michael learned about apples, he could go on to establish himself as a fruit farmer in Tasmania and provide his grandfather with a congenial place to which to retire. For Michael the schoolboy it was good to munch cider apples as part of what his grandfather believed to be a vocational education. It was difficult, however, even with practical men to guide him – and there were practical guides, too, in poultry keeping – to prune the trees on which the apples grew. The first of his 'might have beens', dreamed of by his grandfather, not himself, never looked likely to be implemented.

What most appealed to Michael was repairing and selling second-hand motor cycles, an activity which required little expert tuition. On his first visit to Dartington in the summer before he arrived as a pupil he had been deeply impressed by the sight of Whitney Straight, Dorothy Elmhirst's son by her first marriage, riding a motor cycle; and it was on Michael's own initiative that he went into partnership with another boy to buy and sell them. He enjoyed revving his Triumph on the Devonshire hills – it had cost him 30 shillings – and trying to clip seconds off his own time record on the private roads of Dartington where no licence was needed. Outside the estate he rode an ordinary bicycle, a red Hercules, as fast as he could, for example to go to a cinema in Paignton or Torquay. Whitney, who flew an aeroplane at Dartington at the age of 13, was to become the youngest acting Air-Vice Marshal during the Second World War and a hero of pre-war motor racing. He was also in turn to be a Vice-Chairman of the British Overseas Airways Corporation, of Rolls Royce and of the Post Office. There was work as well as fun in this.

'Without ever ceasing to enjoy myself,' Michael declared years later, 'I gradually learnt year after year at Dartington a most important lesson, or rather the same lesson, several times over, about what I was *no* good at.'[6] There were other lessons. One was draughtsmanship, taught in the architect's office. The most important lesson of all was how to respond to new challenges. Michael had been encouraged, above all, to be adaptable. He used paraffin, not petrol, in his motor-cycle business, taking it from the electricity generator. After a year at Dartington he was awarded a scholarship – he jocularly called it a 'motor bykeship'– to continue his studies or rather his process of learning.[7] The process included making a pair of pyjamas for himself. They did not fit. The legs reached only just below his knees. He had made a mistake in the measurement. The girls at Dartington were particularly amused by his failure as a pyjama maker.

It seems right that Michael, who spent the early part of his childhood in Australia, was talking about his Dartington experiences – not in quite so much detail – to an Adelaide audience, many of whom, far from Academia, were familiar with the kind of childhood pursuits, if not pyjama making, that he was describing. Few of them, however, would have had the child-centred education which he had enjoyed. Leonard and Dorothy Elmhirst embarked on the foundation of their school as part of 'a more comprehensive venture to show that individuals of all ages could have their rights, in the broadest sense, as implied by the American Declaration of Independence'. Australia had had no such Declaration, although it had long been involved in the pursuit of happiness in its own fashion.

There was another element in Michael's own experience, involving a different continent, which influenced the content of 'The Shortening of Childhood and the Lengthening of Education', this time through contrast rather than through continuity. Michael was lecturing in Adelaide after spending most of the previous year in Nigeria, very unhappily, as Visiting Professor at Ahmadu Bello University.[8] The first story that he told his audience in the centenary seminar, which bore the title *Universities in a Rich and Poor World*, came not from England or Australia, therefore, but from Nigeria, where Hausa children were closely controlled by their parents. The family background of Michael's early childhood had been insecure. In Nigeria the family role seemed secure and established. Yet there had been a ten-day strike by university students in authoritarian Nigeria. Something had gone wrong, therefore, with the learning process. Had it not become separated both from the family and from learning?

Michael touched on many questions in his Adelaide lecture, but he held up one British example to his Australian audience, that of 'the new Open University', which allowed students to take degrees whenever they wished to do in their lives and to study for them at their own pace. It was, he said, 'removing or helping to remove some people from rule by the great dictators of modern society, the clock and the time table'.[9] Time, so prodigal in childhood, could no more be left out of a timed Young lecture than place. In this particular lecture, indeed, there was more emphasis on time than on 'openness'.

At Dartington 'openness' was put in a different context. The headmaster, W. B. Curry, who took up his post there while Michael was a boy, quoted H. G. Wells, who had offered the world 'the inspiring conception of the "Open Conspiracy" in [which] teachers may play a dominant part ... Its central idea is that the new world will be created not by politicians, but by men and women of good-will, in large and small groups throughout the world, undertaking the task of creation, wherever their influence extends.'[10]

Dartington, both as a place and as a social enterprise, is discussed in greater detail in a later chapter of this book.[11] For Michael it was the formative experience, and already by 1941 he was contemplating its history as well as its future.[12] For the Elmhirsts the school that they had planned four years before Michael arrived was designed to be 'a little world in itself, carrying on in a real, if elementary and simple way, the activities of the great world around it', and 'like the village community of earlier times, which was in many respects self-sufficing', it had to 'engage in many practical enterprises'.[13] The classrooms of the school were to be 'a farm, a garden, workshops, playgrounds, woods and freedom'. Learning should be through doing, and the Dartington estate was to be the school's workshop. And when classrooms were built in the 1930s, lessons were to be handled in the same spirit. Too many teachers in other schools, the Elmhirsts believed, were continually looking for 'the man in the child' without thinking of what he (or she) is before he comes a man (or woman).[14] And with this intent Dartington teachers set out to respond to children's own interests.

It was not this intent, however, nor the curriculum on offer, which first impressed Michael when, not quite 14, he went to look at Dartington in 1929. What most captivated him was the food. He felt that he had gone to live in a gingerbread house. 'I never felt hungry for four years. And what food. Apple sauce in great bowls for breakfast, piles of cornflakes and giant jugs of milk. Roast beef without gristle, crisp Yorkshire puddings. Bean shoots from China.' Michael could remember having had no sense of guilt that he was eating like this 'while most people in the world' were not even as well off as he had been at his previous schools where he had lived on bread and treacle. There he had always 'longed for the end of term ... Now ... I longed for the end of the holidays.'[15]

The food figured too in the reminiscences of Bertrand Russell's daughter, Kate, who arrived at Dartington five years after Michael with an initial 'terror', quickly lost when she began to feel 'the luxury of the place: a room to myself: delicious food'.[16] Russell's own views on education were set out in his books *On Education Especially in Early Childhood* (1926) and *Education and the Social Order* (1932). If 'knowledge wielded by love' were the basis of education, he claimed, 'the world could be transformed'.[17]

Like Russell – and A. S. Neill, headmaster of Summerhill, doyen of progressive educationists and a friend of Leonard – Kate herself was aware that 'all that American money' at Dartington 'made a difference', as it was to make a difference to Michael.[18] Neill, far away in Suffolk, wrote to Russell in 1931 of 'our millionaire friends at Dartington Hall'.[19] Several pupils came to Dartington from Summerhill, one of them, Dick Jennings, the co-owner of Michael's Triumph; and Neill addressed Dartington pupils and staff while Michael was a boy there. Neill wrote many books, some autobiographical, like his first, *A Dominie's Log* (1915), published in the year when Michael was born.[20]

Boys did not always behave as progressive headmasters wished, and the headmasters themselves were more aware of this than anyone else. While one of the boys who arrived at Dartington in the same year as Kate Russell, Peter Turner, unlike Michael 'a voracious reader', never saw any bullying by either pupils or teachers, others, like Lizzie Davies, a pupil from 1936 to 1941 and later on the staff, did: 'we were terribly bullied by older children'.[21] Michael encountered one of the few real bullies at Dartington in his time, and it was love of food that gave Michael his first nickname, Bell or Belly.

Michael had often been hungry, not only at the first of the two previous private schools he had attended at Bristol, where bread and black treacle had been the staple, but in his own home, where very little money was available for food. He remembered with horror too that before he went to school his grandparents had forced him to eat spinach which may or may not have had the effect of quickening his energies. At the first English private school which Michael attended second helpings were served on the principle of first come first served and there were no fair shares for all: every boy at a long table had an eye on the suet pudding served once a week, and delicate timing was required to get at it.[22]

Michael's Australian grandparents had not served as models for him. He was unhappiest with them, indeed, when both his mother and father were away. He was unhappy too when his parents left him on his own in a creaking timber country house not far from Melbourne, returning home between eleven o'clock and midnight. Before going out they always left behind them a candle which Michael prayed would last until their return. He counted numbers too, only falling asleep (or pretending to be asleep) after they were back. They were cross if he was awake.

We get many glimpses of Michael's early life from his mother's autobiography. She writes, for example, of their voyage across the Atlantic in 1917 – their way of reaching Australia – when baby Michael refused to let her out of his sight. One unforgettable memory for her was of before they set sail: she recalls Michael's 'protesting howl' when her Russian friend Grisha took the pram from her in Hale and 'shoved it up the path to the door'.[23] Michael was 'not so easily deceived as his father', who only learned later of the intimacy of that relationship. She sensed that Michael did not approve. The relationship ended when she made it clear to Grisha, in her own words, that she would never 'desert my son'.

It was a crucial decision for both her and Michael, who has memories of his own concerning particular incidents in his early life. Thus, he recalls vividly the scene when his father left Melbourne docks in 1924 and he thought that he would never see him again. He held tight in his hand two streamers, one yellow and one blue, that his father, following harbour rituals, threw from the deck of the ship on which he was to sail. The breaking of the streamers was a momentous symbol of parting. Yet this particular parting was not to be for long. His mother returned from Australia, but he could not feel very reassured even then, for when he saw his father, the only man who had been allowed to get on the ship before it landed (he had joined a small pilot boat), Michael's first act was to rush down to his mother, who had been having two affairs on the ship, to tell her of her husband's surprise arrival.

There had been one ultimate terror in Australia. While his father was in England Michael was afraid that he might be disposed of altogether by his parents. A local carpenter's family, very kind to him, wanted to adopt him. Michael did not want this to happen and made his views known strongly. It did not happen, but this did not prevent the carpenter from building him a paddle boat out of kerosene cans which on its first ocean trial, with Michael wielding the paddles, symbolically went straight to the bottom. Michael found this 'funny' while at the same time wanting to cry. There was some ambivalence in his attitudes towards his grandparents. He saw too much of them and hated to see his grandfather bullying his grandmother. He felt special gratitude to her – there was no ambivalence there – and he went on doing so.

Apart from separation and hunger Michael had experienced suffering, even cruelty, as a slightly older, somewhat sickly, child, a suffering that was thereafter associated in his mind with injustice. At his London elementary school, one of the two non-private schools which he attended – the first had been in Australia – he recalls his geography master 'standing like a Cyclops ... superimposing the edge of his ruler on the outstretched knuckles of any seven-year old who failed to remember the name of the river on whose banks Rome was alleged to stand' and 'seeing the little smile playing on his lips' before he felt the pain splitting through his hands. Enoch Powell, with his own Australian experiences, was to familiarise the British public with the name.

At his preparatory school in Bristol the headmaster, a classics graduate, left the running of the school to his senior master who was 'a tyrant corrupted by his own almost absolute power': he had 'courtiers' among the boys who fawned on him. All those boys who broke his rules or showed any spirit of defiance he forced to fall into the rear of daily crocodile walks through the city: their coats were turned inside out as a sign of disgrace. Behind the scenes the same master also flogged wrongdoers, who had to strip naked in front of fellow pupils. Their letters home were censored. Not surprisingly, Michael vowed at the age of eight to murder this tyrant if he ever met him again.

Michael's second preparatory school, The Grange at Cockfosters, north of London, a very small school, where one of his immediate contemporaries was Patrick, later Lord, Gibson, was much better, if, as Michael recalls it, more conventional;[24] and while he was there Michael's father, who he felt had hitherto paid little attention to him when he was very young, for the first time took a real interest in what he was doing. Michael was good at games – captain of cricket and soccer – and, indeed, school captain, and for the first time he was aware of family pride. Later, his father would take him into pubs, places that were to play a not unimportant role in his son's life. ('Children didn't seem to be kept out of them then.'[25]) It was Michael's mother, however, who was told by the headmaster when she asked about his future as he was leaving, that 'with the right kind of coaching he had the makings of a really good wicket-keeper'.

There were parental differences about what should happen to Michael next. His head thought that the Naval College at Dartmouth (coincidentally not far from Dartington) might be the best school to attend. His mother, who as in 1917 was a pacifist, was sure that this was wrong. Michael has memories of discussions about such topics and of a few of his meetings with his London grandparents. In 1924 he visited the British Empire Exhibition at Wembley with his grandfather, Daniel Dunlop, who in the same year organised the first of his series of World Power Conferences which was opened by the Prince of Wales.[26] This was a bigger event for his grandfather than Michael knew. It was, indeed, a triumph for Dunlop – and for Anthroposophy – for, as C. H. Gray, the first Secretary of the International Executive Council of the World Power Conference, appointed by Dunlop, put it, when Daniel described the Conference as 'the first' he was showing great vision: 'only his faith gave any grounds for thinking that it would not also be the last.'[27]

Dunlop was, in fact, busily planning Rudolf Steiner summer schools in Britain and discussing with Steiner the idea of a huge international anthroposophical world conference, and the fact that Michael knew little, if anything, of this or of the death of Rudolf Steiner in 1925 is curious. He certainly knew nothing of the Michael prophecy.[28] Instead, he recalls the Dunlops not only as his richest relations, but as his meanest. They seemed insensitive too. He remembers giving them as a Christmas present a little calendar that he had made and their immediately banishing it below a pile of papers that they kept in their lavatory. He also recalls a present that they gave him, a book, *Tales of Old Chelsea*, which was quite inappropriate for a boy of his age. Even *Tales of New Chelsea* would not then have been right.

Despite his belief in the Michael prophecy and his knowledge of Steiner schools, Dunlop does not seem to have taken any interest in the real Michael's education; and when Michael went to Dartington in 1929, a year of depression that tested the chances of survival even of the World Power Conference, Dartington was as far away from the world of the Dunlops as Bethnal Green then was from Michael's world. East London was off their map too.

Given the strength of Michael's feeling about life at Dartington, revealed in many statements made at many points in his life, it is equally revealing to turn to two statements concerning him which were written by his teachers at the end of his first term there. The first referred to his background as well as his aptitudes: 'Michael's parents are both of the Bohemian artist type ... [They] are living apart and the situation has always been difficult for the boy who all along has been quite aware of it.' And then came a surprising sentence, referring to a link between schools to which Michael has never referred in any of his interviews. 'He has been for four years at a small preparatory school run by my brother and only came to Dartington this term.'

The writer, who did not stay at Dartington for long, already appreciated him:

> He is an imaginative child with a great sympathy for the under-dog. He can become completely absorbed in any imaginative work he is doing and at the same time is quite an intellectual child. Having been educated more or less on conventional lines, he is not at all sure what he wants to do with his life, but he has thought considerably about it, since his future is precarious and he knows he must fend for himself. His school fees are at present being paid by his grandfather.

The writer had met Michael while he was at The Grange and had been told by him, not by his mother, that he wished to be either an explorer, a farmer, a diplomat or statesman (not politician). 'I think,' he went on, that 'he is too near the artist in himself to realise the pull that that side of him possesses. But he is certainly a boy who can understand others and whose development along social lines should be easy.'

This was a shrewd judgement.[29] Michael never lost his 'great sympathy for the underdog', and, wherever he has been and whatever he has done, there has always been 'an artist' inside him, an artist determined 'to bring out the artist in everyone'.[30] One of his own schoolboy paintings was of the modern house at Dartington which was to be commissioned for its first headmaster in 1932; it was exhibited in a Design Council exhibition in London in 1999.

A more detailed second school report on him – probably the first was written at mid-term – placed him within a group of his contemporaries, describing him as 'the best', a boy who 'sets a standard for them':

> He might very easily have got spoilt by his quite recognised superiority [the report goes on] but as far as one can see this has not happened. ... In the exams – partly owing to work done at his previous school – he ran a long way ahead of the rest. He comes out best in imaginative work, especially in Drama, in the writing and reading of poetry, and in essays or narratives on imaginative themes. He is not quite so good when asked to make a case for or against a thing, and his judgement is sometimes vitiated by sentimentality. This will be cured by reading, and he should read more widely.

It was quite a long time before Michael rectified this last failing, although he made up for it later. How good he was to prove to be in making 'a case for or against a thing' was to be tested frequently in his later life, although never as a barrister. And there were to be continuing and persistent signs of sentimentality.

The next paragraph in the report was even more to the point:

> He showed up excellently in an experiment I attempted in the last fortnight or so of term. The group ... responsible for all the work done with me (History, English, Social Studies, Philosophy), formed a cabinet with Michael as Prime Minister, planned the work, and took classes themselves, only referring to me when special help was needed. There was a certain amount of muddle and letting down, but much real enthusiasm, and many interesting things done which I could not myself have initiated. Michael is always on the spot, thinks ahead, and brings others back to the point.

The word 'ideas' does not figure in this judgement, but the word 'initiate' does. Michael was said to be 'popular with his contemporaries and with grown-ups', and to be 'a good captain and chairman, with plenty of common-sense and a pleasant sense of humour'. The words 'good captain' belong to the conventional language of school reports. There were not many schools in 1929, however, which would have paid attention on paper to the qualities of a boy of 14 as a chairman, let alone as a Prime Minister.

As far as 'individual subjects' were concerned, Michael, who to his delight had to study no more Latin and Greek after arriving at Dartington, had

> done some interesting craft work, a duck in stone, a lino-cut, some weaving, in all of which he has shown keenness, and has thought a lot for himself. He often attempts to do things ahead of his technical knowledge. Maths, though he has worked well and made good progress, have not been very satisfactory, as he has been working with an older group ... He has done very well in Music, attended most regularly and got quite absorbed in the work. He is doing some sight-reading and is learning to form chords.

As a professional musician Michael's father must have been satisfied when he read this last comment, and both his parents must have been relieved too to learn that 'his health has been good'. Throughout his life, boy and man, Michael suffered from asthma. When he arrived at Dartington he was, in his own words, 'very small for my age and puny and sort of ill',[31] but he gained eight pounds in weight in his first term, reaching six stones one pound, and an inch in height, making him five feet exactly.

Although there were school reports during the first years of Michael's life at Dartington, there was no headmaster and there were very few rules. Yet conventions and traditions were already taking shape there. Michael accepted them. He was something of a conservative rebel, therefore, when in 1931 Curry was appointed from across the Atlantic as Dartington's first headmaster, strongly supported by the Elmhirsts, who thought him 'not only a great educator' but (in American language) as 'an extraordinarily fine human being'. One pupil who did not like him – almost all pupils did – admitted that he was 'the mainspring' of the school. 'Until he came along it just wasn't a school. The real foundation year was 1931, much as we like to celebrate otherwise.'[32]

It was in 1931 that the senior school or 'main school', as it now came to be called, moved into new neo-Georgian buildings at Foxhole, designed by an English architect, Oswald Milne, who was not Curry's choice, and the nursery school moved into new buildings at Aller Park, designed by an American architect, William Adams Delano, who also designed Dorothy Elmhirst's home on Fifth Avenue, New York, and the South Portico of the White House.[33] Curry's house in steel and concrete, High Cross Hill, which now, well restored, serves as a 'showcase' for visitors and houses the Dartington archives, was described by an American in *Country Life* in 1933 as 'probably the most extreme instance in England of the functional type of house associated with the name of Le Corbusier'.[34] In Dartington itself, where Walter Gropius was to leave his impact, it had scathing critics and stalwart defenders.

When Curry arrived, Michael was less interested in new buildings than in the imposition by the new headmaster of a ban on firearms and motor-driven vehicles, including Michael's 'beloved Triumph'. Michael was not the only boy or girl to protest. Demonstrators sat on the roof of the school – forbidden territory – and threw pillows and food down on to the ground in front of the new head's study. 'He was dared to come up and get us down, which he very sensibly did not attempt.' This was, however, only a short-lived school revolution: it lasted only until supper time.[35]

Dartington pupils would not have found it easy to continue the revolution, for even if Curry was not quite the paragon that Dorothy believed him to be, he was difficult to dislike; and Michael, increasingly secure in Dorothy's love, already the right word, began to appreciate his qualities, even though he was eventually to become highly critical of him. He noted later how Curry got rid of all but two of the old staff, how he brought in new staff with good academic credentials, who proved to be good teachers; how he talked well, told amusing anecdotes and laughed loud and long – not least at his own jokes; and how in school affairs he introduced a greater element of democracy.

There was now a Council at Dartington over which Curry presided, curved pipe in hand, which met weekly, hearing complaints and framing what few rules were thought necessary. Curry liked to stimulate argument, considering children as his 'natural allies' – there was no such thing as a problem child, he believed, only a problem parent – and he carried most children along with him. His philosophy classes held in the evenings in his study were open to any child, and ranged over national and international politics as well as Dartington domestic issues. They may have given Michael a taste for philosophy which he never lost, and years later encouraged him to start taking a degree course in it at Birkbeck.[36]

The school for Curry was a community which was not a miniature copy of society as it was – or a preparation for that – but an example of what it should be:[37] and for him, it was a consequential decision, with an eighteenth-century flavour to it, to keep religion out of Dartington on the grounds that religion was not 'a natural appetite in children'. He believed in 'Reason' and in the inherent rationality of human beings, young and old. He believed also, nevertheless, in 'Sound Learning' which he was determined to promote, quoting Sanderson, the reforming nineteenth-century headmaster of Oundle, who in his last lecture had insisted that 'the modern school is not made by the very simple and easy method of abandoning Greek. Nor is it made by introducing Science and Engineering. The modern school does not depend on any method of teaching.'[38] For Curry, who wanted to leave the world a different place from that when he found it, a modern school was 'one which recognises that the social order must be radically changed if civilisation is to survive at all'.[39]

Known simply as Curry to all his pupils, he wrote eloquently on all these subjects, including one book which stimulated considerable attention, *The School and a Changing Civilisation* (1934). But he did not rely on print for his reputation. Under his headmastership school numbers rose from 51 pupils in 1931 to 124 in 1933 and 194 in 1938 – 131 boarders and 63 day pupils. His pupils continued to learn much from each other as well as from Curry and his staff, some of them highly talented. The outside public, which sometimes read about the school in popular newspapers, which in the 1920s and 1930s were fascinated by 'coeducation', then uncommon in private schools, was encouraged to believe that the pupils there, as in Neill's school, were 'revelling in sex'. This was a charge that amused rather than disturbed Michael and his friends, although according to one of them sex was 'one of Curry's headaches'. It was certainly not one of Michael's. He had a girlfriend, 'Irish, attractive', of whom he was fond, but he never 'slept with her'.[40] There were, in fact, few real 'scandals' in the Dartington of the 1930s.

Michael left Dartington in 1933 at the age of 18, a year before *The School and a Changing Civilisation* appeared, returning frequently between then and the outbreak of war, while Curry, a pacifist, was devoting so much attention to the cause of Federal Union, a militant political minority movement, that the school suffered.[41] The year when he left was, of course, a 'historic year' – the year of the advent to power of Hitler and Roosevelt – but it was not an easy year to move to London. One of Michael's contemporaries, Dougie Hart, who arrived in London at the same time – he had entered Dartington at the same time too, in 1929 – wrote unhappily of 'kicking the gutter', from which he was saved by Michael who encouraged him to go back to the Dartington estate and become a wood turner. His father had taught sculpture at Dartington before Curry arrived and had then lost his job.

Whatever his own uncertainties, Michael found more purpose in London than Dougie did, although not at once. He turned to the bar, rationalising later that in the law he would be able 'to use his argumentative abilities' to the full.[42] Perhaps that was an afterthought. The solicitors' firm that he joined in 1933, McKenna and Company, a large and successful business in Basinghall Street, had a direct connection with Dartington, and to that Michael owed his place in it. Fred Gwatkin, a partner in the firm, was legal adviser to Dartington.[43] One of Michael's best letters to Dorothy Elmhirst in Dartington describing his reactions to life in London was written from Grays Inn in 1934. Its common room he called 'rather an interesting place [where] old and fat men are sitting down in old black leather chairs to cups of tea and enormous sausage rolls. A Sikh with a blue turban is writing a letter; an African negro is reading *The Times*.'[44]

Michael's assigned task in the law firm, a task which he hated, had less to do with an understanding of the law than with its often unpleasant enforcement. He entered the debt collecting department – Harrods, the great retail store, was one of the McKenna clients – which, at the least, acquainted him fully with court procedures, including the issue of writs. (This, along with knowledge he acquired of the libel laws, was to help him when years later he launched the Consumers' Association.[45]) Characteristically, he sympathised more with the debtors, including those who had been involved in hire purchase, than with the concerns to whom they owed money – or, indeed, with his employers.

Collecting rents proved 'more fun': they included the rents from brothels, some of them owned by the Church Commissioners. There was only limited fun (a word he often used – and uses) in being a solicitor's clerk, and not surprisingly, the Bar beckoned. Yet his initial studies for the Bar he found boring – 'hopeless' he was to call them. Roman law (back to the classics) scarcely gave him an opportunity for developing his 'argumentative abilities', and there was far too much learning by rote. What he did enjoy was going to the Law Courts, where he spent as much time as he could, listening from the well of the Courts to barristers such as Sir Patrick Hastings, Sir Norman (later Lord) Birkett and Sir Stafford Cripps.

It was while studying law that Michael turned to the London School of Economics, his first university institution. Like many other people in London, most of them older than himself, he was to begin as an occasional, non-registered student, attending classes that he chose.[46] Some took place in the evenings, as at Birkbeck College, with which he was later to be closely associated.⁴⁷ He heard Cripps speak at LSE as well as in the Courts, 'dressed in barrister-black with a smart, spotted tie, the last person you would imagine to be a socialist ... He has a deep voice, of the type which impresses the Court of Appeal. And the personality of a leader.'⁴⁸ His Socialist League, committed to a left-wing Popular Front against Fascism, emphasised, in Michael's words, 'the importance of the middle class in the attainment of socialism'.⁴⁹

LSE was a place to meet people as well as to hear people, and very soon – the exact dates, like many other dates, remain vague in Michael's memory – he decided to take a B.Sc.(Econ.) degree. He did not attend any classes in sociology, which already figured (exceptionally) on the LSE curriculum, with Morris Ginsberg as Professor. Commercial law, the academic subject which drew him there, was taught him (well) by Robert (later, 1945, Lord) Chorley, Professor of Commercial and Industrial Law: it was far more interesting for Michael than Roman law. Some of the economics that he learned (with Abba Lerner as his tutor) he was to find useful later; and Harold Laski's politics lectures, deliberately argumentative in style and with frequent references to civil law, seemed to him more pertinent outside the lecture room than in the examination hall.

The subject which seems to have interested Michael most was social and economic history. He recalls H. L. Beales, pioneer of social history,⁵⁰ Eileen Power, whom I remember too as the most compelling lecturer on the subject that I ever heard,⁵¹ and 'the great Professor Tawney', with whom I too was to work closely as President of the Workers' Educational Association. Michael's debt to Tawney became more obvious after he had finished his LSE studies and taken his degree – and in 1982, while he was briefly associated with the new Social Democratic Party, he was to be the founding Chairman of a Tawney Society.⁵² Long before that, he had got to know Laski better, through the Labour Party, of which Laski was Chairman when Michael joined its Research Department in 1945. For a time a postgraduate student under Laski, he never became a Laski-ite like Ralph Miliband, who in the late 1950s, very different in mood from the 1930s, was to move into the 'New Left' and popularise, if not invent, the noun 'labourism'.⁵³

Michael heard the third member of Labour's intellectual trio also. G. D. H. (Douglas) Cole, long established in Oxford, visited LSE soon after Cripps, with whom Michael compared him, finding him at that time the more 'sincere' of the two. He was 'much quieter'. Yet Cole's belief in socialism seemed to Michael to be based more on his personal feelings than on political analysis. It would only 'come when the time is ripe'. Britain was not in a 'revolutionary situation'. 'Probably the Labour Party would enjoy more terms of office, filling the place of the Liberal Party and being rather more progressive than the Conservative Party before Socialism is reached.' At that time Michael, like many politically conscious undergraduates in the mid-1930s, was weighing the merits of socialism and communism, asking the question whether or not it was feasible to reach and uphold socialism by 'constitutional means'. How could Englishmen ever become revolutionaries when 'the educational machinery was in the hands of capitalists'?

The Elmhirsts were sent details of Michael's questions and the alternative answers he gave to them. Of one thing he was clear – and that was a matter of feeling. He could never 'shoot a "capitalist" or anyone else in cold blood'. As for his analysis, he found it inconclusive. 'How terrible,' he told Dorothy, in whom he confided everything, 'that Michael Young cannot decide! I cannot decide. I feel much more strongly drawn to the Socialist Party, but Communists are certainly more intelligent people.'[54] This was one of the most revealing letters that Michael wrote before he was 20. 'How can you be sure,' he asked in listing the Labour Party's arguments, 'that socialism is the most desirable state of society except by trusting in the decision of the majority?'

As keenly interested in politics before the Second World War as he was to be afterwards – and systematically listing 'pros' and 'cons' on every issue, as he continued to do – Michael found that LSE was the most congenial place for study, although again it was only later that he became aware of the range of its intellectual resources, in anthropology, for example, as well as sociology. He never heard Bronislaw Malinowski, although he heard gossip about him, and it was not until the early 1950s that he met Richard Titmuss, ten years older than himself, who was to supervise his LSE thesis after the war. Titmuss was not then associated with the LSE. After a very different education from Michael's, he had left school at the age of 15, and during the late 1930s was still 'acquiring industrial and commercial experience'. His influential little book, *Birth, Poverty and Wealth*, was to appear in 1943, written, as he put it, in 'the strutted basement of a London house during the bomb-littered winter of 1940–41'.[55]

In the course of Michael's undergraduate work, which was completed before he too lived through some of the same experiences, he still did not read much, but he read more than ever before. He also wrote more, fearing that the formal legal English required in solicitors' letters to debtors might ruin his prose style. He had no intimation that in 1968 an Assistant Lecturer in Sociology at LSE would write a learned article on debt collection, beginning with a sentence – and first sentences are always worth noting – that ran counter to most of Michael's ideas of writing and, perhaps, of debt-collecting: 'The sociological study of deviance seems to be most rewarding when it examines the deviant [debtor or debt collector] as part of a system which generates and enforces definitions.'[56]

Then and later Michael attached great importance to the art of writing. He had had one teacher at Dartington, Raymond O'Malley, who made him aware of how important this could be. O'Malley, who believed that sixth-form teaching was 'a matter in which the teacher must not dominate or predominate to excess', had been appointed in 1932 after an interview with Curry at the English Speaking Union in London.[57]

In London Michael made friends too, some of them people of a different kind from those whom he had met at school, and who had very different backgrounds from his own. His best friend was Ivan Moffat, son of Iris Tree and grandson of the actor Sir Herbert Beerbohm Tree, who lived in a flat in Fitzroy Square, and who, like Michael, joined the LSE – and the Communist Party.[58] Moffat, good-looking as well as clever, and an 'expert on wine and food', was 'successful with women', noted approvingly by Michael. He was a brilliant mimic and 'could make you laugh'. After the United States entered the war he joined the Documentary Film Unit of the American Army, and after the war ended he was to become a Hollywood scriptwriter: one of his film scripts was that of *High Noon*.

Michael's LSE friends, like Moffat, had futures ahead of them which were to be very different from the future which was to be his. Nor were they always futures which they themselves had expected. Yet their paths were often to cross. The friends included Victor Ross, who was to be a key figure in the London office of *Reader's Digest*; Jean (later Dame Jean) Floud, a future Principal of Newnham, three months younger than Michael, who for 15 years from 1947 to 1962 was a lecturer in sociology at LSE;[59] and Douglas Allen, who became a senior civil servant, ending his career as Permanent Secretary to the Treasury. Allen took a B.Sc.(Econ.) in 1938, the same year as Michael, and was to become a member of the House of Lords one year before him.[60] LSE was to make both of them Honorary Fellows in 1978.

It was Michael's non-curricular interests at LSE that absorbed him most – politics and a dash of sport, the latter the more unusual of the two activities at LSE, but one which was never missing from Michael's life. (Victor Ross was a member of the hockey team that Michael captained.) His sporting abilities – cricket as well as hockey – won him a few more votes in student elections than he would have secured on any straight political party ticket. For a few months in 1937 he was Joint Secretary of the Students' Union, having been involved in a heated debate about the junior treasurership; and he was also an officer of the Socialist Society, which at that time, as in Cambridge, was, in his words, a 'sort of pseudonym for Communist'; Jean Floud was its secretary, and Moffat its junior treasurer. In February 1938 he handed in notice of a motion to be debated in the Union, urging the government to do all in its power to preserve the independence of Austria and Czechoslovakia.

Michael and his mother were both members of the Holborn Communist Party, which at that time would have supported the motion, but as a university student he was encouraged by those who pulled the strings of power inside the Communist Party, like James Klugmann, to work from inside the Labour Party. In 'Popular Front' times there were many causes to support, foreign more than domestic, that pulled rank-and-file Socialists and Communists together. The tactic did not appeal to leaders of the Labour Party like Herbert (later Lord) Morrison, who drew strength from the Labour Party's power base in London. For him, the reason why the North St. Pancras by-election in 1937 had been lost by Labour was 'student support of the Communist Party'. Michael, however, had noted that attendances at Labour Party meetings in the constituency were 'ridiculously low' and that it was Communists who 'seemed to be doing most of the work'.[61] Like many of his contemporaries, who shared these views, he thought of going to Spain to join the Republicans in the Civil War, but, given his health, it is no surprise that he was turned down as a volunteer soldier.

Dartington had not prepared him for that – any more than for shooting capitalists in cold blood. Nor perhaps had it prepared him for London life, which in its very different way was just as unconventional as life in Dartington. He was sensitive to its sights and sounds – and even to its graffiti. Passing Madame Tussaud's waxworks in 1936, he noted one piece of advice scribbled on the wall: 'Put Baldwin and Hitler in the Chamber of Horrors'. He went back to Dartington as often as he could, however, and once after a record return trip to London, 'record, that is, for my motor-cycle', in '5 hours 45 minutes', he wrote simply, 'London's rather unpleasant'. During the summer of 1937 he met Labour activists far from London, in Cornwall, including agricultural labourers, surprisingly 'receptive to political propaganda'. There, one 'big raw-boned fisherman' told him that under pressure 'Major Attlee and Herbert Morrison would behave in the same way as Ramsay MacDonald and Jimmy [sic] Snowden' had done in 1931. 'Leaders always let down the rank-and-file.'[62] Such words were not forgotten by Michael.

While studying in London, Michael lived briefly in a flat of his own, his first, in Regent Square next door to John Strachey. He then shuttled backwards and forwards between his father and his Bohemian mother who took a flat in Bloomsbury to 'provide him' with what in conventional language she called 'a home'. Also in her own words, it was a home where 'a stink of tomcats and garbage cans in backyards hit you in the face as soon as you entered the oak panelled hall to climb to our two rooms'. It was very different from the house in Cheyne Row where she had been given a room by her father after her mother's death. She scarcely saw her Anthroposophical father except at breakfast on Sundays, but from her room there she had been able to catch a glimpse of the River Thames. Now, owing to 'her communistic outlook', she found herself losing two out of the four WEA classes which provided her with a small independent income and was driven 'to rely on writing for a living'.[63] Some of her 'men', Michael recalls, were 'less forthcoming than others': one, Philip Henderson, a William Morris scholar, made him pay for his food when the three of them had lunch together.[64]

In her autobiography Edith Young recalled one conversation with Michael that might have come straight out of Anthony Powell. They were discussing why he had decided to take up law as a profession. '"I don't suppose",' he is said to have said, 'smiling quizzically and scratching his brow [body language, including shrugging, that has persisted] "I shall practise as a barrister. A law degree is simply a means to an end; useful for a political career, or for any other profession I may choose later in life".' '"You're determined to succeed?"', she asked him, '"I am, if I can", he confessed. "I've seen enough of you and Gibson to know that your bohemian way of life is not for me. I'm ambitious. I want to leave my mark on life." "Good for you! I'm all for it providing your health can stand the strain." "You don't really approve, do you?" he questioned. "You're disappointed? You'd prefer me to be an artist?" "I believe in you implicitly, Michael"', she replied. '"It's natural that you should react against your parents. I have enough faith in you to know that whatever you do, you will do well."'[65]

It may have been around this time that Michael's Aunt Florence, now living in Achimota, suggested that if he 'went into painting' she might be able to get a job for him there. Yet it was only years later that

Africa was to beckon him. And it was not until 1951 that he was to revisit his relatives in Australia. In 1938, however, Michael's father, with whom he had spent a considerable amount of time in London, returned to Australia, leaving what Michael told Dorothy and Leonard Elmhirst was an 'extraordinary gap': 'I didn't realise it before.'

Gibson had told Michael before he left that he would avoid shipboard 'social activities', but by the time he reached Gibraltar, 'he had been elected to all the Committees'. Before getting off the ship, a 'miracle' had happened: he had found 'a cure for his asthma'. His friend the Reverend Dick Sheppard, formerly Vicar of St. Martin in the Fields and then a Canon of St. Paul's, who had invited him to organise community singing outside the Cathedral on New Year's Eve, had given him a farewell gift, a vaporiser with an electric motor, a German invention. It was not a cure, but it relieved Gibson as it had greatly relieved Sheppard.[66] It was to relieve Michael too. Bronchitis was another of Michael's problems.

One of the London events which Michael had attended in order to hear and see his father (wearing morning dress) was in Hyde Park – a Jubilee Thanksgiving Service in 1935. He had 'kept off the patriotic stuff', but had 'told the people they were privileged to be singing the hymns that the R had chosen specially for the service:'[67] 'I have become used to writing R for the King as the result of learning criminal cases R v Beard,' he told Dorothy and Leonard. In the same letter describing the Service to the Elmhirsts Michael described canvassing for the Peace Ballot, which he had 'enjoyed very much'. The 'general impression' he gained was of 'the amazing stupidity of the ordinary man and woman': 'the children under 16 often had to explain the object of the Ballot to their parents'. 'Our results were quite good – 66 per cent.' '"What is the League of Nations?" we were asked again and again.'

Michael sent an article on the Jubilee Procession to the *New Republic* in the United States, which had published an earlier piece by him on Karl Marx's grave at Highgate, a London suburb where he was to live between 1949 and 1952. In a letter he compared the 'usual Communist May Day demonstration' – with a slogan 'All Out on May Day against the War Menace' – and the Labour Party's May procession the following Sunday, contrasting both with the Royal Jubilee drive to St. Paul's. He watched this from Fleet Street, treating it, like the May Day demonstrations in Moscow, as 'magnificent propaganda'. His reactions were very different from those which he was to express years later at the time of Queen Elizabeth's coronation. Now, after noting how Princess

Elizabeth 'smiled and bowed' (and her mother looked even more 'gracious'), he felt that she 'would obviously benefit from a course at Dartington'.

'It does not make one like another person any more,' he concluded, 'to realise that he (or she) is the product of his environment, etc.' He referred to George V, 'King-Emperor', 'eyes fishily bulging out of an emaciated face', as 'Poor man!' The uniforms did not impress him. The cavalry were clad in gaily coloured uniforms and bearing lances decorated with pennants 'merely to give people the impression that War was a matter of lances and brave flags'.[68]

Michael liked 'events', but he did not find it easy to carry out his studies in Great James Street, Bloomsbury, and in not unconventional fashion he moved for a time to live in Toynbee Hall in London's East End, appearing on the residents' list for the first time in November 1933. Among the other residents were J. A. R. Pimlott, first historian of Toynbee Hall – and author of much else besides, including his pioneering book *The Englishman's Holiday* (1947)[69] – and S. J. de Lotbinière, educated at Eton and Trinity College, Cambridge, who was to have a distinguished career (which had already taken off) with the BBC.

In 1933 Michael went to the Derby with Pimlott – both were wearing berets, not top hats – 'really a great experience' although rain drenched the course. The bookmaker with whom he had placed a winning bet in the main race decamped with 'my and other people's money'. Michael kept his betting book and cards as souvenirs. On this same visit he saw the Wall of Death 'where gum-chewing men and a super-tough girl do the most extraordinary stunts with motor cycles on a vertical wall', and watched pale men with bowler hats wend their way through the crowd with religious texts. 'The wicked shall perish in everlasting fire. Repent ye.' He also saw Prince Monolulu, 'a noted tipster', who nearly always turned up at Communist and other demonstrations in Hyde Park and drew a bigger crowd than the speakers.[70]

Toynbee Hall, then under the lively leadership of its much loved Warden, Jimmy Mallon, thought of itself as an active settlement community in the midst of the local East End community with which it interacted. There 'is no limit to the extent of the participation of the Settlement', we read in the Report for 1937–8.[71] One of the lecturers Michael may have heard at Toynbee Hall's famous Enquirers' Club was Sir William (later Lord) Beveridge, one of the most distinguished former residents and Sub-Wardens of the Hall, who in 1937 had left LSE, where he was Director, in his last years a very unhappy Director, to become Master of University College, Oxford.

Beveridge lectured on 'The Immediate Future of Unemployment', drawing more on what he had written about unemployment in the past than anticipating what he was to say about it in the future.[72] Michael had had dinner at LSE with him (and Mrs. Jessy Mair, the future Lady Beveridge) once, when he met the economist David Champernowne, five years older than himself and 'incredibly shy'.[73] While Michael was in Toynbee Hall Harold Wilson was already working for Beveridge as a research assistant (in 1938), and Pimlott's son, Ben, was to include a chapter called 'Beveridge Boy' in his biography of Wilson.[74]

Michael, who left Toynbee Hall in December 1935, had returned in March 1938 when he was preparing for his B.Sc.(Econ.) finals. Between these two dates he shared Moffat's flat in Fitzroy Square: 'walls distempered buff; grey book cases and cupboards; blue table and bed cover; a red door; red and green cushions; brown carpet; solid books'. 'I like spending the afternoons here.' He also travelled abroad – with help from the Elmhirsts and in the company of Michael Straight – visiting Russia, for example, in August 1935, travelling on a Russian ship, *Sibier*, which was characterised by 'an atmosphere of efficiency' (Michael gave no reasons for the choice of this word, and noted, for example, that the lavatories were dirty and few.) What impressed him most was that first class passengers allowed passengers from the rest of the ship to use many of their facilities. There was an air of 'casualness' and it was all 'very friendly'. Inside Russia his impressions were 'favourable' too. It seemed a 'sane' country (again an odd choice of adjective) with 'reasons for all things' (Curry could have asked for no more), but he had no desire to live there: 'it is a land for melancholy and homesickness.'[75]

Michael's studies for the Bar and for his B.Sc.(Econ.) degree overlapped, and after graduating in 1938 he remained associated with LSE until the outbreak of war. The School was now under a new Director, Alexander (later Sir Alexander) Carr-Saunders, who was an authority *inter alia* on social surveys and who steered the School across uncharted seas. Soon after the outbreak of war it left London for Cambridge, and if Michael been a little younger he would have been part of the exodus. He visited Cambridge on more than one occasion before 1939 to meet Michael Straight who was studying there, but his own direct experience of Cambridge was to come much later. As it was, during the summer of 1939 he was called to the Bar, but the imminence of war prevented him from going into Chambers and trying his hand at being a barrister. Instead, he had a stroke of luck, the kind of luck the value of which he was never to minimise, and once again it was luck that was dependent on his Dartington connection.

Convinced even before the Munich agreement of 1938 that war was near – Michael wrote as early as the summer of 1937 that 'we no longer talk of the next war. The world is already at war'[76] – he felt that he had to sort out his own future. After Munich his legal studies seemed irrelevant to him – and, indeed, to the world. For advice he turned to Max Nicholson, then General Secretary and Editor of Publications of the independent fact-finding and research organisation, Political and Economic Planning (PEP), a man of imagination and vigour who had strong Dartington connections.

Nicholson had been one of PEP's co-founders in April 1931, when the decision to set it up was taken at a conference in Dartington while Michael was a schoolboy, and he had been the author of a 'National Plan' for Great Britain, PEP's inspiration.[77] Born in 1904, he had a long and diverse career ahead of him and, among many things, he was a distinguished ornithologist and in 1980 was appointed President of the Royal Society for the Protection of Birds, a remarkably impressive voluntary organisation, greatly admired by Michael, who thought of it as a model.

PEP named its series of broadsheets *Planning*, and although the word 'planning', then as later, had different meanings even for different members of PEP, all of them agreed that planning was necessary 'to enable the best standard of living to be achieved in every changed situation'.[78] There was 'middle-way' consensus on this. As another co-founder of PEP, Leonard himself in its first year had paid the salary of its first General Secretary and subsequent historian, Kenneth Lindsay, who had known and admired Dorothy Elmhirst before she married Leonard, and in a later phrase of Michael had 'prepared the way for Leonard's courtship'.[79] Lindsay, born in 1897, had been President of the Oxford Union from 1922 to 1923. He lived at Toynbee Hall from 1923 to 1926. He became an 'Independent National' MP in 1933. Leonard served as a member (sometimes Chairman) of the Executive of PEP from 1931 to 1972.

In 1938 Nicholson proved to be the *deus ex machina* for Michael, who eagerly offered to work for him for nothing. First, he persuaded him that he should continue with his studies for the Bar, war or no war; and next, in the lead-up to war after Munich, he invited him, perhaps seeking to humour him, to write a piece for PEP on manpower policy in wartime. Michael treated this as a heaven-sent opportunity, and rushing down to LSE buried himself in a book on manpower policy during the First World War that was recommended to him by the ever helpful LSE Librarian.[80] It dealt mainly with a sequence of official mistakes between 1914 and 1918. Michael also talked in the LSE tearoom to a German refugee economist, Erwin Rotbarth, who was later to become Keynes's assistant.

Michael was a quick writer when the motivation was strong, and he finished off his piece by midnight, choosing a familiar mode of transport, the bicycle, to deliver it to Queen Anne's Gate. He was subsequently to describe what he had written as 'the most influential paper I have ever published'.[81] It was certainly an ambitious piece of writing on a subject of national importance in which Nicholson wished PEP to be involved. He wanted it to be presented in the form of a report to Lord Perth to whom the Prime Minister, Neville Chamberlain, then a villain in Michael's political scenario – there were many others, far more villainous, to follow – had given the far from easy task of making preparations for war behind the scenes. Michael's piece went to the point at once, urging that from the start the armed forces should be recruited by conscription, not by volunteering – no white feathers this time – and that 'reserved occupations' should be scheduled, with those people directly and indispensably involved in the war effort being denied permission to serve in the armed forces.

There was little that was entirely original about Michael's line of thinking in 1938, although there was both in the manner in which he produced his piece and in the trenchant style in which it was written. There were some civil servants and some politicians who were already advocating the measures he recommended. To begin with, however, there was dragging of feet. Unemployment actually rose between September 1939 and March 1940, and it was not until 1941, after a number of 'crises', that there was full realisation of the implications of a manpower policy which would involve manpower budgeting and the conscription of women.[82] By 1945 Britain is said to have had 'the most substantial and comprehensive allocation of its manpower resources of any combatant nation, with the possible exception of the Soviet Union'.[83]

Michael's 1938 paper was published by PEP as one of its *Planning* broadsheets, by then well known and often highly influential. They were produced by voluntary groups, which often included civil servants, and they bore no one's name. Lindsay called their producers 'a living chain of men and women with a will and a purpose'. They covered a wide variety of themes throughout the mid- and late 1930s in what Lindsay described as 'a crusade for continuous change', and they were circulated to subscribers and – it was an essential part of the remit – to people who 'mattered'. *Planning* No. 133 obviously 'mattered', and it was printed within 150 yards of the PEP office with as much speed as it was written.[84] Nicholson immediately sent a copy of it to Lord Perth, and as a result, Michael was offered a job inside Perth's small unit.[85] A few days later, however, he was told that because of his Communist record he could not join it. 'My politics were against me. Researches [sic] disclosed a black mark against my name.'

In disguise this may have been another stroke of luck, for Nicholson offered him an alternative employment at PEP which 'tremendously excited' him, and he was now free to go on researching – in his own way – and writing quite independently.[86] PEP's executive approved his appointment, and in August 1939 he became Personal Assistant to Nicholson, staying on as a PEP Research Assistant at 16 Queen Anne's Gate, the PEP headquarters, after Nicholson had moved from there to Whitehall. The next PEP pamphlet in which Michael was directly involved, *Planning* No. 153, *The Home Front*, was published one month after war broke out. *Planning* No. 156, very pertinently, was to be called *The Role of Research*.

Michael's war-time years were productive, and they were not all of one piece. He was rejected for military service because of his asthma, and there were several occasions during the War, as in 1941, when he had to write that he had been 'ill for a fortnight with my usual bronchial flu'.[87] Yet there were compensations. The handsome house in Queen Anne's Gate was a good place in a good location to make contacts and to discuss issues – not far from Westminster and Whitehall. It also had a club and a bar. PEP members belonged to different parties or to none, and in the year before Michael discussed his future with Nicholson it had produced four major reports as well as its broadsheets – *International Trade* (1937), *The British Social Services* (1937), *The British Health Services* (1937) and *The British Press* (1938). All were influential, particularly the third, which pointed to a 'comprehensive' national health service, and the last, which was the only comprehensive account of the newspaper industry to be published before 1939.

Already in 1939 PEP was deeply interested not only in Britain but in the future shape of Europe and of the world after war ended, the theme that was increasingly preoccupying Curry. Several weeks before war was declared, a Post-War Aims Group was established, not formally incorporated within PEP but drawing on its expertise and methodologies. The drive behind this Group was strong. Planning for war, which had already begun, gave opportunities to the planners that they had never enjoyed during the early 1930s and strengthened the case for planning after the war. It also provided invaluable experience of how it might be carried out.

Once war had been declared, with Chamberlain as Prime Minister, it was believed that the more attractively the post-war prospect was presented to the public the stronger would be the national desire for victory. At the same time, the Labour Party also was preparing a pamphlet, *Labour's Aims in Peace and War*, demanding that 'while planning the war, the Government must plan for peace and a new society ... After the war, the national war effort must be turned to the building of a new Britain.'[88]

These were 'brave words', and there was certainly no sense of a 'phoney war' at Queen Anne's Gate after the war had begun. Instead, there was a release of energy. Michael was one of the drafters of a pamphlet on *European Order and World Order* which attracted the attention of Chamberlain's Foreign Secretary, Lord Halifax, who was always sympathetic to PEP, and who wrote later in the year that he was 'quite certain that the human conscience in this country is not going to stand for a system that permits large numbers of unemployed'.[89] The other draftsmen included Lindsay, R. H. S. Crossman and Julian Huxley, who in 1945 was to be appointed first Director-General of UNESCO, a by-product of the war: a regular member of the BBC's war-time *Brains Trust*, he was always a welcome guest at Dartington.[90]

The urgency in PEP's messages to the public – and to government – at this time is well conveyed in *Planning*, No. 157, *Reconstruction, 1916–19*, which looked back, as Michael had done in *Manpower Policy*, to the First World War. While it was 'incontestable' that 'winning the war must come first', the pamphlet stated, 'planning for subsequent reconstruction' already had 'a great part to play':

> Men are moved by ideas, and no dictator has yet produced, or is likely to produce, a secret weapon in any way comparable with the military power of a compelling idea compellingly stated ... The Nazis have never made the mistake of neglecting to plan ahead or of underrating the force of ideas, and it is these qualities, rather than any material advantages, that have enabled them to seize the initiative from military powers controlling a far larger share of the world's human and material resources.

These comments on National Socialist planning, while not uncharacteristic of war-time thinking, were wide of the mark. None the less,

Michael was right to draw attention to the limitations of improvisation. However brilliant, it could not take the place of planning.[91] Nicholson was convinced that this was the right approach. He wanted the planning to be concerned with bigger units than the nation. In his *European Order and A World Order*, he looked forward to 'some form of federalism' in Europe after the war, just as Curry was looking forward to world federal union.

Nicholson was then bobbing backwards and forwards from Queen Anne's Gate to London University's Senate House which had been converted into the new Ministry of Information, but he was soon to move again – in April 1940 – to the Ministry of Shipping. He never stayed out of Queen Anne's Gate for long, nor did Britain's outstanding retailer, Israel (later Lord) Sieff, partner of Simon (later Lord) Marks in the most highly successful of Britain's retailing businesses, Marks and Spencer. Before and after the war Sieff helped to finance the flow of ideas in PEP, and Michael was to have many talks with him, by 1944 writing that he had now got to like him 'much more than I did before'. 'He seems full of ideas and is very keen that PEP should play its full part.'[92] Next to service to Weitzmann and to the new State of Israel, created after the war, Sieff was prouder of being an original member of PEP than of anything in his life. He was to write in his *Autobiography* of Nicholson's zealous 'application of the intellect to the everyday pressing affairs of men ... blue printing a path to real progress, not preaching theoretical pie in the sky.'[93]

As Arthur Marwick, first Professor of History at the new Open University, was to note a generation later, such a tribute to PEP must be set in context. In seeking to identify areas of agreement PEP was not alone, but unlike some of the other bodies seeking to uncover them it wished to avoid 'dissipation of energies in forming local branches, in holding public meetings and in propagandist activity'.[94] None the less, it was difficult to sound or to appear so detached when the Second World War entered into 'an entirely new phase', as Michael's second broadsheet on *The Home Front*, No. 168, put it (if, remarkably, still mutedly) in the early summer of 1940 after Hitler had invaded the Low Countries and France.

At that time the most familiar voice in the country after that of the new Prime Minister, Winston Churchill, was that of the novelist and playwright J. B. Priestley, who would never have thought that he was dissipating his energies when he embarked on various forms of 'propagandist activity'. Ironically, some of PEP's earlier talk of reconstruction, echoed by Beveridge,[95] had appealed more to members of

Chamberlain's Government, particularly Halifax and R. A. (later Lord) Butler, then an Under-Secretary at the Foreign Office, than it appealed to Churchill, who remained suspicious throughout the War of too much attention being devoted to war aims or to what should happen after victory.

A third phase of the War began after German hopes of invading Britain had faded and Hitler launched an air blitz on London in the autumn of 1940. Living through the daily dangers of 'the Blitz' stimulated Michael for the first time to feel the power of 'solidarity', a feeling that was to shape much of his own post-war thinking and writing. Working in premises which were themselves damaged by air attack – with a greatly reduced staff – Michael was deeply moved by the reactions of Londoners to the Blitz, which at the time were being chronicled by Mass-Observation, another of the innovatory organisations of the 1930s, founded by Tom Harrisson, Charles Madge and Humphrey Jennings in 1937. Madge was to work closely with Michael long after the War when much had changed in both their lives.

For Michael, as for Harrisson, the Blitz was no myth, as some historians have judged it subsequently.[96] It set the terms of his daily life. He was fortified, however, by the fact that Leonard Elmhirst had become Chairman of PEP in October 1939 and that in February 1941 there was an internal reorganisation of PEP which gave him new responsibilities.[97] For a time François Lafitte, only two years older than he was, worked at his side: he was an experienced member of PEP's small staff when Michael arrived. Lafitte, serving on the PEP Executive from 1943 to 1953, was to remain its Deputy Secretary of PEP until 1943, when he started writing regularly for *The Times* on social policy issues. He went on doing so until 1959, when he was appointed Professor of Social Policy and Administration at the University of Birmingham, where he became Dean of the Faculty of Commerce and Social Science in 1965. In 1945 he published *Britain's Way to Social Security*. He was Chairman of PEP research groups on health from 1943 to 1946 and on housing policy from 1948 to 1951.

A month before the reorganisation, Dorothy Elmhirst, visiting London from distant Dartington, as she infrequently did, was struck by the contrast between the grimness of the conditions in which Michael was working and his strength of spirit. She called him 'Michael Youngster' – he had usually signed himself 'Youngster' in his pre-war letters to her – to distinguish him from her son of her first marriage, Michael Straight, and found that at PEP headquarters boards had had to be substituted for windows and that the back windows of the dining room were bricked in. 'Lunch takes place in the lower front room, and there I had a gay meal with Youngster. His report on London has at last been released by Max and now there is hope of publishing it.'[98] The report, *London under Bombing*, was the longest draft that Michael had ever produced. It was the first broadsheet to appear following a brief interruption of the series because of paper shortage and publishing restrictions. Regular publication of *Planning* was resumed in February 1941.

In order to write *London under Bombing* Michael had been involved in 'action', his word, as well as research. 'The most interesting' of his experiences was 'a week spent in the East End with the Friends' Ambulance Unit, who are doing all kinds of welfare work in the districts most being bombed'. For part of the time he acted as an assistant on 24-hour shifts at a Rest Centre.[99] His report also drew on 'information' derived from the formidable, controversial writer on military topics, Basil (later Sir Basil) Liddell Hart, who stayed at Dartington early in the War in part of a furnished house at a very low weekly rent – 'a characteristically generous act on the part of the Elmhirsts'.[100] Liddell Hart made a mistake, not his only one, in thinking that Dartington itself would be bombed.

Before writing the report – and producing a popular shortened version of it for Americans – Michael had given what Dorothy called 'a wonderful talk' at a Sunday evening meeting at Dartington on the problems arising out of the bombing.[101] He drew a familiar general conclusion from his experience. 'Improvisation seems to have worked again, after a fashion ... But improvisation will not take the place of planning, although I imagine that ability to improvise in an unplanned and therefore overflexible system is one of the advantages of a democracy at war.'[102]

As Michael warmed to his themes in his Report – and doubtless in his talk – he introduced specific points of his own, noting inequality in bombed London as well as solidarity. Against the background of 'the drone of bomber engines, the barrage reaching blindly upwards, the bombs tearing the sky, and the final explosion', it was a 'prosaic fact' that the richer London boroughs had excelled with their ARP (Air Raid Precautions) while the poorer boroughs had not. 'Westminster and Kensington ... have been noteworthy for the high standard of their civil defence arrangements, while Stepney has been as noteworthy for its failures.' This was a matter not of will but of wealth.

In face of what he had seen for himself, Michael used his imagination to foresee the possibility of a simplified post-war London government in which the nine wartime ARP groups would be converted into nine electoral districts of a new London Regional Council. He used his imagination too to hint that in order to relieve future transport congestion in London there might be a peacetime follow-through to the 'Help your Neighbour' scheme for motorists – and drivers of motorcycle combinations – living within a 20-mile radius of London. The Ministry of Information, where Kenneth (later Lord) Clark was Controller of Home Publicity during the Blitz, immediately ordered 2,000 extra copies of the broadsheet, and PEP's paper ration was increased.

Whatever the future might hold, there were compensations for PEP and for Michael even in the grim present. On the night of the same visit by Dorothy in 1941 they had walked through parts of London 'with a jagged skyline of broken buildings' above them and, in her words, 'only the sound of your own footsteps in the silent streets'. It was 'like making one's way through a city of the dead. But suddenly we slipped round a corner and through an alley and, there we were, in the warmth of the Brewery shelter – about two or three hundred people in all, sitting on their mattresses or, in some cases, in chairs.'[103] A PEP publication of 1941, *Planning* No. 178, *The New Pattern*, emphasised the neighbourliness of war-time London and the sense of participation. Unfortunately, it went on to observe, education was still a barrier to 'the ideal of learning together': there was 'a fatal class cleavage in the public education system'.

There must have been a marked contrast for Dorothy and Leonard between blitzed London, where Michael lived in Grafton Way in the West End from 1940 to 1949 and where Dorothy kept her apartment, and the bright American cities which the two Elmhirsts visited frequently, lecturing to packed audiences on what life was like on this side of the Atlantic. The first of the trips was made by Leonard, alone, in 1941. A much-read PEP broadsheet, *America and Britain, Planning* No. 171, which appeared in June of that year, before Pearl Harbor, offered a link between the two worlds. It found hope, as Churchill did, in multiplying 'the threads which bind us' and 'creating an inevitable vested interest [would Michael have used this phrase?] among the people of both nations in the continuous strengthening of those ties'. The Atlantic Charter of 12 August 1941, drafted by Prime Minister and President, had some of the qualities of a manifesto. It suggested a more active democracy devoted to common purposes.

By the time that *America and Britain* (*Planning*, No. 182) appeared – and a later broadsheet on *Britain and Europe* – Michael had left Queen Anne's Gate to work in a munitions factory housed in a quarry on the edge of Swindon, owned by the Sperry Gyroscope Company. It was, in his words, a 'key factory in a key area'.[104] 'I have felt keenly,' he wrote to a colleague of Dartington, Kay Starr, before moving there, 'my practical ignorance of industry in my recent work at PEP'. He was quickly plunged into it, given 'scope too for executive action while some of the gaps in [his] education [curiously he called it 'an academic education'] were being filled in'. Michael knew finally and definitely by June 1941, the month of Hitler's attack on the Soviet Union, that he would never be able to join any of the Armed Services or the Merchant Marine – after receiving call-up papers he had failed a medical examination – and in the circumstances he did not judge that it was 'right to sit out my time in the PEP'. He hoped, however, to return to it.

There was much talk then and later in 1941 of an 'industrial front' (before there was talk of a 'second front' to help the Russians), and Michael wanted to be present on or near that particular front-line. The firm he was joining was producing power-operated turrets for guns on small motor torpedo boats. Michael's dreams were more varied than this, however. He even contemplated preparing a series of bulletins on industrial change parallel to the highly successful sequence of bulletins of the Army Bureau of Current Affairs (ABCA), widely discussed by soldiers in their barracks or camps. Moving to Swindon was a jolting experience. 'My life has been so extraordinary since I left London,' he told Kay Starr, soon after arriving there, 'that I have been unable to take stock or to get myself in perspective.'[105]

What most interested Michael was visiting shipyards, where the motor torpedo boats were built, and he would have preferred to be driving one of the boats himself. The person offering him a job 'was not very precise about its nature', but mentioned that to begin with he could spent 'a month on the bench' if he wished and that he could be called 'Assistant Personnel or Personnel Manager'. At the start he was designated a 'progress chaser', directing the production process; and this, a far more interesting label, was one of the most apt of the many designations of him during his long life, not least when he was Chairman of the Social Science Research Council. Years later – by one of the many coincidences in Michael's life – the SSRC was to set up its headquarters in Swindon long after Michael had left it.

'Progress chasing' involved keeping an eye on all questions relating to performance and output, but from the day of his arrival at the factory, housed in a temporary building in a quarry, Michael found himself with the extended responsibilities that had been hinted at. The factory's Labour Manager – Michael did not like that particular designation – had been taken ill, and at the age of 24 Michael was asked to step into his shoes. One of his tasks was to 'acquire labour', implementing part of the agenda he had discussed in national terms in *Manpower Policy*, for about 500 new workers were being recruited each year, many of them women.[106] Some of the key workers were gas fitters, who required to be trained in plumbing, and more than 400 of them were being employed by the firm when Michael left it in March 1942. Only at weekends could he pursue progress chasing single-mindedly into its final phase, abandoning Swindon to sample the uncertain seas of the English Channel.

Michael enjoyed his managerial responsibilities, but disliked bargaining with trade unions ('I was with them really'). It is sad that he did not write an account at the time of what he was doing – as Celia Fremlin of Mass-Observation successfully did at a munitions factory not far away in Malmesbury. He knew that before his arrival the South Western Divisional Controller of the Ministry of Labour said that he had problems all around him, but he was too busy to record his impressions. He was learning for the first time in his life how to work really hard – for up to 12–14 hours a day – a fact which in itself cannot have endeared him totally to trade unionists even in war-time. The main comment of the *Daily Herald* on conditions at Malmesbury as described by Mass-Observation was that 'the girls were grossly – and it would seem indefensibly – overworked'.[107]

In noting this reaction the Labour Party's *Daily Herald* found a message of its own in a year when messages were abundant. 'What is certain is that those who are responsible for maintaining the rhythm of war production in the fifth year of war will find no adequate solution of the problem of war weariness if they ignore the penetrating human facts which are brought to light in such investigations as are recorded in this important book.'[108] That was not quite the language of the *Daily Mirror*, far more widely read than the *Daily Herald*, and, unlike the *Herald*, in danger of suppression in March 1942 when its publisher and editor were summoned to Whitehall to see Morrison, the Home Secretary. This was after the publication of what the Government considered a dangerously offensive Zec cartoon with a caption suggested by its columnist 'Cassandra'.[109]

When in the same month Michael returned to Queen Anne's Gate as Secretary, in effect Director, of PEP, his own morale was high. He had no feeling of war-weariness. His experience at Swindon may well have helped him when he was offered the key post in what was then generally recognised as both an influential and a prestigious institution. In the interim the Secretary of PEP had been David (later Sir Arthur)

Owen, who had been co-Director of the Pilgrim Trust's Enquiry into Unemployment from 1936 to 1937 and who now moved over to Whitehall to become Assistant to Cripps, still an independent-minded Labour politician, who in 1942 seemed, if briefly, to be the man of the moment.[110] Still not rehabilitated by the Labour Party, between 1940 and 1942 he had served as Ambassador to the Soviet Union, and he had now joined the War Cabinet at Churchill's invitation as Lord Privy Seal and Leader of the House of Commons.

There were significant changes of fortune and of mood, however, between 1942 and 1945, and already by the autumn of 1942 Cripps had lost ground, not only in high politics but with the public. His mission in March 1942 to India, which figured so prominently in Leonard Elmhirst's map, failed to achieve his – or the Government's – political objectives, while British military successes in North Africa, culminating at El Alamein in October 1942, raised Churchill's morale as well as that of the public. In these new circumstances Cripps decided to offer his resignation to Churchill, behind the scenes telling his aged aunt, Beatrice Webb, that 'Churchill would not last out the war: he was too old and had no plan for the future, whether within our own country or for the international situation when we had won the war'. Mistakenly, he thought that he (Cripps) would succeed him.[111] He stayed on, however, demoted although still in an important post, as Minister of Aircraft Production, outside the War Cabinet. His time was yet to come – after the war.

Michael notes that at some point between then and the end of the war he urged Cripps at a meeting in Dartington not to join the war-time party of radical protest, Common Wealth, founded in July 1942 by Sir Richard Acland, but to attach himself firmly to the Labour Party which he rejoined before preparations began for the post-war general election. In fact, like other Labour MPs who had been expelled before the war, among them Aneurin Bevan, Cripps was suspicious of Common Wealth blandishments from the start, while being willing at times to flirt with it, and was happy to rejoin the Labour Party. When Common Wealth tried to affiliate to the Labour Party in 1944, the National Executive Committee of the Labour Party refused, describing it (incorrectly) as set up 'by a rich man who decided he would found a Party in order to become a leader'.[112] There were echoes here which Cripps could not have missed. During the 1930s the Socialist League itself had sometimes been dismissed as 'a rich man's toy'.

As the 'tides of war' turned after the victory of Montgomery at El Alamein in early November 1942 and the surrender of the Germans besieged at Stalingrad in January 1943, the popular man of the moment was now Beveridge, a new 'People's William'. Like Curry, he was a strong advocate of Federal Union,[113] and Michael had been in touch with him – and he with the Fabian socialist G. D. H. Cole – after Beveridge, in his own opinion belatedly, had been made Chairman of the Manpower Requirements Committee of the Production Council in July 1940. (His office was in New Scotland Yard.)

Beveridge deputed Cole, a Fellow of his own College, University College, Oxford, to which he had moved as Master after LSE, to manage his manpower survey, which he organised with characteristic assiduity;[114] and late in 1941 Cole received Treasury funding for a Nuffield College Reconstruction Survey, monitoring the impact of war on industrial structure and on the working of the social services and making proposals concerning 'general problems of social and economic reorganisation after the War'. More specifically, Cole was asked by Beveridge to produce a report on the working of the social services 'from the consumer's end'.[115]

In her reminiscences of her husband's life, Margaret Cole noted how the youthful Michael took part in the nation-wide fieldwork, although misleadingly she described him as 'a very new recruit to the barely recognised study of sociology'. That was a comment made only with hindsight.[116] For Michael sociology still lay ahead. Interestingly, however, some of the consumer complaints that Cole's interviewers noted concerned the Prudential Assurance Company, which was to be one of Michael's main concerns in 1950.[117] And Cole was to figure more prominently in Michael's life after the war than during it.

Meanwhile, Beveridge's political influence, which Bevin, as Minister of Labour, was never anxious to encourage, continued to grow during the war (with his views on insurance as a lever) after the Cole project was brought to a halt amid bitter controversy in 1943.[118] Although in June 1941 Bevin had deliberately appointed a different Director-General of Manpower, and Beveridge was 'kicked upstairs' from the Ministry of Labour to the Chairmanship of a newly founded Committee on Social Insurance and Allied Services, this was to be the making of him, for when the Report of his Committee appeared in December 1942, largely his own work, it was an immediate success, selling over a 100,000 copies in a month. Beveridge was to be far less successful in post-war Britain than Cripps, but he now was at the centre of the stage, the place where he always most liked to be.

In retrospect, Michael judged that the height of PEP's war-time influence was reached in June 1941, the month he left for Swindon, when the Minister then dealing with post-war issues, the Labour Party leader, Arthur Greenwood, invited PEP to prepare evidence for the Beveridge Committee; and when the Beveridge Report appeared a PEP *Planning* broadsheet (No. 205) was to call it 'one of the greatest documents in British history'.[119] On his return to Queen Anne's Gate from Swindon Michael went on to acclaim all Beveridge's war-time publications, including his books *Pillars of Society* and *Full Employment in a Free Society*. In 1943 PEP published a broadsheet on full employment (No. 206), *Employment for All*, which treated full employment, as the Labour Party did, as the precondition of all post-war planning. This was the subject too of a book that Michael wrote with Theodor Prager, an Austrian economist in exile, *There's Work For All*.[120]

The evidence submitted by PEP to the Beveridge Committee was set out in the longest PEP broadsheet ever printed, No. 190, *Planning for Social Security*, 52 pages long, which was written by Lafitte, and which was published in July 1942. It claimed on its first page that the effects of insecurity could be 'as deadening as the effects of unbroken security in a Santa Claus state', a phrase that Beveridge himself might have used. 'Mass unemployment must and can be prevented,' the broadsheet declared, adding that there should be 'a national minimum standard of goods, services and opportunities for every citizen' below which no one should be expected to live, whether in work or distress. A single Ministry of Social Security should take over the administration of all income maintenance services. Unlike Beveridge, PEP recommended that the full costs of the new comprehensive social security system should be financed out of taxes. This would avoid the regressive impact of financing the system through an extension of social insurance.

J. M. (later Lord) Keynes, whom Michael met many times during the war and who paid more than one personal tribute to PEP, thought that this broadsheet was 'a particularly good piece of work, one of the best the organisation has ever produced'.[121] Like Beveridge, but even more so, Keynes could be interpreted in many different ways. Michael certainly drew direct inspiration from him. His *General Theory of Employment, Interest and Money* (1936) was now being hailed as a master-text, and in 1943 Michael co-authored an Oxford University Press pamphlet on home affairs, *Will the War Make Us Poorer*? which greatly appealed to Keynes.[122] In the same year he also wrote a PEP broadsheet (No. 188) on Keynesian lines, *Financial Mysticism*. In retrospect, this was as exciting a year for economists – and briefly Michael seemed to be one of them – as it was for the intrepid journalists who were reporting the war on the eastern front.[123]

Keynes, influential though he was, wrote for the few. Beveridge reached the many, and how to deal with his Report divided the Labour Party's leadership, officially working in coalition with Conservatives, from its active rank-and-file. Thereafter, divisions on this and other social policy issues – what their scope should be and when they should be timed – were brought into the open in what was still a period of political truce for the major parties. At the Labour Party's Annual Conference in June 1943 they were fully aired. Michael greatly admired Bevan, the main critic of the Labour leadership, whose wife, Jennie Lee, standing as a Labour independent – and losing – in February 1943 told the electors of Bristol (Cripps's seat was in the adjacent constituency) that she stood 'for every word, every letter and comma in the Beveridge Report'.[124]

The nearer the end of the war loomed after D-Day in June 1944, the more PEP strengthened its coverage of foreign as well as domestic issues. There had been earlier difficulties with some broadsheets, particularly one on France, which had 'an extremely chequered career' and went through many drafts, but there was little sense of foreboding about the shape of the future world in the summer of 1944.[125] It was seldom suggested, for example, that it might be difficult to reconcile Britain's multiple relationships with Europe, on which Nicholson had focused in 1939 and 1940, with the United States and with the Commonwealth. It was after Pearl Harbor that *Britain and Europe* (*Planning*, No. 182) had been published with its message that 'the issue is no longer whether Europe should remain united, but in what form and by what leadership'. *People for the Commonwealth*, No. 226, did not appear until 1944.

Only one war-time broadsheet dealt with Britain's post-1942 ally, the Soviet Union, and this was restricted in its scope, No. 196, *Soviet Planning in Wartime*. It was suggested, however, in one of PEP's books, *Building Peace out of War* (1944) that 'the unity of Europe', a desirable goal, would be 'effected in either one of two ways – either under German, or under British *and* [my italics] Russian, leadership'. There was a dream element in such talk which, *pace* the historian E. H. Carr, then writing for *The Times*, brushed aside the problems of power.[126] 'It is sometimes suggested that a more active British policy in Europe would conflict with the demands of the Imperial connection, as if Britain's role in the British Commonwealth and in a Commonwealth of Europe were in some way mutually exclusive. The contrary is the case. In this dual role Britain will act as a bridge between the Dominions and a revived and more prosperous Europe.'[127]

These were all big themes, emerging from the crucible of war – and Michael wrote about some of them to Leonard Elmhirst when Elmhirst was travelling in India – after the failure of Cripps's mission – looking at a map of India and wondering just where Leonard would be.[128] There were other elements in PEP war-time work that pointed to the themes that would interest Michael most in the 1950s, when, after six years, he left the Labour Party Research Department, his first post after PEP. *Planning* No. 218 (1944) was called *Old Houses*; No. 231 (1945) *Household Appliances*; and No. 242 (1945) *Retreat from Parenthood*. One PEP interest, already articulated, was consumer research, another 'the journey to work'; and a PEP group on domestic service, a subject that fascinated Michael, was chaired by S. C. Leslie, the civil servant in charge of public relations at the Home Office who also proposed that a Central Publicity Unit should be set up after the War. This was a proposal that led directly to the creation of the Central Office of Information.

In the middle of the war Michael had begun to pursue a further and quite different line of his own also, which must have appealed to Whitney Straight. *Planning* No. 208 (1943) was called *International Air Transport*, and a year later Michael wrote his most forgotten book, *International Air Transport*, in a lively *Target for Tomorrow* series. He also wrote about aviation for the *New Statesman*. It was difficult to forecast the expansion of civil aviation in the 1960s and later, but Michael never lost his interest and went on to concern himself in 'space' during the 1980s, setting up an 'Argo Venture' in 1987.[129]

Michael has referred to the 'homely detail', very different from forecasting, that is to be found in many PEP broadsheets dealing with major matters of high policy. In *Planning for Social Security*, for instance, largely drafted by Lafitte, a proposal was slipped in that there should be a Citizens' Advice Bureau in every social security office, an independent unit not managed by the statutory authorities. As Michael and his colleagues made such suggestions, there was a sense that he at least was becoming a Citizens' Advice Bureau complete in himself. Executive Committee meetings were poorly attended in 1944, 'partly' because Sieff had not been able to be present, and Michael looked forward in October 1944 to Leonard's return from India. 'PEP needs you' (as, he added, Dartington did).[130]

The arduous and unremitting work that Michael carried out at PEP, work for which he was paid £750 a year, covered all kinds of assignments, which he outlined in his formidable final report to the PEP Executive in 1945 just before his resignation:

> The Secretary has also had to contend with most of the petty administrative matters which are always coming up. Over many years PEP has become a kind of post office for information and

hundreds of people make use of it as though it were a combination of a PRO, a Labour Exchange and Selfridge's Information Bureau. We may be asked to suggest the names of authors for a series of articles in *Picture Post*, or a series of books in the *Target for Tomorrow* series, speakers for the Reigate Rotary Club or London Co-operative Forum, speakers to talk to RAF units in the Mediterranean, experts to comment on a report on the Pottery Industry, prepared by the Stoke WEA, or a report on the Coal Industry prepared by the Pontypool Social Settlement, or to comment ourselves on a memorandum by Colonel Devereux or by the Reconstruction Director of Bristol Aeroplane Company, or to criticise and to prepare a reading list for Army Education booklets, or to help to start a new magazine or to find a job for someone or to find someone for a job. In the course of a few months literally hundreds of such requests flow into the office by letter, by telephone, and, worst, in the shape of a visitor.

The simplest response would be to say 'Sorry, we can't help' to all the enquirers. But this would be out of the question. We are ourselves helped in large numbers of ways by many people and we cannot refuse our co-operation in return. And we can never feel content to leave the implementation of PEP ideas to the mere publication of the broadsheet. ... If we can in any way help a local Reconstruction Group in Chatham or a town planner in Glasgow, then that too is worth while.

Routine PEP administration is also heavy. There are the printers and publishers to deal with, the proofs of the reports and broadsheets to read. There are the meetings to arrange, bad attenders to follow up, people to invite and people to thank for commenting on any one of the several hundred substantial drafts which leave the office every year. There are newspapers to write to about broadsheets, critics and admirers to appease or congratulate on their good judgement, American and other foreigners to entertain. Again there are hundreds of jobs, but Miss [Kate] Harris [who had left for a time in 1940 to work with Nicholson] and Miss [Marion] Nuttall provide the most competent, indispensable assistance. [Then or later Marion Nuttall, who headed the administrative staff, was known to everyone in PEP as 'Matron'.]

[In these circumstances] the Secretary has tended to become a mere tactician. He has been buried in day to day affairs instead of having time to think about policy and to advise the Executive accordingly. He has had far too little time for what should be his main job, namely mapping out suggestions for policy, assisting drafters and,

> since he is normally the only person who goes to all group meetings, co-ordinating the work of the different groups and drafters. These two years have been a breathless struggle. Without Henry Bunbury it would have been quite impossible to avoid drowning.
>   The conclusions which emerge from this analysis are as follows: firstly and tritely, PEP must employ on its staff only people who can write with reasonable clarity. It is a delusion to think that bad drafters can be trained. Lack of drafting ability seems to be like cancer, incurable except by surgery: two of the worse offenders have left the staff in the last month. There should be a chance to build on surer foundations in the next year. In choosing new staff it should be realised that the only essential qualifications are (1) drafting ability, (2) intelligence.[131]

This was one of the most down-to-earth statements Michael ever made about his range of activities, and he sent a copy of it to Leonard in India.[132] His mind, however, was moving from the duties of the present into planning for the future, and it seemed a natural move rather than a sudden break when he accepted an invitation in February 1945 to take up the post of Head of the Research Department and Secretary of the Labour Party Policy Committee in time for the forthcoming general election.[133]

Michael was invited by Morgan Phillips, Secretary of the Labour Party, who had only recently been appointed to that post and was seeking to strengthen the central office. Now Michael, joining a small headquarters staff at Transport House in Smith Square, could do something new – plan campaigns as well as convene study groups and devise manifestos as well as plan pamphlets. Phillips, an ex-miner, very different from Sieff or the Elmhirsts, who had secured his first paid Party post in 1928 and who was to keep his Secretaryship until 1961, had not been Morrison's first choice for Secretary to replace James Middleton in 1944. Morrison, who had only recently become Chairman of the Labour Party's Policy Committee, would have preferred his friend Maurice Webb, lobby correspondent of the *Daily Herald*, who was defeated by only two votes.[134] Yet installed in his new post, Phillips, with a long career in the Labour Party behind him,[135] was to work closely with Morrison, while resenting, so Morrison claimed, the key role that his 'boss' played in policy-making.

Sieff would have preferred Michael to have stayed in PEP, but there were other PEP colleagues who shared Michael's own view that 'in the long run we should want at PEP someone less politically minded and with other qualities that I don't possess'. Nevertheless, before accepting the Labour Party offer, Michael saw Morrison privately and, when interviewed by Phillips, was promised that he would 'have a reasonably free hand'. Morrison asked him what his criticisms of the Party were, and when Michael hesitated for a moment exclaimed, 'Good God, you must have criticisms. I have got thousands myself.' Phillips added that he was 'determined that a new wind should blow through Transport House'.[136]

Meanwhile, Dartington continued to play a big and continuous part in Michael's life, as it did more briefly in the life of others, people whom he met when he visited it, among them Cole, who spent three months there as a guest 'in a kind of gazebo in the gardens' in 1943.[137] Like Liddell Hart, he was convalescing. Both men were as resourceful in controversy as ever. Both were concentrating on the new world to come. So too was Michael, but he was also deeply interested, as they were not, in the world within a world that belonged to the Elmhirsts. In a letter to them in May 1944 he declared that what he would like 'to get clear first' was the 'purpose' of Dartington: 'I don't mean the different individual purposes but the sum of all these.' As 'an experiment' it required research. 'An inquisitive researcher should be able to irritate and stimulate all the time and use Dartington to get all sorts of valuable results.'[138] 'Could not Dartington "pump blood" into Devon?', he asked. Could there not be a 'Planning Committee with two, three or four on the staff – an economist, a sociologist [the first time he seems to have used this word on paper], an administrator, an agronomist?'

This seminal war-time letter was written one month before D-Day, and before the month was out Michael spent a 'most interesting weekend' with the Directors of Dartington Ltd., who were facing 'big crises'. The future of the Dartington economy brought the whole organisation into question, and there were problems in the school also. By then Michael had come to the conclusion, if reluctantly, that Curry would never be able to set it 'on a new course after the War': it would be essential to link it more closely with 'the state system', and Curry, committed to a belief in private experimental schools, was unwilling to do this. Another aspect of Dartington interested Michael too – its cultivation of the arts. He was deeply shocked, therefore, when in the following month he heard of the death at Dartington of Christopher Martin, who had been deeply involved in cultivating them. 'When we were down at Dartington he seemed so full of energy and overflowing with ideas about the Arts Reports and the future of Dartington. Dartington will not be the same place now. There will always be a gap.'[139]

In 1945 Michael's interest in pictorial art, nurtured at Dartington and now shared nationally by a considerably larger number of people than there had been in 1939, was as great as it was in 1934, when on his first visit to Gray's Inn he described in his letter to Dorothy the great portrait under which he was sitting, or in 1937 when, having left Toynbee Hall, he took up painting again. Until that year he had sent Dorothy a picture every Christmas. It is not surprising, therefore, that Leonard used an image derived from art to explain Michael's move in 1945 from PEP to the Research Department of the Labour Party. It seemed a 'natural reaction', he said, similar to that which Michael had already demonstrated when he wished 'to place a modern painting in the dining room' at Dartington.[140]

Dorothy's reaction to Michael's move in 1945 was different, and in retrospect dangerous. In congratulation she presented him with a silver cigarette box, and each month sent him cigarettes to fill it. He went on smoking them, despite his asthma, until 1957, telling her then that 'one very strong reason' against giving smoking up was that he 'so much treasured this link' with her. 'These cigarettes always seemed better than others.'[141] Fortunately for them both, when at last he gave up the habit all other links remained unbroken.

3
Party Politics

From the vantage point of Queen Anne's Gate Michael had been convinced before his move to Transport House that the Labour Party would win the general election of May 1945. Not everyone in PEP – or in Transport House – thought that it would.[1] It was only after Winston Churchill in a tart exchange of correspondence with Clement Attlee had refused the request of the Labour Party – at its Blackpool Conference at Whitsuntide 1945 – to postpone the general election until the autumn, that the commitment of the Labour leaders to a nationwide campaign was ensured.[2] Party hostilities now began seriously, and in what became an increasingly heated and excited contest Michael took an active part. It was his initiation into party political campaigning. This was the first general election for ten years.

As Michael had already concluded before he moved to Transport House, it was to be no 'khaki election'. Drawing less on his PEP experience than on what he had heard as a rank-and-file member of the St. Pancras Constituency Labour Party from 'men and women in the street', he felt that popular memories of the 1930s would play a bigger part in determining the result than gratitude to a great war leader. What he had heard at the grass roots in other constituencies confirmed him in this conviction. He put his trust in pressure from below, and this inevitably led him also in a new direction for himself.

PEP, deeply committed as it was to the cause of reconstruction, had deliberately kept free from party ties since its inception in a year of economic and political crisis, 1931, and it was its cross-party composition, not the same as 'objectivity' or 'impartiality', that had attracted most of the researchers and writers, busy people, many of them close to power, who had worked for it. Michael had joined them for different, personal, reasons, but inevitably during a war when there was a coalition government in power he had been very close to the centre in Whitehall. He knew all about the war-time 'White Paper Chase', a memorable phrase of Beveridge.[3] But it was not information derived from 'the centre' that had its biggest long-term impact on him, but rather the memory of war-time 'solidarity', a word that figured, along with 'universality', in the argument behind most of the White Papers.

In the light of his experience of war-time solidarity, the sense that everyone was 'in it together', Michael was keen in 1945 to draw on the enthusiasm of millions of people who had often read only summaries of the White Papers in the press. Their mobilisation, he was sure, was the key to the future just as it had been the key to the winning of 'a people's war'. Phillips realised from his own experience that it was the key to winning the general election, which was announced on 23 May, but did not take place until 5 July. Michael knew what public opinion polls were suggesting too. Published in the liberal *News Chronicle* (with PEP connections through Gerald Barry, its editor), they predicted a heavy swing to Labour. Less attention was paid to them by most politicians at the time than was paid to the opinions of a small number of political pundits who were not usually close to the ground.

Joining the central office of the Labour Party in 1945 just at the time when it was preparing for and participating in the general election was a heady, if backroom, experience for Michael, which he had longed for and which he was never quite to share again. He was to recall years later how heady an experience it also was for the Labour Party leaders from the moment that they started addressing 'meetings on the stump'. They had been mainly concerned during the war-time coalition with Cabinet politics. Now, with the end of the 'electoral truce', they had to switch to electoral politics. Michael, close to Morrison, recalls how his 'boss' could 'almost see it [the prospect] change day by day ... My God, we might win.'[4] Clement Attlee, driven around the country by his wife in their old family car, learnt what it was to be cheered by enthusiastic crowds. They wanted to see him as well as hear him.

Michael's opinion of Attlee, whom he did not know well, rose as the election campaign continued. Making the most of his 'natural disposition' he wrote – even exaggerating it – Attlee chose to employ simple, often single, words and sentences. He was as different from Churchill as any rival leader could be, different too from any of his Labour predecessors, including his immediate predecessor George Lansbury, revered in London's East End, whom Michael was to quote often in the future. It was more difficult to quote Attlee, although Michael sometimes did.[5]

Attlee was different also both from Morrison, who had been involved in efforts, backed by Ellen Wilkinson, retiring Chairman of the Executive Committee of the Party, to replace him as leader before the general election, and from Ernest Bevin, who was intensely loyal to him.[6] Morrison, Londoner of Londoners, was still seeking to displace Attlee even after the Labour Party won a landslide victory, capturing almost 12 million votes out of a total of 25,018,393 cast and 393 seats out of 640. Of the 393, 119 were financed by trade unions, a peak figure in Labour Party history, and 23 by the Cooperative Union. No fewer than 126 successful candidates were ex-Servicemen, and there were 21 women.[7]

Michael was outside the range of pre- and post-election personal manoeuvring in the Labour Party leadership, as rank-and-file members of the Party also were; and it seemed crucially important for the Party and the country that the leaders should follow a common strategy in 1945, the strategy reflected in the Party manifesto *Let Us Face the Future*, large parts of which Michael himself wrote after joining the Party's Research Department. He recalled years later in a characteristic phrase that he 'sort of put it together in its final form'.[8] Drafting had begun soon after the Labour Party Conference of December 1944 which had been postponed from the previous May. It was this Conference which set up a new Campaign Committee, chaired by Morrison who, according to Hugh Dalton, another of its members, left Morrison – and through him, Michael – with 'plenty of elbow room' in which to work.

Dalton, busy choosing young Labour candidates for Parliament while manoeuvring about his own position behind the scenes, took Michael to lunch at Marsham Restaurant in Westminster before the Party Conference of May 1945 and before the date of the general election was fixed. 'I don't find him particularly sympathetic,' Dalton wrote, 'but he is quite capable, I think.'[9] Michael was not the kind of young man whom Dalton had in mind. He sought out and liked bright young men in uniform and clever proletarian protégés. (Later, thanks to Michael, they would have been called 'meritocratic'.) They seemed to Dalton to be the likeliest Labour candidates at the forthcoming general election, and at the Whitsuntide Labour Party Conference in 1945 he noted how 'moving' it was to see and hear them.

The Manifesto went down extremely well at this Conference, and both Morrison and Dalton received great ovations, although Dalton, who gave the V sign when he concluded his speech, admitted that the ovation given to Bevin, who spoke on the international situation, was the loudest of all.[10] There had been plenty of argument about the Manifesto, particularly about its title, before it reached the floor. In its first draft it had been called *Let's Face the Future*. Michael, who saw the political relevance even of punctuation, wanted to get rid of the colloquial apostrophe, and after hours of discussion, longer than the Conference debate, the Committee agreed that the title *Let Us Face the Future* seemed to have the right *ex cathedra* ring to it. In retrospect, Michael concluded that 'almost anything the Labour Party said then' was going to carry them through to victory. 'The mood was such that second class documents were going to be thought first class with a star.'[11]

This was doubtless true, and in the left-wing periodical *Tribune*, founded in 1937 to 'recreate Labour as a socialist party', Bevan, its editor since 1941, concluded as early as August 1945 that 'the general election was not an argument with the issue in doubt until all sides were heard. It was the registration of a change which had occurred in Britain before the War began.'[12] Few on the right of the Party or at its centre would have concurred before the drafting of *Let Us Face the Future*, when they had been forced to take account of differences of outlook not between the parties but within the Labour Party itself. At the postponed Party Conference, held in December 1944, a cluster of compromises had been necessary, although the Conference had ended with a reaffirmation of the Party's 'socialist faith', its support for a 'planned economy', and its intent to 'transfer to the State [the] power to direct the policy of our main industries, services and financial institutions'.[13]

The differences, which were covered over, concerned both foreign and domestic policy. The left wing was anxious for the Party to oppose Churchillian foreign policy, particularly Churchill's vigorous intervention against the Greek left. It was a delegate from the St. Pancras Labour Party, Michael's own constituency, who won applause at the December Conference when she had pressed the Party to kill 'anarchic capitalism' stone dead. 'Sir William Beveridge is trying to put forward a new solution, dressing the old wolf in sheep's clothing, but the wolf is still there.'[14]

The 1944 Conference went on to reject a carefully prepared statement from the Party's National Executive on 'Full Employment and Financial Policy', which had included no references to public ownership. It carried instead (without a recorded vote) a resolution proposed by left-winger Ian Mikardo demanding 'the transfer to public ownership of the land, large-scale building, heavy industry and all forms of banking, transport and fuel and power'. This was in line with pre-war Labour Party policy and sharply divided the Labour Party (all shades of opinion) from the Conservative and Liberal Parties.[15]

Let Us Face the Future, published in April 1945 in time for the next Labour Party Conference, had to take account, therefore, not only of Keynesian economics and Beveridge's *Full Employment in a Free Society*, both of which had influenced Michael before he entered Transport House, but of the by then traditional commitment of the active party membership to nationalisation, which Michael accepted without question. As *Let Us Face the Future* went through its different drafts, it reflected both influences. For this reason it should be compared with an earlier policy statement of 1942, drafted before Beveridge, *The Old World and the New Society*, a paper prepared by the Party's Reconstruction Committee at a time when the Party, as a member of the Coalition, was committed to the avoidance of 'intra-party controversies'.[16]

Writing years later, Miliband, a disciple of Laski who was a highly vocal Chairman of the Labour Party in 1945 – behind the scenes he was highly critical of Attlee's leadership – described the tone of *Let Us Face the Future* as 'mild and circumspect'.[17] This was an exaggeration. In drawing a sharp contrast between what would happen in the post-war future and what had happened to the country before 1939, the Party was striking the right note, proving itself strong, not 'mild', and eager, not 'circumspect', appealing alike to the young (the children of the 1930s) and to the old, those who remembered the 'Great War'.[18]

Morrison, to whom Michael was working directly, had been involved throughout the years between 1942 and 1945, when he was a Cabinet Minister, in drawing contrasts between 'old world' and 'new society'. He was seeking too, not unsuccessfully, to widen the appeal of the Labour Party to attract 'the small man' and, in particular, the technicians who had played a big part in the war effort. Significantly there were politicians further to the left, like Cripps and the Common Wealth Party leader, Acland, who shared the commitment to such a strategy.[19] So, too, during the war had the 1941 Committee. To none of them, nor to Ellen Wilkinson, 'Red Ellen', who had established a reputation for fieriness during the Spanish Civil War, nor, indeed, to Michael himself, could the adjectives 'mild' and 'circumspect' be appropriately attached.[20]

A sceptical, if friendly, critic of *Let Us Face the Future*, writing at the time, might well have had Michael in mind – had he known him – when he observed that the Manifesto had 'something of the quality of the resolutions a young man makes when he leaves home for the first time'.[21] One of its most frequently quoted sections, much quoted then and since, dealt with public ownership, the main issue which separated the parties, under the heading 'industry in the service of the nation'. Ambitiously, if in general terms, it called for industry to be organised so as to enable it to 'yield the best that human knowledge and skill can provide'. 'Only so,' it went on, 'can our people reap the full benefits of this age of discovery and Britain keep her place as a Great Power.' This was Morrisonian language, for it was Morrison who before the general election – and when installed in office after it – coordinated nationalisation policy and formulated nationalisation rules.[22]

The Manifesto then became more specific. There were some basic industries that were 'ripe and over-ripe for public ownership and management' – these were listed – and others that were 'not yet ripe'. The latter were not specified – there would have been internal party argument about this, particularly about financial institutions – but the promise was made that the Bank of England would be 'brought under public ownership'. Moreover, even when there was to be no nationalisation of industries, there was to be 'public supervision of monopolies and cartels' and control over industrial location.

The listed industries, at the 'commanding heights' and 'ripe' for takeover, were fuel and power, inland transport, and iron and steel. (Morrison had to make his own compromise on the last of these, the one nationalisation issue which was to disturb post-war Labour Party politics and to rally Conservatives.[23]) Each industry would be 'taken over on a basis of fair compensation, to be conducted efficiently [as a public corporation] in the interests of consumers [a word that did not then mean as much to Michael as it would have done ten years later], coupled with proper status and conditions for the workers employed in them'.

Five other points stood out in what was a key political section of the Manifesto. First, there was a reference to the fact that before the war 'millions of working and middle-class people [note the addition] went through the horrors of unemployment and insecurity'. Second, there was a promise that 'suitable economic controls' would be maintained. 'There must be priorities in the use of raw materials, food prices must be held, homes for the people must come before mansions, necessities for all before luxuries for the few.'[24] Third, there was a recognition that there should be 'better organisation of Government departments'.

Some of the authors of the Manifesto were familiar with current governmental and administrative organisation because of their war-time role in the Coalition, and had worked closely with Labour-minded temporary civil servants, among them Hugh Gaitskell and James Meade:[25] 'the economic purpose of government must be to spur industry forward and not to choke it with red tape'. They, like realists on their left, emphasised the fourth point, that the items in the Manifesto represented only a first instalment of a Labour programme, a point that was later to be emphasised by socialists of quite different kinds, one of them Michael. 'Socialism cannot come overnight, as the product of a week-end revolution. The members of the Labour Party, like the British people, are practical-minded men and women.'

Fifth, and the main condition for the success of all other proposals, there was a declaration that there had to be 'a firm and clear-cut programme for the export trade'. State help would have to be provided to get export industries on their feet and thereby to enable the country 'to pay for the food and raw materials without which Britain must decay and die'. None the less, such help would have to be conditional. Industry had to be efficient and go-ahead. 'Laggards and obstructionists must be led or directed into better ways. Here we dare not fail.' It was at this point that realism was most tinged with optimism.[26] Outdated business organisation coupled with restrictive labour practices were long to outlast the war and the first post-war governments, Labour and Conservative.

The clauses in the Manifesto dealing with the export trade, perhaps less in the minds of most voters in 1945 than the others, were to be forced to the forefront with the end of American lend-lease in 1945. This came as a surprise, and what followed – a controversial loan from America on difficult terms – made the role of the Labour Government far more difficult than even its leaders had anticipated.[27] Followed as it necessarily was by a financial crisis (convertibility of sterling) in August 1947, by which time the American loan was exhausted, it raised Cripps, prepared temperamentally to face further austerity, to a pinnacle of power. President of the Board of Trade, he became Minister of Economic Affairs, a new post, in September 1947 (reducing the power not only of Dalton but of Morrison), and when Dalton resigned in November 1947 he replaced him as Chancellor of the Exchequer.

The electorate was to be further shocked, if not educated, in the process of carrying out that task, and the Parliamentary Labour Party was to be divided: a 'Keep Left' Group was formed in April 1947, which included Crossman, Michael Foot and Jennie Lee. They wanted more socialist control of the domestic economy and a more independent foreign policy, stretching further the differences which had been apparent at the 1944 National Conference before the Manifesto was drafted.[28] The differences should not be exaggerated, however, for on 'welfare' and related issues there remained substantial consensus, as there had been during the war. The relevant proposals in *Let Us Face the Future* were in line with majority opinions expressed in war-time polls, which had run against the Conservatives since 1942.²⁹ Some of them even influenced post-war Conservative policy. After 1945 the Labour Party provided what Paul Addison has called 'a field of force' of the kind that Thatcher was to provide later in quite different circumstances.³⁰ Michael was as much caught within the first field as he was to resist the second.

Let Us Face the Future, the work of a committee, with Michael active behind the scenes, should be compared with J. B. Priestley's highly personal *Letter to a Returning Serviceman* (1945), based on personal experience very different from Michael's which went back beyond the 1930s to 1918. Addressing 'Robert', his chosen reader, Priestley began by telling him that he wanted him 'to remember that I was once a returning serviceman too'. Because of this he knew that a citizen-soldier as distinct from a professional soldier has a conflict inside him. 'One half of him wants to settle up, the other half want to settle down. Sharing the same billet in his mind are an earnest revolutionary and a tired a cynical Tory.'³¹ After this lead-in Priestley began what he called his 'argument'. Coaches had to give way to cars. 'It is useless to try to *un*invent.' History moves. 'People are apt to think that they are standing outside history, instead of moving along in it.'

As a northerner, Priestley could describe 'industrial folk' as 'my own people'. The freedom that mattered most for them – and for him – he maintained, was 'the freedom to have more fun'. Michael, who found time for fun even while he was working long hours of overtime in Transport House, as he had done in PEP, would have subscribed willingly to this proposition. After all, he had been born near Manchester. Since the industrial revolution, Priestley wrote, 'a vast grey dreariness' had 'descended upon our industrial towns'. Now 'the world must reject the age-old belief that life for most men [Priestley did not refer to women] must necessarily be brief, brutish and sad.'

'Modern man' – and Michael would have approved of Priestley dividing history at the industrial revolution – was 'essentially a communal and cooperating man'. Individuals by themselves were powerless.³² The Soviet Union had set an example of what could be achieved before the war and was still committed to the same purpose. 'Whatever their faults, the Bolsheviks had put a hand to the great task and were trying to lift the load of want, ignorance, fear and misery from their dumb millions, while the Americans – as they freely admit now – were living in a fool's paradise of money-for-nothing and martinis.'³³

At this point a strain of anti-Americanism, which Michael, brought up by the Elmhirsts, did not share, was clearly apparent in Priestley. None the less, Priestley, while warning of the 'Hollywood siren', held up the American example of the Tennessee Valley Authority, an example well known to Michael and to the Elmhirsts – their friend Julian Huxley wrote a war-time book about it[34] – to show what Americans could do if they chose. It had transformed a whole area around Nashville 'not for any man's profit but for the general good'. Priestley added that he had felt as deeply moved by a film about TVA as he would have been by 'a noble work of art'.

The task of accomplishing the kind of 'transformation' achieved in Tennessee was a world task. Here Priestley left behind the limited horizons of his pre-war book *English Journey*, to which he had referred earlier in his *Letter* and to which he was to return later, linking what he had to say about transformation with his own thoughts on the future of Britain's export industries, a main preoccupation in *Let Us Face the Future*.[35] 'If we can begin to raise the standard of living in the world's huge depressed areas, notably India and China, [Britain's] marketing problems' would 'shortly solve themselves and the danger of war can be safely passed.'

It was at this conjunction, according to Priestley, who was proclaiming a gospel rather than offering an analysis, that 'idealism and the noblest altruism, on the one side, and ... self-interest on the other, come together and find a common plan of action.'[36] Not well versed in economics, he was unaware of the economic problems that would be encountered through exporting to 'soft currency markets'.[37] For him, an export drive would have an heroic quality about it, as indeed it was to have in the Board of Trade, when Clem Leslie, an Australian, invited Lydia Horton to plan lectures to women's organisations explaining the need to export. During the war she had organised 'Eat more Vegetables' campaigns for the Ministry of Food. She was to figure later as a trailblazer in the history of the Consumers' Association co-founded by Michael.[38]

There was a postscript to Priestley's *Letter* – 'PS Stop Press – the atom bomb has arrived. So I repeat – *There isn't much time*.' In the circumstances of 1945 this PS did not stand out as the most remarkable sentence in his *Letter*, although it was soon to stand out in the light of later left-wing politics after the development of the Campaign for Nuclear Disarmament.[39] Most remarkable was Priestley's full awareness of the counter-claims of privacy and publicity, and his recognition of the realities of choice. It is also interesting to note what he chose to leave out. He had nothing to say about social security or full employment or housing, the last of which was named by most people as the biggest issue for them in the election.[40] Historically too the one great success of the Labour Party in the inter-war years had been Wheatley's Housing Act of 1924.

These were among the themes that Michael had to deal with in the most pressing and most time-consuming of all his first assignments at Transport House – preparing with extraordinary speed a *Speakers' Handbook* for Labour Party candidates, many of whom knew less about the issues than Michael did, but almost all of whom were 'activists' of the type Priestley advocated. He remembers the *Handbook* as 'an incredibly awful looking thing. Sort of blotting paper covers', 'blood red in colour', packed with 'nuggets'. It reminded him, a memory very much of his own, of his Bendigo grandparents searching for gold.[41]

One of Michael's 1945 assignments, broadcasting, was Priestley's own speciality, and with his war-time BBC Postscripts still in the public mind he gave one of the Labour Party broadcasts immediately before the general election. Morrison rightly kept an eye on the role of radio, as he was to do after the election, and under his direction Michael worked with William Pickles, an LSE lecturer, who had been a regular war-time broadcaster, to handle the Labour Party speakers. This was Michael's introduction to the BBC, which was to figure in both his personal and his public life. He had little to say, however, about the part played by broadcasting in the 1945 election when 50 years later he was interviewed about the period by Peter Hennessey, who himself had made a reputation as a broadcaster.[42]

Attlee went his own way in his broadcasting in 1945, uninfluenced by Morrison or any of his intermediaries, and profiting from Churchill's excesses, like his claim that Labour would have to fall back on 'some form of Gestapo'. Such statements, he thought, were influenced by Beaverbrook, the Press Lord for whom neither Morrison nor Bevin had any respect. (Beaverbrook later denied any responsibility.[43]) According to Mass-Observation, the broadcasts created 'disappointment and genuine distress', and seem to have shocked many people who had never voted Labour and who did not wish to see military warfare give way to the kind of political warfare that Churchill seemed to be offering.[44] By concentrating on domestic rather than on international themes, the Labour broadcasters kept nearer to family experience.

Each subsequent general election since 1945, including, not least, that of 1997, places old elections in new perspective. From the vantage point of 1963, on the eve of another Labour victory, when Michael briefly resumed his role as Research Secretary,[45] it seemed to Anthony Howard, journalist, broadcaster and biographer, that the 1945 voter had not so much been casting his ballot in judgement on the previous five years as in denunciation of the ten years before that. 'The dole queue was more evocative than El Alamein.'[46] Yet, as Howard himself noted, uniformed Major John Freeman in a much admired reply to the King's Speech, the first Labour backbencher speech new MPs heard, looked back not to the dole queue but to D-Day. The country was facing 'a battle for peace no less arduous and no less momentous than the battle we have lived through in the past six years ... Today may rightly be regarded as D-Day in the battle for the New Britain.'

A *Tribune* article in April 1945 on *Let Us Face the Future* was entitled 'Into Battle',[47] and its editor, Bevan, soon to be appointed Minister of Health in Attlee's government, the youngest member of the Cabinet at the age of 47, made as much as Priestley did not only of the 'dole queue' but of events at the end of the First World War.[48] So, too, did Tawney, who wrote a learned war-time article, one of his rare incursions as a historian into twentieth-century economic history, on 'The Abolition of Economic Controls, 1918–1921'.[49]

From the vantage point of 1997, after a Labour victory greater in scale even than that of 1945, perhaps what now stands out most in the story of the 1945 general election was the emphasis placed on 'trust'. An American commentator, Robert A. Brady, who visited Britain in 1948 to find out about 'third force socialism', thought the same. He concluded that in making their choice, many electors were confident that 'the Labour Party means it'.[50] They were impressed by the words in *Let Us Face the Future*: 'Labour regards [the] welfare [of the people] as a sacred trust.' The 'Homes for Heroes promise in 1918 to build 500,000 houses in three years had been broken: 'in 1919 they built 700 houses.' 'Learn from the Past'.[51]

In the words of Michael Foot, Bevan's biographer, Bevan's first pamphlet *Why Not Trust the Tories?*, published by Gollancz in 1945, 'recounted the whole story of 1918, sharply drawing all the morals for 1945'.[52] It sold 80,000 copies. Among the future Labour Ministers Michael was specially drawn to Bevan, with whom he had little direct contact, not least because Bevan had been one of the strongest advocates of a speedy end to Coalition government. Another Minister whom Michael respected was James Griffiths, who was in charge of social security. Health and social security had been one of the major PEP preoccupations.

So, too, had 'fair shares for all'. One of the most popular political cartoons of 1945 was one by Zec in the *Daily Mirror* called 'Under the

Counter', which showed an angry couple in civilian dress demanding in a shop called Tory Peace Stores (Very Limited) 'Decent Schools', 'Good Homes' and 'Jobs'. All the goods were shown under the counter stacked in bundles and labelled 'Fruits of Victory Reserved for the Rich and Privileged'. 'What do you mean – you're out of stock?,' exclaims the customer. 'I've paid twice for these goods, once in 1914 and again in 1939.'

Michael, whose memories did not go back as far as the customer's, kept no diary during the 1945 campaign, but he recalls 'a champagne fizz in the air'. And changing the metaphor, with his war-time experience as a 'progress chaser' in mind, he added that after the election victory 'it was like sailing down the Solent with just the right following wind'. He was aware, too, from his PEP experience, that while new Ministers were settling in to prepare promised legislation – with most of the Coalition drafts waiting on their desks – there was 'a rare commonalty between politicians and the civil service'.[53]

The Labour Party Research Department had been hastily improvised before the election, and, as always in his life, Michael found such improvisation 'the greatest fun'.[54] The Department increased in size after the election, however, and became more organised, turning into a kind of propaganda office for the Government, and producing as impressive a flow of papers of its own as PEP. They were all papers with a message, and in difficult times – times which grew more difficult in 1946 and 1947 – it was not easy to get that message across. So long as the Party had a message, Michael was prepared to face up to any difficulties either in the national situation or in his own. It was only when he felt that it no longer had one that he retreated from party politics into ventures of his own. That was round the corner. In 1945 he did not see his compact with the Labour Party as a limited one.

Even in 1945, however, Morrison and Phillips were placing more emphasis on 'organisation' than on message. They realised that the most essential, if not the most stimulating, of political tasks was to get out Labour voters on election day, and that meant having willing constituency workers who were well prepared. This remained an essential task after the election was won, for from 1948 onwards the annual conferences of both parties were preoccupied with the next general election that lay ahead. By 1949 there had been an increase in the number of full-time Labour Party agents in the constituencies, nearly a third of them working in rural and semi-rural districts.[55] Writing a Manifesto was a second priority, although in March 1949 a new Manifesto, *Labour Believes in Britain*, was produced, with the promise of a further and fuller manifesto to come.

From the centre the Research Department produced posters as well as pamphlets, and organised conferences as well as speeches. One of Michael's liveliest colleagues, Michael Middleton, designed the lay-out of the Party's publications: much in demand outside Transport House, he was to become editor of *Lilliput* and later in life Director of the Civic Trust. Another colleague was Denis Healey who, arriving soon after Michael, became head of the Labour Party's International Department. He remembers Michael as 'a sallow intellectual with lank hair and horn-rimmed spectacles, a product of the experimental school at Dartington Hall'.[56]

While working in the Department, Michael returned frequently to Dartington, where he was now a Trustee – he had been guaranteed leave of absence to attend Trustee meetings whenever they were called – but he was more gregarious than Healey. Unlike most of the young men working there, Denis, whom he recalls as a tough and forceful colleague, did not join them in nearby pubs after long hours of work for hours of drinking. Their favourite rendezvous was 'The Two Chairmen', where the work of the day spilt over into informal talk. They were still 'riding high' during the late 1940s at a time when the drabness of post-war Britain and the limitations on individual choice were becoming major Conservative Party themes.

Popular reactions were similar to those that Priestley had predicted. The Labour vote remained high, but many returned Roberts were putting private life first. There was an unexpected 'baby boom' during these years at a time when there were enough houses to give many new families a home of their own. And while in food there were fair shares for all, the shares were small, sometimes smaller than in wartime. Bread and potatoes were both rationed for the first time. The language of austerity was still pervasive – even persuasive – but affluence beckoned.

Outside the circle of Two-Chairmen 'semi-politicians', as Michael now calls them – some of them were to become very 'real' politicians – Michael did not feel deprived. He enjoyed himself at the theatre and in visiting exhibitions.[57] He succeeded in putting 'drabness' in perspective as he welcomed the nutritional merits of a rationed diet, the standard-setting of 'utility furniture', and the cultural role of the Arts Council. He knew that the daily average of calories (and fat) had declined, that protein and vitamin content had increased; that at a *Britain Can Make It* exhibition in 1946 the emphasis was on design; and that the Local Government Act of 1948 empowered local authorities to impose a penny rate solely for the support of the arts.

All these social changes were noted not only in Transport House but in the PEP headquarters at Queen Anne's Gate, where Michael continued to spend time. Thanks to him, the Labour Party used a small office there, and it was he who chose some of the post-war topics for discussion, including how to foster 'active democracy'. (The junior research assistant in charge of the project would answer the telephone 'Active Democracy speaking'.[58]) No successor to Michael was appointed after Denis Routh and Guy Hunter held the Directorship for brief spells,[59] and the small staff included two men with political ambitions who were nursing constituencies, Angus (later Lord) Maude, a Conservative, and James MacColl, a Labour candidate.

Raymond Goodman took over as Director in June 1946, aware of the need for change inside PEP as well as in the country, and Michael enjoyed talking to him. He saw little, however, of his opposite numbers carrying out research in the Conservative Party, where Butler was assembling an impressive team of young 'people', anxious to shape the future, capable of appealing both to young male voters, most of whom were still being conscripted for military service, and to their wives who, while they still queued, were dreaming of forbidden foods. Butler encouraged 'individual flair, imagination and even idiosyncrasy ... provided all concerned were loyal to the party'. They 'did not have to be made from the same mould'.[60] Another proviso, common to Michael and his colleagues, was that they had to work hard. Typically, they were 'overworked'.

The relationship of the two research departments to the two parties was different. That of the Labour Party was responsible to the National Executive, where there was considerable disagreement: that of the Conservative Party was responsible to the party leader.[61] And in the Labour Party politics was powerfully influenced, if not determined, by the trade union block vote. Churchill listened to Butler: Attlee listened to Bevin more than to Morrison. On some policy questions, there was a measure of consensus between both party leaderships. 'Our first purpose,' Butler wrote, 'was to counter the charge and fear that we were the party of industrial go-as-you-please and devil-take-the-hindmost, that full employment and the Welfare State were not safe in our hands.' Testimony of this was provided in an *Industrial Charter* published in May 1947.

At Transport House Michael worked within a frame. Although London-based, one of his regular tasks, paralleled in the Conservative Party, was that of organising weekend and summer schools in the provinces, a task for which Dartington fitted him. His first assignment, however, was to organise propaganda for the campaign for municipal and county elections in 1945 and 1946, the immediate follow-up to the general election; and almost as soon as these were over he was at work on preparations for the next general election. The timetable was never his own. For the 1945 local government elections the Party chose the slogan 'Forge the Link'. Pictures showed chains falling apart. They did, not least in London. Seven Labour Councillors were elected in Westminster in November 1945 for the first time in 40 years.

Michael was not a good speaker, but between elections he had many speaking chores, and it was while addressing the Labour League of Youth at Filey in Yorkshire that he was called back to London by Phillips after the Government had been forced in the summer of 1946 to introduce bread rationing. This was a desperate measure that had never been necessary in war-time, and Phillips provided Michael with a hired aeroplane, the first time he had travelled in such circumstances, to prepare a pamphlet, *Bread Rationing, the Facts*. It was easier to hire the aeroplane than to make the facts sound convincing. One master baker was willing to say that he would go to gaol rather than collect Bread Units (an ugly new term) from housewives.[62]

The food crisis was only one of the crises that the Labour Government had to face. The fuel crisis of February 1947 set back the recovery of the whole economy, which was still based on coal, and again Phillips demanded another pamphlet, given a parallel title, *The Fuel Crisis, the Facts*. People undoubtedly wanted real facts, but Michael realised that in a winter of exceptional cold and family hardships people wanted – and expected – other things too. Spirits could be low. As for the facts, they were confusing. There were considerable sections of the miners who were already dissatisfied with the fruits of coal nationalisation, although wages were higher than they ever had been before.[63] Meanwhile, there had to be massive power cuts throughout British industry because of the coal shortage. For all the propaganda, the machinery of planning was not working either: there was interdepartmental tension rather than coordination. In 1945 finance and economics had been placed in separate departments, with Dalton in charge of the first and Morrison in charge of the second. It was a recipe for trouble.

There were differences of approach as well as of structure. At the civil service level Treasury officials were particularly uneasy about Max Nicholson, Morrisson's Permanent Secretary, and his staff 'trespassing' on their territory; and even after Dalton had left the Exchequer and there was greater convergence, the problems remained. There was still no consensus either on just what planning meant, except the acceptance of the assumption that there had to be 'physical controls' to ensure 'fair shares'. Nicholson was sure that he knew what he meant. After all, he had known what it meant when PEP was founded in 1931 and he had produced his Plan.[64]

Close as he was to Morrison, Michael became increasingly uneasy not so much about the machinery of planning – or the continuation of physical controls – as about the Morrisonian pattern of nationalisation, which Morrison never attempted to modify. Uneasy about what was happening 'at the top', he did not think that it was enough to precipitate Walter Citrine, former General Secretary of the TUC, from Transport House to membership of the National Coal Board and from there to the Chairmanship of the British Electricity Authority, at the same time raising him to the peerage.[65] More searchingly, he questioned also the relationship of Board members, wherever they came from, to the Ministers in charge of policy, in the case of Fuel and Power first Emanuel (later Lord) Shinwell, another of Churchill's most outspoken war-time critics, and then after the crisis of 1947 Hugh Gaitskell, a newcomer to high-level politics.[66]

Little had been done, he felt, to close the gap between 'them' and 'us'. Lord Hyndley, the Coal Board's first Chairman, had spent his life in the coal industry and had long favoured nationalisation. He believed, too, as did Citrine, that 'the welfare' of the miners should be ensured. But Michael wanted miners not just to be 'well looked after' but to have a greater degree of participation in the running of their industry.

He was in sympathy, therefore, with a comment in the *Manchester Guardian* after the fuel crisis of 1947 that the National Coal Board had 'turned out to be little more than another Government Department',[67] and he sympathised with the rank-and-file rather than with 'official' trade unionism when Grimethorpe miners staged a dramatic and economically devastating unofficial strike in the summer of that year. (Arthur Horner, Communist Secretary of the NUM, whom Morrison, for all his continuing horror of communism, a factor strongly influencing internal Labour Party and trade union politics between 1947 and 1950, would have liked to join the Board,[68] and William Lawther, its President, tried in vain to stop it.) The miners attacked the Board as fiercely as in previous generations they would have attacked the owners. Michael, disturbed by what he judged to be the 'remoteness' of the Board from many rank-and-file miners, concluded, although he too was remote from the scene, that the strikers were right.

This cannot have made life entirely easy for him.[69] After all, Transport House was not only the headquarters of the Labour Party but the home of the TUC and of the huge and powerful Transport and General Workers' Union, then dominated by the totally unintellectual Arthur Deakin, Bevin's successor at the Transport and General Workers' Union.[70] In a period when 'unofficial' strikes were common, Michael's unconditional statement that the 'brotherhood of man' was expressed in 'working-class solidarity during strikes' did not appeal to all who called themselves Brothers. He shared the approach of three writers who in 1956 were to publish their *Coal is Our Life*, who noted that 'far from disappearing, the attitudes of suspicion derived from earlier days' continued to flourish. Scarcely a day went by without at least one pit in Yorkshire experiencing a strike.'[71]

Michael was temperamentally attracted to the idea of 'workers' control', a cause that had been advocated years earlier by Cole, whose writings appealed to many young socialists in the post-war years, but the most that Michael could do while at Transport House was to press the case for what was called 'industrial democracy'.[72] And this, too, was a case that was difficult to propound in face of considerable trade union opposition. At the heart of it Bevin, who in anti-Morrisonian mood in war time had described as 'almost intolerable' the prospect of the country being governed by a series of London Transport Boards' (Morrison's model), but he had no sympathy with theories of industrial democracy.[73] When Michael wrote a party pamphlet on the subject in 1948, entitled *Industrial Democracy*, Number One, in a series called *Towards Tomorrow*, it nearly got suppressed by both Morrison and Bevin, for once in coalition, and the first edition, which in Bevin's view did not give the trade unions their proper place, had to be withdrawn. A second edition met some of the official objections, but left Michael uneasy.

Michael fell back on his experiences both at Dartington and at Swindon, while anticipating what he would argue later after he had spent time at the Tavistock Institute of Human Relations where the psychology of industrial relations was a major preoccupation. So also was 'the dynamics of family relationships'. The Institute, supported by many foundations, beginning with the Rockefeller, had been created after the war as a 'sister organisation' of the Tavistock Clinic, founded in 1920.

One of the writers who influenced Michael most at this time was the American psychologist, Elton Mayo, whom he got to know on a visit to England,[74] Mayo's daughter was commissioned by PEP to do the fieldwork for a British study, leading up to a PEP pamphlet *The Human Factor in Industry*. The conclusion of the Hawthorne experiment which Mayo carried out in a Westinghouse plant (did Michael remember his grandfather's connection with Westinghouse?) was that 'better output is in some way related to ... distinctively pleasanter, freer and happier working conditions'.[75]

While he was being drawn towards psychology, Michael was responsible for two other *Towards Tomorrow* pamphlets, both published in 1948 – *Public Ownership, the Next Step* and *Small Man: Big World* – the latter pointing the way to a long, unpublished report, not for the public but for his colleagues, *For Richer For Poorer* (1951). This was Michael's last report for the Party's Policy Committee, which was presided over by Morrison and to which Healey also belonged until he won a by-election in Leeds in 1952 and entered Parliament.

Michael apologised for the length of his report on the grounds that he 'could not allow himself enough time to make it shorter'. For the historian no apologies are necessary. *For Richer For Poorer* is the most interesting and revealing of all Michael's writings, seminal for himself as much as for the historian. In particular, it pointed the way ahead for him, often described somewhat misleadingly as the way from socialism to sociology. The psychology was equally important. Nor were politics ever left out.

While still working in the Labour Party's Research Department, Michael had already found his way into academic social research before the general election of 1950, and had started an LSE thesis, supervised by Laski, on how the Labour Party (and other parties) operated at the local level. The choice of subject emerged directly from his own experience, but for the Party it was a subject of perennial importance, raising questions both of policy and of 'discipline', a word that the Party then used frequently. Studying the subject formally made Michael read more Labour biographies than he had ever read before – they were not in short supply – but they left him dissatisfied. It was of crucial importance, therefore, when in 1951 he switched his supervisor and his subject from Laski to Titmuss, who had just become Professor of Social Administration at LSE, and from politics to sociology, concentrating on the family. In making the switch, the person who influenced him most was not Titmuss but the American sociologist Edward Shils, who had become a Reader at LSE in 1946.

In Michael's own phrase 'he [Shils] changed my life'. 'When he invited me to join his postgraduate seminar over which he presided with irrepressible intellectual *brio*, by some magic and to my surprise he made me feel I was already more of a sociologist than a politician and should make his strange trade mine.'[76] Shils, who wrote a much discussed sketch of American sociology in 1947,[77] left LSE in 1950 to join the newly founded Committee on Social Thought in Chicago, where a year earlier he had become an Associate Professor of Sociology in parallel with his LSE Readership. Michael continued to keep in close touch with him, however, and wrote an article with him on 'The Meaning of the Coronation'.[78] He was to continue to play a critical part in Michael's life as well as in his thinking. A neatly and meticulously reworked set of Shils's lecture notes are the first item in the only surviving black-bound volume of Michael's notes on lectures and books.

In 1947 Michael must have been interested in the fact that during the war Shils, seconded, like many of his most intellectual compatriots, to the British Army through the US Office of Strategic Services, had worked with an English psychiatrist, Henry Dicks, to investigate why the morale of the German *Wehrmacht* had not disintegrated in spite of crushing defeats in battle. This was intelligence work, and the answer that Shils and Dicks gave was that it was not ideology that was responsible, but the existence of a network of individual, institutional and collective associations.

The essay that Michael and Shils wrote jointly on the Coronation, which began with the sentence 'The heart has its reasons which the mind does not suspect', drew on the early experiences of both men. It was in sharp contrast, however, to the first book that Michael wrote while working in the Labour Party Research Department, *Labour's Plan for Plenty* (1947), a Gollancz publication, which he now looks back upon as 'more like an old sepia coloured photograph than a topical yellow-back'.[79] It was, he states, completely unoriginal. Indeed, it might well have been written by someone else. Yet in the light of his other writings, including *For Richer For Poorer* – and of international political history – it is worth a closer examination than he has been prepared to give it.

It reveals a superficially less complex Michael who was content to present the Labour Party as it wished to present itself, reiterating the point made in *Let Us Face the Future* that what was being offered in 1945 was an instalment, not a whole programme. It also underlined, as Cripps was doing, the economic difficulties that stood in the way of full implementation of policy. Michael emphasised that 'planning by persuasion is bound to be more complex than planning by coercion', and urged, as Morrison was urging, that the 'civil servants of socialism' should be 'drawn from industry and science and should be versed in economics and psychology'.[80] Only his reference to psychology suggests a special personal touch, and even that reference merely picked up the work being carried out by Sir George Schuster, a former

National Liberal MP (1938–1945), who in 1947 was made chairman of a Panel on Human Relations within a Government Committee on Industrial Productivity.[81]

There were no references in *Labour's Plan for Plenty* either to sociology or to the family, while in the unoriginal chapters on nationalisation there was little different from what Morrison would have said, except the statement (perhaps with Dartington in mind rather than with Grimethorpe) that 'for every management function there is an appropriate level', and the conclusion that 'the lower the level to which authority can be devolved, the better'.[82] A passage on civil aviation was doubtless also Michael's own, a follow-up to his book on the subject published by the Pilot Press in 1944.[83] Civil aviation would have to be subsidised 'until such time as aviation is no longer an instrument of national prestige'. Unfortunately, Michael offered no forecast of when that time would be. Nor did he anticipate the largely unforeseen popularisation of air travel, including air tourism. Those were years of strict control on currency for foreign travel. The package tour was not yet an item in the unplanned social agenda that was to influence the lives of people more than official social policy.

The sections on education in *Labour's Plan for Plenty* were disappointingly conventional, and there was nothing in the book about innovation in education or about political education. It was unduly optimistic for Michael to claim that as the Butler Education Act of 1944 was being implemented 'we are now well in reach of a unified educational system which will abolish educational privilege'.[84] There were still sharp divisions inside the Labour Party on comprehensive schools.[85] The 'guinea pigs' proposal in the Fleming Report of 1944 that a proportion of entrants to public schools should come from pupils in primary schools with fees paid by their local education authorities was criticised relatively gently, therefore, and the usual hope was expressed that 'there would be a general rise in the quality of education'.[86]

As a contribution to political education *Labour's Plan for Plenty*, published in a year of shortages and crises that gave a hollow ring to its title, was at best informative rather than inspirational. Nor did it raise questions for discussion, which was one of the objects of the Labour Party Research Department, except the big and persistent question printed not in his book but on its yellow dust cover, 'Why doesn't the Government tell the country what it is driving at?' Had Michael put this question there – or was it Victor Gollancz?[87]

The question had been raised by the French intellectual Bertrand de Jouvenel in his still readable study *The Problems of a Socialist England*, which was to be published in Britain in 1950. In his travels across the Channel, de Jouvenel, an Anglophile, who was sceptical about the Labour Government's belief in planning, found 'a certain malaise' among 'those very spirits' who had done most to keep the fires of socialism alight (Cole was one of the people to whom he talked).[88] 'Can it be that something of socialism has been lost on the way? Where are we going?' The word malaise was also used by Bevan in his book *In Place of Fear* a book that greatly impressed Michael after he had left Transport House: 'Boldness in words must be matched by boldness in deeds, or the result will be universal malaise, a debilitation of the public will, and a deep lassitude spreading throughout all the organs of administration. Audacity is the mood that should prevail among socialists.' The word 'apathy' was already beginning to enter political debate.

Michael was probably one of the other people to whom de Jouvenel talked when he visited the Labour Party's Research Department, and there were certainly two passages in de Jouvenel's analysis to which Michael would have responded sympathetically. 'The socialist ideal is not satisfied by an enlightened despotism dispensing benefits through the mediation of a bureaucracy.' 'The true aim of the spiritual guides of socialism is to raise to the highest pitch the feeling of sympathy and the will to mutual help, to bring to birth a fraternal society.'[89]

In *Labour's Plan for Plenty* Michael made nothing of these two points which he was often to make much of later. The furthest he went in his book, following Priestley, was to stress that when socialists stood for freedom, as they had to do, 'the State in a democracy is not the enemy but the servant of liberty'.[90] The State was still the main organising agent for both of them. Just as war-time production had been mobilised for need, so in peacetime it had to be organised through the State to secure 'millions of new houses, thousands of new schools, hospitals and health centres, more and better food, more books and theatres and sports fields'. There was 'no limit to needs'.[91] *Labour's Plan for Plenty* did not explain how the State was to accomplish these beneficent tasks. Indeed, there was more in the book about 'capitalist failure', the title of Chapter 2, than there was about socialist dream. Michael's later views on the role of the State find no place in it.[92]

There was another passage in de Jouvenel that would have appealed to the Michael of later years, the Michael identified in the title of this book. Complaining of 'the static attitude' both of workers and employers, de Jouvenel observed that to call industrialists 'entrepreneurs' was 'fast becoming a joke'. How could they possibly be entrepreneurs? 'Consider the infinity of steps to be taken and approaches to be made to get together the necessary authorisations' for action. In such circumstances, negotiating gifts were more in demand than abilities to identify openings and to seize opportunities. This was another question not raised in *Labour's Plan for Plenty*.[93] Michael still stood loyally by what had been said at the general election of 1945.

All that *Labour's Plan for Plenty* had in common with *For Richer For Poorer*, therefore, was that it centred on an election. The former looked backwards to 1945: the latter looked forwards to a future general election (would it be as early as 1951?), not to the last. It offered a programme which the Labour Party was unwilling to consider seriously, let alone to accept. *Let Us Face the Future* had registered Michael's initiation into the Labour Party: *For Richer For Poorer* witnessed his exit from its headquarters. In between there had been the general election of 1950, when the Labour Party's share of the poll was 46.1 per cent as against the Conservative Party's 43.4 per cent, but when, because of the electoral system, its majority was reduced to eight.

Before writing his swansong Michael published two pieces which were already very different from *Labour's Plan for Plenty* and which deliberately raised a host of questions, some fundamental. One was *Small Man: Big World*, described as 'a discussion of socialist democracy'. The other was a cogent policy document which the public never saw, a paper submitted to the Policy Committee of the Labour Party, 'Social Science Policy and the Labour Party Programme',[94] prepared while the Policy Committee was working on the manifesto for the 1950 general election, *Let Us Win through Together*. This was the sequel to *Let Us Face the Future* and a riposte to the Conservative Party's *The Right Road for Britain*. The latter was itself a riposte to *Labour Believes in Britain*, published between elections in 1949.

'Social Science Policy', which treated the need for more knowledge as 'immense and urgent', had no immediate impact except to create 'some embarrassment'.[95] It listed under seven headings topics which required research. They included 'the many novel problems arising from nationalisation', 'the economic implications of Western Union', 'colonial economic development', 'the optimum size and lay-out of new towns', 'changes in the birthrate, death-rate and the age composition of the population', and 'juvenile delinquency, crime, capital punishment'. The language that it used now sounds dated, but it had a long-term future. Michael, who was to remain deeply committed to research, rescued it from his archives, and almost a quarter of a century afterwards had it reprinted in *New Society*. This was just before

Parliament met after the second general election of 1974, which was won by the Labour Party.

Michael then gave it the title 'What Might Have Been?', and in re-introducing it raised a question of his own about it, which had haunted him since 1950 and which continued to haunt him after 1974.[96] 'How could one make this sort of thing [and it was the stuff of society] the stuff of politics if one agrees that it would be worth trying?' Michael now laid part of the blame on himself as well as on the Labour Party for the failure to make it the stuff of politics. After all, it was he who had written *Labour's Plan for Plenty*. He had written in the paper that 'there is a rapidly growing body of opinion, not least within the Labour Movement itself that more than trial and error are required and that many complex problems will not lead to common sense conclusions'.

Small Man: Big World began with a series of challenging quotations concerning the nature of socialism, and ended with a series of loaded questions for discussion groups, the first of them 'Does the individual feel that he matters far less in the big organisation then in the small group, like the family?', and the second 'Do people regard the authorities of one kind and another as remote and impersonal?' The first introductory quotation came from Friedrich Engels's *Anti-Dühring* (1878) and the last from a Bevan speech in the House of Commons in November 1947. Bevan himself had ended *Why Not Trust the Tories?* (1945) with his favourite historical quotation from the 1647 Putney Debates – Colonel Rainsborough's reply to a Cromwell statement about freedom and property.

'Under socialism,' Engels had written magisterially, 'anarchy in social production is replaced by conscious organisation on a planned basis ... Men's own social organisation ... will then become the voluntary act of men themselves.' Did socialists have to wait for ever for this replacement to happen? Communists, Michael suggested, were, for all their fascination with 'revolution', quite prepared to do so, in the meantime forgetting what the word 'voluntary' meant. Caught up in the intricacies of dialectical materialism, they were incapable of looking beyond 'the dictatorship of the proletariat' to a classless society, and most of them maintained unflinchingly that even that phase could be achieved *only* through violent revolution.

Michael demurred, as he had done in the 1930s, when he raised the same questions, and in 1945 when he helped to draft *Let Us Face the Future*. Yet the fact that he was now thinking on different lines from Morrison as well as from Marx was suggested by his choice of his final quote from Bevan: 'Bigness is the enemy of humanity.' The book

Small is Beautiful by E. F. Schumacher, whom Michael knew and who sometimes visited Dartington, a book consisting of shorter pieces written long before 1951, preceded by a Tawney quote which Michael might himself have used, did not appear until 1973: in one of the chapters, 'Ownership', all the quotations come from Tawney's *The Acquisitive Society*.

While Michael was meditating on the future of socialism between 1945 and 1951, Schumacher, six years older than Michael, was serving as an Economic Adviser to the British Control Commission in Germany, and after that, from 1950 to 1970 (not without a touch of irony) he was to be Economic Adviser to the National Coal Board.[97] He was to find a special place at Dartington after Michael had ceased to be the major influence on its affairs. Schumacher College was founded there, described as 'an international centre for ecological and spiritual studies'.

The other four borrowed passages at the beginning of *For Richer For Poorer* were obviously quotations which had made Michael think (he might have put them down in his black book), with the last of them – a Morrison quote – from a Hobhouse Memorial Trust Lecture delivered at LSE as long ago as 1944 before Michael had joined the Labour Party Research Department. 'I look with keen and genuine anticipation for the extension in the social field of scientific techniques,' Morrison had then told the professors, lecturers and, possibly, students at LSE, although he too, for different reasons, postponed the day, as Engels did. 'I do not think we are yet near to the day when you, the social scientists, will put me, the practical politician, right out of business.'

By 1950 Michael certainly knew as much as he would ever know about Morrison, 'the practical politician'. His other three quotes, therefore, came from people born before his own time who were to provide him with a message which he was never to abandon. William Morris, writing in *Commonweal* in 1889, put Bevan's terse aphorism into historical perspective. The late Archbishop of Canterbury, William Temple, greatly admired by Cripps (and by Elmhirst), one of the first people to use the term 'Welfare State', a term not used in *Let Us Face the Future*, complained in 1942 that 'while the worst horrors of the early factories' during the industrial revolution had been disposed of, 'the wage earners' were still not yet fully recognised as persons.[98]

Were they being recognised any differently *after* nationalisation? was one of the questions *Small Man: Big World* asked. Morris had intimated years before that they would not. 'It will be necessary for the unit of administration to be small enough for every citizen to feel himself responsible for its details', he had written, 'and be interested in them; individual men cannot shuffle off the business of life on to the shoulders of an abstraction called the State but must deal with each other.' To view the State as an abstraction was to view it very differently from Morrison, or, indeed, the other leaders of the 1945 Labour Party, and Michael was later to build on the Morris quote.

His third quote came from Tawney, who had been a friend of Temple and who years later was to provide the direct inspiration for Michael when he spent a short and controversial period outside the Labour Party in the breakaway Social Democratic Party, led by Labour's 'gang of four'. Indeed, he was then to be one of the co-founders of a Tawney Society. In Tawney's *The Acquisitive Society* (1921), a book which along with his *Equality* (1931) had had a bigger influence on socialists (including Bevan) than *Religion and the Rise of Capitalism*, he had written that 'in all cases where difficult and disagreeable work is to be done, the force which elicits it is normally not merely money [Michael had personal reasons for appreciating the 'merely'], but the public opinion and tradition of the little society in which the individual moves, and in the esteem of which he finds that which men value in success.' A new edition of *Equality* appeared in 1951.

Efficient, beautiful; equality, solidarity; macrocosm, microcosm; small man, big society; tradition, opinion – these were some of the pairs of concepts which Michael was weighing in 1950 as he felt increasingly dissatisfied in the Labour Party's Research Department. His own political views were taking shape within the context of his reading outside the struggles of contemporary politics and serious strains within his family. At the top of *Small Man: Big World* and every other Labour Party publication it was firmly stated that 'This pamphlet is like those in the preceding Labour Discussion series intended for discussion within the Labour Party. The Labour Party does not accept responsibility for the views contained in the pamphlet.' Or, it might have added, the quotations and the headings. Clearly in *Small Man: Big World* Michael was very much thinking for himself, although the warning note had an invitation attached to it. 'The Research Department of the Labour Party will welcome any reports from Discussion Groups on this subject.'

Small Man: Big World had six sections, revealing in their titles alone – the democratic dilemma; democratic leadership; democracy in the economy; democracy in the workplace; neighbourhood democracy; and support for social science. In the first section the family was held up as 'the model': 'there is no doubt that democracy can most easily flourish in the family and in other small groups built to the scale of the individual.' The 'great dilemma of modern society' was that while democracy seemed to require smallness, 'efficiency, promoted by the growth of science' often required bigness. There would be 'no solution' to the dilemma in 'going back to some misty past in which the small man lived in a small world' or even in 'substituting William Morris for the Morris car' – or for Morrison. Nevertheless, the size of organisations should be reduced wherever it could be without harming efficiency. Thereby 'the right kind of democratic leadership should be secured'.

In a second section on leadership Michael quoted Laski: 'it is fundamental to the conferance of power that it should never be permanent ... Responsible government in a democracy lies always in the shadow of coming defeat.' That was negative. For the positive, Michael turned outside Britain to David Lilienthal, the ex-Chairman of the Tennessee Valley Authority, a product of the New Deal. 'There is nothing in my experience more heartening than this: that devices of management which give a lift to the human spirit turn out so often to be the most "efficient" methods.'[99] Lilienthal had remained popular in the United States when the tide seemed to be going against the New Deal in 1945 and when the British Labour Government was under attack in the American press. The publisher Clare Luce told Lilienthal in April 1946, 'You are the only living New Dealer – I underline living – who is still popular.'

Negative and positive are well balanced in Michael's third section 'Democracy in the Economy'. 'Those on a champagne standard of life no longer enjoy the respect they once did.' New modes of communication should be opened up, new sources of respect fostered. 'Integrity' mattered. 'There should be as much direct contact as possible between the Government and the rank and file.' The section on 'Democracy in the Workplace' in Michael's pamphlet began boldly with the words 'Industrial democracy has sometimes been equated with Joint Production Committees. This is a superficial view.' 'Industrial democracy requires that every worker should have the opportunity to contribute his utmost to the running of the place in which he works.' This would be good for production. So, too, would reduced scale. Morale was lower on large building sites than on small ones.[100]

Michael did not quite reach the description to be made famous in Schumacher's sub-title, 'A Study of Economics as if People Mattered', but, after all, Schumacher was writing as an economist whose essay on the economics of full employment had been inspired by Keynes.[101] It was psychology that shaped Michael's vision. And psychology – of whatever variety – usually took it for granted that people did matter.

The fifth section of *Small Man: Big World*, 'Neighbourhood Democracy', introduced Michael's growing praise of 'community', a sociological concept with a history that long preceded the emergence of sociology and which in the post-war context was not confined to urban (or rural) sociology. Michael's 'attack on hugeness' began, however, with 'the great city' which represented 'giantism run mad'. Great cities reinforced a 'neurotic sense of powerlessness', the kind of 'powerlessness' which Michael himself was feeling. They should be divided into neighbourhood units. There should also be more new towns. Somewhat surprisingly, Michael quoted the Webbs, not Cole, as he might have done, to proclaim that the sense of solidarity among neighbours was 'a valuable social asset which socialism aims at preserving and intensifying'. They had made this evaluation within the context of post-First World War English social history before they eulogised the Soviet Union.[102]

Michael himself claimed that community associations were multiplying in post-Second World War Britain. The initiative to build 'makeshift centres' had come from below, drawing strength from the enhancement of the sense of community solidarity during the War. The centres, including those dealing with the arts and adult education (the latter were Tawney's favourite places), were of 'far more value than the fine buildings erected *for* and not *by* the people'. Neighbourhood Councils should become the chief instrument of local government. There was no reference to the region at this point in Michael's thinking; and it was not Michael, but the Local Government Boundary Commission, in its report for 1947, which suggested that urban parish councils might have the same responsibilities as 'the most lively councils in the countryside'.[103]

Social scientists, Michael pointed out, taught that the need to love and be loved was as fundamental emotionally as the need for food was physically. Democracy could best satisfy both needs. It would also 'allow aggressiveness to be released in a constructive manner'. 'Hostile impulses [would not be] forcibly repressed and canalised against scapegoats.' Michael, who depended on loving support, including financial support, from the Elmhirsts, had been freed from the process of regular and unremitting psychoanalysis when he wrote these words and was releasing his own aggressiveness in what he believed to be a constructive manner. A spurt of writing was to follow.

If this section of *Small Man: Big World* anticipated Michael's work at Bethnal Green, the last section anticipated his work at the Social

Science Research Council. Called 'Support for Social Science', it began with 'the new social sciences of psychology, sociology and anthropology'. What they offered was not just an analysis of the theoretical virtues of democracy. They were beginning to demonstrate in workplace and community (there was much in the pamphlet about the themes of his *Industrial Democracy*) how democracy can be 'made to work more effectively in practice'. Research based on fieldwork in the social sciences was 'every bit as important', therefore, as research in the natural sciences, indeed, in Michael's opinion even more important. Yet expenditure on it was only 1 per cent of that being spent on the natural sciences.

Not the least important contribution of social scientists to the future, Michael believed – and he was an optimist in this regard – was their support for an optimistic view of human nature. To the question whether or not it was 'Utopian' to put one's faith in an integrated socialist democracy, Michael, looking to Robert Owen as well as the new social scientists, gave the unequivocal answer, yes. The strength of democracy was that it satisfied human needs, first and foremost 'the need to love': 'it gave opportunity for every person to contribute what he can to the welfare of his fellows'.

'New knowledge' derived from the social sciences would enable two strands in British socialism to 'blend' – Fabian socialism, which emphasised efficiency and social justice and the necessity of assembling 'facts', and 'idealistic' socialism, like that of Owen or Morris, which emphasised the dignity of man and of labour. Michael suggested a compromise rather than a blend in a tantalising sentence, one of many such, which began with 'If'. 'If the socialists of the latter persuasion were ready to restrain their more impractical ideas and compromise with efficiency, idealism need not lead to economic collapse and democratic disorder but to a society, built on the model of the family, which is not only more comradely but more efficient.'

Michael's last words in recounting this dream came neither from the Webbs nor from Owen and Morris – nor, indeed, from Marx and Engels. He chose instead the closing words of Lewis Mumford's *The Culture of Cities*, published the year before the outbreak of the Second World War. 'None of us may live to see the complete building, and perhaps in the nature of things the building can never be completed: but some of us will see the flag or the fir tree that the workers will plant aloft in ancient ritual when they cap the topmost storey.'[104]

There was an element of irony in Michael's borrowing of this particular rhetoric. Mumford, one of the best known American writers on cities, also wrote in the same book of the 'insensate industrial town' of the early nineteenth century, describing it as 'a rabbit warren not an organ of human association'. Yet it was during that century that the voluntarism which Michael prized so much had first been forged in the crucible.[105]

There were ten questions at the end of *Small Man: Big World*, constituting a kind of examination paper on socialism, the last of them a question which must be asked in relation to the whole of Michael's work, then and later – 'Have Socialists (capital S) taken too rosy a view of human nature?' The first question, which like almost every other question in the ten, begged many other questions, was to be at the heart of Michael's preoccupations. 'Does the individual feel that he matters far less in the big organisation than in the small group like the family?'

On the first page the family was described as a small group in which everyone could have 'an active part in making decisions and carrying them out: in the big group, like the nation, not everyone can have a direct and continuous say in the way it is run. The common purposes of the small group are more easily understood; in the large group the people at the top tend to get out of touch with those at the bottom, and the small man to regard those at the top as "they", the impersonal authorities with mysterious power over himself.'

Michael had nothing to say about family size, about 'nuclear' or 'extended' families, about single families, or about population as a whole.[106] Yet he did favour 'extending the birth control advice at present given by local authorities and others';[107] and while he was at pains to avoid references to 'problem families', which were to capture more and more public attention later in his life, he conceded, a minor concession, that 'no family is always cooperative'. More to the point for him, 'in most families things are done together. Things are talked over together. Things are often decided together.'

All the questions in Michael's list demanded the Latin prefix *Nonne*: they expected 'yes', as many of Michael's later questions were to do. 'Do people regard the authorities of one kind and another as remote and impersonal? Should there be consultation between the rank-and-file worker and the foreman or other official immediately above him?' 'Are the wish to get more money and the fear of the sack both weaker incentives to work than they used to be?' It would be revealing to have an account of what was being said in the discussion groups which were examining *Small Man: Big World*.

Electors do not answer set questions; they mark Xs on ballot papers. In the two years following the publication of *Small Man: Big World*, Michael and his office were involved in preparing for an election which was to be narrowly won by the Labour Party. The questions posed by Michael have more than historic interest, however, and those, for example, on non-monetary incentives, written at a time when goods were scarce, are basic. They are also topical in the twenty-first century. For Michael, the desire for individual gain was a legacy from the old acquisitive society, but on this occasion, he did not look back historically to the formation of that society (and the role of religion) as Tawney did. Instead, he dealt with contemporary society, as he judged it to be or as it was becoming, poised on the edge of significant social change. Soon 'for the first time' there was what seemed to be plenty of money for substantial sections of the working classes, generated not by Government but by market forces.[108]

In a 'different kind of society' – and this was the kind of society that had not yet emerged – 'the desire for gain might, as some economists have suggested, be sharpened by stimulating people to strive for a champagne standard of life. But most sensible people [and here, having once talked of "a champagne fizz", he was on awkward ground] would probably settle [*pace* Bevan and Jennie Lee[109]] for a glass of Guinness and a bit of leisure to drink it in.' 'Most people [sensible or not?] would obviously like a lot more than they have got; we would still like much more beef with our mustard, and for some people an issue at the next election will be the number of slices in the bacon ration.'

It was, and so was sugar. In September 1949 Lord Lyle and his fellow-directors of Tate and Lyle Ltd. presented Mr. Cube to the public on every packet of Tate and Lyle sugar, accompanied by such slogans as 'TATE NOT STATE'. They had consulted their shareholders, although Morrison claimed that they had not and had warned them 'to be specially careful' of the legal consequences of their campaign. They had moved from packets to posters, and now talked of a petition. The critique of the state, which was to be pursued with determination by Michael, was thus sloganised by a powerful business organisation which on the eve of an election approached the State from an angle very different from his.[110]

In *Small Man: Big World* Michael stated that 'victories in the battle of ideas are more permanent than victories in general elections', but when he suggested that 'those on a champagne standard of life no longer enjoy the respect they did', he was wrong. Fascination in the popular press with Lady Docker and her luxury cars and champagne corks was to demonstrate that 'most people' were not changing their attitudes to ostentatious wealth as quickly as Michael – or Cripps – wished them to do. Before the rise of television the press had long responded to popular curiosity concerning ways of life very different from those most people 'enjoyed'. It was a great omission in *Small Man: Big World* that there was nothing about the role of the media. Priestley had anticipated more clearly than Michael what the media could and would do. In his lifetime the Coronation about which he and Shils had written could become a 'media event' and the Royal Family consider themselves as 'celebrities'.[111]

When it came not to the examination but to the count, the Labour Party won the 'long awaited and closely fought' general election in February 1950, for which another huge *Speakers' Handbook* was prepared by the Research Department. Michael had once more been involved in the preparation of the final Manifesto, *Let Us Win Through Together*, a sequel to *Labour Believes in Britain*, which had been released to the press as early as April 1949 and which had extended the list of industries ripe for nationalisation to include not only sugar and sugar refining but meat and fruit wholesaling, water, cement – and industrial assurance. From the left Ian Mikardo had wished to add to the 1949 list; on the right there were reservations about whether steel should be kept on it. A lively pamphlet, *Keeping Left*, was produced the day after the dissolution of Parliament was announced. It was described in the *Daily Herald* as not 'an alternative programme' to *Labour Believes in Britain*, but 'an agenda for the 1950–55 Parliament'.[112]

Debate within the Party was as intense as debate between the parties, with a compromise being reached on industrial insurance, a compromise on lines suggested by Michael: it was now not to be 'nationalised', but 'mutualised'.[113] For him, if not for most of his colleagues, this was far more than a terminological change. He was becoming increasingly attached to the idea of mutual aid, and personal and family insurance, the province of large and uncontrolled business, seemed the right place to start. Mutualisation appealed too to the Co-operative Insurance Society which had a substantial stake in the insurance business and was alarmed by the word 'nationalisation'.[114]

Another suggestion of Michael's, completely his own, was slipped in and was sufficiently popular with the public in 1950 to be picked out in a Gallup Poll at the very top of a list of favourite items in the Manifesto. It was an idea with a great future – a consumer advisory service. But it was not picked up by the press, and Michael doubts whether any member of the National Executive noticed that the item was there. He notes also, however, that after the narrow election victory the Board of Trade looked into the proposal – two very senior civil servants talked to him about it – before declaring it to be unworkable.[115] Harold Wilson, then President of the Board of Trade, concurred. Gaitskell was by then Chancellor of the Exchequer, so that there may well have been agreement between them on this issue.

'Thank God,' was Michael's later comment. It had been good to keep the State out. Yet for Michael this was to be only the beginning. He knew that the idea of a consumer service along the lines he had envisaged had been found feasible in the United States, and he bided his time. The end product was to be another version of mutual aid, the Consumers' Association, for Michael 'a new style consumers' cooperative', something more than a lobby or what English writers on politics called a 'pressure group'.[116] Later still, however, there was to be a National Consumer Council which Michael was to chair (a Labour Government was back in power) from 1975 to 1977.

The Labour Party majority in 1950 was too small to enable it to carry out even the programme set out in the Manifesto, which through compromise had 'papered over' many cracks.[117] The 'rank-and-file', however, had proved more solid than the Manifesto, as Michael deduced from a local survey he had commissioned in Greenwich of attitudes to the Labour and Conservative election broadcasts. Priestley was felt to have struck a 'reasonable man', non-party note: Charles (later Lord) Hill, the former 'Radio Doctor', whom the Conservatives called their own Priestley, had been deliberately and aggressively partisan. (He coined the most memorable word of the campaign, 'Queuetopia'.) On the morning after his broadcast there was a flood of telephone calls at Conservative Central Office from people who now wished to become active party workers, but according to the Greenwich survey only one person said that he had changed his mind as a result of Hill's broadcast, and he had switched from Conservative to Labour.[118]

There were some interesting local comments, including grumbles that the speakers in general lacked 'fire' and 'drive' and that they were not communicating with the public: 'Mr. Bevin seemed to be talking to Mr. Churchill not to me.'[119] This was the kind of comment that influenced Michael's thinking between then and the next general election in 1951, but it was of less interest to Labour leaders, who were separately pursuing their own destinies, not least Morrison, who was arguing that there had been a shift from Labour to Conservative among some 'middle-class voters', and that in order to counter this the Party should concentrate on a policy of 'consolidation' rather than a new or broader programme.

In sharp contrast, Michael believed that instead it should increase its appeal to 'working-class' voters who in 1950 had voted Conservative, pointing out in a paper which he wrote for a Labour Party *post-mortem* on the 1950 election, held at Beatrice Webb House, Dorking, that according to the Gallup Poll 21 per cent of the total electorate consisted of working-class people who voted Tory.[120] Phillips supported Michael's version of the reasons for electoral defeat, as did Attlee, who acknowledged that there had been 'an enormous anti-Labour vote in industrial areas such as Lancashire'. Yet Attlee, like Morrison, came out of the analysis in favour of 'consolidation'.[121]

By then, both the Labour rank-and-file and Labour leaders – like the press – were already asking the questions 'Who would follow Attlee?' 'How long would he stay?' Gaitskell, the future leader of the Party, was already climbing the slippery pole, and in October 1950 he replaced Cripps, tired as well as unfit, as Chancellor of the Exchequer. The scene was changing more rapidly than the agenda, as several familiar leaders were disappearing from view and those who remained seemed exhausted. In March 1951, Bevin, also unwell, left the Foreign Office, if reluctantly, to die soon afterwards, to be succeeded by his old rival Morrison, the healthy survivor, still busy planning further party manifestos – and for the Festival of Britain – but ultimately himself to lose to Gaitskell in a personal contest for the leadership.

Attlee had to stay in hospital with a duodenal ulcer at a critical point, and in April 1951 Bevan, who had been moved from Health to Labour earlier in the year, for him an uncongenial move, resigned from the Government along with Wilson and John Freeman over National Health Service charges, proposed in Gaitskell's budget. These were only a pretext. A power struggle was in progress, with the 'Bevanites' as they quickly came to be called – they also included R. H. S. Crossman – now aligned against an equally variegated Labour Party 'right'.[122]

Michael, much as he admired Bevan, felt no more taste for such open manoeuvring within the Party, which necessarily involved bitter struggles between MPs and rank-and-file party workers, than he had felt for the Party manoeuvring behind the scenes in 1945, about which he knew far less. The MP to whom he now drew closest was Anthony Crosland, an intimate friend and staunch supporter of Gaitskell, who had won his seat (South Gloucester) in 1950. This was an important alignment.

The two men, different in background and temperament, enjoyed a two-way exchange, which for both of them had a touch of mischievous fun about it: both believed that conservatism was a problem at least as much as capitalism and that the idea of abolishing classes was not 'so chimerical an undertaking as it would have appeared some years ago'. Crosland's widow Susan in a revealing biography of her husband talks of him arguing about psychology and sociology with Michael. They welcomed 'creative tension', but they shared many beliefs, including the need, as they saw it, to develop comprehensive schools and at the same time destroy the 'privilege' of the public schools.[123] Crosland's *Future of Socialism* (1956), which ranged far more widely over current and future politics, was influential in a changing Labour Party.[124]

The Labour Party was to poll its highest total vote at the general election of 1951, its share reaching 48.8 per cent as against the Conservative Party's 48 per cent, but the Conservatives under Churchill won a majority of 17 seats. They were then to remain in power for 13 years, increasing their majority in 1955 to 67. The main victims at the 1951 general election were Liberals: their total vote collapsed. Thereafter, however, there were to be such sharp divisions in the Labour Party that a kind of 'civil war' ensued, at its ugliest at the annual conference of the party at Morecambe in 1952. 'We haven't had so strong hatreds since 1931,' wrote an aged and now uninfluential Dalton. 'Then one section left the Party, but now everyone is staying on.'[125]

Michael was out of the Party Central Office by the time of Morecambe when Party conflicts were revealed for everyone in the country to see. Indeed, long before the general election of 1951 he had lost confidence in the Party whose Central Office he had joined with such confidence in 1944. By way of thanks to him it sent him on a kind of farewell world tour at the end of 1950, looking for ideas, and during the course of it he met Labour or Socialist leaders in Israel, the first country he visited, Australia, New Zealand, India and Pakistan. He also visited Malaya and Singapore. Both in Australia and New Zealand the Labour Party had recently lost power, and Michael interviewed two party leaders now in opposition – Walter Nash, who was to be New Zealand's next Labour Prime Minister in 1957, and Benedict Chiffley, Australia's last Labour Prime Minister, defeated in 1949. To the question why Labour had lost power in their own countries they gave different answers. Nash said that the Party had been in power for 14 years and that this was felt to be enough. Chiffley replied more simply 'God knows'.

It must have seemed very pertinent – if shocking – to Michael when Nash added that he had instructed MPs 'not to be too precise about the future programme'. The Secretary of the Australian Labour Party, Pat Kenelly, must have surprised Michael even more, however, when he told him that Morgan Phillips was 'the greatest man he had ever known'. Ken Baxter, the Secretary/Treasurer of the Australian

Federation of Labour, said his attitude towards the waterfront workers of Sydney was the same as that of Arthur Deakin to London's dockers. It was 'obvious', he said, that the communists were responsible for the troubles, a statement which Michael commented on tersely, 'This isn't so obvious to me.'[126]

On his return to Britain the Party continued to pay Michael his salary until he had finished his completely independent-minded Report, *For Richer For Poorer*.[127] Completed in 1951, it was substantially longer than *Small Man: Big World* and *Labour's Plan for Plenty* put together. Indeed, it was far longer than anything else that Michael had ever written. He had kept a diary as he travelled, but he did not pick up many new ideas from other countries. Nor did any of them figure in *For Richer For Poorer*. While travelling, he had asked relevant questions, however, about class, education and the family and had met members of his own family living in Australia, some for the first time, some in a long-delayed family reunion about which a play might have been written. He often had it in his mind that he might write a play.

The fact that the experience of other countries did not greatly interest Britain's Labour Party leaders mattered less to him on his return than the fact that they were not interested in those few ideas from abroad that he did pass on. They were even less interested in his own ideas, which were many. One of the few members of the National Executive Committee who read *For Richer For Poorer*, Edith Summerskill, doctor as well as politician, told him that it was 'good stuff', 'extraordinary', but she immediately went on to ask him what on earth he was going to do with it. 'It's not right, is it,' she went on, 'for the Labour Party?' Edith, an unflinching feminist, had entered Parliament in 1938 after a famous by-election at Fulham, when Michael was a student. She had kept her maiden name, and she was to chair the Party's National Executive in 1955.

Perhaps Edith, mother of another future Member of Parliament, Shirley, and author of an autobiography called *A Woman's World* (1967), had begun to be fascinated by Michael's draft when she read the first half of the very first sentence: 'You can always find out what a man's wife is like by listening to his opinions on women in general.' I myself when reading *For Richer For Poorer* for the first time was fascinated by the second half of this same sentence – 'and discover people's attitude to the present by hearing their judgements on the past.' 'Historians,' Michael went on, 'if never a reliable guide to yesterday, are always a reliable guide to today, and since it has become as usual for them to question both the fact of past and the inevitability of future progress, as it was for their grandfathers not to, we can infer that their world is not a happy one. Progress is a Comet – the noise comes after.'

It is interesting that one of the rare references to his own children in Michael's writing refers to the Comet, the exciting new British aircraft which had a glamorous but brief career.[128] In *For Richer For Poorer*, after referring to the fact that 'a world new and uncanny' to parents 'is just every day to their children', accepting change without recognising it as such, Michael describes his youngest son, then aged three, returning from London Airport and 'chuffing excitedly around the room making the noise of an engine' and 'shrieking "I am a Comet"'. 'Only when he has become a parent in his turn (Rutherford's successors willing)', Michael goes on (a rare cross-reference to the bomb which preoccupied many socialists), 'and new wonders have reduced the triumphs of the present to insignificance, may he too realise how difficult it was for his parents to accustom themselves to a society being buffeted by the winds of change, and it may be the worse for him if the wind has by then become a tempest.'

Michael's use of this powerful metaphor, powerful even in an age of jet aircraft, long preceded that of Harold Macmillan. Much of *For Richer For Poorer* is concerned with change, and while much of it is future-looking, there is much also about the past (in places a somewhat idealised past); and in the same section as the Comet reference the challengeable proposition is advanced that 'the family is always a brake upon the pace of change, for, as long as children are reared in their parents' homes, parents exert an educational influence upon them which outweighs that of school-teacher or any other outsiders'. This was a proposition which Michael was to repeat in various forms and in various contexts. A very striking sentence that might also have been written by him at any time in his life was: 'If love did not fly out of the window when poverty came in at the door, that was a tribute to the devotion of parents, not to society.'

Interesting sections on education in *For Richer For Poorer* point the way towards *The Rise of the Meritocracy*, which incorporates very similar passages. It is no more possible, however, completely to separate out what Michael says about family and education in this and his other writings than it is to separate out what he says about family and community. It is the family which always provides him with his starting point, a very different starting point from that of either Gaitskell or Bevan – or, for that matter Crossman or Crosland. 'The ordinary, struggling family we take for granted. It is the home of our affections and the anchor of our lives.' 'Why worry about it?' he asks. 'We know in a general kind of way that it is the foundation of society, and we assume that this, the only permanent social institution, will continue to survive unscathed.'

And then, for a moment, in developing his argument in 1951 Michael paused to remember the nature of his would-be readership, the National Executive of the Labour Party. Given that 'the Labour Party should in its policy-making for the future give some prominence to the needs of the family', it should recall that 'it was not until the election of a Labour Government in 1945 that anything effective was done to ease the strain of modern living on the ordinary, workaday family. The National Health Service, Family Allowances, Food Subsidies and the Achievement in Housing are but four of the pillars of the Welfare State which are memorials to the living, not the dead. They are precedents which, I shall urge in the following pages, we should prepare to follow when next a Government is elected, responsive, above all, to the mothers in whose arms the future rests.'

For Richer For Poorer ends with a passage on family values, actually using the word 'values', a word that was to acquire new life in Thatcher's Britain. Its early use should be compared with what has subsequently been said in changing circumstances about family values, not least by the Conservatives, who were saying little about them in 1951. One of Michael's 1951 passages relates them directly to community values:

> The values to preserve and strengthen are the values of the family: words such as 'kind', 'generous', 'gentle', 'liberal', all have a common derivation. The values to preserve and strengthen are the values of the community: solidarity, neighbourliness, and mutual aid. We should not rest until in Britain and beyond people everywhere can say that 'STRENGTH AND DIGNITY ARE HER CLOTHING'.

'Reviving the community would give mothers more help with their lives', and 'neighbourly socialism could become the core of a Third Force in ideas, a faith free from the materialism of the USA and the tyranny of the USSR'. A 'Third Force', not a 'Third Way', but the approach was similar.

In general, finance, the main preoccupation of Gaitskell and Butler, who succeeded Gaitskell as Chancellor of the Exchequer after the Conservative victory of 1951, is dealt with summarily in *For Richer For Poorer*, although there is one reference to 'the monstrous momentum of inflation' and there is one memorable sentence that seemed directly relevant: 'If the national budget is balanced, it will be done at the expense of unbalancing the budget of every poor family in the country.'[129] At no point, fresh from his world tour, did Michael allow 'Butskellite' economics to disturb the flow of his social argument which has a strong anti-materialist undertow. 'In the universe of ideas we cannot look to any Marshall Plan. We can see in America, despite its immense achievements and the strength of the liberal forces which still endure, the results of concentrating on material things to the exclusion of the things of the spirit, the results of putting calculation of profitability before the ideal of human perfectibility.'

In the universe of things – and Michael was unimpressed by the fact that there were more and more of them – 'vacuum cleaners and radios [could not] look after children'. There was a note of irony in his conclusion:

> If British women are suffering from a sense of injustice, that is the greatest chance British industry has ever had, and a sure guarantee that productivity will rise really fast in the next twenty years. Feed it. Circulate more pictures of Elizabeth Taylor in nylons. Advertise the shiny streamliner that would be the envy of Mrs. Jones. Encourage sponsored radio and television so that hour by hour housewives can be persuaded to want far more than they have got. Stoke up the boilers of feminine ambition, and not all Trelawny's men will be able to stand up against the clamour from the kitchen. We will give in – and get down to work.

This was scarcely what to expect from a Labour Party Report, although there were shades of Priestley in it.

It was also scarcely what to expect from the founder of the Consumers' Association. Most surprisingly of all, the 'welfare state', which had done much for the family, was treated very strangely for a Labour Party readership:

> The very name [welfare state] is against it. It must have been invented by a diabolical copywriter who knew that if the nation was not poisoned by the first cold word, recalling the smell of carbolic acid and the tough brown paper of ration books [Michael did not wish to dispense with these], it could be done to death by the second cold word, suggesting the Law Court [Michael knew about this at first hand], the Sanitary Inspector and the Recruiting Office. When the name is so ill-chosen, is there any wonder that many people should find so distasteful the idea that this thing should help the family. The family is small and intimate, real people who sing songs and drink stout together on Christmas Eve [Dickensian: Priestleyesque]: the family is mine. The State belongs to someone else, belongs maybe to itself.

This unforgettable passage is far removed in tone from most of the writing on the 'welfare state' at the time, including that of Titmuss, who was fully aware of the limitations of redistribution through the welfare state and who talked of its 'biases' in favour of the middle classes. It is still further removed from T. H. Marshall's *Citizenship and Social Class* (1950) which has been rightly regarded as one of the seminal books of the period.

It was also just as far removed from Fabian socialism.[130] There was no reference to the family in Cole's revised version of the pamphlet *The Fabian Society* (1947) which stressed that 'the Fabian Society is not simply a part of the Labour Party, but an independent body of persons organised for furthering the socialist cause'. It noted that one of the Society's difficulties in 'these latter days' is 'that there is no longer the same zeal as there once was for selling Socialist literature'.

It is relevant to note in this context that when the Fabian Society made plans to celebrate the anniversary of the publication of its historic volume of *Fabian Essays* (1889), edited by George Bernard Shaw, which had sold out within in a month, it ran into difficulties with both Michael and Cole. It contemplated a new volume of essays, to be edited by Crossman, and Michael was a member of the preparatory group along with Crosland, Roy Jenkins, Mikardo, the Coles (Cole was the Chairman of the group) and Wilson (but not Gaitskell). It also included the academics David Worswick, Hugh Clegg and Allan Flanders and others, some of whom might have been writing for PEP: indeed, Goodman, Director of PEP until 1953, was himself a member.

When the volume appeared, with an introduction by Attlee, Michael's name was not on the list of essayists, and Margaret Cole had to explain in the Preface, which was signed by herself and by Crossman, that her husband had broken his association with the group while it was meeting. So too had Michael. In the policy document that he had prepared for the general election of 1950, which ended with the words 'Need for Social Science Research Council', he had given a warning that if the Labour Party were to focus primarily on improving the standard of living this would be a 'hollow purpose', 'implanted by capitalism with its glorification of greed and competition'. He added that if it were also to focus exclusively on the State it would break with its heritage, still a word that carried awe with it. (Because of the general election of 1950 the Party had not celebrated its own jubilee.)

In his 1950 document Michael this time quoted Cole, who in his *Guild Socialism* (1920) had written, as Morris had written, of the dangers of centralisation and, indeed, of concentration of power.

'Individual men cannot shuffle off the business of life on the shoulders of an abstraction called the State but must deal with each other.' Abandoning talk of 'meld' or of 'compromise', which had figured in *Small Man: Big World*, Michael now complained of the domination of Fabian empiricists over Labour Party thinking. Could not the 'emotionally inspired aims of socialism be clarified with the aid of social science?' Some of it might come from 'the capitalist United States'.

Michael's comments on the family (and to a lesser extent on education) in his notes for a 1950 manifesto – and later in his unpublished *magnum opus* – are important because they lead directly into his later work as a sociologist. They are important too in relation to other writings on socialism soon after the electoral defeat of the Labour Party in 1951. It is interesting to compare both *For Richer For Poorer* and *Small Man: Big World* with, for example, the Penguin Special, Socialist Union's *Twentieth Century Socialism* (1956), described on the cover as 'a challenging and controversial study of the nature of a socialist economic system and the effect it would have on the life of man'. Its authors, not named, as writers of Fabian Society pamphlets and essays were, never mentioned the family once, although they treated socialist values as 'embodied in the ideals of equality, freedom and fellowship'.

When the *New Fabian Essays* appeared, Attlee remarked, as he might have remarked of the *Target for Tomorrow* booklets, that they 'should stimulate thought in the Movement'. 'Several of them deal with the problem of making democracy effective' in a society where 'managerial autocracy' was 'an increasing danger'. Attlee also referred in his introduction to the fact that the essayists were discussing socialist policy 'in the light of very different conditions from those obtaining in the days of their great predecessors', a comment which has since been echoed by almost all his successors as Labour Party leader.[131] Yet Attlee said nothing of the strand in socialism from which Michael, for personal as well as for public reasons, was now drawing strength and inspiration.

Edward Thompson, anti-Fabian and leader of the 'New Left', at the other end of the spectrum from the Socialist Union, was to complain soon afterwards in his remarkable biography of William Morris of Attlee's unwillingness to examine these same strands. He had made no effort to understand Morris, Thompson grumbled, while granting him conventional praise.[132] Attlee, however, had left the centre of the stage before the emergence of the New Left, a political, social and cultural phenomenon, the origins of which, national and international, were well described by Thompson, an ex-Communist, in the *New Reasoner*, one of two periodicals which held the New Left together. The other was the *Universities and Left Review*. There was a parallel New Left movement across the Atlantic, and there were links too with continental European movements.[133]

By the time that Thompson's *William Morris* appeared in 1955 Michael was in Bethnal Green, having spent a year in the Tavistock Institute, where he further developed his knowledge of psychology. When he left Transport House, he was succeeded by Wilfred Fienburgh, a politician of promise who was to die young, killed when his car hit a tree, and to bequeath as his literary testament not a treatise on principles but a novel dealing with party scandals, *Johnny Come Home*.[134]

While at the Tavistock Institute, Michael extended the notes he had made in *For Richer For Poorer* concerning 'love' as 'the necessary, not the only condition, for healthy personality development'. 'Child can be stifled by love if parents do not respect the child's personality. Family should be democratic group, defined as one in which all members are invited to participate in determining ends and means.' The main aim of governmental policy should be 'to help parents to form democratic family groups in which children [are] treated with respect'. There were two types of parent – the 'well-adjusted' and the 'maladjusted' ('feeding to clock', rapid weaning'; 'rapid toilet training'; 'beating – genuinely believing that it is good for child'). The latter should be helped with 'much better advice then he or she receives at present'.

These brief notes point to the undisclosed fact that Michael was not only in the course of further psychoanalysis, but was facing a family crisis of his own. He was in great debt at this time not to a political thinker – or a sociologist – but to his son Chris's psychologist, Dr Winnicott, author of *Through Paediatrics to Psychoanalysis*, published by Tavistock Publications in 1958.[135] Before reaching Bethnal Green, however, via Tavistock Square, Michael had failed to reach the University of Birmingham, when he applied for a job as assistant lecturer in sociology. His friend Charles Madge, one of the founders of Mass Observation, whose first wife was the poet Kathleen Raine, had worked with Michael in PEP in 1943 and had made his way to a Birmingham Chair in Sociology with no better academic qualifications on paper than Michael. One of his publications was a book of poems called *The Father Found* (1941). Madge could not help Michael, however, at a moment when he particularly needed help. His influence in the University was limited. He stayed on at Birmingham, however, until 1970 by which time Michael had established his reputation both as a writer and as a man of action.

In 1954 luck was with Michael, if not with Birmingham. To have been made an assistant lecturer at Birmingham would have been a setback to Michael's developing career, even though it was a lively university, where Halsey was a lecturer from 1954 to 1962 and where Lafitte was to be installed as a Professor in 1959.[136] Instead, he was to benefit from being outside a university and, in the first instance, from carrying out a study of disaster, a report on the Thames floods at Canvey Island in 1954.[137] Familiar as he was with 'crises', Michael found the human story of physical disaster moving and compelling. This was, in a sense, the ideal preparation for a move to Bethnal Green, and in the same year, 1954, his thesis completed, he published his first article on what was to be subject of the first of his two best-known books. 'Kinship and Family in East London' appeared in the journal *Man*.

Theoretical sociology might have led Michael to write about Bethnal Green, but it would never have made him move his office there and to establish an Institute of his own. In fact, it was neither psychology nor sociology that provided the bridge. Anthropology, the last 'social science' that Michael mentioned in his list of relevant aids to policy-making, guided him in his journey. *Man* was a very different learned periodical from the *British Journal of Sociology* which was founded in 1950 by LSE sociologists, many of them involved in PEP, in conjunction with Routledge, publishers who had already established a niche in the social sciences.[138] A year earlier the British Sociological Association had been founded, with Titmuss amongst its first members. That was an academic landmark.

It was Asian and African family studies – and not British studies – to which Michael first turned in his thesis on Bethnal Green; and in the completed thesis he explained carefully how anthropology had 'helped to make more precise the terms for describing the subject matter of the enquiry'.[139] By the time that he co-authored his book *Family and Kinship in East London*, the first product of the new Institute of Community Studies, which appeared in 1957, he had realised that as he and Willmott, his co-author, put it, the vocabulary that anthropologists had employed in describing the societies they studied was 'not necessarily apt in describing our own'.[140] He also realised that sociology was at last making strides in Britain as an academic discipline.

Willmott, eight years younger than Michael, was the first person he attracted to his new Institute. He had worked with Michael in the Labour Party's Research Department. It helped both there and in Bethnal Green, however, that his background and his education were completely different from Michael's. There was no Dartington in his personal history. Before the war Willmott had served his time as an engineering apprentice, and at the end of the war he was a Bevin boy working in the coal mines. While a student at Ruskin College he had written so enthusiastically to Michael about *Small Man: Big World*, enclosing a piece of writing of his own, that Michael invited him to lunch. He had asked him to prepare a dummy broadsheet on 'Nationalisation'. Peter had no typewriter and rang Michael from a public telephone box. Immediately he was offered a job at Transport House.

Having joined the Labour Party Research Department through Michael, Willmott left it a little later. They had no desire to stay in Transport House after the 1951 general election. Yet both of them felt that the Party might be redeemed through the social sciences, and Peter was eventually to take an external degree in sociology and to become Co-Director of the Institute of Community Studies. 'We believed,' Michael recalled – and he was speaking for them both – 'that if only the Labour Government had somehow been in closer touch with supporters, above all working-class supporters, things might have been much better. It could partly be that they just really didn't know what was going on in the minds of ordinary people and we thought that if we could act as interpreters that it really could have an effect.'[141] Michael had already carried out research in Bethnal Green, talking to 'ordinary people'. Now he and Peter were determined to serve as interpreters.

From a background very different from both Michael and Peter, Shils was to hail the Institute for Community Studies as 'the chief achievement of sociology outside the universities' and to salute Michael as 'the first of those Labour supporters who renounced the tired phrases of inherited socialist doctrine and sought contact with reality by other means'.[142] In fact, some of the first members of the Institute were to become University professors, and its emphasis then and later on policy issues, including housing (it wanted research to lead to action), kept it closer to the Labour Party than PEP had been, was or wished to be. Moreover, in setting out explicitly to examine the daily lives and needs of working-class people, the Institute was driven by the sense that their attitudes and activities had been treated inadequately by people in power.[143] Communicating and interpreting started on the spot in Bethnal Green.

Shils, who knew a great deal about power, did not think quite in these terms, although in 1964 he was to contribute a chapter, 'Britain Awake', for a book edited by the geographer Peter Hall called *Labour's New Frontiers*. It revealed how much he owed to Michael, as much, indeed, as Michael owed to him. 'The immediate task ... is to provide the conditions under which latent motivation and capacities can come to life.' Having written a remarkable anti-McCarthy book on 'the background and consequence of American security policies', *The Torment of Secrecy* (1956), the first of a Heinemann series on sociology, Shils was to go on from his Chicago base to take a special interest in intellectuals and in the history and sociology of universities, and to establish as strong a series of links with the right as with the left.

He seldom resorted to jargon in his own voluminous writing, but he may have viewed with a little scepticism, if with basic approval, the sentence in Michael's statement of first priorities for his new Institute that he wanted 'to make social science intelligible to the interested layman'. The reports of the Institute were to be readable, Michael wished, and, as he put it in a draft, 'free from the deplorable jargon that afflicts so much of sociology'. The wish became a promise, and although the Labour Party may not have been redeemed during the 1950s and 1960s this particular promise was.[144]

4
Two Places; One Purpose

Just how research enquiries were initiated, organised and concluded mattered deeply to Michael long before he set up the Institute of Community Studies; and continued to matter deeply long afterwards. If only because of this, it is revealing to compare the opening paragraphs of his doctoral thesis, 'A Study of the Extended Family in East London', supervised by Titmuss and successfully submitted in 1954, with the opening paragraphs of his much later book on *The Elmhirsts of Dartington* (1982), by which time Michael had become a well-known writer – not only of books, but of reviews and pamphlets.

There is a further reason, however, for making the comparison. Superficially there is nothing in common between the two places that have figured most prominently in Michael's life, Bethnal Green and Dartington. One is situated in the countryside far from London: the other is set in the east of the metropolis. They are directly brought together, however, in Michael's mind – and memory – through his experiences in each of them, in Dartington, stretching back to his childhood, and in Bethnal Green, where he was to carry out his researches and set up his Institute. There was interaction rather than juxtaposition – or contrast: he dedicated his *Family and Kinship in East London*, co-authored with Willmott, to 'Dorothy and Leonard'. Willmott had nothing to do with that. Nor could anyone but Michael have claimed, as he did in 1984, that he had been working for most of his life from 'the branch office of Dartington that I set up in Bethnal Green'.[1]

Both thesis and book begin with an evocation of place, and both passages deserve to be quoted in full. The non-thesis-like opening of the thesis has an almost Dickensian flavour to it which can be detected in some of Michael's other writings. The vocabulary is not that of an anthropological or sociological monograph but that of a novel: 'I think we all hope to write like novelists,' he once said, 'if only we could get somewhere like it.'² His opening was intensely personal. 'The fog became thicker as I crossed the canal from Bow':

> and by the time I left the housing office I could not see the ground. When I ended an attempt to crawl away by lodging my front wheels in a shop, I abandoned the old [pre-war] London taxi which was to be colleague for the next year [it had been bought for £40] – and that was when the enquiry began. Waiting until I heard some steps I put my first question: I asked the way to the nearest tube station. 'Search me, mate', came back the voice, curiously loud in the fog. Then a woman spoke from nearer me. 'The Tube? Yes, dearie, you go straight on till you get to the traffic lights. You turn left and you'll see it right in front of you. What a game eh?' With the help of other faceless friends, I felt my way along, tapping my foot against the kerbstones as I went. I am still tapping. So I know when the enquiry began. What I am much less clear about is why. What brought me to the housing office? So far as I can remember, the point of departure for my journey into the fog was an interest in the social services, particularly in housing.³

For the rare reader of both thesis and the Young and Willmott book, like myself, this autobiographical statement, with its disarming 'so far as I can remember', contrasts with the reference in the first sentence of the book to 'the living memory' of the very different kind of people that Michael was to interview. By contrast, the directly related Young and Willmott book which derived from the thesis began quietly and factually with the sentence 'Bethnal Green is part of a country which has been, within living memory, the scene of great social changes, and in this background chapter we shall note their impact upon married couples.'⁴

Michael may or may not have known that what he was writing in the thesis was Dickensian in style, but he did know that Dickens himself knew Bethnal Green. It figured in *Oliver Twist* as the site of the thieves' kitchen, and in a footnote to his thesis Michael quoted the opening sentences of Chapter 21 of that novel: 'It was a cheerless morning when they [Bill Sykes and Oliver] got into the street; blowing and raining hard; and the clouds looking dull and stormy.' In *The Symmetrical Family* (1973), which he later co-authored with Willmott, he was to quote *Sketches by Boz*.⁵

In Michael's thesis the fog that Dickens so often referred to factually and metaphorically returns at the end in a brief section called 'A challenge to social services', the theme which had first taken him east. 'If I have demonstrated that the task of investigation is as formidable as it is necessary,' he wrote in his 'In Conclusion: the Problem of Change', 'I shall have achieved the purpose with which this chapter was aimed. If I have demonstrated that the task of investigation is as necessary as it is formidable, I shall have achieved the purpose with which I crossed the fog-bound bridge into Bethnal Green.'[6] Fog had figured in Michael's early memory. When, sitting on a bollard, waiting to greet his father on his return from Australia in 1924 he was 'very miserable, thinking somehow we'd never get through this terrible English fog. And suddenly my father was behind me and miraculously appeared out of the fog.'

Michael's approach, intensely personal, is less that of a sociologist than of a traveller – this too provides a link with anthropology. He is a traveller who becomes increasingly involved the longer that he continues his journey. Much of the explicit sociology is on the side in the thesis or, as yet, waiting to be investigated. By the time that the book was written with Willmott there was far more published sociology – and there were far more sociologists – but the approach had not changed.[7]

The Elmhirsts, an extremely revealing book, again with a strong autobiographical dimension, turns quickly, like Michael's thesis, to the relationship between family and community, picking up the main theme of *For Richer For Poorer* where it was left off. It was written when Michael was now thought of primarily as a sociologist, but it begins neither with sociology nor with autobiography, but with Michael's first journey to Dartington in 1929.

A helpful travel note is offered for any readers visiting the place for the first time; they might

> drive off the road from London at Buckfastleigh and miss altogether the first indication that they have arrived at Dartington. Only if they take their eyes off the car ahead will they notice a grim stone church standing on its own, with hardly a house in sight, as if some nineteenth-century ecclesiastical planner absent-mindedly stuck it down on paper without venturing out of his deanery; and only if they slow down sufficiently might they see, almost hidden by grasses, the small blue signpost leaning drunkenly to one side:
>
> DARTINGTON HALL TRUST
> COLLEGE OF ARTS
> SCHOOL

Parking in the church car park and continuing on foot they will see a rounded hill topped by a collar of trees and then half a mile away over the top of the bank a sawmill gantry and by its side a box-like building, surely twentieth-century. White. In Devon old buildings are grey. On the left there is an old one in the right colour, very strung out.[8]

The approach to the place that Michael goes on to describe is not dissimilar to that of Leonard Elmhirst who, apart from being a great traveller himself – labelled baggage was always a prominent sight at Dartington – was, in Michael's phrase, 'a one-man Automobile Association ... always ready to suggest routes to anyone'.[9] He was also an authority on past routes, including Roman roads.

Two pages later, we move from place to people, as we do in the Bethnal Green thesis, ending what may be called the prelude to the volume with a basic question:

Our visitors [to Dartington] might be able to piece together a little more by using their eyes alone. But to find out what is happening inside the buildings they would either have to enter them one by one and talk to people or consult the records. Then they would find that the Dartington Hall Trust, despite that notice by the church referring only to a college and a school, owns a textile mill, a glass factory (Dartington Glass, at Torrington in North Devon), a furniture and joinery works, a number of shops, a substantial share in a large building contractor, farms, woodlands, a horticultural department and of course the promised college and school. The Trust, directly or through its companies, employs about 850 people. There are in addition nearly 300 students and nearly 300 pupils. It owns 2,000 acres of farm and amenity land and 1,200 acres of woods. The annual turnover is about £14 million ... How did it all come about? This book tries to sketch an answer.[10]

It was to be an answer to the question 'Why?' as much as to the question 'How?', and Michael answered it not as a sociologist but as a Dartington Trustee.

Travelling back into Dartington's history, Michael began not with the Elmhirsts, but with the ninth-century Saxon Lady Beorgwyn. Normans and Plantagenets follow, their names recorded on 'richly coloured heraldic shields'. He referred more than once to John Holland, Earl of Huntingdon and Duke of Exeter (one of the rooms in the Dartington manor house was still called 'the Duke's Room'), although he did not include Holland's name in his index.[11]

The last occupants of the Manor before the Elmhirsts were the Champernownes, who owned Dartington from 1560 to 1925. None the less, Michael did not linger long over their family history: one of them was the economist, David Champernowne, whom Michael had once met while at LSE.[12] Michael had chosen as the sub-title of his book 'The Creation of a Utopian Community', and although the Elmhirsts gave financial support to Withymead, a retreat for the mentally disturbed, founded by Irene and Gilbert Champernowne – the latter was the Champernowne who would have inherited the Dartington estate if it had not been sold[13] – Michael did not suggest that there was any touch of Utopia in Dartington before the Elmhirsts arrived.

Leonard, born in Yorkshire and educated at Trinity College, Cambridge, had had what Michael, contemplating him across time and place, called 'a succession of narrow escapes from conformity',[14] and had worked in India for four years as a personal assistant to Rabindranath Tagore, a 'tyrant magician' as Leonard later described him, born in 1861,[15] at a community at Santiniketan, the 'place of peace', a would-be Indian Utopia. Before that, across the Atlantic at Cornell University, Leonard had studied agriculture, a subject that was to preoccupy Michael when he turned to overseas education.[16] In the process of learning in an American university Leonard had become more of a Cornell than a Cambridge man; and, most important of all, it was while studying at Cornell that he had met Dorothy.

Their courtship was difficult and protracted, for their backgrounds were quite different. None the less, within the history of Dorothy's wealthy and prestigious family there was already a utopian strain. She was brought up in a mansion in New York's Fifth Avenue, but she had ancestors who had arrived in America on the *Mayflower* and who had established 'a kind of utopian community in the Massachusetts Bay Colony'.[17] When she and Leonard began to work together at Dartington, the community which they established combined ideas and experience from different times, from different places and, not least, from different families.

There were religious echoes as well as ideas, even religious influences, behind the venture, not least when they turned to the arts, although neither Leonard nor Dorothy, like Michael after them, acknowledged any allegiance to credal Christianity. They belonged to a period when such allegiance was being diluted, yet Leonard, educated at Repton before going up to Cambridge, was a boy there when William Temple, a Christian Socialist, later to become Archbishop of Canterbury, arrived as headmaster, and while he was an undergraduate at Trinity he encountered and mixed with evangelical Christian enthusiasts. He might even have taken orders. By 1917, however, in war-time Mesopotamia, not far from the Biblical Holy Land, he was writing to his mother that 'the old creeds, formulas, hymns and doctrines no longer sum up my experience or satisfy my reason'.[18] With Tagore in India, eclectic Hinduism did not tempt him either, although he found Buddhism in some respects an attractive religion, as Michael was to do and his mother and daughter were to do also.[19]

As a child Dorothy copied into her diary the lines 'there is only one true religion – the ministry of the head to the directions of the heart. You need no priesthood here but the priesthood of conscience.'[20] None the less, it was not until after the death of her first husband, Willard Straight, that she turned to mystical religion, beginning with spiritualism and continuing through what came to be called, in the words of Gerald Heard, 'new age' thinkers, men (not women) who were to influence her in the 1930s as they searched for the 'Life of the Spirit'. One of her closest friends of the 1930s, the actor Michael Chekhov (always 'Misha' to her), happily ensconced in Dartington, was a disciple of Rudolf Steiner, a curious link with Michael's grandfather on his mother's side, a link unacknowledged by Michael himself.

Leonard had not scorned the word Utopia. Nor, of course, have most founders of new schools which have set out to be communities. Nor, indeed, did Michael when he joined Transport House or even when he was serving in it. As he himself noted in his account of Dartington, there was a socialist strand as well as a religious strand in the history of utopianism, the two sometimes being confused. He quoted the late Victorian Fellowship of the New Life, out of which Fabianism emerged: one of its tenets was that 'all schools ought to be communities, miniature commonwealths or states, as they were in the middle ages'.[21]

If Dorothy was to spend much of her life searching for manifestations of 'the spirit' – through intuition and impulse more than through scholarship and thought – by 1952 Michael himself had come to devote much of his meditation on socialism to a search for the roots of socialist communitarianism in the years before the foundation of the Labour Party. *For Richer For Poorer* expressed all this while he was starting work on and at Bethnal Green. The words 'Christianity' and 'religion' do not figure in the Young and Willmott index nor, indeed, in their agenda, as they certainly would have done in Charles Booth's or Seebohm Rowntree's social surveys.[22]

History, particularly pre-industrial history, became directly relevant in Michael's search for understanding, as it also had done for Leonard at Dartington (more than for Dorothy). In 1925 Leonard had told the prestigious estate agents, Knight, Frank and Rutley, from whom he and Dorothy heard about Dartington Hall, that he wanted a place which was beautiful ('we're starting a school') and which would make farming pay; and although he mentioned 'historical associations', these came in only last. Very soon, however, he became deeply interested in them, as he did in genealogy. He came to 'love the game of being a detective into history' and introduced into the 'Dartington experiment' – a description, with or without Leonard's inverted commas, which Michael found particularly appropriate – 'the new notion of restoring the past'.[23] He and Dorothy, in Michael's words, transformed Dartington into 'a great household again', as it had been centuries before, 'without the knights, the archers and the huntsmen, but with a strange brilliance of its own', largely derived from the artists who played a big part in the community.[24]

In 1934 after Dartington ideas and experience had transformed his ways of viewing past ideas and experience, Leonard wrote:

> Another Utopia, you will say. Perhaps, but with this difference that economics and psychology have begun to offer us yardsticks of measurement, clumsy as yet, that the old utopias never possessed.[25]

Even more, science, along with economics and psychology, had made a huge difference to the way Leonard, never entirely satisfactorily, conceived of both 'utopias' and managing Dartington. That management, he maintained, would have something to offer the world. 'In everything that we have attempted at Dartington we have endeavoured to secure that element of universality which would make such discoveries as we made there be applicable in principle, at any rate, to any other part of the globe.'[26]

Michael, with his own brief war-time experience of management, was to make many statements in the future about 'yardsticks of measurement' and about 'universality', even using Leonard's vocabulary. Nevertheless, in retrospect he was critical of Dartington's management when he wrote *The Elmhirsts*. There had been a 'poor choice of executives': 'managerial [as distinct from technical] competence was nowhere'. Leonard was not interested in 'experimental systems of management and in attempts being made to make every worker a partner in his enterprise instead of just an employee'. When Michael and Marianne Rigge wrote *Revolution from Within* in 1983, which began with the reflections of a 'manager who was ill at ease behind his desk', there was no place in it for praise or indeed for assessment of

Dartington or Devonshire. There were references in the index, however, to Danish and to Japanese experience and even to Buddhism.

The Elmhirsts appeared only one year before *Revolution from Within* and it was evocative rather than evangelising. For Michael his schoolboy life at Dartington, with its obligatory practical tasks, was the 'first community life' that he had encountered and into which he was drawn very quickly; and later in his life, before, during and after his days at Transport House, he returned to Dartington frequently, school and place, and revisited them as much in his imagination as in his writing. In 1950, for example, he visited Dartington immediately after attending the Labour Party Conference, the first time he had done so. 'Perhaps as a result,' he told the Elmhirsts, 'it [the Conference] seems stranger than ever.'[27] And in 1958, when *Family and Kinship* was published, a very difficult, though highly creative year in Michael's personal life, he found succour and sometimes peace at Dartington.

A year later, he described Dartington as 'the real world, where I belong', with 'everything else a bit unreal'.[28] He was delighted when Sasha, welcomed there by the Elmhirsts,[29] found it possible to understand his feelings, and the two of them lived there – at Hunter's Lodge, a rebuilt house, with a wonderful view – from 1976 to 1981 while he was writing *The Elmhirsts*.

In this book, a labour of love, Michael added important glosses of his own to what Leonard and Dorothy themselves said and wrote about Dartington, and it is this, in particular, which gives it a deliberate autobiographical dimension. The Dartington Utopia, Michael noted, was rural, like other Utopias, 'Utopias do not seem to exist easily in cities.'[30] Within it limits were set to specialisation. 'The community was seen as an agent of reintegration', the means by which the people who composed it could take collective responsibility for bringing together the many different separated aspects of their lives. 'School, arts, workshops, farm, forestry would be organised separately but within the matrix of a larger community to which they [and he] all belonged.' At this point the universalism, dealt with more fully in a later chapter, came in for Michael also.[31] In the Young and Willmott book there an early reference too to the penetration of Bethnal Green 'at a hundred points' by 'the great society'.

Bethnal Green, Michael's own chosen base for research and action, even after he returned to Dartington in 1976, was urban, not rural, part not of a county but of the great metropolis, where there was far more variety (and contrast) than in any other city in the world. The traveller passing through Bethnal Green by road and the passenger going through it by train did not know when he was entering or leaving it.

At neither beginning nor end was there a distinguishing boundary. It was not the appearance of the place, 'cramped, grey, dirty, with all the beauty pressed out of it', that appealed to Michael, but 'the character of the people' who lived there with 'such gusto and humour'. They had 'imposed life' on a 'terrible city environment', and Michael confessed that he felt that when he got away from description he became sentimental about them. He recognised too that during the 1950s Bethnal Green was losing some of its historic integration, not strengthening it: there was an 'exodus'; soon to be followed, although he did not foresee it fully then, by a wave of new immigration.[32]

None the less, in preparing his thesis Michael found a sense of community in Bethnal Green that was linked to family and through family to class and to gender, and his sense that this was powerful enough to make his 'unconscious' 'engage gear'. When asked why he was so drawn to Bethnal Green, he gave as one reason the fact that he was being psychoanalysed at the time,[33] and the appeal of what he found there was powerful enough, he suggested, to have remained 'inviolate' as he continued on his course of psychoanalysis.[34]

His unconscious was engaged too at Dartington, although Michael came to realise, drawing not on his unconscious but on his reason, that at Dartington by contrast with Bethnal Green there was a 'contradiction': 'Leonard never entirely stopped being the squire ... and Dorothy ... the great lady, even though they were surrounded with all the outward forms of limited liability companies, managing directors and accountants.' It was difficult for them to devolve power or for any power that they did devolve to be accepted as genuine by people at Dartington.'[35] For Michael the people of Bethnal Green were, above all and from the start, completely 'genuine'. 'Class' came into his own judgement, at least so he thought in retrospect. He felt that there were 'outsiders', who looked down on the people of Bethnal Green, thinking of them as 'scallywags', whereas 'in some ways they were models for the very people who were disparaging them from their heights in Hampstead or South Kensington'.[36]

While Bethnal Green was in process of change, vividly evoked in the second chapter of Michael's thesis and a little less vividly in the first chapter of the Young and Willmott book, there was much that had not changed, including the strong sense of place, associated with an almost equally strong sense of time. Far more was to change between the 1950s and the 1990s, as Michael was to appreciate and seek to explain.[37] In 1950, extended family housing still rested on a private landlord system that was 'manipulated' by kindred to keep extended families together. And there were only two bus routes in the borough, so that in order to see it you had to leave the main roads behind and walk through the side streets, where the small houses (could they be called cottages?) had red or white doorsteps and curtained windows.

Walking slowly or standing in doorways, Michael learned to 'listen for voices'.[38] And here the people came in. He might have quoted another Young, G. M., who believed in such listening in order to understand historical change, though not, it is true, to such voices as Michael heard.[39] Forty per cent of the people had been born in the borough, and this accounted for their strong attachment to the place. Total numbers had fallen, however, having reached a peak of 129,680 as long ago as 1901. In Young and Willmott we are told simply that 'most of the 54,000 people it contained in 1955 belonged to the "working class"'. Only Michael would have noted that the proportion of the population born in Bethnal Green (40.9 per cent) was almost exactly the same as that in Totnes (40.2 per cent).[40]

The second chapter of the thesis ends, as several chapters in *The Elmhirsts* were to end, with a section called 'The Sense of History':

> People are aware of living in a place which has a distinct character, an identity of its own for which they feel affection, and they are also conscious of a feeling of solidarity with others who live in it. Obviously not all people are equally aware of this sense, but there are enough who are to set the tone for the rest.

History, Michael went on, was a 'binding force in almost any kind of social institution', including a political party or a trade union. And in Bethnal Green when the leader of the dominant Labour Party, which then held all the seats on the Borough Council, then the local authority, stated as his Utopian aim that of seeing Bethnal Green 'become the ideal garden city with everyone working and living together happily', he owed something, Michael suggested, as Morris might have done, to accounts of the parish as it had been in the sixteenth century.[41]

Not surprisingly, perhaps, Michael's salute to history ended with a reference to the Borough Council's souvenir programme for Queen Elizabeth II's Coronation, where the hope had been expressed, a little more modestly, that soon Bethnal Green would recapture 'a suggestion of its former charm and repose'.[42] There was one old building in Victoria Park Square which was to become the address of the Institute of Community Studies. Another old house, Netteswell House, dated back to 1553, and there was one old inhabitant who remembered 'the old days when sheep were grazing where Victoria Park Gardens now are'.[43]

History and myth were interwoven, as they usually are, in the topography of Bethnal Green, a topography of 'turnings' as well as of roads and streets, as much as in the volumes to be found in the Bethnal Green Library, a place which did not figure either in Michael's thesis or in the Young and Willmott book. On the Minerva Estate four of the Council houses were called Achilles, Hercules, Ajax and Priam, while two others were named after Beatrice Webb and Ellen Wilkinson. A main thoroughfare, passing nearby to Victoria Park, was a Roman road. (Leonard Elmhirst would have been interested in its existence.) Within the topography there was an 'even more marked sense of attachment to that bit of it in which people happened to live' than there was to the whole.

There was a sense of romance in all this – as well as of history and myth – although, descending to earth, Michael knew more of the last two characters in the list of Council house names through his own recent history than of the four classical heroes. He had once been taunted by Crosland at a Labour Party weekend conference at Buscot House, the impressive country house of Lord Faringdon, whom he described later as 'a sort of Fabian', when in the course of discussing classical paintings – and the classics – he had mispronounced the name of the Greek historian Thucydides. 'Tony roared with laughter and mocked this sort of hopeless fellow from Dartington who couldn't pronounce a well-known author's name. And I got terribly ribbed over' (a curiously public school expression).[44]

As we have seen, the kind of society that Michael had been forced to learn about at LSE through 'primitive anthropology' in preparation for his thesis was even more remote from twentieth-century life, and he would have had the laugh over Tony there. The five books on the family, referred to in his first footnote, neatly set out in chronological, not alphabetical, order, had obviously been prescribed as necessary reading to bring him up-to-date.[45] (Had Titmuss himself read them?) Firth, who had – indeed he recommended them – once upbraided Michael and Willmott (and he recalled that it was 'good' for them) for not having properly acknowledged the work that he himself had carried out on kinship in Bermondsey.[46]

The method of reaching conclusions employed by social anthropologists obviously appealed to Michael. They had 'done much of their work by systematic study in depth of small numbers of people', and while Michael was not impressed by the way travellers with anthropological training approached interviewing in a British as distinct from an exotic setting – for instance, sometimes switching accents in an attempt to win the confidence of the people to whom they were talking seemed totally misguided as well as funny – he came, like them, to attach importance to information gleaned from formal interviewing as well as from joining in or eavesdropping on conversations. There were few books or booklets or guidance on interviewing at that time, and Michael wrote to Dorothy in 1958 after the Institute had managed to do 800 interviews in two weeks, with 200 more to do in less than one week, stating that the next task was to convert interview reports 'back again into flesh and blood people', first 'making people into words' and always hoping then for 'a creative leap which will make facts into life'.

Michael continued to draw heavily on quotations, as he had done in *Small Man: Big World*, but they now included quotations not from great men of the past but from 'unknown' people in the present. Their representativeness always worried him less than their kernel of content. Sociology as such did not figure in Michael's statement of intent at the beginning of his thesis, where before turning to evidence drawn from the limited number of interviews he had conducted, he offered a painstakingly compiled list of definitions of 'the family' and two diagrams comparing 'the immediate family' and 'the extended family'.

About to describe Bethnal Green movingly – as he was to go on doing for the rest of his life – returning to it for a second major study in his eighties – Michael had to explain specifically in his thesis abstract why he had chosen Bethnal Green as the locus of his studies of 'the family', the heart of his study. He was curiously defensive in his explanation: 'any national survey would have been out of the question. There were not the resources for it.' He added more positively, however, that even had there been, 'it would have been the wrong way to proceed … A national survey might only conceal the differences [between one place and another] which it is the long-run job of research to uncover.'

Again, representativeness was not his paramount concern. At the lowest level – or would he have seen it as such? – there were practical positive reasons, too, for choosing Bethnal Green, reasons of the kind that Elmhirst had looked for when he chose Dartington. 'Official statistics were usually kept for local government units as a whole, and since these were usually kept for local government units as whole [later in 1974, after radical local government reorganisation, introduced by a Conservative government, Bethnal Green was to be swallowed up in Tower Hamlets], the area should be a borough.'

The most practical reason of all, that 'it would be an advantage if some of the necessary work had been done in advance, made it worthwhile to look for an area where 'social studies', had been made in the past. The 'redoubtable' Ruth Glass, wife of Professor David Glass, LSE sociologist and demographer – Michael quoted both her and him in *For Richer For Poorer* – had collected a substantial volume of evidence about the borough during the last years of the war. Along with M. Frenkel, she had written *How They Live at Bethnal Green* for the Association of Planning and Regional Reconstruction.[47] Ruth was a pioneer in detailed urban studies – one on Watling, another, still considered important, on Middlesbrough[48] – and she had strong views on the direction of urban sociology.[49] She was also a vigorous left-wing protagonist of the urban against the rural, Marxist in her sympathies – and prejudices. No Dartington for her, and no Welwyn Garden City, a place which greatly appealed to Leonard.[50]

Nevertheless, Ruth generously placed her files at Michael's disposal. He also collected information from Dr. J. H. Robb, who had written a London University thesis on anti-Semitism in Bethnal Green, which was published in 1954 by Tavistock Publications and given the title *Working Class Anti-Semites*. Michael did not mention in his thesis his own earlier connection with Toynbee Hall which under Mallon's Wardenship had been one of the main centres of resistance to anti-Semitism in the East End during the 1930s.[51] He drew attention rather to the work of Dr. J. H. Sheldon, who had interested himself in the lives of old people in Wolverhampton and who in 1947 had published *The Social Medicine of Old Age*.[52] Sheldon was to become a member of the Advisory Committee of the Institute of Community Studies.

A second geographical centre, a new place to compare with the 'old' Bethnal Green, was a necessary element in Michael's thesis, and in this case the reason for his eventual choice was entirely practical. He might have chosen Hainault, but after consultation with officials of the London County Council's Housing Department he chose Debden in Essex, 'mainly because it was near to the LCC office which would act as a local headquarters'. Having made his choice, he recognised that if he were to present a 'moving picture ... not a still photograph', he would need to interview people both in Bethnal Green and in Debden. 'Deliberately to introduce an element of change into his analysis would also be a valuable discipline, for it would guard against the danger that one would think of kinship as something static.' The project would only be feasible, however, if he limited the interviews to around 50 in each case. (In fact, there were to be 49 interviews in Bethnal Green and 47 in Debden.)

The question which kept Michael 'awake in the day-time' was 'would they [local people] be prepared to cooperate?' 'Would they give information about their family life?' They would, and not only to him but to the interviewers who later worked with him. 'Hearing what they say, knowing what they mean' was the title of the sociologist W. G. Runciman's contribution to *Young at Eighty*, which dealt with interviewing and which paid a tribute to Michael's enviable 'gift for talking to people – old friends, chance acquaintances and survey interviewees alike – in a way which elicits the maximum forthcomingness with the minimum offence'.[53]

The criterion for those interviewed for *Family and Kinship in East London* was that they should have at least two children under the school-leaving age of 15, and from these they were chosen at random, 'by hat', not from the electoral roll, but from housing lists. No letters were written to possible informants either in Bethnal Green or Debden. Michael rejected another idea, that of relying on introductions from local doctors, priests and officials: that would have incurred basic charges of unrepresentativeness which, even given his chosen methodology, he was not to escape. Housing lists were used, not electoral rolls, because they enabled the people he was seeking to be identified in both Bethnal Green and Debden. There were more old people in the former than in the latter, and as part of the overall survey the eleven old people from Bethnal Green who lived in Debden were interviewed too.

Interested as Michael was in the changing role of women and in child rearing as the inter-generational link between women, he followed up a section of his thesis called 'children who earn' with a section called 'old people'. The process of ageing, he acknowledged, 'is one in which members of all generations take part – one thing that everyone in the world has in common, even the pilot of the Comet. [Back to the same image.] Each moment makes all of us that much older. But our needs depend on the stage we have reached in our journey [once more note the metaphor] and the resources available to meet them on the stage reached by the other members of the family who are our travelling companions.'[54]

The sections on women, which Michael was to follow up later, have gained in interest since the thesis was written. 'Mother and daughter,' he wrote, 'have a bond possessed neither by father and daughter nor by mother and son. Whatever else they do, their most important role in life is that of child bearing and child rearing.' He did not dwell on the possibilities of child bearing and child rearing ceasing to be considered as women's 'most important role in life', although he acknowledged, none the less, that changes in techniques of child rearing and housekeeping made the common element less important.[55] Forty years later he was to note more fully than he did at the time – in the light of later social change – how Bethnal Green men suffered because they were excluded. 'There was a fairly horrible kind of vicious circle at work' since men 'kept a lot of their own money for themselves ... the women needed to bond together even more closely ... There were wonderful things about it and dreadful things.'[56]

The first encounters with people from the chosen 'sample', male or female, young or old, began on the doorstep, described by Michael as 'this formidable frontier'. While very few people refused to cooperate, many were suspicious at first, unready 'to answer a lot of questions about their private lives' unless they could 'approve the purpose of the enquiry'. Interpretation would have been impossible had they remained silent. But even when they began to talk, Michael had to make it plain to them that he had nothing to offer in return: in particular, he was not in a position to influence their chances of securing a house from the local authority, their supremely practical object. To win people over, he felt it necessary to explain that even if they themselves would not benefit, the results of the enquiry could 'help' somebody else.

Michael admitted that in 'assuming' that this was the reaction he might have been putting into the mind of the respondents 'something which is solely in my own mind'; and this note of self-criticism was to be taken up by some of the critics of his own and Willmott's work. Yet Michael was particularly sensitive throughout his thesis to this particular danger. In one of his most remarkable passages he talked of 'passing over from the realm where quantitative measurement has some meaning to a shadow land where one repeatedly sees one's own face without realising it.' This was another of his moving images, already quoted in the first chapter of this book, but worth repeating in its particular context.[57]

The brief abstract, less than two pages in length, which Michael was required to attach to his thesis, made little or no reference to some of the policy issues that had most concerned him when he began to write it, although in the text, after having described on page 1 the pea soup fog which enveloped him when he first arrived in Bethnal Green, he noted next his special interest in housing, and his concern about the social impact of 'the public housing estates [that were] springing up everywhere around the cities of Britain'.[58] None the less, he had no desire to confine himself within houses and gardens, old or new, and, almost at once he turned back to the 'extended family'.[59]

In the text of the thesis, in a passage doubtless written earlier, Michael pointed out that what had most drawn his attention to the housing estate was the extent of the extended family. Since the estates had been built, in the main, for families with young children, he had asked the people he had been interviewing two questions – What about their relatives when they moved there? What about old people? Who looked after them? How did they respond to changes in housing layout and community? He could get no answers to such questions in any books about housing or from housing policy makers and administrators. (He did not mention architects.) Housing experts took it for granted that the family meant the parents and their children. Michael did not. He wanted to consider as well as grandmothers and grandfathers, 'uncles and aunts, cousins and nephews'.[60]

When Michael picked out as the fifth of his headings in his abstract the bold theme of his last chapter, the eleventh, 'In conclusion: the problem of change', he was searching for motives, conscious and unconscious, both in the initiation of change and in resistance to it. He was to note later how successive Ministers of Housing, attempting to deal with the post-war housing shortage, had done the same when they turned from demography to psychology and argued that the growth of demand for housing was due not only to an increase in the number of families but to the unwillingness on the part of families who in the past had shared dwellings to go on doing so in a time of full employment and high wages. Demography was not enough: psychology (with economics) was a necessary key.

His conclusion to what he called a report, not a thesis, was highly personalised, although it carried with it a challenge to social science which heralded his future role as Chairman of the Social Science Research Council:

> While I was writing this report I felt like a man standing tiptoe on a narrow ledge. The facts were so precarious, the reach so ambitious. To widen the ledge is work for many climbers. And yet if the ledge is to be widened and extended in the right direction it is necessary to begin by straining and stretching even further upwards. One may fall off. Or one may be able to catch a glimpse of the way.

Psychology was relevant there too: he himself was always in danger of losing his personal bearings. 'The problem of change,' he went on briskly, abandoning his imagery of climbing, was 'perhaps more fundamental in this kind of research than method.'

Michael confessed in his thesis that methodology 'bristles with difficulties, most of them stemming from the besetting problems of how to get really intimate with a family chosen at random. Yet the first thing is to decide what one wants to find out, and only then to consider whether it is possible.' What had that 'first thing' been? Instead of mentioning housing, which he might have done given not only his future interest in the subject but also his work for the Labour Party and the importance of the issue at the general election of 1950,[61] Michael focused again, as he did in his thesis abstract, on kinship. 'I hoped to show that kinship was a subject; and that there was something to investigate.'

His thesis was divided into three parts – the environment and the family; the internal working of 'the system'; and the housing estate, with the final chapter not so much drawing the different parts together as pointing to the future. For him, as for most later social researchers, more than one social science was involved. Economics had been more in the minds of Ministers of Housing than psychology, as it had been of Cripps and as it was to be in the minds of Ministers, Labour or Conservative. Yet Michael, while recognising the importance of economics, occasionally explicitly, seldom gave it priority.

Nor was he content with sociology, a word that he rarely used in his thesis. Once, however, after observing that 'the conflict felt by women who both want and do not want children must surely be an important influence upon the personalities of their offspring', he added, 'This is where sociology begins to become psychology.' He drew on history also. 'If in Bethnal Green mother and grandmother, not to speak of aunts, and older sisters, might share the maternal function', in 'the aristocracy, at the other extreme ... children quite commonly have several mothers too, Nannie taking the place of Grannie.' Might he have had Dorothy in mind?[62]

Two out of five of Michael's appendices, probably defensively, dealt with methodology – 'selecting the samples' and 'the kinship diagram and questionnaire'. There was one kinship diagram for the husband and one for the wife. Occupations were given in them. In the questionnaires standard questions had been asked about the frequency of contact with relatives named in the kinship diagrams. Michael stated that he was following a 'biographical approach' through 'life histories' which he associated with Firth whom he was later to have appointed to the Social Science Research Council.[63] Michael also compared his kinship diagrams with heraldic family patterns set out in the 1952 edition of *Burke's Landed Gentry*.

In both cases the morale of a family was influenced directly not only by its marriages but by its mobility. An interesting appendix to the thesis dealt with questionnaire answers given by 33 families who had removed *from* Debden, nine of whom chose to go back to Bethnal

Green. 'Loneliness' was the reason most often given and/or a wish on the part of daughters to get near once again to their mothers. In one case, the Debden wife did nothing but cry and cry: she had lost two stones in weight since living in Debden. Whatever the reason offered by the people who returned, the largest number of removals took place between one and two years after arrival.

Geography, like social history, was soon to be transformed as an academic subject, a transformation which had to be taken account of by the Social Science Research Council,[64] and it was one of the social sciences that Michael wrote about in his thesis without ever considering it explicitly, except perhaps when he looked briefly at the relationship between geographical and social mobility, a relationship also examined briefly by David Glass.[65] Michael quoted Glass's opinion, which he shared, that 'actual movement itself may, save in special circumstances, destroy or distort kinship associations, with possible personal and social deprivation. We need to encourage [physical] mobility for the advantages it offers to individuals and to society; but we also need to avoid, as far as possible, such disadvantages as may follow from having a social structure in which the status relationships between individuals in successive generations will be far less stable than at present or during the past half-century.'

The relationship between geographical and social distance was abundantly clear to Michael, who was also aware of the significance of 'mental maps'. Debden was separated from Bethnal Green, 12 miles away, by only half an hour on the Central Line tube train but by 'an age in behaviour'. Michael's description of wind-swept Debden was as vivid as his description of foggy Bethnal Green. 'Instead of the fierce loyalty of the turnings there are the strung out streets in which everyone is a stranger. In Debden the bevy of groups which surround the household has disappeared.' The household had become 'geographically isolated'.

It was not only the visitor who felt himself to be a stranger at Debden, as Michael himself had felt, if briefly, when he first entered Bethnal Green. At Debden the inhabitant felt it too. 'You're English, but you feel like a foreigner here.'[66] Michael recognised, of course, that middle-class families could 'straddle distance with the aid of the car and the telephone'. He included a footnote on the same page. 'The effect of the telephone on kinship relations is just one more of the subjects which need investigation.' Cars and telephones ['mobile' telephones were not yet envisaged] were status symbols in working-class Bethnal Green, but already in Debden they were being acquired by working-class people. In *Family and Kinship* he pointed out that whereas in Bethnal Green there were only 13 residential telephone subscribers per 1,000, in Debden ('Greenleigh') there were 88. '"There are only two things that I think are essential when you live on an estate", said Mr. Berry, "one's a telephone, the other's a car".'[67]

Michael's general conclusion at the end of his thesis was that 'many more questions have been supplied by this enquiry than answers given', and in its very last pages he raised both practical and abstract issues in an attempt to relate facts to values.[68] In the kinship system of Bethnal Green, the 'little world' in which the wife moved 'require[d] that a higher valuation shall be placed on duty than on freedom'. The wife, who has or may have had choice of husband – that is her freedom – is 'enjoined to follow her duty to her family, particularly to her family of origin, and this means obeying the rules which prescribe the behaviour proper to her relations with her various kin according to their degree'. 'Where the family of marriage is dominant ... a higher valuation is placed on freedom than on duty. The one family relationship into which freedom of choice does enter – that is the relationship between husband and wife – is stressed as the most significant of all, and [it was] glorified by the wife [who was] given to romantic love.'

By the time that Michael, working closely with Willmott, had turned his thesis into a book, the forces of change, which had been the subject of the last chapter of the thesis, had further reshaped both Bethnal Green and Debden, the latter disguised in the book as Greenleigh. Just as significant as far as the book was concerned, Michael's own position had changed too after he had decided to set up the Institute of Community Studies in Bethnal Green, which for many years was to be co-directed by Willmott. It was never to be out of his mind.

The Institute was an independent, non-profit-making body, constituted in law as a charitable trust, and before its inception Michael had had both PEP and Dartington in mind.[69] He conceived of the purpose of the Institute as that of carrying out 'research in the "social sciences" which would at the same time add to basic knowledge and illuminate practical questions of social policy'. There was another link with PEP here, as well as with what Michael had written while at Transport House. Unlike PEP work, however, work at Bethnal Green would be carried on not by groups of experts brought in from outside and reporting anonymously, but by the Institute's own identified researchers carrying out organised field studies.

The five-page typewritten draft proposal for an Institute had nine headings – the last of them finance and staff. Three or four people would constitute the permanent staff; and in order to set them to work with 'some minimum continuity of employment', about £5,000 a year would be needed, spread over a period of at least three years. Michael expressed himself 'fairly confident' that if such initial support were forthcoming, the publications of the Institute would 'by then be good enough to make it fairly easy' to raise further money. The double use of 'fairly' is interesting, although Michael was to prove himself exceptionally adept at ensuring that initial support could be found. In this case he put his trust in future income derived from publications: they should be important and attractive enough to sell. He wished to make sociology accessible, and that meant making it readable. 'Every effort will be made to keep reports [the same noun again, going back to PEP] free from the deplorable jargon which afflicts so much of sociology.'

The second paragraph in the Draft Proposal was called 'Family and Community', and under the sixth heading, 'Projects', it was made clear that these would focus, as Michael's thesis had done, on the family, 'not only because of the obvious relevance of the family to social policy [particularly housing], but also because the extent and grouping of family relationships had been much neglected in the sociological description of contemporary industrial society.'[70] The Institute was to provide the means of making Michael's thesis public and turning it from an individual into a cooperative venture. There would be a focusing upon 'one critical stage in the life cycle of the family – the point when the young man gets married and leaves home'.

A further question to be considered was 'What happens when the children of working-class parents succeed in rising into the middle classes?' Michael was not alone in identifying a 'social gap' which demanded as an 'outstanding need' 'studies of family and community in the working classes'. 'Britain is still in significant respects two nations composed of the working classes on the one side and the expanding middle classes on the other, and there is consequently a very real danger that the one class will not understand the other.' Failure of communication [was] particularly serious in so far as it affects the social services.' 'If the middle class people who draw up policy for the social services do not understand the needs of working-class people these services will fail to achieve their purpose.' Michael's own experience at Transport House had helped to shape this conclusion.

The issues raised in *The Rise of Meritocracy* were already present in the paper and, far more precisely, those raised in *Family and Kinship*. There was a reference to 'a study of the migration from Bethnal Green to a new housing estate at Debden in Essex, on which the author of this note is at present engaged'. In general, more had to be done through such studies 'to find out about the community'. There were different aspects in such exploration.

Other items figured in the draft proposal which began with a paragraph on 'the prevention of distress'. 'The welfare state recognises that it is the common responsibility of all to relieve the material distress of anyone. What is much less widely recognised is the need not only to relieve distress but to prevent it.' The draft explicitly left out economics. 'The pressure to channel the very slight resources of social science into economic enquiry is now greater than ever since the U.S. Government's decision to set aside large counterpart funds for research on human problems in British industry. [The size of these was exaggerated.] These problems are vastly important, but if they alone are regarded as of sufficient importance to justify investigation the whole research effort of the country will become dangerously unbalanced. The maintenance of the family and community is surely no less necessary than the maintenance of industrial progress.'

The contrast so drawn was to lead a Conservative Government 20 years later to reach the opposite conclusion about the direction of national research policy. Under the aegis of Sir Keith Joseph economics was to come first.[71] What Michael was proposing in 1953 was so clearly expressed without compromise that it clarifies across time the diametrically opposed approach which itself was to be equally clearly expressed by Joseph and Thatcher. In 1953, six years before Thatcher became a Member of Parliament, Michael was pointing out plainly, ending up with capital letters, that the response to his memorandum would test whether or not money would be forthcoming for social research which 'did not bear the label PRODUCTIVITY'.[72]

'Distress', even 'material distress', and 'poverty' were related, but were not the same, and Michael's draft focused explicitly on 'the prevention of distress' and on 'the social gap'. 'A pennyworth of prevention of distress was better than a pound of cure'; 'how much better to help families to stay together than to run institutions for the young victims of broken marriages. How much better to build new houses than sanatoria for people suffering from tuberculosis caused by overcrowding. How much better to expand opportunities for old people to stay at work than welfare services which will make their enforced leisure tolerable.' The examples were only examples. Determining how to prevent distress required research which so far had 'not been done'. It also, of course, required financial resources, and Michael, while aware of how much his Institute needed by way of resources, did not even attempt to tot up national requirements.

Within the 'Projects' that Michael listed two were associated with resources as well as with ideas. 'Rural community' was given special importance because of its possible Dartington connections – and Dartington provided small but important pump-priming funds (£4,000) through the Elmgrant Trust, of which Michael was to become a Trustee, as he still is. In August 1953 he thanked Dorothy and Leonard for deciding to make 'this new research venture of mine possible on the scale I had hoped for. How many times have you been decisive in my life.'[73] The second project rested on financial support from Shils, who wished to carry it out himself. How were Oxford and Cambridge related to provincial universities? 'Do the provincial universities get the rejects?' 'Does the failure of academic staff to get appointments at Oxford and Cambridge jaundice their outlook?' 'What could be done to improve the quality of the relationship between staff and students?' 'How does England compare with Scotland and Wales?' While the questions related to Michael's past (Birmingham) and his future (Cambridge), Shils, as much at home in Tolstoy's Russia or Goethe's Germany as Attlee's England, was its initiator. Michael recommended him to the Elmhirsts as the son of an immigrant to the United States. There were other coincidental links of the kind that Michael liked. 'In Bethnal Green we are now interviewing a lot of Jews who fled from Russia at the beginning of the century like Shils's father, who became a cigar-maker in Philadelphia.'[74]

The fourth heading in Michael's memorandum, 'Jobs Not Being Done', referred to the universities in a different context: 'very little field research is coming from that quarter'.[75] With a touch of irony, however, in the year when the draft proposal for a new Institute was being prepared, Michael suggested at the annual weekend PEP Conference (to the horror of some people present) that PEP should be disbanded since it had by then carried out the work which it had been set up to do. His suggestion, which was designed to shock, was not surprisingly rejected on the grounds that there remained matters on the PEP agenda which required attention. In fact, Michael's new Institute did not take the place of PEP: it worked beside it.[76] There were to be future points of convergence also. In 1975 PEP was to publish an edition of *Planning* (No. 552) on 'Voluntary Services in Society', and two years later the premises of his Institute were to be designated a Mutual Aid Centre.[77]

Many of the sub-headings in Michael's draft proposal relating to Bethnal Green had been set out in his thesis. Yet there were to be as many differences between Michael's thesis and the book, the first product of the Institute, which he wrote with Willmott, the first person to join him at Bethnal Green, as there were between PEP and the new Institute. Moreover, the book, when it appeared in 1957, did not even mention the thesis, and the draft proposal itself, which had very little to say about methodology – less than the thesis – mentioned Bethnal Green only twice.

First, Michael explained, he had chosen Bethnal Green because it was a working-class community. Second, premises were available in Bethnal Green at Oxford House, directed by Alan Jarvis, a 'lively' nineteenth-century East End social settlement with a religious foundation, its mission 'the salvation of the godless poor'. While not all the work of the Institute would be carried on there, Oxford House was 'ideal' as a centre. Toynbee Hall, where Michael had been a resident, seemed to him 'too stuffy' during the early 1950s.[78] By contrast, Oxford House was 'always full of people, always being visited: social work students, community youth work students, university theological students' were active there, one of them an LSE student, Peter Duke, who was to be Jarvis's successor.[79]

'Research workers would be able to learn [there] from the resident staff and from the students who are in daily touch with the lives of local people'; and the overheads of secretaries and administration could be shared with Oxford House, which 'might be able to provide rent free accommodation for the venture'. Michael had met Jarvis while writing his thesis, and it was Jarvis who first introduced him to the phrase 'oral sub-culture' which he used in his thesis, but which did not stick in the Institute's vocabulary. Jarvis's name was to appear with that of Titmuss above the heading on the first batches of Institute of Community Studies stationery.

To translate the ideas in the Draft Memorandum into action Michael needed the support of an Advisory Committee. Titmuss was among the first names that he proposed, which also included Jarvis, Shils, Elmhirst, Tawney, the name that appeared so often in Michael's life, and Barbara Wootton, who was then President of the British Sociological Association and a Governor of the BBC. Tawney and Wootton did not accept. Titmuss did and became Chairman.

Within this group Michael was conscious of the distinctiveness of his relationship with Shils. Believing that Shils knew London 'like a taximan' – no compliment could have been warmer – he felt at the same time that he was 'handicapped as a sociologist by being an academic'. 'He models his clothes on German Professors of the 1920s.'[80]

While Michael's prospectus for the Institute irritated some sociologists – there were still not many of them in Britain – it appealed to Shils, who provided a personal grant to the new Institute on an annual basis, from a personal grant which he had received from the Ford Foundation, and which he could dispose of as he wished. In his diary Peter Townsend, who was to follow Peter Willmott to Bethnal Green, described meeting him for the first time. 'He looks rather like a root that has been buried deep in the earth ... He tended to talk too much, but the range of his ideas made one want to whistle through parted lips ... He is certainly one of the two or three best sociologists in the world.'[81]

Michael's plan to finance the Institute by grants from educational and charitable foundations provided him with a challenge that drew out new qualities in him. He was thereafter to become as famous for his capacity to raise money as for his power to generate ideas.[82] For him the two always went together. There was never any lack of ideas, most of them his own, but each one needed financial backing. Michael knew how to raise it, and he preferred to do this himself. It was the socially committed Joseph Rowntree Memorial Trust which provided the first general support grant for the Institute, offering longer-term security to keep the Institute running, and Joseph Waddilove, Executive Officer of the Joseph Rowntree Memorial Trust from 1946 to 1961, later to be called Director, was to become a member of the Institute's Advisory Committee and (later) to join the Social Science Research Council under Michael's leadership. One of Waddilove's main interests was housing, but he was also to serve on the Public Schools Commission (at Michael's suggestion?) in the late 1960s.[83]

The Institute achieved a greater sense of permanence when roomy premises in Victoria Park Square were acquired from Peter Benenson, who had tried and failed to become the local Labour MP. The premises at Oxford House had been provided at considerable rent and an alternative site soon seemed desirable. Number 18, which came to Michael's attention when he saw a removal van outside it, was an old and attractive Queen Anne house looking out over public gardens, and was secured first at a low rent and then as a purchase at the low price of £5,000. It was only two minutes walk from the Bethnal Green underground station, and was next door to the Universities Settlement, of which John Peterson was Warden. When he acquired No. 18, did Michael think of the PEP premises in Queen Anne's Gate, and did he appreciate the symbolic importance of the first word in the half-letters, half-numbers telephone number – ADVance 3952?

Peterson, keenly interested in what was going on around him,[84] provided the first members of the Institute with lunch, and for a time the Institute's address was given on the stationery as University House, 18 Victoria Park Square. Another friendly nearby Settlement – this was Settlement country – was St. Margaret's House, where Audrey Harvey worked. One of the places where they all ate together was a working-class café 'with bacon and eggs and so on'. Bethnal Green Hospital was just along the road. And this was to become more relevant later than it was at the time as the Institute became increasingly interested in questions relating to health (both attitudes and policy), questions not raised in the draft memorandum.[85]

Old though the Institute's house was, years later it was to be described by two of Michael's closest assistants, Wyn Tucker and Sue Chisholm, who was to become its Manager, as 'The House that Michael Built'.[86] They were to be two of its mainstays. When Sue Chisholm became Michael's personal secretary in 1971, she pictured 18 Victoria Park Square on her arrival as 'buzzing with the coming and going of interviewers'. Her predecessor was Daphne Piccinelli. One of the first people to sleep in one of the bedrooms in the house was Naomi Sargant, who in 1962 was to marry Andrew (later Lord) McIntosh. It was McIntosh, made a peer in 1982, who was to call that other, even older house where Michael found a place in 1978, the House of Lords, 'that curious and indefensible institution'.[87]

By 1957, when *Family and Kinship in East London* appeared as the first publication of the Institute, it was not only the Bethnal Green address on the stationery of the Institute which had changed. Above all, the description of the Director was no longer the same. In 1953 he was described as BSc and Barrister-at-Law; by 1957 the PhD had been added. The composition of the Advisory Council had changed too. It now included Madge, who was to succeed Titmuss as Chairman, Sheldon, and Geoffrey Gorer, author of *Exploring English Character* (1955).[88] There were no politicians, but there was one prestigious academic figure, Carr-Saunders, Director of LSE, who as early as 1927 had co-authored *A Survey of the Social Structure of England and Wales*.[89] Later the psychiatrist Morris Carstairs, who in 1974 was to become Vice-Chancellor of York University,[90] was added, along with William Wallace, Chairman of Rowntrees Ltd.

Michael was to summon similarly prestigious – and knowledgeable – advisory committees in his future organisation building, and some he was to make Trustees. The direction of the organisations, however, was always his own. So, too, was the inspiration. For their success

Michael owed much to the three people whom he quickly attracted to join him. Known as the three Peters, after the initials of their first names, they were also three pioneers. Peter Townsend and Peter Marris were friends who had met while undergraduates at Cambridge, and came from backgrounds as different from Willmott's as from Michael's. Townsend, however, had been working for PEP, through which he met Michael, Titmuss, whom he judged 'the best man on social affairs in this country',[91] and Brian Abel-Smith, who became a close friend.[92] At this time Marris was working in Kenya as a District Commissioner, writing to Townsend about the Mau Mau disturbances there. All three men were to leave an immediate impact on the activities of the Institute – in a sense, although Michael would not have liked the word, to establish it – and they were all to go on to make significant personal contributions to social policy as well as to sociology.

Townsend, who did not meet Willmott until February 1954, was ready for a change in 1953, a year when he was responsible inside PEP for influential issues of *Planning* dealing both with social security and education.[93] In May he turned down an invitation from Professor W. J. M. Mackenzie of Manchester University to become an Assistant Lecturer in the Department of Politics and Social Administration, preferring the idea of researching, and before joining Michael wrote an article which was accepted by the *British Journal of Sociology* on 'Measuring Poverty', a subject which he was to make his own.[94] Townsend in his own words looked forward to 'genuine, as opposed to pseudo-research, no months wasted fighting what is and what is not to be published, no paternalism from a hierarchy of nominal superiors, a chance of joining a pioneering concern, studying persons as opposed to institutions'.[95] The Institute in Bethnal Green seemed a perfect place.

The research project which he discussed with Michael was concerned with old age in Bethnal Green, and it was Townsend who was largely responsible for securing a grant from the Nuffield Foundation which made it possible for him to join the Institute.[96] Michael gave him the good news in a telegram on 23 December 1953 – it 'garnished the Christmas scene' – and he left PEP and joined the Institute at the end of February 1954. Michael was ill with asthma on the day that Townsend arrived in Bethnal Green, and Townsend has drawn a vivid picture of him a few days later – not in Bethnal Green but at his home, near Regent's Park:

> I am always impressed by Michael's energy and originality of thought, and his ill-health is a great handicap. On this occasion he

sat up in a red dressing gown, habitually lifting his horn-rimmed spectacles and rubbing the corners of his eyes, drawing his knees up to him and then stretching them again, and occasionally he spat apologetically into a mug by his side. The high ceiling, coloured terracotta red, the pearl grey walls, and the large yellow lampshade with its smooth, wooden base shaped like a bottle lent a curious atmosphere to our rather academic discussion. We are studying kinship and community structure – almost virgin territory in this country – and the problem is not so much original ideas, of these there are many, but dividing the fields of activity, using the right techniques of interview and shaping a background of sociological theory.[97]

By then Townsend had already carried out a number of pilot interviews of his own for his book *The Family Life of Old People*, and with some trepidation had addressed the Bethnal Green Council of Social Service at the local Town Hall.[98] 'The audience was made up mainly of trade unionists, social workers, teachers, youth club and settlement leaders, with one or two barristers and borough councillors among them.'

Townsend liked Bethnal Green 'with its stalls, jellied eels, boiled sweets, bootlaces in packets, fish and chip shops, crazy ironmongers, second-hand clothing shops, old woven coats shining with age, stolid resigned men and women waiting in doctors' surgeries'. Once, while working in Bethnal Green Library, he observed an old man 'in a greasy mac ... reading *The Meaning of Eternal Life* by Canon Raven'.[99] Yet for Townsend, as for Michael, it had black elements too: interspersed among its colourful markets and its rows of terraced cottages were grim sentinels of Victorian solidity, gloomy blocks of flats built around the turn of the century. They were not yet confronted with what they judged to be incongruous twentieth-century high rise.

Townsend's account of Michael in bed in 1954 should be compared with Michael's description of Townsend at work in the Institute, surrounded by huge sheets and boxes of information, 'ticking and thinking and making notes'.[100] Rooms were shared, and there were, he said, no computers or even calculating machines, only hollerith cards relating to the 200 people interviewed. This was 'cottage industry sociology'. None the less, what Townsend was doing was 'in the best tradition of English social empiricism, Mayhew, Charles Booth, the Webbs and Rowntree', although he too, like Michael, acknowledged the influence on him of social anthropologists who had 'set high standards of intensive fieldwork and imaginative analysis'. He began explicitly with individuals in their families and their comments on themselves, their relatives and their neighbours, concluding that 'provision for old age has emerged as a 'problem' largely because of the loosening of family ties ... Whereas families used to accept responsibility for their old people they now expect the state to look after them.'[101]

This last comment moved beyond empiricism at least in its implications. Yet Michael, Townsend and Willmott wanted to stick close to comments made in their interviews. And conscious as all three were of their lack of research experience in sociology, a point stressed by Marris, the fourth member of the group, they all began by trying to learn more about interviewing techniques from the sociologist Margot Jefferys.[102] They learnt much also from Ann Cartwright, who was later to leave a tenured post and join the Institute as a treasured member of its growing full-time staff in 1960.[103] Approaching health care through the experiences of patients (as consumers) and general practitioners, she fully appreciated, as Michael was to put it, how important it was to make the 'creative leap' which would reconvert 'facts' into 'life'. Social research was 'a strange job'.[104] She knew how to cope with it.

When Willmott went to carry out his first interview, it seemed – and he too used Dickensian language – like entering Fagin's kitchen. Thereafter he brought his whole family into the process. His wife, Phyllis, a hospital almoner and later editor of *Social Work*, was one of the interviewers, and in the preface to the paperback Pelican edition of *Family and Kinship in East London*, which appeared four years after the Routledge and Kegan Paul edition in 1962, Willmott recalled the words of his small son, who attended a Bethnal Green school, and returned one afternoon to corroborate their main finding. 'The teacher asked us to draw pictures of our family. I did one of you and Mummy and Mickey and me, but isn't it funny, the others were putting in their nannas and aunties and uncles and all sorts of people like that.'[105]

Children figured prominently in the Willmott world. Townsend describes a horde of them swarming round the old taxi bought for £40 and asking for a ride. As the taxi started they pushed it on its way with the words, 'You'll give us a ride now, mister, after 'elpin yer.' 'We bowled down the street with at least a dozen urchins hanging on by their fingers, all cheering madly.'[106] There were more children than some Bethnal Green mothers would have liked. Michael and Willmott quoted one memorable interview. 'When one husband said to us, "We wanted the baby", his wife retorted, "You may have, love; I know *I* didn't". Asked later in a second interview if she wanted more children, she said "I don't want them, but you can't tell. You ought to ask him (pointing at her husband) about that. He's the guv'nor".'

Interviews had never been so directly quoted before. Indeed, the most important differences between Michael's thesis and the book that he and Willmott were to co-author derived not from the fact that it was written in partnership or from the context in which thesis and book were written, but the increase in the size of the sample interviewed. In the book the electoral register was now chosen as the base, and one name in every 36 was taken from it for a 'general sample'. In addition, a smaller 'marriage sample' was taken of couples with young children, all of whom were interviewed more than once.

Michael and the three Ps succeeded far more than Titmuss suggested in a somewhat guarded foreword to *Family and Kinship* (1957):

> The Institute of Community Studies, as a collective name to embrace the activities of a small group of social investigators, perhaps claims too much. However, when work was begun in 1954 by the initial group of three students of contemporary social problems, stimulated and led by Michael Young, no member of the team could think of anything better.

In fact, Michael has always been good at choosing names – he was to be consulted by other organisation makers, including me – and the name Institute of Community Studies was a memorable name made to last. Titmuss added the modest hope that the Institute's studies would 'make some small contribution to correcting the present unbalanced views about the British family'. They did far more than this. Not least, they achieved what had been the most distinctive claim behind Michael's venture – that of making sociology seem both relevant and readable.

The novelist Kingsley Amis was not alone in appreciating *Family and Kinship in East London* which he saw as a readable supplement to Richard Hoggart's *The Uses of Literacy*.[107] The *New Statesman* wrote specifically that 'the general reader will find it [the book] full of meat and free of jargon'. The *British Medical Journal*, familiar with Sheldon's work, called it 'charmingly written, engaging, absorbing'.[108] *The Economist* found it 'interesting but depressing'. The modern East End emerged as 'a still cosy and chummy place, one in which a kind of robust Dickensian fellowship continues to flourish without its old accompaniments of poverty and bad drains'. Greenleigh, however, had a 'tragic' quality about it if the relatively small sample taken at an early stage in its growth was a reliable indicator.[109]

The reviewer who wrote these words may have been thinking of the last somewhat inadequate policy-related sentence in the book:

> If the authorities regard that [community] spirit as a social asset worth preserving, they will not uproot more people, but build the new houses around the social groups to which they already belong.

In other parts of the section of the book on Greenleigh what the reviewer called the 'tragic quality' was missing. There was, indeed, more emphasis on what has subsequently come to be called 'consumerism', something very different from the consumer guidance in which Michael believed.[110] It began on arrival:

> The house when the builders leave it is only a shell. The house when people move into it comes to life. They bestow an authority upon it, even vest it with a kind of personality: up to a point it then decrees what they shall do within its walls. The house is also a challenge ... When they make a first cup of tea after the removal van has driven away and look around their mansion, they are conscious not only of all they have got which they never had before but also of all the things they need which they still lack.

There was nothing about advertising in this analysis. Even before the great burst of television advertising in the late 1950s, which chronologically accompanied the writing of *Family and Kinship*, 'the struggle for possessions' was 'one in which comparisons with other people are constantly made.'

After the move of home had taken place, 'the understandable urge to acquisition' could easily become 'competitive'.

> People struggle to raise their all-round standards ... and in the course of doing so, they look for guidance to their neighbours. The later arrivals have their model at hand. The neighbours have put up nice curtains. Have we? They have their garden planted with privet and new grass seed. Have we? They have a lawn mower and a Dunkley pram. What have we got? The new arrivals watch the first-comers, and the first-comers watch the new arrivals. All being under the same pressure for material advance, they naturally mark each other's progress. Those who make the most progress are those who have proved their claim to respectability, Greenleigh style.[111]

Whatever might be said of the merits of Greenleigh's styles, there was at least one optimistic passage in *Family and Kinship*, overlooked by the reviewer, which had not been anticipated in Michael's thesis. For some residents in Greenleigh, where 'the fresh air hits you when you come out of the station', Michael and Willmott had noted that the new estate was thought 'better for the kiddies'. 'Even when they left their kin with regret, the people were not deserting family so much as acting for it, on behalf of the younger rather than the older generation.' There were also continuities in the relationship between mothers and daughters: nine out of ten girls interviewed stated that their mothers were keener than their fathers that they should stay on at school.[112]

There was a section of the book on the spread of television sets too ('the telly' had been given only one mention in the thesis). 'I think the telly is spoiling family life,' Mrs. Dray complains. 'We always meet at Mum's on Sunday evenings and we all used to talk and laugh, but now automatic at 8 the lights are turned off and we all sit in silence.'[113] Yet for more of the people interviewed television compensated for the absence of amenities outside the home, and served to support the family in its isolation. 'The telly keeps the family together. None of us have to go out now.'[114] Old people living on in Bethnal Green could find scope for compromise. Even the 'telly' could be put in its place. Townsend describes one widow's small kitchen where there was a television set with two Toby jugs below it and a budgerigar in a cage standing on top. There were photos of the two sons on the walls, 'one in police uniform'.[115]

The men's world was to change as much as the women's between the 1950s and the 1990s, not only in the East End, which was to become the subject not of interviews but of a popular television soap opera, *EastEnders*, with an audience of millions from all social classes. There was certainly to be no shortage of stories there. Already in the mid-1950s, however, when women's magazines were flourishing, a Greenleigh wife could say, 'My husband has given up the beer since we moved and he doesn't go to football matches any more.' The 'telly' was not the sole cause, as it seldom was the sole cause of anything. In Bethnal Green there had been one pub for every 100 dwellings, and for many men the bar in the pub had been 'as much a part of their living space as the room in their home'.[116]

Some of the quotes in the Michael and Willmott book were the same as in the thesis, but people interviewed were now given carefully chosen names. In tribute to Michael's greatest mentor, one family was called Tawney, and in tribute to one of the co-authors' guides, another family was called Jefferys. There was no Mrs. Shils, but there was a Mrs. Firth. There was also a Mrs. Cole. The names Mrs. Banks, Mr. Banton, Mrs. Florence and Mrs. Gould would be noted by other English sociologists, if not by non-sociologist reviewers of the book.

Naming was recognised as being important in Bethnal Green itself. About half the informants interviewed came from families in which the eldest children were named after their parents.

There had been a break, however, since the 1930s as names began to be taken from other sources, particularly Hollywood, the influence of which was strong before television. Cinemas figure little in *Family and Kinship*. Yet during the war and just afterwards they were at the peak of their popularity. Writing more generally, Michael and Willmott could note perceptively how the change in 'customs of naming' was 'one of the few social changes which can be measured quantitatively'.[117]

There was only one person untouched by family in *Kinship and Community*. 'I was found by a policeman as a baby in Finsbury Park,' said Mr. Head, 'and taken to Barnet Union. I lived there until I was 16. They gave me two suits then and turned me out. My mother got away with it. She was never traced. I was only a baby then, so I wouldn't have known what a mother was, would I? Children don't remember or know things.' Michael would have empathised with the situation – he felt let down by his own parents – but would never have reached the same conclusion.

Townsend's *The Family Life of Old People*, which offered his own picture of Bethnal Green, focused attention on problems not elaborated in Michael's thesis, many of which Townsend wished to follow through. One of his memorable, if not surprising, conclusions was that 'solidarity with relatives, neighbours and friends [as distinct from relatives] was strongest in some of the older streets ... People there talked, though very generally, [as Michael did] of the community as a family.' One woman said of life in a street which had been destroyed in the war, 'We was all one family. I think they are like that in these little turnings.' 'The trend in family life' seemed to be towards 'mutual aid, partnership, financial independence and personal freedom' in marriage. The conclusions of the Institute's researchers thus converged. Their methodology, of course, was the same.

Townsend had an excellent turn of phrase: in the words of Sheldon, who wrote an introduction to it, *Family Life* had 'the "true tang" that comes only from direct human contact'. He was just as interested in the lives of particular individuals as in the structure and dynamics of Bethnal Green's three-generation families which were held together by 'the ties of blood, duty, affection, common interest and daily acquaintance'. Thus, after having described most of the old people he visited as 'short in stature ... some lined and bent and rooted like withered trees, others swift and spruce and sly as the experienced fox', he picked on a woman who in her early sixties had resigned herself to her room, her stick, her black cat and her fire, and a man in his late eighties who had not seen his doctor more than three times in ten years and who 'moved swiftly about the house and the neighbourhood'.[118]

In the light of Townsend's later work, the most important chapter in *The Family Life of Old People* (Chapter XII) was called simply 'Poverty'. It began modestly – 'One of the possible consequences of retirement is poverty' – although it quickly went on to indicate what was to become Townsend's distinctive approach. 'Most studies of poverty in Britain over the past 60 years have concentrated only on the cost of maintaining some standard of subsistence needs ... Households were felt to be so much below the poverty line.' 'Why research has been restricted to this approach is puzzling – although it probably explains why a philosophy of payments on the basis of subsistence has been written into the nation's social security scheme.'

Soon Townsend was to leave the Institute (at Titmuss's invitation) to work at the London School of Economics, following a life pattern clearly of his own making. Independent-minded and with a strong will, Townsend had already known exactly what he wanted to do when Michael invited him to join the Institute. Now he saw opportunities elsewhere. From the start he had been specially drawn to Titmuss,[119] who appreciated the quality of his research and his commitment to it and who worked with him on Labour Party policy on social insurance, including pensions, the subject which had most interested him when he joined the Institute from PEP.

His two years at Bethnal Green seem short in retrospect, but they were formative. Before he left, he felt that there were tensions, even disagreements. For Townsend Michael seemed a 'somewhat insecure and vulnerable person', 'unpredictable' but 'indestructible', a Director who did not like it when 'things didn't go his way', yet 'looking in too many directions at the same time, some of them associated not with kinship research but with consumer organisation'.[120] He also wanted 'to come in very heavily' when he read his colleagues' drafts, as in Townsend's opinion he did when he read the manuscript of *The Family Life of Old People*,[121] criticising both style and content. At the same time in the affairs of the Institute he often left Willmott 'holding the baby and running the show'.[122] Townsend went on participating in the show. After finishing his book he carried out interviews for other Institute projects, including an interview with three old women living in Stepney who were alive when Beatrice Webb carried out her interviews for Charles Booth. 'The connection and continuity were quite evident.'

Townsend's career blossomed after he left the Institute and moved outside the range of Michael's and Willmott's influence, going on himself to combine research and action, founding the Child Poverty Action Group in 1969 with Frank Field as its first Director,[123] and becoming Chairman of the Fabian Society in 1983.[124] He had an academic career ahead of him also, as his friend Marris was to do. He was to become Professor of Sociology at the new University of Essex in 1963, where he did much to justify the University's declared commitment to the social sciences, and in 1982 he moved to a chair in Bristol.

Looking back at his years in Bethnal Green, Townsend recalls most vividly his talks with Marris, 'a very articulate and a very sensitive person', who according to Michael was the most fluent writer of reports that he had ever met, writing slowly but getting what he wrote right first time. For Townsend, who was a fast writer and completed *The Family Life of Old People* in two years – it took a year for Routledge to publish it – Marris had contributed more 'in a direct sense to [his own] research than anyone else, by doing part of the interviewing as well as advising on the planning of the report'.[125] He was to employ the Institute's interviewing techniques in places far away from Bethnal Green, like Lagos in Africa, the continent which was later to fascinate Michael.[126] He was to stay with the Institute until 1973, when he moved over to the newly founded Centre for Environmental Studies, and in 1976 he was to cross the Atlantic to become a Professor of Sociology in California and later at Yale.

Marris's study *Widows and their Families* (1958) produced a surprising conclusion given that the other studies carried out in the Institute had pointed to the strong attachment of married women to their mothers. Widows were not drawn more closely into the kinship circle, but tended to be withdrawn from it. They were keen to maintain their independence and suffered from emotional reaction to bereavement, a subject which was to fascinate Michael later in his life. Michael was particularly impressed by the fact that Marris's research led immediately to action. Sensitive to the loneliness of widows in Bethnal Green, he had proposed clubs for them, a proposal immediately taken up not in Bethnal Green but far to the west of London in Richmond. There was soon a cluster of CRUSE clubs. Significantly, two later books by Marris, who wrote novels as well as sociological studies, were called *Loss and Change* and *Meaning and Action*.

Writing about the Institute almost 40 years later, Marris, who did not mention CRUSE, began by singling out methodology. The three Ps along with Michael – all 'apprentices' in sociology – had introduced a 'new technique', 'their own technique' based on a 'blend of direct observation, random sampling and long open-ended interviews', and the 'life stories' in the books that emerged from their interviews carried most of 'the interpretive argument' in them. 'The tables, many of them relegated to an appendix, provided numbers in support.'[127] At the time, Willmott in an appendix had tried to explain their intent as well as their methodology. 'We have tried, in what we have written, to respect the appropriate statistical procedures and to avoid bias or tendentiousness. But the extent to which the final account is a personal interpretation, shaped and coloured by our own interests and sympathies, predispositions and unconscious prejudices, should be borne in mind by the reader.'[128]

Some readers who were academic sociologists were highly critical of this approach, complaining that the samples were too narrowly drawn, that the quotations and the statistics were not fully integrated, and that the statistics were used not to draw out conclusions but to illustrate answers already reached. They may or may not have fully borne in mind – what Michael and Willmott had to say about 'personal interpretation': they were unsympathetic to it. Nor had they much to say about the mission of the Institute to direct attention not only to the conclusions of research, expressed in intelligible language, but to the social action that should follow from them. Some of them, as Marris suggested, preferred relating conclusions to 'theory' not to policy, believing that sociology, if it was to establish itself as an academic subject, required a firm theoretical foundation. But this was by no means a general stance among sociologists. The situation as far as academic sociology was concerned was confused in the 1950s. Even inside the LSE, where there were more differences of approach and of personality than there were in the Institute, doubts about the Institute's approach to kinship and community studies were based on something more than concern for the autonomy of university sociology departments and for their necessary dissociation from social work or social administration.[129]

When the complaints first made in 1957, often in hushed voices, were echoed and formulated nearly ten years later, this time with no hushing, the main critic was a University of Sussex sociologist, Jennifer Platt, who (by a coincidence?) had been a pupil at Dartington School.[130] She was teaching and researching in a university which was not organised on departmental line and had no autonomous department of sociology (or of other social sciences, like economics, anthropology and psychology) to protect, so that she could not be accused of academic selfishness. Praising both what Michael and Willmott had to say about theory in *Family and Kinship in East London* and accepting their 'Demeter tie' hypothesis concerning women, she concentrated her critique on methodology. There had been too little use of multivariate analysis. The combination of a small sample, intensively interviewed, and a general sample led to bias: 'the usual procedure of illustrating the total data with examples is reversed ... the anecdotes are illustrated by occasional figures.' There were too few tables.

In unorthodox but useful fashion, Michael and Willmott reviewed Platt's book in *New Society*, in a review called 'On the Green'. They denied that they distrusted large questionnaires except as a means for eliciting straightforward information and declared that they had been right to rely on a small number of interviews in depth in order to identify which questions they should ask in interviewing the big sample. They had been interested in the vocabularies of the interviewed (their 'patterns of linguistic observation') and in their 'sets of mind'. Most forcefully, they challenged – in my view rightly – Platt's suggestion that it was a mistake to concentrate on Bethnal Green and to write with 'warmth' and 'sentimentality' about its people without at least comparing them with people in other places.

A historian, like an anthropologist, finds no difficulty in appreciating the need for 'micro-studies' of particular places, whether or not they are in some way 'representative'. Yet this does not seem to reach the heart of the matter. The use of the word 'illustrated' in Platt's account of the normal practice of sociologists suggests a distaste for 'story telling' and with it a distrust in some of the other community studies, rural or urban, of the period. Only at this point was there a certain defensiveness in Michael and Willmott's reply: instead of defending the genre, they emphasised that when they carried out their researches they were not sociologists to begin with but sociologists in the making. They even welcomed Platt's version of a school report: 'the Institute's methods have shown recently some marked improvements; let us hope that these will be maintained and further developed'.

By then the Institute had broadened its scope as it recruited new researchers and produced more books, not all of them about Bethnal Green. It had also produced revealing school reports of its own in 1961 and 1962, which were published in the *Sociological Review*. It had been involved in self-assessment even earlier. Townsend, in what he called 'a philosophical debate' on 'the aim of the Institute', had initiated an exchange of internal memoranda, arguing that the Institute had too many aims and needed 'ballast'. The fundamental aim of the Institute should remain what it had been – 'to answer the question, how important in our society is the extended family of three or four generations ... The basis of individual fulfilment rests on life membership of an active family of three generations.'[131]

Like Marris later, Townsend posed such questions within the context not only of society but of academic sociology. The Institute had made 'a compromise between statistics and readability, which can only be understood in the context of the present state of sociology, ranging from the absurd mathematics of the survey exponents to the woolliness of the social philosopher.'[132] 'Must we emphasise the interest of "doing good" and of "understanding ourselves" too self-consciously' was one of the questions raised at Bethnal Green. 'We must be "other-directed",' was the response.[133]

Four years after Townsend left Bethnal Green to join Titmuss, Michael himself moved to Cambridge to teach sociology as a Fellow of Churchill College, having tried unsuccessfully to take up a post first in Birmingham and then in Nuffield College, Oxford. It was in the year when he moved that the fourth report of the Institute appeared in the *Sociological Review* in July and was subsequently reprinted. It stated that it was still not the time for summing up the results of the research conducted so far, but it went on to identify 'as frankly as possible' those 'peculiar features of an independent research institute' which differentiated it from the university departments of sociology which were 'responsible for the bulk of sociological research'. (Were they?) The two main advantages were said to be that members of staff could devote their full time to research (might there not be a loss there?) and that people of experience could be employed even if they lacked what universities might consider to be proper academic qualifications. The University of Sussex, founded in the same year as the Report, was already widening the range of occupational and age backgrounds of the first academics it was appointing.

The disadvantages were acknowledged too. The Institute was playing no part in 'training the younger generation of research workers, and so ensuring the continued accumulation of knowledge on which progress in the subject depends'. There was no cross-fertilisation. 'Not only does a university atmosphere encourage the highest academic standards, but it also provides an opportunity for discussion in different disciplines. A small institute like ours is perhaps liable to become ingrown, and to engage in a continuous "internal dialogue" whose circularity is much plainer to those outside than to those within.' Last, but not least, there were financial worries. 'None of the staff can ever be established or given a long-term contract as they could be in a university: this is because there is no guarantee of funds.'

There were pluses in community links, largely then missing in Oxford and Cambridge, if not in Sussex, and it was entirely appropriate that another researcher at the Institute, the social historian Ralph Samuel, discovered qualities of vitality in working-class communities everywhere and encouraged them to revel in their own history. He also knew how to tap nostalgia in the 'history workshops' that attracted large numbers of people who had never studied history before. Later, Michael was to ask him to write the history of the Institute. 'I am greatly looking forward to [doing it],' he told Michael in 1982, adding that he had become interested not only in the people who had been interviewed by researchers in the Institute or the researchers who studied them but in other initiators, individuals not communities: it struck him from a reading of Mark Benney's *Almost a Gentleman* (and Benney was then a popular, now neglected, figure both with some British and some American sociologists, including David Riesman) that 'Ed Shils's sojourn at the LSE' had been pivotal.[134]

Samuel was not to complete his studies of the Institute. Nor did he ever put together the interviews which he amassed during the early 1960s on Bethnal Green's teenagers at the opposite end of the age spectrum from Townsend's pensioners. Nevertheless, while he was at work in an East End which he loved and to which he belonged, Samuel succeeded in turning 18 Victoria Park Square into a kind of sociological club for teenagers long before it was transformed into a mutual aid centre. Inevitably, this work raised questions of style as well as of income, status, family and community. Willmott used large parts of the material in *Adolescent Boys of East London* (1966).

Another early recruit to the Institute, more controversial than Samuel, was Brian Jackson, a Yorkshireman, who was deeply impressed by *Family and Kinship* and who wrote to Michael to discover whether there could be a place in the Institute for a study of his own on the West Riding. The result was not only a book, *Education and the Working Class* (1962), 'difficult to write', which he completed in co-authorship with Dennis Marsden, but a relationship which drew Michael into an expanding network of educational activities.[135]

Jackson wanted to focus on Huddersfield (Marburton), then in the course of physical and social change, near the moors but with 'a rough, sexy, violent world just round the corner';[136] and in 1968, a year when there was more obvious sex and violence than there had been six years before, he wrote a second book, *Working Class Community*, which was to be criticised sharply by a greater number of sociologists, among them J. A. Banks, himself from a provincial background, than Michael had ever been forced to confront. In fact, Jackson's second book was – and is – highly readable, and it is revealing to note the differences that had occurred in Marburton (and the author's analysis of them – and of himself since the publication of *Education and the Working Class*. It pays special attention to the media, noting that the 'more popular they are, the more they muffle their presentation of working-class life with a ring of images and attitudes quite as formidable as the old invisible wall'.[137]

Chapter 10, 'Change and Community', ends with the question as to whether the old working class community was going anyway'? There were links here with 'consumerism' and the consumer movement, chronological as well as thematic, for the magazine *Which*? first appeared in 1957, the same year as *Family and Kinship*, and during the late 1950s Michael, criticised for this by Townsend, was spending as much of his time on the Consumers' Association, launched in Bethnal Green, one of his great achievements, as on family and kinship.

The first guiding spirits behind the Association were Ray and Dorothy Goodman. Ray, an economist, was Michael's successor as Director of PEP; Dorothy, an American, working, like Michael, on a postgraduate degree whilst living in London, provided the main initial driving force. Whilst they were in London, Michael himself, in his own words, was 'a sort of passenger', a role that he soon totally changed.[138] The first impulse behind their efforts was practical. Dorothy wanted to install central heating in their home (well in advance of British taste at that time) and found that there was no British equivalent of American *Consumer Reports* which gave information about comparative efficiency, quality and price. There were, indeed, impressive American precedents for a consumers' journal. Since 1936, *Consumer Reports*, a venture well known to the Goodmans, had provided American consumers with information based on research.[139] It was not only Americans, however, who had blazed a trail. Another country with experience in the publication of influential consumer reports was Sweden.

Michael did not take over the organisation of a Consumers' Association until the Goodmans left England for the 'affluent society' of the United States in 1956, bequeathing him various filing cabinets dealing with consumer reporting, but once he had taken over he galvanised it into active life. This was a busy and exciting time in his life culminating for him in the first appearance of *Which?*, for which there were no initial supporting funds. Indeed, Michael and the small group of friends, including friends of the Goodmans, owed £60 in unpaid bills.

The man who thought of the name *Which?*, an inspiration (names like *Consumer* and *Value for Money* were rejected), was Paul Fletcher: when he named it to Michael over the telephone, it seemed like a 'moment of revelation'. The first person who set out to make the Association work was Peta Fordham, who found people to work with her for nothing. She got the Public Analyst of Birmingham to write a report on aspirin. Fordham soon left, however, and Eirlys Roberts, imaginative, resourceful and indefatigable, a journalist married to a barrister, was brought in as editor. She had worked as Press Officer in the Treasury, and it was she who was to write the history of the Consumers' Association for its 25th anniversary.[140] While the Association was in its first phases Michael, designated Director, bombarded her with 'an uninterrupted stream of new ideas'.[141]

Faith in the future of consumer organisations was not unaccompanied by anxiety. Michael had been told that, whatever the situation might be in the United States or in Sweden, consumer reporting in Britain would run into legal difficulties. He knew, too, that any 'slips' in reporting would leave him and his colleagues liable to prosecution. He had been advised, however, by Gerald Gardiner, a future Labour Lord Chancellor, that a British Consumers' Association would not be 'against the law', and this gave him as much confidence as he hoped consumers would derive from reading the published reports.

Of course, it was plain that most of the members of a Consumers' Association and the readers of a new consumer magazine would be middle-class, not working-class, consumers. They would live neither in Bethnal Green nor in 'Greenleigh'. They would include a large proportion who had never heard of Robert Owen. Already other people were catering for them too. Elizabeth Gundrey, a journalist on the *News Chronicle*, was editing a magazine called *Shoppers' Guide* for the British Standards Institution, a voluntary non-profit-making body incorporated by Royal Charter, and another journalist, Marghanita Laski, whom Michael know well, was writing articles on consumer products in the *Observer*. Gundrey, Laski and Roberts set an example by writing clearly and without jargon. And in that respect *Which?* followed the same path as the Institute of Community Studies.

Even though in retrospect, at least, the time seemed ripe for a consumers' journal, not least because 'there was money about' – in Roberts's words, 'Many people bought with gay abandon. Many others were afraid of being swept away' – publicity was necessary if *Which?*, first circulated like one of Michael's Research Department Reports, was to take off. Before the Goodmans left Britain, a meeting in the House of Commons to describe it had failed to interest either Government or MPs. Now Michael turned to Lord Francis-Williams, friend of and Press Adviser to Harold Wilson, who agreed to chair a launch meeting at the Waldorf, which was well attended and enthusiastic, but not at all reported: the journalists present were as concerned about 'reprisals' as Michael had been. The breakthrough came when Michael approached François Lafitte, who was then writing *Times* leaders, and it was he who persuaded a woman's correspondent of *The Times* to insert a note on the new Association – it was very brief – stating that the membership fee would be ten shillings a year.

There was an immediate response. Subscriptions poured in, and within a month there were no more worries about debt. There was an American cheque too from the American Consumers' Union, responsible for *Consumer Reports*: it had refused to help until it saw the look of a number of *Which?* that dealt with aspirin, electric kettles and cars. Reporting on aspirin turned out, in Michael's phrase, to be 'very, very easy'. Reports on samples of branded aspirin products were provided free by the Public Analyst: they all turned out to be the same. Electric kettles were more difficult. Michael's faith in the venture was fortified when on a reconnaissance visit to Sweden he secured from a Swedish motoring magazine the right (free) to reports of tests made by its staff on two European cars. This was consumer territory which he himself knew about intimately. (But what about aspirin?)

Receiving the cheque from America enabled Michael to appoint Roberts as editor, and Philip Barbour, treasurer of the Institute of Community Studies, to hire a few paid staff, among them Fietje Baukema, who had once ridden in the Dutch cycling team in the Olympics (she used to cycle to buy electric light bulbs for testing) and Edith Rudinger. When the subscriptions first poured in, the Association was operating from the University House Settlement address, and a group of volunteers gathered to paint an empty garage next door and turn it into a one-room office. *Which?* was soon successful enough to move out of the East End to bigger offices in Holborn, with Barbour using his Morris Minor to carry the files and equipment on three journeys. Meanwhile, Michael Rubinstein became the Association's first lawyer and other recruits came from both the Civil Service and the Labour Party.

Recalling these hectic beginnings, Michael fondly remembers another early event. One day a taxi arrived at Victoria Park Square in

Bethnal Green – an event in itself, for not many taxis, except the old £40er, made their way there – and a stranger asked for the office of the Consumers' Association. 'Is it here?' He was told yes and invited in. Immediately he ordered ten copies of *Which?* for the Board members of Marks and Spencer in Baker Street. There were echoes of Israel Sieff in this. 'I've never had such an immediate success in anything that I've done,' Michael was to recall.[142]

Continuity in the consumer enterprise was provided for Michael first by his successor in charge of the Research Department at Transport House, Wilfred Fienburgh, and later by Jeremy Mitchell, who had worked with Michael in the Research Department and was employed on market research by ICI when Michael invited him to join the staff. He was interviewed by Roberts. He recalls that when he had first discussed consumer reports at supper with Peter and Phyllis Willmott in 1954 Peter had expressed scepticism when shown American reports dealing with patent medicines, cars, refrigerators, washing machines and 'even hunting rifles'. 'It would never work here.'[143]

It did, quickly reaching a membership of 10,000; and at its peak membership was to reach over one million. Its staff became more organised – with project officers, directed by Caspar Brooke, who arrived from the *Economist* Intelligence Unit (another interesting link), developing a system of checking and verifying sheets and of answering letters. As it grew there were to be many side-ventures and offshoots. Thus, in 1962 the first quarterly supplement *Motoring Which?* appeared and later in the year the first *Drug and Therapeutics Bulletin* was published. Also in the same year the Association, which by then had moved its premises for the fourth time in four years to 14 Buckingham Street, Charing Cross, bought the *Good Food Guide*. Raymond Postgate, its editor, was the brother of Margaret Cole, another curious link, and having established the *Guide*, which he published from his home, he was happy to sell it to Michael. This was the start of a substantial Consumers' Association publishing business.[144] The *Good Hotel Guide* and the *Good Holiday Guide* followed.

Michael gave up his chairmanship on becoming Chairman of the new Social Science Research Council, handing it over in 1965 to Jennifer (later Dame Jennifer), wife of Roy (later Lord) Jenkins, while remaining as President. By a coincidence rather than a 'curious link', Roy Jenkins was then Minister of Aviation, a subject which had always interested Michael.[145] There was a new Director also. Brooke had resigned, to be succeeded by Peter Goldman, who had been head of the Conservative Political Centre, set up by Butler. This was another coincidence.[146] There was a final coincidence. The Consumers'

Association was then located in Holborn, not far from where Michael himself was to move when he became Secretary of the Social Science Research Council. Before moving over, Michael had initiated the most important offshoot of the Consumers' Association, the Advisory Centre for Education (ACE), founded in July 1960, with a journal *Where?* as the counterpart of *Which?*. Another much later offshoot was the College of Health (1983), based on self-help groups, which developed more on the lines that Michael envisaged for the Consumers' Association itself when it was founded: its journal evolved into *Which Way to Health?*.[147]

Long before then, the Institute of Community Studies had established itself in the health field. One of the early people working on it even before Ann Cartwright joined the staff was Enid Mills who was studying mental patients and, when they had them, their families. Studying ex-patients discharged from Epsom Hospital to Bethnal Green, she added a new use to 18 Victoria Park Square. The ex-patients often set up self-help groups and some of them could be seen in the small garden outside the house or in the square waiting for or just having finished their interviews. In Michael's phrase 'she had very good material'.[148]

Health as a subject of major interest in all families was placed in the same category as education after Cartwright joined the Institute. Meanwhile, however, education had been clearly identified as the first follow-through of the Consumers' Association. 'The subject of this new venture [ACE] was chosen because no public service affects the welfare of every family, and of the nation, more than education.' There was a public stake too. Yet as in the case of the Consumers' Association, it was middle-class rather than working-class parents who were initially most interested in what *Where?* had to offer, and Michael was seizing on a theme, 'choice', which was to appeal to the right rather than to the left during the 1970s and 1980s. 'One of the paradoxes of modern life is that as the country gets richer and the range of choice increases, we may feel not so much free but more confused.' Michael went on to refer to section 76 of the Education Act of 1944: 'pupils are to be educated in accordance with the wishes of their parents'. The section was 'hedged round with qualifications', but it used the word 'right'.[149]

ACE was smaller than the Consumers' Association. Of its first 2,000 members, recruited during the first four months, more than half came from the South-East, including London, and only 222 from the North. The overseas figure was 94. By the end of its first year it had nearly 5,000 readers and 200 new members were said to be joining each week. The subscription in the first year was kept at 10 shillings.[150]

There were difficulties in managing it. Michael turned first to John (later Lord) Vaizey, a friend of Crosland who was keenly interested in education, who set about organising it on highly respectable lines, choosing among his Honorary Vice-Presidents (with Michael's full blessing) Mrs. (later Lady) Dora Gaitskell, Mrs. Jo Grimond, wife of the Liberal Leader, Lady Kilmuir, wife of the Conservative Chancellor, H. D. P. (later Sir Desmond) Lee, Headmaster of Winchester College, Miss (later Dame) Diana Reader Harris, Headmistress of Sherborne, and Eric (later Lord) James, High Master of Manchester Grammar School. Among the others some were particularly prominent in the cause of 'educational advance' – John (later Sir John) Newsom, formerly Education Officer of Hertfordshire, and A. D. C. Peterson, then Director of the Department of Education, Oxford University.

Vaizey and Michael agreed on this list. They were not able, however, to establish a satisfactory working relationship. Michael found him in general 'too Establishment', and for temperamental reasons failed also to develop a satisfactory relationship with the Centre's first full-time Secretary, Tyrrell Burgess, who, after graduating from Oxford, where he was President of the Union, had become a teacher and then news editor of the *Times Education Supplement*. Burgess was to produce *A Guide to English Schools* and *Education After School*.[151] When the Centre moved from Bethnal Green to Cambridge, it was reshaped by Brian Jackson, who attracted volunteers to work with it and left his imprint on all he did, seldom without controversy. He was capable of generating as much opposition to his organisational methods from his colleagues as from his competitors, just as he was in provoking scorn from reviewers hostile to the methods employed in his books. On first seeing him Michael judged him bright and brilliant, but difficult: in particular, he did not seem to engage in conversation. It might have been as difficult to work with him as with Vaizey or Burgess, but this proved not to be. 'Don't know that I could deal with you,' Michael told him at his interview, 'but as long as you don't have to work from my office, you can be your own fellow and do what you like.' When ACE moved from Bethnal Green to Cambridge and Michael in the reverse direction the relationship became closer.

Jackson was one of the last appointments to the staff of the Institute for Community Studies before Michael took up his university post in Cambridge, but it was Michael himself who wrote a number of seminal articles for *Where?*, which for a time Sasha edited. As a family enterprise it is as valuable a source for the historian of education, old and new, in the 1960s as *Which?* is for historians of the 'consumer society'. Its first number included articles on 'Prep schools for boys – how to choose one' and 'University overseas – how to go to one'. There was another practical article, 'Boarding schools – how to get grants', along with an article on 'Education at home'. In the first number there was an article close to Michael's own experience: 'Progressive schools – how to choose them'. There was also an article in No. 11 on 'Rudolf Steiner Schools for normal children' and in No. 14 on 'Painting for young children'. There was a fashionable turn to 'Italic handwriting' (also in No. 15) and a focusing on a major middle-class worry, 'Word Blindness', in numbers 16 and 17. Other early copies of *Where?* included 'Nursery schools, how to find one' (No. 2), 'Boarding schools for girls' (No. 2), 'Diploma technology – how to get one' (No. 2), 'How to set up an adventure playground' (No. 3).

General educational themes soon became more prominent, and Nos. 9, 11 and 12 included news and addresses of officers in the Association for the Advancement of State Education. One issue (No. 12) included an article on 'Comprehensive schools – choosing one'. There was also an article on 'Grammar Schools – selection in different areas' (No. 11). Meanwhile, 'Encyclopedias – are they worth buying?' (No. 15) strayed into territory covered in *Which?*. 'Teaching by television' was one of the topics covered in No. 11: it was followed by 'Programmed learning and teaching machines' (then much in the news) in No. 13.

Issue No. 14 announcing Michael's latest venture, the National Extension College,[152] also included an article on his oldest venture 'Motor mechanic – becoming one'. In the next number there was an article on 'Oxbridge stranglehold'. Michael's concern for international issues was reflected in 'Voluntary Service Overseas' and 'African schools – links with' (No. 14); and in 'Universities of the Commonwealth – cooperation with' (No. 16). In picking out these he was not only reflecting his own interests. He was appealing to a new generation who wanted – through education – to get out of little England and into a 'big world'.

5
Merit and/or Solidarity

Education, the driving force behind ACE, had not figured at the top of Michael's preoccupations while he was in charge of the Labour Party's Research Department, although in *Labour's Plan for Plenty* he stated that 'of all the social services, education is by far and away the most important'. It did not stand out prominently, however, either in the Party's election manifesto of 1950, the last with which he was directly concerned, or in the next manifesto of 1951, the first to appear after he left Transport House.

None the less, in *For Richer For Poorer* Michael dealt with education at some length, beginning with the most topical of images:

> The educational system is rather like that strange water chute at the Festival of Britain. Do you remember it? Most people flood straight through the ordinary schools and out to a job at 15. Some are lifted a little way up and, joining the horizontal scheme, flow with a slight clatter through the grammar schools to the lower reaches of the middle class. Others are hoisted higher and out through the provincial universities to merge with the flood waters from the public schools in the middle reaches. Yet others are scooped well up into the air and with a tremendous splash are disgorged into the learned professions where they flush the upper reaches. For the upper class there is a more curious chute of different design, with narrow channels leading straight from Nanny to New College.

The imagery is refreshingly different from that of the ladder which Michael himself used frequently in *The Rise of the Meritocracy*, where he describes 'the educational ladder' as being also a social ladder. 'The scruffy, ill-mannered boy who started at five years old at the bottom [was that really the type even at five?] had to be metamorphosed, rung by rung, into a presentable, more polished and more corpulent as well as a more knowledgeable lad at the top.'[1]

Michael's main point, he added, was a different one: the home was as much an educational influence as the school. In the future he was to explore the implications of this for the working classes of Bethnal Green. Now, at this point in his argument, he focused more generally on those 'above' and those 'below'. For the 'superior class', as in the past, it remained better to start work with no passport at all than with a passport signed by a schoolmaster. Birth was more relevant than merit. 'The same man was always at the head of the table.' The word 'table' was to require a new meaning as educational issues become prominent on the political agenda within the next decade.

Most of Michael's comments on education and the criterion of merit rather than birth were included during the 1950s in the section of *For Richer For Poorer* which dealt with the class system. He suggested there that the system was held together by its ends, at one end the 'upper class', at the other the 'working class' with 'its own institutions and loyalties'. Both were gripped by birth. Yet there was an increasing need in the national interest to break the pattern and to deploy all available talent wherever it was to be found. Kenneth Lindsay had calculated back in 1924 that the ability of at least 40 per cent of the nation's children was being 'denied expression'.[2] In 'a classless society', Michael insisted, the 'aristocracy of birth' would have to go. 'If only because of the state of the economy in a world of competition ... we have to get rid of the feudal class structure as quickly as we can. Every young man with the capacity to design a better tin tack or soup-spoon, prevented from exercising his talents by lack of education, is a loss to the nation. We shall need every ounce of ability we can find.' 'Talent imprisoned is a spirit failed.' The 'funeral of feudalism' would be the one funeral at which 'the mourners will wear scarlet'.

Michael was to expand on this point, placing it in its historical context in the last pages of his LSE thesis where he claimed that it was 'one of the axioms of an industrial society' that a person's social status 'should not be ascribed by birth but achievable by merit'. The strength of the proposition, he went on, could be judged by the simultaneous acceptance of death duties and of scholarships on the part of society. Neither was new. What was newer, however, was a growing sense, inevitably involving strain, that job and status should not be ascribed by 'birth into a particular sex any more than into a particular family: women should be as free as men to achieve what status they can on their own merits'.

The implications of that led him deep into psychology. He did not expand at that stage on the politics. Instead, he concentrated on what he saw as a new danger. An aristocracy of birth or wealth, plutocracy, would be replaced, he feared, by an aristocracy of intelligence, 'no less galling because it is not hereditary'. And given this 'danger' – for that is how Michael saw it unequivocally, without spelling it out as fully as he was to do in *The Rise of the Meritocracy* – 'what was needed immediately was to reduce the difference between top and bottom by giving, not a few selected children, but every child an education in a common school [he also used the word "comprehensive school"] which would give him and her access to the treasures of culture and knowledge which should be everyone's possession.' Michael did not identify different forms of knowledge or hint at the emergence of a 'knowledge society', but instead referred back to William Morris: 'I want to be able to talk to any of my countrymen in his own tongue freely, and feeling sure that he will be able to understand my thoughts according to his innate capacity; and I also want to be able to sit at a table with a person of any occupation without a feeling of awkwardness and constraint being present between us.'[3] Michael quoted also the 1899 Charter of Ruskin College: The student was 'to be taught to regard the education which he receives, not as a means of personal advancement, but as a trust for the others. He learns in order that he may raise others, and not rise out of the class to which he belongs.'[4]

Michael might have referred back to Tawney too, for despite the lack of attention devoted to education in the Labour Party political manifestos of 1950 and 1951 there was one relevant Labour Party pamphlet of 1951, *A Policy for Secondary Education*, which reflected a strand in Labour Party history which went back via Tawney to Morris. This strand was strongly in evidence in 1951 in the Education Committee of the London County Council, which consisted of unflinching advocates of the comprehensive school. For them, as for Michael, there was nothing utopian about the conception of a common school. Such schools flourished in the United States, Australia and New Zealand, where they were taken for granted.

For Michael it was not enough, therefore, 'to open careers to the talents'. This was 'a poor unambitious ambition', already achieved in great measure in 'new countries'. Equality of opportunity was not sufficient. In Britain there was already too much competition between children – and their status-seeking parents – for the limited number of places in grammar schools, making life in primary schools 'like the inside of a pressure cooker'. Dartington had avoided all that.[5] At this point Michael could not resist a dig at the suburbs. 'The tension in some suburban streets before scholarship results were announced resembled that of a crowd [the imagery became awkward at this point, for suburbs lacked crowds] waiting for the last trump'.

> The sturdiest protagonists of equality of opportunity do not customarily anticipate that they or their children will be amongst the rejects or reckon with the fact that those who have the chance to rise and then fail to do so are likely to be more frustrated, and more humiliated, than if they had never had the chance at all. Nor should we overlook the danger that if [a very big 'if'] all the able people were skimmed off by the schools, and routed into white collar jobs, none would be left as leaders of the manual workers, to fight for their interests and interpret their needs. Had Keir Hardie and Arthur Henderson been safely shepherded into learned professions, the gain of the professions would have been the loss of the Labour Movement and society. How many working class students at Ruskin College are, one might ask, keen to return to their old jobs?

Did he have Peter Willmott in mind when he wrote these words?

'A danger foreseen is half avoided,' Michael concluded, with a gloss that 'it would be irrelevant further to explore the subject of social mobility in any detail'. Meanwhile, 'although we cannot hope to equalise status, we can seek to narrow the difference between the top and the bottom. A famous start has been made towards doing this as far as incomes are concerned. ... Lazarus is sitting at the table. But income is not all. There is also ... education.'

Detail on schooling was to be left to the pages of *The Rise of the Meritocracy*, and by the time that Michael wrote it he had studied more fully current approaches to a system of intelligence testing. Merit was being identified with intelligence. The conclusions of Cyril (later Sir Cyril) Burt, born in 1883, who from 1913 to 1922 had been Psychologist to the London County Council, were still in fashion: the intelligence tests he depended upon and other techniques which he had devised had been used widely during the Second World War and were familiar to most ex-servicemen.[6]

Michael was fascinated by intelligence testing, but unimpressed. In *For Richer For Poorer* he identified more directly than he was to do in *The Rise of the Meritocracy* what kind of a 'classless society' he wished to see. Admitting that he might be 'leaving solid ground quite behind and disappearing into the upper air', he placed 'diversity of values' uppermost:

> Socialists, it has sometimes been said, stand for equality. It would be better said that they are against inequality. We have sought to remove extreme inequality, not because we wished to make men equal but to show that they were not ... Socialists have attacked the class system not only because it was difficult to justify existing inequalities by any test of reason or justice, but because it was impossible in a society founded on such simplification, to cultivate diversity of values.

The 'classless society' to which he aspired, in line with these earlier socialists, was a society where there would be greater rather than less diversity. It would be polychrome, not monochrome:

> Were we to evaluate people not only according to their wealth, their occupation, their education and their power, not only according to their intelligence and manual skill, but according to their kindliness, their courage, their imagination, sensitivity, honesty, sympathy and humility, there could be no classes. Who would be able to say that the scientist was superior to the manual worker, the University professor without children superior to the porter with admirable qualities as a father, the Chairman of the Board superior to the lorry-driver with unusual skill at growing roses?

Eight years elapsed between the writing of these words and the publication of *The Rise of the Meritocracy*, which appeared at just the right time in 1958, one year after *Family and Kinship in East London*, and which purported to be an LSE doctoral thesis written by a different Michael Young. Yet there had been no change during this eight-year period in his outlook or in his conclusions.

Throughout the 1960s, when the subject of education was as much at the centre of policy-making as it had been in the period of fictitious history covered in *The Rise of the Meritocracy*,[7] Michael was to follow the same approach, while gaining in experience in the field through initiating or participating in movements for educational advance and reform. He knew that he was living in an exceptional time: as John Vaizey was to put it wittily in 1962 at the beginning of his Penguin Special on Education, 'somewhat to the surprise of the academic profession it now seems that education is important'.[8]

Like the Victorian Liberal politician, John Morley, who in the 1870s described education as a 'unifying national cause', Michael realised that 'progress [in education] was, as always uneven', and that it required a particular convergence to turn it into a national cause. Both the potential of education to stir and to unify the public and its unevenness in doing so were facts that had subsequently stood out in the history of educational change, and it was with a reference to the 1870s that Michael began *The Rise of the Meritocracy*. Its first sentence read: 'The 1870s have been called the beginning of the modern era not so much because of the [Paris] Commune as because of Mr. Forster [and his Education Act of 1870].' The 1960s was to be another of the rare decades when education was a 'focalising issue' that captured the headlines, and Michael was to be in the thick of it.[9]

It was not only newspaper headlines that made education news. Periodicals did the same, notably *New Society*, first issued on Thursday, 4 October 1962, following in the wake of the *New Scientist*, which was six years older. They were produced by the same firm, which was owned by Max Raison who had been managing director of *Picture Post*, an interesting link with war-time radicalism. Michael wrote frequently for *New Society*, first edited by Max's son, Tim, and although it did not break even in its first three years, within ten it had a circulation of 37,000. 'As it created a new audience it created a new market place.'[10]

Even earlier, a prestigious Victorian publication, the *Nineteenth Century*, now called the *Twentieth Century*, became a quarterly forum, and under the editorship of Richard Findlater it followed 'a dominantly sociological approach in the broadest sense of the word'. Its 'ruminations on fashion', characteristic of the decade, gave details of what was 'in' and 'out'. Education, 'higher' and 'lower', was said to be in a mess in a special issue devoted to it in 1963, but it was clearly 'in'. Michael was a member of its editorial advisory committee. So was I. It very rarely met, but it watched over all signs of educational change and of resistances to them.[11]

That was the immediate context, covered more fully in the next chapter. The title of this chapter, however, takes *The Rise of the Meritocracy* out of its immediate context. Like the Consumers' Association, it is a product, with a history behind it as well as in front of it, which has retained its relevance in contrasting circumstances.[12] Indeed, unlike much of the writing on education of the late 1950s and 1960s – and there was no break between the two decades – it is quoted during the 1990s as much as it was at the time. This is not so much because it was a book set in the future but because it probed beneath educational structures and policies to the basic issue of the role of 'merit' in society and the limits, real and potential, to its influence.[13]

'The axiom of modern thought,' Michael said of the future world that he was discussing, was that 'people are unequal', and it followed from this axiom, 'as a moral injunction that they should be accorded a station in life related to their capacities'. What were the implications? Educational structures and policies have changed more than once since the 1950s and 1960s, sometimes for demographic or economic reasons, sometimes through the pull of fashion. Society has changed in such a way too since the 1950s and 1960s that *The Rise of the Meritocracy* is in certain respects a more telling work when there is a 'New Labour' government in power, by no means doing all that Michael would wish, than when Old Labour held office – for far longer periods of time or old or new Conservatives.

At the time when *The Rise of the Meritocracy* appeared, the periodical *Time and Tide*, long defunct, described it as 'a fountain gush of new ideas',[14] and the fact that the ideas are now familiar does not blunt them. They could, of course, be treated selectively then as now. Conservatives had as much reason for drawing on them as socialists. The blurb of a new American edition of *The Rise of the Meritocracy*, which appeared in 1994, put in simple form only half of what Michael had to say – 'You need intelligence rating, qualification, experience, application and a certain caliber to achieve status. In a word, one must show merit to advance in the new society of tomorrow.' The point had been made forcefully by Daniel Bell, employing Michael's word: 'The post-industrial society, in its logic, is a meritocracy.'[15]

The other half of what Michael had to say in his 'essay', as he called his book more than once, was explained briefly by him in his introduction to the same 1994 American edition, where he left context, both locational and temporal, out of the picture and emphasised the universality of his theme:

> The book was ... intended to present two sides of the case – the case against as well as the case for a meritocracy. It is not a simple matter and was not intended to be. The two points of view are contrasted throughout. The imaginary author has a shadow. The decision ... was, and is left to the reader.

He or she would have 'to make up his or her mind on one of the great issues of modern society'. If that sounded portentous, Michael expressed the hope that in reaching a decision the reader, 'he or she', would also 'have a little fun'.[16]

There was little 'fun', however, in the last pages of *The Rise of the Meritocracy*, written as it purported to be by a 'funless' Michael Young who was never to live to see his thesis appear in book form. Before it was published he had met his death at a new 'massacre of Peterloo' in

2034. In a final footnote on the last page of the book we read 'since the author ... was himself killed at Peterloo, the publishers regret that they were not able to submit to him the proofs of his manuscript, for the corrections he might have wished to make before publication.' We are not told exactly what happened at this twenty-first century Peterloo. Did the meritocracy win – at least in the short term – as the old order won at the earlier Peterloo? What happened later on? Were there to be new 'myths', a word Michael used elsewhere in the text, centred on the new Peterloo?

The other Michael, a sociologist who set out painstakingly to live up to the 'conscience of the sociologist' – the real Michael at his least playful – believed in advance that 2034 would not be a 1793 but 'at best an 1848, on the English model' of that year of revolutions. 'Nobody had been killed then.' He envisaged 'nothing more serious than a few days' strike and a week's disturbance'. Are we to deduce that Michael II was a bad forecaster, despite all his care in seeking to demonstrate that the rising discontent which led up to 2034 had 'deep roots' and was not simply, as the Government tried to claim, the result of 'administrative errors'? In any case he disclaimed any intention in his thesis of 'predicting the course of events next May'. The real Michael, who had just finished his own thesis, must have enjoyed writing the last sentence of the final footnote – there was an obvious touch of fun there: 'the failures of sociology are as illuminating as its successes.'[17]

In his thesis the other Michael had admitted that the meaning of 2034 was 'not certain'. 'Only the historians of the future will know, perhaps even they will not agree?' The phrase, the 'deep roots' of history, was referred to on the second page of the thesis and repeated on the third page from the end. There is as much history, general and specific, as futurology in *The Rise of the Meritocracy*, which traces step by step as a historian would – the thesis writer was a '*historical* sociologist' – the process through which Britain became a meritocracy. In the beginning was the aristocracy and hierarchy. Then came industry and inequalities of class. 'The soil creates castes, the machine manufactures classes.' After that came meritocracy and new élites, the latter a word that Michael used frequently in the book.

'Today [2033],' he concluded, 'we have an élite selected according to deserts, with a grounding in philosophy and administration as well as in the two S's of science and sociology.' It had had no grounding, however, in communications or in public relations; and in this respect the real Michael's sense of what the rest of the twentieth century would be like went somewhat astray. Politicians, not least Labour politicians, were to have more grounding in communications and in public relations than in science or in sociology. There were no spin doctors in *The Rise of the Meritocracy*.

The *New Oxford English Dictionary* did not include an entry on meritocracy. The *Longman Dictionary of Contemporary English* did, defining 'meritocracy' in 1978 as 'a social system which gives the highest positions to those with the most ability' or, more particularly – and perhaps in relation to Michael's book more relevantly – as 'the people who rule in such a system'.[18] (Ironically Longman had turned down Michael's manuscript when he submitted it to them for publication.) The other Michael, the doctoral student, had specialised at school in the period of British history between 1914 and 1963, and after leaving school he acknowledged his debt to his sixth-form master, Mr. Woodcock,[19] for first pointing out to him 'how revealing a study of that time could be for an understanding of the progress man has made in the last century'. The publisher's reader at Longman quite extraordinarily took Michael's book to be itself a real PhD thesis, 'fair warning' for Michael 'that the book if it ever saw the light of day was going to be misunderstood'.[20]

Influential though *The Rise of the Meritocracy* was to be, unlike *Family and Kinship* it was a difficult book to get published – with or without 'the fun'. Michael 'hawked it around from one publisher to another – eleven of them in all – before, by a coincidence, he met Walter Neurath, who with his wife – both of them refugees from Germany – had founded Thames and Hudson. Mainly concerned with art and uninvolved in sociology, Neurath published *The Rise of the Meritocracy* 'out of friendship'.[21] It proved, however, to be an excellent business proposition, and was to be translated into at least nine languages, French, German, Italian, Spanish, Dutch, Danish, Norwegian, Swedish, Finnish and Japanese. In London it was published in paperback by Penguin in 1961 along with *Family and Kinship*. In themselves, these two books, which were completed in trying circumstances, guaranteed Michael's long-term fame.

He was confident in the literary genre which he had chosen – and he thought of it as 'satire' – but there were some critics who expressed doubts about his choice after it appeared, not all of them as flattering as the reviewer in *Time and Tide*. Thus, Richard Hoggart who had described *Family and Kinship in East London* in *The Observer* as 'valuable', did not like 'anti-Utopian satire' any more than he liked the other Michael Young, the doctoral student. (Subsequently cultural historians were often to put together Michael's Bethnal Green and Hoggart's Hunslet.[22]) Works such as *The Rise of the Meritocracy* seemed to Hoggart 'dangerously accommodating' to their writers. 'Once the initial theme has been found, structure presents no complex problems.' The works tended towards 'a sort of invented embroidery of notions, moving out from their given and realistic base into elaborate but telling fancies'. For Hoggart, who obviously found little fun in *The Rise of the Meritocracy*, its interest fell off before the end. What Young had had to say was 'sufficient only for a good short squib'.

Michael had shown his own good public relations sense when in the autumn before publication of the book he had arranged for extracts from his essay to be printed in *Encounter*, then jointly edited by the English poet Stephen Spender and the American intellectual Irving Kristol.[23] The extracts concentrated, as most of his reviewers were to do, on the triumph of meritocracy rather than on the revolt against it, and the first extracts picked out began not with futurology but with history. 'In feudal times the country was governed by neither caste nor class, rather by a combination of both. For hundreds of years, blood shared power with brain.' And only then was there a shift in the selection of extracts with those relating to the future being planted in the present.

> The fundamental change of the last century [the twentieth], which was fairly begun before 1963, is that intelligence has been redistributed between the classes and the nature of the classes changed. The talented have been given the opportunity to rise to the level which accords with their capacities, and the lower classes consequently reserved for those who are also lower in ability. The part is no longer the same as the whole.

Such extracts printed in *Encounter* were well chosen to tempt the reader to turn to Michael's whole book which, like *Encounter* itself, had an Anglo-American appeal.[24]

In the same number of *Encounter* there was an American article by W. H. Whyte on 'the City Eviscerated' and a long review by John Strachey of J. K. Galbraith's *The Affluent Society*, a book which influenced socialist thinking in Britain, including the thinking of Michael's friend, Crosland, one of the people whom Michael thanked in his acknowledgements.[25] That was the immediate intellectual context. Strachey, ex-Marxist, who had once been Michael's neighbour,[26] looked back to Veblen, stating that *The Affluent Society* was written from 'a completely American standpoint', but when he added that it was 'a study, at once massive and intricate, of what happens to a society which chooses personal self-enrichment as its national goal or ideal', he was implicitly, though in no sense intentionally, comparing it with *The Rise of the Meritocracy*, a supremely English book, equally intricate but not massive, a study of what happens to a society which chooses merit as its criterion.[27]

In the same number of *Encounter* another supremely English volume edited by David Glass, *Social Mobility in England* (1954), was described in a lively and critical review article by Barbara Wootton, as having 'an Oliver-Twistish effect'. Glass and his colleagues, she said, had caught a glimpse of a 'brave new world' where social mobility would be increasingly determined by education. *Social Mobility in England* made no attempt to focus on this as a 'theme', as Michael did, although Glass himself suggested that improved educational selection might 'divide the population into streams which many may come to regard – indeed already regard – as sheep and goats'.[28]

The papers which Glass included in his much quoted volume answered only a limited number of the questions raised by Michael, and they included no paper on the social distribution of intelligence. 'One hopes,' Glass wrote, 'that fresh inquiries into the relation between educational mobility on the one hand and the distribution of intelligence on the other will presently follow to settle this issue.' The issue was not to be settled, but in *The Rise of the Meritocracy* Michael was able to speculate about the issue by turning not, as Glass and his colleagues did, to data derived from past life histories, most of it statistical, but to an imaginative picture of the future.[29]

It was a very English picture, although on the very first page of his book Michael referred to 'similar trouble' to that in England 'in the other provinces of Europe'. There had, however, in his opinion (or in the opinion of both Michaels) been distinctively British rather than European causes of twentieth-century change. (He did not separate out Scotland, although the obstacles to change were mainly English.[30]) Britain's economic problems and the need to compete internationally with bigger rivals had been the spur. It was 'for the sake of survival' that Britain turned step by step to a meritocracy which was geared to one task only – the achievement of maximum productive efficiency.

This was precise focusing. H. G. Wells's new samurai in his book *The Modern Utopia* (1904), mentioned, along with George Bernard Shaw, by Michael the thesis writer, had had broader purposes in view. When authors like Wells and Shaw were contemplating the society of the future earlier in the century, they were writing before the threat to Britain's economic power had seriously intensified. It was, however, already being discussed.

One of the publishers who turned down Michael's text, Chatto and Windus, in Michael's opinion smaller and less 'stuffy' than Longman, expressed willingness to publish *The Rise of the Meritocracy* if it were rewritten in the form not of a thesis but of a novel 'on the model of Aldous Huxley's *Brave New World*', and Michael took a year trying to do so before Leonard Woolf rejected it for Chatto. Michael's own doubts about his manuscript were different, however, and began with the word 'meritocracy' itself. A friend who was a classical scholar warned him that since 'meritocracy' was half Latin and half Greek he would be 'laughed to scorn' for using it. She was wrong. After all, the word 'television', which became one of the best known new words of the century, fell into the same category – and had initially been criticised for the same reason.[31]

Television was Richard Hoggart's main preoccupation around the time that *The Rise of the Meritocracy* was being discussed, for in 1960 he had been made a member of the Pilkington Committee on the future of broadcasting which very sharply criticised the Independent Broadcasting Authority and the commercial companies, deriving their profits from advertising, which had been set up to provide an alternative service to the BBC. This experience led him to point to an alternative social outcome from that depicted by Michael:

> One could, I think ... with relevance and point, imagine ... an unequal society in which 'equality', far from being discredited, had *formally* been allowed to rule in fantastically diverse areas of experience; a society so generally prosperous that material differences between people would be exploited only, but intensely, to rouse marginal rivalries; a society which would show little variety, not simply because it would be rigidly stratified according to IQs, but because ... 'the bland would lead the bland', a society in which a second Peterloo would be unlikely, because the few dissidents, whatever their class or IQs, would have no common emotional language in which to communicate with almost anyone else.

The violent ending of *The Rise of the Meritocracy* left Hoggart cold.

It is not difficult for reviewers to suggest alternative scenarios, and Hoggart, with more nostalgia in his make-up than Michael, was the more pessimistic of the two. Moreover, he appreciated more clearly than Michael how significant the media – and public relations – would be in the Britain to come. For his part, Michael was right to appreciate that people of power in the mid-1950s, an 'Establishment', would feel flattered to be told that in the future, however much talk there might be in their own time of 'the rule of the people' (and he might have added 'mass culture'), it would be 'the cleverest' who would rule in the twenty-first century. 'Some people like to congratulate themselves on being like aristocrats but going one better by earning power and prestige on merit.'

En passant, another '*ocracy*', along with 'aristocracy' and 'plutocracy', was mentioned by Michael, George Bernard Shaw's 'mobocracy', a word which continued to have unfavourable undertones after the word 'mob' had largely been supplanted by the word 'masses'.[32] 'This haphazard mobocracy,' Shaw had written as late as 1948 'with characteristic pungency', 'must be replaced by a democratic aristocracy: that is, by the dictatorship, not of the whole proletariat, but of that five per cent of it capable of conceiving the job and pioneering in the drive towards its divine goal.'[33] Shaw put his trust in the 5 per cent without asking what methods they would employ to achieve that goal.

The other Michael discussed some of these in his thesis as he tried – at greater length – to identify what methods would be used by the leaders of the protest movement emerging within a meritocratic society. He gave a special place to women as he had done in *Family and Kinship*. It was women from more than one social class who stoked the fires that burnt in 2034, a point noted at the time by a different reviewer, Boris Ford, in the *Spectator*.[34] Hoggart did not mention women once in his review, even when he was discussing the scope for a 'common emotional language'. Nor, surprisingly, did Michael in the introduction to his 1994 edition. Yet the other Michael found 'a strange blend of women in the lead and men in the rank and file' on the eve of the new Peterloo – with some of the old of both sexes thrown in. There had been an equally strange alliance, too, 'for the only time within living memory', between 'a dissident minority from the *élite* with the lower orders', the right term (as 'mob' was) to use within the context of *The Rise of the Meritocracy*. The uprising of 2034 was far more, therefore, than a thoughtless outburst produced by despair.

The other Michael had realised this not through his knowledge of sociology but of history. The quarterly Populist journal of the future was called *Commonweal*. Back to Morris![35] And in dealing with the 'the young and ravishing' he looked back to the Suffragettes, 'the first women to come to the fore in left-wing politics'. Lady Avocet, a Populist leader, went further back still in time in her own version of history: she liked to compare the meritocracy which she was fighting against with the Mohicans who took away the best young men and women from a conquered tribe and then reared them as members of their own families. The name of one of her colleagues was plucked from the real Michael's personal history: she was called the Countess of Perth.[36]

A brief section on 'the modern feminist movement' represented the other Michael's attempt at sociological analysis. Intelligent women could ally themselves with 'the aged men' who represented low IQ workers in the Technicians' Party. 'The old men were attracted to the young girls and perhaps now and then it happened the other way round as well.'[37] 'Shaggy young girls from Newnham and Somerville', places the real Michael scarcely then knew, 'instead of taking the jobs as surveyors and scientists for which their education fitted them, scattered to Scotland and Newcastle to become factory workers, ticket collectors and air hostesses.' In 2009 they captured *The Times*, turning it for a few months into a popular newspaper. (The real Michael did not foresee, as Hoggart might have done, that Rupert Murdoch would have done this long before.) Biology had to be taken into the reckoning too. Child rearing was difficult to relate to professional advancement, and there was 'mental tension in all those women who could not feel that child rearing is (as it is in fact) one of the noblest occupations of them all, especially when it is part time.' (Was this the real Michael speaking?)

'Women have always been judged more by what they *are* than by what they *do*, more for other personal qualities than for their intelligence,' the other Michael wrote. 'It is therefore understandable [as it would have been to the real Michael] that they should wish to stress their own virtues, only regrettable that in this the quality [now an obsolete expression[38]] have joined with women of no more than ordinary ability.' Beauty came into the reckoning too (and here the other Michael, unlike the real Michael, said that he did not understand why). Faced with advice given by Professor Eagle and eugenicists to enter into 'intelligenic marriage', picking their partners for their IQs, women of high IQs coined the slogan 'Beauty is achievable by all'.[39]

Women did not figure prominently in any of the reviews of *The Rise of the Meritocracy*, none of which seem to have been written by a woman. (Barbara Wootton had, however, herself entered into a non-intelligenic marriage.) The *Economist* reviewer was more favourable to Michael than Hoggart had been, although he accused Michael of retreating 'behind a smokescreen of entertaining jibes'. Having considered other parts of the book, he hoped that, like the 'anti-Utopias of

Huxley and Orwell', *The Rise of the Meritocracy* would become 'part of the common coin of discussion'. The reviewer took most seriously the other Michael's argument that what would happen in the future would depend on economic imperatives, and he did not pay much attention either to the revolt or the rebels (men and women) or to the sense of hope that Young himself saw in it, a sense of hope that surely made *The Rise of the Meritocracy* far more than an 'anti-Utopia'.

The reviewer thought instead that the evolution of a meritocratic system, for which the *Economist* was pressing and on which the *Encounter* article had concentrated in its selection of text, had been 'beautifully worked out' in *The Rise of the Meritocracy*. This was 'the way we are going', and the reviewer liked it.

He was less impressed, not surprisingly, by what he took to be the real Michael's comments on the economic, if not the social, implications of his story. Given the drive for maximum productivity, embarked upon for economic reasons, clearly set out by Michael, would 'a mania for capital expansion' have driven down the standard of living of the untalented in the late twentieth century? Surely (and he was right in this) it would have raised it. Were there not prospects of 'common material welfare' too? Perhaps surprisingly, the reviewer did not mention 'consumers' as such: then nor did either of the Michaels. Hoggart was nervous about how the untalented would react to economic (and technological) change: the *Economist* reviewer welcomed the prospect of their reacting positively. They would demand more. He was of the sensible opinion that if there were really to be space travel in 2033, a possibility that greatly interested Michael, and air conditioning, both of them referred to, it would be unlikely that there would be 'no hint of better food'.

The reviewer did not mention atomic energy which Michael placed in his future. In his book the 'modern Gladstones' were at Harwell, not at Westminster, and there was a European Atomic Authority.[40] By a coincidence, the year of publication of *The Rise of the Meritocracy* was the year of the Campaign for Nuclear Disarmament's first Aldermaston march. There was no hint of any future protest sequence following on after this in *The Rise of the Meritocracy*. Nor, despite brief references to electronics and automation, was there any intimation of encounters with computers, even though 'weather control' had also been achieved, at least partially, by 2033. Michael also envisaged a Social Science Research Council in existence in 2033, and it was this Council (with obviously greater powers than the real Michael's Council was to have in the 1960s) which advised the Prime Minister 'to bring on autumn a month earlier' that year in order to limit popular discontent.

In his conclusion the reviewer showed that he did not share Michael's values. 'What will, what should be, the relations between [post-meritocratic] classes thus constituted and divided?' 'How can democratic institutions survive when the masses can no longer generate gifted leaders? How can common human properties be preserved. Belief in the *carrière ouverte aux talents* and belief in human solidarity may not be reconcilable. But they are going to take a lot more reconciling than the French Revolution thought; or the nineteenth-century radicals; or the early twentieth-century socialists. Mr. Young evades the task; he does not even seem to recognise it. [Untrue.] But he had strikingly demonstrated its necessity.'

It is interesting that one year after *The Rise of the Meritocracy* appeared, when Michael was almost the only British sociologist to be mentioned in an American survey of *Sociology Today*, he was referred to in another final footnote, that to Seymour Martin Lipset's chapter on Political Sociology, as a sociologist concerned not with conflict but with stability.[41] In *The Rise of the Meritocracy* the other Michael had claimed that 'progress has ever been born of conflict'. Lipset's reference, however, referred not to *The Rise of the Meritocracy* but to the article on the Coronation which Michael and Shils had written together and which had been sharply criticised by a conflict theorist, Norman Birnbaum.[42] The only link between that article and *The Rise of the Meritocracy* was that the other Michael's thesis refers to an 'Elizabethan age', a description that did not pass into history.

The fortunes of hereditary monarchy in an age of change were to be far more complicated than any futurologist could have envisaged. So too were the fortunes of *the* family, royal or not. Curiously, Michael was not referred to in the chapter on the sociology of the family in *Sociology Today*.[43] Yet some of the most interesting passages in *The Rise of the Meritocracy* relate to the family – to 'ancestral capital', even 'ancestor worship' – 'feudalism and family go together' – and to the family as a 'pillar of inheritance'. For Michael, the strength of the family as an agency of resistance to change lay in the working-class as well as in the upper-class societies of the present as well as in the aristocratic societies of the past and the uneasy 'intelligent' and 'unintelligent' sectors of twenty-first century society. The 'intelligent' – or at least a section of them – were then to conclude dangerously, under the influence of a Cecil, a delightful touch in the light of what was to happen in 1998 to hereditary peers, that 'any loss of effectiveness in the meritocracy will be more than outweighed by the benefits of making it hereditary'. The shock had been profound for the other Michael: 'extremism on the right has always led to extremism on the left.'[44]

The family in 2033 remained for Michael 'still much the same kind of institution [as it had been in 1958 or indeed in "feudal times"], inspired more by loyalty than reason'. 'The home is still the most fertile seed bed of reaction.' There was an 'inevitability', therefore, about 'family opposition to progress'. And while 'reason' might influence the structuring of the family (and its size) – eugenics suggested 'intelligenic marriages' in the twenty-first century after there had been a 'eugenic campaign' to persuade high IQ males that to mate with a low IQ woman was a 'waste of genes'. There was resistance here from women. Many of them, as we have seen, objected to the whole idea. 'Where,' they asked, was 'the romance in a intelligenic marriage?'

There was insight here on the real Michael's part, and experience, as there was in Michael's prescient forecast of the future role of sport, passive as well as active, in the twenty-first century, although he did not touch on the fascinating question as to whether interest in sport, like 'beauty', could or might cross the new class or caste lines based on IQ. Concentrating on 'the low IQs' he suggested (in the disguise, particularly thin at this point, of the other Michael) that the 'Mythos of Muscularity' was one of five factors which had 'saved' society from some of the dangerous consequences of 'depressing the status of the inferior and elevating that of the superior', a subject which had 'engaged the full attention of social science'.

Handicrafts, gymnastics and games had become the core of the curriculum in twenty-first century secondary modern schools, pointing to 'education for leisure', if it could be so called. Each night sports were displayed on the 'screens in [people's] own homes' (a rare reference to television, but an outcome realised long before the end of the twentieth century). 'Inferior' people, as defined by the new system, 'esteemed physical achievement almost as high as we of the upper classes esteem mental'. The use of sports to divert or to pacify was reinforced by the fact that the English love of sport was 'traditional'. Secondary modern schools were not breaking with the past when they incorporated sport into their basic curriculum. The public schools had done it first.

The other four factors making for stability included organised adult education, not described as 'continuing education', a term then little in use, but depending on regular checking of IQs which in the last phases of *The Rise of the Meritocracy* was under threat; 'the application of scientific selection to industry', including the setting up of a new Pioneer Corps, carrying out civilian rather than military tasks; the hope parents placed not only in their children but in their grandchildren (a footnote referred to a fictitious future article of the real Michael Young in the *British Journal for Sociology* of 1967);[45] and, not least, stupidity.

There were echoes here of Walter Bagehot, the influential nineteenth-century editor of *The Economist*. The 'inferior' in society, who might have other 'sterling qualities', not least 'duty to their families', were 'incapable of grasping clearly enough the grand design of modern society to offer any effective protest. Some are sulkily discontented, without being too sure what to do about it, and find their way to the psychologist or priest. Most are not, for they know not what is done to them.'

Stupidity for Bagehot had preserved an aristocratic society based on deference: for Michael it would – or might – preserve a meritocratic society. In 'the grand design' of that society domestic service had an important place too. The Clauson Committee, which reported in 1988, took the view that a third of all adults were unemployable in the existing economy. They were capable only of meeting one need: for personal service. And that became acceptable when 'the inferior knew that their [meritocratic] betters had a greater part to play in the world, and beyond [a remarkable extension], and were glad to identify with them and wait on them'. The Home Help Corps, enrolled as a national institution, had 'topped the ten million mark' by the year 2000. 'Every private employer had to pay the wages laid down; provide sanitary living space; release the servant two nights a week to attend a sports club run by the Corps; pay for a refresher course every summer; and not demand more than forty eight hours a week, except with permission from the local office.'

There is as much psychology as there is sociology in *The Rise of the Meritocracy*. Some of it was homespun, like 'all babies are creeping socialists and some never grow out of it' or 'no age is more acquisitive than adolescence'. Some of it was clinical. Psychiatric treatment was available in every factory. The tension suffered by women who pursued their jobs with no time for child rearing, following their profession rather than their 'biological vocation', was known to the real Michael who had been suffering from acute tension himself during the mid-1950s when he began what proved to be a liberating burst of writing. Most of the psychology in *The Rise of the Meritocracy* was, however, strictly operational in character. At the core of 'social advance' was more sophisticated intelligence testing at school and at work, followed by a mode of measuring effort at work,[46] and the introduction of 'merit money' in 2005, the year of an Equalisation of Income Act, a landmark date.[47]

'Intelligence and effort together make up merit ($I + E = M$).' There was nothing new in this proposition, Michael insisted, 'only in the way in which it was formulated'. In consequence, the word 'workers' became a discredited word, and the Labour Party, which had made possible the breakdown of pre-meritocratic society in the name of equality – this was straight history in *The Rise of the Meritocracy* – changed its name to the Technicians' Party, a word which came to have in it just as much magic or, at least, strength. 'There is ordinarily no one as stolid as ordinary British technicians. They are the salt of the earth.' Herbert Morrison had made a direct appeal to them in 1945.[48]

The process of improving the testing and the measurement of intelligence had been challenged by sections of the Labour Party of the 1950s – and here, too, Michael dealt with history as it had been – although there had as yet been no discrediting of the pioneering Burt, who had defined intelligence as 'in-born, all-round intellectual ability ... inherited or at least innate, not due to teaching or training ... intellectual, not emotional or moral ... uninfluenced by industry or zeal'. It was, he held, 'general, not specific, i.e. not limited to any particular kind of work', but entering into 'all that we do or say or think'. For Burt it could 'fortunately' be measured with 'accuracy and ease'.[49] For the future Michael that was a premature verdict. True accuracy and ease were only achieved after the invention of the computer.

In no other place in the real Michael's writing was the computer, instrument of so much subsequent social change, so spotlit. Already, however, in an earlier passage, he had referred to 'cyberneticists' (in inverted commas) who 'had realized that man would best understand his own brain when he could imitate it'. He had also referred *en passant* to managers' offices in the 1960s where there were cocktail cabinets in the cupboards and nothing 'so vulgar as a digital computer'.

There are interesting sections in *The Rise of the Meritocracy* on factories and management which should be related to the real Michael's own experience and to his other writings. One section was called 'Factories Cease to be Schools'. Self-made men had prided themselves in 'the distant past' on the fact that they owed nothing to school education: 'the school's shame was the factory's pride'. Gradually, however, with the nationalised industries leading the way, education had become a main determinant of managerial recruitment, and 'eventually every forward-looking company had teams of talent scouts combing the universities and grammar schools'.[50] And, once in work, managers were paid not on the basis of seniority but of 'merit rating'.

Such processes were to be pushed further forward in the twentieth century than even the future Michael anticipated, although whether it was genuine talent that was being discovered or true merit rewarded remained open questions.[51] Nor was the history of business perks, including lunch expenses, quite to follow his line of prediction.

History and fiction did not converge as completely as information and entertainment. Nor was there ever any likelihood that an Equalisation of Income Act would ever be passed. It is fair to add that we have not yet reached the year 2005 when in the future Michael's history it eventually reached the Statute Book.

Less than ten years ago it might have seemed that the point where history and fiction would most diverge would be a Labour Party switch against 'comprehensive schools'. In *The Rise of the Meritocracy* this took place soon after the point in time when Michael was writing, and was complete by the 1980s. There were few signs of any switch until the late 1990s, and even then David Blunkett's limited moves met with resistance. History and fiction diverged sharply too in 1989. In the future Michael's thesis that year saw 'the scientific leap of the century', 'Bird's pi-computer': that year, historically, was to see the collapse of the Soviet Union. With the new computer it was now possible to rely for reference purposes on a common unit of intelligence measurement: it had a constant IQ of 100. This was a landmark date, but already by then all adults with IQs of over 125 belonged to the meritocracy. It was before 1989 that in 'an interim' or 'transitional' period the failure of comprehensive schools, chronicled in a book of the future, Dr. Nightingale's *Social Origins of the Comprehensive Schools* (n.d.), had become plain; so obvious, indeed, to the future Michael that it did not seem 'to require explanation'.

The real Michael, however, believed in such schools and devoted a considerable portion of *The Rise of the Meritocracy* – here he was writing for himself on the basis of his very recent reading, summarising what now seems to be a somewhat dated debate among his own contemporaries. Foreign readers must have found what he had to say on this subject, particularly its local ramifications, difficult to follow even at the time.[52] English readers may have found out more than they already knew. Asked years later whether *The Rise of the Meritocracy* had helped to 'promote' 'the comprehensive idea', Michael replied simply 'No, it didn't',[53] but when asked the supplementary question, 'Do you feel things have developed in this direction?', he replied equally simply 'Yes', without going into any reasons.[54]

Two of the real Michaels contemporaries figure prominently in this context, real and fictitious, both under their own names, in *The Rise of the Meritocracy*, although only the second name appears in his list of acknowledgements. Eric James, arguing as early as 1951 that testing worked, that intelligence mattered more than birth, and that grammar schools were the schools of the future, not of the past, was revered as a prophet in the other Michael's pages;[55] while the young Crosland, whose book *The Future of Socialism* (1956) is mentioned in a footnote, figures prominently, decisively indeed, in the fictitious history of the other Michael. No longer young (and granted a knighthood), Crosland is 'persuaded' that the battle for national survival – economics had priority – would be 'won or lost in the "A" streams all the way from the nursery to grammar school'; and, once persuaded, it was he who made public money flow into education, benefiting both teachers and students. In the real 1990s this argument was still being advanced, not least in New Labour circles.

The real Crosland thought quite differently, and although money flowed into education in the 1960s it never flowed in the quantities described in *The Rise of the Meritocracy*. The real James, who had become High Master of Manchester Grammar School in 1945 at the early age of 36, thought consistently on meritocratic lines that the other Michael greatly admired. He had clearly expressed his views, which the real Michael never liked, by the time that *The Rise of the Meritocracy* was written, and he was to figure, somewhat curiously, as a colleague in the real Michael's later life, chosen by him, in the newly formed Social Science Research Council in 1965. Having left Manchester Grammar School to become Vice-Chancellor of the new University of York, at Michael's suggestion he was to be made Chairman of the SSRC's Educational Research Board.[56]

In all the references to real history in *The Rise of the Meritocracy* the Second World War, what Michael calls 'the Hitler War', was never far away from his thinking – and feeling. It was then that psychological selection had first been tested. It was then that Butler's Education Act had been passed, making secondary schools free. 'Although it was introduced by a Conservative Minister in a Coalition Government', we read in *The Rise of the Meritocracy* that 'the purpose was that of the Labour Party. After that, children were educated according to their "age, ability, and aptitude", those with greater ability getting more education.'[57] Butler was to be one of the Prime Ministers in *The Rise of the Meritocracy*, although little is said in the book about most of the post-war problems, above all the national economic problems, which were to preoccupy him without his ever becoming Prime Minister.[58] In 1965 he was to become Master of Trinity College, Cambridge.

The same problems were to preoccupy Michael himself in *Labour's Plan for Plenty* and lay behind the whole meritocratic argument advanced in *The Rise of the Meritocracy*. How (or whether) to deal with the public schools which Butler had helped to save and which for many socialists were anachronisms was to draw Michael back into Labour politics in the 1960s. The public schools had been the subject of a famous war-time report, the Fleming Report, which appeared two months after Butler's Education Bill had been given its third reading: it had recommended that those independent schools that chose to do so should offer 25 per cent of their places to qualified pupils from primary schools, who would then be granted a bursary by the Board of Education or local authority.[59]

Some socialists had been to public schools themselves. Most Conservatives wished to preserve them. In the other Michael's thesis they largely got rid of themselves, a solution that would have greatly appealed to the real Crosland. 'Private schools did not have to be abolished; the best of them abolished themselves. Wide-awake public school headmasters worried about the stupidity of the children they were attracting, and as the drift of events [a curious choice of expression for either Michael] became clear, and as the Treasury became more open handed, [they] solved their problems by negotiating with the State for inclusion on the roll of "grant-aided boarding grammar schools".' Eton, not surprisingly, set the pace: in 1972 it reduced its entrance age to eleven, and undertook to accept 80 per cent of Queen's Scholars. 'Where Eton led, others followed.'

Grammar schools, not known from the inside by Michael, figure prominently as the favoured agents of change in *The Rise of the Meritocracy*, and that is why in the book Crosland's conversion to a belief in their excellence is of such significance. In historical fact, he was to see no more future in them than in the public schools. Whatever the future of socialism, he would have found a future unthinkable in which Walsall Grammar School could be superior to Rugby.[60] A capital levy to make change possible would have been more thinkable, however, as would the integration of Rugby in the national educational system. And such events were outlined in the future Michael's chronology. It was 'a sixth Labour Government, with Crosland and Hughes [Bill Hughes, in the real Michael's time Principal of Ruskin College] working as a team' in the two key ministries.

Hughes, if the identification is correct, belonged to a college designed for trade unionists, the college attended by Willmott.[61] For the most part, however, Michael, present or future, had little good to say of the trade unionists in *The Rise of the Meritocracy*. They had abandoned ideology and traded power for status: the last strike took place at Leamington in 1991. Their 'ponderous, carefully rehearsed reflections [Michael was reminiscing here, not forecasting] had no more influence upon their colleagues than a peashooter upon an astro-rocket'. The civil servants were bound to win out, and by the 1980s they knew more of the state of opinion in the factories through their intelligence system ('sociological surveys') than did the trade union stewards who worked in them. 'The union leaders seldom have the insight to see that the courtesy with which they are treated is pure formality [in the meritocratic age].' In Bagehot's terminology they had become part of the 'dignified' rather than the 'efficient' working of the constitutional system. Trade union leaders do not figure in the forces of revolt at the twenty-first-century Peterloo.[62]

Change for Michael had been made more rapid, as it had been for Bagehot, by the fact that on the surface there had been no change at all. This had happened with the Commonwealth – and with the monarchy before 1958. In *The Rise of the Meritocracy* it had now happened not only with the 'Labour Movement', politicians as well as trade unionists, but with Parliament. Significantly when we are first introduced to the Prime Minister he is speaking in the House of Lords. Along with the civil servants the 'vital House of Lords', stripped of its hereditary peers, and consisting of women as well as men, 'chosen from the most eminent people in the realm', was a bulwark of the meritocracy. 'Skipping all the intermediate styles of democracy as some countries have jumped straight from railways to rockets, aristocracy was by one brilliant stroke made instrument of the meritocracy. The hold of the Lords of Parliament was assured in the period covered in *The Rise of Meritocracy* when by a constitutional convention the Ministry of Education was in all cabinets reserved to the upper chamber.'[63]

The House of Lords looks vulnerable at the end of *The Rise of the Meritocracy*, the penultimate section of which is called (by the other Michael) 'A Rank and File at last'. The reaffirmation of hereditary succession was as calculated to undermine the meritocratic system as was the alliance between intelligent women and a labour rank-and-file. 'In defiance of trade union leaders, trade unionists (and their allies) came from all over the country, and particularly from the North of England and Scotland.' The other Michael, brought up in Manchester, as the very young real Michael was, found this particularly disturbing. The hostility of the discontented towards London was 'a sinister aspect of the agitation, too much played down by government sociologists'. Stevenage, Kirkcaldy and South Shields were among the centres of discontent. Both Westminster and Whitehall were under threat. Yet for the other Michael '*déclassé* people' could never be more than an 'eccentric minority'.[64]

The analysis of discontent that he offered clearly depended on the musings of the real Michael – down to the final footnote. 'Family discontent' was at the heart of it. There were other immediate 'real' causes – for example, the threat not only to adult education but to school teachers posed by the increasing capacity of psychologists to predict IQ at earlier and earlier ages. In 2000 the age was nine, in 2015 four, in 2020 three. The justification for a common education in primary schools for everyone up to eleven had been that 'no one could be quite sure of the ultimate value of any boy or girl' and socialists had been the first to appreciate this. 'But when ability could be tested and identified at the age of three, there was really no point at all in the brighter children going to the same co-intellectual [a good word] school as others who would almost inevitably retard their development.'

There were teachers in the other Michael's account who argued that, given that it had been discovered that the right age was three, it was necessary to pretend that it was not. 'Children cannot be condemned so early: they will cease to strive when they know that no effort will prove the psychologist wrong, except within a small margin of error. They must be given the stimulus of hope; so must the teachers, and so also, above all, must their parents.' To have handled such deception would have required very clever spin doctors indeed. And it is difficult to see how a society based on such a colossal deception could have survived.

The two Michaels concur that 'any sociologist must admit the strength of the [teachers'] argument', but was it the future Michael or the real Michael who added that 'equality of opportunity has for so long been the ethos of education that it will not do to abandon it overnight' and that 'so important is social cohesion that we shall have to make haste slowly'? The trouble was – and fictitious history sounds like real history at this point – 'science does not move slowly. Three was not the [age] limit.' A Nobel prize winner, Dr. Charles, experimenting at first with rats, had shown that the intelligence of children could at last be safely predicted from the intelligence of their forebears. At Eugenics House records had been kept from the 1950s onwards on the intelligence of babies. 'The study of obituaries' too had become 'a recognised branch of sociology'.

We are back to birth again and back to the idea of an hereditary aristocracy. New twenty-first century Conservatives saw Charles's 'discovery' as a means of terminating 'the pandemonium of social mobility'. Equality of opportunity could become an outdated idea. Not all contemporaries agreed that it was, but had they pursued the matter they would have had to acknowledge that within a meritocracy there could be as much argument about the implications of new biological knowledge as there would be within a democracy. They had no means of 'weighing the gravity of the issue'. This was sound prophecy. Biotechnology was to raise more profound issues than intelligence testing, and a newspaper headline of 1997 could read 'Scientists discover gene that creates human intelligence'.[65] In 1999 there was to be protracted debate about genetically modified agriculture – and the responsibilities of government for monitoring its use were among the most topical of issues when this book was being written.

The issues of biotechnology, touched on briefly in *The Rise of the Meritocracy*, have proved to be too important to be left to biotechnologists. 'Experts' did not always agree, and the best of them were employed not by the State – for the real Michael that was the Leviathan – but by huge multinational business concerns. The economic, the moral, the aesthetic converged, just as words, numbers and images converged in digital technology.

Religion as a guide through 'moral mazes' did not figure in *The Rise of the Meritocracy*. Neither Michael saw it in that way. There was a touch of the sinister, however, in Michael's mention in his thesis of experimental work at a Volunteer Maternity Centre at South Uist and at far-away Ulan-Bator. He quickly returned to politics, observing, perhaps ominously too, that public opinion surveys of the 2020s were 'fired more by a sentiment of opposition to the Conservatives than by a sentiment of loyalty to the Populists'.

The Populists had a manifesto, or what they called their Charter: History returns here too. It was drafted at Leicester, and while the future Michael calls it 'a strange document with its echoes from the past in the quotations from the now long-forgotten Tawney and Cole, William Morris and John Ball' and does not quote from it (his ending moves very fast), he does quote in italics the last paragraph from an earlier Chelsea Manifesto of 2009 drafted by a local group of the Technicians' Party which had attracted little attention at the time. The words in it about 'the classless society' echo the words of the real Michael in *For Richer For Poorer*:

> The classless society would be one which both possessed and acted upon plural values. Were we to evaluate people, not only according to their intelligence and their education, their occupation, and their power, but according to their kindliness and their courage, their imagination and sensitivity, their sympathy and generosity, there could be no classes. ... The classless society would also be the toler-

ant society, in which individual differences were actively encouraged as well as positively tolerated, in which full meaning was at last given to the dignity of man. Every human being would then have equal opportunity, not to rise up in the world in the light of any mathematical measure, but to develop his own special capacities for leading a rich life.

Some of the people who drafted this manifesto would have been alive when the future Michael, who found it 'archaic', was writing his thesis on *The Rise of the Meritocracy*. He was upset by the fact that they appeared to accept the view of culture propounded by the then 'almost forgotten' nineteenth-century poet and critic Matthew Arnold. (Perhaps surprisingly neither Hoggart nor Ford mentioned this reference.) Arnold had wanted all men to live in 'an atmosphere of sweetness and light, where they may use ideas ... freely – nourished and not bound by them'. The future Michael's comment is in the real Michael's style. 'Oh God, oh Galton!'[66] Eugenics, not poetry.

What might have been one of the most interesting reviews of *The Rise of the Meritocracy*, because of its author, Peter (later Lord) Shore, appeared in the *New Statesman*. Shore was not only one of Michael's successors as head of the Labour Party's Research Department, following on after Fienburgh. He was also to become Labour MP for Tower Hamlets which included Bethnal Green, the centre of Michael's Institute of Community Studies. There was no doubt either about his IQ – or that of well-known members of his family – or about his Balliol education. In his review Shore concentrated almost entirely on the rise of the meritocracy and failed completely to mention the rebellion of 2034. He referred to Michael's 'harsh and pessimistic vision of the world', while admitting that it was, in his view, 'not implausible'.

His main point was that it would be a 'pity if the argument of Michael's book were misinterpreted. 'It is not an argument against the selection of talent, still less a defence of inherited privilege. Essentially, it is a plea, to use Michael Young's own words, that "equality be more than opportunity", that it should include power, education and income, that equality should be made the ruling principle of social order.' 'If the aim is a better society and not just a more efficient one, these are words to remember.'[67]

Such a didactic judgement left out all the point-counterpoint, all the originality and all the sophistication in Michael's book and, not least, the fun. It is these that have made the book continue to live. And it gives an added interest to it, as it does to George Orwell's *1984*, that it continues to stimulate thought about how far what was projected in it has proved true. The economic imperative is as strong as it was in 1958.[68] We have never been able to evade 'the relentless facts of the modern world'. None the less, it would be difficult, given 'material progress', expressed in consumption patterns, to argue as the other Michael argued that 'we are all poor, and shall always remain so, because the demands of a scientific age are insatiable'. As a result socialism of the 'traditional' variety has been pushed aside, if never destroyed, by the spokesmen of 'new Labour', as conscious as Michael's meritocrats that socialism can be a brake rather than an accelerator.[69] The 'working class' has 'crumbled from within' even if it has never been 'sated by conquest'.

The course of change in the Conservative Party – and the rise of Thatcher and Thatcherism – were outside the range of Michael's vision in *The Rise of the Meritocracy*, although before she became Party leader she was Secretary of State for Education and Science, as he might have predicted. John Major's proclamation of a 'classless society' might have been predictable also,[70] although when interviewed in 1994 Michael still saw a 'greater impetus towards meritocracy' in the Conservative Party than in the Labour Party – 'it's something they have agreed on'. He stressed then that his own 'message' in 1958 had been misunderstood. 'He had written *The Rise of the Meritocracy* as 'an attack'. 'Meritocracy ... would be a more wounding stratified system than perhaps had been known since the days of slavery but people have taken it that I was lauding this society and working to push it ahead and arrive as quickly as possible.'[71]

Individual educational 'progress' in the early twenty-first century is measured as precisely as it can be more often than would have seemed likely during the decade after *The Rise of the Meritocracy* was written, and the 'results' are expressed in league tables as the fortunes of football clubs are. It is inspected to a degree that was not even contemplated in the other Michael's thesis. Meanwhile, teachers, still underpaid, do not take easily either to inspectors or to politicians. Grammar schools have not become central to the educational system, nor have there been 'weekly pay days' encouraging pupils to stay in them. Far from paying wages to university students, grants were first sharply reduced and then for most students, now offered loans, abolished. The agent was to be Michael's friend Tessa (later Baroness) Blackstone, Minister for Education, who, like her new Labour Cabinet colleagues had concluded that it was only by pursuing this policy that the numbers of individuals involved in age-based higher education, far larger than was contemplated in *The Rise of the Meritocracy*, could be supported. The Treasury has never become 'more open-handed'. 'Miserliness' has never given way to 'munificence'. After the country has reached a historical millennium, not charted in the chronology of *The Rise of the Meritocracy*, we cannot recall any twentieth-century date in real past history, as the other Michael could, when 'with education reformed, some people imagined they [already] they had matriculated to the millennium'.

6
Education for Change

There was more about school education in *The Rise of the Meritocracy* than there was about university education, although the relationship between the two was recognised as crucial. So also was the relationship between educational change and social change, and there was plenty about that. There was a higher education department in ACE, which organised a summer school in Brighton, and an enquiry was launched into university entrance.[1]

Around the time that Michael left Transport House it had been assumed too that university development could be safely left to a non-political University Grants Committee, financed directly by the Treasury, although the Association of University Teachers and the Association of Scientific Workers had made public statements about education and research. So, too, had official committees. The Barlow Committee, set up in 1945, had called for significant university expansion, including the foundation of at least one new university. At the school level it had been assumed also that Butler's Education Act of 1944 had laid the foundation for current 'educational advance', leaving a way open, but not necessarily *the* way, for comprehensive education.

There were, of course, considerable numbers of people in most parts of the country who were committed to further educational advance at all levels, some of the most active of them members of the Workers' Educational Association. The title of its magazine was *Highway*.[2] Many of them were teachers and members of local education committees, and there were strong pressure groups in favour of comprehensive education, particularly in London, where the Education Committee of the Labour-controlled London County Council included comprehensive schools in its development plan of 1947.[3] Recalling the mood of this period, Martin Wilson, Chief Education Officer of Shropshire from 1936 to 1965, far from London, described what was happening from the vantage point of Shrewsbury, as 'the last grand flourish and fanfare of local government'.[4]

The results, however, were limited, and after cuts in planned expenditure on education were imposed in 1949 (under a Labour government), the *Times Education Supplement*, dedicated to educational advance under the editorship of H. C. Dent, wrote sadly that 'the realisation of some of the fondest hopes of teachers must recede yet further into the future than before'.[5] In the two years between then and the defeat of the Party at the general election of 1951, the time when Michael left Transport House, increased expenditure on defence, the result of the Korean War, and an alarming drain on gold and dollar reserves had checked further educational advance. And there were further cuts to come, with Butler, Chancellor of the Exchequer in Churchill's new government, responsible for making them.

Disagreement on the question of whether or not to concentrate educational advance on the creation of comprehensive schools was a source of division inside the Labour Party as well as between it and other political parties, but it was accompanied by a broad consensus between the parties on the general aims of educational policy and on the practical steps necessary to implement it. There was little new thinking about the weaknesses of 'the tripartite system' in secondary education (grammar, secondary modern, technical),[6] when technical education was not catered for on a significant national scale. Direct Grant grammar schools (with Manchester outstanding) were treated separately from the rest, although their numbers were reduced. The public schools, charging fees, were left to themselves.[7]

The one innovation, known to more people since than any other, was a new examination, the GCE, with 'O' (Ordinary) and 'A' (Advanced) levels, devised to come into effect in 1951, although at the time the eleven-plus examination, separating one section of the greatly enlarged age-group from the other, was known to far more people than the GCE. The chance of 'winning' an 'eleven-plus' to move on to a grammar school varied remarkably in different parts of the country. How a child fared in the examination, which now included an 'intelligence test' element, powerfully influenced chances for life as a whole.[8]

This was the scene when *The Rise of the Meritocracy* was being written, but it was a scene that was already changing when from the real world the real Michael in his own journal *Where?* wrote a prescient paper in the autumn of 1962 with the memorable title, 'Is Your Child in the

Unlucky Generation?'. It was a paper that was characteristic of the new decade in that it dealt more with universities than with schools. 'Children born in the war have had comparative peace at school,' he began. 'Children born in the early years of peace, after their fathers came out of the Forces, have had to struggle through schools packed with others of the same age.'

'Will the last scene be the same as the others [as they "moved upwards"]?' Michael asked. There were now more children than demographers had predicted, and the result was imminent crisis in higher education. 'In 1965 children who stay on at school will be besieging the universities. The number of 18-year-olds at school is expected to jump more than a third in the single year between 1964 and 1965. Are the universities ready to meet the crisis? They have, after all, had much more warning than the schools.'[9]

Before considering Michael's answer, his article must be placed not only within the context of *ACE*,[10] but within that of national debate on education in which issues were raised other than those which he outlined. One was what came to be called 'educational technology'. Early in 1962 a new Research and Intelligence Section was set up in the Ministry of Education, which had as one of its tasks the coordination of policy on educational broadcasting, including television, which was seen as a promising agency of educational expansion. In July 1963 Sir Edward (later Lord) Boyle, Minister of State for Education, with a seat in the Cabinet, told the Postmaster-General that he had now concluded that 'in the long term at any rate, a separate [television] channel for a direct teaching service [would] be required',[11] and an interdepartmental working party was set up in January 1964 to report on 'the technical, financial and organisational' implications of educational broadcasting. The Working Party continued to meet until the Conservatives lost power.

By then an important meeting had been held in July 1962 at Hamilton House to plan 'an educational advance campaign'. The main initiative came from the National Union of Teachers, with the support of the WEA, and no fewer than 54 other organisations constituting a 'broad front' which, it was believed rightly, would soon become even broader. The NUT, which had opposed the introduction of independent television, had already concerned itself with questions relating to the media and to the impact of television, in particular, on children, concentrating in the first instance on its negative effects.[12] Now there was increasing emphasis on the need for positive action.[13] A great meeting was to be held in the Albert Hall as a climax of a national campaign – and *The Economist* offered invaluable media support[14] – but it was at the local level that the campaign was most successful. It drew in many people who had never before been involved in education struggles.

The campaign was a dramatic prelude to a decade when expenditure on education, calculated as a proportion of gross national product, was to increase by nearly 50 per cent.[15] In *The Rise of the Meritocracy* the 1970s, not the 1960s, was picked out as 'the marvellous decade'. It was in the last months of Macmillan's Conservative Government, however, that responsibility for university finance passed in April 1964 to the Ministry of Education, which was given additional duties and renamed the Department of Education and Science. The same Government also set up a teacher-centred Schools Council for the Curriculum and Examinations to replace the Secondary School Examinations Council, a sign that interest was growing in curricular and pedagogical themes as well as in quantitative change.[16] Boyle also reconstituted the Central Advisory Council for England and Wales.

Part of the reason why the main emphasis on 'educational advance' during the early 1960s was not on schools, as in *The Rise of the Meritocracy*, but on higher and adult education, was that significant changes had already taken place in schools before the debate began. The 'secondary modern school' was on its way out even more than the grammar school. Meanwhile, most schools now had bigger sixth forms. More girls were seeking places in universities. Meanwhile, the total number of comprehensive schools of all types rose from 262 to 1,100 between 1965 and 1970, amid continuing fierce argument about 'streaming' within them.[17]

With Labour back in power after 1964, the raising of the school leaving age from 15 to 16 was postponed by the government in 1968 as part of a package of economy measures;[18] and it was to be under a Conservative Government (with Thatcher as Secretary of State for Education) that the school leaving age was at last raised to 16 in 1972. By then there had been a 'student explosion' in higher education during the 1960s, 'common to all the countries of the advanced world'.[19] The number of full-time students in British higher education rose from 170,000 in 1959/60 to 339,000 in 1969/70, when for the first time in history expenditure on education, £2,300 million, exceeded that on defence.[20]

During the late 1950s the UGC, the body then responsible for the oversight of university education, was basing its recommendations for this increase in university numbers not just on demographic forecasts – the movement of 'Bulge' as it was called, the increase in the number of children in the university age group[21] – but on the influence of 'Trend'. This was conceived of as an ensemble of educational, social and economic forces influencing the demand for higher education from within the family as well as from within the school – what Michael called 'motivation'. A significant proportion of university entrants was now coming from families where no member of the family had ever been admitted to a university before.[22]

Public demand for skilled manpower figured in all the 'educational advance' equations also. It was estimated in 1959 by Solly (later Lord) Zuckerman, Chief Government Adviser on Science, who had been a member of the Barlow Committee on Scientific Manpower in 1945, that by 1970 the number of qualified scientists and engineers trained each year would have to be doubled;[23] and in the same year questions of justice ('access') as well as of need ('wastage') were raised in the important report of a Committee chaired by Geoffrey (later Lord) Crowther, editor of *The Economist* from 1938 to 1956, which argued that 'there was hardly one amongst the advanced English-speaking countries which would profess itself content with so small a trickle as one in eighteen continuing in full-time education into the later teens.'[24] There was nothing new in such argument, only in the up-to-date statistics.

It was a major proposition of the most influential of all the official Reports of the 1960s, that produced by Lord Robbins and his Committee in 1963 – it had been set up two years earlier – that the lower the social class, the greater the degree of educational wastage.[25] This was a proposition which had been placed in its social context in yet another report of 1963, that chaired by a publisher, former Chief Education Officer for Hertfordshire, Sir John Newsom, *Half Our Future*. Demanding in its first chapter 'Education for All', it dealt with the education of children of 'average and less than average ability': their fate depended, in the Committee's view, not so much on 'administrative action' as on changes in attitudes. And there were various links with Robbins.[26] It was in the institutions examined by Robbins that the teachers of the 'Newsom children' would be trained, and it was from 'Newsom homes' that increasing numbers of 'Robbins children' would come. How many there should be was a matter of contention. A vocal minority clung to the slogan 'More means worse'.

Newsom argued, as others did, against the view that there was a limited 'pool of ability', putting his trust in the proposition that 'everyone can be given some understanding of the social order and his own place within it, some insight into the ways of thinking that have shaped the modern world, some habit of creative response to the arts, some basis for a personal sense of values'.[27] Michael might well have been a member of this Committee which was dealing with some of the issues raised in *The Rise of the Meritocracy* had a Labour government then been in power.[28] Instead, he was to serve with enthusiasm on a later official Committee set up in the year when Robbins reported and chaired by Lady Plowden, the first committee to report on the education of primary school children since the famous Hadow Reports of 1931 and 1933.[29] Tessa Blackstone, then an Assistant Lecturer in Social Administration at the London School of Economics, was not alone in seeing the Plowden Report as 'in a fundamental sense ... an extension of the philosophy embodied in Hadow thirty-five years earlier.[30]

Lady Plowden, who was not the Government's first choice, had been appointed to the Central Advisory Council for Education by Boyle at a time when a third of the country's educational expenditure was then being devoted to primary education. It was a subject of interest to all sections of the public and she was asked to consider 'primary education in all its aspects, and the transition to secondary education'. Hers was a bold choice. She was then far less well known than her husband, who from 1956 to 1964 chaired a Committee of Enquiry into Treasury control of public expenditure.[31]

The Plowden Committee produced yet another historic (and in this case, in retrospect, highly controversial) report, far more controversial than the Robbins or Newsom Report, which has subsequently been judged to be particularly characteristic of the late 1960s. Indeed, it was described at the time as the primary schools' Robbins'.[32] Its opening lines read (and Michael might have written them):

> At the heart of the educational process lies the child. No advances in policy, no acquisitions of new equipment have their desired effect unless they are in harmony with the nature of the child, unless they are fundamentally acceptable to him.

From an early date in their lives, the Committee maintained, children shared 'a strong drive towards activity in the exploration of the environment', impelled by 'a curiosity, especially about novel and unexpected features of ... experience'. Yet they were not all alike: there were 'differential rates of development'.

As a consequence – and this had financial implications which were never fully recognised by Government[33] – there had to be an increase of individual as against group or class tuition within the classroom. Class teaching should cease to be the norm, and it should cease to be formal. 'Streaming' within infant, junior and middle schools should go. Earlier in the decade Boyle had asked the National Foundation of Educational Research to look into the subject of streaming, but two inconclusive interim reports which it submitted on the subject were of little help in determining policy.[34] It clearly had an impact on the 'leaving intentions of school pupils', including 'early leaving' which had been a topic of concern since the 1950s.[35]

The Plowden Report, which dealt with one end of the educational spectrum, was based on what its secretary, Maurice Kogan, then a lively young civil servant, later to become a Professor, called 'hot knowledge':[36] it was he who was 'particularly keen' to have Michael as a member of the Plowden Committee which received no fewer than 465 pages of submission from outside bodies. Kogan added that the presence on the Committee of Professor A. J. Ayer, the Wykeham Professor of Logic at Oxford, and others (Michael?) would guarantee that the 'hot knowledge' of the practitioner and administrator would be subjected to 'the informed critique of the sceptical philosopher and professional social scientist'. Whether the critique inside the Committee was adequate quickly became a matter of controversy. An early critic from outside was Lionel Elvin, former Principal at Ruskin College, who had served on the Robbins Committee.[37]

As far as teachers were concerned, Plowden herself recognised problems. Recalling her role as Chairman years later, she said that she had been fully aware of the dangers of huge numbers of inexperienced young teachers, recruited as part of a crash programme to cope with a serious shortage, entering overcrowded primary schools.[38] Moreover, there were obvious variations of quality among existing teachers, and particularly head teachers.[39] One of the main purposes of the Committee, as it envisaged them, was to set out 'the best practices that could be found in primary schools with a view to encouraging others to follow them'.[40]

Among the 197 recommendations of the Plowden Committee four of the most important were that there should be a greater use of teachers' aides (the Committee attached much importance to their use, which was unpopular with teachers' unions); that there should be 'community schools' in all areas, with a more direct involvement of parents;[41] that 'a start should be made as soon as possible' on a massive expansion of nursery education; and that Educational Priority Areas should be set up. The last recommendation was very much Michael's own, thought out and, despite obstacles, brought into operation in partnership with Halsey, the sociologist who was then working for Crosland in the Department of Education and Science. From the start the new Social Science Research Council under Michael's leadership was directly involved.[42] Great emphasis was placed on 'action research': the Educational Priority Areas would provide information that could subsequently be used far more widely.[43]

A policy of positive discrimination was to be followed whereby greater public resources and assistance would be allotted to areas where pupils were 'the most severely handicapped by home conditions.[44] At first, 2 per cent of the most socially handicapped would be involved; in five years 5 per cent. The Government accepted this proposal, which involved extra expenditure, but although additional Treasury Grants were asked for by the Plowden Committee, funding between 1968 and 1971 was minimal.[45]

Michael, who had a host of ideas relating to almost every item on the Committee's agenda, found serving on the Committee one of the most absorbing tasks of his life, and warmed to its enthusiastic but controversial child-centred approach to primary education: Dartington was all the time in his mind. He visited schools, met teachers and administrators, forming his own judgements on the quality of both the schools and the teachers. Among the administrators one man whom he greatly admired was Sir Alec Clegg, since 1945 Director of Education for the West Riding of Yorkshire. Like Michael, he was keenly interested in the content of primary education and its place in a life-long educational process.[46] He was also a well-known figure at Dartington. For both of them, as Young put it, 'some of the enthusiasm that had once gone into socialism of the old sort had emigrated into education of the new sort'.[47]

By the time that the Plowden Report appeared in January 1967 – and it sold nearly 70,000 copies in a year – the national political situation had been transformed, along with much else since it first met, including the situation in higher education at the other end of the educational spectrum,[48] and, not least, Michael's own personal position. After Labour's return to power in 1964 he failed to become Chairman of a commission on the future of the public schools, but had been appointed as first Chairman of the SSRC in 1965.[49] Crosland, who appointed him, found the Plowden Report 'anodyne'. It must have been one of his biggest differences with Michael.

The situation in higher education had begun to change substantially long before Plowden and, indeed, long before Robbins. The first of seven new universities launched by the UGC, Sussex, had taken in its first students two years before Newsom reported. In his stirring article in *Where?*, published in 1962, and elsewhere Michael discounted the work of the UGC, carried out quietly behind the scenes, but active and enterprising in its recommendations; and his references to the new universities, which were planned separately and were deliberately not all of one pattern, were somewhat unfriendly.[50] They cost too much and were in the wrong places. Nor, in his view, would they be ready by 1965 to meet the numbers crisis. Michael failed to appreciate their attractions, curricular as well as locational, to both teachers and students, or the intensity of the commitment of some of the people in them to changing the curriculum of universities as well as to increasing the number of students.[51]

They too thought of education as a social enterprise, backed but not controlled by a strong UGC, then operating in what in retrospect was its classic form[52] – and they fully appreciated the need for educational innovation at the school as well as at the university level, far more, indeed, than most members of the Robbins Committee or its Chairman, for years a key figure at the LSE, who was to become first Chancellor of the new University of York with Eric James as the first Vice-Chancellor. York, a university which had been launched earlier, fictitiously, by Michael in *The Rise of the Meritocracy*, was different from the rest, although it was built on a new campus outside the city, as were Sussex, Essex and Lancaster.

By the time that the new universities were being built, Michael had become a well-known figure in the shifting world of education, approaching a wide range of educational issues, including the uses of technology, from the vantage point not of a new university but of the second oldest university in the country, Cambridge. His move there was an important step in his life. Having learnt in 1958, before any new university received its Charter, that Cambridge was hoping to create a chair in sociology after a battle to establish the subject, which he believed was largely 'student-led', he decided to show interest in the possibility of moving there. By then Townsend had already left the ICS for the LSE, and this had added to Michael's restlessness.[53] There were other factors too. Willmott seemed to Michael to be capable enough and ready enough to safeguard the interests of the Institute in Michael's absence. And so he was, 'common sense incarnate' as Michael was to recall him nearly 40 years later on after his death in April 2000.[54] Having become Deputy Director in 1960, he was made Co-Director four years later, and from 1970 he was also Chairman, moving in the latter year to become Director of the Centre of Environmental Studies. With Phyllis at his side, keeping a daily journal, he was never just a caretaker. He produced a long and varied list of books and articles, the first of them about what was then said to be the largest housing estate in the world at Dagenham.[55]

Like much else in his life, Michael's move to Cambridge, 'the heart of Academia', and his subsequent increasing public involvement in the process of 'educational advance' was inextricably bound up with his own personal history. It took place after the breakdown of his first marriage to Joan, a painful and protracted experience, including a distressing spell at the Center for Advanced Study in the Behavioral Sciences at Palo Alto, in California and his second marriage in 1960 to Sasha Moorsom, herself a Cambridge graduate, who had studied at Girton; she had taken a double first in English and had made her undergraduate mark as an outstanding student actress. When Michael first met her in 1958 in a BBC studio the programmes for which she was responsible included one on 18+ pressures and one on poverty. She and Michael were subsequently partners in all his enterprises.

It was Shils, however, who having played such an important part in the successful establishment of the ICS at Bethnal Green, now served as the intermediary between Bethnal Green and Cambridge. He had encouraged the campaign to establish sociology in Cambridge, knowing that it met with considerable resistance from economists, within the faculty in which it would be organisationally located. Fortunately, for Michael, by the time that he moved there, Shils was closely associated with King's College which welcomed the advent of the subject. Its Provost, Noel Annan, was one of the interviewing panel that after a formal interview offered Michael a University Lectureship in Sociology (not a Professorship) in 1960.

His name was well known to the panel through his two recent books, both of them still in the news, but he seemed sufficient of a maverick for them to insure against future problems by appointing a second lecturer alongside him, David Lockwood, described correctly by Michael as a 'real sociologist'.[56] Twelve years younger than Michael, he too was a graduate of LSE and lectured there from 1953 to 1958, the year of publication of his book *The Blackcoated Worker*. Michael saw little of him in the two and a half years that he remained in Cambridge, where both of them, in his phrase, were 'kind of a bit lost in the thickets of economists'.[57]

Michael delivered his lectures as he was required to do, but he still felt restless, not secure, and he was drawn relentlessly, deeper and deeper, into educational politics (with the Consumers' Association on the side) rather than into sociology. The fact that he was made a

Fellow of Churchill College, Cambridge's newest college, still in course of construction, influenced his attitudes as much as the fact that he was a university lecturer. Indeed, the College was to be drawn into his educational plans more than it was into the development of Cambridge sociology. It too had a complex pre-history, bound up with the struggle to establish (with business support) postgraduate technological education. Coincidentally, like Michael, it might have been located not in Cambridge, but in Birmingham.[58]

Michael found his formal role in the University uncongenial, even though he had an important part to play if sociology were to establish itself in Cambridge. He was disturbed by what he considered to be the 'complacency' of most Cambridge dons (and many 'students'), in his view 'so pleased with themselves for being there' and knowing and caring little for what was happening elsewhere. He was untouched, therefore, by any Cambridge spell. Indeed, only one spell was still cast on him – that of Dartington, the same spell as that cast on Leonard Elmhirst, who was a Cambridge graduate. For Michael, the past in Cambridge, unlike the past in Dartington, seemed to be a 'great weight' on the institution. 'The stones that embodied the history, although they were the great glory of the place, were ... helping by making the history so vivid to make the place even more conservative than it would have been any way.'[59]

Had Michael been working in a new university, he might have approached the educational issues of the 1960s somewhat differently and with greater hope of success. As it was, Cambridge seemed to him to be hostile to the dynamics of expansion. There was an obvious moral. 'More people ought to be got into the place'. Yet there was an odd ambivalence in this answer, for if Cambridge had been the 'bleak' place Michael found it to be (and this was a personal reaction, not shared by most of its undergraduates, let alone its Fellows), why should other people flock to it? Michael put the question on one side, however, and proceeded, with what he later called 'green-ness', to develop the idea that there should be two universities of Cambridge, one for term time – the Cambridge as it was and had been – and one for the vacations, the Cambridge as it ought to be.[60]

Michael believed, as Crowther and *The Economist* did – he was at one with them in this – that one of the worst examples of educational 'wastage' in the 1960s was wastage of academic buildings; and at least two Cambridge dons, Peter Laslett, Fellow of Trinity College, with a plenitude of ideas of his own about university reform – and much else – and Hugh Morrison, Senior Tutor and Vice-President of Churchill

College, a classicist, listened carefully to what Michael had to say. Laslett had much in common with Michael both temperamentally and in his ideas: Morrison was influenced more by what was happening in new universities. Most Cambridge dons, however, for good as well as for bad reasons, were opposed to any dual university plan whether or not it involved them. So, indeed, were most supporters of educational change outside Cambridge, like myself.[61] It did not help Michael's case that in putting his plan forward for a 'dual Cambridge' he used the word 'campus', not then an acceptable term in the University and in most others except the new ones.

If Sussex was dismayed to be called in sections of the press 'Balliol by the sea', it did not help Michael (or Laslett) when the 'other university' he was planning was called 'Battersea University in King's Parade'. That was because an unabashed Michael, undeterred by most of the obstacles, first looked outside Cambridge to the Battersea College of Advanced Technology for a 'second academic staff' to teach in his second university. There, not surprisingly, he found ample support, particularly among scientists, who were drawn to the idea of working in the great Cambridge laboratories.

Only a far less ambitious scheme proved practicable – with the scientists left out. After protracted negotiations with the Cambridge Extramural Board of Studies, an academic teaching symposium was held in Churchill College in March 1963, the first event of its kind to be held there.[62] The participants were warned that the College was 'still in process of construction and certain minor inconveniences will have to be accepted'. Most College rooms at that time were in temporary huts on the western edge of the site. It might have been Sussex.

Ensured the support of Morrison and of Major-General Hamilton, the Churchill College Bursar, Michael (along with Laslett) had found it possible to attract 50 students, half of them school teachers or teachers in technical colleges. The youngest was 19, the oldest 52. Three were Nigerians.[63] Just as important, they had attracted as lecturers, again ironically, some of the Cambridge economists who had stood in his way when he dreamed of sociology establishing itself in Cambridge. They welcomed the chance of teaching highly committed mature students on a one-week residential course. Like the students, they were prepared to start work at 8 am and work on until midnight, and the lecture subjects on offer included 'The Common Market' and 'World Economic Development'.

The first tutors included a future Nobel Laureate in Economics, Richard Stone, then Professor of Finance and Accounting at Cambridge,[64] Richard (later Lord) Kahn, like Stone a Fellow of King's

College, and a disciple and friend of Keynes, and Kenneth (later Sir Kenneth) Berrill, who was to become Chairman of the University Grants Committee in 1969 and Chairman of the Council and Pro-Chancellor of the Open University in 1983. The right collective noun for this group of tutors was galaxy. Yet Michael, down-to-earth, felt that the College charged students too much for their accommodation – 2s 6d for breakfast and £3 10s for a double room for a week.[65]

This conference, not quite the right noun to apply to it, sounds as romantic in retrospect as it did at the time, and it left a deep mark on Michael. It also had far wider public ramifications for him and for educational advance. It made it possible for Cambridge – the place, more than the University – to figure on the future map of adult distant learning long after a disillusioned Michael had left Churchill College in 1963 to return to Bethnal Green.[66] The National Extension College, an offshoot of ACE, founded by Michael and Brian Jackson in the autumn of 1963, while a Conservative government was still in power, was to remain there, committed through the years to 'open learning', which, from the start, through an Open University, had been Michael's goal.[67]

Michael's article in *Where?* in the autumn of 1963 had been a call to action. 'So far nothing has actually been done. We have therefore decided to act ourselves' he told his readers, not all of whom had bought *Where?*. 'With no full-time staff of its own', it would depend on part-time teachers from other institutions, including the Universities of Cambridge, Keele, Bristol, Harvard and Hull (in that order) 'as well as from the remarkable College of Arts and Technology in Cambridge'. They and their scattered students learning at a distance would constitute 'the Invisible College of Cambridge', to be called the National Extension College (NEC).[68] 'Without any official grant, its equipment would come from the sort of far sighted people in industry who supported nineteenth century civic universities'. Its students would profit, as the Open University was to do, from a conjunction between changes in education – and the demand for it – and the technology of communications.

How the NEC, which was to spawn the International Extension College (IEC),[69] came into existence and how it related to the Open University, the most innovative of all the new universities of the 1960s, demands study in detail. So, too, does Michael's personal contribution to its history. He was not, however, the only person pressing for a new kind of university which would use modern technology to broaden student access. Thus, in 1960, Professor Sir George Catlin, father of Shirley (later Lady) Williams, who had made his academic career across the Atlantic, specifically suggested what he called a 'University of the Air',[70] recalling too that as first Labour Minister of

Education after 1945, Ellen Wilkinson, well known personally to Michael as Shirley herself later was to be,[71] had envisaged the use of radio frequencies to transmit lectures to a wide audience by such eminent academics as Huxley and Hogben.

Just as specifically, R. C. G. Williams, Chairman of the Electronics and Communications Section of the Royal Institution of Electrical Engineers, who had long advocated the importance of educational television, had pressed in 1962 for a 'Televarsity', offering 'an academic link between student and teacher',[72] while at least one Director of Extramural Studies, based in Nottingham and speaking and working from inside the very varied adult education establishment, Harold Wiltshire, believed that experiments on these lines were urgently necessary and diligently set about planning them.[73] The WEA, of which I was then President, was increasingly, if critically, aware of the potential of electronic communications.[74] Meanwhile, Michael had shaped his own opinions on education, and on television, and on the relationship between the two, before Harold Wilson became Prime Minister.

How much Michael knew of the proposals of Catlin and of Williams or of the enterprise of Wiltshire is not certain; and he was never in close touch with the WEA. What is certain is that in his seminal article in *Where*? 'Is Your Child in the Unlucky Generation?' he had already included a substantial section of his text to which he gave the title 'Open University'. It followed two sections outlining possible methods of meeting the educational 'crisis' – creating universities based on research stations, like the Atomic Energy Establishment at Harwell and the Royal Radar Establishment at Malvern, where teachers were already available; and making fuller use of existing facilities to take in more students, as Crowther had suggested.[75]

Turning some universities into double-shift universities was very much Michael's own idea; and in the second of these sections he mentioned evening as well as vacation shifts, noting that LSE had long offered evening lectures, as had Birkbeck. London University, which had on its rolls a large number of external degree students, none of them taught by it, many of them studying for the B.Sc.(Econ.) degree, which Michael himself had taken internally, was very much in his mind in his third section when he turned to examinations and degrees. His 'open university', like his short Cambridge courses, would prepare people for external degrees of London University.

Michael displayed a remarkable warmth of enthusiasm for London University at this time in his life because of its record in granting external degrees. In another article in *Where*? he drew attention to Statute 4 in the University's constitution of 1836, setting out the purposes of the university, calling this a 'classic statement'.[76] He found it 'strange', however, that London University had failed to provide teaching for its own 'beneficent' external degrees which provided a world-wide as well as a national qualification. (He had not looked at the history of examinations.) 'All the civic universities in England and Wales [not quite true], as well as the University Colleges of Africa and the West Indies, at one time entered their students for this Degree, and it has also given an opportunity to many thousands of people in Britain unable to gain admission to a university.' In 1961 no fewer than 13,000 students qualified for university entrance were registered for an external degree.

As for those enrolled abroad, the External Registrar of London University was responsible for thousands of people 'who will one day be amongst the rulers of Africa, Asia and the West Indies', opening up a vision of power as well as education, and one shared at the time by the then External Registrar, L. E. Ball. Not all the faculties of London University or its graduates were so enthusiastic: officers and officials of the University were seeking to stop granting them. The idea of creating new universities in the Commonwealth was proving far more attractive, as it had been in Britain, and London University was playing an important part in the creation process as was the British Vice-Chancellors' Committee.[77]

The article 'Is Your Child in the Unlucky Generation?' referred not only to external degrees but to correspondence colleges, citing the experience of the Soviet Union, which had 'developed higher education more rapidly than anywhere else': in 1961 the majority of all new entrants to higher education there were working in correspondence colleges. In Britain 'the failure of orthodox higher education to adapt to the "revolution of rising expectations"' had given the correspondence colleges their chance to expand.[78] They were already catering for 250,000 'pupils', but they would have to be reformed on Soviet – and American – lines, Michael believed, if they were to help solve Britain's educational crisis.

'The inadequacy of teaching' in them, exposed in *Which*? in the month that the NEC was announced,[79] was partly responsible for 'poor results in the external examinations'. In the Soviet Union, by contrast, the correspondence colleges, which Michael had visited, had 'premises all over the country', which the students were encouraged to attend in order to make use of library and laboratory facilities. There, too, they could discuss their reading with resident tutors.[80] In the United States educational television was, he believed, well developed.[81] Many universities had their own closed-circuit television stations for full-time students and open broadcasts for external students. 'If TV and radio courses were arranged to tie in with their written work and reading, correspondence college students would be a great deal better off than they are now.'

Michael's article ended with a section on 'National Extension Colleges' – in the plural. 'To make use of ... overseas experience a new centre is needed – a National Extension College – to act as the nucleus of an "open university" and to work closely with London's External Registrar.' With a special government grant (this was never to be obtained) the College would organise new and better correspondence courses for the External Degree, promote lectures and residential schools and, not least, 'teach by means of television'. 'The National College would work with the BBC and ITV [Michael did not see the choice as either/or] to secure programmes for its students.'

There was no reference in the article to the almost always bitter argument between BBC and ITV about both the motivation and the organisation of such programmes or the politics of a fourth channel, an argument which more than once reached Cabinet level.[82] Michael, unaware of the extent of the squabblings which went on also in Whitehall, found it just as difficult to work with the top échelons of the BBC, familiar to Sasha, as to work with Cambridge University.[83]

Before the NEC was founded, Michael had acquired in Laslett an invaluable ally, whom he had not met before taking up his post in Cambridge. Most important for their alliance, Laslett had had broadcasting experience with the BBC and had watched with an eagle eye what he considered to be the erosion of BBC Third Programme policies. He was taken seriously in Broadcasting House, as the Third Programme Defence Society had been,[84] and his criticisms were monitored and recorded. Michael was less well known there, although he was close to Prudence Smith, a BBC producer, and before he married Sasha in 1960 he had already established broadcasting credentials at a time when television, not radio, was becoming the dominant medium.

It was Laslett who set up and chaired a Cambridge Television Committee and who with Michael took the decision to move into this daunting territory. He visited the United States in 1962 at the instigation of ACE, one of several enlightening foreign visits in his life (China was to figure later on his map) – through Michael some of his costs were borne by the Elmgrant Trust – and he returned convinced that educational television was 'the one new thing that we can still call upon to expand and to adapt British education to the needs of the late twentieth century'.[85]

In April 1963 Laslett attended an Anglo-American conference on education by correspondence and television, organised at Ditchley by the Oxford University Department of Education, then directed by A. D. C. Peterson, in conjunction with Gene Rietzke of Capitol Radio, Washington.[86] This was one of the rare occasions when Oxford entered Michael's story, for he too was present, as he was at a second Ditchley conference in May 1964 at which the two Ministers in Wilson's new government who were directly responsible for higher education took part – Lord (Vivian) Bowden, Director of the Manchester College of Science and Technology, and James Boyden, who had a special interest in correspondence education, and who during the previous Parliament had introduced an abortive Private Member's Bill to regulate correspondence colleges.[87] A Ditchley working party, presided over by Michael, went on to draft a report, 'Towards an Open University' which was published in *Where?* (Autumn 1964) and which stands out as a landmark text.

Between the two conferences Laslett was the main driving force behind a 'milestone' series of six educational television programmes put out not by the BBC but by ITV in October 1963.[88] 'Dawn University', the name given to the series, was broadcast by Anglia Television, 'a brave and enlightened gesture', made possible because it had the full backing of the Independent Television Authority: indeed, it was the Authority which gave Laslett a small grant of £500 to set up the preparatory organisation for the series and which arranged to have the programmes broadcast nationally through its networking system. This was the first time that it had claimed air space in its own name.[89]

From 21 to 26 October 'Dawn University' broadcast 'straight' lectures by distinguished Cambridge dons, including Fred Hoyle, an astronomer well known to television audiences, who lectured on 'the Mathematics of Violence' – much of his broadcast was concerned with a topic that was to gain in importance, violence at football matches – and Raymond Williams, Lecturer in English Literature, one of the spokesmen of the 'New Left', whose academic background was in adult education and who had become deeply involved in studies of communications.[90] David Grugeon, a London teacher initially seconded to ACE and later to become Director of Educational Services in the Office of Continuing Education at the Open University, was one of the main organisers, and D. A. W. Wade was the technical organiser.

At the same time – and this was an equally imaginative venture – closed circuit television lectures were broadcast for two days by Cambridge University and the new University of East Anglia, which was then starting its first academic programmes, and for one day by Cambridge and Imperial College, London. These lectures, related to seminars, were designed to see whether universities could work together effectively in the use of television. They were described by Laslett as a 'rough, brash experiment' from which 'an enormous amount was learnt ... in three days'.[91]

It was estimated that 200,000 viewers saw the Dawn University programmes, nearly double the then University population of Great Britain. In order to examine their impact Laslett, who, like Michael, believed, perhaps too fervently (as did the first staff of NEC), that educational television had to prove itself – in fact, it was never required to do so – organised the taking of a sample of viewer and listener reactions. He had the support of TAM, ITV's market research organisation. The sample (64 per cent were women, about half of them housewives) was drawn from respondents to a coupon placed in the *TV Times*, none of whom was over the age of 59: the biggest age group was that between 20 and 29. Leaving aside students, only 17 per cent of the viewers had had a university education. A third of the viewers were in minor clerical jobs, and 6 per cent were unskilled manual workers.

Only a few of the Cambridge dons who had been involved in the broadcasts believed that the lectures had been beyond the grasp of the listeners, and some of the respondents stated that they had been impressed most of all by the simplicity of the plain lecture form: it was 'just as if they were all doing a lecture at a college'.[92] Most listeners and viewers preferred listening in the early morning to late at night, suggesting to Laslett that Ulster TV's *Midnight Oil* was broadcasting at the wrong time.[93]

Laslett now spoke of a 'University of Britain' – there was no shortage of alternative titles at this stage – which would deliver a complete televised first year university course, backed by residential schools and correspondence kits, a form of educational integration that was later to be adopted by the Open University and commended in Africa and other parts of the world by the International Extension College. Television by itself was not deemed to be enough. And in many parts of the world radio was still the dominant medium.[94]

The overseas models that Laslett and his colleagues had in mind when considering the British scene were the American 'Sunrise Semester' and the Chicago Television College. 'We have every indication,' Michael wrote, 'that large numbers would gain by the creation of a television-based university. There is no possibility whatsoever that conventional universities will meet the needs of this audience [the audience attracted by the Anglia programmes], but the core of it can be turned into a serious student body: the unwalled University of the Air lies within sight.'[95]

It all seemed rosy, but the scale of any independent British venture quickly had to be reduced when support from the independent television companies proved in practice to be strictly limited. As for the BBC, suspicious of, when not hostile to, any rival broadcasting enterprises, it was moving slowly, concentrating primarily on 'further education' and on 'adult education', territory which was familiar to it but largely unfamiliar to Michael. Yet John Scupham, a well-known figure in educational circles, including adult education and the WEA, believed as passionately in 'educational advance' as Michael. In 1963 he had been made the BBC's Controller (Education), a new post, created in another sign of the times by the BBC's brilliant but controversial Director-General, Hugh (later Sir Hugh) Greene, much admired by the young television producers who listened more prudently, if not convinced, when the word 'education' crossed the lips of 'the DG'.

Scupham was a member of the Newsom Committee, yet when Laslett approached him for BBC help in November 1962 he replied that 'this is just the type of operation which the Corporation might find most difficult, both financially and because of restricted technical resources'.[96] Scupham wished to push beyond radio into television, but, despite the support of Greene, continued to meet with tough and always irreverent opposition from other senior BBC officials involved with television production and administration. 'Who's to be master?', one of them, Donald Baverstock, asked. Scupham had left the Corporation by the time that BBC Further Education became a separate television department in 1965, headed by Donald Grattan.[97]

There were other institutional barriers to experiment in the early and mid-1960s. Thus, when in the summer of 1963 before the NEC was set up Michael applied to the Post Office for a licence to use the sound radio services of a commercial company, Rediffusion Ltd., for a limited educational venture, to be run by the Advisory Centre for Education in conjunction with the University of Hull, the Post Office ruled, after consulting the BBC, that the venture would not be possible since it 'would be regarded as an experiment in local sound broadcasting'.[98] 'The proposal to provide lectures from local sources for transmission over local relay networks,' Charles Curran, then the BBC's Secretary and later to be its Director-General, told B. L. Savage of the Post Office, 'would seem to us to perilously close to origination of programme material by the networks, which we have consistently opposed on ground which are familiar to you.'[99]

Michael did not know of the BBC's long-standing resistance to Rediffusion[100] but, even had he known, he would still have applied for permission to carry out this experiment. Hull would have been a good place at which to begin. The Vice-Chancellor of the University, Brynmor (later Sir Brynmor) Jones, was one of the few Vice-Chancellors who was interested in the possibilities of television, and later he was to serve on the Planning Committee of the Open University. In February 1963 he had been invited by the UGC to prepare a report on *Audio-Visual Aids in Higher Scientific Education*, which appeared in 1965.[101] Michael did not use the jargon phrase 'visual aids', which was a favourite phrase of the Nuffield Foundation – and of Boyle, an enthusiast for their use.[102]

In looking outside Cambridge to universities like Hull and Keele, Michael recognised that while with difficulty Cambridge had supported one pioneering experiment in distance education, it 'was distinguished from most other universities by having no university television centre, no plans for one and little interest in their obvious utility'. Many dons there did not even have television sets, and those who did were sometimes treated with contempt by their colleagues. The most promising institution in Cambridge, the 'remarkable College of Arts and Technology', did not belong to the University.[103]

A direct approach by Michael to the University College of Keele failed. It had a unique four-year degree programme (unique to England, not to Scotland), and Michael had suggested that it should broadcast the whole of its distinctive foundation year courses.[104] He did win some support, however, from Imperial College, London. He also persuaded the Midlands Region of the BBC, better geared to school than to university broadcasting, to broadcast experimentally six weeks of radio programmes based on the GCE 'O' level syllabus. A year later, the course was offered nationally under the title *After School English*. While Michael was busy contacting both BBC and independent companies, Harold Wiltshire was launching integrated courses made possible by ITV. They were carefully monitored.[105]

Michael, like Laslett, believed that every local experiment would bolster the case for a new national institution, and the opening of the NEC, which he had sketched in his 1962 article, followed closely after the Cambridge Television Week in October 1963.[106] Yet television, which Brian Jackson called the 'great stimulant', was not to be the rationale of the College. The core of its activities, as Laslett had suggested, was to be 'a combination of means of communication', with 'correspondence' by post as a sustaining operation.

A major article 'Announcing the National Extension College', which appeared in *Where?* in the Autumn of 1963, was a sequel to 'Is Your Child in the Unlucky Generation?'. 'The College,' Michael told his readers, 'is designed for distinctive students: it will, therefore, have to use distinctive methods.' Learning at a distance was possible, he went on, only if the 'most ancient communications device, the post', was employed.[107] 'The newer devices for sending messages over a distance – the magnetic tape, the telephone, the moving picture, radio and television – are too new to have been used systematically for instruction on any large scale. ... From this range the new College will have to choose.' There might also be (and this was an accurate prediction) 'a new sort of book'. The Internet was then beyond the powers of any forecasters.

This article, however, was 'future oriented' and can be thought of in retrospect as a contribution to the public discussion, still limited, on a University of the Air which followed Wilson's speech, of great historic importance, delivered at a Labour Party rally in Glasgow on 8 September 1963, in which as Leader of the Opposition he outlined proposals 'on which we are working, a dynamic programme providing facilities for home study to university and higher technical standards on the basis of a University of the Air'. In his article Michael noted Wilson's 'very welcome' Glasgow speech, delivered at the start of his pre-election campaign, which he called a 'similar proposal' to his own.[108]

The term 'University of the Air' was picked up at once by the press, as Wilson had wished. From then onwards the name and the freight that it carried with it passed into politics as well as into education.[109] Leaving aside Catlin, it was not, however, the first sign of interest within the Labour Party in 'similar [or related] proposals'. Among the recommendations of a higher education study group appointed by Gaitskell, then Leader of the Labour Party, in March 1962 and chaired by Lord (Stephen) Taylor, a friend of Michael's, was the setting up of an experiment in educational broadcasting for adults involving both the BBC and the ITA.[110] The secretary of the study group, which reported to the National Executive of the Labour Party, was Howard Glennester, another old friend of Michael's, who worked in the Labour Research Department at Transport House, and who knew of Michael's plans. Other members included Crosland, Vaizey and Boyden.[111]

Published in March 1963, the Taylor Report opened with the words 'The reform and expansion of higher education is one of the most urgent and important questions before the nation', and went on to recommend, although it was not its main recommendation, a 'University of the Air'. Speaking of 'the Battle of the Bulge', it also proposed a large number of new city universities integrated into 'the main stream of community life'. The 'University of the Air', conceived of not as an institution but as a series of courses, was to be a cooperative venture drawing on the facilities both of the BBC and ITA. Wilson talked at Glasgow of a 'new educational trust'.

In February 1963, Frank Barlow, Secretary of the Education Group of the Parliamentary Labour Party, had written to Hugh Greene stating that several members of the Group wished to visit the BBC to discuss educational television. They did so later in the month at a time when the Conservative Government's Inter-Departmental Working Party on educational television was itself deeply involved in talks with Greene and his staff.[112] At the meeting with Barlow and his colleagues Greene was not present. Scupham, who was, reacted to the Labour victory at the general election, which followed in the Autumn, by producing an internal BBC memorandum in which he stated that it had been prepared 'in the conviction that education will be overwhelmingly the most important domestic problem for as far ahead as can be seen ... we are still in the early stages of a social revolution'.[113]

The precise chronology of events (which stopped short of 'social revolution') is complicated, but important to record. Wilson, who had prepared an undelivered speech on the subject of educational television in the Spring of 1963, had become interested in the educational uses of television while travelling abroad in the United States and the Soviet Union before he became Leader of the Opposition on Gaitskell's death in January 1963.[114] He had learnt much about the American situation in Chicago from Senator William Benton, owner of the *Encyclopaedia Britannica*, who in October 1963 had prepared for him a memorandum on university television. Wilson also studied a report published by Television International Enterprises which outlined the various educational uses of television throughout the world – in schools as well as in universities.

A few weeks after his Glasgow speech, he introduced the subject in a policy statement at the Labour Party Conference held in Scarborough. 'The strength, the solvency, the influence of Britain, which some still think depends upon nostalgic illusions or upon nuclear posturings – these things are going to depend upon the speed with which we can come to terms with a world of change.'[115] These were words that might have been written by Michael. Questions of efficiency (through research[116]) and of justice were involved. 'We simply cannot as a nation afford to cut off three quarters or more of our children from virtually any chance of higher education.' The University of the Air would offer a second chance to those who had previously missed out. Not surprisingly, *The Economist*, given its earlier stance, strongly backed Wilson – although it was one of the few periodicals or newspapers to do so. 'It is one of the best things he has done, and provides a real hope that he is not going to be inhibited in his approach to higher education by Labour's formidable and orthodox tail of supporting academics.'[117]

In later years Wilson was consistent and, more important still, persistent, in striving for what he was to regard as the crowning achievement of his governments, the 'brainchild' for which he would be most remembered.[118] Yet the institution which emerged, the Open University, was different in significant respects, including organisation and academic direction, from that which he had outlined in 1963 one year after Michael had drawn attention to the need and had referred to the title. It was just as different too from the institution which Michael had canvassed. The NEC was not to be its embryo. Indeed, Michael had little to do with the subsequent evolution of an idea, which in its inception was exciting, if for most people vague.

Thus, when he produced an early paper on the subject in March 1964, Michael left open the size of the institution, its cost, its broadcasting arrangements and its range of courses.[119] And that was after he had made his brief return to the Labour Party's Research Department on the eve of the general election of 1964, when the then head of it, Shore, left to fight a seat in the constituency which included Bethnal Green.[120] It was a short-lived, if eventful, episode, however, and Michael, having sparked off a number of innovatory ideas, played no part in the general election of March 1966 which increased Wilson's precarious majority.

Despite all the talk – and all the paper – and the prominence of the idea at the Labour Party Conference of 1964, the 'University of the Air' did not figure in Labour's general election manifesto. It was an idea which appealed neither to leading officials in the Department of Education and Science, particularly those who had been close to Boyle, nor to a number of leading Labour Party politicians, among them Crosland and Jenkins, the latter a future Chancellor of the University of Oxford, then Crosland's main political ally inside the Labour Party. Nor did this situation change. Throughout the 1960s, close as the idea was to Wilson's heart, it met with resistance from both quarters – and from the Treasury over which Jenkins became Chancellor of the Exchequer.

As a result, the Open University was never allowed to compete with other items in the Labour Party's programme for higher education. Nor was it integrated into an overall programme. It stood on its own, with its finances insecure to the last. Wilson himself stated categorically in *Labour and the Scientific Revolution* in 1964 that it 'was not a substitute for our plans for higher education ... for new universities ... or for extending technological education'. One important Cabinet discussion as early as February 1965 in which it does not seem to have been mentioned put it in a different context, however. Crosland concurred with the opinion of his predecessor, Michael Stewart, that the Government should create no additional new universities or 'promote' any further 'institutions to university status with the possible exception of a university in the north-east of England'.[121] Michael would have been interested in this last 'possible exception': he had even contemplated locating the NEC in the North-East. He would have been interested too in the fact that the minute of this discussion followed a minute on the Comet: 'agreed that Comet should be adopted as a replacement for the Shackleton 11'.

As planning the Open University continued, without too many Cabinet minutes, what was being planned remained entirely separate from the non-official plan of the institution which Michael had created, his NEC: like Wilson's University of the Air, it went through many changes during the 1960s, at times even placing itself, under the ebullient direction of Brian Jackson, in opposition to the evolving Open University. Like the Consumers' Association, it had to fend for itself without any official grant, sometimes describing itself as an 'information cooperative' as well as a teaching centre and at times offering 'a range of promising vistas ... so vast as to be almost dizzying'.[122] Jackson sometimes called the NEC 'Karl Marx College, Cambridge.'[123]

An offer which the College made to the Wilson Government to make 'freely available' 'all the experience we gather' was never accepted. But this may have been an advantage, as the Consumers' Association had discovered. Funds came in easily at first. After Michael's *Where?* article of September 1963 had been reprinted in the *Guardian*, readers of the paper donated £1,000 to support the new venture, while another £1,000 came from the Elmhirst Trust. Once the College had been brought into existence, it secured an indispensable grant of £10,000 and a loan of £10,000 from the Gulbenkian Foundation, one of many grants that the Gulbenkian Foundation was to offer Michael.

Grugeon was the NEC's first Administrator – still on secondment – and Michael was its Chairman, with much in practice being left to Jackson, who moved to Cambridge in charge of ACE after Michael had left it. Its first address as a Visible College was that of ACE, 57 Russell Street, Cambridge, a room nine-feet square in 'two condemned workmen's cottages round a pub'.[124] In 1965 it appointed as its first Director of Education Hilary Perraton, who went on to succeed Grugeon, and who figures prominently in the later history both of the NEC and the IEC.[125] Its Treasurer, Howard Dickinson, was shared with ACE and ICS. The College never became 'the nucleus' of the Open University as Michael had originally hoped.[126] Its negotiations with the emerging University were difficult, but it had a zest and a style of its own and it was to prove itself a great survivor.

'The students we have in mind,' Michael stated in retrospect, were people who were seeking 'a second chance', people who 'cannot in the ordinary way see their teachers in the flesh'. Courses would start on 1 January 1964, allowing ample time for student registration. They would be of three types – courses at university level (or at pre-university level to secure relevant entry qualifications), with London University external degrees as the objective; courses for housewives with young children, including one on 'Pre-School Play Groups' and one for play group supervisors;[127] and vocational courses, among them courses on business mathematics and electronic engineering.[128] With the opening in mind, a day conference for 30 would-be NEC tutors was held at Churchill College on 14 December 1963. It was addressed by Laslett, Willmott and Jackson. Another residential student course was held in Churchill College, and residential courses in Mathematics and English were offered at Keele.[129]

Equipment for the College was initially provided, as Michael had wished, by 'far-sighted people in industry', In particular, the Pye Company, located in Cambridge (a company with which the BBC had long been on bad terms), would supply a 'language bus', 'a mobile language laboratory' and 'special instructional radio sets to be assembled by long-stay hospital patients'. From further afield US Industries Inc. supplied teaching machines (much in vogue, if not in use, at that time),[130] and more modestly Crédit de Paris supplied courses in French. The double decker bus soon made its presence felt as it toured schools, colleges and businesses in East Anglia.[131] Again, Michael was aware of an international dimension to what he and his colleagues were doing. 'If all goes well, we hope in 1964 to build a similar bus for teaching English in Africa.'[132]

There was to be a different kind of venture in July 1964 when the College took an existing television series, Rediffusion's *Towards 2000, The Britain We Make*, which focused on the social implications of technological change, and added a twelve-part correspondence course so that the serious viewer could deepen his knowledge of the matter covered in the series.[133] It had been approached by the executive producer Guthrie Moir only six weeks before transmission. Michael's own 'future orientation' and his interest in forecasting made this a congenial link-up: one of the 'lessons' was 'the Development of Clock Technology, Clocks and Measurement of Time', another 'The Study of a New Town'.[134] A second series in 1965, still part of the *Towards 2000* project, called 'Design for Living', included programmes on 'functionalism in architecture' (without reference to tower blocks) and 'on the influence of new materials on the things we see'. The penultimate programme was called 'Mass Demand and Mass Production'.[135]

None the less, despite the imagination, enterprise and professionalism of *Towards 2000*, it did not prove to be a successful course in terms of enrolment: one College report described it as 'spectacularly unsuccessful'. As John Griffiths, then Executive Director of the NEC, put it, 'it appears that there is little demand for a serious pattern of supporting correspondence study for a non-vocational general interest TV series'.[136] Griffiths had been drawn to the NEC by Michael, who offered him the post of Executive Director after he had been the runner-up in 1964 in interviews for the post of Director of the Consumers' Association. He accepted it on Michael's personal invitation, the kind of invitation which it was difficult to refuse. 'Although I never had any intention of being involved in education the radical in me responded with enthusiasm.' He accepted at once.[137]

One course that was a success was *After School English*. This was backed by the Oxford Delegacy for Extra-Mural Studies, whose Secretary, Frank Jessup, had been Head of the Rediffusion Panel of Advisers for the *Towards 2000* series[138] put on a residential course in 1965, which pointed the way for a series of GCE courses, including English and Mathematics at 'O' and 'A' level, the consequence of the takeover of the University Correspondence College in Cambridge, 'lurching the NEC towards formal education. There was little time and energy for the scatty, entrepreneurial leaps into the educational dark which characterised NEC's first two years.'[139]

The taking over of the University Correspondence College in Cambridge, founded in the 1880s by William Briggs, had seemed a remarkable, if characteristic, stroke of luck. One of the correspondence

1 Entrance to the courtyard, Dartington Hall, 1925. The little girl is Christine Gilpin.

2 Michael's oil painting of High Cross House on the Dartington Hall Estate, 1931.

3 Michael's wartime work pass, 1941.

4 The Institute of Community Studies, Victoria Park Square, Bethnal Green.

5 A street of Bethnal Green interviews, 1950s.

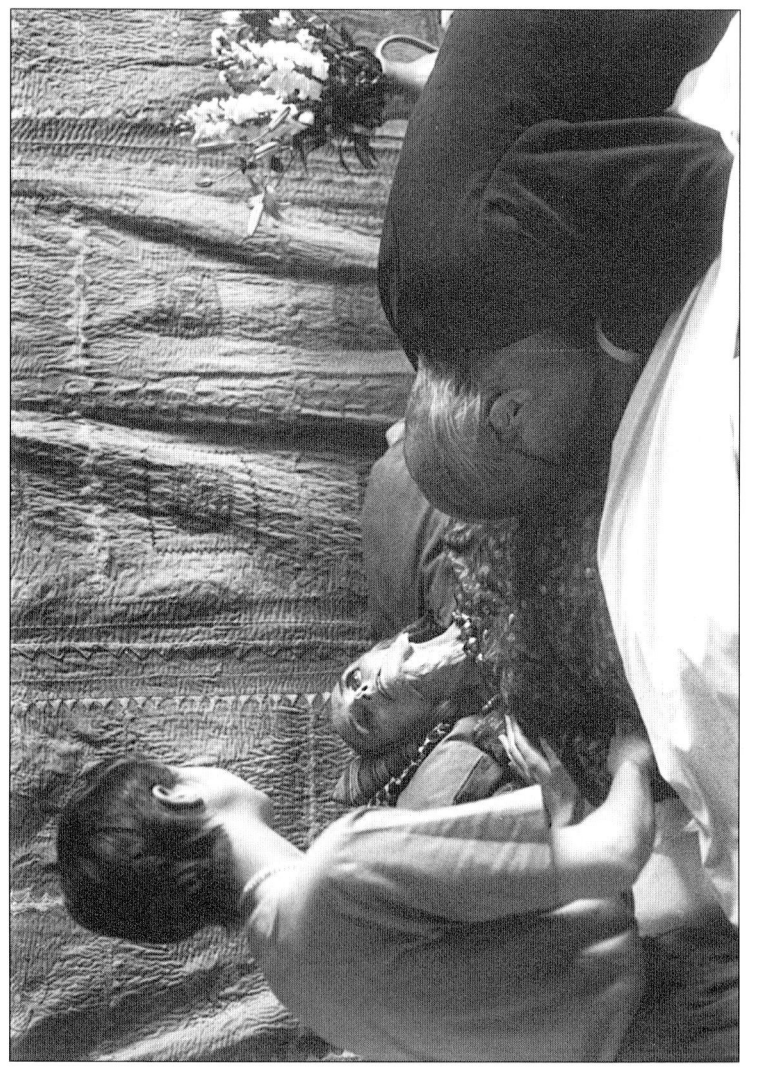

6 Sophie, Sasha and Michael, 1993.

7 Michael Young with his daughter, Gaia, October 1998.

8 Michael with students, study week, School for Social Entrepreneurs, June 1999.

9 Michael Young, June 2000.

colleges cited in the *Which?* survey of current provision, it was a privately funded, non-profit-making organisation, and the oldest college of its kind in Britain.[140] In October 1963 it made over to the NEC all its assets, 'lock-stock-and-barrel' – and they included a Victorian Gothic terrace building overlooking Parker's Piece.

This was a dramatic as well as momentous turn of fortune, although fortune's wheel was soon to turn again. Michael, along with Jackson, became members of the William Briggs Trust, alongside three members of the Briggs family, and three days later the three Briggs Trustees resigned and Jackson became Chairman. At the beginning of 1964, therefore, before Labour won the general election, the NEC already had a staff of about 50 people, a building, a range of available UCC courses, including a course for London's B.Sc.(Econ.) degree and for other external degrees. Most of the staff were to leave and most courses were quickly scrapped as out-of-date, but there was £60,000 in new resources and, most important, a register of students working with the College and paying for their courses.[141]

In 1967 there were 7,000 new students – in four years 12,500 had passed through or were still passing through the College – but there were serious financial problems. There had been a small financial surplus for the first time that year, but there were cutbacks in 1968, when the problems became so serious that there had had to be a reduction in staffing, and the second Executive Director, David Baron, had to warn that 'while a progress report on educational venture should not start with finance', in practice in the case of the NEC 'finance had tended to be largely the master'.[142] Tightening up continued through 1969 even after new Trustees had been appointed, and an NEC Trust Ltd. set up.

The imposing first list of Vice-Presidents included Newsom, Zuckerman, Bowden, Vaizey, then Professor of Economics at Brunel University, Elvin, now Director of the London Institute of Education, Baroness Gaitskell, Bullock, Master of the new St. Catherine's College, Oxford, Herman (later Sir Herman) Bondi, a future Master of Churchill College, and the Roman Catholic Archbishop of Liverpool. With them there were three ex-Vice-Chancellors – Lord Fulton of Sussex, the only man to chair in parallel BBC and ITA committees on adult education, Sir Charles (later Lord) Morris of Leeds, a close friend of Fulton, and Sir James Mountford of Liverpool, who had a long connection with the Leverhulme Trust and was chairman of the Leverhulme Committee which made awards to individuals.

There were also several heads of schools, including public schools, among them Sir Desmond Lee, Headmaster of Winchester and Diana (later Dame Diana) Reader Harris, Headmistress of Sherborne. The list deserved the name of galaxy, as the list of lecturers at the first NEC 'conference' had done. Yet they were busy people, many of them preoccupied elsewhere, and at that stage in educational history, when fund-raising was not a necessary qualification for Vice-Chancellors and heads of colleges, most of them lacked the gift of raising money.

They faced a more serious problem than that. By the time that the Extension College Trust was set up, the Secretary of State for Education and Science had appointed a Planning Committee of the Open University in September 1967 – with an equally impressive roll call of names – in order 'to work out a comprehensive plan for an Open University as outlined in a White Paper of February 1966 and to prepare a draft Charter and Statutes'.[143] And that came as a climax rather than a start. Since February 1965 the care of the 'University of the Air' project had been in the more than capable hands of Jennie Lee, Nye Bevan's widow, after Wilson's initiative was in danger of stalling.[144] Nominally in the first instance a Parliamentary Under-Secretary of State, unlike anyone in that position, past or present, Jennie had direct access to the Prime Minister. It was invaluable. Her responsibilities covered the arts too, and she discharged them thoughtfully and, above, all, effectively, using every art of her own in the process.[145]

Her first committee, appointed in the Summer of 1965, was described as 'advisory': its 13 members were appointed by herself, and she herself served as Chairman. They were called upon 'to consider [very specifically] the educational functions and content of a University of the Air, as outlined in a speech made by Mr. Harold Wilson at Glasgow on 8 September 1963'. Laslett was a member of this Committee, as were Brynmor Jones, Peterson, Scupham, Wiltshire, Annan, by then Provost of University College, London, and Norman Mackenzie of the University of Sussex. They had all been appointed as individuals and not as representatives of interests.

The second Planning Committee of 1967 was different in composition and approach. Hard working and at the same time imaginative, it included members who had definite interests to advance or protect. It was chaired superbly by Peter Venables and worked through sub-committees, including one on the curriculum and degree courses.[146] While reaching key decisions about the structure of the Open University, it deliberately left detailed planning to the future Vice-Chancellor and academic staff of the new institution: this was at my suggestion, as Vice-Chancellor of a new university suspicious of

Planning Committees extending their time and powers. The Committee thereby freed itself from unnecessary detail, while giving academic depth to the whole venture, unanimously supporting Jennie Lee's effort to guarantee 'excellence' while at the same time ensuring that there would be ample scope for initiative and flexibility on the part of the new University's faculty and staff.

None the less, important though this Planning Committee was for the future of the Open University, it was the first advisory committee, described by Jennie Lee as an 'informal group',[147] which had greater political importance. Its report was never published, but for political reasons it was prepared with speed – the group met six times in less than two months – in order to figure prominently in the Labour Party manifesto for the general election of March 1966. Wilson gave it his full approval, referring to it (if in somewhat cautious language) in a speech at the tenth anniversary dinner of the Independent Television Authority on 16 September 1965. He deliberately chose that occasion: his relationship with the BBC at that time was awkward on both sides.

In the following month the Report was presented to the Ministerial Committee on Broadcasting, a formidable backstairs body within the Cabinet, working behind the scenes and deeply involved in discussions concerning the financial future of the BBC. From now onwards the 'University of the Air' became the 'Open University', a term which Michael himself, like the Advisory Committee, greatly preferred.[148] There was much, however, that he disliked about the way events were unfolding – and more that he knew nothing about – as Jennie Lee set about realising her own dreams. At her insistence, the new university was to be a 'full university' with degree-granting powers. It would provide 'genuine equality of opportunity to millions of people for the first time', but they would all be offered 'the best', as Bevan had promised when he launched the National Health Service in 1947.

The Advisory Committee accepted her vision. In setting out to realise it, she was unobtrusively backed by Ralph Toomey, whose backstairs role was in its way as important as that of Wilson, who stood by her throughout in public and in private, or of Wilson's 'wise man' and her friend, Lord Goodman, who was invaluable at critical moments in matters relating both to education and to the arts. After the general election of 1966 a further White Paper on Broadcasting, issued in December, stated firmly that no allocation of frequencies to a fourth television service would be authorised for at least three years because of 'the possibility that the network would be required for a specialized service of educational television'; and the final outcome after what seemed to be endless discussions was an arrangement between the Open University and the BBC which still lasts.[149]

Michael was not a member either of the Advisory or of the Planning Committee. He chose not to join the first, and he was not invited to join the second. There was no chance that he ever would be. The first decision was his and was based on a miscalculation – that the NEC could be converted into an Open University: he was unhappy about the terms of reference of the Committee. Yet his decision also reflected the fact that his time was in demand elsewhere: he was working with Crosland on the future of the public schools, and later in the year he was to become Chairman of the new Social Science Research Council.[150] Jennie wrote to him shrewdly that she had 'wanted very badly to have you on the Advisory Committee, but I understand perfectly that it is just not possible for anyone as much in demand as you are to fit in all such requests'.[151] Jennie knew how closely he was working with Crosland, who was not one of her great supporters inside Wilson's government.

Michael was later to write correctly that from the moment that Jennie Lee took charge of the project he was out of the mainstream.[152] At the time, in a letter of March 1966, he had written that he 'only wished' that he were more centrally concerned with the 'University of the Air' than he was. 'But I am afraid I am now very much on the fringe. Not that anyone knows what is really going to happen. If Jennie Lee does go back to the same post after the election, then she will probably continue to be the main mover.'[153] She did so continue, and as Michael was to recognise later, when all had been worked out, there would have been no Open University without her.

While it was being worked out, Michael tried to explain why the NEC did not become the 'nucleus' of Jennie's new institution. 'To a politician's eye,' he explained, 'the modesty of the [NEC] venture, the offbeat interest in building for students' expressed needs rather than in providing standardised education, and the desire to be perpetually innovating, were all likely weaknesses. And to a determined and experienced Minister there was the other road of simply cutting into government and demanding resources to create a new, but well endowed and high status university.'[154]

Such an explanation, which focused on the political process, did not do justice to the innovatory role of other busy people who were in the mainstream, most of them less of politicians than Michael was, or to their own positive attitude towards student needs. There was a touch of envy also in the reference to the new university being well endowed.

In fact, it always had to fight for its resources, which did not come from the DES. Even after the appointment of Walter (later Lord) Perry, formerly Vice-Principal of Edinburgh University, as its first Vice-Chancellor in June 1968 – indeed, even after it had secured its Royal Charter in July 1969 – its funding was insecure.[155]

It was determined to take in its first students in January 1971 (1968 had been the year first mentioned), but at the very last hurdle it was not certain how it would fare after the general election of 1970, when a new Conservative government took over with Edward Heath as Prime Minister and Thatcher as Secretary of State for Education and Science.[156] That had been one general election which Wilson (though not Michael) expected the Labour Party to win. It was crucially important that Thatcher gave the Open University her approval. It could not move ahead.

Michael did not seek to explain why she behaved as she did. Jennie's trust in a 'high status university' helped, but Michael would have preferred to see a 'less pretentious' college which cared nothing about status but devoted itself imaginatively to what he called 'flexi-learning', much of it at a sub-degree level.[157] 'We [and he was speaking for Jackson as much as himself] would have preferred to have avoided the whole idea and style of a university altogether and build a cheaper, more many-sided college whose hallmark was its concern with the established academic style.' Michael was uneasy too about the way in which the Open University had been devised by committees: although he looked for big names to give weight to his own activities, he did not expect them to make big decisions. He preferred 'experiment' by individuals and small groups, led by himself.[158]

Michael's individual contribution to the initiation of the idea of the University was recognised, and after the new institution had been founded on Jennie's lines, not his, he and Wilson were the recipients of the first two Honorary Degrees conferred at its first degree ceremony. By then Michael was prepared publicly to recognise Jennie's unique leadership role, although in accounting later for the remarkable success of the institution he paid most attention to the University's 'dedicated students': they demonstrated the kind of enthusiasm that he had spotted among the first 'mature students' that he had attracted to Churchill College in 1963 and thereby engendered confidence in others. He was to note in 1994 that 'the OU confidence level is all the more striking because it stands in such sharp contrast to that in the country's schools' and in 'ordinary universities' too.[159] Wherever he travelled, not least in Africa, he always carried this message with him.[160] He wanted the appeal to be from below, not from above.

Dealing long after the event with the period between 1965 and 1969, Michael ignored the fact that the NEC and the incipient Open University were sometimes in conflict with each other. Indeed, while professing the necessity for cooperation, the College was sometimes in uneasy alliance with bodies which for varied reasons and often in unison were seeking to hold back the progress of the University. They included the National Institute of Adult Education, the WEA (under a new Presidency), and, most important in terms of internal politics, the Association of Municipal Corporations, the County Councils Association and the Association of Education Committees, all of them bodies which then carried great political weight.[161]

None of them objected to an Open University *per se*. All, however, deemed its imminent start 'premature' and asked for more open planning in which they themselves could take part. All feared its impact, particularly its financial impact, upon them. Very wisely, Jennie took no advice from interested groups when she set up her first Committee, and it was on the grounds that the NEC was an interested party that she did not include Jackson on it.

Their fears, freely expressed in the press, which was largely hostile to the scheme, left Jennie unmoved. Her single-mindedness proved as effective as her enthusiasm, and by 1967 she was able confidently to include erstwhile critics, notably Sir William Alexander, then an ex-General Secretary of the Association of Education Committees, on her new Planning Committee. Dr. Eric Briault, then Deputy Education Director of the Inner London Education Authority, was one of the few people to serve on both of her committees. There were no people on the Planning Committee who were not prepared to work with a sense of urgency, and Venables, responsive to the mood – indeed, he shared it – ensured that work proceeded as quickly as possible.

In 1967, after the Open University's Planning Committee had been appointed, the NEC produced a document, 'Towards an Open University', which it still hoped would have an influence on policy. Two sections of the document, one of them Michael's Ditchley Conference Report, another Jackson's report on the College between 1963 and 1967, looked backwards: one, newly written, listed 'proposals for cooperation between the Open University and the NEC'. By then the gap between the plans that were being made for the Open University and the ideas behind the NEC, set out most fully in Michael's Ditchley Report, had widened, and there seemed little chance of the College being given public funds to strengthen its organisation by appointing Directors of Correspondence and Programming, of Broadcasting, of a Student Advisory Service, and of Research, the last of these, in Michael's opinion, particularly important.

Michael attached great importance too to a report of an inspection of the NEC carried out by Dr. John Blackie, formerly a Schools Inspector, which had been financed by the Dartington Hall Trust and had a Preface by Lord Bowden.[162] Yet it came out too late for the Open University's Planning Committee to consider. Michael had laid particular emphasis on courses at different levels, and, above all, on teacher training: the Planning Committee did not. Nor was the Planning Committee interested in the Bachelor of Commerce and Bachelor of Pharmacy degrees which the College had projected. Instead, it was devising one single Bachelor of Arts degree, with options both as to choice of subjects and the time taken to study them.

Michael still referred to London University, although he now believed that the new institution should have its own power not only to teach but to examine: the Planning Committee wanted it to be granted these powers by Royal Charter, a device which Michael never mentioned. It was the device that had been used by John Reith when the BBC was converted from a Company to a Corporation in 1927.[163]

Jennie herself did not hesitate to use the word élite: she rejected any idea of 'a poor man's University of the Air'. As she exclaimed in an important speech in the House of Commons in 1965, 'If we are to mount a really élite corps of lecturers – and nothing less than that has any relevance – and if we want a university of the air ending with a definite qualification which I should like to be nothing less than the external degree of London University ... one of the preliminary things that we must do is to find out where people would be able to study in peace and quietness.'[164] She wanted the broadcast programmes to be given in peak time and not early in the morning; and it was only after protracted discussions with the BBC on this subject, with Goodman as mediator, that she partly – but only partly – got her way.[165] En route she had told Parliament, in language which related directly to Michael and Laslett, 'we want no dawn patrols'. She also resisted 'utopian' demands to extend the new institution's influence. Michael talked of 'under-developed countries': the Planning Committee stuck to Britain.

In 1967, however, there was some contact between Michael and Jennie before the first Vice-Chancellor of the Open University was appointed. There were members of the Cabinet – possibly including Wilson – who would have liked Michael to obtain the post, but Jennie did not want him. Instead, she offered him a second-in-command position as Director, even suggesting before any other names were mentioned that he would be the one who would actually run the place. Probably she expected Michael to say no. He did.

After Perry was appointed, however, Michael invited him to Cambridge to meet the various people associated with him in the NEC – and elsewhere – and Nevill Mott gave him dinner at Caius College of which he was to become Master. It was then that Michael suggested Milton Keynes, a new town with a great name (half way between Cambridge and Oxford) as a centre for the new University; and when Perry showed interest in this highly imaginative idea Michael, the same night, telephoned Lord (Jock) Campbell, Chairman of the Milton Keynes New Town Corporation and a proprietor of the *New Statesman*, to raise the matter. In Michael's version Campbell 'jumped at the opportunity ... and was after Walter the following morning, and it happened'.[166] In retrospect, Michael claimed that 'Walter turned out much better than I would have been'.[167]

In parallel discussions Jackson and the Trustees of the NEC met Perry on 26 September 1968 after they had submitted a plan for possible cooperation earlier in the year and had received a visit from the Ways and Means Committee of the embryonic University on 25 March. The meeting was friendly, but it soon became abundantly clear that the sole task that the new University expected the College to undertake – and it would not be granted a monopoly in it – was the provision of 'gateway' courses.[168] 'The Vice-Chancellor was sympathetic to the idea of a gateway college, preparing students to enter the Open University, but he did not see how the NEC could become the sole preparatory body, except perhaps in its use of 'correspondence and broadcasting' facilities. No special funds could be made available. The Open University was still on the Civil List estimates and was not grant-aided.[169]

An interesting and important article of 1971 in *Where?*, both backward- and forward-looking, provides a climax to the story, a still unfinished story, told in this chapter. Written jointly by Laslett, Jackson and Michael, it was entitled 'On the Air: the End of a Phase'.[170] In two days' time, the authors began, Professor Michael Drake, a demographic historian, 'will give the first TV lecture' for the Open University. Just seven years before Hoyle had given the first of the 'Dawn University' lectures at 7.15 am. The reminiscences took account of the fact that 'what had happened at Cambridge' was 'only one of the series of movements and events which finally gave birth to the Open

University'. They referred to Wiltshire, the two Ditchley conferences and the years since 1963, 'packed with further experiments and consistent lobbying'. They also referred to Wilson, but not to Jennie Lee.

Most interesting of all, perhaps, the reminiscences recalled (and it had not been made much of at the time) that on the Thursday morning of the historic 'Cambridge Week', hard on the heels of a Dawn University lecture on 'Concentration', the Robbins Report on Higher Education had been published.[171] It had received far more enthusiastic press notices than either 'Dawn University' or the Open University, and the Conservative government, which was soon to give way to Wilson's, gave it its immediate approval: Alex Douglas Home (earlier and later Lord Home), who had succeeded Macmillan as Prime Minister, five days earlier, had waved the Report in his hand and assured the nation – on television – that it would be implemented soon.[172]

Thereafter, in the words of John Carswell, the civil servant then responsible for university finance, 'the Press, the public, the political parties, were full of enthusiasm for higher education, especially university education. Money flowed in abundance.'[173] Not quite so abundantly, however, as the money that flowed in *The Rise of the Meritocracy*. Nor, indeed, as abundantly as some of the new (and old) universities demanded or, indeed, required. Nor did it flow into either 'traditional' adult education or innovative open learning.

What the Robbins Committee had had to say on the convergence of communications changes and educational changes, the most important conjunction of the 1960s, had been unoriginal, unimaginative and flat:

> The second experiment that we think may prove practicable and of considerable potential value in this emergency is the establishment by some universities of correspondence courses. Here we draw on what we saw and learned in the Soviet Union. It would be necessary to ensure that the numbers registered for any particular course were such that the university teachers concerned could maintain proper contact with their students throughout the course and give them intensive teaching in the university itself in the summer vacation period. We think it likely that television as a technique of educational communication, may be found to have considerable potential value as an ancillary both for part-time and correspondence study.[174]

This was scarcely a clarion call. Nor, indeed, was the Robbins Report a clarion call to those new universities which owed nothing to it.

Jackson, Laslett and Young, in describing this Robbins paragraph, put it devastatingly simply: 'That was not quite the idea.' They also drew attention to divergences of outlook at a time when there was a quest for a new consensus.

> A Conservative believes that education should start from the universities and work downwards, a Socialist that education starts with the children and works upwards. If this be true, the Robbins Report, admirable though it is in so many respects, is fundamentally a Conservative document.

Michael conceded that 'the Socialist can go a long way with the radical Conservative': both could support the Robbins Report 'as much as the Beveridge Report'. Leaving communications technology on one side – and there could be consensus on that – 'where they part[ed] company was over selection', selection at 18+ (or later) as well as at 11+. This was the link with *The Rise of the Meritocracy*. According to Michael, Wilson's University of the Air, if 'properly managed', could have as many external students by 1970 (one year before its actual opening) 'as there will be in all the ordinary universities combined'.

The last part of the 1971 article, that which looked forward, treated what had already happened as no more than a 'phase', and made a plea for a *continuing* revolution in higher education, a 'perpetual dynamic'. 'It would be a sad reduction of ambition if all [that] we did were to welcome the Open University and watch it settle in its seat as a kind of extra-mural visitor, well below the salt.' And sadly that was the reaction of a majority of University Vice-Chancellors who, resenting the fact that the new University was funded directly by the DES and not through the UGC, delayed Perry's admission to the Vice-Chancellors' Committee.

Three lines of future action were suggested by Michael, Laslett and Jackson. First, the Open University was 'uniquely placed to mount – in action – a public critique of university education'. 'All its negatives' should 'be turned into positives'. Second, the University should press hard to attract working-class students: it should not concentrate on the professional middle class. Third, it should assist in the provision of open learning abroad. 'If Nigeria built a new school every week from now on until the year 2000, she would still not have a network of schools as good as that which William Forster inherited in Britain in 1870', the year of the first National Education Act.

For a mixture of public and private reasons, as there had been ten years earlier when Michael moved to Cambridge, the third of these objectives now seemed to him to be the most important, and he decided to move again himself, not permanently, but on a series of travels. A year before the first Open University broadcasts, which were extremely well received – and which, open to everyone as they were, had a large overspill audience – he had given up the Chairmanship of the NEC (Mott took his place) in order to devote the whole of his time to creating and developing an International Extension College. Africa beckoned. He too was entering a new phase, as Chapter 8 of this book reveals.

Before turning to it, however, it is necessary to look back in Chapter 7 at his years as Chairman of the Social Science Research Council. He was just as interested in educational change then as he was earlier and later in his life, and much in the chapter is directly or indirectly concerned with it. Yet the research that he supported personally as well as in his role as a strong Chairman of the Council was broader in scope. 'Society' was its remit, and many of the programmes that the Council supported were designed to stimulate innovative social enterprise in explicitly different spheres.

7
Necessary Research

Michael was soon to move into a bigger world. Yet before he did so he saw his dream of a Social Science Research Council become a reality with himself in charge. He had already brought it into existence unobtrusively and fictitiously in *The Rise of the Meritocracy*, although he did not date its inception. Before that, one section of *Small Man: Big World* had been headed 'Support for Social Science', and before that, leading back into a time largely forgotten in the 1960s, the context of the last chapter, he had been intimately involved in the preparation of two relevant Labour Party memoranda on the subject in June and October 1948 (RD 118 and RD 172), which set out two basic propositions: 'the need for more knowledge is immense and urgent' and 'more knowledge means more research'.[1]

The first memorandum, RD118, had been approved by the newly-formed Scientific Policy Committee of the Party, which held its first meeting in May 1948 and which initiated RD172. It referred to the support given to the idea of a Social Science Research Council, particularly by the Association of Scientific Workers, but concluded that it would be 'unwise' to set up a Research Council responsible to the Lord President. Nor did it favour a national survey of research projects at that time. 'Economics apart, the social sciences in the narrower [sic] sense – sociology, social psychology and social anthropology' – were still 'very much at the beginning', and a central directing body entrusted with the task of 'surveying nationally all problems requiring social science research; and of arranging for the highest priority projects to be carried out by existent research agencies in universities or elsewhere, or alternatively by its own research units', might do more harm than good.[2]

This was scarcely a promising start. The second memorandum, RD 172, sent to Nicholson in October, written by Michael and revised by Nicholson, was far more positive. Recognising 'the need for more knowledge' to deal with 'an immediate crop of urgent economic and social problems' which it listed, it praised the work of independent institutes and urged that since 'the Labour Party [had] always been concerned with the human consequences of development in the natural sciences' it was 'now time' for 'the aid of the social scientists [to] be brought to the assistance of all those who wish to improve the welfare of mankind'.[3]

There were touches both of Michael and of Nicholson in this paper, which recommended the setting up of a Council acting both as a clearing house for information and as a channel for public funds. Yet Morrison, having received it and discussed it with Nicholson, decided against the recommendation, as did Cripps, Chancellor of the Exchequer, to whom Morrison referred it. While that did not end the matter, further pressure behind the scenes was equally unsuccessful.

On 31 May 1949 Morrison met a deputation led by Laski, who warned of what came to be called a brain drain of social scientists to the United States, but once again the case for an SSRC was turned down. Treasury opposition remained forceful, and in the last resort decisive. Morrison, who did not seek to resist it, publicly confessed in 1959 to the House of Lords, to which he had moved after the fall of the Labour Government, that one reason why he did not persist in arguing for a Council was he did not know just what the words 'social sciences' meant.[4]

He was not alone in this. And some who more or less knew – some of them were economists – were sceptical about the use of the word 'science'.[5] One natural scientist who was not was Lord Adrian, Master of Trinity College, Cambridge, and in 1959 President of the Royal Society. As a physiologist he spoke strongly in favour of a 'Human Sciences Research Council'. He had put forward the idea five years earlier when he was President of the British Society for the Advancement of Science.

Research does not seem to have figured prominently in Michael's many talks with Crosland during the late 1950s and early 1960s before the Labour Party won the general election of 1964. Public school reform did. Crosland, who had been an Oxford tutor in economics, had not once mentioned research in *The Future of Socialism*, where there were three footnote references to Michael's work.[6] Nor did he in an article in *Encounter* in July 1961, called 'Some Thoughts on English

Education',[7] the first version of his book *The Conservative Enemy* (1962), where he argued that 'the public schools offended against "the weak", let alone "the strong" ideal of equal opportunity: they offended even more against any ideal of social cohesion or democracy'.[8] For Michael as for Crosland, public school reform was always on his mind, whatever the major items on the political agenda, and before he became Secretary of State for Education and Science in 1965, Crosland asked Michael to prepare a behind-the-scenes report on the future of the public schools, nominally for the Fabian Society. They were both enthusiastic about the idea of a Royal Commission on the Public Schools, Crosland, knowing as a leading politician that abolition of the public schools *tout court* was 'politically out of the question'. One of its tasks would be to examine an idea put forward by Vaizey that an 'Educational Trust' consisting of 'independent and impartial persons' should oversee their transformation.[9]

Placed in office, however, Crosland found it difficult to persuade senior civil servants, who were sceptical about the idea of an 'educational trust', that a Commission should be appointed with the remit of advising on the best way of integrating the public schools into the state system. In his own words, 'they rightly challenged me on whether there was any possible compromise solution which a Commission could recommend [in relation to the full integration of private and public schools in one system] and which stood a chance of acceptance on both financial and political grounds'. With Michael's backing behind the scenes, Crosland held his ground, 'insisting' on a Commission, but he got his way only to realise 'at the end of the day' that 'much of their scepticism eventually proved justified'.[10]

It was against this background that Crosland took a decision that changed the course of Michael's life. In his own changed circumstances he felt that Michael was not the right person – nor did he have the necessary 'weight' – to act as Chairman of a Commission, and completely in character, he did not hesitate to tell Michael himself. Instead, he offered the post to Newsom, and made Michael Chairman of the new Social Science Research Council. None of the reasoning (or feeling) behind this switch was made public, of course. Indeed, in public Crosland could still state, apparently firmly, in March 1965 that 'we must either have a proper reform of them [the public schools] or not at all'.[11] In private, according to his widow, he was coming to view the public school situation as 'a strictly intractable problem' and at this stage of his political career turning his back on 'reforms that could not be made now'.[12]

Irrespective of his judgement that Michael would not be the right person to chair the Commission, he had no confidence in its success, for he knew by the Spring of 1965 that not everyone in his own Party – or, indeed, in the Cabinet – was willing to treat public school reform as a priority, however it was approached. When he first raised the issue in May 1965 with the Cabinet Social Services Committee after having taken over from Michael Stewart as Secretary of State, it was formally decided that 'the moment was not propitious for stirring up another major row, and that action should wait till the autumn'. Stewart, a long-standing advocate of comprehensive schools, did not wish to touch the subject of public schools, and before moving from the Department to the Foreign Office, he never even acknowledged the full report on them that Michael had prepared.[13] Crosland had to give a stalling reply to questions in the House of Commons, therefore, before conducting 'a leisurely series of meetings' at which he said that he 'would listen rather than talk'.[14]

In Michael's long-term interest, therefore, it was important for him that he should be offered the Chairmanship of the SSRC, which had a future ahead of it, and to which there was no opposition in Parliament from either side: when Crosland announced it on 2 June 1965, a leader in *The Times* read 'The Social Sciences Arrive'.[15] On the question of public schools, however, there were always party political differences, and the Chairmanship of the Public Schools Commission, with an awkward remit, was a thankless task. Crosland deferred the announcement of Newsom's appointment until December 1965 after Michael had taken up his new post.[16]

None the less, Newsom did his best. His Vice-Chairman, David Donnison, was a colleague of Michael's; and one of the members of the Commission, who shared many of Michael's views,[17] particularly on educational expansion, was Vaizey – who for a time had been in charge of ACE:[18] he was to be sufficiently impressed by one public school, Eton, to send his son there. Like Michael, Vaizey attended a small and informal education group which met in Crosland's house. 'I suppose they were mostly academics,' Crosland recalled, 'although the atmosphere was completely non-academic.' As one of the academics myself, I confirm his recollection.

The group gave Michael an opportunity to learn what was going on in Whitehall and to question Crosland at critical moments, as during the week after he had delivered an influential speech at Woolwich to the Association of Teachers in Technical Institutions, which hardened the lines of a 'binary system' between universities and polytechnics. The scheme had been recommended to him by Toby (later Sir Tobias) Weaver, his over-powerful and opinionated Deputy Under Secretary of State in charge of higher education.

Another member of the same informal group – and of the Public Schools Commission – was Annan, educated at Stowe, who figures so prominently at different points in the background of Michael's life. There were two comprehensive school heads on the Commission also, W. F. Hill of Myers Grove at Sheffield and H. G. Judge, who was later to become Head of the Institute of Education in Oxford. Bernard Williams, later to become Provost of King's College, Cambridge, then married to Shirley, was the almost obligatory philosopher in the Commission's midst, with a more difficult task than Ayer had on the Plowden Committee.[19]

Characteristically Crosland was frank (or 'rude') – as he was to all his friends and to many of his associates – when, having told Michael that the public schools were somebody else's business, he also told him, not entirely jokingly, that while the SSRC was 'all yours, and you can experiment where you like', he would warn the other members of the new Council at the start that 'you're a wolf in sheep's clothing. And so you won't be able to run away with it too much.'[20] Crosland duly kept his word when he spoke at the first meeting of the new SSRC in February 1966. But did the members, all of whom had been appointed following discussions with Michael, need to be warned? How many of them had read his new book *Innovation and Research in Education*, the first book he had published for some years, which set out very clearly his views on research and presented the case, incontrovertible as Michael saw it, for 'linking research and innovation'?

Education at all levels and in all types of institution (and outside them) was the main area on which Michael focused when he looked both for this vital link and for an equally vital link between research and action. His Institute of Community Studies had already made a few sociological studies in education, produced as numbered volumes in the Institute's series, published by Routledge and Kegan Paul – B. Jackson and D. Marsden, *Education and the Working Class* (1962); P. Marris, *The Experience of Higher Education* (1964); and B. Jackson, *Streaming: An Education System in Miniature* (1964).[21] Before going further, however, it seemed desirable to stand back and ask the question: 'What sort of research is going to be most worth doing in the next ten years?' In Michael's opinion there were no 'objective' criteria.[22] He believed also that given that 'innovation research' was most 'needed', teachers and administrators were 'as necessary to it as professional researchers' were and could do a 'great deal themselves on their own'.[23]

Universities did not figure directly in this agenda, although they were to figure prominently in the formal agenda when Michael became Chairman of the new SSRC. They were difficult institutions to handle even for a conventional university professor, and they were wrestling at this time with the problem of the relationship between teaching and research. Thus, at the Home Universities Conference of 1966 – and these conferences were important annual events – the Vice-Chancellor of Brunel University, a former College of Advanced Technology, asked why 'universities with all their research experience' did not try to find out why there were some students who wanted to stay on one side of the binary line, now defined and defended by the Department, rather than the other. 'Why do we not do more research on ourselves and on the problems which intimately concern us?'[24]

Michael's book, written before he was caught in the thickets of officialdom, started with a reference to Wells, who had never been to a university and who had treated schools as 'instruments to restrain not innovate',[25] and ended with appendices on educational research in the Soviet Union (by W. D. Wall) and 'educational research in the light of Australian experience'. There was an ambitious reference to five possible new Institutes – for Teaching Method; Child Development; Special Education; Research Method; Innovation ('to deal with "fashion" and the spread of innovation'); the relations between home, community and school; Technical Education, Teacher Training; Economics and Planning of Education ('including in the underdeveloped countries; and Higher Education'). Different ways of directing these were outlined, and there was a brief reference to the Heyworth Committee which, Michael stated, was expected to recommend the setting up of a Social Science Research Council.

It was the existence of this Committee, appointed by a Conservative Government, and the timing of its Report which made it possible for Wilson's Labour Government of 1964, with its tiny overall majority of three, increased to 98 at the general election which he called in March 1966, to launch the SSRC. Although party politics had not been involved, the setting up of the Committee had been protracted and contested – by civil servants more than by politicians – with the Treasury the main, but not the only, source of opposition. Strong political support had been necessary, and it had come from both Conservative and Labour Members of Parliament.[26]

R. A. Butler, whose path and that of Michael often crossed, had recognised the need for research in the immediate post-war years, research directly related to policy-making;[27] and now, having moved to the Mastership of Trinity College, Cambridge, he was even talked of as a possible Chairman of the new SSRC. The Conservative politician who played however, the front-line part, in the appointment of the Committee was Lord Hailsham, Lord President of the Council, who in 1959 had also been given the new post of Minister of Science when it was split off from Education.[28] There were other politicians who were helpful when necessary. Thus, W. F. 'Bill' (later Lord) Deedes stepped in and gave useful behind-the-scenes help, as he often did, in the autumn of 1962.

It mattered substantially that the Chairman of the Committee that prepared the Report on social sciences, Lord Heyworth, former Chairman of Unilever from 1942 to 1960, had long been interested in research as, indeed, had Unilever, which had a strong research department, that was directly involved in social as well as in product research.[29] He had served as a member of the National Coal Board from 1949 to 1955, when Michael knew of him, and, more immediately of relevance, on the University Grants Committee from 1954 to 1958, where he was close to Murray, its Chairman.[30] Most important of all, as Chairman for 21 years of the Leverhulme Trust, which gave invaluable support to individual and collective researchers – the level of support was dependent on the scale of Unilever profits – he was committed to education and to research by the terms of the first Lord Leverhulme's will,[31] from which the Institute of Community Studies itself had directly benefited.[32] In 1967 Heyworth was to be made a Visiting Fellow at Nuffield College (a centre of research in the social sciences), one of four, among them Morrison, who remained far more sceptical about the social sciences than Heyworth ever was.[33]

The influential Heyworth Report, very much a product of its times, was different in content and in intention from the draft paper which Michael had written for the Labour Party in 1948 when he headed its Research Department.[34] Yet the fact that Wilson acted so quickly after its publication seemed in tune with the times. It owed something too, of course, to the fact that a number of Labour Members of Parliament, when in Opposition, among them Judith (later Dame Judith) Hart, had been putting pressure on Hailsham. They felt that the Party itself was committed.

One of the members of Heyworth's small Committee – its smallness added to its influence[35] – was Annan, who in 1966 was to move from Cambridge to London, where he became Provost of University College and, from 1968 to 1971 Vice-Chancellor of the University of London. Another member, Charles (later Sir Charles) Carter, economist, first Vice-Chancellor of the new University of Lancaster (1963), and the Chairman of the Centre for Studies in Social Policy, was to figure in

Michael's future. He was to play a key part in 1978 in the amalgamation of CSSP and PEP, the affairs of which never ceased to concern Michael, within a new research body the Policy Studies Institute (PSI), an amalgamation which Michael did not like.

A third member of the Heyworth Committee, added late, was Sir Austen Bradford Hill, who had made his mark as a pioneer in statistical and epidemiological research leading up to the identification of smoking as a cause of cancer of the lung. Michael had been sufficiently impressed by his findings to give up smoking.[36] That was a link of a unique kind.

The other two members of the Heyworth Committee were not known to Michael – Sir Charles Wilson, a former Oxford tutor in politics, who in 1961 had moved from the Vice-Chancellorship of the University of Leicester to the Principalship and Vice-Chancellorship of the University of Glasgow, and Dame Mary Smieton, Permanent Secretary of the Department of Education and Science from 1959 to 1963, one of the few women to hold that post. She had met Heyworth through the University Grants Committee, but when she joined his Committee as an ex-civil servant she was moving into new and unfamiliar territory.

She was not alone in this. When Crosland asked Michael to be Chairman of the new Council which the Heyworth Committee had recommended, he did not find many officials in the Department of Education and Science who knew much about the subject of research or were particularly interested in it, even those who had cooperated with Michael fully when he was writing his report on the public schools.[37] The Secretary of the Heyworth Committee, A. B. Cherns, was well informed, however, and had his own angle: he was Head of the Human Sciences Section at the Department of Scientific and Industrial Research,[38] and was later to join Michael as Scientific Secretary of the new Council before leaving to take up a Chair in Sociology at Loughborough University. That was before Michael himself moved on in 1969.

The Heyworth Report noted in a chapter called 'History since 1945', one of nine, that while a previous committee, the Clapham Committee, had reported against the idea of a Social Science Research Council in 1946 on the grounds that the universities were 'short both of staff and of the resources they needed to pursue their research',[39] this was no longer true. By then there were far more social scientists too. In 1946 out of 889 university professors only 35 held chairs in the social sciences, defined (in somewhat strange order) as 'economics, economic history, anthropology, industrial relations, social science, social psychology, demography, economic statistics, commerce, sociology and political science'. Twenty years later, the comparable (or nearly comparable) figure was around 200.

A different area of research concern, research leading up to the formulation of public policy, was just as important, if not more important, to Michael in the 1960s as it had been when he had headed the Labour Party's Research Department. Meanwhile, Clapham's recommendation that an Interdepartmental Committee on Social and Economic Research should be set up had not been effectively implemented. The duly appointed Committee, known as the North Committee after its Chairman, the Registrar-General for England and Wales, had been charged with the duty of surveying and advising upon research work in government departments, but it had been granted no power to administer research funds, nor had it succeeded in encouraging the 'consumers' of research, as it called them, those concerned with the application of research results, to list problems which they considered required investigation.[40] It had not met since 1960: some government departments had not even heard of it. Bureaucracy, as Michael well knew, was not favourable to new initiative. It disturbed too much. This had become all too obvious in the difficult discussions between different government departments which preceded the appointment of the Heyworth Committee.[41]

Before proposing a Social Science Research Council, the Heyworth Committee, as aware of the importance of enterprise as Michael was, collected evidence (300 submissions were received), held five informal seminars, and met for 29 days, including no fewer than 60 sessions of formal oral evidence. It meditated on the perceived differences between 'social sciences' and 'social studies' – more than a matter of language – and after recognising how difficult it was to draw 'definite boundaries between the social sciences' and other studies, it drew attention to 'the interdependence of the disciplines' and the need for 'multi-disciplinary research'.

One of its inevitably more superficial sections, included largely for 'the benefit of the layman', related not to such 'multidisciplinary' or 'interdisciplinary' studies but to the content and methodologies of the individual 'disciplines' themselves. Economics, which at first the Treasury wished to exclude from a Research Council agenda, came first, and sociology, according to the Report 'the discipline which people find most puzzling', came third. Yet, as was noted later in the Report, while the number of departments of economics (and psychology) had grown only steadily in recent years, sociology departments had grown with explosive force, extending 'from two or three centres to practically every University, including the new Universities and Colleges of Advanced Technology'.

Sociologists studied 'society in the large', the Committee reported, and 'the building up of a body of theory' was regarded as being of 'extreme importance'. The point was not pursued far, but it was clear that the kind of sociology that the Committee was seeking to describe was not quite Michael's: it might have been helpful if it had examined and outlined what that was. In the description of social anthropology that followed Michael must have been surprised to read, picked out as an item, that one of the signs of a switch of interest in social anthropology from 'underdeveloped societies' to contemporary British society was an 'enquiry into kinship structure in a middle class area in London', that carried out by Firth.[42] What of Bethnal Green?

The section on 'social administration' did refer, however, to 'the adjustment of families who have been resettled in the New Towns', while in a later section on 'administration' we learn (the source is not given) that, as in Molière's play *Le Bourgeois Gentilhomme*, the administrator, whether he knew it or not, was 'using methods and techniques to help him deal with his work and solve problems that a social scientist would recognise'. In a brief note on social psychology that followed, the subject was described as a discipline which covered 'the same problems as sociology, but emphasises the behaviour and reactions of the individuals who make up the group, institution or class which is being investigated'; and in a separate note on geography, not included in the list of outlined subjects, it was stated that there had been 'difficulty in developing 'the social side', but there had been a growth in "area studies"'. At that time, there were already the first signs of an increasing interest in environmental studies, linking the social sciences with the biological sciences, although these were not mentioned.[43] Five years later, this would have been impossible.

There were no references to history in the Heyworth Report, although it is the historian rather than the theoretician who will now take the greatest interest in these comments of the 1960s on the state of particular disciplines. Meanwhile, in 1965, a *Penguin Survey of the Social Sciences*, claiming that 'we are all sociologists now', commented on the special relationship between history and sociology and the 'wide-open frontier' between them, and reached the conclusion that 'whatever partners sociology may have (and these could usefully include philosophy or political science) it can and should retain its autonomy'.[44]

The Heyworth tour round the disciplines ended with law, included under 'social studies' in the University Grants Committee's categories. It had, of course, been Michael's starting point in the 1930s,[45] but, as Heyworth noted, there was still 'no centre for the encouragement of the study of law as a social science'. (There was no Law School on American lines either.) Education, however, Michael's main field of interest, was deliberately left within the remit of the Council as he had wished: the Committee rejected the demand for a separate Council of Educational Research (para. 158), which had been put forward by a 'Committee of Nine', set up by the Heads of University Departments and Institutes of Education.[46] 'The research disciplines in education are predominantly those of the social sciences,' the Committee concluded, 'and if the social scientists in the educational field were cut off from the mainstream this would detract from the contribution which they can make.'

In *Innovation and Research in Education* Michael had given a number of reasons for taking the line that the Heyworth Committee was to follow. First, a 'shortage of professional researchers' was not restricted to education: it applied to all the social sciences, so that if there were suddenly 'a great accretion of money for research', it 'would not follow that very much more solid work could be done'. Second, the prestige of educational research was so low that an 'SSRC concerned with social sciences as a whole should help a little to raise its standing', that is if the SSRC was prepared to devote funds to it.[47] It was not the Heyworth Committee that could guarantee that, however; only the new Council itself.

By far the most useful sections of the Heyworth Report – and, above all else, Heyworth wanted his Report to be useful – were those which surveyed, with relevant statistics, trends in 'postgraduate training'. They demonstrated forcefully, as Michael often had done, that the social sciences and 'related disciplines' were far behind both the humanities and science and technology. An Appendix gave details of grants 'earmarked' to universities between 1947 and 1958 under the terms of the Clapham Report: outside the London School of Economics, which was the main centre (£316,000), Cambridge came second with £89,950.

Another Appendix tabulated research institutes outside universities, eight of which (out of 18) had been founded since 1952. The Institute of Community Studies, which was described as having a staff of seven researchers and two administrators, had had grants of £25,300, all from Foundations, and came tenth in terms of total revenue. The Tavistock Institute of Human Relations, with a staff of 50, had received more income 'from Foundations, Industry, Government and subscriptions' (£157,310) than any other listed organisation, including

PEP, founded far earlier, which was said to have received £70,285. PEP then had a research staff of twelve, three senior administrators and three consultants.

The Tavistock Institute had produced its own paper *The Development of Research in the Social Sciences in the United Kingdom* which laid emphasis on 'field-determined' problems and on students acquiring 'deeper knowledge' of 'the nature and modification of human abilities and character'. Michael was familiar with this approach. It had influenced his own thinking. Looking ahead, the paper had postulated that 'first the biological and then the behavioural sciences would lay claim to a greater share' of public research funding, although mathematics, too, might require 'greater resources because of the cost of computer development'. Meanwhile, a range of independent institutes should be set up, including 'Natural Resources', 'Family and Household', 'Community and Region', and 'Developing Countries'.

The Heyworth Committee was favourable to independent research Institutes without classifying them as the Tavistock Institute tried to do, or going quite so far as Michael did when he identified research with innovation. The Institutes tended 'to pioneer research in special fields of a multidisciplinary character', the Committee observed: their approach was often 'fresh', and because they were financed almost entirely project by project, 'a certain standard of competence' had to be reached if funds were to be secured. 'Most of them [had been] formed in response to social issues of recent origin and therefore [drew] together people with a particular interest in one branch or another of social reform.'

There had been no reference to such institutes in two relevant numbers of PEP's *Planning*[48] in 1950 and 1951, and at that time there had been no Institute of Community Studies. Now Michael could claim through his study of research and innovation – admitting that he was 'no doubt even more prejudiced on this question than on [any] others' – that 'independent institutions' could do very important work, supported by groups of distinguished businessmen, public servants and professional economists.[49] Michael mentioned not only his own Institute, but PEP, the Tavistock Institute of Human Relations and the NIESR, which had been founded in 1938 as a non-profit-making body under the Companies Act of 1929. It was best known for its economic forecasts, but it also published *The National Economic Review*.[50]

Part II of the Heyworth Report, called 'Discussion and Recommendations', which ended with the recommendation that a

Social Science Research Council should be set up, recognised the need for 'independence' both in research and in organisation, without using the word. It set out some particularly pertinent observations which must have appealed to Michael. 'Problems in government or industry do not usually present themselves to administration in a fashion which at once shows how they could be clarified by research in the social sciences. The need, therefore, is for social scientists to work at points where problems first emerge and to help identify and deal with them.' Such problem orientation rather than orientation by discipline was beginning to characterise Institutes and Centres being created in some of the new universities.

The Committee countered some of the arguments against a Social Research Council. Would not its field be 'too wide'? No: there was 'a growing interdependence of the subjects'. Was it not possible for research to continue and expand on the basis of contracts, backed as far as Universities were concerned by UGC finance? No: 'Research Councils do not merely provide funds for a residue for research otherwise unsupported. Their duty is to keep under review the development of the science in their field.' Could not the British Academy do the job? No: 'the social sciences need more than a research grant programme, and it would be inappropriate to expect the Academy to perform the wider functions we are now describing.'

Not the least interesting paragraph in the Heyworth Report (No. 161), at least for a biographer of Michael, dealt with the Chairman of the proposed SSRC, to be appointed by the Secretary of State for Education and Science. From the outset he or she 'would have to establish, without question the independence and integrity of the Council. The goodwill and trust of Government, the universities, industry, and other users had to be won, and for this reason the Chairman had to 'be clearly independent and of sufficient eminence to obtain respect'. He would have 'a lot to do, particularly at the outset, establishing contacts with Government, with the other Research Councils, the University Grants Committee, the Universities and Research Institutes, and with user organisations; setting up sub-committees, devising an appropriate headquarters organisation, and finding the people to staff it. These considerations imply a full time appointment or, at the least, one [member of staff] with a minimum of other commitments.'

It was deemed essential that the part-time members of the Council, who would be discharging other tasks outside the organisation, 'should include a majority of social scientists together with men of practical experience in commerce and industry – management and trade unions – and from time to time, local government, voluntary agencies, and other areas of application of the social sciences.' Attention should be paid in their choice to 'the special needs of different parts of the country'. There should be no governmental representatives on the Council, but civil service departments should provide assessors.

The main model was clearly that of the University Grants Committee, which Heyworth knew well and on which he had served with distinction, although the three existing Research Councils were also in his and his Committee's mind. The Medical Research Council, which had acquired its Royal Charter as long ago as 1920, had set up a Social Medicine Research Unit in 1948 and had funded an Applied Psychology Unit in Cambridge, while the Department of Scientific and Industrial Research (DSIR), created in 1916, had shown an increasing interest recently in 'economic and sociological studies'.[51]

Prepared to concern itself with costs as well as with objectives, the Heyworth Committee proposed an SSRC expenditure, not all of it new, of £600,000 in the first year of operation and in the second year of £1,100,000. In the fourth year the figure would reach £2.26 million. There was more than a touch of rhetorical flourish in the final sentence in this section of the Report: 'It is our conviction that the additional expenditure by Government that we recommend will in the course of time be more than repaid by improvement in the efficiency of the national economy and the quality of our national life.' The Tavistock Institute's proposed figures had been more rhetorical than those of Heyworth. Estimating that £2.5 million was already being spent on support for social research, it suggested that this figure should rise to £25 million, £13 million of which should come from public funds.

Within five months of the publication of the Report of the Heyworth Committee the new Council received its Royal Charter, and at an informal meeting held in November 1965 Heyworth met Michael and most of the future members of the Council that he was to head, telling them that he had encountered interest and goodwill towards the new institution 'in all sorts of places'.[52] On this historic occasion Michael spoke too of his own aspirations and plans; and at the beginning of the following month by Order in Council the new body was given powers to operate, as was the new Science Research Council, within the framework of a Science and Technology Act, the new piece of Labour legislation, strongly Wilsonian in flavour, expressing his belief that there was an urgent need to develop new knowledge, particularly in technology, as well as to use to the full the nation's 'pool of ability'.[53]

Michael took great pains to find the right people to work with him on what was a completely new kind of assignment, as he did in all his labours, seeing more than 60 'possibles', yet the trade unionist on the Council, Len (later Lord) Murray, Head of the TUC Research Department, who was later (1973) to become General Secretary of the TUC, was not Michael's own choice but Crosland's. Nor did Michael then know the businessman, W. Campbell (later Sir Campbell) Adamson, an industrial General Manager who was to become Director of the Confederation of British Industry in 1969. Both were (at different times) Visiting Fellows of Nuffield College, and both had links with the University of Sussex.

Murray was to become a member of 'The Next Thirty Years' Committee', a novel SSRC committee to which Michael, who thought of it, attached particular importance. Could Murray have forecast what would happen to trade unions in the thirty years ahead? Could Adamson have foreseen the intricate complications of 'Britain in Europe'? Michael was to describe Adamson as one of the three best committee chairmen he had encountered. (The other two were Beveridge and Morrison.) In retrospect, he considered the 'laymen' on his Council 'a more powerful group ... than on any other Research Council, but by no means powerful enough to stand up to the professional phalanxes'.[54]

The academics on Michael's new SSRC, many of them well used to chairing bodies themselves, some members of 'professional phalanxes', included Titmuss and Firth from the LSE, with both of whom Michael had worked as a postgraduate pupil, not as a colleague. T. H. Marshall, author of *Citizenship and Social Class*, was one of the most widely read sociologists in the country: Michael was not to find him easy. The representative of politics, considered a 'wise man', a favourite word in the 1950s and 1960s, and to be related to Europe as well as to Britain in the 1990s, was Bill Mackenzie, an ex-Oxford don, who was to move from Manchester, where he had been Professor of Government since 1949, to Glasgow to join his Oxford friend, Charles Wilson. The representative of social psychology, Marie ('Mitzi') Jahoda, then of Sussex University, well known on both sides of the Channel and of the Atlantic, was the wife of the MP Austen Albu, who, having pressed hard for the foundation of the Council, was now from 1965 to 1967 a Minister of State in the Department of Economic Affairs: he was an active critic of 'bad management' both in industry and in government.[55]

G. D. N. Worswick, an Oxford economist and a committed socialist, became Director of the NIESR in 1965: he was the co-editor of a valuable volume *The British Economy, 1945–1950* (1952). There was another well-known Oxford figure, the historian, Alan Bullock, who had chaired the National Advisory Committee on the Training and Supply of Teachers in 1963. Sir William Hart, Director-General and Clerk to the Greater London Council, was a former Fellow of Wadham College (1926–47), the Oxford College that would appoint Claus Moser as Warden in 1978. James Drever, Professor of Psychology at Edinburgh University, a member of the Robbins Committee, was to become Vice-Chancellor of Dundee University in 1967. R. G. Lipsey, Professor of Economics at the University of Essex since 1963 – he had taken his doctorate at LSE in 1957 – was the writer of a much used textbook, *An Introduction to Positive Economics* (1963): his new university was specialising in the social sciences as a deliberate policy.[56]

Moser, soon (1967) to become Head of the Government Statistical Service, had been Professor of Social Statistics at LSE since 1961, and was to be a leading figure in British musical life: a friend and protégé of Robbins, he had been Statistical Adviser to the Robbins Committee. He was to become Chairman of the Royal Opera House, Covent Garden in 1974. Years later, when Warden of Wadham College, Oxford, he was to be Chairman of a non-governmental Commission on Education, backed by the Leverhulme Foundation.

Apart from Michael himself, the only representative of 'Education' on the SSRC was Lord James, the only name to be found (and quoted) in *The Rise of the Meritocracy*. James's meritocratic views were different from those of Michael, who came to regret that he had ever suggested his appointment. Yet they both attached great importance to teacher training, and James was to serve as Chairman of an official Committee to Inquire into the Training of Teachers in 1970–71. His Report was as controversial in 1972 as anything that Michael had ever written.[57]

None of these first members of the SSRC was close to Crosland, although Murray represented his trade union link, essential to his political career. He had anticipated Michael in criticising James, bringing in Plato as Michael did not.[58] None of the members had political careers ahead of them, although Bullock, biographer of Ernest Bevin (not chosen to serve on the SSRC as a historian), was a Liberal who was to chair a government Committee of Enquiry on Industrial Democracy (1975) which came to a number of conclusions which were similar to those which attracted Michael and which, like his, disturbed trade union leaders.[59] Like Titmuss, who died in 1973, he was to stay on the Council of the SSRC for only a short period, but he was to serve from 1966 to 1969 as Chairman of the Schools Council, another body that joined Wilson's institutional constellation.[60]

The first formal meeting of the SSRC, chaired by Michael and attended by all its 14 members, took place on 21 January 1966 at its somewhat drab new headquarters, State House, High Holborn, which were shared with the Science Research Council. In an address to it, which was the basis of a press release, Crosland, speaking as 'an ex-teacher of the Social Sciences' – Harold Wilson could have said the same – claimed in language similar to that which Wilson was using (and Heyworth) that investment in 'this field' – he mentioned no figures – would produce 'considerable dividends in many aspects of national life and well being'.[61] This thought always made Michael uneasy. While he recognised that the prospect of dividends seemed to offer the best argument for supporting the new Council, he found the concept of direct 'benefits' elusive, particularly in the short run. How quickly such dividends would accrue would be bound to influence opinion, on the biggest of all issues – and he was not sure that it had been finally settled – as to whether there should continue to be a Council at all.

Michael was right to be concerned, for when he addressed the Parliamentary and Scientific Committee of the House of Commons in July 1966 – after an 'elaborate dinner' – he was given what he called later 'a dreadful grilling' – the MPs (and they must have included people who had willingly accepted the setting up of the SSRC in the brief and unanimous Parliamentary debate) 'kept asking me for three hours why any more ... taxpayers' money should be spent on the social sciences'. 'Some of the MPs seemed to be as hazy as Morrison had been in 1946 about the nature of the social sciences. They were thought to be something to do with the social services and social work. Like many others, they [the MPs] were surprised that economics was a social *science* at all.'[62]

So far, there had been little talk either among MPs or outside Parliament of the differences between 'useful' and 'useless' research, although the differences were touched on in 1966 in a Committee headed by Dr. Jeremy Bray, a Labour MP, keenly devoted to the study of science policy.[63] For him and for Michael, apathy and ignorance seemed greater dangers to success than opposition in these first years of the SSRC. Even the dazzling talk of high technology appealed only to a minority of the population, and the social sciences could command far less attention than technology.[64]

Ominously, perhaps, the BBC devoted more attention to the foundation of the SSRC than did the press, with the notable exception of *The Times*. None the less, as Michael recalled years later, 'there was much in our favour. The economy was apparently in permanent crisis, but not so economists, and still less some other social scientists. Within the expanding universities the great boom of the 1960s in the social sciences was well under way.'

In the second Annual Report of the Council it was noted that the number of full-time students admitted to 'social studies' faculties had increased by an estimated 62 per cent between 1962/63 and 1966/67 – 'and by very much more' in certain individual studies, such as sociology and psychology – whereas the total number of students in all subjects had increased by just over 50 per cent.[65] This in itself seemed ominous rather than encouraging to observers who doubted the 'healthiness' of this boom. They were to become vociferous, however, only after the economic and political crisis of 1973–74 when the 1960s were being surveyed in retrospect.

The five objects of the SSRC, set out formally and extremely generally in its Charter, all looked to the future. They were based, not on Michael's definitions, but on the earlier recommendations of the Heyworth Committee. The first was 'to encourage and support by any means research in the social sciences by any other person or body'. The second, 'without prejudice to the foregoing paragraph', was 'to provide and operate services for common use for carrying on such research'. The third was 'to carry out research in the social sciences', and the fourth 'to make grants to students for postgraduate instruction in the social sciences'. The fifth was 'to provide advice and to disseminate knowledge concerning the social sciences'.

Great attention was attached to finding the best postgraduate students – the 'seed corn' of the future. Immediately, therefore, the choice and care of postgraduate students in the social sciences, which accounted for half the SSRC budget, was taken over from the Department of Education and Science. There would be difficulties. 'We were almost bound to make a mess of it,' Michael was to recall later.[66] Yet he delighted in the challenge of doing new things, as he always did, and enjoyed most his first months in the Council. Briefly he had been the only member of staff, and he had had the illusion of freedom, 'hardly less sweet' because he was aware that it was an illusion.[67] He had chosen himself to be paid only half-time, and in the rest of his time with the Council he was also able to work – or rather, as always, to overwork – for the other half in the Institute in Bethnal Green and in Dartington. Having 'settled in', if not settled down, he was quickly entangled for the first time in his active life within the mesh of a huge institutional complex, accountable to Parliament for all his Council's actions.

There may have been more than an illusion of freedom in that Crosland made it known in 1966 that in his dealings with the new Council he would not be seeking 'for the time being' the advice of the Council for Scientific Policy and would leave the SSRC to operate on its own. Nevertheless, Michael had to deal at once, in his own Council's interest, with the other Research Councils, learning in the process about academic relationships that hitherto had been completely unknown to him. He also had to ensure 'liaison' (including exchange of papers) with the University Grants Committee, presided over at that time by Sir John (later Lord) Wolfenden, a very different kind of person from himself or indeed from his predecessor, Murray, who was now a provider of private research funds through the Leverhulme Trust.[68]

In an effort to find his way through the labyrinths of power, in which he was recognised at once as one of the chief powerholders, Michael turned first to Sir Harold Himsworth, the Chairman of the most prestigious of the Councils, the Medical Research Council: in evidence to the Heyworth Committee it had declared that it was of 'primary importance to promote social studies in universities'.[69] In 1965 Michael visited one of the MRC's Working Parties and discussed at some length with Himsworth, eleven years older than himself, the relationship between reporting and decision-making. Not surprisingly, therefore, Michael invited Himsworth to address the second meeting of the SSRC. In retrospect – and doubtless at the time – Michael judged him 'a wonderfully persuasive advocate for the best of the traditional procedures'.[70]

There were others who were at Michael's side to carry out the traditional procedures, particularly Cherns, who was appointed the first Secretary of the Council, and the 'ever genial' H. C. Rackham, who had been Assistant Secretary in charge of external relations in the Department of Education and Science. What neither of them – nor Michael – could do then was to stop the Council staff from growing in numbers, so that by the Spring of 1967, when the SSRC was said to be 'coming to grips',[71] the total number of staff, most of them transferred from other Research Councils, had reached 30. By the Spring of 1968 it had risen further to 47 and by the following spring to 63. It was difficult in these circumstances for Michael to ensure that all the members of this staff shared his purposes, let alone his dreams. Yet it was they, not he, with whom applicants for research funding had to deal directly. In the beginning Michael had known all the members of his office staff as he did at Bethnal Green, and in retrospect he singled out 'the invaluable Hilary Clay, who combined dealing with

Studentships with handling Management and Psychology, and Dorothy Butterworth, who combined Research Grants and Economics'.[72]

By 1968 each sub-committee had a full-time Secretary and there was a Scientific Secretary, Jeremy Mitchell, whom Michael had earlier recruited for the Consumers' Association and who had stayed there until 1965 when he joined the National Economic Development Office. In appointing him Michael was establishing his own continuity – this time following non-traditional procedures.[73] There was, of course, a Finance and Establishment Officer, G. J. Sheppard, although it was not until January 1967 that a Budget Committee was appointed, and this did not meet until June. It regarded the 1968/9 grants figure of around £2 million, almost double that for 1967/68 (£1,129,000), as a base-line for 'a steep increase' during the following four years, reaching a target of £5 million for 1972/73. In fact, the Government approved a budget of only £1.7 million for 1968/69, Michael's last year as Director.

More difficult to deal with, perhaps, than the increase in the numbers of staff or the limits to funding[74] was the increase in the numbers of academics associated with the Council. Many of these were members of 'subject' sub-committees – initially there were eight of them – which operated on similar lines to the recently introduced UGC sub-committees. It was not easy in the academic disciplines to identify a community peer group, and as the SSRC extended its constituency, it did so at considerable cost. The choice of members of particular sub-committees sometimes raised eyebrows, more often it created jealousies. As the fascinating Report of the Council for 1968/69 put it, after Michael had ceased to be Director, 'the Research Council idea was a novel one to the community of social scientists [was it really a community?], and the first necessity [even before the establishment of subject sub-committees] was to make it clear that there was no intention of trying to take over from individual scholars responsibility for deciding the direction of their research.'[75]

The Council's approach, therefore, was, in the first instance 'producer-oriented', an orientation diametrically opposed to Michael's. 'Its policies were guided very largely by the existing academic interests of those engaged in the various social science disciplines – the improvement of their instruments of research, the perfecting of their methods and the furtherance of research themes which were already well established.' It took time to go further and to identify pressing research and training 'needs' as part of a 'research strategy', however the needs were defined.[76] Nor did it help that there was a lack of basic information. In consequence, the Research Council under Michael's direction, prompted and guided the collection of relevant data. That was one of its main functions.

It is far from self evident, however, that organisation of sub-committees by 'subject' or 'discipline', the UGC's way, was the best way of proceeding for the SSRC. It would have been better, Michael came to believe – and some believed it at the time – to start not with disciplines but with 'problems', in particular those that required an interdisciplinary approach, and to create sub-committees accordingly. By 1967, when a Committee on Social Science and Government had been set up, designed both to close gaps in knowledge of the social sciences and to plan an agenda for the future, which would draw in a range of government departments, his belief came to be shared by others, including some who were less concerned than he was with translating research into action.

In the early circumstances it was wise to decide to rotate the membership of the subject sub-committees, but there was little change in membership in the second year of the Council's life, when it increased its size by one. Half the members were then being appointed for one year, and a half for two years, with the new members of the Council including the statistician Professor Sir Roy Allen, who replaced Moser when the latter became Director of the Central Statistical Office, Lewis Waddilove, well known to Michael, who from 1946 to 1961 was in charge of the Joseph Rowntree Memorial Trust,[77] the economic historian (first Cambridge, then Oxford) Professor H. J. (later Sir John) Habakkuk, and the geographer Michael Chisholm, Reader in Geography and from 1972 Professor at Bristol University, then the most thriving university centre of geographical studies.

The last two represented 'disciplines' originally left out of the organising scope of the SSRC, but now welcomed to its ranks as Crosland had promised such disciplines would be.[78] Before they were appointed, the SSRC turned to committees chaired by two senior scholars to give advice. That on economic and social history (other kinds of history were excluded) was headed by Professor E. M. Carus-Wilson and that on geography by Professor Emrys Jones. The latter sub-committee, identified as Human Geography and Planning (the study of geography was split), had as one of its members Michael's friend Peter Hall, who kept them united, and it quickly organised a symposium in conjunction with the Centre for Environmental Studies on 'The Future of the City Region', in which Michael himself took an active part. The Labour Government had set up Regional Planning Councils, and the subject of regional planning had become directly related to policy studies.[79] Michael (and Hall) were to take it up again through the Social Democratic Party and the Tawney Society.[80]

One of the recurring themes at the symposium, dear to Michael, 'the diversity of human needs and life patterns on the one hand, and on the other hand the circumscribed range of choice that the majority of people are able to exercise', was to be one of the themes of *The Symmetrical Family* (1973), and one of the speakers was Michael's co-author Peter Willmott, who had prepared a background paper, 'The Influence of Some Social Trends upon Regional Planning'. Michael doubtless had Bethnal Green in mind when he suggested that there should be continuous rather than sporadic monitoring of new housing schemes and other developments, including new roads:

> An attempt should be made to find out before ... change [was brought about through planning] what people of various kinds who would be affected by the proposed change wanted; and then at various time-intervals after the change the same or similar people should be asked about their reactions to the change after it had been made and whether and how they had altered their preferences.[81]

Civil servants concerned with housing and planning were usually the last people who wanted this.

From the start, symposia and conferences were very much part of Michael's vision of what the new Social Science Research Council should be doing, and they brought into his *dramatis personae* young as well as established scholars, including people whom he had never previously met. At the symposium on 'The Future of the City Region', for example, two of the speakers were Professor Tom Burns of Edinburgh University,[82] a sociologist who did not fit into any obvious group of sociologists – he spoke on 'urban life styles' – and Dr. R. Pahl, Lecturer in and later Professor of Sociology at Kent University, who doubted, on the basis of studies in London's commuter belt, whether measurable indicators – kind of housing, range of domestic appliances and so on – really revealed 'true patterns of life'. There could be malnutrition in families where there were all the outward symbols of affluence.[83]

It is worth recording that in the same summer as this symposium a conference was also held on social indicators, and that in *The SSRC Newsletter*, which quickly became a valuable channel of communication, an account of it immediately followed the account of the 'Future of the City' conference.[84] Two invited French participants from the Commissariat Général du Plan had been unable to be present at the conference at the last moment, but Americans were.[85] So also was

Moser, who, as new Director of the Central Statistical Office, announced plans to bring out a series of regular reports called *Social Trends*, the first number of which appeared in 1970. It has subsequently proved invaluable to sociologists and historians alike. So, too, has a later publication, *Social Attitudes* (1982 onwards), which has gained in importance as sociologists and historians have turned, often controversially, from 'facts' to 'perceptions'.

In his closing remarks at the symposium Michael pleaded for the inclusion of a 'research opportunities' appendix in all future social reports. 'This would encourage researchers outside government to work out some of the chains of cause and effect – the relationship between, say, indicators for delinquency and those for education, housing and real income.' Whether 'chains of cause and effect' was the right term is open to question: there were always intricate interconnections. The word 'network', like the word 'trends', was being used increasingly at this time, applied not only to interconnections but to networks of information and to networks of people.[86] 'Multi-media' had not yet entered the vocabulary: 'networks of people' was a neutral term.

The openness of these early SSRC conferences and the publication of reports on them reflected Michael's sense of the importance of openness in all the Council's dealings. The idea of getting 'outsiders' to address Council meetings was very much his own. So, too, was appointing laymen like Waddilove as well as academic specialists, to join the Council; and as early as the Council's second meeting, names of other possible speakers were considered, including Bertrand de Jouvenel,[87] Dr. Alexander King, Director for Scientific Affairs in OECD, who had become an authority on the evolution of science policy, and C. D. (later Sir Christopher) Foster, Director General of Economic Planning at the Ministry of Transport.

Questions relating to transport, which came to interest Michael, were often at the core of policy-making in the 1960s, as they were to be 20 years later. This was the age of Buchanan (roads) following on after the age of Beeching (railways).[88] (The first motorway had been opened four years before Beeching.) There were some transport policy-makers and researchers who thought of their field as essentially technical, and there were research bodies which followed this approach. The SSRC was right to appreciate the human context of all technical development in transport and to start by looking at 'what [was] happening in urban and regional development rather than at what transport systems could or could not do'. These, however, were not the words of Michael but of one of his successors as Chairman, Sir Douglas Hague, in 1986.[89]

Michael heard different voices on transport and other matters in the 1960s. Indeed, differences of approach were evident when almost all social policies were being discussed. He never tried to silence any of them. Instead, he welcomed dissent. Examining the names of the first appointments to the Council or to its sub-committees or, indeed, those of their subsequent renewals or replacements, no charge of nepotism could ever be made. Michael had few personal friends on the subject sub-committees, which included some people who were suspicious of him. The only two people close to him before 1965 were François Lafitte, a member of the sociology sub-committee, and Jean Floud, a member of the psychology sub-committee, who was also serving on the Educational Research Board of the Tavistock Institute. The sociologist J. H. Goldthorpe was well known to Michael too and was directly interested in his work, and along with Michael Mann organised a lively conference on Social Stratification and Industrial Relations in the Autumn of 1968, which was chaired by T. H. Marshall.

The scholarly calibre of most of the members of the sub-committees was beyond doubt. Edmund (later Sir Edmund) Leach, Noel Annan's successor as Provost of King's College, and Professor H. M. Gluckman from Manchester University were on the first social anthropology sub-committee. D. N. (later Sir Norman) Chester, active and determined Warden of Nuffield College, Oxford, was on the political science sub-committee, along with Bernard Crick, future biographer of Orwell, who moved from LSE to Sheffield, and later to Birkbeck. On the economics and social studies sub-committee was a man with a future, Professor A. A. (later Sir Alan) Walters, appointed to LSE in 1968, who was to pass into history through his later political special relationship with Thatcher as Personal Economic Adviser from 1981 to 1984 and again in 1989.

Named last in the politics list in the first Report of the Council was another man with a future – Andrew Shonfield, who was present at the Conference on social indicators and who was to succeed Michael as Director in 1969. Like Michael, Shonfield was an able and imaginative non-academic, a journalist by profession and was treated warily, therefore, in some academic circles. From 1961 to 1968 he was Director of Studies at the Royal Institute of International Affairs and from 1965 to 1968 he was also a member of the Royal Commission on Trade Unions, headed by Lord Donovan, a body to which Wilson attached special importance.[90]

Shonfield set out some of his views in a forthright article ('forthright' was the best adjective to apply to him) in *Encounter* in June 1967 in which he expressed serious doubts about the efficiency of a Royal Commission as 'the traditional method of inquiry in the circumstances of the second half of this century'. Like Michael in this respect at least, he focused on the country's 'relative slowness to respond to change'. Its essential feature, he suggested, was not 'absence of energy in the conduct of government but failure of intellectual rigour in performance'.[91]

One subject area which was difficult from the start was psychology. It posed organisational problems which were familiar to Vice-Chancellors of universities, including Sussex, where Jahoda knew them well; and it required a Working Party of the SSRC, the Science Research Council and the Medical Research Council to decide how to divide the subject nationally. The SRC would be responsible for 'experimental psychology', the MRC for psychological research in relation to health 'in a broad sense', and the SSRC for social and developmental psychology. This was a despairing division which in the light of his own experience made no sense to Michael.

One of the most interesting members of the SSRC's Psychology Panel was Hilde Himmelweit, Professor of Social Psychology at LSE since 1964. Her knowledge of communications was immense and wide-ranging, and she had written one of the most discussed books of the 1960s, *Television and the Child*, two years before the decade began. She must figure prominently in any historical account of the period – at the centre of several (indeed, many) networks of public (and personal) communications. She was a friend of Lord Goodman, and was to become a member of the Annan Committee on the Future of Broadcasting in 1974, while through its years of early growth – and crisis – she served as a Trustee of the International Broadcasting Institute (later the Institute of International Communications), a body which then had a highly articulate and impressive Third World membership. Himmelweit was fully aware of the international dimension of the communications revolution – and, indeed, of most current social thought and action.

The first task of the subject sub-committees (along with other specially appointed groups, some of them organised on PEP lines) was to investigate the current state of research in their fields and to identify the main gaps,[92] but within a very short time, their main task, under the umbrella of the Council as a whole, was operational – that of dealing with the large and rapidly increasing number of applications for research grants. At first, these were considered by the whole Council, but there were felt to be so many of them in 1967 that powers were delegated to the Chairmen of the subject sub-committees to deal with applications for amounts of up to £2,000, one-sixth of the applications received: hitherto these powers had been reserved for urgent cases. In all, just over half the applications were approved (after some had been referred back), and these accounted for a third of the monies requested.[93] Most of the applications involved joint funding, and universities contributed the salaries of their full-time staff working on the project.

A minority of grants went to research centres, such as the Institute of Community Studies, that were not financed by the UGC. There the SSRC was able to pay salaries, overheads and computer time. Michael did not apply for or accept any grants for the Institute while he was Chairman. The SSRC was not authorised to carry out research by its own staff, even when it required to collect information that was necessary to its planning: it had to put out all research to outside contract. In 1968 it awarded contracts to study *inter alia* student loans schemes outside Britain (with particular reference to Scandinavia) and the career patterns of statisticians and economists.

Some of the applications were cross-disciplinary and had to be referred to more than one sub-committee, and from the start attention had to be paid also to 'peripheral studies' beyond the limits of those allowed for in the first remit. Michael, under pressure from inside government to approve the setting up of a new Environmental Research Council in parallel with his, was successful in keeping at least part of this inter-disciplinary field within his Council's remit, working in cooperation with the Centre for Environmental Studies, set up by the Government in Regent's Park, London, in 1966.[94]

Within the Council there were three other initial groupings besides the subject sub-committees, and these were to be added to later. The first was an Automation Panel, headed by Dr. A. T. Welford, who was not a member of the full Council: his panel had been set up by the DSIR in 1964,[95] and in his final report, published in March 1967, he urged the need for further seminars: 'the study of the human and social implications of technological change is potentially a productive field of research which has been very little explored'.[96] The second and third groupings Michael thought of as 'counter-committees', free from specialist bias. The first was concerned with 'management and industrial relations' and the second with education.[97]

The first of them was chaired by Adamson, and included among its ten members the trade unionist Sir William Carron, A. J. M. Wilson from the Tavistock Institute, who knew Michael well, Allan Flanders of Nuffield College, and Raymond Nottage, Director of the Institute of Public Administration. Like other *ad hoc* committees on management and industrial relations appointed by Wilson, it faced what proved to be insurmountable tasks, and despite its freedom from specialist bias, it did not achieve useful results. No answer to the deep-rooted problems of industrial relations was to be found there. Its Assessor, the shrewd and experienced economist Sir Alec Cairncross, close to policy-making – and as interested in policy-making in retrospect as he was at the time – perhaps ominously for Michael, came from the Treasury.

Michael was not familiar with the term 'Assessor', which had never previously entered his vocabulary, but Assessors could have ideas, and Cairncross was never lacking in them. He was soon to become Master of St. Peter's College, Oxford (1969) and Chancellor of Glasgow University (1972). He was also President of the Royal Economic Society from 1968 to 1970 and a member of the Councils both of PEP and of the NIESR.[98] No one was to take a greater interest in contemporary history, a subject which was the topic of an exchange of views between Michael and Peter Laslett.[99] Should a Centre be set up? In due course it was.

The second of the groupings, the Education Research Board, which had been proposed by the Heyworth Committee and which was chaired by Lord James, did not meet until March 1966. It was anxious to avoid any duplication with the National Foundation for Educational Research, whose Director, W. D. Wall, introduced an SSRC Seminar in March 1968 with a percipient paper on 'Future Trends in Education', acknowledging that 'there are so many things outside education which may effect future trends within it that it is necessary to make some kind of selection'. Education should be related to differential wants and needs over the 'whole life-span', and that would demand 'a tremendous development in guidance'. The school would become 'a community institution with very wide educational functions'.

James himself was 'uncomfortably aware of how much educational research makes virtually no impact on the schools',[100] and whatever other differences he had with Michael, he did not discourage him from putting forward imaginative and important ideas of his own, like that of 'educational priority areas'. The words, often shortened to EPAs, were Michael's own too.[101] He appreciated the need to increase the education budget. In *Innovation and Research in Education* Michael had quoted an MP who had noted that in 1962/3 DSIR had spent more on research into glue than the nation spent on research into education.[102]

'Action research', to be carried out in order to ensure that special treatment would be accorded to children in places where the total environment was unfavourable to their education and put them at a disadvantage, cost a lot of money, and the setting up of the priority areas depended on funding from the DES as well as from the SSRC.

Michael succeeded in securing such funding in cooperation with Halsey, who shared his sense of priorities in other fields also, and who from within knew the DES at first hand when discussions began.[103] Yet at first Crosland (at one of the private seminars held in his home soon after the publication of the Plowden Report – Toby Weaver was one of those present) told Michael and Halsey that there were no funds available. This was not the last word. In the discussions that followed, the idea of the SSRC being involved was mooted by Michael,[104] and after further discussions Halsey became Director of the project. This was the Social Science Research Council's first major investment in action research. Its share in the outlay was £75,000, that of the Department of Education and Science £100,000.[105]

On Michael's advice the Council decided to monitor research in five educational priority areas – Birmingham, Dundee, Liverpool, London and the West Riding of Yorkshire (Manchester had been the first Northern choice): uniform criteria of measurement were to be applied to very different environments. SSRC participation was justified by Michael on the grounds that it was highly desirable that when a new development was being planned in the social sciences 'it should be tried first on a pilot basis so that faults [could] be corrected and money saved before the change becomes general'.[106] He was to be consistent in advocating such strategies both as a member of the SDP and in the 1990s when new Labour came into power.

The share of the Department of Education and Science in the EPA scheme was to be devoted to buildings, but Michael did not feel that if it were restricted in this way it would capture the public imagination. He made efforts, therefore, to suggest to the DES that some of the funds which Crosland made available for buildings should be transferred to aid 'local action'. It did not help that when Crosland left the Department he was succeeded by Gordon Walker, whom Michael had never admired, but while ruling out a reallotment, Gordon Walker wrote sympathetically and helpfully to Michael that he understood his reasons. He added that he hoped that the SSRC had made progress with 'thinking about a "poverty programme" and that he would be very glad either [to act] jointly with the Council or to complement your own projects'.[107]

It was after receiving an official letter from Gordon Walker that the SSRC supported its own involvement in the EPAs Scheme.[108] But there were many hurdles to cross, before the West Riding (with Clegg's invaluable help) led the way in implementing it. The nub of it, as Halsey put it, was 'to encourage parents to join in the educational process. To foster the partnership between home and school it [was] necessary to move in both directions – to take education into the home and to bring parents into the school.'[109] Michael might have used the same words.

Halsey was also a member of a new SSRC Panel on Poverty Studies, created in March 1967, to which Gordon Walker referred. It was set up to deal with research on a subject which the Institute for Community Studies had pioneered from its beginnings. Townsend, however, was not a member. The Chairman was David Donnison, now a professor at the LSE, who addressed the whole Council on the subject in June 1967, the month when his Panel produced its first report. It had been given the formidable (if unoriginal) task of clarifying 'the character of poverty and its extent; identifying the main problems, examining the contribution that the different social science disciplines could make to understanding [its] causes, and assessing the efficacy of different policies for its relief'.

There was a curious sense of going round in circles at this time. When Donnison had been made Vice-Chairman of the Public Schools Commission, which Michael had hoped to chair, Crosland had drawn a forbidding picture of the Secretary of State having to go round talking to public school headmasters as his predecessor had done.[110] That was just what Donnison himself was now doing after succeeding Newsom as Chairman in 1968. Handed what one public school headmaster called a poisoned chalice, he had to face the whole Headmasters' Conference to which all public school headmasters belonged. It might well have seemed easier to deal with poverty research than with public school education.

Donnison's poverty report was less of a survey of existing 'literature' than an action programme, relating research on poverty to 'expected economic, social and administrative trends' and calling for the setting up of a research unit, independent of government but in close touch with government departments, which would conduct a continuing programme of interdisciplinary studies concerned with poverty. This proposal was not implemented, despite discussions with the government, but the report of the Panel was published for a wider audience, and there were exchanges of views behind the scenes between Michael, the Panel members and Gordon Walker.

In 1967 the first report of the Poverty Panel was discussed at an important weekend conference which Michael organised at Warwick University to examine future research strategy. It was important in the history of the Council since it raised the fundamental question as to whether the Council could and should initiate social research as well as respond to requests made from outside. There was an even bigger related question too. Could and should the Council support collective as well as individual research through newly established Centres? If it were to do so, specific governmental approval would be required.

Among the other reports calling for action, that of one of the first sub-committees – the Committee on the Next Thirty Years – was closest to the hearts both of Michael and Crosland, the latter unimpressed by the Treasury's approach to economic forecasting. Its remit was wide, although it modestly set as its first task consultation with potential users of research in industry, government and the social services about what kind of problems and new developments might arise in the future within the conventional span of a generation. Its second task, more difficult, was to identify what research might be usefully undertaken to influence major necessary decisions of policy. The Committee was to change its name in 1968 to the Committee on Forecasting.

At that time there was great public interest in this field. The word 'futurology' had been invented by Aldous Huxley after the Second World War, and now in the 1960s it became something of a buzzword. In 1963 Denis Gabor, keen student of computers, not yet thought to be the key to everything else, spoke of 'inventing' the future, and in the same year across the Channel de Jouvenel's *Essai sur l'art de la conjecture*, *Futuribles*, was published. It began, like *Innovation and Research in Education*, with a reference to H. G. Wells,[111] and an English translation soon appeared in 1967.

A year later, the British periodical *Futures* was launched, aimed at people working on futures research as well as people in government and management who were required to make long-term policy decisions; and in 1974 N. Cross, D. Elliott and R. Roy edited an Open University book of readings, *Man-made Futures*. By the 1970s there was a reaction, so that in 1972 Krishan Kumar, author of *Prophecy and Progress* (1978), could write in *Futures* of 'inventing the future in spite of futurology'.

Michael's own essay on 'Forecasting and the Social Sciences', which he published in book form – it was the first essay in the American collection of his essays, *Social Scientist as Innovator*[112] – followed de Jouvenel, whom he quoted, in pointing to the difficulties in 'the art of conjecture'.[113] He also forecast that 'the overall demand for professional forecasters is going to grow steadily for the next thirty years'. There were now more 'almanacs for the millennium', a phrase of George Eliot that he quoted, than forecasts based on the social sciences. He did not foresee how few of the latter there would be in the 1990s as a new millennium approached. He chose a motto from

T. S. Eliot at the head of his essay. People have to reconstruct the past and future continuously in their mind in order to do service in a moving present: 'And every moment is a new and shocking valuation of all we have been.'

Not surprisingly, Michael noted past mistakes in forecasting, 'predictions falsified', among them 'failure to allow for other people doing the same thing as oneself'. Taking examples of mistakes in studying manpower, housing and automobiles, he urged the need to draw not on one forecast but on independent alternative forecasts. He also stressed the importance of considering 'society' as 'a whole' – 'its parts are inter-related even if the manner is still not understood' – and of charting cycles as well as sequences. Such an 'engagement with forecasting' was 'some counterweight to all the other pressures bearing the other way, towards institutional specialization'.

Given the agenda of the Committee on the Next Thirty Years, Michael considered it important to link the SSRC with other scientific bodies, particularly the prestigious Royal Society; and in 1967 a joint symposium, informal in character, was held at which social and natural scientists discussed 'technological devices' that were likely to be 'socially significant' by the end of the century. The venture would not have been possible had it not been for the fact that the then President of the Royal Society, Sir Patrick (later Lord) Blackett, was himself keenly interested in the social context and social role of science, as was its Biological Secretary, Sir Ashley Miles. The Physical Secretary of the Royal Society, Professor M. J. Lightfoot of Imperial College, opened the symposium with a paper on technological developments.

In retrospect, the resumés of the papers that were read – and they did not peer very far into the future – are far less impressive than the names of the scholars present. The first prediction in Gabor's paper on the economics of abundance was that 'things cannot go on much longer as they are going now': Lord Bowden's paper on 'Education' called the Berlin Wall between East and West Germany 'a complete success from the point of view of the politicians who built it'.[114] Other participants included Sir Isaiah Berlin, Sir John (later Lord) Cockcroft, Lord Florey, David Glass, Sir Bernard Lovell, Sir Peter Medawar – and Professor Shils.

If the Committee on the Next Thirty Years and its offshoots provided Michael with his most interesting assignment as Chairman of the Council, the method of choosing postgraduate students in the social sciences provided him with his greatest difficulties – until routines had been established. Nearly half the SSRC's budget went towards postgraduate training in the social sciences: how to use the money most effectively was a challenge in itself. The officials of the new SSRC were far more familiar with the existing procedures than he was or, indeed, most of the members of the Council. Hitherto, postgraduate research awards had been dealt with in two different ways. The Department of Education and Science and the Scottish Education Department distributed their awards in national competition, while the Science Research Council employed a quota system under which quotas were distributed to university departments on the basis of their expectations of candidates' performance in their finals examinations. Which mode should the Council choose?

The competitive system was open: the quota system was protective and favoured established departments, leaving new institutions at a disadvantage. Yet it was the second system that the SSRC decided to adopt on Michael's recommendation in its first year of operation. He and his colleagues believed that it would encourage departments to make forward plans for training and research in the assurance that they would have adequate numbers and finance.[115] The forgone alternative, national competition, would have allowed the preferences of postgraduate students themselves to be taken into account from the beginning and would have allowed what were coming to be called 'free market forces' to operate. It would have enlivened the approach to research and could have been accompanied, as the Heyworth Committee had suggested, by special arrangements being made to initiate and develop subjects where there was felt to be a 'national' need.

On a lower plane it might also have saved the Council from some of the bitter controversy and intervention from outside which preceded an early change in arrangements in 1967. Matters had come to a head in July 1966 when a weekend conference of social scientists on the subject of postgraduate training was held at the University of Kent, attended by over 200 people, including representatives of most university social science departments and some independent research institutes, a number of university registrars – and a few students.[116]

Apart from Michael there were four other main speakers, Robbins, Wolfenden, George (later Lord) Porter, then Professor of Chemistry at the University of Sheffield and a future Director of the Royal Institution and President of the Royal Society, a unique dual qualification, and Dr. Clemens Heller, Secretary of the International Social Science Council. This was a top-heavy arrangement. There were three other foreign speakers outside the British academic establishment, Professor W. Baumol from Princeton, Professor J. Westerstahl from the University of Gothenburg, and Dr. V. Ahtik from the École Pratique des Hautes Études in Paris. Michael attached special importance to the last of these foreign institutions with which he had established a special relationship.[117]

Michael remembers the Kent conference as a turning point in his Chairmanship: he had never before seen so many angry people in one hall together.[118] 'For a great variety of reasons, almost to a man and woman they thought they were not going to get their proper number of postgraduate awards from this new and *dirigiste* organisation.' He was terrified, he recalled later, before the conference began, but after the ordeal was over 'it almost seemed downhill much of the way from then on'.

A wide variety of suggestions were made for improvement, and although some of them were mutually contradictory, the discussions were of great assistance to the Council when it came to revise the scheme for 1967/68. They also provided Michael with a peripatetic as well as with a continuing education, for during the following six months he spent much of his time, 'in a slightly obsessional way', devoting himself to 'the wierdly fascinating details of the new scheme', going round from one university to another with his Development Officer, Adrian Moyes, to 'conduct miniature public hearings'. He learned more at first hand then about universities than he had learned in the rest of his life before he became Chairman.

The Conference had revealed that there were serious problems not only in handling postgraduate awards but in communicating between State House and the universities, and one significant by-product was the *SSRC Newsletter*, launched late in 1967, as invaluable a source for historians as it was for the academics of the time. 'The *Newsletter's* correspondence column,' Moyes promised, 'will keep staff in State House in touch with the people they serve'. His hope, soon realised – and here he was echoing Michael – was that the *Newsletter* would also become a 'forum for discussion', a medium of ideas as well as of practical information.[119] Soon 6,000 copies were being circulated in university social science departments and research institutes, and 2,000 copies more in central and local government and in commerce and industry.

By the time that the first *Newsletter* appeared, the system of awarding postgraduate studentships had settled down. Michael had talked privately with Professor Barry Supple, then Dean of Social Studies and Pro-Vice-Chancellor at Sussex University and later to be Director of the

Leverhulme Trust, who stressed the need to take into account student preferences in 'a kind of shadow pricing mechanism'[120] – a conclusion already reached by Worswick and which was shared by a majority of the Professors who were present at the Kent conference.

Awards continued to be based on quotas, but potential candidates were asked at which university department(s) they would prefer to undertake their postgraduate studies. Departmental bids and students' preferences were submitted to the Council in February, and the Council's subject sub-committees used this information as their main guide in allocating departmental quotas. The total number of awards available was 535. The changes were set out in the Council's booklet, *Postgraduate Training in the Social Sciences*, designed to give students – as well as their professors and tutors – better information on which to base their choice of university department.

In 1968, when the SSRC was allotted 901 new postgraduate students, it made a careful review through its subject Committees of the taught courses which were then on offer, taking into account level, scope, power to attract students, quality, duplication and staffing. Nearly two-thirds of the 1968 award-holders started their postgraduate work at a university other than that at which they took their first degree. The distribution of students by subject demonstrated the pull of sociology among the social sciences, with economics a strong second and politics and international relations a powerful third. Education was low on the list and statistics was at the bottom. About one-third of the students selected had taken their first degrees in non-social science subjects.

When Michael retired from the SSRC in February 1969, its postgraduate scheme had succeeded in its original purpose, and this was a major achievement. Yet he had no desire to go on for a further term that was offered him, and would have retired at the end of December 1968 if his successor, Shonfield, had been able to take over immediately. In terms of the Council's history the change of command in 1969 – if that was the right word – was significant, but continuity was not broken. The four new members of the Council had all been members of its sub-committees. Burns, Leach, Professor R. C. O. (later Sir Robin) Matthews, then Drummond Professor of Political Economy at Oxford and joint editor of the *Economic Journal*, and Professor J. Tizard, Professor of Child Development at the London Institute of Education, succeeded James, Firth, Lipsey and Marshall. Matthews was to be Shonfield's successor when he retired in 1971. For Michael there was continuity of a quite different kind. He missed his last meeting of the Council in order to return to Dartington for Dorothy Elmhirst's funeral.

As far as the postgraduate scheme was concerned, there were limits to the Council's beneficent *dirigisme*. The review of courses that it had carried out covered only taught courses: it did not include postgraduate work based on a thesis. The independence of universities was retained intact in that sphere. It was appreciated, although little could be done about it, that the standards of performance determining degree classification – the basis of admissions into the Council scheme – differed significantly in different disciplines and, indeed, in different universities.[121] There was also a high fall-out rate once postgraduate research had begun or rather when it was well advanced. There was still much to sort out when the Council was asked by the DES to take over the burden of handling postgraduate courses with a training emphasis in management, planning and other social sciences: these had been hitherto been supported by local education authorities.

Most of these awards were lower in value than Council awards, and the request to the Council by the Secretary of State to take them over was not entirely popular with the local education authorities, the most responsible of which had hitherto spent much time choosing between well-qualified local applicants. To lose their powers seemed to them to be 'the thin end of the wedge'. They were right to be concerned.[122] Their independence in many spheres was to be greatly diminished in the future. This would have been a possible theme for the Next Thirty Years Committee as it was for Michael in the 1980s when as a member of the SDP he interested himself deeply in issues of local government.

Michael had written a farewell note to the Council, which appeared in the *Newsletter* in November 1968. Its title, 'The SSRC – Towards the Second Three Years', looked to the future rather than the past. Yet Michael began with the Heyworth Committee and the subsequent setting up of the Council, asking flatly, 'Who became any less sceptical about the social sciences just because a new Council had been set up?' And he gave his own frank answer. 'Certainly not the majority of politicians and civil servants who control the money. They have learnt about the oddities of human affairs from peculiar first-hand experience. They are not natural champions of the view that these affairs might, even in small particulars, yield to a scientific approach.'[123]

Nevertheless, Michael discerned some shift in attitudes since 1965, themselves part of the same shift which had earlier produced the SSRC. Three official enquiries – Donovan's Royal Commission on Trade Unions, the Seebohm Report on Local Authority and Allied Personal Social Services, and the Fulton Report on the Civil Service – had each acknowledged the importance of research and the need to pursue it further.[124] The last of these had encouraged Michael most, not only because he was aware of the importance of the civil service in policy making as well as in administration, but because the Fulton Report covered all aspects of government when it stressed, as PEP might have done, that 'research is the indispensable basis of proper planning'.

> The staff of Planning Units should develop close contacts with the appropriate experts both inside and outside the service. They should be aware of, and contribute to, new thinking in their field. They should also be trained in, and have the capacity to use the relevant techniques of quantitative analysis.

Fulton had just ceased to be Vice-Chancellor of the University of Sussex when his Report appeared.

'My guess is,' Michael commented, that the Fulton Report along with the other two reports would 'hasten ... official recognition of the value of social sciences'. Before he made this guess, however, he had encouraged the Council – with Government support – to strengthen liaison between civil servants and academics and had invited government departments to appoint Academic Liaison Officers, 35 of whom had been named by the end of 1968. He had also set up a cross-disciplinary Social Science and Government Committee, consisting largely of Council members and members of Council sub-committees, among them Professor E. Grebenik of the University of Leeds, who was to be the first head of the Civil Service College set up after the Fulton Report.

Michael had also explored the possibilities of providing links with Members of Parliament and their Select Committees, mentioned specifically when the Social Science and Government Committee was set up. Indeed, he had invited Ian Mikardo, who would not have been everyone's choice, to write a short article for him on the opportunities and the problems of doing so.[125] The Social Science and Government Committee had already taken the initiative in exploring how far the House of Commons Library could be of use to social science research and in serving MPs. A Council conference held in the Library in November 1968 was the first meeting of outsiders ever to be held there.

Surprisingly, perhaps, given the statistics of growth set out in the annual reports of the Council, Michael was 'less sanguine' that there would be proper support in future for training and research in the universities and institutes, It was necessary to persuade government not only of the importance of research, as the three Reports he noted had attempted to do, but of the necessity of supporting social science work in universities. Thereafter, the need for funds would grow. 'Although we may be cheap [and he was thinking comparatively, with other Research Councils in mind], we are not as cheap as we were. It is no longer possible to do "research" with no more equipment than a pencil sharpener.' Increased funding was urgently needed: cuts, more likely, would be disastrous. 'It would be folly indeed to cut back support for the infant now that it is three years old.'

The diversity of the research grants made in 1968 reflected the range of concerns now taken up by social scientists. The first three projects in the alphabetical list of institutions receiving them on behalf of individuals were 'politics in Aberdeen' (£4,340), 'tents in North Africa' (£1,428), and 'management style and organisation structure in the smaller enterprise' (£14,820). The last of this trio went to Ashridge Management College. Birmingham received a grant requested by Madge (£4,782) for a study of 'the attitude and behaviour of change of art students while at college'. A few art colleges were on the frontiers of student protest, a phenomenon that Michael did not have to confront directly.

SSRC grants in response to applications were not enough, Michael believed, and he pointed to three signs that indicated that in the future the SSRC would no longer follow the largely 'responsive' role in relation to research projects that had been envisaged for it in most governmental circles. One was the Educational Priority Areas schemes. Another, with a long-term future, was an SSRC Data Bank at the University of Essex, directed by Professor A. M. Potter, with Dr. D. J. G. Farlie as Deputy Director. The Data Bank would have three objectives – to collect, 'clean' and store data; to provide information about it; and to analyse and reproduce it. The Bank had a 'national character' and was to have a National Council to guide it. It would also have a working Research Unit to give advice and assist in survey research. Third, the Council had taken initiative in planning (on the advice of its Panel on Race Relations) to set up a Race Relations Unit under its own aegis. Government consent was required for this, as it was also for a Committee on Industrial Relations.

There was a Unit in Race Relations in existence at Sussex University, headed by a Caribbean, Fernando Henriques, but it was not to survive. Before it closed, however, a person who was to figure later in Michael's life, Nicholas Deakin, later to become Professor and Pro-Vice-Chancellor at Birmingham University, had been appointed to it. He had written his doctoral thesis on the history of race relations in the East End of London.

Race relations was a subject of global importance which had a distinctively British stance because of British imperial history and the late twentieth-century legacy it left behind it when large numbers of Commonwealth immigrants arrived in Britain. Michael was to interest himself in the local legacy of Empire in Bethnal Green, but he now took up his own world agenda, described in some detail in the next chapter.

8
A World Agenda

Michael had always had a world agenda. He was never either parochial or nationalistic, as he proved even before joining PEP. *For Richer For Poorer*, the seminal text in his writings, was the product of a world journey. Throughout the 1940s and 1950s he watched American elections as keenly as British elections, and inside Europe he compared British politics with the politics of other countries, particularly Sweden.[1] He believed also that the United Nations Organisation was a necessary instrument of world order and required grass-roots support. Significantly in 1960, his pamphlet *The Chipped White Cups of Dover* started not with domestic policy – or with consumers – but with 'internationalism and reform'.

'Growing awareness of the world outside Britain' had to be reflected in British party politics, he argued. It was not. The Labour Party had been internationalist before the War. Now it had shrunk 'not just into a nationalistic party, but more into a Little Englander party. Witness Labour's attitude to Europe both before and after 1951.'[2] At the end of the Suez decade Britain was 'too drab in relation to Europe' and 'too selfish in relation to Africa and Asia'. A move had to be made to offer leadership not through power but through 'world reconstruction'.

In *The Chipped White Cups of Dover* the sections on Africa and Asia were more interesting than those on Europe – or on the United Nations. They began with the proposition that 'in some ways it should be easier to strike up a new relationship with Asia and Africa than with Europe'. They were 'in some part English-speaking continents, and we know more about them. Yet the way by which we had got to know more about them – through the politics (and economics) of empire – threatened rather than assisted future understanding.' One of the first tasks of 'a party of reform with a world outlook' would be to dispose of 'residual wooden headed jingoism'.

These lines were written at a point in history when, as Michael saw it, the memories of service in 'the old Empire' were stronger influences on attitudes to foreign policy in the minds of the influential few than the presence in Britain of immigrants who had been born in it. Indeed, immigration did not figure at first in his world picture, and although he mentioned Notting Hill *en passant* it was in the context not of immigration but of an opinion poll taken at the time of Suez.[3] In fact, SS *Empire Windrush* had landed at Tilbury Docks from the Caribbean as early as 1948 and there were disturbances at Notting Hill in 1958. The first change in the nationality laws was to be made in 1962.

In *The Chipped White Cups of Dover* Michael urged Britain to give a lead through the Commonwealth, 'a free association of peoples', and to send out to the Third World (not so described in the pamphlet) trained Britons 'particularly agriculturists with knowledge about the tropics' and 'linguists of all sorts', to give support in development projects: one section of his pamphlet was called 'The Poorest He'. Working together would be 'a great international experiment'.

Michael was to devote a large part of the next ten years of his life not to politics, which were uppermost in his mind after Labour's defeat at the general election of 1959, but to education and research; and it is interesting to note that these two subjects figure prominently in the sections on foreign policy in *The Chipped White Cups of Dover* before being referred to (more briefly) in the later sections on 'Reform at Home'. 'Indians and Arabs' studying in Britain too often had 'to put up with racial prejudice in their leisure time and with indifference in their places of study', and students who came to Britain from developing countries should be given a better training. 'We have not taken the trouble to devise special courses devoted to their needs which are (in many subjects) quite different from ours. Let us have an "Asian" university in York and an "African" university in Brighton, where overseas students would be in a majority and where the staff would know Africa and Asia as well as they know Yorkshire and Sussex.'[4] There should also be 'an International Service Organisation modelled to some extent on President Roosevelt's Civilian Construction Corps, in place of National Service which is soon to be defunct'.[5]

Michael's pamphlet ended with a demand for research on matters of urgent concern to developing countries.[6] Indeed, it was just as important, he claimed, as education. And he spoke in language which members of the Labour Party could easily understand. 'What was needed was a gradual shift of research effort from perfecting more destructive weapons and more refined electronic equipment to the problems of agriculture and the means of controlling the growth of population in Asia and Africa.'

There was nothing original about this analysis, but the way in which Michael set it out so clearly reveals that his future world agenda was already there in outline in 1960 while he was teaching in Cambridge. It did not become an action agenda until ten years later, but Michael was not silent on any of its main points during the intervening decade, a distinctive decade and one of the most fascinating in world history as it was in British social and cultural history.

Before it had proceeded far, in 1963, one year after the foundation of the National Extension College,[7] PEP published an interesting number of *Planning* on 'The Shape of the Sixties' in which it pointed out that 'despite the high hopes and brave efforts of the late forties and fifties', there had never been 'so many very poor and hungry people on the earth', nor had 'their numbers ever been multiplying so fast'.[8] The United Nations had just launched a 'Development Decade', and Michael wrote an article in the *Observer*, as part of a Freedom from Hunger Campaign, in which he appealed for voluntary funding by seven-year covenant, stressing yet again the importance of education, training, 'research and demonstration'.[9] Two countries he mentioned specifically were Tanganyika and Sarawak, as they then were.

By a coincidence, it was in the year that these first seven-year covenants came to an end – and the year when Labour lost another general election[10] – that Michael activated his own world agenda, choosing as his agency for action an International Extension College, the natural extension (the right word) to the National Extension College, which was registered in 1971 as a non-profit-making organisation under English charity law. Thereafter, implementing a world agenda always came first for Michael, although this did not mean that he ever abandoned his national (or local) agenda or stopped writing on subjects concerned with kinship and community (or a wide range of other subjects).

What the activation of his agenda did was to force him to reallocate his time. Travel took up more and more of it, and he became very familiar with the interiors of jumbo jets which took him from continent to continent. Africa for him was never a dark continent. As he put it in 1998 to Kate Gavron, who was working with him on a new book on Bethnal Green, a difficult and protracted exercise, 'I have been buzzing around in Africa for nearly thirty years. In total, it amounts to perhaps five of those years – in hundreds of short visits and some long ones.'[11]

None the less, Bethnal Green remained his continuing base, a Bethnal Green where Bangladeshis were becoming an important element in the local population, a demographic and social change that made a new study of Bethnal Green very different from the old one.[12] (An independent Bangladesh came into existence – after war – only in 1971.) And Dartington always remained in his mind wherever he travelled. He tried to establish international links with it while in Africa, particularly, but not exclusively, through the arts.[13] An important conference, concerned with African educational policies, was held there in 1977. This was the year when Victoria Park Square was designated a Mutual Aid Centre, with Michael as its founding Chairman.

For Michael the local and the global, a word which established itself only later in the century, were never opposites. Nor did he lose interest in Europe (or Australia) as he turned to Africa (and Asia). He wrote an interesting think-piece called 'Dilemmas in a New Europe' in 1972 in a book with the characteristic title (for that date) of *The Future of Tomorrow*, which began with a consideration of the forecast recently made by Herman Kahn and Anthony Wiener, *The Year 2000*.

Back in the past, G. K. Chesterton, a writer whom Michael never quoted, once remarked in a brilliant essay that 'the man who lives in a small community lives in a much larger world. He knows more of the fierce vanities and uncompromising divergences of men.'[14] That is not how Michael saw the relationship between small and large, although he was to learn more about 'vanities' and 'divergences' in Bethnal Green – and Dartington – as they changed during the 1970s and 1980s. Yet the language of 'the fierce' and 'the uncompromising' was never his. Instead, he carried his ideas of 'mutual aid' and educational 'extension' from Bethnal Green around what he called in a letter to Richmond Postgate 'the common universe which we inhabit'.[15]

Postgate, who in the 1970s was Controller of Education at the BBC after Scupham, was the brother of Margaret Cole and Raymond Postgate. He worked with the National Extension College on the Gateway courses, which were all that was left of the unfulfilled partnership between the National Extension College and the Open University. In the same letter Michael thanked Postgate for his cooperation in the Gateway courses, 'especially at moments of crisis which I suppose are inevitable in any organisation, or at any rate every one which is alive'.[16]

There was no coincidence in the choice of timing for the preparation and publication of Michael's world agenda and for the setting up of the International Extension College. Indeed, like his visits to Africa, they were quite deliberately timed. The British Open University started its degree course broadcasts in January 1971.[17] A year earlier, an African leader who was to be frequently quoted by Michael and the IEC, Julius Nyerere, President of Tanzania (which had not gained its independence when *The Chipped White Cups of Dover* was published), had declared 1970 'Adult Education Year'. (He also wished his country to move to universal primary education in 1977.)

Already during the last years of the 1960s large numbers of Third World visitors had travelled to Bethnal Green or Cambridge seeking advice on correspondence courses and the use of radio in distance learning from the National Extension College. Some were seeking support, particularly human support, as well as advice. Could the College provide the names of people willing to help on the spot, the kind of people Michael had identified in *The Chipped White Cups of Dover*?

In most of the countries from which the visitors came there was pressure on government, sometimes unprepared for it, to provide correspondence courses: in some of them there were business organisations that were doing so. In all countries there was an interest in the use of radio in education: the age of television, a more expensive medium, had not yet arrived. Moreover, international agencies were already involved. Foundations, particularly the Ford Foundation, were anxious to help. UNESCO and the Commonwealth were drawn in too, as later was the European Economic Community.[18] An interesting book on American attitudes to Third World education appeared in 1977: the opening essay in it was written by the first Rector of the United Nations University, James Hester.[19]

Michael, wary as ever of all universities, had distinctive advice of his own, and he responded positively to the appeal of his visitors when they arrived in Cambridge. The first step, as he saw it, was to promote an exchange of information so that they could learn from each other as well as from the NEC. At the very least, the sharing of experience would reduce waste. At the most, it would generate new action so that the very word 'extension' would now acquire a double significance. Substantively it would cover, as it had done inside Britain, the attempt to reach large numbers of people who for whatever reason had not been able to take advantage of formal education. This had been the rationale of the NEC (and of the Open University). Chronologically, the word 'extension' could now be applied to Michael's own interests and to those of the NEC.

The three-fold combination in open learning that the NEC and the Open University had pioneered – radio (and when possible television); correspondence; and personal tuition – was to be commended through the medium of the International Extension College, a deliberately small but well-focused agency, operating in Africa (and Asia). Already there was education by radio in some countries, as there were correspondence colleges, but separated as they were from each other they were incomplete. It was the combination which he offered that would be innovative, particularly when backed by an element of personal tuition. Broadcasting by itself would leave gaps between broadcasts. Nor would it be easy to achieve feedback. The quality of correspondence courses was often in doubt, and there would be an undoubted improvement in quality if radio set standards. Personal tuition by itself, the third element in the combination, which the NEC had pioneered and which the planners of the Open University regarded as an indispensable element in the mix, was expensive. Nor was it easy to find the right tutors.

Good organisation would be necessary to make the combination work. It was not merely a matter of technology or of pedagogy. The Open University was to pioneer the idea of 'open learning', sometimes contrasted with 'open teaching'; and if there was a need for good teaching there was also a need to avoid 'learning by rote' unless this was for identifiable reasons appropriate. The opportunities in Africa and Asia seemed almost limitless, for there were far larger numbers of people than there were in Britain without any formal education, some of them illiterate, who were enthusiastically seeking it. In this situation IEC as an extension of NEC, modest in scale, ambitious in purposes, wished to concentrate not on the provision of degree courses through distance learning institutions (or distance learning departments of other universities), (relatively) old or new, but on what were sometimes dismissed by university administrators as 'sub-degree courses', particularly practical courses of a vocational kind or in agricultural development. Schools could not be neglected either – nor, sometimes a top priority – the training of school teachers.

One incentive in moving into Africa was that the possibility of real innovation appeared to be substantial, particularly in the field of rural education. Michael noted, for example, the literacy and social development campaigns by radio in Tanzania, which was to run four such new campaigns between 1970 and 1975, including one on health and one on nutrition. He enjoyed picking people to work with him, the first of them Tony Dodds, straight from Tanzania, and in turning to Africa first he found exactly the right colleagues. They all believed that formal education could and should don 'seven league boots'.[20]

Dodds, born in 1938, a history graduate (from Oxford), had been working since 1964 in Dar-es-Salaam, first as an Assistant Resident

Tutor and then as Resident Tutor in Adult Education when Michael first met him; and while there Michael had appreciated on the spot the pedagogic and economic value of radio in education in developing countries.[21] He had set up an institute in Tanzania's southern highlands at Mbeya, which by a coincidence (Michael called it 'an occult link') had figured in Leonard Elmhirst's life.[22] When later in the 1970s Dodds visited Calcutta for the first time, representing the IEC, a West Bengali woman, committed to the same cause as he was, told him that Michael had been inspired by Tagore and Santinitekan and that he, Dodds, therefore, was 'the great grandson of my movement'. She detected a familiar kinship relationship.

There was nothing occult about Michael's link with Hilary Perraton, who on arriving at the National Extension College had worked with a small Inter-University Research Unit. Having completed its initial work, it now turned its attention from British universities to the world scene;[23] and in the late 1960s it was beginning to make overseas contacts, the first of them not with Africa but with the University of Guyana. It was said to be easier for university teachers there and, indeed, in the Caribbean area as a whole, 'to find out what is happening at British or American universities – where many themselves graduated – than about teaching or researching in other parts of the tropics'.[24] Michael wanted there to be a network which was not dependent only on universities in 'advanced countries', a term he would never have used; and he discussed future plans with Brian Jackson whom he knew would not think about them in stereotyped fashion.[25]

Looking for financial support to extend his international involvement, Michael made his first visit to Africa in October 1970, two months before formally resigning the Chairmanship of the NEC, which he had held for seven years, and handing over to the Cambridge physicist, Mott. Thereafter, he was always in the thick of the action, whether in Bethnal Green or in Africa or travelling between the two, conscious throughout of how much he owed to his colleagues whether they themselves were 'in the field' in Africa or back at IEC headquarters in Cambridge. They too were learning as he was, although even in the very first stages of learning they were often called 'experts'. Some did become experts, capable in often difficult political and economic circumstances of winning the confidence of Africans (or Asians).

Michael clearly explained his views on the timing of his African involvement in a letter that he wrote in December 1970 to Brian MacArthur, then Features Editor of *The Times*, after his first visit to Mauritius and Africa in October. He had not heard then whether or not the Ford Foundation, sympathetic though it was, would provide funds to support IEC projects. The IEC, he said,

> would be the counterpart to NEC as it was in 1963, except that it would be entirely international in scope. A recent trip of mine round Africa has convinced me that the need for multi-media teaching is much greater there at the secondary level than it is here. We are hoping for an initial grant from *War on Want* to get it started. We are proposing to announce the setting up of it on January 7th. In the issues of *Where?* published then there will be an article on NEC and the OU. The OU goes on the air for the first time on January 10th, I think.
>
> The question is whether if we supply you with all the stuff in plenty of time you could possibly manage a feature article on NEC-OU-IEC and mentioning *War on Want* at about that time, preferably on the *Where?* publication day? I would especially value it because I very much need something like this, preferably not written by me, to send off to the people in the three key countries for it – Nigeria, Botswana and Mauritius – whom I'm hoping to persuade to establish the first new-style correspondence college in the African area. I shall need to keep as much pressure as I can to get anything off the ground, ie into the air. Any chance?[26]

This was one of a number of similar or related letters that Michael sent around the same time to everyone that he thought might be of help from Postgate to the Labour ex-minister Anthony Greenwood.[27]

In his letter to MacArthur, whom he knew would be sympathetic, Michael referred to possibilities of support from British charities for a 'pilot experiment for an international university of the air'. He may not have known at the time that in the month when he wrote to MacArthur a group of experts, including Walter Perry and a number of others from Britain, had held a conference in New Delhi on the feasibility of setting up an open university in India.[28]

Such an article did not appear, but by the time that the first British Open University programmes were broadcast – with considerable publicity – Michael was ready for action, and in February 1971 he embarked on a second strategic visit to Africa, this time very carefully planned in advance. The preliminary visit which he had made to Mauritius and Africa in October 1970 was conceived of by him as a 'prospecting' visit. Sasha, born in South Africa, now accompanied him, a great source of strength. For her there were memories that he could not share. Yet, brief though the visit was, it greatly widened his own experience.

In Mauritius nothing had been settled on his first visit in talks with Sir Harilal Vakjee in the Speaker's Office,[29] where Dartington figured on the agenda as well as the IEC: he did not see either the Prime Minister, Sir Seewosagar Ramgoolam, or the British Governor, Sir Len Williams, an ex-Labour politician, who was out of the country. The last time Michael had seen Williams was at Transport House during the Labour Party preparations for the 1964 general election. He wrote to him, therefore, before finalising a second visit, describing Mauritius as 'your wonderful island', and at the same time he wrote also to Greenwood about seeing the Prime Minister, explaining that on his second visit he would be accompanied by Donald Chesworth, a Greater London Councillor, a future Director of Toynbee Hall, and an active figure in War on Want: Michael had designated him as a Trustee of IEC.[30]

On his way back from Mauritius in October 1970, Michael paid his first visit to South Africa, where it seemed ironical that the British official who met him at Johannesburg Airport bore the name badge Mr. Marx.[31] While in Johannesburg he met members of the small and determined – but much harassed – South African Committee of Higher Education, known then and later by its initials, SACHED. The Committee had been formed in 1960 by Anne Welch, and ten years later it had taken over a commercial correspondence college which in April 1970 was renamed the Turret Correspondence College. Michael warmed at once to the members of SACHED's organising group and their ambitions: they were, he reported, 'brave, realistic and practical', seeking to give as many Africans as possible 'dignity through knowledge'. He was particularly impressed by David Adler, SACHED's Research Officer.

The organisation had raised sufficient funds with which to work, but any kind of work with black students in South Africa raised 'immense' difficulties. 'Their students are frequently picked up by Special Branch and questioned about the staff. Students can only be seen one at a time. If there were two together, that would be a breach of the law about unlawful assembly. The students are working under conditions difficult even to imagine, often without even candle light in their huts in some shanty towns.'

Michael went on to note that he had 'left out' of his report 'the terrible stories' he had heard about apartheid and its human consequences. 'Several of the people I saw are waiting for one of their friends to be arrested and tortured to the point where they mention their own names – in which case they suffer the same fate. It is a country in which liberals have no immediate hope to counter their fear and disgust. Only the long-term hope that perhaps through education and living their liberal values can they help to prepare the leaders of a different South Africa even if it does not come about till the next century.'

From Johannesburg Michael went on to Botswana, where he met David Crawley, Lecturer in the School of Adult Learning, stationed in Gaborone – he had just arrived from Tanzania – Peter Hunter, newly appointed Professor of Adult Education at the University of Lesotho, and Potlake Molefke, Director of Botswana Radio, which covered only a small part of the country: there were only 8,000 licences. Other government officials present included Mark Thompson, Senior Education Officer, Planning, who was on secondment (thanks to Alec Clegg) from the West Riding of Yorkshire Local Education Authority.

It was a government official who was not present, however – he was on leave in London – who proposed that a Botswana Correspondence College should be set up with a grant from UNESCO. As Educational Planner in the Minister of Finance and Development Planning, John White had recently produced a report on the experiences of correspondence education in Zambia, Malawi and Rhodesia (as it then was). By luck, his 'boss', as Michael called him, Peter Landell-Mills, Chief Planner, had been a pupil of Michael's in Cambridge in charge of a team of young economists, and in Michael's opinion anything that he decided was likely to take effect.[32]

Michael considered that a university institution would be senseless on economic grounds: Botswana was 'a poor country the size of France and with a population the size of Leeds'. The meeting convinced him, however, that if Crawley were to be given charge of a 'Correspondence-Plus' College, taking over in January 1972, he would make it a top priority; and in those circumstances it might be called a 'University of the Air'. (A Botswana translation was to be sought.)

The new institution would be located inside the University of Lesotho. While this had the disadvantage for Michael of being in the 'white settler' belt, it would probably have at least one advantage: it could recruit staff more easily.[33] The first students to be recruited would be people who could not get into secondary schools because there were no places for them.[34] Their teachers would be drawn from school teachers in the country, but they themselves would require training. A new radio transmitter would be built to ensure national coverage. A Research Officer would be appointed as early as possible 'to assess the whole project and to write a series of reports about its progress'. Throughout there should be an emphasis on feedback.

For IEC two questions would arise – how much of the curriculum could be prepared in England and how much of it could be shared with other countries. It would obviously be wasteful to have multiple course-writing teams doing exactly the same thing in different places at the same time. Yet some courses would have to be specifically associated not with particular languages and cultures but with particular places.

Michael's discussions on matters of this kind in South Africa had been much to the point. SACHED spokesmen had said that they would like to have the complete range of NEC courses with permission to adapt them for their own needs, and that they would like someone from the IEC to spend a short time in Johannesburg, helping with course preparation – for instance in mathematics and science. They told Michael that they feared that London University, in which he had once placed so much trust,[35] would soon terminate its external degree programme and they dismissed as Afrikaner the University of South Africa, UNISA, a correspondence university, which had 30,000 students. It was not for them a suitable alternative.

They also told him – and it was a point of fundamental importance – that if the IEC were to set up an African centre, for example, in Nairobi or in Addis Ababa, Turret would not be able to communicate with it by post. 'Letters would be stopped.' They could communicate with London, however, and years later in 1980, when Turret was serving as the base of a distance learning programme with six centres and catering for 1,200 students, it acquired a SACHED Education and Training post box – and more – in the United Kingdom.

The British body to which SACHED now reported what it felt to be its most urgent needs, provided it, when it could, with financial and promotional support. Ten years later, the first item it supported in 1990, when the South African political situation had changed – and when priorities in funding could be clearly identified – was the provision of bursaries for 125 part-time students.[36]

With his African conversations of October 1970 in mind, Michael returned with Chesworth to Africa, via Mauritius, in February 1971, ending his journeys with an exploratory visit to Nigeria, accompanied by Dodds, in April/May. Agreement was soon reached about a Mauritius College of the Air, which constituted a model, following talks with both the Prime Minister and the Minister of Education. There were to be reciprocal obligations. The Mauritius Government promised to provide facilities for student learning courses and to second experienced personnel from the Audio-Visual Unit in the Mauritius Broadcasting Company and from the educational services: IEC promised to raise £20,000 a year for the first five years of the College's life.

Michael himself was to direct the College for its first nine months, backed by Philip Baker. Dodds was to succeed him. There would be Trustees who would plan College strategy: according to it, the felt and expressed needs of Mauritius would be paramount. Emphasis was to be placed on the measurement of 'successes and failures' by 'systematic recording and research', a regular requirement for Michael.[37] On the financial side donors for the College were found relatively quickly – War on Want, Oxfam, Christian Aid, the United Nations Association and Freedom from Hunger, the last of these earmarking its support (and Michael had no difficulty in agreeing to this) for education in agriculture. Research and how to pursue it was to prove to be more difficult.

Given the pledges and the outline plans, the Mauritius College of the Air Act was passed in December 1971, although operations were not to begin until later in 1972, with 1972–3 designated as a pilot year. Before Michael left, the College was opened (and shown on television on 28 August 1972), and in the following month it was officially inaugurated by the Prime Minister. The first IEC staff had arrived in May. Three senior tutors had been seconded by the Ministry, and three audio-visual officers had been seconded by the Mauritius Broadcasting Corporation, one of them a television producer. There had also been a course writers' workshop directed by Perraton, described as Co-Director of IEC. The detail is interesting because this was a new beginning, the kind of beginning that Michael delighted in. What followed in Mauritius and Africa was not always a story of success, but it was always a story of imagination and effort.

Perraton remained based in Cambridge: Dodds, who became Director after Michael left, had oversight over IEC's African activities as well as responsibilities for Mauritius. He was to remain in Mauritius until September 1974 when he moved to Nigeria as Director of the Correspondence and Open Studies Unit of the University of Lagos.

The Mauritius courses were of various kinds. In Michael's mind a top priority was the provision of distance learning in 'the poorest rural areas' and in Rodrigues, the poorer, dependent island off Mauritius. For the Ministry of Education, however, top priority had to be given to courses for Cambridge School and Higher School Certificate examinations, described by the Ministry as being part of a Mauritius 'tradition': the pupils were studying mainly in private and independent secondary schools which were also deemed to be 'traditional' in Mauritius. Only a 'new mathematics' course, based on an 'O' level NEC extension course, was non-traditional in content.

The genuinely innovatory courses, described as 'more experimental' than the others, were in Rural Development, and these were offered in cooperation with the Ministry of Agriculture and the Ministry of Economic Planning and Development. There was also a course in Office Management, written by a member of the School of Administration at the University of Mauritius. A sixth course in Creole, complete with tapes, was also introduced, the only course in the prospectus which it was hoped would raise funds for the College. It was devised by Philip Baker, who also played a main part in the preparation of the rural development programme.

Teaching the new courses had not proceeded far when Geoffrey Dench, who visited the island at Easter 1973, wrote a revealing report for IEC on research priorities at the Mauritius College of the Air, admitting frankly that in practice politics mattered as much as technology or pedagogy, and that research was difficult to carry out: 'the overall situation in Mauritius' was such that where there was a 'divergence of interests between action and effective valuation' action had to be given priority. Furthermore, within whatever research programmes were possible there were problems associated with the demand for immediate feedback: 'short-term monitoring of an activity confuses any longer-term monitoring of the same activity'.

The fact that it had been decided that the independent secondary schools themselves – and not the College – should decide whether or not to participate in the Cambridge School and Higher School Certificate scheme, had in itself made it inevitable that there would be difficulties in drawing reliable conclusions about the effectiveness of the courses taught. 'It would have been much better either to select schools on a random (or stratified) basis or to have included *all* schools immediately.' 'Only in those circumstances [politically impossible] could a properly experimental evaluation be carried out.'

Dench went further and questioned whether it had been wise to think of 1973 as 'an experimental year': 'the first year (pilot year, trial year or whatever) should not be treated as critical, for subsequent years were bound to be very different'. Not only had there been some teething troubles, for example in teaching and in marking, but the very novelty of the courses provided in the first year could have had 'both specific and general effects on examination results, negatively as well as positively'. There had also been 'statistical hazards'.

Dench's conclusion, which he realised would apply to other Colleges outside Mauritius that might be initiated by the IEC, was that it would not be an easy task through research to demonstrate the effectiveness of modes of teaching – 'and certainly not a quick one'. 'The choice of means of communication [in education] seems likely in practice to be determined in most countries by economic considerations (of relative costs of alternative media) and on a whole constellation of political judgements about which groups in society should be, and desire to be, the audience for the communications.' There would inevitably be 'political allies' and 'political enemies' as choices were converted into action, and there would always be a continuing need for acceptable cost accounting.

Dench went further. If there were to be advances outside the examination-based school system, as Michael wished, it would be necessary to carry out 'anticipatory or base-line studies' before decisions were made: without them it would be 'very hard to gauge what the real demand' for such courses was. And it would be important, too, before decisions were made, to ensure that courses offered were 'matched by desirable employment prospects': Mauritius itself was 'a veritable graveyard of good intentions'.[38]

Mauritius was not as exceptional in its educational structures as some of the people from outside who visited it or, indeed, worked there, sometimes believed. As Dench realised, the colonial and surviving post-colonial structure in Mauritius – and elsewhere – implied dependence on an élite who had much to gain from placing emphasis entirely on traditional academic goals; and where there was more than one ethnic group in a colony or ex-colony the formation and renewal of an élite necessarily entailed competition *within* ethnic communities as well as *between* them. Leaving ladders on one side, the sense of an 'academic race' fostered 'anti-communal intellectualism'. Michael accepted this diagnosis. At this stage in his thinking universities were part of the problem, not agencies which could help to solve it.

Given that Michael saw the Mauritius College of the Air as a pilot experiment and planned to create other colleges in Africa and in other parts of the world, the last section of Dench's report, 'Implications for IEC research policy', was particularly important – and not only in relation to research. 'The efficiency of 3-way teaching' as a pioneering model had to be analysed in broader terms, within the context of 'developing economic and political structures' as a means of increasing educational output or changing educational directions.

The first progress reports on the Mauritius College of the Air, prepared largely for its Trustees, revealed difficulties as well as successes. The first 50 television sets to be loaned to schools by the Mauritius government were stranded in London by a dock strike. The use of Creole in classes of non-school teenage girls following the social biology courses 'ran against the intense linguistic sensitivity of the island'. Yet by the Summer of 1974 it could be claimed that classes had been 'modernised' and that the College, having completed its pilot projects, was 'moving into full operation'. It also attracted interest far outside the island. An Open University Professor visited the College *en route* eastwards for the Seychelles. The Director of the Institute of Education at the University of Dacca in Bangladesh travelled westward to look at the College. Staff of the College visited Australia.

Links with Africa were strengthened too. The University of Nairobi had set up a Correspondence Course Unit in Kenya which offered courses for the Kenyan Junior Certificate of Secondary Education: they were devised, as courses in other parts of Africa were to be, mainly for unqualified primary school teachers, and used both radio and correspondence.[39] The International Extension College was not involved in them – they were started before it was founded. Nor was it directly involved in the setting up at Nairobi of an African Association for Correspondence Colleges in 1973. Yet it followed developments everywhere as closely as it could, and while the Association, in which the Mauritius College of the Air participated, proved unsuccessful, the fact that it had been created at all seemed to be a sign of progress.

The most hopeful African country was the richest, Nigeria, then enjoying an oil boom, and it was Lagos, the city to which Peter Marris had travelled more than ten years before, when it was already changing fast, which was the next capital city to which Dodds travelled on behalf of IEC in June 1973. He was following up a request for assistance in the development of a University of the Air at Ahmadu Bello University in Zaria, a new campus in the largely Muslim region of the North. It was after this visit that Michael extended his own African experience by spending many months, accompanied by Sasha, at Ahmadu Bello, taking the place of Lalage Bown, a highly experienced adult education tutor and professor who was returning from Africa, a continent which she knew better than anyone that I have known, to spend a period of study leave in Scotland.

Coinciding, as it did, with one of the most difficult – and depressing – years in twentieth-century British social history (but a year also of great political excitement), Michael's stay at Ahmadu Bello was itself difficult and depressing, confirming his distaste for university environments, whatever the particular circumstances might be. 'I didn't want to get involved in university level education,' he wrote in January 1974, 'but to do as much as possible about non-formal education in rural areas'.[40]

The results of efforts to provide such non-formal education were themselves to prove disappointing over the years, but from the very start there was a difference between meeting demands and identifying needs. Indeed, even before IEC became involved, it had already been shown that the meagre funds devoted exclusively to non-formal development education were often being wasted 'for lack of a clear strategy, good planning and workable administrative arrangements'.[41] Michael, however, was learning for himself the hard way at first hand, and when he contemplated what passed for educational strategy in Nigeria he was depressed rather than inspired: no fewer than six new universities were being contemplated by the Northern States of Nigeria alone. In boom conditions this seemed a misdirection of effort.

Sasha drew on her experiences of Nigeria in a novel, *In the Shadow of the Paradise Tree*. Michael had no such outlet, however, and felt stranded – and wasted – in a 'ludicrous campus where nothing of Africa was touching you'. None the less, frustrated though he was, he made some useful contacts and carried out a research survey with Dodds of 73 students, all teachers on study leave who were taking B.Ed. degrees. The average age of those interviewed was 29. Most of them came from farms. They were all hoping for 'higher status and more reward', suggesting that there was 'a general rule that aspirations rise to match opportunities'. They were an élite (or part of an élite) 'in formation'. He was not blind to the fact that if a successful College of the Air were set up in Nigeria, it would give a great boost to the creation of similar colleges or universities in other parts of Africa and that would put the College in 'the big league', a curious expression for him to use.

Seeking a different approach, he asked characteristically whether what was wrong was not just bureaucracy but the lack of an inspirational ideology. He sought, therefore, to find out what was happening in the countryside in other parts of the world, including Latin America, where radio seemed to be effectively used for development purposes, and China; and, having asked Perraton to find out about rural polytechnics in Kenya, he wrote on the same day to Denis and Edna Healey, who had just visited China, seeking information about what they had seen of adult distance learning in the Chinese countryside.[42] He felt that 'no one [in the world] would get very far with a rural biased education unless there's a pretty strong ideology behind it'. Nyerere, who was turning to China rather than Britain as a model, had come to the same conclusion.

Michael was no more able to answer his own questions about ideology, very similar to those he had raised in the 1930s as a young student in London, after he visited China himself towards the end of the decade in 1979. He was a member of a party which included David Attenborough, seeking to film the giant white panda, and the novelist Iris Murdoch: 'I wish,' Michael wrote, that 'I had her powers of observation.' What most struck him at the time as an observer was not how fast things were moving politically in China, but how slowly people were moving physically. Bicyclists rode 'at the same slow steady pace as though they had been rolled up on an endless conveyor belt'. And pedestrians walked slowly too. There was metaphor in that. But it did not need metaphor to explain another aspect of the cultural situation. Books in English in libraries and bookshops had been withdrawn in 1949.

Michael was in China at a distinctive moment in its long history, but when he was received by Deng Ziau Ping, who was carrying forward policies that would transform the economy, Michael found him 'not in the least charismatic'. He concluded that the Chinese regime was a gerontocracy, but suspected that it might be undermined in time by 'the most meritocratic system he had ever seen, let alone imagined'.[43]

By the time that Michael visited post-Cultural Revolution China Africa seemed somewhat less promising territory for innovation than it had been in 1970 when he first landed in Mauritius, and he never went back to it for as long a 'chunk' as he did in 1973. Nevertheless, having returned to Britain and plunged himself back into British politics, he threw all the weight of his influence and energy into a conference, described as a 'workshop', that was held at Dartington in September 1977 to discuss development and distance education in Africa and IEC strategy. He was intimately involved, too, in the preparations for the workshop, giving comradely 'orders' to his British colleagues – like 'Tony, your chapter – literacy campaigns have been left out even where functionally related to agriculture', or 'Tony – would you write to the Tanzanian Minister a letter to go off with an IEC workshop paper saying you hope whatever else he reads on plane, he will be able to read the paper' on radio schools in Bolivia.

Among his other comments in a particularly illuminating letter to his colleagues were 'Even at this late hour should we invite the Federal

Adviser from Lagos? I suppose nothing would happen thereafter' and 'Nothing said about any Tanzania campaign after health one. Have they been dropped? If so, we are probably going to be unlucky with our workshop.'[44]

A discussion paper prepared by the IEC team began with a quotation from Nyerere and a statement relating what was happening in Africa to what was happening in Britain and elsewhere:

> It has in the first world become almost fashionable in recent years to decry education and all its works. Many of the contemporary criticisms have force. But we want to make it clear at the outset that for our part we are in this respect old-fashioned: we do not subscribe to the current vogue. We are only engaged in education at all because we believe in it and in [its] liberating potential. Education is to do with power. People without education are at the mercy of those with it ... Power is also freedom. Education is a means of gaining power; and hence freedom which should be everyone's right.

In order to fulfil the full promise of education, low-cost distance learning was a necessary mode. UNESCO had estimated in 1972 that the number of illiterate adults had risen between 1950 and 1970 from 700 to 783 million. Unless more economical methods of providing education could be found, 'the extent of present inequalities between rich and poor countries, between men and women, and in the poor countries between urban and rural people, may actually grow for the rest of this century. If this happened the world would in this respect not be making progress but moving backwards.'

In this discussion paper Michael was playing the role of 'progress chaser', used in a different sense and in a very different setting from war-time Swindon. But in both settings quality counted as well as quantity, and, in order to achieve that, 'live people' were needed and not just technology. Policy-makers had the remit of dealing with teacher training, where quality obviously mattered, with adult education and with non-formal education. There were appendices to the paper dealing with each item in their remit, and Nigeria was especially picked out as a land of opportunity.[45] The perspective, however, was 'global'. Thus, there were references to radiophonic schools, used in Colombia as early as 1947, to farm forums in Canada, dating back to an even earlier period in the 1940s, and to BBC listener groups arranged earlier still (but later discarded) in the 1930s. A metaphor of a railway train was used, a train that not only moved at different speeds, but often jolted, but the tone of the paper was optimistic.[46]

Three years after the workshop, Michael, as Chairman of the IEC – and still its prime mover – joined with Perraton, Dodds and Jenkins in writing a book, still valuable – and far more than a record – called *Distance Teaching in the Third World*. It had as its arresting sub-title 'The lion and the clockwork mouse', characters in an Aesop fable, quoted at the beginning of the book with little explanation of its relevance in the text. This was clearly a very different kind of mouse from the computer mouse that would become familiar around the world as computers in successive generations made their way around it. As for the lions, they were not quite symbols of empire, although the legacy of imperial rule was directly relevant to the educational experiences described and analysed in the book.

'Traditional' forms of education, indigenous or imposed, could not meet the needs and the hopes of the future, they argued, quoting a well-known passage about change by A. N. Whitehead already a generation old, in his *Adventures in Ideas* (1942). Traditional forms of education assumed that change was 'a slow process and that values and ways of doing things will change only a little from generation to generation', but 'we are now living [and there was a touch of exaggeration here] in the first period of human history for which this assumption is false.' Michael and his colleagues were offering an invitation to participate in adventures in action. Change was treated as a social enterprise.

The adventure was on the frontiers, and although modern technology was the instrument of change, 'the barefoot technologist of education [was] partner to the barefoot manager and the barefoot doctor':[47] 'If you have the technology without the face-to-face groups, then in educational terms nothing much may happen. If you have the groups without the technology something will happen, but it may happen better with the support of broadcasting.' While in Nigeria Michael (and Dodds) found in the then Director of Nigerian Broadcasting, Christopher Kolade (a friend of mine through the International Broadcast Institute) one of their strongest supporters.

There was no reference to South Africa in *Distance Learning in the Third World*, for in 1980 it was ruled through apartheid, and the Anti-Apartheid movement, British and European, concerned as it was with basic human rights, tried to keep visitors out of it. None the less, Michael had continuing contacts with SACHED,[48] and in 1976/7 the IEC helped to set up an emergency programme of education for refugees after many of them had poured into Botswana following the Soweto uprising. It also supported a South African extension unit in Tanzania. The refugee problem was serious in other parts of the world, too, and in 1971 the IEC, still in its infancy, drew up plans for a project to assist Bangladeshi refugees in West Bengal during the war between India and Pakistan.

Twelve years later, under Michael's inspiration, it proposed a World Refugee College, and although this was never brought to life, the IEC participated in educational projects for Namibians in exile, for Ethiopians and Eritreans in exile in the Sudan (through a Sudan Open Learning Unit), and for Somalis, never sure of their future.[49] The problems seemed at times insuperable, but through such activities it drew attention, as Michael had done years before, to the role of education not only in the process of development but in the horrors of a disaster.

With the great turn of events in South Africa, beginning with the release of Nelson Mandela on 11 February 1990 and the new freedom to operate of the African National Congress, Michael, in his own words, 'leapt back' to South Africa which he had first seen in 1970.[50] He was subsequently to visit it frequently and to get to know many South Africans inside and outside politics, in the process of learning at first hand both of opportunities – some, well known to others too, like the educational preparation of the diverse people whom the country needed – and the problems that made preparation difficult. On his part patience was needed as well as imagination. He not only needed to persuade, but also to ensure that ideas, even when accepted, could be implemented.

When he had gone to Nigeria in 1973 the political situation had been difficult – the rule of the generals set the terms – but the economic situation had been favourable. When he went to South Africa in 1990 the political situation was exciting, but the economics were the economics of recession. In both countries there were necessary – and often inhibiting – rounds of negotiations.

In post-apartheid South Africa 'the need for second chances [in education] is so great that the situation can only be likened to that after a major war'. These words of a 36-page interim report from the IEC, written in June 1991 by Michael, Dodds and Tony Morphet, and given backing from Brussels, began with its major recommendation – the setting up of a South African Institute of Distance Education, SAIDE.[51] The recession made this more important rather than less. 'The people who would for the first time have fair educational opportunity are amongst the people who would bring about educational expansion.' 'For the moment' there was more point in 'an education-led economy than in an economy-led education'. But Michael, as always, while aware of the moment, looked far beyond it. He referred to the US GI

Bill of Rights, urging that its provisions should apply to victims of apartheid.

He and his colleagues also proposed the setting up of a Foundation for Basic Education. There should also be a pilot project on rural development. To ensure imaginative but practical planning full use should be made of Turret, the body he had first encountered in 1971: it should provide 'the initial core of the new South African Institute' and with an Independent Examinations Board figure at the centre of a network of bodies providing support for literacy and other work as 'part of an emerging alternative system of Basic Education for adults'.[52]

The IEC had been asked to prepare this report by John Samuel, Director of SACHED and African National Congress head of Education, but the approach and proposals suggested in it were not acceptable to a section of COSATU, the trade union connected with the ANC – its representatives wanted to send delegations to Cuba and China – and in Michael's words were subsequently 'scuppered'.

A quite different proposal was to be made by Michael after several visits to South Africa, including one in 1995 where he visited Robben Island, the island where the first Portuguese explorer landed in South Africa in 1488, and where five hundred years later Mandela and other ANC leaders had been locked up for twenty years and more. In 1991 Michael had focused his attention on South African adults, 'the lost generation'. Now in 1995, still deeply concerned with them, his rethinking began in the small primary school which he found in the island. It was only 45 minutes away by slow boat from Cape Town and 25 minutes by fast boat. (He characteristically drew attention to the time difference in an article on his visit in the *Guardian*.[53])

For Mandela and his comrades in gaol the island, so near and yet so far from the mainland, had been known as 'the University'. Mandela had taken external examinations there. Why not turn it now into an Open University? The word 'open' would have a special significance in this unique context. 'It had been known as the university,' Mandela wrote, 'not only because of what was learned from books or because so many of our men earned multiple degrees ... [but] because of what we learned from each other. We became our own faculty, with our own curriculum, our own courses. We made a distinction between academic studies which were official, and political studies which were not.'[54] 'We transformed Robben Island into the University of the ANC.'[55]

Why not transform it again? For Michael, this was the case *par excellence* of 'mutual aid', the theme of the next chapter of this book. Why not turn the island not only into a museum but into a place of modern studies, a university whose main purpose would be to give effect to the government's pledge to offer redress to the people of South Africa who missed the educational opportunities to which they were entitled. Whether or not it will be so transformed is still 'unfinished business', the theme of the last chapter in this book.

9
Mutual Aid

Looking back over the decade from 1970, when he had decided to follow a world agenda, and 1980, which saw the publication of the co-authored *Distance Teaching for the Third World*, Michael compared, as, indeed, he had done earlier in the decade, what was happening in the Third World and in Britain. In both places it had been a difficult decade which had broken sharply with the 1960s after the international oil crisis of 1973. Just as darkly, there seemed likely to be a still bleaker 'or at any rate a more difficult' period ahead both for education and for social policy.

In an interesting, undated and confidential memorandum of ten typed pages for the ACE, probably written in 1976, the year when he ceased to be Chairman and became President, Michael struck a personal note. Over the last few years he had

> been out of touch with education in Britain and instead [had] been in Africa trying with my colleagues Tony Dodds and Hilary Perraton to spread teaching by the methods of the NEC and the Open University [they were now fully paired in his mind] and incidentally also trying, not yet with much success, to get from a distance a different view of education from in Britain.[1]

He concluded that there was perhaps most reason for scepticism about the prospects of the Third World which had 'for the most part taken over the educational systems of the colonial past'. 'So much energy' was being put into 'quantitative growth' in the numbers of people being educated that not much was being 'left over for qualitative improvement'.

A friend of his in Mauritius, the country where he had started his African adventure, was trying to modernise her school's curriculum and was proud because she had managed to persuade the history teacher 'to take a great step towards the present'. She was now 'going to concentrate on 18th-century English history rather than 17th-century'. 'Modernisation' even of such a limited kind was being held back by poverty. 'If they manage in the next decades, considering their rates of population increase [he did not at this point refer to the burden of debt] to maintain the proportion of children at school at the present levels, they will be doing well.' Some countries did not do well, and the 1980s was a more difficult decade than the 1970s. UNESCO estimated in 1995 that in no fewer than 14 countries a smaller proportion of children of primary school age were going to school in 1992 than in 1980. Over the same period Africa's total debt as a proportion of gross national product soared to the point that it exceeded gross national product.

The answer for Michael remained what it had been before he even went to Africa. 'The need is for an alternative to school which is both cheaper – a cardinal point – and more related to the needs of agriculture and of rural life.' 'Ministers of Finance are more likely to look on education as a virulent modern plague which the poor have caught from the rich.' What he and his colleagues in the IEC had been trying to do was to make sense, conceptually to start with, of an education based on informal, non-school small groups consisting of people of all ages without special buildings and without professional teachers.' In other words, the only way out – was by mutual aid.

Michael's ideas about 'mutual aid' had been consistent and comprehensive since he set out his first thoughts in *For Richer For Poorer*. Indeed, he had successfully urged the implementation of a 'mutual aid' scheme as early as the general election of 1950 when he secured the substitution of the word 'mutualisation' for the word 'nationalisation' in the section dealing with insurance in the Party programme. And after the general election of 1951 had been lost, the failure of his proposals for a consumer service operated by government to advise consumers about the merits of goods and services on the market pushed him further in the direction of mutualisation.

Michael's first conception of the Consumers' Association in 1956 was that it would provide a way of 'empowering people' (a phrase to be much used in the future) 'if they were joined together and put their resources together ... holding their own up against the giant State'.

This concept was related in his mind to the operative principle of the Cooperative Movement, formulated more than a century earlier, the century the Mauritius school teacher did not yet reach, at a time when the power of the State was not strong. For more than a century the pursuit of this principle, the history of which greatly interested Michael, had served as a distinctive strand in socialist history.[2] Michael wanted the new Consumers' Association to give people not only information but a 'spirit of confidence' that would enable them 'to combat the fraudulent claims of advertisers and the self-interested salesmanship of commerce and industry'.[3] In a broad sense his purpose was political.

For a brief moment in 1960 it became narrowly political after the failure of the Labour Party at the general election of the previous year. Michael's pamphlet *The Chipped White Cups of Dover* (1960), already referred to, sub-titled *A Discussion of the Possibility of a New Progressive Party*, which would make an explicit appeal to consumers. It was published by another Michael venture, Unit 2. Its perspectives were long-term. A section called 'Reform and the Consumer Interest' began with the words: 'Politics will become less and less the politics of production and more the politics of consumption.'[4]

Michael's 'new party' would cease selling consumers 'short weight, measure and number',[5] get rid of resale price maintenance (Edward Heath would do this), amend the Shops Act to allow Sunday opening ('when the women are free, the shops are shut'), abolish licensing hours and introduce a decimal system. Heath was to do the last of these, too, as he was to take Britain into the European Community. *The Chipped White Cups of Dover* demanded immediate entry into the Common Market in 1960 when it was still young, without pointing to the obstacles in the way. This was a highly controversial issue for a Labour Party, led by Gaitskell, who was passionately opposed to Britain's entry. At the same time Michael pressed for consumer action in relation to nationalised industries and social services. 'Private enterprise cannot wholly disregard what consumers want. The threat of bankruptcy preserves some respect for the customer [was that the only motive?] But there is no such sanction in the public sector.'

Both education and health were singled out among 'social services'. Why should a notice appear outside the main gates of a school 'NO PARENTS ARE ALLOWED INSIDE THIS GATE unless they have business with the Head Mistress, By Order of the Governors of the School'? Why should doctors and hospital administrators reply to critics, 'Never mind the endless waiting in the Out-Patients Department' – implying that 'We know best what is good for you?' There was to be no College of Health at Bethnal Green until 1983, but within ACE, Michael unhesitatingly used the term 'Parent Power'.

The *Chipped White Cups of Dover* did not mention 'mutual aid' as such, and it concluded with the words, 'Labour could still be the new progressive party – if it satisfied the conditions that any reforming party must satisfy'. By 1964 Michael clearly thought that it did – or at least could – and found it curiously satisfying to be back for a time in Transport House during the general election of that year, despite the fact that Len Williams seemed 'concerned all the time to avoid offending anyone. He calls himself not the Admiral but the Chief Engineer of the Party'. 'I imagine,' Michael added, '[that the Chief Engineer is] ordinarily concerned not to upset anyone on the upper deck.'[6] He was offered an opportunity from the upper deck himself when he became Chairman of the SSRC after a Labour government had been returned to power.[7] None the less, consumers were very much on his mind in 1964 itself when he made an interesting and important speech 'Consumers and the Quality of Life' which showed how his mind was working. Against the background of the more materialistic and individualistic society which was developing fast through the action of market forces he focused more on the position of the poor than that of consumers in general.

The Consumers' Association had grown far more quickly than even Michael had forecast, and in 1964 it had a membership of over half a million, regularly supplied with valuable information on a wide range of products and services. Yet from Michael's angle of vision 'the poor', shut out from that range, were not getting any 'information service on the merits of goods and services that we [the consumer organisations] are trying to present to the public'. They were exploited in two ways, therefore. They had less money to spend, and what they spent their money on gave them less value. New forms of action were needed. People now had to be organised 'as parents, as patients, as passengers'.

This had been the explicit approach from the start of ACE. 'Only when more knowledge is gathered about the education system will we be able to enlighten our members adequately.' Michael and his colleagues were required to be both recipients of information and suppliers. There had to be interactivity. He expressed the hope, also, that the Centre would make 'national surveys' covering 'the questions and suggestions in the minds [not only of members] but of parents in general'.[8]

For Michael such research was always a necessary ingredient in policy-making, and on the eve of becoming Chairman of the SSRC and relinquishing his Chairmanship of the Consumers' Association, he pointed out clearly the differences between market research and social research. Without in any way dismissing the role of individuals like Mark Abrams who were involved in market research and who saw its limitations – he was to bring him into the Council – he suggested that the Consumers' Association itself should conduct research to discover not only what its members thought and felt, but on what was thought and felt by 'consumers at large'. It was not enough to treat people simply as 'customers', as both producers and advertisers were already doing. Yet it was a practice that was to spread until it reached the railway station and the airport.

Before resigning as Chairman of the Consumers' Association, Michael had set up a Research Institute for Consumer Affairs, a charitable sister organisation to the Association: like many of the associations he created – this was his pattern – it was organised on a small scale but had big ambitions. Under the direction of Brian Groombridge, as deeply interested in education and in life-long learning as Michael was, the Institute planned to investigate how those consumers, the large majority, who had little or no individual choice, were dealt with when confronted by monopolistic business or by nationalised industries. Two of its reports were on London Stations and on Estate Agents. There were also reports on 'British Cooperatives' and 'Elderly Consumers'. That on London Stations, based on observers' comments, had what seemed then to have a utopian flavour to it. Stations could become 'popular places to linger in ... a place to enjoy a coffee at all times of day and night, a place to take your girlfriend on a wet afternoon.' Parts of the Utopia were to be realised under commercial auspices.

The Research Institute worked closely with other bodies. For example, a project on equipment for disabled people, managed by Michael Dunne, was funded by Duncan Guthrie, head of Action for the Crippled Child, and by James Loring, director of the Spastics Society. Such cooperation flourished in the early 1960s as Caspar Brook, strongly backed by Michael, set up 'grass-roots' consumer groups that would *inter alia* publish magazines reporting on local supplies of goods and services. In 1962 14 independent local groups were set up, making a total of 50, and in 1963 a Federation of Consumer Groups was created. By 1965, there were 93 such groups, of whom 10 received grants from local authorities. Many of them dealt with local services, including refuse disposal.[9] Nor was that the end of the story. It was after Michael had ceased to be Chairman that Peter Goldman developed Consumer Advice Centres.

Meanwhile Michael, who remained as President until 1993 when his title was changed to that of Founding President, continued to develop and advance his ideas on consumption in general and on its relationship to 'mutual aid'. Thus, in 1970 he made an interesting and important speech at Baden in prosperous West Germany to the International Organisation of Consumers' Unions, placing consumers' associations in their economic context.

'We have nearly all come into existence in the last ten or twenty years,' he began, 'children of the affluent society':

> In the industrial countries of the West we have been *called* into existence by the fastest growth in consumer prosperity that the world has ever known, in order to meet one of the needs created by the 'consumer society', as Marcuse and other vocal critics of modern industrialism have contemptuously called it. This society generates an ever more bewildering variety of goods and services. Our organisations are needed so that consumers can benefit from this variety instead of being overwhelmed by it.

Herbert Marcuse (1898–1970) was at the height of his surprising popularity in Germany and in the United States at this time. A founder of the Frankfurt Institute of Social Research, he taught at Harvard and other American Universities before becoming Professor of Philosophy at the University of California, San Diego in 1965. A hero of the student radical movement, Marcuse attempted to integrate Marxism and Freudianism in *Eros and Civilisation* (1954) and *One Dimensional Man* (1964). His most memorable contribution to the language, if not the most convincing, was the phrase 'repressive tolerance'.

Consumer organisations would not be needed, Michael went on, 'or at any rate not just in their present form', if 'the affluent society' ceased to exist of 'even if it drastically altered its character'. Would it? This was 'a vital question for us to ask ourselves if we are to be prepared for any changes that may come.'

Michael's answers – and he began with economics – must have surprised some of the participants in the conference and they must be related to their German context. It was 'impossible to rule out completely the possibilities of a world slump on a 1930s scale'. While governments had 'learnt [back to Keynes] how to deal with deflation', they had not yet learnt how to deal with 'its opposite, inflation'.

Michael did not clearly foresee the conjunction of high inflation and high rates of unemployment, soon to be Heath's nightmare. Nor did he fully examine the extent to which supermarkets would affect not only the structure of retailing, but the psychology of individual and family behaviour; and when he pointed out that 'the affluent society *could* also end if consumers stopped wanting to get richer', the example that he chose would have seemed dubious even at the time to advertisers of cars who were familiar with market research. 'A man without a car gets great pleasure out of the first one he buys, but if he already has not got one but two cars he might actually refuse a third if he is offered it free.'

At that point Michael switched from economics and psychology to manners and morals:

> When one sees some families at their restaurant tables, looking too well-fed already, eating their way through course after course with imperturbable fortitude, showing no sense of blanching even at the end of what looks like a massive endurance test, one may have to remind oneself that they too have a physical need for food and drink. But Nature is always ready to remind us of the point if we miss even a couple of meals in a row.

By way of qualification of his argument he returned to one of his own favourite themes. 'People do not only accumulate commodities for themselves; they do so also for their families. The family transforms selfishness into altruism. Within it, people are not only striving for their own enrichment: they are striving for it on behalf of their dependants, and this itself gives another twist to the acquisitive spiral.'

In an interesting section of his address Michael turned to the social costs of production and consumption, suggesting that consumers' associations did not draw enough attention to them. For example, 'when in our journals we say that a particular detergent or typewriter or refrigerator is good value for money we do not allow for its social costs any more than the manufacturer does if he can possibly avoid doing so. We do not attach a social cost tag to the detergent declaring that on top of its price in the shops should be added the cost of polluting a river or a lake.' He went on to distinguish between the costs 'caused' by producers to consumers and those caused by consumers to consumers, taking the car, always near to the centre of his social preoccupation, as his example. An individual's car 'gets in the way of others, and makes them go slower, exudes fumes and noise for others to endure, and at the worst adds to the total kill of people slaughtered on the roads.'

Michael concluded that, whatever the problems, a 'consumer society' would continue to exist, but that the number of its critics would grow through the resistance to it of what would be at first small scale minority groups, 'not only in California': 'Students, hippies, beatniks and drop-outs', were the nearest thing to revolutionaries that the modern western world can show'. And having dwelt on the environmental costs that were to influence majority as well as minority opinion – and action – in the 1970s and 1980s, he ended neither with the rich nor the poor, but with a prescient plea for 'the consumer movement of the world' to join forces with the growing conservation movement. He had a personal message for himself also on the eve of leaving for Africa. 'Unless a more determined effort is made to reduce the social costs of congestion, the desire of people to move speedily around the earth and find something worth waiting for at the end of their journeys is going to become increasingly self-defeating.'

On returning from Africa, Michael was quickly drawn back into British consumer politics, which were themselves influenced by national politics, but in a Sunday newspaper article called 'The Unacquisitive Society',[10] which he wrote in cooperation with Tony Lynes, Frank Field's predecessor at the Child Poverty Action Group,[11] he concentrated not on any of the issues that had arisen or were arising in relation to the consumers' movement suggested by the title, but on the failure of large numbers of people to take up the welfare state benefits to which they were entitled. 'In an increasingly acquisitive society,' he suggested, '[these people were behaving in] a most unacquisitive way.' The article drew to the attention of Barbara (later Baroness) Castle, who became Secretary of State for Social Services after Labour returned to power in 1974, a *Poverty Report, 1974*, which Michael himself had edited: the research was the work of Chris Trinder of the Department of Economics at Essex University. For *The Poverty Report, 1975*, he was to carry out research himself (with support from the Leverhulme Trust) in Camden, Hackney and Bethnal Green.

The two Reports insisted that those people who were dependent on social service benefits were not 'scroungers' and that those people who refused to take up their benefits for whatever reason should be told about their rights. 'Politicians and administrators in different Government departments had created a jungle' and unless Wilson's new Labour Government made 'a determined effort to clear it away', there would be only one conclusion to draw: 'it does not really want the poorest people to enjoy their rights'. In 1975 he noted that more efforts had been made 'to put precept into practice' than had been the case 'for a long time'. Yet it was still 'the old story' of 'forwards and back'.

He drew international comparisons also, beginning with two unknown individuals among the dependent poor in Britain and Germany, Miss Semple, a 36-year-old London spinster, an epileptic, who had earned nothing for 17 years and whose only joy left was music, and Frau Langer, an 80-year-old widow in Dortmund. The German woman was the worse off of the two. Her problem was not just money but isolation. She had never had a holiday in her life.[12]

The handicaps of the poorest in both countries were linked – money, housing, health, isolation; and in England the experience of means tests had been 'so uniformly depressing as to provide a powerful argument for the call of the Child Poverty Action Group for the steady elimination of means-tested support.[13] The model was the attendance allowance for disabled people, which Lynes had hailed as a necessary advance in 1974.

In many ways the benefits jungle was to become even more thicketed between 1975 and 1995, and Michael, while aware that State action was still necessary, paid more attention after 1975 to 'mutual' than to State aid. The Labour Party was to be divided on such issues which were to be debated in the House of Lords (with Michael present) on the eve of the departure of most of the hereditary peers from the House. They remained issues close to his heart in a new millennium.[14]

There had been many political as well as personal switches of fortunes and attitudes during the last quarter of the twentieth century, which began with Wilson's resignation on the grounds of ill health in 1976 and his replacement as Prime Minister by James Callagahan, who chose Denis Healey as Chancellor of the Exchequer. Forced to take what were also unprecedented economic decisions before and after calling in the International Monetary Fund, trade union resistance, much of it unofficial, was aroused and after a 'winter of discontent' (1978–9), the Labour Government, dependent on Liberal votes in parliament, was defeated by the Conservatives, led by Thatcher, at the landmark general election of 1979. Twenty years later, with 'New Labour' in power under Tony Blair, the balance of forces had been strongly influenced by her. She had affected both major parties, not one, just as the Labour governments of 1945 and 1951 had influenced Conservative thinking about the welfare state. She herself, however, ceased to be Prime Minister in 1990, after a long and increasingly controversial spell in office.

It was during Callaghan's prime ministership that Michael, who was to be offered a peerage by him in 1978, was made Chairman of a new National Consumer Council, with two familiar figures acting as intermediaries – Jeremy Mitchell, who in 1966 had been brought into the SSRC by Michael, and Shirley Williams then Secretary of State for Prices and Consumer Protection. Both knew Michael well: he was their first choice as Chairman for a post to which considerable political importance was attached and which carried with it membership of the National Economic Development Council.[15]

As in many stories in the book, there were ironies. It was Heath, not Wilson or Callaghan, who had brought consumer interests back on the political agenda when in 1972 he appointed Geoffrey (later Lord) Howe to a new post of Minister for Consumer Affairs at the Board of Trade, and it was on Howe's and Heath's initiative that the first Fair Trading Act was passed in 1973 and the Office of Fair Trading created. It was Callaghan, not Wilson, who had appointed Williams to the new Secretaryship of State against her own wishes and the wishes of a substantial section of the Labour Party, who would have preferred to have seen her in the Department of Education and Science where she had served before 1970. His reason was said to have been that she had been too vigorous a supporter of British entry in the European Community during the referendum.

There was another change in the political spectrum when Roy Jenkins, having been defeated by Callaghan in the parliamentary election for the leadership of the Labour Party which followed Wilson's resignation, was made President of the Commission of the European Community in 1977. Michael was on the 'pro-European side' of the Labour Party whatever such political switches there were.

During the two years in which he served as an active Chairman of the NCC, he steered it along the lines that he had recommended since the early 1960s, paying particular attention to the consumer needs of the disadvantaged and not restricting his interventions to the private sector. The Council produced a series of spotlight reports that included subjects like the price of fuel, then supplied by nationalised industries, tenancy agreements and rent arrears. The first of these subjects was particularly difficult to handle and pitted Michael against bodies which he would usually have supported. In the long-term interests of conservation of resources through energy saving, the Council recommended that fuel prices should rise: in the short-term interests of poor consumers a National Fuel Poverty Forum demanded cheap fuel now.

How to deal with rent arrears took Michael into the past, rather than into the future, back to a topic he had first encountered – in a very different capacity – when he left Dartington for London in 1933.[16] There was a kind of autobiographical symmetry here. In the whole of his long life no better illustration of how he related ideas to action via research can be found than his work as Chairman of the Consumer Council. And one publication of the Council, *For Richer For Poorer*, echoed the title of his seminal unpublished work of the 1950s.

After leaving the Chairmanship of the Council Michael chose to make his maiden speech in the House of Lords on consumer matters in a debate opened by Lady (Elaine) Burton, a former Labour Member of Parliament. Like her, he felt that Callaghan's Government was not willing to give teeth to consumer bodies like the one that he had chaired, particularly when asking for consumers' protection against 'State monopolies protected by the Stated and by the law'.[17] Michael was to speak on consumer questions on several future occasions from the benches of the House of Lords, first as a Labour peer, after 1981 as a Social Democrat and then once again, after 1991, as a Labour peer. Whatever his party label, he continued to relate consumers' interests to the democratic rights of citizens. Thus, in 1982 in a debate on a Supply of Goods and Services Bill he lent his weight to the idea of extending consumer protection available already for physical goods to contracts for services because 'consumers can so much more readily be "done down" over services than they can over goods'.[18]

Three years later, having so often queried the power of the State to ignore consumers' interests, particularly in relation to public services (many of which were now being privatised), he directed attention to the power of the State as itself 'an enormous consumer'. Was it a 'good one?' No! 'If the purchasing power of public authorities [were] used quite deliberately to improve the efficiency of British industry, so much could be achieved. If such powers were properly deployed, perhaps we would see fewer reports from the Consumers' Association ... about the technological inferiority of British products.'[19]

Before leaving the chairmanship of the National Consumers' Council Michael had decided that the consumer movement 'needed a mutual aid wing to it',[20] and in 1976 he began planning a Mutual Aid Centre at 18 Victoria Park Square. It was so designated in 1977, the year that he left the Council. There was a legal resemblance between the two, Council and Centre, in that they were both companies limited by guarantee, although neither of them employed the words 'company' or 'Ltd' in their title. It had been Michael's idea that the National Consumer Council should be set up in this form: it was not brought into existence by legislation, and its finance was arranged through annual grant-in-aid. He favoured the same form for the Centre, although it received no kind of annual grant-in-aid.[21]

The pertinent link now, not legal, was between the Institute of Community Studies and the Mutual Aid Centre, which had a common address and which both depended on his leadership. Company status for the Centre made it easier for him and his Trustees to handle overhead costs and expenses and to transfer revenue from one charitable enterprise managed from Bethnal Green to another. There was flexibility. At the same time, the fact that Centre and Institute had the same Trustees (except Willmott) ensured unity of direction, if not democracy.

The Centre, which lacked any hierarchical structure but which depended on allocation of space to meet (or to try to meet) the requirements of the different bodies housed there, had cooperation as its philosophy. It was not the kind of cooperation, however, that was represented by the Cooperative Society which Michael tried in vain to galvanise at its local level, seeking to foster not only a sense of participation but of innovative entrepreneurship of the kind that in the 1990s was to infuse his School for Social Entrepreneurs. For most people in the 1970s as in the 1950s cooperation simply meant 'the Coop'; and, like Crosland before him, who, chosen by Gaitskell, had been secretary of a Commission on Cooperation in 1958, Michael wished to put life into it, starting with the London Cooperative Society. The Crosland Report had appeared at a time when the retail trade as a whole was in the course of a transformation which left the Cooperative movement behind, making it look obsolete and vulnerable.[22]

By virtue of his role in the consumer movement, Michael was one of the nine Presidents of the Society for Cooperative Studies which in 1983, a quarter of a century on, was to produce an interesting number of its *Bulletin* devoted to the Report. By then he had much experience of his own to record: the Mutual Aid Centre in Bethnal Green initiated a series of regeneration plans during the late 1970s, which included giving shoppers in every store information of a kind that would then have been considered 'unbusinesslike' in private supermarkets, like displaying *Which?* – and information on nutrition. Improving management by recruiting from outside as well as from inside the cooperative movement and ensuring that Boards of Directors would concentrate on policy-making, leaving managers to manage was Michael's hope: some of the people who had been behind 'the modern consumer movement' would recognise the value of this. There would be a 'mutual gain'.[23]

'Mutual' was becoming one of Michael's key words in the late 1970s as it had been in 1950s, when he pressed for mutualisation, and in 1969, when he had been a contributor to a *New Society* Open Group pamphlet called 'Social Reform in the Centrifugal Society', where he did not hesitate to use the term 'consumer syndicalism'. The other members of the Open Group included Willmott, Marris, Hall, Paul Barker, then the editor of *New Society*, John Maddox, editor of *Nature*, and Brian MacArthur. Among the proposals, put forward in the pamphlet 'in the interest of debate', was an Equity and Incentives scheme. There was also a brief section on Overseas Aid, and a cross-reference to Marcuse.[24]

This was a pamphlet that should be considered along with *The Symmetrical Family*, written by Michael and Willmott and published in 1973 while Michael was spending much of his time in Africa: two years later it was to appear in Penguin as a paperback. It rested on survey information from a far wider area than Bethnal Green. Hall, who considered it the best book Michael and his co-authors had ever produced, praised it not only for its content but because it was 'suffused with an extraordinary humanity … untrammelled by too much sociological theory or fashionable intellectual constructs'. In a century when academic research had 'replaced the novel as major form of social observation and creative writing', it was 'surely a major literary achievement in its own right'.[25]

Examining as it did, among much else, the distribution of cars in London – and they were taken as visual as well as social indicators – it dealt with far more than numbers. For example, we learn at the start that 'on the Hyde Park side of Sussex Gardens most of the cars parked at night were new. One minute and many years away … they were mostly of mid-century design, standing outside cheap hotels and houses so shabby they might not have been painted since Hitler fell.' The index reference to cars in *The Symmetrical Family* had subheadings 'cleaning and maintenance as leisure activities; driving as a leisure activity; effect on housing; husbands as drivers of; of managing directors; ownership, class and leisure; parking; and [a characteristic Michael entry] reducing effects of seasons'. A footnote on motorways (p. 61), which were not mentioned in the index, notes that 'our survey showed that car owners were naturally more favourable than others to the new motorways proposed for London'. It also referred to an article by Willmott and Young, 'How Urgent are London's Motorways?'.[26]

The first big effort of the Mutual Aid Centre was concerned with cars, the Milton Keynes OK Service Station Ltd (the letters Ltd were used here), a motorists' cooperative specialising in Do It Yourself servicing, repairs and advice as well as selling everything that a conventional garage would sell. The idea was borrowed from Sweden and adapted in the community garage purchased for £250,000 in the new town that was also the centre of the Open University. There was something quintessentially entrepreneurial about the venture, designed to culminate in a chain. Brixton was the second location. The directors included Tony Flower, who had his office at 18 Victoria Park Square, and who, while self-employed was acting as Deputy Director of the Institute of Community Studies. In the mid-1990s the turnover was over £400,000 a year.

The second such social entrepreneurial activity concerned the recycling of domestic appliances and furniture, and the first cooperative workshop, Brass Tacks, opened in Hackney. Others followed in Lambeth, Greenwich and Southwark. The most successful of all the 'mutual aid' activities was 'Language Line', launched in 1990, a telephone interpreting service for the large numbers of people in Bethnal Green who did not speak English.[27] It subsequently extended its business outside and by 1995 had a turnover of over £1 million a year. It had also widened its range to include a translation service. It had an important place in a long-term Bethnal Green strategy. If funds were necessary for other activities, it was ripe to be 'privatised'.

The strategy looked beyond Bethnal Green itself. The Consumers' Association was not the only organisation to leave Bethnal Green once it had become a going concern. Another was the College of Health, set up in 1983 and designed explicitly to encourage National Health Service patients to discuss openly and fully their experiences as 'consumers of health care'. It operated *Healthline* and *Waiting List Clearing House*. The idea behind the College is said to have occurred to Michael while he was in Guy's Hospital for a cancer operation. While there, he met a surgeon, Ian (later Lord) McColl, who gathered his patients around a table, offering them tea and biscuits and asking them what they thought of the care they had received or were receiving while in hospital.

The person who cooperated most closely with Michael in this venture was Marianne Rigge, daughter of a general practitioner; and the success of the College, which subsequently moved from 18 Victoria Park Square to another part of Bethnal Green, owed much to her and to the publicity given to the College in the *Guardian* by Malcolm Dean, editor of its Wednesday *Society* supplement, who also contributed to *Young at Eighty*. His contribution was called 'The Architect of Social Innovation'. It drew an implied distinction between social innovation and voluntary organisation. The idea of a 'voluntary sector' was emerging and in 1996 was to be examined fully by an independent commission headed by Nicholas Deakin, working from a Birmingham base.[28]

Marianne Rigge, who was Secretary of the Mutual Aid Centre, had previously worked with the Consumers' Association, and was co-author in 1977 with Michael of the second published paper of the Mutual Aid Press, *Mutual Aid in a Selfish Society*, which referred to other small-scale mutual aid activities associated with the Mutual Aid Centre, including a parent–teacher cooperative in a Cambridge village school and a domestic appliance repair cooperative in Shrewsbury. Such cooperative activities were related in the paper to the principle of cooperation as well as to the practice of cooperative production and consumption. Beginning with the Webbs and Cole, the co-authors examined what they and others took to be the weaknesses of the British cooperative movement, and in conclusion urged the need 'to bring back to a selfish society some vital elements of mutual aid and some vital elements of altruism'. 'Since the rivers of selfishness are always in flood the banks need to be very high. To erect any defences is what society is for.'

Society, however, was 'fragile'. Where were 'propagandists for altruism' to be found? 'In the colour supplements? Padding about in empty chambers and deserted cooperative meetings rooms?' The authors had failed to mobilise support for reform candidates at the last democratic election before the London Cooperative Society was taken over by Cooperative Retailing Services. On the opposite side (and the pamphlet was Manichean in the sharpness of its contrast) the 'legitimaters' of greed were 'everywhere in evidence'.[29] One section of the paper was devoted to the 'new consumerism which starts with the family' and went on to outline the work of the Pre-School Playgroups Association and of voluntary bodies concerned with the interests of particular groups of patients, like the Multiple Sclerosis Society and the Cancer Aftercare and Rehabilitation Society.

There was also a section on housing, a subject that had been dealt with frequently, not always in the same way, in some of Michael's earlier books. His influence could be discerned behind in the Housing Act of 1974 which introduced a system of Housing Association grants. Another piece of recent Conservative legislation charted was that setting up the Office of Fair Trading and the Department of Prices and Consumer Protection.[30] There were highly critical references, however, to the kind of socialism for which the Labour Party had stood between 1945 and 1950 – and for which a large section of the Party still stood.

Nationalisation under the control of great public corporations had been a 'misguided way' of substituting common for private ownership. 'State socialism' was discredited. 'Cooperative socialism is not: it can still offer a constructive way forward.'

In the year when the Mutual Aid Centre was formally established in Bethnal Green, Michael had written an interesting article for *New Society*, where he had many allies among both writers and readers, called 'Toward a New Concordance' in which he suggested in his first sentence, not for the first time, that conventional politics were becoming obsolete. There were few compensations, however, in social forces beyond or beneath politics. The modern *leitmotif* of society itself was 'acquisitiveness' which made people both greedy and hypocritical. It was a society that was becoming more violent too, and this in time was to preoccupy politicians as well as the public. So also was 'racism'.

Michael mentioned 'Enoch' in 'Toward a New Concordance', without considering how many poor inhabitants of Bethnal Green had warmed to what Powell had to say in his 'rivers of blood' speech. But in 1979, a year of dramatic political change, after having carried out a survey not of Bethnal Green but of Hackney, he noted above all else 'the growing violence being done to people and property' in Hackney.[31] 'Things were so bad that many of the older people, white or black, would not go out at all at night, and they did not necessarily feel safe even at home.' The title of a later article, which he published in 1981, was 'Never Go Out After Dark'.[32] In it he referred to the appointment through the Mutual Aid Centre of a Neighbourhood Warden Organiser for a housing action area in Hackney 'to do some of the work that caretakers used to do'. It described for the benefit of *New Society* readers that the Mutual Aid Centre, a 'sister body' of the Institute of Community Studies, 'which all its readers must have known about', was concerned not so much with research as with action. For example, it had started a workshop at Dalston Junction to train young unemployed to repair and refurbish furniture and domestic appliances, artefacts of the 'consumer society'.

Acquisitiveness was easier to reflect upon than violence, since there had been 'compensations for it especially for women' and for violence there were none. 'Socialism, in Michael's opinion, had gained its major victory not in industry, but in the home, where 'the real proletariat' was being 'slowly liberated'. There had been another victory too, just as significant: more and more women were migrating from the kitchen to the workplace. As a result of an alliance been socialism and acquisitiveness the old socialist vision was fading and past politics would wither away. Michael appreciated also that since both men and women could claim that in their desire to raise 'standards of life' they were motivated by love of their children, parents could claim that they were in alliance with altruism even when they were acquisitive.

Michael maintained in his 'New Concordance' article that only if the family became 'symmetrical' – with men returning to the home as women left it – could the family tip the scales against 'acquisitiveness'. 'If people put less demands on themselves [to become materially better off] and became less strenuous about what to squeeze out of their limited time in each day and on earth', discordance in society would 'gradually give way to a new concordance'. The last sentence in this revealing article, similar to the first, showed that Michael was arguing with himself, 'I said I was an optimist.' Was he? He was certainly unwilling to abandon his sense of struggle, which was to increase after Thatcher became Prime Minister two years later. Thereafter, until she lost power, he need not argue with himself. He need only argue with her.

New Society had chosen as the sub-heading for his article of 1977 'Politics is Only Part of Life. And will it be a smaller one in future with personal relations more dominant and more just?'[33] This was the wrong way of putting it on the eve of a 'winter of discontent' and a general election that changed the political agenda. The optimism that he wished he could justify in 1977 was not the kind of optimism that the Labour leadership could possibly share. Yet it was to be a different leadership after 1979 following the defection of the 'gang of four' (Jenkins, Williams, David Owen and Bill Rodgers) – Europe was a major difference on which they broke away – and, later, the rise to power of Neil Kinnock.

When Michael wrote his next book with Marianne Rigge, *Revolution from Within – Cooperatives and Cooperation in British Industry* (1983) he too had broken not only with the Labour leadership but with the Labour Party, and for a brief spell he was optimistic about the prospects of the new party which he believed might break sharply away from the past and realise his own major objectives through genuinely open discussion, backed by serious research. Indeed, in reply to a letter he wrote to Williams in December 1980, she sent a warm reply identifying as far as she could her own experiences with his:

> I must say that one of the great things about you is that you're always ready for something new. As you know I'm probably as deeply wed to the Labour Party as Tony Crosland was, and the whole idea of making the break is one that I find utterly appalling.

But we shall have to see what this year brings. I suspect it's likely to be rather a decisive one.

Michael suspected – or more than suspected – the same. It was the main reason why he joined. On joining he asked to be described as 'Founder of the Consumer Movement in Britain, co-author with Herbert Morrison of *Let Us Face the Future* in 1945'.[34]

Inevitably, however, he found himself at odds with some of his old Labour Party friends, particularly after he had not only joined the Gang of Four but on his own had founded a Tawney Society which was a rival to the Fabian Society.[35] For some Fabians – and other Labour Party members – the name of Tawney was being exploited for political purposes of which 'the great Tawney' would never have approved. For them too David Owen was the arch-traitor in the story, while for Michael it was he alone of the Gang of Four who did not want to have the Social Democrats 'absorbed', as Michael came to see it, into a bigger Liberal Party.

David Donnison, then Professor of Town and Regional Planning at Glasgow University, was one of the first of his old colleagues to protest. Writing to Michael in forceful fashion in 1980 from a city which he described as 'politically unforgiving and unforgetting', he drew a distinction between the 'relatively non-political south', where the SDP was winning converts, and politicised places and areas outside it. Michael replied disarmingly – although the reason he gave in his reply would have aggravated many people inside the SDP, including Owen. While he was sorry that they disagreed, he told Donnison, he 'certainly' did not feel 'that strongly' about it himself and that he would give him his reasons later.[36]

Michael was to list these reasons publicly in 1987 in a remarkable pamphlet *The Chipped White Cups of Steel* which appeared after the general election of that year when it had become clear that the SDP and the Liberal Party would cease to act in alliance as they had done since 1980 and would now amalgamate to form the Liberal Democratic Party. This was an outcome, the result of democratic votes, which Michael resented and bitterly opposed. He thought that the Liberal leader David (later Lord) Steel, a man in a hurry, had forced the pace. He had joined the SDP 'gladly', Michael stated, not because he had discarded what he thought of as 'the basic principles of the Labour Party', but because 'with its combination of watered-down policies and fired-up mutual antagonisms it had itself gone a long way towards abandoning them'.[37] Already he was preparing for his return.

Comparing *The Chipped White Cups of Steel* with *The Chipped White Cups of Dover*, there were more signs of continuity in Michael's thinking than of contrast, although in the first he was putting forward the argument for a new progressive party and in the second he was writing after he had become disappointed with the record of the new, professedly progressive, party which he had 'gladly' joined. He noted irony too as well as contrast. *The Chipped White Cups of Dover* was turned down by the Fabian Society, then presided over by Williams. *The Chipped White Cups of Steel* was turned down by the Tawney Society, which he himself had founded in 1981. As a result, it was published, as the first pamphlet had been, by Unit 2, 'a publishing house with only a cupboard in it'. It was very much Michael's own cupboard. 'After this,' Michael explained, he intended to speed up Unit 2's publication rate and publish the third pamphlet before the end of the century. It has still not appeared.

On joining the SDP Michael served briefly as Acting Director of the Policy Research Department, but he refused to apply for the advertised job of Research Director of the Party and founded the Tawney Society instead, with Tony Flower at his side. This was because he had already concluded as early as May 1981 – after the first Policy Conference of the new Party – that it was not going to convert itself from 'a negative into a positive' force.[38] And that was before it began to win a series of by-elections (Williams won the first, dramatically, at Crosby) and before it proclaimed on the day of its first anniversary that at the next general election it would offer the country 'not just a change of government but a change of system'.[39] It was also before a Statement of Principles, *A Fresh Start for Britain*, was published. This was drafted by a Working Party of Liberals and Social Democrats, chaired jointly by Steel and Williams, which recognised that 'our Parties', while sharing 'a common concern about Britain's political and economic future, stem from different traditions and have their own identities'.

The National Steering Group of the Party had already set up a number of policy committees as it attempted 'to develop strategic policy proposals across the board', and Michael, who found it difficult to restrict his interest to only one of them, served on the committee concerned with urban Policy which was chaired by Williams.[40] He worked very hard as a member, soliciting information from councillors, administrators, academics and friends in many different cities, including Manchester, where one of his correspondents, Charles Hill, was willing to persuade people 'to carry out a local survey on similar lines to that undertaken in Hackney'.[41]

It was not as a result of his work with this group that Michael came to feel that the Party was not working on the right lines, but as the author of an SDP Open Forum pamphlet *Bigness is the Enemy of Humanity*. This for him was the oldest of themes, but when he completed his draft he met with criticism not only for its content but for his method of handling it. The first sharp attack came from Wayland Young (later Lord Kennet), who objected to Williams about a number of specific points in it, including suggestions, as he, the other Young, interpreted them, to dismantle the national electricity, gas and water distribution networks. Wayland Young disliked the tone of the pamphlet too and the use of phrases like 'No doubt the government would rather build prisons than schools'. Another Michael, Michael Heseltine, had also been attacked in the pamphlet, aggressively in Wayland Young's opinion, as was a great figure from the past, Edwin Chadwick, the founding saint of 'all public health people', just the people we want to appeal to.

Michael defended himself on each of these points in a tripartite argument that involved Williams,[42] but he moved to the attack also, objecting to being criticised for comments in an Open Forum publication which was designed to arouse discussion:

> Open Forum papers are not meant to be statements of party policy which you are expected to agree with all along the line ... They are intended to be statements by individual authors, not committing the party, which will show that a wide range of personal views is not just tolerated, but encouraged. You seem to be upset because you don't agree with me when you should be pleased. The paper has already, at any rate between the two Youngs, achieved its purpose of stimulating discussion.[43]

Michael had said the same during the late 1940s when producing discussion documents for the Labour Party. But he did not deal with another point raised by Wayland Young – that it had been a mistake for Michael to hold a press conference on the pamphlet, the first in the Open Forum series, 'on which much hangs', without even being able to give printed copies to the press.

It was against this background that Michael developed the Tawney Society, calling it 'our own Bow Group'. It would, he said, 'make for excitement', and it did. As Tony Flower wrote in *Young at Eighty* in an essay called enchantingly, borrowing from R. A. Butler, 'The Art of the Possible':

> Helping to start the Tawney Society was my first job with Michael, and my first lesson in how to grab a headline. Naming the Society after the great Labour philosopher was either a very good idea or an extremely bad one, depending on which Party you were in at the

time. But in putting the Society on the map it was a stroke of genius.[44]

Such a Society needed not only press publicity but its own organ of internal communication, and the first number of the *Tawney Newsletter*, issued in April 1982, three months after the Society came into existence, stated plainly that the Society had two main functions – first, to provide a forum for collective study of policy issues and, second, to 'give a platform to individuals with something stimulating, constructive and (we hope) original to say both about the philosophy and the policy of the party'.

Under the first heading the first Tawney Society Conference had already been held at Croydon on the subject of 'centralisation' under the chairmanship of Tyrrell Burgess, reunited with Michael on this issue: among the people who had attended from distant places there were groups from Manchester and Cardiff. The second conference, already being planned for June, was to be in Havering, and was to offer the occasion for starting the East London Tawney Society: the Havering branch had already shown initiative in carrying out local opinion surveys, starting a 'community newspaper' called *Community View*, and 'womaning' a Complaints Switchboard. The *Newsletter* went on to underline the importance of 'mutual aid' without using the term. The SDP, it said, was not brought into existence simply to 'breathe new life' into central or local government, but 'to encourage its members to take an active part in voluntary bodies and to set up new ones'.

The first Tawney Society pamphlet had already appeared – Hall's *Investing in Innovation*, a good Michael-type title, criticised sharply in the first letter to appear in the *Newsletter*; and the second was by Michael, *Inflation, Unemployment and the Remoralisation of Society* (1982). The title of the fourth pamphlet, written in partnership with Hall, *The Middle of the Night*, he had already used. It recalled Hackney, 1981. The content, however, was different.[45]

There were also to be *Tawney Papers*, the texts to be sent in by local members. These were not to be generally circulated, but to be purchasable on demand. One already received was by Glenna Robson and the Manchester Housing Policy Group, *Housing Problems and Policy*. Interested as he was in these topics, Michael took the chair at one of two joint meetings with Liberals. Organised by the Society and the Liberals' counterpart society, Arena, its subject was 'New Forms of Enterprise', and the rendezvous was the National Liberal Club in Whitehall.

The research function of the Society was to be linked 'where possible' to 'direct action and experiment', and the first group of projects were to be concerned with local government. The choice of this theme was stimulated by the Conservative administration's 'attack on local independence and on local government spending'.[46] Another project was headed 'Cost of Leaving the EEC', an interesting title if only in the light of Thatcher's views on Europe and the complex future impact of the subject on both Parties. 'If the Labour Party were returned to office, one of its acts might be (according to some of its members certainly would be) to pull Britain out of the EEC. [For Michael it] would be well for this to be countered, as far as it can be, well before the Election.'

For a research society there was a strong, if not surprising, stress on elections throughout the period of Michael's Chairmanship. Tawney Pamphlet Number 4, *The Middle of the Night*, stated that the Society stood on 'the radical wing of the SDP': was sub-titled 'suggestions towards the Election Manifesto'.[47] Its second section was called *Incomes Policy*, and much of the pamphlet was devoted to arguing the case for such a policy of the kind which had been pursued by Wilson, Heath and Callaghan, but which Thatcher had explicitly rejected.

Before writing it, Michael had corresponded with the economist James Meade, who congratulated him on having created the Tawney Society. 'If there were to be a Liberal/Social Democrat Government after the next general election' – and at this early point Michael seemed optimistic about the chances – it would be judged 'more than anything else on the extent of its success in implementing such a policy' which needed to be worked out at once.[48] Meade agreed with Michael that it would be 'to misunderstand the task' of a future government to 'place all the blame for inflation', as Thatcher had done, politically successfully, on the acquisitiveness of trade unions. 'Outside the unions there are also masses of people ... behaving like trade unionists even though they abhor the name.'

Other sections of *The Middle of the Night* dealt with social security, fringe benefits, reducing unemployment and industrial democracy. Meanwhile, another pamphleteer, Ronald Dore, active in the affairs of the Institute of Development Studies at Sussex University, had entitled his pamphlet *An Incomes Policy Built to Last*. Dore was one of the people who served on the first Provisional Committee of the Tawney Society, along with Tom Forrester, who had been President of the Students' Union at Sussex University and who was fascinated by the new technologies of Silicon Valley. Other members of the committee included Burgess, Dean, Martin Minogue, one of Michael's regular correspondents, Julia Neuberger, and Helen Price.

On the eve of a 'truly momentous' national party conference it was essential, the editors said, to decide 'what sort of SDP' was wanted and needed:

> Very rarely in political history can it be truly said that a cause and a party stand at some critical juncture ... The autumn of 1982 is surely one of these few occasions.

Europe had been the major matter of division within the Labour Party in the 1970s, but after the Falkland Islands War the world became the stage; and the last section of *The Middle of the Night*, called 'The World Around Us', rightly accused both the Labour and the Conservative Parties of pretending that 'the rest of the world is an island, Britain the mainland'. It added, however, that the SDP should clearly beware of EEC integration for integration's sake. 'It is by no means obvious that many government functions are better run from Brussels.'[49] David Owen was to follow this line after the end of the SDP.

The most important characteristic of the SDP for Michael and Hall 'in sharp contrast to the two older parties of the left and right', was that it was not 'a class party'. There was more than a whiff of Richard Acland's Commonwealth Party in such statements,[50] just as there was a recurring whiff of that Party when by-election victories, peak events for the winners, were announced. Yet there was more emphasis on 'right to choose' than there had been in Acland's speeches and writings; and some of the issues picked out as particularly relevant, not least choice, were to be picked up in turn by the Conservative Party more than by the 'old' Labour Party.

The 1983 election was won decisively by Margaret Thatcher and the Conservatives, and the Social Democrats made far less headway than by-election results had suggested. The Labour Party, however, which had been led from the left by Michael Foot, gradually set about reorganising itself from within further encouraging Michael to begin looking back to the party which he had left. In 1983 itself there was already a forlorn note to the last letter that he wrote to Eirlys Roberts in the summer after she had suggested that he should convene a meeting of the Consumer Policy Group:

> I would gladly convene a meeting as you suggest but I don't think the moment is right. The discussions about whether the SDP should merge with the Liberals etc. are getting more active now and I am afraid no one's going to be interested in policy questions for a bit.[51]

Roberts's letter had been set on paper headed European Research into Consumer Affairs, ERICA. She was its Chairman.

In 1987 after another Thatcherite election victory Michael's *The Chipped White Cups of Steel*, which did not focus on Europe, none the less had a section called 'Need to Join the World', which recognised as David Owen, then sole SDP leader, did, that 'to shape purely national policies in a world society' was 'bound to be fraught'. Referring back to 'British nationalism, even jingoism', exploited by Thatcher in the Falklands crisis, and taken up by the popular press, Michael insisted that the world society of the future 'should not be dominated by the polyglot cosmopolitan grey sameness of globalism'. He hated sameness.

The word 'globalisation' was to become as fashionable, not least among sociologists, as any word of the late twentieth century had been, but the media, which had more and more to do not only with the making of new words but the ordering of new agendas, were not mentioned in *The Chipped White Cups of Steel*. This was a serious omission. It was through headlines in the press and images on the television screens and not in the pages of well-written pamphlets that perceptions of Britain and the world were being formed, and 'perception' itself was to become a new buzzword, not least among politicians.

Within a Thatcherite political context *The Chipped White Cups of Steel* plainly maintained that if 'a fourth [Thatcher] victory' was considered possible, there could only be one proper course for those who wanted 'to shift Britain into a different direction'. They would have to organise an electoral 'working arrangement between Labour, Liberals and the SDP'. What distinguished Michael from the majority of his SDP colleagues, however was that he still did not believe that such an arrangement could be brought any nearer by 'submerging the SDP into an alliance with just one of these elements, the Liberals, on their own'. That, of course, was just what was to happen, although there were bigger things too to happen, including the fall of Thatcher, yet another Conservative victory under John Major at the next general election in 1992, and the emergence after it of what came to be called 'New Labour' leadership first under John Smith and then under Tony Blair.

It was not Michael's political analysis which makes *The Chipped White Cups of Steel* interesting to historians, but the repetition in it of an argument used in *The Middle of the Night* which sounded to some like 'pure Thatcherism':

> The consumer should be sovereign – as he or she is, at least in theory, and much of the time in practice, in the private marketplace. Choice of service should be built in as a principle. This means

that the customer must be able to choose between schools, colleges, specialists, bus systems, and different forms of public housing – just as now with cars, television and holidays abroad.

The approach to this proposition was none the less totally anti-Thatcherite. Michael saw 'mutual aid' as just as essential as consumer choice in a society where the gap between rich and poor was widening. He sharply criticised 'enfeebling' cuts in government spending and looked forward to a time when 'welfare state and welfare self help' would flourish together in partnership: they were not substitutes for each other. Some of the 'mutual aid' associations within his range of influence drew on the state or on local authorities: some did not. Ironically again, some State help came from the Manpower Commission, set up by Thatcher's government and then abolished. There was no irony for him in the fact that she had actually strengthened the State while freeing the market. It was in order to check 'the new concentration of power' that mutual aid would have to be both devolved and publicly supported.[52]

Only ten years earlier, Michael had considered the possibility of life having less politics in it.[53] Now he was demanding more intervention to redress injustices. Yet he still attached more importance to ideas than to structures. 'Organisations run on the wheel of ideas, and first we have to get them right.' This might have been the motto of a new periodical publication which he launched in 1988, *Samizdat*, an oddly named centre-left magazine, which was planned during the year before the wall dividing Germany fell.[54] Its first editor was Ben Pimlott, and Tony Flower, who succeeded him, was managing editor and producer. Its object was to succour 'a new popular front of the mind'. 'It is an open question,' Michael pronounced, whether 'Gorbachev has benefited Thatcher more than Kinnock.'

That was the kind of question which its contributors liked asking. They included Bernard Crick, identifying the place of Orwell in the radical tradition, Paul Hirst discussing Cole, and Robert Skidelsky, then a member of the SDP and soon to become an SDP (and later a Conservative) peer. He was renowned then for his biography of Keynes. One of the articles in the first number (by Colin Ward) was called 'Self-Help and Mutual Aid'; and for Michael, looking at the world from his vantage point in the Mutual Aid Centre, it was this which remained at the core of any radical programme.

Outside party politics, to which he quietly returned, Michael had two other concerns which none the less overlapped with rather than replaced his political preoccupations. The first, which was not his own idea but which was linked to all his ideas, was the University of the Third Age, usually abbreviated to U3A, a response not to the electoral timetable but to long-term social trends. The second, very much his idea, was the Open College of the Arts, which he might have founded at any time in his active life, the purposes of which transcended time. The two concerns were connected, involving both Bethnal Green and Dartington. There was a thriving Devon branch of the University of the Third Age. (The full title misled some people who confused Third Age and Third World.) Meanwhile, preparations for the Open College of the Arts, which overwhelmed the staff of the Mutual Aid Centre in the East End, were largely carried forward by people in Dartington.

The English U3A, 'de-centralising, de-institutionalising and de-professionalising',[55] was born in neither place but in the other place that figured on Michael's map, Cambridge, where the first public meeting took place in the Guildhall on 20 July 1981. Laslett, whose interests in both education and ageing were deeply rooted, was the man behind its founding. Yet there was a Dartington link even there, for Laslett, who was carrying out work on 'The Education of the Elderly' in 1979, with the help of the National Extension College, had received a grant from the Elmgrant Trust to explore what was happening in France, where a Federation of Third Age Universities had been founded in Toulouse in 1973.[56] It was he, as interested as Michael was in action as well as in research, who convened the landmark meeting where Michael was one of the people present. Another was Eric Midwinter, a friend and colleague of Michael who had long been involved in community and mutual aid projects and who had directed the Educational Priority Area Project in Liverpool. Completing a network of links, he had been Head of the Public Affairs Unit of the National Consumer Council.[57]

Laslett wrote an essay on *The Education of the Elderly in Britain* in 1980 and in the same year drafted, as Michael might well have done, what he called *An Educational Charter for the Elderly*.[58] Distance learning was mentioned explicitly. The motto was 'Education is NOT just for youth'.

The University of the Third Age in Britain drew on French conceptions of what the Third Age is without accepting them. For the French, the first age is an age of learning, the second an age of working and parenting, and the third an age of living when a sense of fulfilment can be combined – 'can' is a necessary verb – with a sense of exploration. Only the 'Second Age' sounds definite within this schema, rather like secondary education in older schema of an age of learning (or being taught), cut off sharply (often by examinations) from primary education at one end and at the other with an entry into university education or into 'the world of work'.

Such a phase model gives a special significance to the 'Third Age', an age not of innocence but of experience when patterns of work and leisure are blurred and where paid work and 'gift work' – work done 'for the love of it' – can be combined.[59] Yet it is only a model, and the pattern that emerged in England was characteristically English, 'Broad Church' in character, with an emphasis on local decision-making rather than on a national system.

A National Committee came second, not first, supported in time not by the State but by the Nuffield Foundation. A Forum on the Rights of Elderly People, the work of which was co-ordinated by Dianne Norton, had been created in January 1981, and Norton went on to become Executive Secretary of the first National Committee. Michael was made Chairman. The first programme activity was an Easter School in March 1982. By then, Age Concern, a national body with interests that were not primarily educational, was also involved. It was not until 1983, however, that, following Michael's formula, a Third Age Trust was registered as a company limited by guarantee which later in the year was recognised too as a charity.

The first representative national conference and general meeting of U3A was held at the University of Keele in 1984, and flexibility was guaranteed when a motion to put a lower age limit on membership was heavily defeated. At the same conference Sir Roy Shaw, formerly a Professor there and Director of the Arts Council, delivered the first Third Age Lecture.[60] One of the most interesting groups in England was based on Totnes, where it emerged from a 'New Horizons Project for Mature Redundant Workers and Early Retired Persons', supported by the Nuffield Foundation and the European Social Fund.[61]

The Open College of the Arts, a distance learning venture, originally with a Devon base, also had European support, but the idea behind it went back deep into Michael's life and was closely associated with the experience of Dartington. The first memorandum relating to the College – and it was written by Michael and Hilary Perraton – gave it a far more ambitious title, however – 'a European Open University for the Arts and Crafts'.[62] Ideas about its structure and its programming were abundant, all of them based on Michael's belief that the artist could be 'brought out' in everyone, an idea which he shared with many others, ancestors and contemporaries.

Asked why it was so late in his life that he set out to translate the idea into action, Michael confessed that he had felt that the translation might be very difficult.[63] He also knew that it would cost a substantial sum to launch it. He had four groups of people in mind – those with no experience, those with some and wishing to extend it, those wanting to understand art and appreciate it without 'doing' it, and school children, very much a group on its own.

He quickly found a Director – Ian Tregarthen Jenkin, retired Principal at Camberwell and Curator of the Royal Academy Schools. Offering him the 'pioneering' post after discovering his enthusiasm, he talked of a 'marriage between British excellence in distance learning and the equally marked excellence in the arts and crafts'. In a 'post-industrial society there were growing numbers of people whose lives would be enriched if they were able to express themselves creatively.'[64] By the time that Jenkin summoned advisory groups, the title of the proposed institution had been shortened to the European University for the Arts and Design, but it remained as ambitious a project as ever, and by the time that he took up his post officially on 1 September 1986 it was only slightly less ambitious. The word University was now changed to College.

It was not until November 1986 that the name 'Open College for Art, Design and Crafts' was used, and by then the word 'Open College' had become familiar in a broader context. In 1981 the Manpower Services Commission, which gave useful, sometimes invaluable, support to many 'mutual aid' groups, had launched an 'Open Tech', and in July 1986 an Open College was announced, a collaborative national venture which was supported initially by a grant of £32 million, but was required to become self-financing after a limited time. Richard Freeman left the NEC to become its Director in January 1987. It seemed then, although the expectation was falsified, that the NEC would suffer. Might not this, however be an opportunity for OCA?[65]

Michael's ideas for OCA courses seemed limitless. They were also extremely diverse, including, for example, the idea of a garden design course, complete with multi-media elements that included a kit box containing among other items 3D glasses to look at cut-out scenes of a suburban garden, soil analysis equipment, and a rain gauge. Continuing with a garden metaphor, Jenkin had to prune such ideas, assisted by Ralph Jeffery, formerly in charge of the Art and Design Inspectorate. The result was one basic course, 'Foundation for Art and Design', prepared by ten people with Sasha as editor.

The course was planned in Devonshire, not in Bethnal Green, but long before the first students began to work on it in January 1988 the staff at the Institute and Centre in Bethnal Green were under continuous pressure, answering telephone calls and arranging for the printing of materials. Wyn Tucker received hundreds of letters a week, and Tony Flower designed the first course books. Meanwhile, part-time tutors were being recruited, a remarkable group, and over 1,200 students signed up for the first year.

Michael insisted on adding more courses for the second year, and although the Open University was unwilling to help and the Open College restricted the help that it gave, the range of courses was duly widened. Sasha was of immense importance both at the centre and in keeping in regular contact with a number of regional tutorial centres, some in Colleges of Art and Arts Centres, some in artists' studios and craftsmen's workshops. Not all parts of the country were covered: there were many blank areas on the map. Michael wanted to know everything that was happening or being thought through. 'Do forgive me for writing and from such a distance,' he once wrote, not untypically, to the Director. 'Seven thousand miles away I may be, but in spirit I am in the next room and thinking about OCA.'[66]

Soon the place that Michael was thinking about had changed, and that was his own idea. The College was moved to Yorkshire to the outbuildings of the historic home of two other Elmhirsts, Alfred and Gwen, close friends of Michael, keenly interested in education.[67] Not far away from Wentworth Woodhouse, the great Fitzwilliam mansion, the world of industry was not far away either. When the move took place the Director changed too, Jenkin giving way to David Davies, already deeply involved in the project, who remained in the post until 1998. Michael himself, who continued to have ideas (one was to build a cathedral), handed over the chairmanship of the Trust to Bob (later Lord) Gavron in January 1991. Yet he went to Yorkshire as often as he could, watched with interest as the College grew, and worried restlessly when its finances were precarious.

From the start the fees paid by the 'students' (the term was never quite the right one) were inadequate to cover expenses. The Elmgrant and Elmhirst Trusts were helpful. So, too, were other Trusts. Over the years they were to include the Gulbenkian Foundation, the Carnegie United Kingdom Trust, the Paul Hamlyn Foundation, the Rayne Trust, the David Cohen Family Charitable Trust, the Clore Foundation,[68] the Midas Trust, the Robert Gavron Charitable Trust, and the Foundation for Sport and the Arts (for office computers). There were also individual donors, some anonymous. Some donors who supported the Open College of Arts would have supported none other of Michael's projects. (This was, of course, true in reverse.) The membership of the College's Board of Trustees remained impressive over the years. It included, among others, Alec Bernstein, Graham Greene, Patrick Nuttgens, Barry Till, Lady (Simone) Warner and Naomi Sargant. Michael continued as a Trustee after he ceased to be Chairman. There was also a parallel Academic Committee, responsible for monitoring old courses and deciding on new ones. Some courses required attendance at designated local centres.

Most of the mutual aid projects described in this chapter continued into the 1990s, and new ones were added. All are unfinished. How long they will last depends on the energies of individual people and groups, how much time they are prepared to devote to their voluntary tasks, and what talents they bring to them. Their scope changes with social trends that they can help to identify, like ageing, or on economic circumstances, which are beyond their control, including the level of employment and of the national income. They all raise policy questions, in particular, the extent to which the State or local authorities and through them public funding is involved.[69] Within the context of this book, however, they are interesting as well as important in that they are integral elements in Michael's biography as they would certainly have been in any autobiography he might have cared to write.

10
Unfinished Business

The title of the Stamp Memorial Lecture in 1984, delivered by Lord Rayner, an ally of Thatcher, was 'The Unfinished Agenda', and his opening sentence might have been written by Michael. 'As organisations grow larger, the natural drift is towards inertia and away from dynamic response to new challenges and opportunities.'[1] Notwithstanding, whatever may be said of organisations – and not all of them respond in that way – it is certainly not always the case that as individuals grow older there is a 'natural drift' of the kind described.

As this last chapter reveals, Michael never showed any signs of 'natural drift'. He was as purposive as ever, although he experienced much suffering and in 1994 the death of the person, Sasha, who meant the most to him. The chapter relates his purpose directly and indirectly to time – and to change – while reaching back through memory, as he often chose to do, to the origins and development of his earlier initiatives. It constitutes something of a summary, therefore, of finished as well as unfinished achievement. Because of this it might have been the longest in the book. As it is, it is the shortest. In part, this is because Michael's plans, as open and exciting as they ever had been, are still in the process of being worked out. In part, however, it is because many of the themes, which will now be familiar to readers, are the same as in previous chapters, with some of them, however, gaining new relevance in a new millennium. Dartington and Bethnal Green are still on the map and will remain on the reader's map. For the new millennium, where some of the themes already set out are gaining a new relevance, Michael has ventures in mind which draw on his memory and his experience. Thus, before the millennium began he was hoping in 2000 to raise enough money through the Phoenix Educational Trust, which he had created, to put up a building for two independent schools which had sprung out of Dartington School. It would be the first new building designed for a progressive school for over 50 years.

There are two reasons of a different kind for the relative shortness of this chapter. The first is basic. As a historian used to 'updating' my own work, I cannot yet see the political history of the present in historical perspective, nor, indeed, foresee within a global context the likely social or economic fortunes of Britain. They rest largely on the United States, but Europe figures in all the many relevant equations. Solving them now is impossible. There are too many unknowns, too many unresolved organisational choices. Futurologists are of even less help than historians.

The second reason is that since Michael forges ahead with his projects, old and new, some of them on a large scale, like the School for Social Entrepreneurs, some of them intimate, confidential and in course of negotiation, what he himself is saying (or will say) about them matters far more than what a historian – or biographer – can say at this point in history. He is thinking of writing a last book called *Letter to Gaia*, the daughter of his last marriage with Dorit Uhlemann in 1995, and this will be essential reading for all who look to him for the kind of assessments of past, present and future which he has so frequently offered in the past.

In the absence of a letter to Gaia, autobiography should take over, and in lieu of an autobiography reviews and oral interviews rather than the last chapter of this book. The interviews are often revealing. Michael told one interviewer in 1995 that he did not feel any older than he did when he was 19, 'perhaps less old really'. He had 'no less energy', he added, 'mental energy anyway'.[2] Certainly, six years later his physical expressions had not greatly changed – his shrugs of the shoulder, his raising of his eyes, his smiles – although there were perhaps more looks of concern, even frowns.

Going beyond *Young at Eighty* in my own researches I have been the most persistent of his interviewers, seeking from time to time to get him to identify his own priorities, and attempting to place in limited perspective his views on time, on age, and on birth, life and death. As always he sees these not as exclusively personal views but as expressions of cultural values, and public documents, like *The Age Shift*, complete with up-to-date statistics, produced by the Department of Trade and Industry in 2000, have to be added to lists of sources that historians must consult. 'Down with Age' was the title of an interesting article that he wrote in the *London Review of Books* in 1990 which ended with the sentence 'the ageless society would be a far-reaching liberation in the brave new world of the twenty-first century.[3]

There is much in this chapter about life and death which goes forward in time beyond *Young at Eighty*, now a dated book. And what is said about them, while not new, is striking. One of his books, co-authored with Leslie Cullen, was called *A Good Death*. Yet it was five years earlier than its publication and four years before Sasha's death that he delivered a lecture on 'Death and Modern Culture' at the University of California, Santa Barbara, in 1990, not far from the crematorium which Evelyn Waugh had satirised in *The Loved One*, and two years after that he wrote the article on death in the *Encyclopedia of Time*, edited by Jan Macey. The subject was already in his mind.

None the less, in this chapter, as in the ones that precede it, there is always return to resilience and enterprise, and both time and timing are more important to him than ever. 'Time is Right', the title of one of his articles written in the late 1970s, reflects a continuing preoccupation, although in this particular case it concerned the idea of a magazine for the over-fifties (or sixties) which was taken over by *The Oldie* and Saga not by Michael or Mary Stott, for many years editor of *The Guardian*'s women's column whose picture appeared alongside his own at the top of the article.

Michael's determination not to be a slave to time was accompanied by a determination that others should not be either. His Presidential Address to the British Association for the Advancement of Science in 1990 was called 'Liberating the Old and Young: The Case for an Ageless Society'. How clock time is related to other time had long been one of his personal and public preoccupations, even before he reached what he would never himself have called late 'middle age', and he both lectured on and wrote books about the relationship as early as the 1980s. He also founded in 1983 an interdisciplinary body to discuss it, the Association for the Social Study of Time, ASSET, one of his memorable acronyms. 'Time is becoming popular,' he wrote in 1985, 'so much so that authors are finding themselves hard put to find new ways of playing with the word.'[4]

A book of essays produced by ASSET, *The Rhythms of Society* (1988), co-edited by himself and Tom Schuller, bearing the words 'Report of the Institute of Community Studies', served as a prelude to *The Metronomic Society*, Michael's most original and penetrating book, which followed later in the same year, published simultaneously in the United States and England by the Harvard University Press and Thames and Hudson, the publisher of *The Rise of the Meritocracy*. Michael once described the book (mischievously?) as 'recreational reading', but he now regards it as the best book that he has written.

It had been longer in the making than any other of his books because of the nature of the research which he carried out concerning both the rhythms of 'daily life' and historical cycles, short and long. In writing it he had consulted scholars from a variety of disciplines. As early as 1971 he had published an article in *Nature* in collaboration with the physicist John Ziman, 'Cycles in Social Behaviour', and in 2001 he was working with Ziman again on the relationship between 'habit' and 'change' and the role of fashion.

He had recruited Schuller to work alongside him in 1983, and in a memorable essay in *Young at Eighty*, wittily entitled 'My Time with MY', Schuller described his first characteristically informal interview with Michael, who had driven up 'fast' (four hours) to Oxford to see him after he had been observing nurses on night duty in Torquay Hospital: he was in the first stages of 'rhythm' research for *The Metronomic Society*. After he had rushed back to Torquay again to study the nurses' next nocturnal round, Schuller was left to ponder on 'a fragmentary research outline, an unfinished plate of digestive biscuits' (dear to Michael), and a recollection of 'concentration, will power and gentle energy'. 'Rhythm, which Michael was so committed to exploring as a fundamental characteristic of life, was harder to discern.' There was, however, an invitation to join the ICS, where he was to stay for two years.[5]

The book that Michael and Schuller wrote together in 1991, *Life After Work*, had an element of irony in the first part of its title: Michael never stopped working. The word 'retirement did not exist in his vocabulary. Michael had already used the second part of the title, "The Arrival of the Ageless Society" although he was not entirely happy about it. He had also referred to existing society or an "age-locked society", a modern variant on the class system which would one day be unseated. Indeed, "liberation" might prove to be the great social revolution of the next [21st] century', outdating by far what has been achieved by the women's struggle.[6]

There was no element of irony in the title of the article, also written in 1991, in which Michael wrote these words. It was called 'The Slaves of Time', and in it he described the state as the spider who both spun the web of 'entangling age-stratification' and 'pounced on malefactors'. He attacked the state for turning itself into Father Time, decreeing when people should start and be able to leave school, when they can draw a pension and when they can have sexual intercourse, buy alcohol, marry, vote, get a concessionary ticket on the buses and trains and much else besides.

This libertarian message was not concerned only with the state. In 1994 Michael identified 'hurry sickness' as a contemporary malady. 'Modern clocks are always slow – it is always later than you think. Never has there been so much to do, and so little time to it.'[7] And he put himself in the middle of the picture, as he had done when he left PEP in 1944, writing to me in 1997 that 'a day in the life of MY' was as 'hectic an affair' as ever, 'with ongoing commitments which I ought to cut down, and am doing, but not fast enough'. 'It is mad to do reviews, but I do some to make me read the book.'[8]

While Michael was contemplating the rhythms of time, the rhythms of contemporary world history were changing too, and at the end of the 1980s a sequence of events in Central and Eastern Europe ended in the dramatic collapse of the Soviet Union. The character and the extent of the historical transformation two centuries after the French Revolution were often misinterpreted at the time because of the headline drama. Was it really a death – the death of Marxism? Was it a birth – the birth of democracy? It proved to be neither, and much that happened later between 1989 and 1998 required cyclical as well as sequential explanation. There was a major political change in Britain too in 1997, loosely related to the changes of 1989 and 1990 to which Thatcher thought that she had contributed, when Tony Blair became Prime Minister with a large Labour majority. With his experience of elections Michael could look back to 1945 and draw long-term comparisons, some of them 'lessons'.

The themes of this chapter, like the themes of the book, all interconnect. Thus, in a different sphere of his experience, when on his initiative in 1995 a steering group was set up, with the support of the Leverhulme Foundation, to plan an International Research Foundation for Open Learning, Hilary Perraton was appointed as project director, returning from a post in the Caribbean.[9] All the experience of the National Extension College and the International Extension College, still as active as Michael was, lay behind the venture, which was launched appositely by Michael in a regional jubilee Open University Lecture at Churchill College, Cambridge in 1994. Place and time were right. In it he stressed that if the next twenty-five years were to be 'as brilliant as the previous twenty-five or more so', research and reflection on open learning would have to be 'encouraged in a large way'. A 'revolving core of people' would need time to 'think, study and experiment in new practices'.

With this in mind he called his Research Foundation for Open Learning 'a look-out tower'. It would have an international, not a national remit, with Deakin University in Australia within its orbit, Athabasca and Laurentian in Canada, and Indira Gandhi in India. In order to launch it, funds would be required from charitable trusts, 'like Ford and Rockefeller, Nuffield, Rowntree and Leverhulme, Sainsbury and Esmé Fairbairn and the Volkswagen and Agnelli Foundation'. The field would have to be 'the whole of open learning and not just that bit of it which operates in higher education'.

In prophetic mood Michael went on to raise a few of the issues which would be examined by the Foundation. The first set of issues concerned schools, especially secondary schools. They were 'in trouble' and seemed to be getting deeper and deeper into it every year. Children were growing up more quickly than they did – sexually and socially – and teachers were 'having to struggle with ever less biddable pupils who feel like conscripts even if they are not'. At this point Michael was back to the argument that he had advanced years before in South Australia: while childhood had been shortening, education had been lengthening. By contrast, adult students were volunteers. Had any country got 'the balance right between school and adult education'? It was not a new question.

With or without research – and Michael did not succeed then in raising the research funds he requested – he foresaw that in the next century there would be a 'major reform'. There were echoes of *The Rise of the Meritocracy* here. The entitlement to funded education should remain, but people should be able to take their ten years of post-primary education at any time in their lives: it should not be confined to the years from 11 to 21. To set the ball rolling, the Open University should get rid of all entry bars on age. 'Given that adulthood comes earlier, should there not be equality, centred on the age of 16 as a start?' At the other end of the spectrum the University of the Third Age, the success of which Michael noted with pride, had wisely decided that there should be no minimum age for participation.

Another set of issues that Michael raised – and these were old ones – concerned the 'underprivileged'. One third of the entrants to the Open University were not then formally qualified in terms of their educational record to enter other universities, and it was that 'final third' to Michael which seemed 'crucial to the name of the Open University and its basic principles of open access'. More of the unemployed, more people living in inner cities and more members of ethnic minorities needed to be brought in. The £2 million then being spent by the Open University on financial assistance to poor students was, in his opinion, far too little. Research was needed to identify blockages: regional pilot schemes needed to be supported too. It remained one of Michael's objects to encourage such schemes, whatever their subject matter. It was 'a recipe for inertia' (and apathy) to suggest – as many people did – that the whole country had to be treated as one when educational, social and arts policies were being advanced. He continued to believe that establishing priority areas or zones was the best way of proceeding.

It was sad for him, therefore, to be forced to recognise that objections to this approach would come more from the left than from the right and more from 'old Labour' and trade unionists than from Blair's 'New Labour' or from energetic post-Thatcher Conservatives. There were ironies here, as there were in all the politics of the period covered in this book. It was particularly ironical, for example, that it was Conservatives with very different values from Michael's own who took the lead in 1999 in criticising the Labour government's decision (following an Inspector's report) to place Summerhill progressive school on trial. In a brief House of Lords discussion it was Michael's Conservative namesake, Baroness Young, of a contrasting political persuasion from his own who – from an Oxford base – described the school as 'in many respects a pioneer of many educational ideas which have subsequently been incorporated into mainstream school teaching and practice'.[10] Baroness Young was to become active and well known on a very different set of issues with the next year. She was adept and effective in mobilising opinion.

Lady Young had many supporters – and equally angry enemies. Meanwhile, a group of prominent people gave their support in 2000 to the establishment of a new Michael Young Centre for Open and Distance Learning in Cambridge, 'to meet the growing need for greater choice and support for adult learners'. The Chairman of the appeal to raise funds for it was Sir Kenneth Berrill, and the patrons included the Director of the LSE, Anthony Giddens, a sociologist and Reith Lecturer in 1999, Betty Boothroyd, Speaker of the House of Commons, and my successor as Chancellor of the Open University, its Vice-Chancellor Sir John Daniels – and Nelson Mandela. Giddens's theme as Reith Lecturer was 'globalisation', a concept which divided the world bitterly as well as brought it together, raising all kinds of questions that cannot be ignored in exploring either past or future.

The Michael Young Centre now exists next to Homerton College and IEC is about to be located there alongside NEC. Cambridge is still on Michael's map, therefore, as well as Dartington and Bethnal Green. In 2000 IEC won a contract of just under £500,000 for the reworking of

London University External Degrees, another culmination of a long involvement by Michael in the issue. IEC was involved too with the Bangladeshi Open University, and Michael has proposed imaginatively that it should open an outpost in the East End's Brick Lane.

If the lecture to the Open University gave Michael the opportunity both of looking to the future and recalling the past, a lecture that he gave in 1990 under the auspices of the Economic and Social Research Council gave him the opportunity of looking back further still into a different period of his life. This was the first such ESRC Lecture, delivered in December 1990, *A Haven in a Heartless World*. Its sub-title was 'the future of the family', but it dealt briefly also with the past and the future of the ESRC. Michael's uppermost feeling a quarter of a century on, like that of some of the other first members of the SSRC, was surprise that the Council had survived. He accounted for it, he said, not only 'by dint of struggles waged by their successors', 'but in the manner that any institution survives, by successive waves of new people coming on the scene and both filling and varying the roles of their predecessors'. 'At last we can now say the SSRC is dead, long live the ESRC.' Moreover, he went on, no one, 'or hardly any one', would now resent the S giving way to the E since (a rare admission for Michael, or was it?) the E had a fair claim to be considered 'the queen of the social sciences.'[11]

The content of the lecture, sub-titled 'The Future of the Family', took Michael still further back into the past than his days at the SSRC. He referred to the ICS surveys of the 1950s, mentioning Willmott, Townsend and Marris, before turning to 'the changing family' and 'the public debate about family policy which has been generated in the run-up to the general election'. Michael saw 'nothing worrying' about marriage being 'tailored' to people rather than people being tailored to marriage, and welcomed what he called 'a great liberation from a host of cramping restrictions'. Yet he ended his lecture with a critique of the effects of so-called material progress on family life, quoting words of the nineteenth-century American critic of society Ralph Waldo Emerson, 'If I keep a cow, the cow milks me.' In an acquisitive society parents suffered from cross-pressures, while children were taught too early 'the great game of choice' that they were going to have to play throughout their lives.

What still mattered most for Michael, as it always had done, was the fate of children, whether parents were married or unmarried or divorced, and the key social indicator was the proportion of children living with both natural parents, married or not. In his lecture

Michael's picture of the Bethnal Green of the 1950s focused on the particular place, as he had done 40 years earlier. Bethnal Green then had been 'not exactly a moral gymnasium', but 'local kinship was supported by a moral code which if it sometimes stunted growth and self-expression was a powerful force all the same'. It was not an exaggeration to say that 'the home was a haven in a heartless world'.

There seemed more than an element of irony for me, however, when in the last stages of correcting the proofs of this book I read accounts of the funeral in Bethnal Green in October 2000 of the last of the Kray Brothers when the bedazzled congregation heard Frank Sinatra singing 'My Way'. One of the wreaths read 'Free at Last'.[12] And Michael was still leaving the criminal side of the East End out of his picture in 1995 when he and Leslie Cullen, a Research Officer at ICS, produced their book *A Good Death*, largely a 'family study', based on interviews. The dying East Enders whom he and Cullen were describing were all 'going through the same sort of experience' at a particular moment in general history 'and in their own', a conjunction that 'all of us, unless we die on the instant, are likely to have'.

The two 'general forces' determining attitudes and behaviour among their East Enders were the state of medicine and the influence of individualism on character. Religion, which once would have been central in people's lives, had been dealt with briefly in an earlier chapter, 'The After-Life', and was dealt with only briefly again in the last chapter when funerals in two churches were compared. Yet religion could still colour rites of passage in Bethnal Green. At the Kray funeral 16 black limousines, led by two horse-driven flower hearses, crossed Victoria Park, and the Evangelical preacher, despite the Sinatra song, in his valedictory address called Kray 'a man in search of God'.

There was a very different message at the ending of *A Good Death* which drew deep on Michael's own experiences, findings and thoughts (with references to Freud, to Durkheim, and to the philosopher who most appealed to Michael when he studied philosophy late in life at Birkbeck, David Hume).

> If the essential link between death and birth, and the way the linear spirals into the cyclical is acknowledged ... the search could be on for new kinds of observance which could be relevant to the world which the movers of science and technology have built. This would involve taking death out of the closet and casket into the open and dealing with the fear of it by other means than courage

or at least not by that alone ... It is not by courage alone that the dead will be saved.

Like all Michael's writing, there was nothing detached about this general prescription. As he memorably ended his preface, 'I am very far from being a dispassionate student of dying and death'.[13]

Michael was already contemplating a return to research on Bethnal Green when he delivered his SSRC lecture, and during the last decade of the twentieth century he reflected on all the changes that had taken place there, realising that further research, some of it comparative, was needed. He carefully observed both the politics of Tower Hamlets in which Bethnal Green was now situated, and the new kind of society which was emerging there, a society with a completely changed ethnic distribution. In 1994 the Nuffield Foundation gave him a grant for a preliminary study of racial tension in the area. There was a need for it. As long ago as 1978 the Bethnal Green and Stepney Trades Council had produced a booklet with the title *Blood on the Streets*, and Michael was now re-examining old presuppositions as well as old interviews.

By 1997 he had prepared a chapter outline for a new book, an 'internal document' which pointed to the need for a comprehensive new study. 'Time is the enemy,' Michael wrote to me when he sent me the outline to study. It drew heavily on the detailed research of Kate Gavron who had been writing an LSE thesis, as he once had done, in her case on Bangladeshi girls living in the district. She had visited Bangladesh in 1994. Team research proved difficult for ICS, although Michael attached central importance to further detailed study of Bethnal Green when he suddenly and surprisingly announced in 1999 that he was giving up as Director of the Institute in 2000, and advertisements appeared for the post that only he had ever held. No suitable applicant appeared, but Michael said that he hoped to hand over to a successor in 2001 who would preside over a new survey.

A Good Death relied on limited Bethnal Green evidence, but it also had a characteristically practical side to it. Appendix III consisted both of essential information about counselling, hospices and similar home care facilities – listing sources of medical help and social and financial support, and 'information for careers'. Much of this information, which covered cancer and AIDS, was taken from 'Facing Death', a booklet prepared by Colin Murray Parkes for the National Extension College. There was also references to an article in *Which?*: 'What to do when someone dies'. CRUSE figured too, as did Language Line. When bereaved persons were 'dazed' or 'numbed', they needed 'help with the simplest decisions', but they also needed time: time in which to sit back and 'take in what ha[d] happened'.

Appendix IX of *A Good Death* drew attention to one of two organisations founded by Michael in 1994, an *annus horribilis* for him, the year of Sasha's death, the National Funeral College. Designed to promote thoughtful attitudes towards bereavement in funeral directors, cemetery and crematorium managers, and people officiating at funerals, it had as its Director the Rev. Dr. Peter Jupp, a priest resident at Duddington, a Lincolnshire parish. Michael was its first Chairman, soon to be succeeded by Professor Malcolm Johnson, and it had a small advisory group to guide it. The annual Phoenix Fund competition for projects that help old people gave it limited financial support. Its most striking publication was a Dead Citizen's Charter.

The second new organisation that Michael created in 1994 was the Family Covenant Association, concerned not with the last 'rites of passage' but with the care of children, which had concerned Michael earlier during the 1990s when he set up Education Extra (1992), the operating title of a Foundation for Children's After School Activities Ltd (1991), and the National Association for the Education of Sick Children (1993), a title which spoke for itself. It developed from within the Open School and was set up to secure proper educational provision for hospitalised children. Michael, from inside his own family, was personally well aware of the necessity for it.

The Family Covenant Association started from the premise that while 'families don't necessarily need children, children *do* need families'. Obviously all was 'not well with the nation's children'.

> There is joy and achievement. But there is also distress and pain. This is brought home at fairly regular intervals by the train of tragic children thrust into sudden prominence by the media. Their figures are haunting. They come like so many others from families which have broken down, families which have been plunged into poverty, schools which are in disarray, an economy which has left so many young people without jobs.

Many of the remedies could not be found by individuals: they were 'matters of general policy'. 'Collective ills' required collective action. But there was much that individual parents could do.

A new focus on 'parenting' was necessary. 'The combined force of single parenthood, children being born out of wedlock, divorce, remarriage and the rest' meant that only about half the children in Britain would experience a 'conventional' childhood by the year 2000. At the beginning of the twenty-first century Michael, still pondering on the implications of this, was attaching increased importance to the role of grandparents and the possibility of organising them in the task of grandparenting. When the Family Covenant proposals were utmost in his mind he asked whether ceremonies could not be devised which would activate and promote child care. 'Welcoming children' could be associated with a commitment to their future welfare. The Family Covenant Association was set up for children whose parents did not, for whatever reason, put their trust in baptism, bringing in grandparents (and friends) as well as parents as Michael was to do even more strongly in 2000. There would be a legal side also to the work of the Association – clarifying for unmarried parents living together the law relating to inheritance and property.

The Director of the Family Covenant Association was Rosie Styles, and, having brought it into existence, Michael, who was far more than a nominal Chairman, wrote a joint pamphlet with Tony Flower in 1995 called 'How to Make a Family Covenant', 'a new way of expressing commitment' which explained the background of the Association as well as its purposes. The introduction to it had three sections – 'A New Way of Expressing Commitment'. 'The Need for Rites of Passage' and 'What is a Family Covenant?' Dickens was mentioned near the beginning.

The word Covenant, which did not have 'the same significance as it does in the Bible', was 'mainly, but far from exclusively, for unmarried parents and their children'. There was 'nothing to prevent parents' who had already been baptised 'from going in for the Covenant thereafter, if they wish'. An ordinary baptism, Michael felt, did not 'feature parental commitment in the way that the Covenant does'. 'Parenting' mattered to Michael profoundly as he pondered over the meaning of rites of passage, a subject which his anthropologist friend Mary Douglas had treated as being of the most profound importance. Her essay in *Young at Eighty*, the last in the collection, was called 'To Honour the Dead'. Elsewhere she referred to 'the poverty of our rituals [today]' and 'their unconnectedness with each other and with our social purposes'.

It was Michael's main purpose, as he put it in a undated memorandum, 'The Family Covenant', 'to honour the living' while affirming the dignity of death. Both last and first rites of passage needed to be restored, securing 'a decent measure of fraternity'. We are back to an assertion of Michael's treasured old value, which he had always considered alongside 'equality'. Continuity should be established between the dead and the living. Death could (and should) 'regenerate morality and human solidarity'. In *A Good Death* too he used the same phrase 'a decent measure of fraternity'.

It was children, however, on which he concentrated most, as he was to do in 2001, when they so often stole the headlines for often appalling reasons. Children were being dealt with 'indecently' in the broadest sense of the adjective. If the twentieth century was ending as 'the century of the child', he wrote sadly in 1999, 'it was happening the wrong way round'. 'Joy and achievement seem to be overwhelmed by distress and pain.' The figures of 'tragic children', to be thrust more and more into prominence in the media, were haunting. They came from 'families which have broken down, schools which are in disarray, an economy which has left so many people without jobs'. The twentieth century was ending 'not as the century of the child but as the century of child neglect'.

The pattern of this last chapter in this book is being dictated by Michael, although he does not know it, for I am trying, as I said, to see the world as he sees it. It is a chapter that will end, as this book began, with the School for Social Entrepreneurs, which in 2000 and 2001 has been placed on a new basis, with negotiations, local and national, and interviews, public and private, continuing. It was ideas, however, that governed the process. In 1997, before the School opened, Michael told me that ideas were still 'flowing like a flood' and that he could not 'deal with them all'.[14] Paul Barker, when editor of *New Society*, had chosen the image of fire rather than of flood to describe how Michael's mind worked, calling him 'a pyrotechnician of ideas and organisations'.[15]

Some of Michael's ideas concerned his oldest preoccupation – housing. The Mutual Aid Housing Association, leading Michael back to what was a still older source, was now the most practical of his projects, if only because from the uncertain vantage point of 1997 there seemed to him to be hope in housing policy being introduced by Blair's New Labour government. Meanwhile, the Housing Corporation had given an indispensable grant of £40,000 for a survey.

Michael had already made a contribution of his own when he projected a housing scheme far from Bethnal Green in industrial Bradford, a city with a huge Asian population, which had hitherto not been on his map. In inner city Bradford an Undercliffe Mutual Aid Housing Association, a small local group of tenants, equity sharers and owner-occupiers was founded. Drawn from poor housing, some of them 'already practised the mutual aid which is the essence of fraternity'. The law could not 'compel people to be neighbourly', but they could be encouraged 'by expectation as well as example'. A 'mutual aid' clause would be incorporated in all the tenancy agreements at Undercliffe and in all deeds of sale of properties to owner-occupiers. Choosing the words of his announcement about the Association with care and characteristically turning them into a public pronouncement, Michael spoke of an 'Undercliffe Declaration', a pronouncement which recalls in style, if not in content, the Chelsea Manifesto in *The Rise of the Meritocracy*.[16]

It was a Declaration which laid stress on the 'big idea' of 'fraternity', insisting that equality and fraternity (or liberty for that matter) are 'never meant to be in conflict'. They are 'complementary'. A rallying call of the kind noted by Annan followed,[17] accompanied by exclamation marks. The trumpets sounded: 'Come in Undercliffe! Come in a thousand Undercliffes!' The Declaration included a topical political plea. 'New Labour could rediscover its roots in an older Labour tradition of mutual aid which is as relevant today as it ever was.'[18] Michael always has his eye on politicians. There is always a present tense, but it is usually followed by a conditional.

There were other clarion calls too in the mid-1990s. The Open College of the Arts made many of them, not just calls for money. It was in some ways the most interesting of Michael's preoccupations, given the Dartington connection with music, dance, painting, pottery and sculpture, his own long and deep interest in paintings, Sasha's enthusiasm for the project and her invaluable assistance in developing it, and the disdain that both of them felt for ubiquitous manifestations of 'materialism'. He told one of his interviewers in 1994 that his 'ideal society' would be one in which 'every person was an artist and wanted to be'.

At the most profound level the arts were 'a sort of twentieth-century vehicle of the religious impulse', working through 'a sort of church where people need to be themselves and so something to themselves if possible'.[19] He believed that the progress of the College owed most to the fact that 'students' and their tutors could think and feel in this way. There was a link here with the Family Covenant: rites of passage too had once affected everyone, and surrounding each rite there was a heritage of art.

The College was in both organisational and financial difficulties in 1997, but thanks largely to a grant from the Lottery Fund, which arrived at just the right time, Michael could claim that 'things are looking better [now] than at any time since the College was formed'. The anniversary was celebrated with a party in the House of Lords, where Michael found valuable allies. By then no fewer than 33 courses were on offer: in 1988 there had been one.[20]

The newest course was 'Understanding Dance', and the range of courses, described as 'courses for everyone', now included art and design, garden design, in Michael's mind from the beginning – 'I had hoped cooking would figure too' – interior design, painting, drawing, sculpture, calligraphy, textiles, singing, creative writing, creative reading, photography and video production. The courses followed a variety of methods, including use of a video produced by the public television station in New York, WNET.

The motivations of the students were as diverse as the range of courses and the range of learning materials and methods on offer. David Davies as Director of the College until 1998, believed that a legitimate aim of students was to obtain an Open College of the Arts degree in the arts just as students could take a degree in academic subjects through the Open University. But not all students wanted to do this. Some had professional careers in mind. One student following the video course was taking the first step to what he hoped would turn a hobby into a full-time occupation. The number of such full-time occupations was increasing, some in a cyberworld falling outside the range of Michael's own experience. But for a 97-year-old foundation student, Irene Chapman, present at the House of Lords party, the ten courses that she had followed were all different and that was their fascination. She had no academic or professional aims in mind.

'For me,' Michael commented, 'she was like an ancient mariner who had started her journey into the unknown with no sealed orders.' This was a literary metaphor that Davies, a former oceanographer, would understand and appreciate, and it was used by Michael's friend Peter Hall in Book One of his *Cities in Civilisation* where he offered what he called a Navigator's Guide. Michael, who always paid close attention to what Hall said or wrote, admired the students of the University of the Third Age because they were like Irene Chapman. They did not need degrees and they had retired from their professions. When in September 2000 he was presented with a plaque at the Annual General Meeting of U3A at the University of East Anglia (far more acceptable to Michael than a medal) he considered it the greatest of honours. Laslett, Midwinter and he were honoured as founders. By then there were 480 branches of U3A and an enrolment of 200,000 was being forecast within two years.

Michael thought of himself, like the students and researchers he cared for, old or young, as a mariner moving out into the unknown, not always with a map or even a compass to guide him. He never believed that it was enough to see the future in terms of technology, including communications technology. He made this point, often eloquently, in almost all his lectures, which for him were public statements with policy implications. Technology of a domestic variety – and electronics – had 'individualised' activities within the home, and some homes were now 'automated'. Some of the 'miniature machines' in use there had been the subject of informed articles in *Which?*. As a result 'the family', the unit which had fascinated Michael since the 1950s, was 'giving way to the individual within it'. This was not the first time that he had made the point, but it was the first time that he had made it since the coming of the Internet and the large-scale development of digitalisation. That (with whatever long-term ramifications it might have) he had not forecast.

Many of Michael's long-standing preoccupations converged at this point, including his preoccupation with time. 'People are more and more jumpy [and he had people like himself in mind], more and more aware of other places in the world where they might be, with other men, or other women, at other meetings, and other conferences, in other beds, on other moonlit nights. They are made continuously aware of what they haven't the time for, and the major tactic used to deal with the time-famine – doing more things at once – like making love and simultaneously listening to a Bartók quartet on the hi-fi are liable to be self-defeating, as all members of the Senate of the Open University will know for themselves from their every night experiences. They are always missing out on the cadenzas in the scherzo.'

This characteristic passage, so unlike the kind of observation that most sociologists make, Michael described as a 'digression'. Yet for him it was far from a digression. Crossing the boundaries not between country and country but between present and past, Michael went on to refer not only to one of the most familiar of all his themes – the effects of the industrial revolution on relationships, sensibilities and aspirations – but to what for him was still 'the central problem' of modern politics – that of 'the small man in a big world'. The problem would get 'a sharper edge' in the next century with the big world getting bigger while at the same time getting 'miniaturised down to the size of a computer programme'. None the less, his conclusion was optimistic. There could be a deliberate response 'of an opposite kind ... against the worldwide trend, encouraging students to work together as well as separately, not just in some schools and tutorial groups but as a necessary part of their courses ... The new Open University course on family and community history could point the way.'[21]

A penultimate passage on Open University tutorial centres looked back long before the industrial revolution to classical Athens – a rare historial journey for Michael to make – 'when a tiny community without any technology in it shone with an intellectual brilliance which has never been matched in the technological world. One of the greatest of modern philosophers, who would by no means have been dwarfed in the Agora, was the Scottish philosopher, Hume. For him fellow feeling was what kept humanity together, as it did for Michael. If he had been guided at Birkbeck College to move forward from Hume, not to Kant (as he was), but to Coleridge (as he was not), he might have noted that for Coleridge 'mutuality', a reciprocal relationship, had its genesis in the sense of touch just after birth. We are back to psychology – and to autobiography.[22]

In a lecture that Michael delivered to the British Association in 2000 he went back to 1945 – or rather, what followed the Labour victory – to see if anything could be learnt from such recent but largely forgotten history. At once he was caught up not in empirical investigation but in interpretation. He described what followed 1945, usually considered as 'an age of austerity', as 'a golden age' of full employment without inflation – with 'a relatively equal society' and a 'belief in the future'. He concluded that there was much to learn about 'principles'. 'Equity in the distribution of incomes' and 'the importance of public service' stood out. Since the 1980s 'deprivation for the poor' had been taken for granted in a competitive market, shaped by technology, indexing welfare benefits to prices instead of wages had reinforced market trends: the shift to indirect taxation had been deliberate. Michael's emphasis on economics was couched in stronger language than that which he had employed in 1945 itself and in the years that followed it, and there were new emphases. Poverty reduction should begin with children. New Labour's goal was the end of child poverty in 20 years. Was that not too long to wait? There was a 'middle-age trap' too. 'An incredible 2,600,000 people over 50 but under retirement age' were out of work in 1999. The New Deal 50 Plus had recognised the problem. But it was 'on much too small a scale'.[23]

Michael's main complaint was that while something had been done – and more promised – to raise the bottom, very little had been done 'at the top end' and that 'self-interest' in a naked form had 'not exactly added to social cohesion'. 'We seem to be into a new golden age, not for equality but for booty.' Private enterprise had become the icon. And here Michael broadened his attack to include not only the suggested privatisation of air traffic control, a subject on which he also spoke in the House of Lords debate in the winter of 2000, and the London Underground but Ofsted and the privatisation of prisons. Public service was denigrated. He was sorry for Herbert Morrison in his grave. During the late 1940s Michael had been critical of Morrison's approach to the setting-up and management of public corporations. Now he suggested that 'if Labour had won the 1950 election with a convincing majority, it might have gradually freed itself from the straitjacket of the old public corporation and favoured a variety of different kinds of common, and cooperative enterprises'. 'Mutuality' might have become, as he had wished, the order of the day.

As it was – and Michael did not examine the force of the 'might' – governments had denigrated the people on whom they depended, particularly teachers, 'a lasting campaign and a bitter one', and had destroyed local government. 'Mobilise local people, including the poor, and give them their head and something really valuable might come of it.' At all these points in what amounted to a new Young manifesto, Michael was suggesting an alternative to New Labour, not treating it as the culmination of a process which had started with the rise of the SDP. Gordon Brown's budget of mid-2000 had come, however, at a crucial time and was a 'sign' that the government was responding to pressures from the rank and file. Michael was more critical of the Treasury than he ever had been, but Brown's appeal in January 2001 for voluntary action, was very much along Michael's line. 'A new era of active citizenship and an enabling State is within our grasp.'[24]

Psychology rather than economics came in only at the very end of Michael's lecture. The material progress of the twentieth century had not made people happier, but more uneasy. And even economists had come to realise this. The *Economic Journal* had organised a symposium on economics and happiness, and there had also been an international conference on the subject in Oxford in which economists had participated. There was, 'strange as it might seem', a 'World Data Base of Happiness'.[25]

Michael returned finally to themes raised in *The Rise of the Meritocracy*. 'Were we to evaluate people, not only according to their intelligence and their education, their occupations and their power, but according to their kindliness and their courage, their imagination and sensitivity, their sympathy and generosity, there could be no overall inequalities of the sort we have got used to.' It was the conclusion of a long lifetime. Michael had never been willing to get used to anything. He expected his social entrepreneurs 'to bring to social problems the same enterprise and imagination business entrepreneurs bring to wealth creation'. But that was not his language but that of Tony Blair who in 1997 promised to back 'the thousands of social entrepreneurs' who were around in every community.[26] That is now history. Michael's motto still is 'Let Us Face the Future'.

The School for Social Entrepreneurs, 'for the high-minded and the hard-headed', had good news to report as this book was going to press. Ably directed by John Cornford, who for Michael became an invaluable colleague, it played a leading part in a seven-partner consortium, the Foundation for Social Entrepreneurs, which bid successfully against powerful competitors for a £100 million Lottery Fund grant from the Millennium Commission. The shared mission of the consortium is the same as that of the School – 'to invest in individuals as a driving force to regenerate social capital across the UK'.[27] Its motto is the same as Michael's: 'We believe that there is a new movement at work in our society that can make a difference.' 'Making a difference has always been Michael's own purpose, and the new impetus given in late 2000 to the School that he founded will make a difference in many places far from Bethnal Green.

Although the scale of the consortium is unparalleled in Michael's direct experience, the grants the consortium will handle in all parts of the country will be on the human scale that he has always favoured. In the School's 2000 Report it was stated that 'people learn best about entrepreneurship by taking entrepreneurial action themselves', that the School was 'rather like a family' and that 'the only certainty about human society is that we will never get it right'. There was no jargon there, and no hype, no false expectations. One of the founder students, Alastair Wilson, claimed that through working in the School he had been offered 'a rich insight into the behaviour and techniques which separate the well-intended from those who do'.[28]

Afterword: The Last Victorian?

Many of the themes set out in this book and outlined in the Foreword are still topical, discussed more indeed during the first years of the new millennium than they were in the mid-twentieth century. They even hit the headlines, as Michael himself sometimes does.

I have described him throughout the book as Noel Annan did – very much a man of his own time, identifying and influencing the processes of change, planned and unplanned. As he contemplates his own life, however, Michael feels now that he would like to escape from his own time, not only into the future but into the past; and, somewhat surprisingly to me as a committed critical historian of Victorian Britain, he has come to regard himself less a man of his own time than the last Victorian.

Born only fourteen years after Queen Victoria's death, Michael was not drawn into the revolt against the Victorians associated, above all, with Lytton Strachey. Nor did he emerge from a background where it mattered much whether you shared in that revolt or sympathised with it. Dartington was scarcely a Victorian institution, however, less so, indeed, than Bethnal Green with its alleys and its fogs was a residually Victorian place.

Michael can provide a variety of reasons for his self-judgement. First, he has a conscience, and so did the Victorians. Second, he dislikes 'materialism', and so did some of the most influential Victorians. Third, he is suspicious of the state, and so were most Victorians. Self-help and mutual aid went together. Cooperation was one Victorian response to industrialisation. Fourth, there were many Victorian social entrepreneurs who were driven as much by enterprise as industrial entrepreneurs were, the kind of social entrepreneurs in demand to shape the twenty-first century. Fifth, and perhaps most important, Michael himself, as Martin Bulmer put it (see above, p. 23), has been an explorer of society who has written from outside a university context. As a sociologist, he was in the tradition of Charles Booth and Seebohm Rowntree. He did not depend on a salary and he did not expect a pension. He was concerned, as they were, with research through survey, and like Rowntree, in particular, he wanted research to lead to the formation of public policy.

Michael's statement, quoted in the Foreword, that 'everything derives from research' ended with the words, not quoted there, 'so it is all very empirical'. Whatever else may be acceptable in his self-judgements, this last phrase is not. Research is not all empirical, and since Michael is highly intuitive, the ideas that he translates into organisations, are translated in complex, not simple, ways, even when the research seems empirical. His ideas have infuriated as well as inspired. There has been no one like him, although he has often had co-authors in writing his books and co-workers in pushing his projects, and his relationships with them have not been uniformly good. He may be completely Victorian in that – and in his capacity to dream as well as to think.

As a historian of Victorian Britain I have always questioned the tendency of commentators, including some fellow historians, to generalise about Victorian character and Victorian values. I have not only distinguished between early, middle and late periods in what was an exceptionally long reign, but between different people in each period, wishing that for some periods I had had oral evidence, some of it based on interviews. For me there was no one Victorian prototype. None the less, if we were to try to identify 'representative' Victorians and draw comparisons between them and us, Michael, in some respects, had more mid-Victorian than late Victorian qualities. It would be late Victorian characters, however, like Havelock Ellis and H. G. Wells, whom we would have to bring into the picture.

Michael is like Wells in that they are both time travellers, critical of their own times. But was Michael ever as critical of his own times as Wells was when four years before Michael was born he described 'the Victorian epoch' as 'a hasty trial experiment, a gigantic experiment of the most slovenly and wasteful kind'? Victorian people were 'restricted and undisciplined, overtaken by power, by possessions and great new freedoms and unable to make any civilized use of them whatever'.

Wells was gloomy about the twentieth century when he reached old age, although there were many signs of 'social progress' that he had foreseen, as Michael, as interested in the future as Wells was, did also in twentieth-century rather than Victorian fashion.

It is not possible to summarise his achievements as a projector of ideas and organisations more finally than was attempted in the last chapter. Perhaps the most telling way of ending this Afterword, therefore, is to go back in time, but not as far as the Victorians, and quote from a handwritten letter written by Dorothy Elmhirst to Michael from Dartington on Sunday, 28 April 1957. Close as they were they communicated in entirely non-Victorian terms at a time when a revival was in full swing. Dorothy had just been reading *Family and Kinship in the East End*:

> I've had such a good time reading your book that I can't believe that it could ever be hard work to make sociological studies, still less to read them. Yours is a study of *living* people, who come and go all through – rather like a novel and at times like scenes from a play. I feel I know the individuals – they seem to ... greet me.

'Michael,' she went on, 'this is an important book – and it achieves something that Chekhov [no Victorian] used to talk about – the art of saying serious and profound things in a light vein. This is a great achievement. ... You know what it means to me.' The words were written more than forty years ago. They still carry across all the divides of time. At this time no other words are necessary.

Notes

1 In Lieu of an Autobiography

1. George Orwell was one. Yet 'ironically', as one student of Orwell has observed, 'a writer who asked in his will for no biography has gotten several' (J. Rodden, 'Personal Behavior, Biographical History and Literary Reputation: The Case of George Orwell' in *Biography, An Interdisciplinary Quarterly*, Vol. 12, Summer 1989).
2. M. Young and M. Rigge, *Revolution from Within: Cooperatives and Cooperation in British Industry* (1983).
3. The sub-title of the book is 'The Arrival of the Ageless Society'.
4. NLSC Interview by Paul Thompson, 12 May 1990.
5. V. Brome, 'Practising What You Preach' in G. Dench, T. Flower and K. Gavron (eds.), *Young at Eighty* (1995), p. 94.
6. Tessa (Baroness) Blackstone, 'The Birkbeck Presidency' in *Young at Eighty*, pp. 52–3. 'Putting Michael together with Roger Scruton,' she writes, 'would have been interesting, but a trifle risky.' This was one of the many 'might have beens' of Michael's life which has often involved risks.
7. See below, p. 150.
8. A. Bullock and O. Stallybrass (eds.), *Fontana Dictionary of Modern Thought* (1977), p. 400.
9. It still did not figure in the third edition of *The Shorter Oxford English Dictionary* (1973). Nor did the words 'meritocrat' or 'meritocratic'. Five years later, however, the word 'meritocracy' was given an entry twice as long as 'meritorious' in the *Longman Dictionary of Contemporary English*.
10. See below, p. 161. For China viewed as a gerontocracy turning into a meritocracy, see below, p. 274.
11. Young and Willmott, *The Symmetrical Family* (1973), p. 9, p. 1. P. Hall, *Cities in Civilization* (1998). For Michael's connection with Peter Hall, see below, pp. 240–1.
12. See below, Chapter 8.
13. *The Rise of the Meritocracy*, Ch. 1, which is called 'The Clash of Social Forces'.
14. The sector and the range of organisations within it is clearly identified at the Hauser Center at Harvard University. For the practical side of the parallel, well known to Michael, see F. Setterberg and K. Schulman, *The Complete Guide to Managing the Non-Profit Organization* (1985). See also Michael's draft, *School for Social Entrepreneurs, Application from the Institute of Community Studies* (1996).
15. D. Bell, *Social Scientist as Innovator* (1983).
16. Inaugural Speech, 5 January 1998.
17. P. Drucker, *Innovation and Entrepreneurship* (1989), p. vii. See also his book *The Leader of the Future* (1997). The Peter E. Drucker Foundation for Nonprofit Management held its first conference in 1991: the seventh in

1997 was devoted to 'Mastering the Tools of Change'. Two papers were delivered on 'The Social Enterprise of the Future'.
18. For changes in values, attitudes towards value systems and the political (and professional) use of the term 'Victorian values', see out of a huge literature – in chronological order of appearance – J. A. Banks, *Victorian Values: Secularism and the Size of Families* (1982); J. Walvin, *Victorian Values* (1986); G. Marsden (ed.), *Victorian Values* (1990); and E. Sigsworth, *Victorian Values* (1991). In a television interview of 1983 Thatcher described Victorian values as the values 'when our country became great'.
19. *The Times*, 9 October 1997. Queen Elizabeth was addressing the Pakistani Senate and National Assembly in Islamabad.
20. See below, p. 84.
21. *NS*, 23 May 1963.
22. GP Interview by Jane Gabriel, 22 March 1994. See also M. Young and M. Rigge, *Mutual Aid in a Selfish Society* (Mutual Aid Papers, No. 2, n.d.) and below, Chapter 8.
23. R. Williams, *Keywords* (1976), p. 76. For the variety of uses, see D. J. Smith, 'Research, the Community and the Police' in P. Willmott (ed.), *Policing the Community* (1987).
24. T. B. Bottomore, *Sociology – A Guide to Problems and Literature* (1962), p. 20. See also 'What is a Society?' in A. H. Halsey (ed.), *Trends in British Society since 1990* (1972 edn.), pp. 4–9.
25. So did Willmott. See his *Community Initiatives, Patterns and Prospects* (PSI, 1989), where he noted attempts to eliminate the word and quoted Margaret Stacey, who had carried out an early community study of Banbury.
26. See below, Chapter 9.
27. *CR*, Interview with Peter Hennessy, 1995, pp. 88–9.
28. See his pamphlet, *The Chipped White Cups of Dover* (1960) and below, p. 259. The Gallup Poll percentage figures were 25 per cent yes, 38 per cent no, and 37 per cent don't know. There would have been higher percentages in favour at a by-election as opposed to a general election. Michael had wartime by-elections in mind when he made this statement, and he canvassed for Sir Richard Acland, leader of the war-time Common Wealth Party (see below, p. 57), who stood as an Independent Labour candidate at the Gravesend election of 1955. None the less, Michael had been 'happily helping' Herbert Morrison at the Labour Party's Central Office in the general election of that year. 'One part of me is still the politician' (Letter to Dorothy Elmhirst, 27 May 1955).
29. Quoted in A. H. Halsey, *No Discouragement* (1996), p. 44.
30. See below, p. 78.
31. For family as well as for academic reasons these were difficult years (see below, p. 192). There were compensating happy times abroad on both counts, particularly in France. In the *Sunday Telegraph*, 21 July 1991, Sasha described how she first 'fell in love with Provence in 1951 when [she] was a penniless student'. She and Michael subsequently acquired a sequence of houses in the same area, hoping to go on visiting there as often as possible. The Youngs were planning a trip when Sasha died in 1994.
32. See above, p. 2.

33. Letter to Sir Rex Richards, then Director, the Leverhulme Trust, 10 February 1992. For the historian of sociology, Martin Bulmer, Michael was a 'scholar outside the university', in this respect, at least, having more in common with Victorian students of society, like Charles Booth, or critics of how it worked, like William Morris, than with his twentieth-century contemporaries. He has had 'less connection with universities than any other social scientist of his generation'. ('A Scholar outside the University' in *Minerva* (1985). See also, for Bulmer's perspectives, his *Essays on the History of British Sociological Research* (1985).)
34. The first new organisation that Michael ever contemplated, while he was studying law in London in 1935, was a 'real London Dartington Society', in this case Society with a capital S. (Letter to Dorothy and Leonard Elmhirst, 5 May 1935, written in the Common Room of Gray's Inn.) The Society would be 'composed of members who for one reason or another have an interest in Dartington', including not only parents and former pupils, but individuals who at one time had worked on the Dartington estate, and, above all, 'people living in London who are interested in Dartington, wish to hear about its activities and meet its products'.
35. See above, p. 18.
36. *Social Scientist as Innovator*, pp. 253–4.
37. GP interview, 22 March 1994.
38. Letter from Samuel to Michael, 5 January 1982.
39. There is a Samuel-like ring to a few passages in his unpublished work *For Richer For Poorer*, a seminal study written earlier while Michael was head of the Labour Party's Research Department, in the knowledge that it would never be published by the Party. 'The history of Britain is the history of a million families like the Thomases. Recalled in the memories of people still alive, in the fly-leaves of Family Bibles, in old photographs and pictures are the changes which have made our society what it is.' The introductory section of this text was called 'Neighbourly Socialism'; the first part 'The Pressure of Progress on Parents'; and the third part 'Parents in Poverty'.
40. *The Rise of the Meritocracy* (1958), Ch. 1; foreword to *The National Extension College, Catalyst for Change* (1980). 'That or something like it,' he goes on, 'is certainly true of many institutions: they do tend to ossify. They suffer from a hardening of the categories. But the National Extension College is most universal. It was born by enterprise out of zest, and it has stayed that way throughout all of its 25 years.'
41. *The Metronomic Society* (1988), p. 18. Another remarkable phrase in the same book is 'Time is imminent in everything ... you cannot catch it because you already have it.' The title of one of Michael's reviews – of Nigel Calder's *Time-scale: An Atlas of the Fourth Dimension* (*NS*, 8 March 1983) – was 'History Lesson'. He suggested that the word 'history' would have been better than the word 'atlas' in Calder's title.
42. *The Rise of the Meritocracy*, p. 86.
43. *The Symmetrical Family*, p. 65.
44. Foreword to the American edition of M. Young and P. Willmott, *The Symmetrical Family* (1973), p. xii. Michael and Willmott noted that they were turning more explicitly to 'theory' in this book, having read W. G. Runciman's *Relative Deprivation and Social Justice* (1966).

45. *Ibid.*, pp. 108ff. See Vance Palmer, *The Legend of the Nineties* (1954). Its beginning is topical: 'A romantic aura always hangs over the last days of a dying century, for those who look back on it. (p. 9). For the continuation of Vance Palmer's work, see R. Ward, *The Australian Legend* (1958).
46. Gabriel Productions (GP), Interview, 22 March 1994. The last phrase echoes Dorothy Elmhirst who often used the word 'wonder' whether she was talking of art or of gardens (*The Elmhirsts of Dartington*, p. 245).
47. Young is not mentioned in the brief account of the 1930s in K. S. Inglis, *This is the ABC* (1983).
48. E. Young, *Inside Out* (1971), p. 161.
49. Typed note by Miriam Walkington Young (1942).
50. R. Lovett, *History of the London Missionary Society, 1795–1875* (1899), pp. 398ff.
51. T. H. Meyer, *D. N. Dunlop* (1992).
52. For the combination, see the popular account by Ron Landau, *God is My Adventure* (1935).
53. See R. F. Foster, *W. B. Yeats, a Life* (1997), p. 33. Yeats was interviewed by Dunlop for the *Irish Theosophist*. When asked about his prophecies Yeats replied that 'the power of England would not outlast the century' (*Irish Theosophist*, 15 November 1893).
54. See Mayer, *op. cit.*, p. 365, where the author refers to 'the sun spheres of Michael's reign'.
55. See below, p. 26.
56. M. Young and P. Willmott, *Family and Kinship in East London* (1962 Penguin edition), p. 113.
57. See below, pp. 110ff.
58. See below, p. 42.
59. 'An Invisible Wind' in *New Society*, 21 June 1985.
60. See S. C. Easton, *Rudolf Steiner: Herald of a New Era* (1980). In *God is My Adventure*, Landau explains that Steiner did not want his clairvoyant powers to be thought of as taking the place of knowledge of the world and its history by other means.
61. Letter of 27 May 1958.
62. Letter of 17 August 1946.
63. *The Elmhirsts of Dartington*, p. 4.
64. *Ibid.*, p. 323.
65. *Ibid.*, p. 61.
66. GP Interview, 22 March 1994.
67. See below, p. 131.
68. *Ibid.*, p. 159
69. M. Young and L. Cullen, *A Good Death. Conversations with East Londoners* (1996). In the preface, p. ix, Michael describes his reactions to Sasha's dying.
70. *Guardian*, 26 June, 1 July 1993.
71. Young and Cullen, *op. cit.*, In applying to the Gulbenkian Foundation for a grant to assist the research, Michael referred to Peter Marris's book *Widows and Their Families* (1959), one of the books produced in the first seven years of the Institute of Community Studies in Bethnal Green. See below, p. 143.
72. Letter to Dorothy Elmhirst, 11 October 1958.

73. S. Moorsom and M. Young, *Your Hand in Mine* (1994), p. 8. Sophie found her own pattern too. She went on to complete a professional course in nursing and to work in an adolescent cancer ward.
74. The *Sun*, 6 January 1998.
75. Prince Kropotkin (1842–1921), born in Moscow, welcomed the First World War because he believed that it would destroy the power of the State. The book of his that exerted most influence in Britain – and on Michael – was *Mutual Aid: A Factor of Evolution* (1902).
76. See below, Chapter 9.
77. Review of *Social Scientist as Innovator*, introduced by Daniel Bell (1983), in *Minerva*, Vol. XXIII (1983).
78. There is an interesting article by Barbara Goodwin, 'The Other Owen and Utopian Socialism', in the journal *Samizdat* which Michael launched (May/June 1990, pp. 10–11). In the issue of *Samizdat* where Goodwin wrote there were articles by David Miller on Tawney and Paul Hirst on Cole.
79. See below, p. 51.
80. 'The Dead Citizen's Charter' speech when Michael launched the National Funerals College, 11 June 1994.
81. Madge was five years older than Michael and had been educated at Cambridge. His first job was reporter on the Daily Mirror. In 1947, three years before becoming Professor at Birmingham, he was Social Development Officer in the New Town of Stevenage. In the 1950s and 1960s he made many technical assistance visits to Asia and Africa. He published and edited *Pilot Papers* (1954–9). His first wife was the poet Kathleen Raine.
82. Laslett, born four months after Michael in 1915, has been a Fellow of Trinity College, Cambridge since 1953. He founded the Cambridge Group for the History of Population and Social Structure in 1966 and wrote *The World We Have Lost* in 1965.
83. Letter to the *Guardian*, 18 October 1971.
84. Barker, born in 1933, was educated in Yorkshire at Hebden Bridge Grammar School and Calder High School, and at Oxford. He began his writing career on *The Times* in 1959.
85. From 1991 to 1993 Runciman chaired the Royal Commission (by then a rare constitutional device) on criminal justice. His writings on sociology are voluminous. See also his *Confessions of a Reluctant Theorist* (1989). Michael described his *Treatise on Social Theory*, vol. 2 (1989) as 'a classic' (*New Statesman*, 24 February 1989).
86. Midwinter, born in 1932, was Director of the Liverpool Education Priority Area project and Head of the Public Affairs Unit of the National Consumer Council from 1975 to 1980.
87. Halsey, born in 1923, was Lecturer in Sociology at Birmingham (with Madge) from 1954 to 1962, and was Professor of Social and Administrative Studies in Oxford from 1978 to 1990. He was Reith Lecturer in 1977, publishing *Change in British Society* (1978), which has gone through various editions.
88. Hall, born in 1932, was educated at London University and has served on many official committees. See below p. 381.
89. Born in 1933, McIntosh was created a peer in 1982. He became Deputy Government Chief Whip in 1997.

90. Quoted by A. McIntosh, 'Michael in his Peer Group' (*Young at Eighty*, p. 143).
91. *The Elmhirsts of Dartington*, p. 6.
92. M. Bulmer, 'A Scholar Outside the University', in *Minerva* (Spring 1985).
93. E. Young, *op. cit.*, p. 77.

2 Michael When Young

1. A. H. Halsey, 'Education and Ethical Socialism' in *Young at Eighty*, p. 129. See also Halsey's autobiography, *No Discouragement* (1996), p. 132.
2. University of Adelaide, Centenary Seminar (1974).
3. 'The Increasing Obsolescence of Childhood Education' in *The Times Saturday Review*, 9 January 1971; 'Liberating the Old and the Young', Presidential Address to the *British Association for the Advancement of Science*, 23 August 1990.
4. See Tawney's leader in the *Manchester Guardian*, 15 May 1946 and B. Simon, *Education and the Social Order* (1991), pp. 98–9. For Michael's views, see *Learning Begins at Home* (1968). For Townsend, see below, pp. 133ff.
5. There is a good but brief autobiographical account in David Gribble (ed.), *That's All Folks: Dartington School Remembered* (1987), pp. 11–14.
6. 'Progressive Education at Dartington', the eighth W. B. Curry Lecture delivered at the University of Exeter, 7 June 1984.
7. *The Elmhirsts of Dartington*, p. 157.
8. See below, pp. 272ff.
9. For Michael and the Open University see below, pp. 203ff.
10. W. B. Curry, 'The School' (1941), quoted in M. L. de la Iglesia, *Dartington Hall School, Staff Memories of the Early Years* (1996), p. 12. Wells, of course, was as fascinated by time as Michael was. One of the people to write about Wells was Michael's friend Vincent Brome, *H. G. Wells* (1951).
11. See below, Chapter 4.
12. Letters of 27 October 1942 and 8 May 1944 to Dorothy and Leonard. In the first of these he refers to his having persuaded Leonard in August 1941 'to allow me to start going through some of the old Estate papers'. The second letter begins: 'I have been wanting for some time to join the discussion about the future of Dartington.'
13. *The Elmhirsts of Dartington*, p. 98.
14. This was Gribble's summary of Rousseau's teaching. See his book *Considering Children* (1985).
15. The *Elmhirst of Dartington*, p. 159.
16. Gribble, *op. cit.*, p. 31.
17. In 1927 Russell and his second wife, Dora Black, started a school for young children, which they managed until 1932.
18. *The Elmhirsts of Dartington*, pp. 174–6. In different times, years later in 1950, William K. Elmhirst was to make Neill a small covenant of £1000 a year for seven years.
19. *The Autobiography of Bertrand Russell, 1914–1944* (1968), p. 187.
20. See his *The Problem Child* (1926), *The Problem Parent* (1932) and *The Problem Teacher* (1939). His *Hearts not Heads* appeared in 1945. His book on

Summerhill (1937) was translated into 15 languages. His last book, *Neill! Neill! Orange Peel!*, largely autobiographical, was published in 1973, two years before his death.
21. P. Turner and L. Davies (Piper) in de la Iglesia, *op. cit.*, p. 26, p. 55.
22. Food figures prominently in the highly readable autobiography of Frank Giles, future editor of the *Sunday Times*, another pupil at Michael's second school, *Sundry Times* (1986). When Giles was given a specially nourishing cream diet on health grounds, the other boys looked on 'with envy and malice' (*op. cit.*, p. 4).
23. E. Young, *op. cit.*, p. 91.
24. Giles, one year younger than Michael, recalls it as 'slightly cranky' (*op. cit.*, p. 4).
25. NLSC Interview, 12 May 1990.
26. T. H. Meyer, *D. N. Dunlop, a Man of His Time* (1992), pp. 202ff. This was the first conference after the First World War which was attended by both German and Russian delegates. Dunlop persuaded the Prince of Wales to open it after telephoning St. James's Palace and being granted an interview.
27. *Ibid.*, p. 203. See also *The Times* obituary of Dunlop, 5 June 1935.
28. See above, p. 63.
29. The comment is taken from a collection of typed comments in his School Box. Of another pupil, a girl, described on the same page, the writer, who reveals much about himself, says, 'The effort to re-make herself has been very fruitful. She is now much more self-conscious ... I have a recent dream of hers.'
30. This is the title of the piece in *Young at Eighty* by David Davies, who was appointed Director of the newly founded Open College of the Arts in 1989. He had been Director of the Dartington North Devon Trust.
31. NLSC Interview, 12 May 1990.
32. P. Turner in Gribble, *op. cit.*, p. 25.
33. Foxhole included an assembly room, a gymnasium, a library and kitchens, as well as bedrooms for children and houseparents.
34. M. Girouard (ed.), *House for Mr. Curry, A. Miscellany* (1996), first published in *Country Life*.
35. *The Elmhirsts of Dartington*, p. 161.
36. See below, p. 78.
37. *The Elmhirsts of Dartington*, p. 167. Cf. the remark by Leonard Elmhirst's Indian friend, Rabindranath Tagore, with whom he had worked closely: 'Childhood should be given its full measure of life's draught ... The young mind should be saturated with the idea that it has been born into a human world which is in harmony with the world around it.' ('My School' in A. Chakravarty, *A Tagore Reader* (1961), p. 218.)
38. Wells wrote an account of Sanderson's life and influence, *The Story of a Great Schoolmaster* (1924). Sanderson died in 1922 at the age of 65.
39. Quoted in de la Iglesia, *op. cit.*, p. 12.
40. NLSC Interview, 12 May 1990.
41. He published *The Case for Federal Union* (1940). For the background, see C. K. Streit, *Union Now* (1939) and *Union Now with Britain* (1941) and W. I. Jennings, *A Federation for Western Europe* (1940).
42. NLSC Interview, 12 May 1990.

43. *The Elmhirsts of Dartington*, p. 110. Michael does not mention McKenna and Company in his index to this book, although there are two references to the firm, the other on p. 227.
44. Letter of 30 October 1934.
45. See below, p. 97.
46. R. Dahrendorf, *LSE, A History of the London School of Economics and Political Science, 1895–1995* (1995), esp. pp. 296ff, 'Remembering the Student Days'. Michael is not mentioned.
47. See above, p. 2.
48. Letter of 30 October 1934.
49. See B. Pimlott, *Labour and the Left in the 1930s* (1977), and S. Burgess, *Stafford Cripps, a Political Life* (1999), Ch. 9.
50. For an invaluable survey of the tangled strands of social policy before Michael became interested in them, see H. L. Beales, *The Making of Social Policy* (Hobhouse Memorial Lecture, 23 May 1945).
51. Eileen Power, described by José Harris in her biography of William Beveridge as 'brilliant and beautiful', listed her recreations in *Who's Who* as travel and dancing.
52. See below, p. 297.
53. See R. Miliband, *Parliamentary Socialism: A Study of the Politics of Labour* (1961) and 'The Sickness of Labourism' in the *New Left Review* (1960). 'Labourism', though not the name, figured in Michael's *The Rise of the Meritocracy*. For an interpretation of the history of labourism, see W. Thompson, *The Long Death of British Labourism: Interpreting a Political Culture* (1993).
54. Letter of 30 October 1934.
55. R. M. Titmuss, *Birth, Poverty and Wealth* (1943), p. 9. For Titmuss's early life, see the fascinating account by his daughter, Ann Oakley, *Man and Wife: Richard and Kay Titmuss, My Parents' Early Years* (1996).
56. P. E. Rock, 'Debt Collection' in *The British Journal of Sociology* (1968), pp. 176–91. In the same number of the *Journal* there was a review of Talcott Parsons's *Sociological Theory and Modern Society* (1967). That represented a very different kind of sociology from Michael's.
57. For O'Malley's views and for his personal assessment of his experiences at Dartington, see de la Iglesia, *op. cit.*, pp. 27–33.
58. Communism had been present at Dartington. One member of the staff, Fred Sneyd, who arrived in 1934, stayed on until 1951. His views were Communist, but he did not join the Communist Party until 1941. See *ibid.*, pp. 41ff. In the Dartington syllabus of the 1930s there was also a subject called 'sociology', taught by Bill Hunter. It was described by O'Malley as 'a mixture of all sorts of things' (*ibid.*, p. 28).
59. From 1940 to 1946 Jean Floud was Assistant Director of Education in Oxford. In 1956 she was co-author with A. H. Halsey and F. M. Martin of *Social Class and Educational Opportunity*. In 1970 she was made a member of the Social Science Research Council after Michael had ceased to be its Chairman.
60. Allen entered the Board of Trade in 1939 and from 1940 to 1945 served in the Royal Artillery. He took the title Baron Croham of the London Borough of Croydon.
61. Letter of 9 February 1937.

62. Letter of 29 July 1937. For Michael's own temperamental 'rank and filism' see below, p. 81.
63. E. Young, *op. cit.*, pp. 157–9.
64. Letter of 11 December 1997.
65. In a letter to Dorothy Elmhirst, 11 October 1958, he thanked her for having 'represented the powers of love' for him since he first met her and Leonard and had become 'a sort of child in your family'. He added that his mother had 'forbidden achievement as it made her jealous'.
66. Letter of 4 January 1938.
67. Letter of 7 May 1935.
68. Letter of 14 May 1935.
69. Pimlott, like Kenneth Lindsay (see below, p. 47) and a later friend and colleague of Michael, François Lafitte (see below, p. 51) were undergraduates at Worcester College, Oxford, where on their visits back I met and got to know them well.
70. Letter of 7 June 1935.
71. Toynbee Hall, *Report 1935–8*. For the role of Toynbee Hall, not far from Bethnal Green, see J. A. R. Pimlott, *Toynbee Hall, Fifty Years of Social Progress, 1883–1934* (1935) and A. Briggs and A. Macartney, *Toynbee Hall, the First Hundred Years* (1989).
72. Beveridge's *Unemployment: A Problem of Industry* (1909) contrasted significantly with his *Full Employment in a Free Society* (1944). For an invaluable assessment of his life and work see J. Harris, *William Beveridge* (1977: rev. edn., 1997).
73. Letter of 1 February 1937.
74. B. Pimlott, *Harold Wilson* (1992), Ch. 4,
75. Letter of 21 April 1935 from Kiev.
76. Letter to the Elmhirsts, 29 July 1937.
77. *Weekend Review* (February 1931). This new periodical, with a brief life, was edited by Gerald (later Sir Gerald) Barry, who was to become editor of the *News Chronicle*. He directed successfully the Festival of Britain in 1951. Nicholson was secretary of its organising committee.
78. J. Pinder (ed.), *Fifty Years of Political and Economic Planning* (1981), *passim*, and *Planning*, vol. xvi, no. 300, 1949, *A Record of the Early History of PEP*.
79. See K. Lindsay, 'Early Days of PEP' in the *Contemporary Review* (1973) and 'Dartington's Heritage' in *Voice*, 18 August 1997; *The Elmhirsts of Dartington*, p. 282.
80. H. Wolfe, *British Labour Supply and Regulation* (1924). The author was a poet as well as a civil servant. In retrospect the Government's Military Service Bill of January 1916 can be seen as crossing 'a new threshold' in the relationship of the state with 'ordinary citizens'. (J. Stevenson, *British Society, 1914–45* (1984), p. 64).
81. M. Young, 'The Second World War' in Pinder, *op. cit.*
82. See A. Briggs, *Go To It!* (2000) which charts with illustrations the history of manpower and womenpower during the Second World War.
83. Stevenson, *op. cit.*, p. 445. See also A. Calder, *The People's War* (1969), p. 236, p. 269, pp. 291–3 and pp. 547–8. For the First World War, see A. Marwick, *After the Deluge* (1965), pp. 56–62, 168–71. For the failure of

the French to follow a national manpower policy in war time, see *Planning* No. 161 (1940), *Economic Priorities in War*.
84. *Manpower Policy* (1938). No. 131 had been called *Planning for Defence*, and No. 132 dealt with a subject which Michael had learned much about at Dartington, *Bringing Science to the Farm*, a subject close to Elmhirst's heart. PEP invented the now forgotten slogan 'Eat More Science' (Pinder, *op. cit.*, p. 43). There were continuities in Michael's interest in rural development. See below, Chapter. 9.
85. Letter of 15 May 1939. 'I have just telephoned Max who says that he sees no reason why the job shouldn't go through.'
86. Letter of 21 June 1939.
87. Letter of 4 February 1941.
88. Published in 1940, the pamphlet is quoted in P. Addison, *The Road to 1945* (1977 edn.), p. 73.
89. *Ibid.*, p. 122. The same views were being expressed by R. M. Barrington-Ward, the Tory-radical deputy editor of *The Times*, who was to be appointed editor in 1941. 'The duty of *The Times*,' he declared, 'is to prepare for the great social changes inevitable after the war.' (D. McLachlan, *In the Chair, Barrington-Ward of The Times, 1927–1948* (1971), p. 179.)
90. *Ibid.*, p. 48. Michael asked Huxley after the war why UNESCO could not build its own laboratory to deal with nuclear power. It would have seemed extraordinary then that Britain would leave UNESCO in 1985 explicitly on Thatcher's instructions. See T. L. McPhail, *Electronic Colonialism* (1987), pp. 277–80.
91. Letter of 19 November 1940.
92. Letter of 11 July 1944.
93. *The Memoirs of Israel Sieff* (1970), p. 169. See also *ibid.*, p. 192 and *The Times*, 19 January 1943, where it was stated that 'to PEP belongs the credit of founding itself expressly upon this belief'.
94. *Planning*, No. 71, March 1936, quoted in A. Marwick, 'Middle Opinion in the Thirties: Planning, Progress and Political "Agreement"' in the *English Historical Review* (April 1964). See also R. Lowe, 'The Second World War, Consensus and the Foundations of the Welfare State' in *20th Century British History* (1990).
95. Harris, *op. cit.*, p. 354, quotes a Beveridge letter to Halifax on 4 March 1940, suggesting that a reconstruction programme would not only avoid the economic catastrophes of the 1920s but would provide psychological encouragement to soldiers and workers.
96. T. Harrisson's *Living Through the Blitz* is 'free of mock heroics'. It was published posthumously in 1976. Harrisson's account (p. 59) begins with Stepney and includes an appendix on the Coventry Blitz. Like PEP publications, all Mass-Observation reports were anonymous.
97. Letter of 4 February 1941.
98. Quoted in Pinder, *op. cit.*, p. 88.
99. Letter of 19 January 1940.
100. *The Memoirs of Captain Liddell Hart*, Vol. II (1965), p. 258.
101. Letter from Dorothy to Leonard Elmhirst, 12 October 1940.
102. Letter of 19 November 1940.

103. Letter from Dorothy to Leonard Elmhirst, 19 January 1941, quoted in *The Elmhirsts of Dartington*, p. 308.
104. Letter to Mrs. Kay Starr, 22 June 1941. Michael was offered the position on 22 May.
105. *Ibid.*
106. For a later interpretation of this aspect of the war, see S. L. Carruthers, 'Manning the Factories: Propaganda and Policy in the Employment of Women, 1939–1947' in *History* (1990) and A. Briggs, *Go To It*.
107. Mass-Observation, *War Factory* (1987 edn. with a new introduction by Dorothy Sheridan), pp. 3, 120.
108. Quoted in *ibid.*, p. 4.
109. See H. Cudlipp, *Publish and Be Damned* (1953) and Calder, *op. cit.*, pp. 287–9. Morrison was supported by Ernest Bevin. Within a few days of the summons 'Cassandra' joined the Army.
110. Owen worked closely with Cripps and went on to become Deputy Secretary of the Preparatory Commission of the United Nations.
111. B. Webb, *Diary*, 26 October 1942.
112. A. Calder, 'The Common Wealth Party, 1942–1945' (PhD thesis, University of Sussex), p. 293. The Party won stirring war-time by-election victories. So, too, did Independents. Thus, in March 1942 an independent businessman won a by-election at Grantham. His opponent, Air Chief Marshal Longmore, had served in the Middle East. Margaret Thatcher, aged 17, was then living at her family home in Grantham.
113. *Peace by Federation* (1940) was the first of a series of Federal Tracts, and in May 1940 Beveridge flew to Paris with Lionel (later Lord) Robbins and Barbara (later Lady) Wootton for an international conference of Federal Union.
114. The best account of the Survey is by G. D. N. Worswick, 'Cole and Oxford, 1938–1958' in A. Briggs and J. Saville (eds.), *Essays in Labour History*, Vol. I (1960), pp. 25–43. (Worswick was later to cross swords with Michael, see below, p. 234) See also J. Harris, 'Did British Workers Want the Welfare State? and G. D. H. Cole's Survey of 1942' in J. Winter (ed.), *The Working Class in Modern British History: Essays in Honour of Henry Pelling* (1983).
115. Cole produced a threepenny pamphlet on *The War on the Home Front* and a sixpenny pamphlet on *War Aims*. Later in the war he was to be responsible for no fewer than four Left Book Club books published by Victor Gollancz, including *My Dear Churchill; Europe, Russia and the Future; Great Britain in the Post-War World*; and, most topical of them, *The Means to Full Employment*.
116. M. Cole, *The Life of G. D. H. Cole* (1971), p. 23.
117. See below, p. 96.
118. Michael had known of the argument between Cole and the Government. He had seen the economist Henry (later Sir Henry) Clay, the Warden-to-be of Nuffield College, where the Cole project was housed, and had discussed cooperation with PEP. (Letter of 25 September 1942.) Clay was also Chairman of the Executive Committee of the National Institute of Economic and Social Research, founded in 1938, taking over from Lord (Josiah) Stamp after the latter was killed in an air raid in 1941.

119. *After the Beveridge Report* (1943). For the relevant *Current Affairs* pamphlet, published by ABCA, see Major Richard Bennett, *A Weapon Against Want*, 4 November 1944.
120. Compare Harris, *op. cit.*, and Beveridge's autobiography *Power and Influence* (1953). The best narrative account of Beveridge's work and the contemporary reactions to it is Addison, *op. cit.*, Ch. VIII, 'The People's William'. For later reactions, diverse and contradictory, see J. Hills, J. Ditch and H. Glennester (eds.), *Beveridge and Social Security: An International Retrospective* (1994). Beveridge's wife Janet wrote her own account, *Beveridge and His Plan* (1954), which Harris rightly handles critically (*op. cit.*, pp. 35ff).
121. Quoted in *Fifty Years of Political and Economic Planning*, p. 93.
122. His co-author was Sir Henry Bunbury. (See above, p. 21) See also the most Keynesian of all PEP broadsheets, *Planning*, No. 160, *Paying for the War* (1940).
123. *Ibid.*, No. 188, *Financial Mysticism* (1943).
124. Quoted in Addison, *op. cit.*, p. 226.
125. In a letter written to Leonard, 25 September 1942, Michael noted how the arrival in Britain of the French socialist André Philippe had changed the situation. Philippe reported that the German occupation had 'created a new spirit in Frenchmen which [otherwise] would not have been brought about in decades'.
126. See E. H. Carr, *Conditions of Peace* (1942) and for Carr's account of the historical background *The Twenty Years Crisis 1919–1939* (1940).
127. *Building Peace out of War* (1944), p. 17, p. 19.
128. Letter of 15 August 1944.
129. See *Young at Eighty*, p. 236. Aims shifted from creating space colonies to founding a National Space Museum.
130. Letter of 19 October 1944.
131. *Fifty Years of PEP*, pp. 95–6.
132. Letter of 13 January 1945. He added that he was 'arranging to get some of the younger Labour Party and also Communist Party people here for a couple of lunches'.
133. Letter of 22 February 1945.
134. Morrison might not have become Chairman had not Hugh Dalton, the previous Chairman of the Policy Committee, preferred to move over to the Chairmanship of the Party's International Committee: he hoped to become Foreign Secretary.
135. He had become Secretary and Agent to the West Fulham Labour Party in 1928 before taking up a similar Agent's post in Whitechapel in 1934, and in 1937 he had joined the Party's Central Office as propaganda officer. After a brief spell in the Ministry of Information in 1939, he had returned to the Party as Organiser for the Eastern counties.
136. Letter of 22 February 1945.
137. M. Cole. *op. cit.*, p. 249.
138. Letter of 8 May 1944.
139. Letter of 15 August 1944.
140. Letter from Leonard to Dorothy Elmhirst, 4 March 1945.
141. Letter of 13 October 1957.

3 Party Politics

1. Arthur (later Lord) Henderson, described by Hugh Dalton as 'one of the best electioneering judges of our times', said that although he was 'not as optimistic as some people, he thought we should win at least 80 seats. This would mean a Conservative and Liberal majority of not more than 75'. 'My own estimate hasn't settled down yet,' Dalton wisely added. 'I am still thinking in terms of a very wide possible variation.' B. Pimlott (ed.), *The Dalton Diaries* (1986), p. 864. John Pimlott was Morrison's private secretary at the Home Office in 1944 and kept this position after Morrison became Lord Privy Seal and Deputy Prime Minister in the Labour Government of 1945.
2. For the lead-up to the Blackpool Conference and the attitude of the Labour leaders and of the Labour Party's National Executive to the timing of a general election (June or October), see Labour Party National Executive Committee, *Minutes* (1945), p. 256; A. Bullock, *The Life and Times of Ernest Bevin*, Vol. II (1967), Ch. 12; *Dalton Diaries*, 18 May 1945; and H. Dalton, *The Fateful Years* (1957), p. 459.
3. William Beveridge, *Power and Influence* (1953), p. 330. For the sequence of the 'white paper chase', which included education as well as social security and health, see A. Marwick, *Britain in the Century of Total War* (1968), pp. 314–27, and N. Timmins, *The Five Giants: A Biography of the Welfare State* (1995). The 1944 White Paper on *Employment* (Cmnd. 6527), promising action to secure and maintain 'a high and stable level of employment', endorsed by all parties, was the key document. Before Attlee told the Labour Party's Whitsuntide Conference of 1945 about the letter from Churchill suggesting an election in the autumn, he had asked Churchill to insert the sentence in it, 'In the meantime [until the election] we would do our utmost to implement the proposals for social security and full employment contained in the White Papers we have laid before Parliament.'
4. 4 *CR* (1995), pp. 80–98. In a speech to the Sociology Section of the British Association for the Advancement of Science, 11 September 2000, Michael placed 1945 in historical perspective. There is a summary in the *Guardian*, 12 September 2000, headed 'Ghosts in a Manifesto'.
5. In 1945 Michael mischievously (and unfairly) compared Attlee with a Huddersfield bank manager in a J. B. Priestley play whose 'exaggerated character was that he would say nothing except in one word and in monosyllables. If he tried anything else it would have been disastrous, because it would not have fitted him.'
6. B. Donoughue and G. W. Jones, *Herbert Morrison, Portrait of a Politician* (1973), pp. 340ff. Compare the bland and misleading comment in Morrison's *An Autobiography* (1960), p. 236, 'I was disturbed to learn that moves had begun to propose me as Leader of the Party in place of Attlee. I promptly took steps to see that these activities stopped.'
7. The Liberals, who put up 307 candidates, won 12 seats and lost 64 deposits. The Common Wealth Party, which put up candidates in 23 seats, lost them all, and there were 16 lost deposits. The Communists, who won 2 seats, one, Stepney in London's East End, lost 12 out of 21 deposits.
8. *CR*, p. 82.

9. Pimlott, *op. cit.*, p. 858.
10. *Ibid.*, p. 862.
11. *CR*, p. 82. The future Labour Prime Minister, then Lieutenant James Callaghan, serving on a ship in the Indian Ocean, never saw the manifesto and had to make up his own. See K. O. Morgan, *Callaghan: A Life* (1997), p. 52.
12. *Tribune*, 3 August 1945. The comment left out some of the obvious sting in 1945 Labour politics. Cf. Pimlott, *Hugh Dalton* (1985), p. 360. 'In theory the election manifesto offered ... a distinctive break with the past ... In reality the break with the past had already occurred.' R. B. McCallum and A. Readman, in their pioneering study of an election, *British General Election of 1945* (1947), p. 269, quoted an opinion poll which noted that 84 per cent of the people voting had made up their minds how to vote before nomination day.
13. *Report of the 43rd Annual Conference of the Labour Party*, 11–15 December 1944, pp. 160–8.
14. *Ibid.*, p. 37. Bevin, who at the time of the setting up of the Beveridge Committee had wished it to concentrate on 'administrative issues rather than policy', called the Beveridge Report 'this Social Ambulance' scheme. (Bullock, *op. cit.*, Vol. II, pp. 225–6.) See *Lloyd George's Ambulance Waggon: the Memoirs of W. J. Braithwaile*, edited by Bunbury (1957), with a commentary by Titmuss.
15. For the origins of 'Full Employment and Financial Policy', approved by Labour's National Executive on 17 April 1944, see Pimlott, *op. cit.*, pp. 395ff. 'We all know what to say on F[ull] Employment,' Dalton wrote after an informal meeting early in 1944 at which Gaitskell, Evan Durbin and Douglas Jay were among those present. 'The trick is to say it well.'
16. Memorandum on 'Platform Propaganda', Labour Party National Executive, *Minutes*, 9 April 1942.
17. Miliband, *op. cit.*, p. 278.
18. J. Parker, Secretary of the Fabian Society (1939–45), who was elected MP for Dagenham in 1945, described *Let Us Face the Future* as 'a positive Reconstruction Plan', 'gradually worked out as a result of research and discussions over the previous fifteen years' (*Labour Moves On* (1947), p. 26).
19. See above, p. 57.
20. See B. Vernon, *Ellen Wilkinson* (1982). Michael felt that the adjectives 'mild' and 'circumspect' might have been applied to another of the draftsmen of *Let Us Face the Future*, Patrick Gordon Walker. He found him too 'right wing', and this remained his opinion.
21. E. Watkins, *The Cautious Revolution* (1950), p. 30.
22. See Donoughue and Jones, *op. cit.*, pp. 354–6, and K. Middlemas, *Power, Competition and the State*, Vol. I, *Britain in Search of Balance, 1940–1961* (1985), p. 61, p. 185.
23. Already before the break-up of the Coalition, Churchill, in a speech at the Conservative Party Conference in March 1945, had described the Labour Party's 'sweeping' nationalisation proposals as threats to 'the whole of our existing system of society ... borrowed from foreign lands and alien minds' (*The Times*, 16 March 1945). For a vigorous response by Bevin in a speech at Leeds, see Bullock, *op. cit.*, pp. 369ff. Bevin saw

private monopolies as 'a danger to the state, a positive danger to the community'.
24. *The Daily Herald*, 27 July 1945, claimed that 'the Labour Party stands for order as against the chaos which would follow the end of public controls'. In the same number there is a reference to an East End doctor's placard placed in the street 'This is the hour of triumph of the common man'.
25. Their role was appreciated by some of the senior permanent civil servants like Sir Edward (later Lord) Bridges, who praised their 'notable service, not only in helping to guide the country's war effort, but later in shaping our post-war policies and organisation'. (Quoted in Pimlott, *op. cit.*, pp. 468–9.) See also D. N. Chester (ed.), *Lessons of the British War Economy* (1951), published under the auspices of the National Institute of Economic and Social Research.
26. For a critique both of the realism and the optimism, see Correlli Barnett, *The Last Victory: British Dreams, British Realities, 1945–1950* (1995).
27. Twenty-three Labour MPs, including Callaghan, Foot, Lee and Barbara Castle, voted against the Government on the acceptance of the Loan on 13 December 1945. The terms had been negotiated by Keynes. See L. S. Pressnell, *External Economic Policy since the War*, Vol. I (1986); J. C. R. Dow, *The Management of the British Economy, 1945–60* (1964); and A. Cairncross, *Years of Recovery: British Economic Policy, 1945–51* (1985).
28. See J. Schneer, *Labour's Conscience, The Labour Left, 1945–1951* (1988).
29. Addison, *op. cit.*, p. 264; see also his 'By-Elections of the Second World War' in Cook and Ramsden (eds.), *By-Elections in British Politics* (1973), pp. 178–9; and F. V. Cantwell, 'The Meaning of the British Election' in *Public Opinion Quarterly*, Vol. IX (1945). Until 1964 there was no publication dealing exclusively with polls, the title of a new international quarterly which had Henry Durant, Director of the Gallup Poll, and Mark Abrams on its editorial board.
30. Addison, *op. cit.*, Epilogue to the 1994 edition, p. 282.
31. J. B. Priestley, *Letter to a Returning Serviceman* (1945), p. 5. '[Don't] allow them to inject you with Glamour, Sport, Sensational News, and all the other De-Luxe nonsense, as if they were filling you with anaesthetic' (*op. cit.*, p. 31).
32. See A. West, *The Mountain in the Sunlight: Studies in Conflict and Unity* (1958), p. 169. See also *J. B. Priestley* (1988) by Michael's friend Vincent Brome.
33. *Ibid.*, p. 24.
34. J. Huxley, *TVA, Adventure in Planning* (1943).
35. Priestley dealt at some length with Swindon, well known to Michael, in his *English Journey* (1934), pp. 36–43.
36. Priestley, *Letter*, p. 26.
37. See B. W. E. Alford, *Britain in the World Economy since 1880* (1996), pp. 129ff. 'During the export drive [which was highly successful] complacency over the prospects of international competition was easily clothed in the rhetoric of "Made in Britain"' (p. 199).
38. E. Roberts, *Which? 25* (1982), pp. 9–10.
39. See below, p. 169. The first CND march to Aldermaston did not take place until 1958.
40. Addison, *op. cit.*, p. 267.
41. NLSC Interview, 12 May 1990.

42. Hennessey was interviewing Michael in a television series for Channel 4, *What Has Become of Us?*. See also Hennessey and A. Seldon (eds.), *Ruling Performance, British Government from Attlee to Thatcher* (1987).
43. Addison, *op. cit.*, p. 265.
44. For the issues behind the campaign, see R. B. McCallum and A. Readman, *op. cit.*, Ch. 3, and Mass-Observation, file report 2268, 'Report on the General Election', October 1945. For the campaign, see A. H. Booth, *British Hustings 1924–1950* (1956), Ch. 10. For the broadcasts, see A. Briggs, *The History of Broadcasting in the United Kingdom*, Vol. IV, *Sound and Vision* (1979), pp. 622ff. For a historical judgement, see H. Pelling, 'The 1945 General Election Re-considered' in the *Historical Journal* (1980).
45. See below, p. 283.
46. A. Howard, 'We Are the Masters Now' in M. Sissons and P. French (eds.), *Age of Austerity* (1963), p. 16.
47. M. Foot, *Aneurin Bevan*, vol. II (1973), p. 501.
48. Before the election Bevan had demanded (in not dissimilar fashion to Thatcher 30 years later) 'the complete extinction of the Tory Party and twenty-five years of Labour Government'. (Quoted in Foot, *op. cit.*, p. 505.)
49. *ECHR* (1943).
50. R. A. Brady, *Crisis in Britain* (1950), pp. 39–40. Two of the institutions Brady mentioned in recording the list of people whom he had interviewed in writing his book were PEP and the Research Department of the Labour Party. Young was not mentioned by name.
51. These words were printed in capital letters in a Party pamphlet called *Why the Tories Won't Build the Houses and Labour Will*. Bevan was in charge of both health and housing. By 1947 there were 260,000 houses under construction and a further 90,000 under contract. The two responsibilities, both difficult, were divided in 1951 when Dalton took over the latter after returning to the Cabinet as Chancellor of the Duchy of Lancaster.
52. Foot, *op. cit.*, p. 500. At Dundee in 1918 Churchill had said: 'We have got to do something on a bigger scale than ever before. The three great factors are land, communications and power and the three children, food, housing and manufacture. So long as the railways are in private hands they may be used for private profit. We cannot organize the great questions of land settlement, new industries and the extension of production unless the State has the control of transportation' (V. Brome, *Aneurin Bevan* (1953), p. 159).
53. *CR*, p. 84.
54. Yet note his reactions when he went back to 'the hideous corridors' of Transport House, in 1964. See below, p. 266.
55. H. G. Nicholas, *The British General Election of 1950* (1951), p. 28. There were 245 full-time agents in November 1949, and 279 on the eve of the general election in February 1950. By then, however, the Conservative Party had the larger and more highly trained constituency organisation.
56. D. Healey, *The Time of My Life* (1995), p. 12.
57. NLSC, Interview 12 May 1990.
58. *Planning*, No. 263, *Clubs, Societies and Democracy* (1947); No. 265, *Public Relations and the Town Hall* (1947); and No. 291, *Local Elections, How Many Vote?* (1948. See also J. Pinder (ed.), *Fifty Years of Political and Economic*

Planning (1981), p. 105. Bunbury produced a *Current Affairs* bulletin in September 1941 called *Voluntary Associations* which began with a sentence which might have been written by Michael. 'British people when they want to get something done have a way of forming a Society or Association or Union to do it.' See also F. Prochaska, *The Voluntary Impulse* (1988).
59. Hunter was to reappear briefly in Michael's vistas when both men turned to Africa to extend educational provision there. See below, Chapter 9.
60. R. A. Butler, *The Art of the Possible* (1971), p. 139.
61. See R. T. McKenzie, *British Political Parties: The Distribution of Power within the Conservative and Labour Parties* (1955), p. 559.
62. Quoted in S. Cooper, 'Snoek Piquante' in Sissons and French, *op. cit.*, p. 41.
63. See *Current Affairs*, 4 October 1947, *Spotlight on Coal* by Mark Benney, who had worked as a Pit Relations Officer, described as an 'experimental job'. See also H. Wilson, *A New Deal for Coal* (1945). For an interesting and relevant retrospective note, see T. Blackwell and J. Seabrook, *A World Still to Win, the Destruction of the Post-War Working Class* (1985), pp. 77–8.
64. See also Nicholson's book *The System* (1967). A later PEP publication, *Planning* No. 499 (1967), written by Samuel Brittan, *Inquest on Planning in Britain*, dealt with the demise of Labour government planning in the 1960s. The word 'inquest' seemed appropriate. Yet the word 'planning' remained vague. 'It would be a great mistake,' Brittan said, 'to spend too much time on a search for a single true meaning of "planning".' One 'safe' sense of the word was 'a set of policies which together make up a credible strategy for achieving a stated objective'.
65. His main duties in the British Electricity Authority concerned a statutory Welfare Commission. His responsibilities at the National Coal Board were wider. See Lord Citrine, *Two Careers, A Second Volume of Autobiography* (1967).
66. For an authoritative account of the fuel crisis, see W. Ashworth, *The History of the British Coal Industry*, Vol. 5, *1946–1982* (1986), pp. 130ff.
67. Quoted in Sissons and French, *op. cit.*, p. 249.
68. Donoughue and Jones, *op. cit.*, p. 355.
69. The terms 'workplace history' and 'rank and filism' were introduced into historical discussion in the 1980s, by J. Zaitlin, 'Rank and Filism in British Labour History: a Critique'. See also Zaitlin's article 'From Labour History to the History of Industrial Relations' in the *EHR* (1987), pp. 159–84.
70. The Labour Party, the TUC and the TGWU had been in the same office building, built on the initiative of Bevin, since 1928. The TUC moved out to Great Russell Street, Bloomsbury, in 1958, leaving the TGWU and the Labour Party together until 1978.
71. N. Dennis, F. Henriques and C. Slaughter, *Coal is Our Life* (1956), p. 64.
72. In *Local and Regional Government* (1947), p. 250, Cole criticised the civil service, never criticised by Attlee or Morrison, not for 'its lack of brains – of which it has, I think, a fair share, but for its failure to sympathise with the workings of democracy'.
73. Quoted in Bullock, *op. cit.*, p. 338. In 1975 Bullock was to chair a divided and abortive Committee of Inquiry into Industrial Democracy, which reported in 1977. It included Jack Jones, successor to Bevin, Deakin (and

Frank Cousins). A majority recommended an equal number of trade union and shareholders' representatives on the boards of private companies with over 2,000 workers. (See K. O. Morgan, *Callaghan, A Life* (1997), pp. 560–2.)
74. Letter of 15 March 1947.
75. See above, p. 82 and E. Mayo, *The Human Problems of an Industrial Civilization* (1933). For the British story see *Planning* No. 260, *Men, Management and Machines* (1947) and No. 248, *The Human Factor in Industry* (1948). See also A. Flanders, *Management and Unions: The Theory and Reform of Industrial Relations* (1970).
76. Michael's obituary of Edward Shils appeared in the *Guardian*, 8 February 1995. Cf. the unsigned *Daily Telegraph* obituary, 8 February 1995. See also below, pp. 131ff for the impact of Shils on the Elmhirsts and his role in the founding of the Institute of Community Studies.
77. *The Present Situation in American Sociology* (Pilot Papers, 1957).
78. *The Sociological Review* (1953). Michael's first academic article, 'Distribution of Income within the Family', directly related to his thesis, had appeared the year before in the *BJS*, Vol. III (1952).
79. NLSC, Interview, 12 May 1990.
80. *Labour's Plan for Plenty*, p. 11. Cf. p. 19, 'Modern economists, under the influence of Keynes, have given powerful reinforcement to the moral considerations which have impelled socialists to condemn inequality of income.'
81. See G. E. Schuster, *Private Work and Public Causes* (1979). From 1947 to 1966 Schuster was a member of PEP's Council of Management and from 1966 to 1978 a member of its Board of Patrons.
82. *Labour's Plan for Plenty*, p. 56.
83. See above, p. 151.
84. *Labour's Plan for Plenty*, p. 119.
85. See below, p. 157.
86. *Labour's Plan for Plenty*, p. 119.
87. Gollancz, born in 1893, is a key figure in Labour history and in the diffusion of left-wing ideas. In 1937 he had founded the Left Book Club. In 1951 he was to establish the Association for World Peace, the forerunner of War on Want. His autobiographical memoirs include *My Dear Timothy* (1952) and *More for Timothy* (1953).
88. *In Place of Fear* (1952), p. 5.
89. De Jouvenel, *The Problems of Socialist England* (1950).
90. *Labour's Plan for Plenty*, p. 9.
91. *Ibid.*, p. 27.
92. For an important discussion of the role of the State, see J. Harris, 'Society and the State in Twentieth-Century Britain' in F. M. L. Thompson (ed.), *The Cambridge Social History of Britain, 1750–1950* (1990). See also Mark Abrams, *The Welfare State* (*Current Affairs* pamphlet), January 1951, which in its teachers' notes stated bluntly 'The State now looks after family welfare because the family is unable to do so itself.' This sentence appeared in a section called 'the historical view'.
93. For a brief account of the balance of opportunities and obstacles in 1947, illustrated with effective graphics, see M. Abrams, 'The State of the Nation' (*Current Affairs* (August 1947)).
94. See below, p. 220.

95. See Labour Party, RD/172, marked confidential, 'Scientific Policy Committee, the Social Sciences', October 1948.
96. *NS*, 2 November 1974.
97. For an early Schumacher essay which was as different from the later Schumacher as *Labour's Plan for Plenty* was from *For Richer for Poorer*, see his 'Public Finance in Relation to Full Employment', in F. A. Burchardt (ed.), *The Economics of Full Employment* (1945).
98. W. Temple, 'The State', quoted in C. I. Schottland (ed.), *The Welfare State: Selected Essays* (1967), p. 23. For the term 'welfare state' and its historical and social orientation, see *inter alia* A. Briggs, 'The Welfare State in Historical Perspective' in *European Archives of Sociology* (1961), reprinted in *Collected Essays*, Vol. II (1985); S. P. Aiyer (ed.), *Perspectives of the Welfare State* (1966); T. H. Marshall, *Citizenship and Social Class* (1949); R. M. Titmuss, *Essays on the Welfare State* (1958); and D. E. Ashford, *The Emergence of Welfare States* (1986).
99. D. Lilienthal, *TVA: Democracy on the March* (1944). Quoted in *The Journals of David Lilienthal*, Vol. II (1964), p. 36.
100. Michael quoted N. M. Davies, *Industrial Psychology* (April 1948), D. Chapman, 'Increasing Production: a New Approach' (*The Listener*, 15 July 1948), and an American textbook, *The Dynamics of Industrial Democracy* (1942).
101. For the most cogent short economic analysis of the Labour Government's choices, see J. E. Meade, a war-time civil servant, *Planning and the Price Mechanism* (1948).
102. S. and B. Webb, *A Constitution for the Socialist Commonwealth of Britain* (1920) and *Soviet Communism, a New Civilization?* (1935).
103. See Michael's article in *NS*, 29 January 1970, 'Parish Councils for Cities'. By then the Maude Commission, which carried out considerable (if selective) research, had made suggestions for sweeping changes in local government.
104. L. Mumford, *The Culture of Cities* (1938), p. 493.
105. *Ibid.*, Ch. III. Mumford did include a short section called 'Resistance to Barbarism'. For an alternative scenario, see P. H. J. Gosden, *Self-Help: Voluntary Associations in Nineteenth-Century Britain* (1973) and A. Briggs, *Victorian Cities* (1964). Michael was doubtless drawn to some of the sections in Mumford's last chapter, particularly 'From a Money-Economy to a Life-Economy', 'Modern Housing by Communities' and 'The School as a Community Nucleus'.
106. PEP produced three issues of *Planning* on these themes in 1946, No. 251, *Population – A Challenge and a Choice*; No. 254, *Mothers in Jobs*; and No. 255, *The Unmarried Mother*.
107. *Social Science and the Labour Party Programme.*
108. For working-class reactions, see Blackwell and Seabrook, *op. cit.*, p. 88. 'Because it was felt to be a real liberation, people did not pause to wonder whether a succession of shifting images, conceived in the shadow of the market-place might not be as imprisoning in its own way as those tight cells of terraced houses under the shadow of the factory chimney.'
109. See P. Hollis, *Jennie Lee* (1997), pp. 223–4.
110. H. G. Nicholas, *The British General Election of 1950* (1951), pp. 71ff.

111. See D. Dayan and E. Katz, *Media Events* (1992). The Coronation is dealt with specifically.
112. Quoted in Nicholas, *op. cit.*, p. 78.
113. Healey has recalled a pre-election discussion at Shanklin, where insurance was an item on the agenda. The compromise 'mutualisation', as he remembered it, was accepted without any definition of what the word meant. (Healey, *op. cit.*, p. 128.)
114. Nicholas, *op. cit.*, p. 51, where he quotes a *Daily Express* headline, 'The MU Swallows the Pru'. See also Michael's 1950 Labour Party Discussion Pamphlet, 'The Future of Industrial Assurance: Labour's proposals for mutual ownership by the policyholders'.
115. NLSC, Interview of 12 May 1990.
116. See below, Chapter 9, where the story of the Consumers' Association is told more fully within the context of mutual aid.
117. S. Haseler, *The Gaitskellites: Revisionism in the British Labour Party 1951–1964* (1969), p. 49.
118. For the Greenwich survey see M. Benney, A. P. Gray and R. H. Pear, *How People Vote: A Study of Electoral Behaviour in Greenwich* (1956).
119. '1950 Election Broadcasts' (Labour Party Archives R/4, June 1950). For a later verdict, see P. Addison, 'Attlee' in the *New Statesman*, 17 December 1982. 'Committed as they were to working-class welfare, they [the leaders] had no interest in redistributing authority ... Orders and injunctions flow[ed] down from on high, and Labour leaders expected the people to respond.'
120. Interest in this section of the electorate was to increase in the 1960s. See, for example, R. T. McKenzie and A. Silver, *Angels in Marble: Working-Class Conservatism in Urban England* (1968).
121. Labour Party Research Department, 350, April 1950, 'Notes on the Findings of the Public Opinion Polls'; Morgan Phillips Papers; National Executive Committee, *Minutes* (1950), p. 119.
122. See B. Brivati, *Hugh Gaitskell* (1996), p. 118; Foot, *op. cit.*, p. 326; and W. Wyatt, *Confessions of an Optimist* (1985), p. 211. The so-called 'Keep Left' Group was responsible for the 1950 pamphlet *Keeping Left*. It was after the Bevanite split, however, that *Tribune*, then edited by Foot, published its pamphlet, *One Way Only*, which quickly sold out.
123. Susan Crosland, *Tony Crosland* (1982), p. 54.
124. See also C. A. R. Crosland, *The Conservative Enemy* (1962).
125. B. Pimlott, *Harold Wilson*, p. 179; Dalton, *Diary*, 29 September, 1 October, 1952.
126. Diary Notes, 23 February, 6, 21 March, 8 April 1951. Israel Sieff, who read the Diary with great interest, told Leonard Elmhirst that until reading it he had not realised 'how Anglo-Saxon Michael was'.
127. In a letter of 27 November 1952 Morgan Phillips thanked Michael on behalf of the NEC for 'all the work which you have done for the party, first as a Research Secretary and latterly as a Research Advisor'.
128. It follows the statement: 'For those born since the Second War, television and jet planes and radar will for ever be part of the accepted order.'
129. Some of the most interesting sections of the Report concern the balancing of the second of these budgets and the role of husbands and wives in family budgeting. During the 1970s and 1980s Michael wrote forcefully

about the perils of inflation. See, for example, his *Inflation, Unemployment and the Remoralization of Society* (1982), a Tawney Society pamphlet.
130. See in addition to Titmuss's major works, a 1951 broadcast 'Family Problems in the Welfare State' (*The Listener*, 15 March 1951) which was quoted by Michael in *For Richer For Poorer*.
131. R. H. S. Crossman (ed.), *New Fabian Essays* (1952), pp. vii–ix.
132. E. P. Thompson, *William Morris, Romantic to Revolutionary* (1955).
133. See E. P. Thompson, 'The New Left', in *The New Reasoner*, Summer 1959, and the book he edited in 1960, *Out of Apathy*, one of a New Left Books series launched in 1959 with Norman Birnbaum as general editor. The Communist split after the putting down by Russia of the Hungarian revolt in 1956 was only one, if the most important, landmark date in the story. See also P. Anderson, 'The Left in the Fifties' in the *New Left Review* (1965).
134. Michael organised a Trust Fund to support Fienburgh's wife and family. In 1955 Fienburgh had written a book *25 Momentous Years* for the 25th anniversary of the *Daily Herald*. The first chapter was called 'Bitter Froth' and the last 'And for Tomorrow?', which referred (p. 189) to Wilson's 'blaze of controls'. 'We are still far from attaining our aims,' he concluded. 'It is no blue-printed, constricted and controlled society we seek to build, but one breathing adventure and enterprise' (p. 202). Fienburgh was succeeded in 1959 by Peter (later Lord) Shore.
135. A series of broadcast talks by Winnicott, *The Child and the Family* was published in book form, also by Tavistock Publications, in 1957, as in the same year was *The Child and the Family, First Relationships* (1957). In 1958 *The Child, The Family and the Outside World* appeared in Pelican. For another relevant Tavistock Publication see A. K. Rice, *The Enterprise and its Environment* (1959) which outlined 'a theory of organisation applicable alike to industrial and non-industrial enterprises'. Treating 'resistance to change' as 'a natural phenomenon of all living organisms', Rice stressed that 'real differences – whether person-centred or task-centred – should be neither heightened nor suppressed by the fear of organisational change'.
136. For the Birmingham University of this period, see A. H. Halsey, *No Discouragement: An Autobiography* (1996), Ch. V.
137. 'The Role of the Extended Family in a Disaster' in *Human Relations* (1954).
138. 'The Meaning of the Coronation' had been published in the oldest British journal of sociology, *The Sociological Review*, first published in 1908 and in 1953 taken over by the new University College of North Staffordshire, later the University of Keele. See P. Collison and S. Webber, 'British Sociology, 1950–1970: A Journal Analysis' in *The Sociological Review* (1971) and for the longer-term historical background, P. Abrams, *The Origins of British Sociology, 1834–1914* (1968) and M. P. Carter, 'Report on a Survey of Sociological Research in Britain' in *The Sociological Review* (1968).
139. He referred in a footnote to a list of six books by anthropologists, including *We, the Tikopia* (1936) by Professor Raymond Firth, to whom he talked at LSE, and A. R. Radcliffe-Brown and D. Forde (eds.), *African Systems of Kinship and Marriage among the Nuer* (1951). He added to the list the American sociologist Talcott Parsons's 'Kinship System of the contemporary United States' in his *Essays in Sociological Theory* (1949).

140. M. Young and P. Willmott, *Family and Kinship in East London* (Pelican edition, 1962), p. 12.
141. NLSC, Interview, 12 May 1990.
142. E. Shils, 'On the Eve: a Prospect in Retrospect' in M. Bulmer (ed.), *Essays on the History of British Sociological Research* (1985).
143. P. Willmott, 'Resolving the Dilemma of Bigness' in *Young at Eighty* (1995), p. 2.
144. There was an interesting discussion on the question of the language of sociology in *Encounter*. In December 1965 Runciman wrote an article 'Sociologese' to which Shils replied in the number for June 1967. 'Many sociologists are ignorant of the traditional language of educational discourse,' Shils concluded, 'but so are many other professional persons with highly specialised education.' 'The language of a generally educated public is crumbling.'

4 Two Places; One Purpose

1. 'Progressive Education at Dartington, 1930s to 1980s' (M. B. Curry Memorial Lecture delivered on 7 June 1984 at the University of Exeter).
2. NLSC Interview, 12 May 1990.
3. Unpublished PhD Thesis, 'A Study of the Extended Family in East London', p. 1. Characteristically the thesis is undated both on its bound cover and inside.
4. M. Young and P. Willmott, *Family and Kinship in East London* (1962 paperback edition), p. 17. Michael would have been interested in an article years later by Jeff Porter in *Open History*, the quarterly magazine of the OU History Society (March 1999) on 'Bethnal Green in 1871: Immigrants and Natives', originally submitted as a course essay. It was largely based on an analysis of data in the 1871 census, but it took the form of a historical survey.
5. *The Symmetrical Family* (1973), p. 38. For post-1945 novels of the East End see H. Pollins, 'East London in Post-war Fiction' in *East London Papers* (1961).
6. NLSC Interview, 12 May 1990.
7. See Chapter 7.
8. *The Elmhirsts of Dartington*, p. 1.
9. *Ibid.*, p. 326.
10. *Ibid.*, p. 4.
11. *Ibid.*, p. 105.
12. Champernowne, a Cambridge (King's College) graduate, was Director of the Institute of Statistics in Oxford from 1945 to 1948, and a Fellow of Nuffield College from 1948 to 1959. He had worked during the War from 1941 to 1945 as Assistant Director of Programmes in the Ministry of Aircraft Production. In 1970 he became Professor of Economics and Statistics at Cambridge.
13. Born in 1884, he was the ninth child of Arthur Champernowne, Victorian squire of Dartington. In 1950 Leonard told a Withymead doctor that he and Dorothy were 'entirely in sympathy with their [the Champernownes'] work'. (Quoted in *The Elmhirsts of Dartington*, p. 212.)

14. *Ibid.*. p. 31.
15. Leonard's phrase in a letter to Tagore, quoted in *ibid.*, p. 87. For an anthology of Tagore's writings see *A Tagore Reader* (1961), edited by A. Chakravarty, who served as Tagore's literary secretary from 1926 to 1933.
16. See below, Chapter 9.
17. *The Elmhirsts of Dartington*, p. 99.
18. *Ibid.*, p. 27. Later, Leonard described with relief how 'the old religious enthusiasms, austerities, burnings and striving' were 'gone' (*ibid.*, p. 91).
19. See above, p. 17 and below, pp. 115, 117.
20. Quoted in *The Elmhirsts of Dartington*, p. 45.
21. *Ibid.*, p. 133. The quotation comes from W. H. G. Armytage, *Heavens Below* (1966), p. 154, where he is quoting *Seed Time*, the quarterly journal of the Fellowship of the New Life. For the links with the Fabian Society see W. Knight (ed.), *Memorials of Thomas Davidson* (1907). When Davidson read a paper on 'The New Life' in October 1883 to a group of people who subsequently founded the Fabian Society, one of the people present was Frank Podmore, later a biographer of Robert Owen. Another was Havelock Ellis. For relatively recent appraisals, see N. and J. MacKenzie, *The First Fabians* (1977), pp. 21ff; A. M. McBriar, *Fabian Socialism and English Politics, 1884–1918* (1962), pp. 1–13; and R. J. Harrison, *The Life and Times of S. and B. Webb, 1858–1905* (2000).
22. The word 'churching' figures in the index of *Family and Kinship*, however, and in the text on pp. 56–7. It refers to the custom of going to church as soon as possible after confinement for a service centred on thanksgiving for the birth of the child. One mother who did go to be 'churched', which Young/Willmott associate with the notion not of thanksgiving but of childbirth making mothers 'in some way unclean', comments, 'It's the Mums. It's not that I actually believe in it, but I'd get an uneasy feeling if I didn't do it. You don't like to break tradition' (*loc. cit.*, p. 57). For Michael's interest in secular rituals as a substitute for traditional religious rituals, see p. 316. For Booth's interests in religion within a survey context, see R. O' Day and D. Englander, *Charles Booth's Note Books Reconsidered* (1993). A Charles Booth Centre for Social Investigation was subsequently set up at the Open University.
23. *The Elmhirsts of Dartington*, p. 113, p. 128.
24. *Ibid.*, p. 119.
25. *Ibid.*, p. 100.
26. *Ibid.*, p. 102. For Michael's persistent search for universalities, see his lecture 'From Universities to Universalities', given at the University of Swaziland, 23 October 1998.
27. Letter of 3 October 1950.
28. Letter of 11 April 1959.
29. Letter of 11 October 1958.
30. Michael was quoting a note by Leonard Elmhirst, 'Time Budget, 1934–5', a revealing description (*ibid.*, p. 102). Michael mentioned in this context the work of Patrick Geddes, Ebenezer Howard and Frederic Osborn, but not that of Lewis Mumford (for whom, see above, p. 93). 'Leonard did not like large cities.' Michael also criticised the building of a new town, Becontree, 'on a wide area of the best market garden land in Essex' (p. 257).

31. Young and Willmott, *op. cit.*, p. 25.
32. See below, p. 310.
33. GP Interview, 22 March 1994.
34. Letter of 5 May 1951.
35. *The Elmhirsts of Dartington*, p. 321.
36. GP Interview, 22 March 1994.
37. See below, p. 310.
38. Unpublished thesis, pp. 24–5.
39. See A. Briggs, *Collected Essays*, Vol. II (1985), pp. 257–8. G. M. Young had a strong visual sense too: 'everyone of us lives in a landscape of his own' (*Last Essays* (1950), pp. 130–5).
40. *Family and Kinship*, p. 13.
41. A footnote referred to M. Rose, *The East End of London* (1951), p. 4.
42. Michael noted 'a kind of shrine' in one of the Bethnal Green 'turnings' which encased a war memorial, a Union Jack and two pictures of the Queen. For Michael's account of the Coronation, see above, p. 84.
43. Unpublished thesis, p. 38.
44. NLSC Interview, 12 May 1990.
45. See above, p. 107.
46. R. Firth, *Two Studies of Kinship in London* (1956). GP Interview, 22 March 1994.
47. *Contact: Britain between West and East* (1946).
48. R. Glass, *Watling, A Social Survey* (1939) and *The Social Background of a Plan: A Study of Middlesbrough* (1948). The adjective 'redoubtable', which I might have used myself, is Geoff Dench's in *Young at Eighty*, p. 182. Ruth's first husband was Henry Durant, pioneer of opinion polling. See the interesting obituary of Ruth in *The Independent*, 13 March 1990. PEP produced a pamphlet, *Watling Revisited*.
49. In 1958 Ruth founded the Centre of Urban Studies at University College, London, with which I was closely connected. Its chairman was the architect Sir William Holford. For her views on urban, rural, suburban and 'new towns', see her UNESCO Report of 1955, *Urban Sociology in Great Britain, a Trend Report*. For my own work on Middlesbrough, see *Victorian Cities* (1963), Ch. 6.
50. In 1929 Leonard wrote to a Cambridge friend who was working in Welwyn Garden City, 'some time I want you to come down and see our embryo Welwyn in Devonshire' (quoted in *The Elmhirsts of Dartington*, p. 258). In fact, one basic and obvious difference between Dartington and the garden cities was that it was more like a village than a town (*ibid.*, p. 259).
51. See Briggs and Macartney, *op. cit.*, pp. 121–2.
52. For Sheldon see below, pp. 134, 138, and G. Wolstenholme (ed.), *Lives of the Fellows of the Royal College of Physicians of London*, Vol. VI (1982), pp. 402–6. Michael read Sheldon thoughtfully. He had concentrated, he wrote in his thesis, on 'the services received by old people'. 'Are there any other studies,' he asked, 'which show not what they receive, but what they give?' The Social Medicine Unit of the Medical Research Council had touched on the question.
53. *Young at Eighty*, p. 85.
54. The idea of 'travelling companions' was to appear in a different form in *The Symmetrical Family*, Ch. I.

55. For some of the implications of this approach, followed also in *Family and Kinship*, Chapter 2, 'Mothers and Daughters', see G. Dench, 'Tracking the Demeter Tie' in *Young at Eighty* and below, pp. 144–5. The phrase 'Demeter Tie' was to be used in *The Symmetrical Family*, pp. 91–3, where it was contrasted with the Oedipus Conflict between son and father. For Dench's further thoughts on 'the problem of men', see his *The Frog and the Prince* (1994).
56. GP Interview, 22 March 1994.
57. See above, pp. 3, 10.
58. See above, pp. 15, 75.
59. Dwelling throughout on the contribution made to this subject by anthropologists, he even mentioned the Chinese kinship system, referring to Wong Su-Ling's *Daughter of Confucius* (1952).
60. He referred in a footnote to an article on different definitions of the family by Barbara Wootton in 'Am I my Brother's Keeper?' (*Agenda*, May 1944) *before* the social service legislation of the Labour Government.
61. Health was a less important issue, although it gained in importance in Michael's mind as it did in national politics. See pp. 87, 88.
62. A footnote after 'maternal function' refers the reader not to Dartington but to Samoa. See M. Mead, *Coming of Age in Samoa* (Pelican edition, 1954). This was one of the most widely read anthropological books of the 1950s.
63. R. Firth, *We, The Tikopia: a Sociological Study of Kinship in Primitive Polynesia* (1936). The 'ideal', Michael observed, 'would be to witness the birth of a number of people and then follow them through until their death.' This ideal, 'Chasing a Cohort', which was to be followed by medical researchers, was then deemed to be 'obviously unattainable' in social sciences, although the Social Science Research Council was to encourage longitudinal studies. Firth, a New Zealander, born in 1901, was to be knighted in 1973. In 1959 he published *Social Change in Tikopia*.
64. See below, p. 240.
65. D. Glass, *Social Mobility in England* (1954), p. 25. The same passage was quoted in *Family and Kinship*, p. 170.
66. Cf. A comment of 'Mrs. Banks', living in Bethnal Green, in *Family and Kinship*, p. 51. 'Strangers are all right, but you prefer your own every time.'
67. *Loc. cit.*, pp. 158–60.
68. One question concerned housing, treated as 'the chief agency of social change' just because 'a better house brings with it a different style of living'. Did married couples who considered themselves less dependent on kin adapt themselves to changes in housing more effectively? 'My belief, like so many other statements in this report,' he wrote, 'is one which cannot be tested.'
69. Unpublished 'Draft Proposal for the Establishment of a London Institute of Community Studies' (1953).
70. M. Young and P. Willmott, 'Institute of Community Studies' in *The Sociological Review*, July 1961.
71. See below, p. 242.
72. Michael referred to the Schuster Panel, but not at this point to the National Institute of Economic and Social Research, founded in 1938, or to the idea of a Social Science Research Council. See below, Chapter 5.
73. Letter of 18 August 1953. Michael referred to his arrival at Dartington, to LSE and PEP and financial help with his psychoanalysis. This was 'the

biggest project yet'. He was writing his letter on the edge of a cliff in South Devon where he was on holiday.
74. Letter of August 1953.
75. The draft memorandum referred to the Clapham Report and the loss of an earmarked grant from the University Grants Committee. It thus connects with Michael's demand for a national scheme of social research before and after 1953.
76. Lord (Eric) Roll et al., *Fifty Years of Political and Economic Planning* (1981), p. 118. This was the first annual conference attended by a new Director-Designate of PEP, Richard Bailey, who remained as Director until 1964.
77. The full title of *Planning*, No. 552 by R. Clarke and R. Davies – the authors of PEP's broadsheets were now identified – was 'A Chance to Share: Voluntary Services in Society'.
78. NLSC Interview, 12 May 1990.
79. Mandy Ashworth, *The Oxford House in Bethnal Green: 100 Years of Community Development* (1994), p. 5. One of its pre-First World War heads had been the pacifist Rev. Dick Sheppard, later Vicar of St. Martins-in-the-Fields and Canon of St. Paul's, who gave good advice to Michael's father.
80. Letter of August 1953.
81. *Diary*, 9 March 1954.
82. See R. Gavron, 'Making Money for Other People' in *Young at Eighty*, pp. 117–20.
83. See below, pp. 240, 242. Waddilove served on the Milner Holland Committee on Housing in Greater London from 1963 to 1965, and a year later became a Trustee (and later Chairman of Trustees) of Shelter. He also chaired a PEP group on Housing Associations in 1962. In 1954 he had published a book, *One Man's Vision*.
84. Townsend described him giving a 'rousing talk' on 'Housing and Behaviour in Bethnal Green' (Diary, 15 March 1954).
85. There have been many subsequent changes of stationery.
86. *Young at Eighty*, p. 69.
87. *Ibid.*, p. 150. McIntosh's chapter is called 'Michael in his Peer Group', Naomi's 'Consumer Power as a Pillar of Democracy'.
88. Based in part on comments from readers of the newspaper *The People*, Gorer's book included chapters on 'people and homes', 'friends and neighbours', 'going out' and 'growing up'.
89. Ten years later, Carr-Saunders produced a new edition – his co-author was D. Caradog Jones – and in 1958 the two co-authors were joined by C. A. (later Sir Claus) Moser in a further *Survey of Social Conditions in England and Wales*. Another social surveyor was Cole, along with his wife, who produced *The Condition of Britain* (1937). For his war-time Nuffield College survey in which Michael participated, see above, p. 58. In 1951 Seebohm Rowntree, known to Dorothy Elmhirst before she married Leonard, and G. R. Lavers published their third social survey of York, *Poverty and the Welfare State*. For a different strand in the history of social surveys see M. Abrams, *Social Surveys and Social Action* (1951). For nearly quarter of a century from 1946 to 1970 Mark Abrams was Managing Director of a company, Research Services Ltd.
90. Carstairs was the BBC's Reith Lecturer in 1962, taking as his subject *This Island Now*.

358 *Notes*

91. *Diary*, 27 January 1952.
92. *Ibid.*, 10 September 1953. Abel-Smith, then employed by the National Institute for Social and Economic Research, wrote a Fabian Society pamphlet on social security in 1954. Later in the year Townsend met Beveridge whom he found 'surprisingly misinformed' about what was happening to social security.
93. *Planning*, Nos. 358, 9, *Schools under Pressure*. Townsend wrote an article on the subject of education, 'After the Deluge', in *The Times Education Supplement*, 29 January 1954, arguing that the system of education envisaged in 1944 could not be achieved unless the proportion of teachers in the working population was doubled from 1 to 2 per cent.
94. *BJS* (1953). In 1965 he was to co-author 'The Poor in the Welfare State' and *The Poor and the Poorest*.
95. *Diary*, 30 December 1953.
96. He and Michael visited Nuffield Lodge in October 1953. 'At first our reception was cool,' Townsend noted, but at the end of the meeting it seemed almost as if the two people they saw (the Secretary and his Assistant) would be sympathetic to the proposal. 'Now everything depends on a Trustees' meeting in three weeks time' (*Diary*, 22 October 1953).
97. *Diary*, 18 February 1954.
98. *Ibid.*, 21 October 1954, 14 December 1954.
99. *Diary*, 9 March, 23 April 1954.
100. NLSC Interview, 12 May 1990.
101. 'The Family Life of Old People' in the *Sociological Review*, Vol. 3, December 1955.
102. Michael had met her while a student at LSE.
103. It was she who introduced Wyn Tucker to Michael and the Institute. See above, p. 34.
104. Letter to Dorothy Elmhirst, 27 May 1955.
105. *Family and Kinship in East London* (Pelican edn., 1962), p. 14.
106. *Diary*, 9 March 195?
107. See below p. 163.
108. *British Medical Journal* [to insert]
109. *The Economist*, 3 August 1957.
110. See above, pp. 96–7.
111. *Family and Kinship*, p. 132.
112. *Ibid.*, p. 148.
113. *Ibid.*, p. 106.
114. *Ibid.*, p. 117.
115. Townsend, *op. cit.*, p. 15.
116. *Ibid.*, p. 228.
117. Willmott and Young, *op. cit.*, p. 113.
118. Townsend, *op. cit.*, p. 14, p. 127, p. 154. The second of these passages is followed by an account of an old people's 'outing' to Brighton on a cold grey day. Four hundred people travelled there in eleven coaches.
119. Townsend wrote later of Titmuss that he was the only person he knew who brought 'his most tenacious beliefs into the open for all to survey. We all like to think we can be critical of our own society. Richard asks questions about things everybody else accepts' (*Diary*, 1 August 1954).

120. NLSC interview (with Paul Thompson), December 1997.
121. 'He has always taken the line that this is my book ["about the same subject and people" as his] and until now has left me to get on with it', 'but now he appears to be trying to edit mine down to the last detail'. 'Now he is trying to be Director in an editorial as well as an executive capacity' (*Diary*, 14 October 1956).
122. NLSC interview, December 1997.
123. Field, then a teacher in further education, was Director from 1969 to 1979, the year he entered Parliament, becoming Minister of State (Welfare Reform) in the Department of Social Security after the Labour victory in 1997. His tenure in office was as short as his commitment to welfare was long. He is an important figure in the *dramatis personae* of the twentieth century and will demand a full biography.
124. Townsend's later writings include *Sociology and Social Policy* (1975) and *Poverty in the United Kingdom* (1979). He was a co-author of *Inequalities in Health* (1980) and editor of *Labour and Equality* (1980). Returning to his first theme, which he never forsook, he wrote *The Family and Later Life* (1981).
125. P. Townsend, *The Family Life of Old People* (1957), p. vii.
126. *Family and Social Change in an African City: A Study of Rehousing in Lagos* (1961). This was an Institute publication. For Michael and Africa, see below, Ch. 9.
127. 'Knowledge and Persuasion: Research of ICS' in *Young at Eighty*, p. 75.
128. Dealing with the passages they quoted from their interviews, Michael and Willmott stated that 'Their comments are quoted [to a historian, at least, they are far more than this] solely as illustrations, partly because we are interested in individual people and partly because this research, which is for us a work of apprenticeship in sociology, is merely the first of a series of family studies' (Young and Willmott (1957 edn.), p. xix). This passage was not incorporated in the paperback edition.
129. Marris, *loc. cit.*, p. 77.
130. J. Platt, *Social Research in Bethnal Green: An Evaluation of the Work of the Institute of Community Studies* (1972).
131. 'The Aims of the Institute', No. 3, 17 January 1956.
132. *Ibid.*, 26 November 1956.
133. *Ibid.*, 17 January 1956.
134. Letter to Michael from Ralph Samuel, 5 January 1982.
135. The book was difficult to write because it was 'a venture largely into territory very little known' (*Education and the Working Class*, p. 225). The authors could have chosen any place. 'We chose Marburton. To have gone elsewhere would have strengthened our claims to distance and "objectivity" and these are qualities we value deeply and have tried to attain in this report. [Note the word.] But against this there seemed so much to be gained by facing the paramount fact that we were dealing with people and not things' (p. 3). The book was based on a survey of 88 'working class children'.
136. *Education and the Working Class*, p. 224.
137. B. Jackson, *Working Class Community* (1968), p. 118.
138. NLSC interview, 12 May 1990.

139. Kellen described such organisations before the Second World War as 'pressure groups, employing so far as their limited means permit, pitiless publicity to combat deceptions, false claims, false pretences, [and] poor quality' (*loc. cit.*, p. 142). An American periodical *Consumers' Research*, published by Consumer Research Inc., went back to 1928, and a year before that a little book by Stuart Chase and R. J. Schlink, *Your Money's Worth*, had asserted that 'if a million citizens could be persuaded to invest one dollar per year for verified facts about their purchases, wonderful things could be done'.
140. E. Roberts, *Which? – 25 – Consumers' Association, 1957–1982* (1982).
141. J. Mitchell, 'A Triptych of Organisations' in *Young at Eighty*, p. 10.
142. NLSC Interview, 12 May 1990.
143. Mitchell, *loc. cit.*, p. 10. The third organisation in his triptych was to be the Social Science Research Council. Michael was to make Mitchell Secretary. See below, p. 239.
144. Postgate, who had written *The Common People* (1938) in partnership with Cole, had edited *Tribune* in 1940 and 1941, and was employed as a temporary civil servant in the Board of Trade from 1942 to 1950. His *The Plain Man's Guide to Wine* appeared in 1951.
145. See above, p. 85.
146. See *Which?*, November 1965.
147. See below, p. 293. In her book *Which? 25*, p. 23, Roberts stated that she could not think of any paper or magazine which owed – or owes – as much to its reader-members as *Which?*. 'It was not that they wrote it, and *Which?* rarely published their letters. But they offered free the benefit of their experience and expertise, and it is hard to see how *Which?* could have managed at all without them.'
148. NLSC Interview, 12 May 1990.
149. *Where?* No. 19.
150. Report to the Elmgrant Trustees, September 1961.
151. NLSC Interview, 12 May 1990.
152. See below, p. 203.

5 Merit and/or Solidarity

1. This memorable passage ends with the boy acquiring a new accent, 'the most indelible mark of class in England'. The ladder image is raised again in the chapter on work, 'From Seniority to Merit'.
2. K. Lindsay, *Social Progress and Educational Waste* (1924). See also L. Hogben, *Political Arithmetic* (1983). 'We may investigate how far the progress of occupational recruitment is based on special aptitude for a particular occupation, and the problem of political arithmetic is then to estimate the remediable wastage due to defective social organization.'
3. *Art, Wealth and Riches* (1883).
4. In his introduction to the 1994 American edition of *The Rise of the Meritocracy* Michael quoted J. J. Rawls, *A Theory of Justice* (1972): 'Resources should go to education not "solely or necessarily mainly according to their

return as estimated in productive trained abilities, but ... according to their worth in enriching the personal and social life of citizens, including ... the less favoured."' See also Michael's article in *Dissent*, Fall 1973, 'Is Equality a Dream?'.
5. Progressive schools figure once in *The Rise of the Meritocracy*. It was they which had abolished prefects. The prefect system had often converted into a life-time awe of the older children by the younger. It was at the base, therefore, of the seniority system. *Seniores priores*.
6. Michael did not mention Burt by name in *The Rise of the Meritocracy*. He included a section called 'Progress of Intelligence Testing' in his Chapter 3 where he referred to 'continuous growth in the efficiency of selection methods'. 'Very few laymen could at first understand that intelligence was not an abstraction, but an operational concept.' See N. Black and G. Dworkin (eds), *The IQ Controversy* (1976); L. J. Kamin, *The Science and Politics of IQ* (1976); and G. Sutherland, *Ability, Merit and Measurement: Mental Testing and English Education, 1880–1940* (1984).
7. See below, Chapter 6.
8. J. Vaizey, *Education for Tomorrow* (1962), p. 7. On the cover of the Penguin the word 'Education' was printed in far larger letters than 'for Tomorrow'. 'Futures' (see below, p. 249) were not yet in fashion.
9. See below, Chapter 6. See also A. Briggs, *Collected Essays*, Vol. III (1991), pp. 231–45, where there is a reprint of a talk given to the History of Education Society in 1971. See also my introduction to the reprint of F. Adams, *History of the Elementary School Contest* (1882). Compulsory education was not a feature of the 1870 Act as Michael suggests. That came in 1893.
10. *NS*, 10th Anniversary Special Issue, 5 October 1972.
11. *Twentieth Century*, Summer 1963, 'What's In What's Out' 'Education', October 1963.
12. There were different strands in the previous history which went back to the idea of 'a career open to the talents'. In American sociology the strand led back before Talcott Parsons, *The Social System* (1951) to K. Davis, 'A Conceptual Analysis of Stratification' in the *American Sociological Review* (1942) and K. Davis and W. E. Moore, 'Some Principles of Stratification' in *ibid*. (1945). See also T. Parson, 'A Revised Analytical Approach to the Theory of Stratification' in R. Bendix and S. M. Lipset (eds.), *Class, Status and Power* (1954).
13. For its application to post-war communist societies in Eastern Europe, see W. D. Connor, *Socialism, Politics and Equality* (1979), reviewed in the *New York Times*, 15 April 1979, under the heading 'Some More Equal than Others'. For Britain, see M. Dean, 'The Social Disorder of Merit', written after John Major had set the goal of a classless society, in the *Guardian*, 31 December 1990. 'The book worked,' Dean reported. 'It helped abolish the 11 plus, made the left think more carefully about equal opportunity, and prompted more support for a pluralistic society.' See also Dean's article in *Young at Eighty*, pp. 105–11.
14. *Time and Tide*, November 1958. For Western Europe, see T. Husén, *Talent. Equality and Meritocracy* (1974).

15. D. Bell, 'The Meritocracy and Equality' (*The Public Interest*, November 1972). Quoted in Michael's introduction to the 1994 American edition of *The Rise of the Meritocracy*. See also Bell's book *The Rise of Post-Industrial Society* (1973).
16. Introduction, p. xvii.
17. At an earlier point in the other Michael Young's thesis he had observed that 'in the balanced view of sociology we have to consider the failures as well as the successes. Every solution of one is a rejection of many.'
18. For the other Michael, in an interesting footnote to Chapter 1, 'the origin of this unpleasant term' [meritocracy], like that of 'equality of opportunity' was 'obscure'. (He might have added 'welfare state' or 'Establishment'.) 'It seems to have been first generally used in the sixties of the last [20th] century in small-circulation journals attached to the Labour Party, and gained wide currency much later on.'
19. Michael took the name from the trade union leader, George Woodcock, Secretary of the TUC. He joked with names in this book as in *Family and Kinship in the East End*.
20. M. Young, Introduction to an American (Transaction) edition of *The Rise of the Meritocracy* (1994), p. xi.
21. *Ibid.*, pp. xi–xii.
22 Hunslet was described vividly, with a plenitude of quotations, in R. Hoggart, *The Uses of Literacy* (1957).
23. *Encounter* (October 1958).
24. Interestingly, the extract from *The Rise of the Meritocracy* printed in *Social Scientist as Innovator* (1983) came not from the beginning but from the end of the book.
25. Others included Irving Kristol, Vincent Brome, Margaret Cole, Jean Floud, Geoffrey Gorer, A. H. Halsey, Peter Marris, Edward Shils, Prudence Smith, R. H. Tawney, Peter Willmott, Leonard Woolf, Dorothy Elmhirst and Joan Young.
26. See below, p. 191.
27. See *Encounter*, October 1958. Strachey's review was called 'Unconventional Wisdom'.
28. D. V. Glass (ed.), *Social Mobility in England* (1954), pp. 25–6. See also B. Wootton, 'Social Prestige and Social Class' in *BJS*, Vol. V, No. 4 (1954).
29. There were to be many empirical studies attempting to measure the incidence and consequences of 'class inequality' in education. See, for example, J. Murphy, 'Class Inequality in Education: Two Justifications, One Evaluation but no Evidence' in *BJS* (1981) and 'A Most Respectable Prejudice: Inequality in Educational Research and Policy' in *ibid.* (1990), and A. E. Heath and P. Clifford, 'Class Inequalities in Education in the Twentieth Century' in *Journal of the Royal Statistical Society* (1990).
30. 'Above the cosiness of Lords [cricket ground], the exclusiveness of Ascot [races], and the somnolence of the Federation of British Industries loomed the shadow of the clever foreigner.'
31. See A. Briggs, *A History of Broadcasting in the United Kingdom*, Vol. IV (1995 edn.), p. 1. The critic was C. P. Scott of the *Manchester Guardian*.
32. See A. Briggs, 'The Language of Mass and Masses', reprinted in *Collected Essays*, Vol. I (1985).
33. Postscript to the 1948 edition of *Fabian Essays*, 'Sixty Years of Fabianism'.

34. 'Rule by Merit', *Spectator*, 21 November 1958. Ford did not take kindly to Young's 'satire'. 'It operates at a comparatively simple debating level, and he has little command of the undertones of irony, let alone of the verbal compression, that one associates with Swift.'
35. *Commonweal* first appeared in 1885. Morris was ejected from its editorship in 1890.
36. See above, p. 49.
37. A footnote to the other Michael then ran 'Dr. Puffin of York University [which did not exist when the real Michael wrote] asserts that on a count he made at the Populist Convention at Leicester, women ... numbered sixty-two per cent of the delegates, the rest being men with the old predominating.'
38. So too is 'quality press'. 'Quality of life' has survived, even becoming in 1999 a Conservative slogan.
39. Interestingly, David Riesman, the American sociologist, picked out this point in his 'Notes on Meritocracy', which appeared in the number of *Daedalus* (Summer 1967) that was devoted to Daniel Bell's project *Toward the Year 2000: Work in Progress*.
40. There was a need for psychologists at Harwell, however, besides physicists. An advertisement of the 1990s for a personable endocrino-psychiatrist is quoted in Chapter 7, 'Rich and Poor'.
41. R. K. Merton, Leonard Broom and L. S. Cottrell (eds.), *Sociology Today, Problems and Prospects* (1959).
42. 'The Meaning of the Coronation' in the *Sociological Review* (1953). Lipset quoted the critique of the paper by Birnbaum, 'Monarchs and Sociologists', *ibid.* (1955).
43. W. J. Goode, 'The Sociology of the Family' in *ibid.*, pp. 178–97. The writer quoted Malinowski – and Eileen Power – but made no references to Peter Laslett or other British writers.
44. One of the books revived by the new right was T. S. Eliot's *Notes Towards the Definition of Culture* which had appeared in 1947. Some of Eliot's words had obviously left a deep impression on the real Michael, particularly 'An elite, if it is a governing elite, so far as the natural impulse to pass on to one's offspring both power and prestige is concerned, if not artificially checked, will tend to establish itself as a class. But an elite which thus transforms itself tends to lose its function as an elite, for the qualifications by which the original members won their position will not all be transmitted equally to their descendants.' This was one of the observations that influenced how Michael drafted his chronology of change in *The Rise of the Meritocracy*.
45. M. Young, 'The Role of the Extended Family in Channelling Aspirations' in *BJS*, March 1967.
46. A footnote refers to one finding in Professor H. J. Eysenck, *Uses and Abuses of Psychology* (1953).
47. Chapter 7, 'Rich and Poor', is a key chapter, dealing with 'the reform of the money structure'. The 2005 Act eliminated all the prices and incomes arguments which were to bedevil the Labour and Conservative Parties in the 1960s and 1970s after *The Rise of the Meritocracy* was written and which were to shape the programmes of the Social Democratic Party.

48. See above, Chapter 3.
49. *How the Mind Works* (1933), pp. 28–9. See also his war-time 'Inquiry into Public Opinion regarding Educational Reform' in *Educational Psychology* (1943 and 1944). For the first serious critique of Burt's conclusions, see P. E. Vernon, 'Intelligence Testing' in the *Times Educational Supplement*, 1 February 1952. With the use of intelligence testing during the Second World War in mind, a footnote in *The Rise of the Meritocracy*, Ch. 6 refers to the book by Vernon and J. B. Parry, *Personal Selection in the British Forces* (1952). For the later 'exposures' of Burt, see L. S. Hearnshaw, *Cyril Burt, Psychologist* (1979).
50. Michael introduced 'the ladder', a favourite metaphor, in this context. Employees had 'ladder plans'. He quoted the *Report of a Committee of Enquiry into the Electricity Supply Industry* (Cmnd. 9672, 1956), Citrine's industry. 'Employees in the industry are considered to be on a common ladder, rising as openings occur, and in open competition according to experience and ability for the particular vacancy.'
51. See, for example, 'A meritocracy that makes a mockery of toil', *The Independent*, 18 January 1997, which deals with 'star-led' industries. The widespread use of the word 'industry' to relate to entertainment or leisure has revolutionised the conceptions of and organisation of both. Heritage also became an industry in the 1980s. Television already was. So was 'sport'.
52. For example, three pages are devoted to the so-called Leicester experiment which extended study at a 'common school', a primary comprehensive, to 15, leaving selection to take place then, not at 11. Leicester was on Michael's mind when he wrote *The Rise of the Meritocracy*, and there is a footnote reference in it to S. C. Mason, *The Leicester Experiment* (1957). Michael sited the original source of his Populist Party in Leicester. In his fictional future 'the Leicester hybrid never bloomed'. For the 'reality', see D. K. Jones, *Stewart Mason, the Art of Education* (1988) and N. Pye (ed.), *Leicester and its Region* (1972), Ch. 21. For the 'comprehensive' argument, see R. Pedley, *Comprehensive Education, A New Approach* (1956).
53. GP Interview, 22 March 1994 with Geoff Dench.
54. *Ibid*. This is the most revealing interview relating to the origins, content and impact of *The Rise of the Meritocracy*. It covered not only equality and fraternity but the role of women. When Dench asked whether Michael had been influenced by his work on Bethnal Green (and the role of women there) he replied 'No'.
55. E. James, *An Essay on the Content of Education* (1949) and *Education for Leadership* (1951). James was cited along with the American President of Harvard, J. B. Conant, in the section on education, but he figured too in the sections on work. 'No longer will industry or commerce be able to recruit at fifteen or sixteen boys who, as in the past, are of a quality to work their way up to positions of the highest managerial responsibility.' Packing a point of his own into a later long footnote, the real Michael noted how the Co-operative Movement had singularly failed to learn this lesson. See below, p. 291.
56. See below, p. 246.
57. For the balance of the Act and its longer-term political implications, see Simon, *op. cit.*, pp. 73ff. See also for different interpretations R. G. Wallace,

'The Origins and Authorship of the 1944 Education Act' in *History of Education* (1981); and K. Jefferys, 'R. A. Butler, the Board of Education and the Education Act' in *History* (1984). For H. C. Dent, writing at the time, as for the future Michael, the Act was 'the greatest measure of educational advance since 1870 and probably the greatest ever known' (*The New Education Bill, what it Contains, What it Means, and Why it Should be Supported* (1944)).

58. See his book *The Art of the Possible* (1971) and the biography of him by Anthony Howard, *Rab: The Life of R. A. Butler* (1987).
59. *The Public Schools and the General Educational System*.
60. For an even stronger version of the real Crosland's views on education than that set out in *The Future of Socialism*, see his book *The Conservative Enemy* (1962).
61. See above, p. 108.
62. The careers of the fictitious trade union leaders, Lord Wiffen (born 1957) and the very real trade union leader, Ernest Bevin (born 1881), are set out in a section called 'Fall of the Labour Movement'. 'The excellent qualifications of the former' (IQ at 11 plus 121: Bevin's was not given) contrasted with the fact that 'Bevin had no education worth the name'. Wiffen's IQ fell, however, as he rose to trade union power, and when he was raised to the peerage at the age of 64, the age when Bevin became Foreign Secretary, it was 116. When at the age of 76 he was working as an Assistant Lecturer at Aston Technical College, it was 104. This is another interesting choice of location, as interesting as that of York, given the development of Colleges of Advanced Technology (under Crosland) and the later transformation of Aston into a University. Peter (later Sir Peter) Venables was to be the key figure there. He was also to be first Chairman of the Council of the Open University. See below, p. 210.
63. The Labour Party had played its part in the establishment of this convention. Ironically, the person whom both Michaels chose to suggest that this was what would happen was 'Anthony Wedgwood Benn' who in *The Privy Council as a Second Chamber* (Fabian Society, 1957) had written that Labour's objection to the House of Lords did not 'stem primarily from the weakness or unfairness of the system of creating peers so much as from the absurdity of the inherited element'. 'The Labour Party ended up as active for reform as their opponents,' the other Michael wrote, 'Selection largely replaced election.' The story was not to be quite so simple, but it is still unfinished, as are many of the stories brought to a conclusion in *the Rise of the Meritocracy*.
64. The other Michael quoted with approval earlier in his thesis 'Fenn's first maxim for the student of historical sociology – "where goes power, there go I".'
65. *Daily Telegraph*, 31 October 1997.
66. Francis Galton (1822–1911), cousin of Charles Darwin, set up a Galton Chair of Engineering at the University of London. Two of his most influential books were *Inherited Genius* (1869) and *Natural Inheritance* (1889).
67. *New Statesman*, 29 November 1958. Shore's review, 'More than Opportunity', discussed two books, the other, *The Boss* by Roy Lewis and Rosemary Stewart. It began, like the first chapter of *The Rise of the Meritocracy*,

366 *Notes*

with the Victorian acceptance of Sir Stafford Northcote's recommendations that the Civil Service should recruit by competitive examination.
68. The other Michael wrote of Chinese competition in the last decade of the twentieth century, following Russian competition, which, in fact, never mattered. He refers to 'the battle in the 1990s against making Chinese the second language in schools'. The failure to do so was 'an interesting example of continuing conservatism in a profession whose primary role is discouraging it'.
69. Cf. the other Michael's note on how while 'the socialists collapsed as an organised force, the same thing did not happen to the sentiments they expressed'.
70. For Michael's response, see his article 'Beyond the Chatter' in the *Guardian*, 24 July 1991. One section of *For Richer For Poorer* was called 'What Do We Mean by a Classless Society?'. It distinguished between 'equality of opportunity' and 'equality'. In one passage (reminiscent of Marx's praises of capitalist bourgeois achievements) he hailed the Boulder Dam, the Volta Dam and the Mulberry Harbour as 'some of the monuments to "equality of opportunity"'. See also N. Bosanquet and P. Townsend, *Labour and Equality, A Book of Specialist Papers* (Fabian Society, 1970).
71. GP Interview of 22 March 1994, with Geoff Dench. For Peter Saunders, writing in *Sociology* (1995) 'the meritocratic hypothesis', in relation to Britain, had not been disproved. See 'Might Britain be a Meritocracy?'. Saunders was using John Goldthorpe, not Michael, as his reference authority.

6 Education for Change

1. Report to the Elmhirst Trustees, September 1961.
2. See my article in it, 'Education to Improve Education' (1958).
3. *The Organisation of Comprehensive Secondary Schools – some preliminary suggestions for the consideration of teachers* (1953). In that year 14 comprehensive schools were complete in various parts of the country, and 23 local education authorities out of 146 had one or more comprehensive schools planned.
4. M. Wilson, *Epoch in English Education, Administrators' Challenge* (Sheffield City Polytechnic Papers in Education Management (1984)), p. 24.
5. *Times Educational Supplement*, 4 November 1949, quoted in B. Simon, *Education and the Social Order, 1940–1990* (1990), p. 121. See also H. C. Dent, *Secondary Education for All* (1949). There is an excellent summary of the role of the *Times Educational Supplement* in a special edition to celebrate its 75th anniversary in 1985.
6. *The New Secondary Education* (HMSO, 1947). 'The name "secondary modern" was part of the brave new world hoped for after 1944'. *Ibid.* (19 June 1959). For an early criticism of the system, see Lady Simon, *Three Schools or One? Secondary Education in England, Scotland and the USA* (1948). Lady Simon, critic of the system, lived in Manchester and played an active part in its local government. In 1938 she had written its history, *A Century of City Government* (1938).

7. For an evaluation of the period, see R. Barker, *Education and Politics, 1900–1951, A Study of the Labour Party* (1972); D. W. Dean, 'Planning for a Post-War Generation: Ellen Wilkinson and George Tomlinson at the Ministry of Education, 1945–1951' in the *History of Education* (1986); H. D. Hughes, 'In Defence of Ellen Wilkinson'; D. Rubinstein, 'Ellen Wilkinson Reconsidered'; C. Benn, 'Comprehensive School Reform and the 1945 Labour Government' in the *History Workshop Journal* (1979); and P. Wann, 'The Collapse of Parliamentary Bipartisanship in Education, 1945–1953' in the *Journal of Educational Administration and History* (1971). See also the valuable collection of papers and essays drawn from the period in H. Silver (ed.), *Equal Opportunity in Education* (1973).
8. In 1953 the Labour Party's manifesto *Challenge to Britain* proposed the abolition of selection at eleven. In 1957 the National Foundation for Educational Research, started in 1945 (there had earlier been an Education Research Fund), estimated that 78,000 children out of 640,000 were wrongly allocated by the eleven-plus examination.
9. Michael delivered a BBC Third Programme talk in 1959 called 'Pressure at 18 plus'. In 1959 he proposed to the Labour Party's Youth Commission, set up by Gaitskell, that 5,000 'adventure' travelling scholarships should be provided each year for the young.
10. See above, p. 87.
11. R. Toomey, 'The Early History of the Open University', an authoritative unpublished paper (n.d.). Ralph Toomey was Jennie (later Lady) Lee's admirable senior civil servant at her side at the setting up of the Open University. See below, p. 211.
12. *Times Educational Supplement*, 11 November 1955, observed that 'there never was anything quite like television for setting the jeremiah on edge'. In November 1960 the NUT organised a large-scale conference on 'Popular Culture and Personal Responsibilities' at Church House, Westminster. Brian Groombridge, who was to play an important part in educational broadcasting through television, prepared an influential report.
13. Unpublished Report of an Exploratory Meeting held at Hamilton House, 3 July 1962. Campaign for Educational Advance, 'The Objects of the Campaign' (Working Paper No. 12 (n.d.)).
14. See, for example, *The Economist*, 24 August 1963, 'Ministry for the 18-Plus. How should the Government organise itself for a massive expansion of higher education?'. Among the 'facts' revealed in the campaign were that about 5,000 boys and girls with the necessary qualifications to enter the universities in 1963 would not be admitted (a figure provided by the Association of University Teachers) and that in 1957 (the source was *Where?*) only 6.5 per cent of the girls at Oxford and Cambridge were from working-class homes. The cost of educational research was no more than 0.2 per cent of what the Government spent on education.
15. In 1953 spending on education was 2.7 per cent of the gross national product (P. J. D. Wiles, 'The Nation's Intellectual Investment' in the *Bulletin of the Oxford University Institute of Statistics* (1956)).
16. For the beginnings of the Council, founded on the recommendation of a Working Party appointed by Boyle in July 1963 and chaired by Sir John

Lockwood, see M. Kogan, *The Politics of Education, Edward Boyle and Anthony Crosland in conversation with Maurice Kogan* (1971).
17. B. Simon, *op. cit.*, p. 298. See also for the beginnings of the trend, the Penguin by R. Pedley, *Comprehensive Schools* (1963). For the content and tone of the surrounding controversy, see M. Cole, *What is a Comprehensive School?* (n.d.); B. Simon, *The Common Secondary School* (1956); R. Pedley, *Comprehensive Education, a New Approach* (1956); and H. Rée, *The Essential Grammar School* (1956). For a retrospect, see I. G. K. Fenwick, *The Comprehensive School, 1944–1970* (1981).
18. Lord Longford, then Lord Privy Seal, resigned from the Government on the issue.
19. E. G. Edwards, *Higher Education for Everyone* (1982), pp. 51–2. The decision to extend the school leaving age to 15 had been taken in 1947 only after a 'battle in the Cabinet'.
20. Simon, *op. cit.*
21. The number of 18-year olds rose from 642,000 in 1955 to 963,000 in 1965.
22. See Peters, *op. cit.*, and J. Carswell, *Government and the Universities in Great Britain* (1985). For an early critique of university policy and indirectly of the UGC (not based on essential knowledge that was unavailable to him), see G. C. Moodie, *The Universities: A Royal Commission* (Fabian Society, Research Series, No. 209, 1959).
23. Cmnd. 902, *The Report on Scientific and Engineering Manpower in Great Britain* (1959).
24. The Central Advisory Council for Education (England), *15–18, A Report* (1959/60), p. 316. Crowther was subsequently to become first Chancellor of the Open University. For the various well-publicised and influential reports of the CAC, see A. Corbett, *Much to Do about Education (Council for Educational Advance, 1968)*.
25. Cmnd. 2154, *The Report of the Committee on Higher Education* (1963). R. Layard *et al.*, *The Impact of Robbins* (1969). For wastage, see J. L. Gray and P. Moshinsky 'Ability and Opportunity in English Education' in L. Hogben, *Political Arithmetic* (1938) and J. E. Floud (ed.), *Social Class and Educational Opportunity* (1956).
26. *Half Our Future: A Report of the Central Advisory Council for Education (England)* (1963). Newsom had published *Willingly to School* in 1945 and *Education for Girls* in 1948. A determined school builder, he was said to have gone round Hertfordshire with a trumpet in one hand and a trowel in the other. (Quoted Kogan, *op. cit.*, p. 24.)
27. *Ibid.*
28. After the publication of the Newsom Report, Sir Herbert Andrew, Permanent Secretary at the Ministry of Education, prepared a paper for Boyle introducing a fictitious family, the Robinsons, 'the least able, those who really were going to be troublesome' (Kogan, *op. cit.*, p. 139). Three Robinson children 'from the bottom quarter of ability' were mentioned in the Newsom Report (p. 60, note 5).
29. Central Advisory Council for Education, *Children and Their Primary Schools* (1967), Vol. I, *Report*, Vol. II, *Research and Surveys*.
30. T. Blackstone, 'The Plowden Report', in *BJS* (1967). Tawney had been a member of the Hadow Comittee to which he often referrred.

31. Plowden was to serve as Vice-Chairman of the Governors of the BBC from 1970 to 1975 and Chairman of the Independent Broadcasting Authority, the successor of the Independent Television Authority, from 1975 to 1980.
32. *Times Education Supplement*, 13 January 1967.
33. See below, note 36. Crosland, Secretary of State for Education when the Plowden Report appeared, wrote in a Cabinet Paper of 25 February 1966 of his 'troublesome relations with the Central Advisory Council (England) under the chairmanship of Lady Plowden, which was appointed by the previous Government to review primary education and the age of transfer to secondary schools' (C/66/43, 25 February 1966, 'Comprehensive Reorganisation and Raising of the School Leaving Age'). Finance, however, was not uppermost in his mind. He could not possibly accept a proposal which Plowden would be making – that transfer from primary to secondary school should take place at the age of 12 because it would interfere with his plans for comprehensive reorganisation 'varying to meet local needs' as set out in his landmark circular 10/65. Crosland did not reappoint the Committee after the publication of the CAC's eleventh report.
34. Half the funds of the National Foundation, which was founded in 1947 as a by-product of the 1944 Education Act, were provided centrally, half by local authorities.
35. Ministry of Education, *Early Leaving* (1954), which laid most emphasis on the effect of home environment. See also E. Fraser, *Home Environment and School* (1959). For a post-Plowden analysis, see J. Ford, *Social Class and the Comprehensive School* (1969).
36. M. Kogan, 'The Plowden Report Twenty Years On' in the *Oxford Review of Education* (1987). See also his book *The Politics of Educational Change* (1988). Other members of the Committee included Donnison, Titmuss's successor as Professor of Social Administration at the LSE, Mollie Brearley, Head of the Froebel Institute at Roehampton, and J. M. Tanner, Reader and later Professor of Child Health at the Institute of Child Health, London University, all familiar names in the world of education.
37. The main critique of the Report was to come a generation later in the 1990s, spanning Conservative and New Labour Governments. In 1969 C. B. Cox and A. C. Dyson edited *Black Paper Two*, which included a paper by R. Lynn, 'Comprehensives and Equality: The Quest for the Unattainable'. During the 1990s the critique was taken up in the popular press.
38. B. Plowden, '"Plowden" Twenty Years On' in the *Oxford Review of Education* (1987).
39. The Committee placed 10 per cent of primary schools into the two top categories of excellence – the top 1 per cent were 'pacemakers and leaders of educational advance', but 28 per cent were 'run of the mill', and 5 per cent 'markedly out of touch with current practice and knowledge and with few compensating features'. Only 0.1 per cent were 'bad'.
40. M. Kogan, 'The Plowden Report Twenty Years On'. One of the co-editors of the number of the *Oxford Review of Education* in which his article appeared was Halsey.
41. The Plowden Committee, setting the pattern for the use of research in the preparation of an official Report, commissioned enquiries into the effect of parental attitudes towards education on child development, turning to the

Government Social Survey and to the Manchester Institute of Education. The social class of parents was shown to be an inadequate predictor of the educational attainment of their children. We are back in the world of *The Rise of the Meritocracy*.
42. See below, p. 247. The possibility of injecting extra resources into schools or areas which were educationally deprived had been considered earlier by the Newsom Committee (*Half Our Future*, Ch. III).
43. For Michael's role in securing funding for the Educational Priority Areas as Chairman of the SSRCl, see below, pp. 247.
44. Whole chapters of the Plowden Report were devoted to community schools and to educational priority areas. There was another chapter on immigrants.
45. The comment of the *Times Education Supplement* when it appeared (13 January 1967) ended with the words 'Lady Plowden and her committee have produced ways of spending public money and convinced us that they are admirable, if only the nation can first earn the money.'
46. See Clegg's four autobiographical articles in the *Times Education Supplement* (1974) and the book he edited in 1972, *The Changing Primary School*. For Boyle, Clegg 'carried weight simply by sheer force of being who he was, the person he was'. (Kogan, *op. cit.*, p. 136.) He was also 'the spokesman of the less fortunate of our society'.
47. Quoted in *The National Extension College: A Catalyst for Educational Change* (1990), p. 2.
48. The metaphor of the spectrum was never entirely appropriate. During the 1960s parallels were drawn between the creative processes in primary education and in university education. There was a great arc linking them. It was the secondary schools in between which were then most criticised, although the Schools Council nationally, despite its cumbrous constitution, and the appointment of local authority Advisors were instruments of change. See A. Briggs, 'The Map of Learning' in D. Daiches (ed.), *The Idea of a New University* (1962).
49. See below, p. 223.
50. Compare Daiches, *op. cit.*, and the Reith Lectures by Albert (later Sir Albert) Sloman, the first Vice-Chancellor of the University of Essex, *A University in the Making* (1964). Annan was Chairman of the Planning Committee at Essex. One of the members of the Sussex Planning Committee was the Cambridge physicist Sir Neville Mott, who was to play a part in Michael's story. See below, p. 219.
51. Michael had relatively little to say about the changing curriculum in the early or mid-1960s, but in 1970 he wrote an interesting conference paper, 'An approach to the study of curricula as socially organised knowledge', reprinted in R. Brown (ed.), *Knowledge, Education and Cultural Change* (1973).
52. See K. Murray, *Recollections* (1992), especially Ch. 7, for the Chairman's attitudes and experiences. Each member of the UGC would have presented a different version. All greatly admired Murray's chairmanship.
53. See above, p. 148.
54. Michael wrote his obituary for the *Guardian*, 10 April 2000.

55. *The Evolution of Community* (1963). Others included *Local Government Decentralisation and Community* (1987) and *Community Initiative* (1989), both published by the Policy Studies Institute, as was *Police and Community* (1987). They were described as 'discussion papers', a phrase that rang many bells.
56. Lockwood was to become Professor of Sociology at Essex University in 1968 when Townsend left for Bristol. He co-authored three volumes with J. Goldthorpe on *The Affluent Worker in the Class Structure* (1968–69), necessary reading for students of *The Rise of the Meritocracy* and of Michael's other writings. In 1973 Lockwood became Chairman of the Sociology and Social Administration Sub-Committee of the Social Science Research Council.
57. NLSC Interview, 12 May 1990.
58. The complex story is well told in J. J. Walsh, 'Postgraduate Technological Education in Britain: Events Leading up to the Establishment of Churchill College, Cambridge' in *Minerva* (1994). Walsh was a former Registrar of the University of Leeds.
59. NLSC Interview, 12 May 1990.
60. See the text of a speech to the Open University, 15 April 1994.
61. David Daiches (see note 48) was a Fellow of Jesus College, Cambridge before deciding to move as a founding father to Sussex in 1961, believing that it would not be possible to reform Cambridge's divided English faculty.
62. The story of Churchill's involvement is briefly told in M. Goldie, 'Churchill College and the Origins of the Open University' in *Churchill Review* (1994), pp. 44–6. A Conference Room had been designated in Whittinghame Lodge, a newly acquired house in Storey's Way.
63. For Michael's later link with Nigeria see below, pp. 265ff.
64. Stone, earlier in his career a Director of the Department of Applied Economics (1945–55), pioneered model-building in economics. His book *The Role of Measurement in Economics* (1951) was followed by *The Measurement of Consumers' Expenditure and Behaviour*, 2 vols (1954, 1956), which touched Michael's own field of interest.
65. Paper on 'The Prospects for Open Learning', 13 April 1994.
66. Churchill College itself might have been more profoundly affected. Very early in the story Michael tried to persuade the College to create a 'Vacation University' there (letter to the Master, 20 October 1961 accompanied by a paper): 'I would willingly speak to the paper at the next meeting of the Governing Body.'
67. See the 25th anniversary publication, *The National Extension College a Catalyst for Change* (1990), pp. 2–7, 'Dreams, 1963–64'; and 'Responsibilities, 1964–1967'.
68. *Ibid*. See also a typescript (n.d.) by Michael and Jackson called 'Story of the National Extension College'.
69. See below, pp. 203ff.
70. G. Catlin, 'A University of the Air' in the *Contemporary Review* (1960).
71. See below, p. 296.
72. R. C. G. Wilson, 'A Television University' in *Screen Education* (1962) and 'The Next Twenty-Five Years of Television', a Lecture to the Royal Institution of Electrical Engineers, 31 May 1962.
73. See H. Wiltshire and F. Bayliss, *Teaching Through Television* (1965).

74. As President between 1958 and 1967, I encouraged the Association to take a positive approach to television, a subject which greatly interested me. I was responsible for its pamphlet *Viewing and Learning* (April 1964).
75. G. Crowther, *Schools and Universities*, a lecture at LSE (1961).
76. *Where?* (Autumn 1964), 'Towards an Open University'. This was the longest article to appear in *Where?*.
77. See S. K. Bailey (ed.), *Higher Education in the World Community* (1975).
78. For the potential, see S. Cotgrove, 'The Forgotten Tenth' in the *Spectator*, 17 May 1963. See also J. Margeson, 'Emerging University' in *ibid.*, 24 May 1963.
79. *Which?*, May 1963, reporting a Consumers' Association survey, found standards 'deplorably low'. Existing courses in basic subjects such as English and Mathematics were 'uninspiring': 'material was often drearily presented, sometimes cramped and badly duplicated'.
80. Michael quoted an American source on the Soviet Union, N. de Witt, *Education and Professional Employment in the USSR*. In post-Sputnik days this report was published in 1961 by the U.S. National Science Foundation. See also the article in *Where?* which Michael wrote in 1963, along with Christina Farrell, 'Who Uses Correspondence Colleges?' (Autumn 1963).
81. Michael quoted W. Schramm (ed.), *The Impact of Educational Television* (1960). Schramm was the recognised doyen of American University teachers of communications.
82. See A. Briggs, *A History of Broadcasting in the United Kingdom*, Vol. V, *Competition*, Ch. VI, 'Education, Politicians, and Pirates', pp. 471–9. There was considerable suspicion inside the BBC of plans for an Institute of Educational Television, proposed in the Autumn of 1961 by David Hardman, a former Labour MP and Minister, and of ITV conferences on educational television in Norwich and in London early in 1962. The suspicion was even more evident whenever ITV spokesmen talked of a separate educational television channel, a proposal disliked in the Ministry of Education and dismissed by the Pilkington Committee on the Future of Broadcasting, of which Hoggart was a member (see above, p. 163), which reported (Cmnd. 1753) in June 1962. Boyle was to change his mind on it.
83. One of the pioneering ITV companies was Ulster Television which put on a series of university television midnight lectures, *Midnight Oil*, in 1962.
84. The Viewers' and Listeners' Association had subsequently been founded by him in 1960, the heir to the Sound Broadcasting Society, with T. S. Eliot as President.
85. See P. Laslett, 'Teaching by Television' in *Where?* (Winter 1963).
86. See F. Hunter, *Community Power Structure* (1953).
87. For a report of the April conference see *Universities Quarterly* (1963).
88. M. Young, undated paper, 'Dawn University'. See also *Where?* (Summer 1964), where the word 'milestone' was used.
89. Joseph Weltman, a former BBC Talks producer, a man of enterprise, who became first Education Officer of the ITA, made the most of this point.
90. See R. Williams, *Communication*.
91. P. Laslett, 'Linking Universities by TV' in *Where?* (Summer 1974).
92. The most successful academic to perfect the form was the Oxford historian A. J. P. Taylor, who used neither notes nor visual illustration.
93. *Where?* (Summer 1964).

94. See below, p. 263.
95. *Where?* (Autumn 1963).
96. Quoted in Briggs, *op. cit.*, pp. 476–7.
97. For Scupham, see his BBC Lunchtime Lecture, *Broadcasting and Education* (November 1963). An important internal paper by him 'The Future of Educational Broadcasting', was considered by the BBC's Board of Management in January 1964. Scupham remained in his BBC post until his retirement in July 1965. See his book *Broadcasting and the Community* (1967), esp. Ch. VII. See also J. Robinson, *Learning Over the Air: 60 Years of Partnership in Adult Learning* (1982).
98. A. Wolstencroft to Young, 16 August 1963: Young to Wolstencroft, 21 August 1963.
99. Quoted in Briggs, *op. cit.*, p. 477.
100. See Briggs, *The Golden Age of Wireless*, p. 132.
101. UGC, Press Release, 13 February 1965. One of the proposals in the Report was for 'a national library of recorded material'.
102. In a Preface to the Newsom Report, which greatly impressed him, Boyle, who was an active Deputy President of the WEA and Pro-Vice-Chancellor of the new University of Sussex, had written in a curious, but intelligible, phrase that the 'essential point is that all children should have equal chance of acquiring intelligence'. He may or may not have read *The Rise of the Meritocracy*.
103. *Where?* (Autumn 1963).
104. One of the first Principals of Keele, George (later Sir George) Barnes, had been the BBC's second Head of Television.
105. See Briggs, *op. cit.*, pp. 492–3.
106. See above, p. 198.
107. Michael paid a tribute in *Where?* (Autumn 1963) to Pitman, the inventor of the most successful system of shorthand, who only a few years after the penny post had been introduced began to teach shorthand by postcard.
108. The WEA, *Viewing and Learning* (1964), *loc. cit.*, described Wilson's 'University of the Air' as 'a bold and imaginative idea'.
109. *The Times*, 10 September 1963. According to Brian MacArthur, later editor of *The Times Higher Education Supplement*, founded in 1970, Wilson deliberately included a reference to a University of the Air in his speech because he knew that if he concentrated mainly on Scottish affairs his speech would not be reported outside Scotland.
110. Its Report was to be called *The Years of Crisis, Labour's Policy for Higher Education*.
111. Wilson set up a parallel committee on further education and polytechnics. He also wrote a foreword to the Taylor Report, 'a plan for action'. 'A policy for higher education can be pious, platitudinous – and worthless – or vigorous, stimulating and clearly argued. This report is clearly of the latter type' (*ibid.*, p. 5). The Report included a section called 'the right to higher education'.
112. See Briggs, *op. cit.*, p. 491. There were strong differences of opinion within the Working Party, reflecting differences in the approach to the subject of different government departments, and no agreement was reached before the final meeting of the Working Party on 9 September 1964.
113. See Briggs, *op. cit.*, p. 486.

114. Speech at the First Congregation of the Open University at the Royal Society, 23 July 1969.
115. H. Wilson, 'Labour and the Scientific Revolution'.
116. Industry should be so organised that it would apply 'the results of scientific research more purposively to our national productivity effort'. He did not mention social science research. This section of the speech, with its focus on productivity, would not have been written by Michael.
117. *The Economist*, 14 September 1963. Cf. *The Times Education Supplement*, 13 September 1963, which was hostile, 'Where are we to get the money? Where are we to get the manpower?'
118. H. Wilson, *The Labour Government, 1964–70, A Personal Record* (1971), p. 685.
119. Michael (Supplementary Note of 2 April 1992) records that while he was in the Research Department Wilson asked him to write a speech for him on the University of the Air, which he did. It was never delivered.
120. See below, p. 266.
121. CAB 128/39, 1 February 1965. It was agreed at this meeting that there would be no SISTERS (specialised high-power institutions for scientific and technological education) but that priority in educational expansion should be given to Colleges of Education. On the aircraft front a decision on the controversial TSR-2 'should be deferred for a limited period'.
122. *The National Extension College, A Catalyst for Educational Change*, p. 3.
123. *Ibid.*, p. 2.
124. *Ibid.*, p. 3.
125. In 1967 Alan Charnley became the College's second Director of Education.
126. For his views, see his article in N. Paine (ed.), *Open Learning in Transition* (1988).
127. A Pre-School Playgroup Association was formed. It was not found possible to use a course that had been introduced in New Zealand.
128. The tutors for the business mathematics course were Gordon Pask and Brian Lewis of Systems Research Ltd. The course on electronic engineering was to be provided by Capitol Radio Engineering Inc. of Washington D. C. Criticisms of existing mathematics courses were listed in *Which?* (October 1963).
129. In September 1964 a residential school on economics was held at Leeds University (*Where?*, No.18 (Autumn 1964), 'Progress Report on the National Extension College').
130. Michael was assisted in dealing with teaching machines by Dr. Austwick of the Teaching Machine Research Unit at Sheffield University.
131. The bus was first used to teach French to Cambridgeshire's pioneering County Colleges. In September 1964 it moved into West Suffolk. Language courses were devised from material invented and tested at Harvard University by Professor I. A. Richards.
132. This hope was not realised. Nor did such a bus figure in Michael's later African activities, which did not touch the Francophone areas.
133. *Where?*, No. 18 (Autumn 1964).
134. See above, p. 15 and below, p. 312.
135. Rediffusion brochure, *Towards 2000* (1965). A book on the series was written by Bryan Magee.

136. Quoted in *The National Extension College, A Catalyst for Educational Change*, p. 32.
137. Undated note by Griffiths, 'Origins of he OU'. The Consumers' Association post went to Peter Goldman.
138. J. Jenkins and H. Perraton, *The Invisible College* (1980), p. 2.
139. *Ibid*. See also K. Harry (ed.), *Higher Education through Open and Distance Learning* (1999).
140. Wells had been one of its part-time tutors, so, for a time, had I. Wells was reputed to have written *The Time Machine* there.
141. Shortly after the transfer, the lease of the building fell in and was compulsorily purchased by Cambridge City Council (which gave generous compensation). Sadly (not least for the Victorian Society), it was razed to the ground so that a new multi-storey car park could be provided. The College moved to 'a shed and pre-fab' in Shaftesbury Road which was leased from the Cambridge University Press and after that (briefly) to an early Georgian mansion, Fitzwilliam House, which it shared with ACE. It subsequently moved to Brooklands Avenue. (*The National Extension College: A Catalyst for Change*, p. 6.).
142. Quoted in *ibid*., p. 8.
143. Cmnd. 2922 (1966), *A University of the Air*.
144. Toomey, *loc. cit.*, discusses the failure of ministers to find funds for ambitious versions of the possible university before Jennie Lee took over and scrapped less ambitious schemes like an experimental service produced by the BBC which Greene hoped would lead up to a College of the Air. The Department of Education and Science and the Treasury were at loggerheads with each other, and Crosland wrote to Lord Normanbrook, Chairman of the BBC and a previous Head of the Civil Service (23 March 1965) regretting that the scheme had not been acceptable to the Government.
145. See P. Hollins, *Jennie Lee, A Life* (1997), esp. Ch. 11, 'The Open University'.
146. I was Chairman of the sub-committee on the curriculum, which recommended a credit system and gateway courses. Michael had realised how important a credit system was. See 'Towards an Open University' in *Where?* (Summer 1964), p. 27.
147. The phrase was used in the letters she sent inviting people to join the Advisory Committee. She wrote to Michael (16 June 1965) describing it as 'hell's own job trying to keep the Committee from becoming too large'.
148. There is an important Cabinet paper, 'The Open University', by Sir Burke (Later Lord) Trend, the Head of the Civil Service (MISC 124/66/1), 19 October 1966 summing up the position to that date. It reported that the Secretary of State for Education and Science had favoured the new title which Trend considered might be thought 'more accurate, though less emotive'. 'I understand,' he went on, 'that the National Extension College have already adopted this title for themselves, and there may be some risk of confusion.'
149. Cmnd 3169 (1966) *Broadcasting*. For the complicated political background to the White Paper, see Briggs, *op. cit.*, pp. 517–18.
150. See below, p. 223.

151. Letter of June 1965, quoted in typescript by Young (n.d.) 'The Open University: MY's Contribution'.
152. For a brief account of the mainstream, see Perry, *op. cit.*, and A. Briggs, 'The Role of the Open University', the first Ritchie Calder Memorial Lecture, November 1985, reprinted in *Media in Education and Development*, March 1986.
153. Quoted in Jackson and Young, *Story of the National Extension College*.
154. *Ibid.*
155. On 27 January 1969 Boyle, then Opposition spokesman on education, more friendly to the Open University than many of his colleagues, stated in a Conservative Central Office Press Release that 'the Opposition cannot hold out any prospect at this time that funds of the order of an annual rate of £3.7 million [as mentioned in the Report of the Planning Committee] can be counted on for the future'.
156. See Perry, *op. cit.*
157. For 'flexi-learning' and 'flexi-study', see R. Freeman in Paine (ed.), *op. cit.*, pp. 37–8.
158. 'The Open University: MY's Contribution', where he contrasted the ideas which were 'in accord' with his as the Open University took shape and those of its ideas of which he disapproved.
159. M. Young, 'The Prospects for Open Learning', 13 April 1994. 'As long as morale remains high, the OU will be set fair to continue its progress.' He added that its staff would have to avoid 'self congratulation' and 'smug over-assurance'. 'Nothing fails like success if it makes anyone think that any right formula has been, or ever will be found for open learning.' 'The danger could be especially great if the OU thinks of itself as being part of the mainstream instead of being a different and essentially innovatory body.' By then the Open University was part of the mainstream in that it was financed not directly but out of the higher education budget allotted to the Department of Education and administered by the Universities Funding Council, the successor to the University and Polytechnics Grants Committee.
160. See below, Chapter 9.
161. Their critique, was expressed forcefully in letters to *The Times*, a newspaper which was hostile to the idea of the Open University.
162. Briggs, *The Birth of Broadcasting*.
163. *Report of an Inspection of the National Extension College carried out between February and December 1969*. See also B. Jackson, *National Extension College, 1967: Four Years Work and the Future* (1967).
164. *Hansard*, House of Commons, 2 April 1965. This debate was initiated by Richard Buchanan, MP for Glasgow, Springburn, and during the course of it another Glasgow MP said that this was fitting since Wilson had made his first speech on the subject there. Two Conservative MPs who were deeply involved in broadcasting and communications, Geoffrey (later Sir Geoffrey) Johnson Smith and Christopher (later Sir Christopher) Chataway, claimed that the idea of the Open University was 'inflated' and that the very concept of it did not convey 'anything very realistic or practical'.
165. Burke Trend's paper (see above, note 148; Cabinet Papers, MISC 124 66/1) refers to 'the elimination of requirements for peak hour viewing' agreed to

in talks between Goodman and Greene which substantially saved costs. Spare hours on BBC-2 would be used. Trend added helpfully for the benefit of the Broadcasting Committee, 'since so much importance was earlier attached to the requirement for peak-hour viewing, the Committee may wish to consider how far the absence of such viewing time would handicap the prospects of the University'. The new proposals also envisaged the use of some 60 local radio stations, not yet in existence.
166. M. Young, 'Origins of the Open University: Supplementary Note', 2 April 1992.
167. *Ibid.*
168. Other possible modes of cooperation were ruled out in a letter from D. V. Stafford, Secretary of the Open University Planning Committee, to Jackson, 16 May 1968.
169. NEC, Note for the Trustees, 26 September 1968.
170. *Where?*, (January 1971), pp. 5–7.
171. Cmnd. 2154 (1963), *Higher Education*.
172. See R. Layard *et al.*, *The Impact of Robbins* (1969).
173. J. Carswell, *Government and the Universities in Britain* (1989), p. 52. The phrase recalls passages in *The Rise of the Meritocracy*.
174. At the time Michael drew attention to this paragraph, which may have been inserted only after his intervention, in an article in *NS*, 28 November 1965, 'Robbins and Equality', in which he suggested that the effects on equality of the Report were inconclusive.

7 Necessary Research

1. See above, Chapter 3.
2. *The Social Sciences*, RD118, June 1948. The National Institute of Economic and Social Research, founded in 1938, while favouring coordination did not wish to have a new official body created, and the Council on the Future of Scientific Policy founded in 1945, had ruled that he social sciences were outside its field of action (CAB 132/51). It was assisted after 1947 by an Advisory Council, but this too (after discussion) did not change the position.
3. 'Scientific Policy Committee, The Social Sciences', RD172, October 1948 (revised).
4. *Hansard*, House of Lords, 26 November 1959.
5. RD172 had urged that if a Council were to be set up 'it would not be justifiable to include amongst its members an overwhelming proportion of senior economists'. All social sciences had to be represented since they had much to offer. It was 'true that the social sciences are relatively to the natural sciences rather immature, but this is a case not for refusing them support, but for giving them the maximum possible support. No infant thrives unless it is well nourished.'
6. *The Future of Socialism* (1956), p. 235. One of them read, 'An aristocracy of talent is an obvious improvement on a hereditary aristocracy, since no one is in fact denied an equal chance. Yet I do not believe, as a personal value judgement, that it can be described as a just society.' The chapter in which this appeared was called 'Is Equal Opportunity Enough?'.

7. This was the last of a series of five articles, where Crosland also referred to Lord James, to Vaizey and to Raymond Williams. His third article dealt with economic growth.
8. *The Conservative Enemy* (1962), p. 80.
9. *Encounter*, July 1961, pp. 56–7.
10. Quoted in Kogan, *op. cit.*, p. 177.
11. *Times Educational Supplement*, 1 March 1965. Crosland had used the adjective 'radical' instead of 'proper' in an otherwise identical sentence in *Encounter*, July 1961.
12. S. Crosland, *Tony Crosland* (1982), p. 142.
13. Stewart left the Department of Education and Science and took over the Foreign Secretaryship after Patrick Gordon Walker, Wilson's nominee, had failed to win a seat at the general election or at the next by-election. Gordon Walker was to succeed Crosland in 1968. See below, p. 247.
14. Cabinet Papers, Public Schools, Memorandum by the Secretary of State for Education and Science, C(65)88, 30 June 1965.
15. *The Times*, 3 June 1965.
16. Cabinet Papers, C(65)155, Nov. 1965, which sets out terms of reference in an Annex.
17. Two of Donnison's book were *Housing Policy since the War* (1960) and *The Politics of Poverty* (1982).
18. See above, p. 152.
19. See above, p. 189.
20. NLSC Interview, 12 May 1990.
21. Those reports had been in the list of references in *Innovation and Research* American books were prominent, among them J. S. Bruner (who was later to move to an Oxford Chair), *The Process of Education* (1961); the Fund for the Advancement of Education, *Decade of Experiment* (1960); J. W. Getzels and P. W. Jackson, *Creativity and Intelligence* (1962); and M. B. Miles (ed.), *Innovation in Education* (1964).
22. M. Young, *Innovation and Research in Education* (1965), p. vi.
23. *Ibid.*, p. vii.
24. Home Universities Conference, 'The Universities and the Future Pattern of Higher Education', 9–10 December 1966.
25. H. G. Wells, *The World of William Clissold* (1933).
26. The pressure was sustained, but so was the resistance. When on 4 April 1961 the Labour MP Austen Albu introduced a debate on the subject in the House of Commons, which won support on both sides of the House, the support was not echoed in Whitehall.
27. See above, pp. 175–6.
28. Welcoming Hailsham's appointment, the Labour peer Lord Taylor, who was to play an important role in the formulation of Labour Party policy on higher education (see above, p. 203), pressed for the creation of a Social Science Research Council (and other new agencies) in a wide-ranging speech in the House of Lords, 9 December 1959. See also an article by Taylor in *The New Scientist*, 11 February 1960.
29. See C. Wilson, *Unilever, 1945–1965, Challenge and Response in the Post-War Industrial* Revolution (1968), Ch. 4. By 1965 Unilever had no fewer than eleven major research establishments throughout the world (*ibid.*, p. 65). For the approach to Unilever strategy in the Third World, see M. Zinkin,

three of whose chapters in his *Development for Free Asia* (1956) were called 'Change and the Contented', 'The Crisis of Development' and 'Innovation and the Responsibility of Business'. In the fourth part of his book, called 'Social', there were chapters on 'education', 'cooperation and credit', 'community projects', 'equality' and 'the economic consequences of equality'.
30. In its quinquennial report for the years 1951–7 (paras. 88–93) the UGC drew attention to the increasing importance of the social sciences.
31. See A. Briggs, *The Story of the Leverhulme Trust* (1991).
32. See above, p. 209.
33. D. N. Chester, 'Nuffield College' in *Geoffrey Heyworth, a Memoir* (1984). See above, p. 146.
34. See above, p. 83 and Cmnd. 2660, Department of Education and Science, *Report of the Committee on Social Studies* (1965).
35. The Treasury did not succeed in securing a Treasury member of the Committee, which it had tried to turn into a condition of belatedly supporting the idea.
36. See above, p. 65.
37. There was no enthusiasm for the Council among civil servants involved in school education, but those involved with the responsibilities for science were better informed, as was Sir Maurice Dean who had responsibilities for the universities. In the backstairs civil service politics a key role was played by Sir Frank Turnbull, who after acting as Secretary of the Office of the Minister for Science, a new post, from 1959 to 1964, became Deputy Under-Secretary of State in the Department of Education and Science in 1964. Differences in civil service attitudes towards the idea of the new Council had to be resolved by a mediator, Sir Harry Campion, Director of the Central Statistical Office before the Heyworth Committee was appointed.
38. In 1963 Cherns had produced a paper on 'Organised Social Science Research in Britain' in *Social Sciences Information* (1963).
39. Cmnd. 6868 (1946), *Report of the Committee on the Provision for Social and Economic Research*. The Clapham Committee added that any new funds should be provided not through a new body but through the University Grants Committee.
40. *Second Report*, Cmd. 8091 (1950).
41. One Department which was not enthusiastic about the idea of a Council was that of Housing and Local Government. Later, it was to press for an Urban Planning Research Institute.
42. See above, Chapter 4, note 46.
43. There was one paragraph (159) on the demand for a Research Council for Planning or Built-Environment Studies, but the Committee concluded, as Michael was to do, that 'a further Council would exacerbate the problems of communication'.
44. J. Gould (ed.), *Penguin Guide to the Social Sciences 1965* (1965), pp. 12–13. A chapter by R. Fox, with a promising title 'Prolegomene to the Study of British Kinship', made no reference to Michael or to specific studies on kinship and community. There was also an essay by Daniel Bell, 'Twelve Modes of Prediction'.
45. See above, pp. 41–2.
46. *Proposal to Establish an Educational Research Council*.

47. Young, *op. cit.*, pp. 123–5.
48. The record of governmental provision for the social sciences had been well surveyed, *Planning*, Nos. 321 (1950) and 323 (1951). They noted that although 'almost all the subjects on which PEP has worked in the past have been matters which do not impinge directly on PEP as an institution', this issue did. 'Policy decisions, whether by Government or by the charitable foundations, might affect its own future.'
49. Young, *op. cit.*, pp. 117ff.
50. For a brief history, see *The National Institute of Economic and Social Research, Jubilee Year, 1938–1988*, and K. Jones, *Sixty Years of Economic Research* (1998). Among the books it sponsored was J. C. R. Dow, *The Management of the British Economy, 1945–60* (1964). Dow, seconded from the Treasury, formulated a scheme to produce regular forecasts for the British economy. The first issue of the Institute's generally welcomed *Economic Review* appeared in 1959. It was followed by a significant expansion of research.
51. The DSIR was about to be transformed into a Science Research Council following a recommendation by Sir Burke (later Lord) Trend, Secretary to the Cabinet, in an independent report on *Science in Civil Life*. In its *Report for 1948–9* (Cmnd. 8045 (1950)) it had noted that 'there are many subjects bordering on the scientific sphere, including questions of quality control, consumer need research, cooking systems and standardisation, which an industry might ask its Research Association to undertake.'
52. SSRC Archives, *Note of an Informal Meeting, 11 November 1965*.
53. *Ibid.*
54. Draft Note by Michael 'SSRC, the First Years' (undated).
55. Albu had been Works Manager, Aladdin Industries, Greenford, from 1930 to 1946.
56. Sloman, *op. cit.*, p. 32: 'Our second school is that of Social Studies [note his choice of word] ... Social studies are at last gaining recognition in this country. We need more research in every aspect of modern societies, whether it is education, old age, or economic growth.'
57. In a contribution to a volume edited by W. R. Niblett, *The Expanding University* (1962), James stated cautiously that 'there seems no real reason why the link between teachers' colleges and universities should not become closer, and why more students at them should not receive some degree from their associated universities'.
58. *The Future of Socialism*, pp. 268–71, where he challenged James's demand for education for leadership – 'high intelligence, an intensive academic education, integrity, courage, judgement, stability, tact and perseverance' (with as a footnote) 'the qualities, evidently, of a successful headmaster'.
59. Like Michael, he was to join the Social Democratic Party.
60. See above, p. 186. The Council, which ran into criticism from the right and inside the Department of Education, was dissolved in 1982. It had welcomed the Plowden Report) which it called 'a quarry from which information of great value and importance will be drawn for years to come' (FEAC 12/67).
61. SSRC Archives, *Report of the Meeting of 21 January 1966*.
62. SSCR, 'The First Years'.

63. *Fourth Report from the Estimates Committee (Sub-Committee on Economic Affairs), Session 1966–7, Government Statistical Services*, HC246, December 1966. The work of this Committee was noted favourably in the *Report of the SSRC, 1 April 1966 to 31 March 1967*, p. 5. In 1966 a new Council for Scientific Policy took the place of the old Advisory Council, in the words of Sir Patrick (later Lord) Blackett, 'the main decision body for matters scientific'.
64. None the less, there was no shortage of rhetoric. See, for example, the address at the end of the decade by Sir John Taylor, President of a newly founded Research and Development Society, to the Royal Society of Arts in 1970 (*Journal* (1971), pp. 15–27). It was called 'New Horizons in Research and Development' and began with the complacent assertion that 'we are at the beginning of changes as important as those instituted in the Classical era of Greece, or the New Learning of the Elizabethan period … There is a growing belief that people matter more than things.'
65. Social Research Council, *Annual Report, April 1966–March 1967*.
66. 'SSRC – the First Years'.
67. *Ibid.*
68. See above, p. 226.
69. As recently as 1962 Himsworth, unlike Murray, had opposed the setting up of an SSRC suggesting that the country should wait for ten years.
70. NLSC Interview, 12 May 1990.
71. This is the phrase used at the beginning of the first published Report, March 1967, covering the first full financial year of operations.
72. SSCR, 'The First Years'.
73. See Mitchell's account in 'A Triptych of Organisations' in *Young at Eighty*, pp. 9–15. Mitchell noted tensions in the SSRC and the presence in it of people who were 'suspicious of a polymath, whose intellect ranged so widely over disciplines in which he had no formal training'.
74. He had to stop some of the members of the Council from demanding extra funds that he knew would not be forthcoming.
75. *Report of the Social Science Research Council, April 1968–March 1969* (1969), p. 11.
76. *Ibid.*
77. See above, p. 133.
78. None the less, in making the promise Crosland added that any financial support for them would require his 'specific approval'.
79. In 1967 the Conservative government had produced two plans for 'Development and Growth', including the so-called Hailsham Plan for the North East. When Wilson created a Department of Economic Affairs in 1965 Ten Regional Planning Councils were created. (See G. E. Cherry, *The Evolution of British Town Planning* (1974) and T. M. Couling and G. C. Steeley, *Sub-regional Planning Studies: an Evaluation* (1975).)
80. Hall had been an Assistant Lecturer (and later Lecturer) at Birkbeck College from 1957 to 1966 when he became Reader in Geography with reference to Regional Planning at LSE. In 1968 he became Professor of Geography at Reading University, a post which he held until 1989. In 1964 he edited *Labour's New Frontiers* and he was the main author of *Europe 2000*, an action plan of the European Cultural Foundation. He was to be Chairman of the Tawney Society from 1983 to 1985.

382 *Notes*

81. *Social Science Research Newsletter*, November 1968, p. 12.
82. Tom Burns became Professor of Sociology at Edinburgh in 1965. He was later to carry out fascinating sociological studies of the BBC.
83. In 1967 Pahl put together a group of academic specialists and policy-making planners interested in the outer edges of London's expansion. It included Emrys Jones. *The Symmetrical Family* was to cover the 4,000 square miles of the larger Metropolitan Region.
84. The article was written by David Allen, secretary of the Conference, who was a member of the staff of the SSRC.
85. Arrangements were made for an American team of three participants in the symposium to return to the United States via Paris where they could meet their French counterparts who had also prepared a report on social indicators.
86. See J. Clyde Mitchell, *Social Networks in Urban Situations* (1969).
87. See above, pp. 85–6.
88. Colin (later Sir Colin) Buchanan, Urban Planning Adviser to the Ministry of Transport from 1961 to 1963 was Professor of Transport at Imperial College from 1963 to 1972. See his *Mixed Blessing, The Motor in Britain* (1958) and *Traffic in Towns* (Ministry of Transport Report, 1963). Michael approached the subject completely differently. See, for example, Young and Willmott, 'How Urgent are London's Motorways?' in *NS*, 10 December 1970.
89. Hague used them in the course of sharp questioning on the Council's allocation of funds to transport research by members of the Transport Sub-Committee of the Select Committee of the House of Lords on Science and Technology in 1986 (*Minutes*, 4 November). When he stated that 'research was still going on as though it was still in the 1960s', 'a golden age when things were developing in phase', he did not do justice to what had been said or written then.
90. Shonfield was particularly interested in French planning experience, which he discussed at length in his important book *Modern Capitalism* (1965).
91. 'The Pragmatic Illusion: the British Formula for Muffling Public Purpose'. After Britain entered the European Community in 1971, Shonfield was to describe it as a 'journey to an unknown destination'.
92. A series of booklets was published after a decision had been deliberately taken that they should be published and not kept confidential. They covered subjects like political science and economic history.
93. *Report of the SSRC, April 1968–March 1969*, p. 16.
94. Its Director, A. H. Chilver, was Professor of Civil and Municipal Engineering at University College. The Centre, which had ten Governors, was funded also by the Ford Foundation. It began work in April 1967. Associated with it was a London University Research Unit for Planning Research. Its Chairman, appointed by the Minister of Housing and Local Government, was Lord Llewellyn Davies, architect and Labour peer. Titmuss was a member. So, too, was the great benefactor, Max (later Lord) Rayne.
95. It reported in May 1967 after it had commissioned a report from P. J. Sadler, Director of Research at Ashridge Management College, on recent and current research. It had also held two seminars. The topic was of major long-term importance.

96. 'Research in Relation to Automation and Technological Change', March 1967.
97. SSCR, 'The First Years', p. 5.
98. There was a UGC Assessor on the full Council and an SSRC Assessor on the UGC.
99. Letter from Laslett to Michael, 30 January 1967.
100. *SSRC Newsletter*, February 1978, p. 19.
101. The words 'positive discrimination' were used in quotes too (para. 174(I)). Boyle welcomed the idea and the words (*Hansard*, House of Lords, 6 March 1967).
102. *Innovation and Research in Education*, p. 121. He got the reference from S. Wiseman, *Education and Environment* (1964). A lecturer at York University, Wiseman also wrote *Examinations and English Education* (1961).
103. See A. H. Halsey (ed.), *Educational Priority, EPA Problems and Policies*, Vol. I, Report of a research project sponsored by the Department of Education and Science and the Social Science Research Council (1978). A valuable MA thesis of the University of Leeds, 'The Origins of the EPA at Denaby: The Anatomy of a Decision' (1975) by D. H. Dodds goes into detail on the basis of careful research, including interviews. Those interviewed included Halsey, Clegg and Boyle.
104. Michael had already thought of following up Plowden with the help of the ACE, but negotiations broke down (letter from Michael to Halsey, 20 October 1970). For the SSRC idea, see also Michael to Crosland, 30 August 1967.
105. *Report of the SSRC, April 1968–March 1969*, p. 14, p. 16.
106. Letter to Crosland, 30 August 1967.
107. Letter from Patrick Gordon Walker to Michael, 1 October 1967. In further dealings with the DES on the EPAs Michael's contact was with Ralph Toomey, then an Assistant Secretary in its Planning branch. For Toomey, see above, p. 366.
108. CP 17/68. The Educational Research Board of the Council set up a small committee to consider it which included Sir Lionel Russell, Chief Education Officer for Birmingham from 1946 to 1968. Once again there were convergences as there was in the case of Toomey's involvement. Russell had served as a member of the University Grants Committee from 1954 to 1963, when it was evolving its plans for expansion, and between 1968 and 1973 he chaired an enquiry into Adult Education in England and Wales.
109. Halsey, *Educational Priority* Vol. I (1978), p. 91.
110. See above, p. 223.
111. He referred to a Conference held in January 1902 at the Royal Institution on 'The Discovery of the Future'. Jouvenal called Wells 'an author whom I often read, known and loved since my youth'.
112. Daniel Bell, who edited *Social Scientist as Innovator*, was deeply involved in futures research. See his 'The Year 2000 – the Trajectory of an Idea' in *Daedalus* (December 1967). See also his stimulating article 'A Report on England: The Future that Never Was', in *Public Interest* (Spring 1978).
113. See M. Young (ed.), *Forecasting and the Social Sciences*. The other essayists included de Jouvenel, Abrams, whom Michael had invited to become a full member of the Committee, Foster, Hall and Tony Lynes, Secretary of the

Child Poverty Action Group. In 1974 Michael co-authored an article with Lynes, 'The Unacquisitive Society' in the *Observer*, 17 March.
114. There is an account of the symposium in the *SSRC Newsletter*, February 1968.
115. A questionnaire was sent to the social science departments in all universities to find out the size of their postgraduate schools and their expectations of appropriately qualified candidates for awards in 1966/7.
116. SSCR, 'The First Years'.
117. In 1967 the Ecole Practique asked for nominations for a British scholar to work there for a period of not less than three months and not more than a year, and, after advertisement, Peter Laslett was nominated by the Council as Visiting Professor. He spent three months in Paris in 1968 working on family reconstitution. For the work of the Cambridge Group for the History of Population and Social Structure, which Laslett initiated and headed, which involves family studies, and which was given Council support, see E. A. Wrigley and R. S. Schofield, 'A Social Survey of the Past' in *The SSRC Newsletter*, February 1968, pp. 16, 18.
118. SSRC, 'The First Years'. See also an article by Michael written just after the Kent Conference, 'Postgraduate Awards' in *NS*, 24 July 1966. One section was called 'The Puzzle'.
119. The first item in the first Newsletter was 'Postgraduate Awards 1967' (*SSRC Newsletter*, November 1967).
120. SSCR, 'The First Years'.
121. *Report of the SSRC, April 1968–March 1969*, p. 12. In 1969 a six-month contract was awarded to the Social Research Unit at Sussex University, under the direction of Dr. P. J. M. McEwan, to examine and analyse the relevant data.
122. For the SSRC's reasons for accepting the responsibility, mainly that research and training belonged essentially together, see *ibid.*, p. 30.
123. *SSCR Newsletter*, November 1968.
124. Cmnd. 3623 (1978), Cmnd. 3703 (1968) and Cmnd. 3638 (1968).
125. *SSRC Newsletter*, February 1968.

8 A World Agenda

1. In 1952 he wrote to the Elmhirsts (letter of 7 November) describing the Republican victory as 'very much worse than the Tory victory here'. In October 1944 he had written in a letter to Leonard in India, opened by the censor, that 'the greatest aim of all must be to maintain the United Nations unity, but at the same time I would like to lose the "emphasis on the Nations"'.
2. *The Chipped White Cups of Dover* (1960), p. 3.
3. For British social history seen within this framework, see A. Briggs, *A Social History of England* (1999 edn.), pp. 337–9.
4. The examples were deliberately chosen by Michael. In fact, the new University of Sussex, which had not yet taken in its first students – they arrived in 1961 – was to be the first university to create a School of African and Asian Studies alongside a School of European Studies. Lord James had not yet taken over York.

5. The reference to Roosevelt is interesting. See above, pp. 11, 37. John Kennedy, who became President of the United States in 1961, introduced his own scheme for overseas service, the Peace Corps. Britain's Voluntary Service Overseas (VSO) was launched in 1958. See *VSO Annual Review 1982–3*, 'VSO, 25 Years of Volunteering'.
6. An Institute of Development Studies, government-backed, was set up in Sussex in 1965, following a recommendation by Sir Andrew (later Lord) Cohen.
7. See above, p. 206.
8. PEP, *Planning*, 25 April 1963. It added later that 'attempting to preserve a fictitious British status as an independent Great Power' was 'an exercise in anachronism which is best left to General de Gaulle'.
9. 'Hunger: Seven Years of Self-Denial' in the *Observer*, 24 March 1963. The British United Nations Association had just advertised a covenant scheme to which the name SUN (Support the United Nations Campaign) was attached. The failure of the campaign was attributed to its organisation. (See W. Tucker and S. Chisholm in *Young at Eighty*, p. 71.)
10. Michael won a bet with Brian Jackson that 'Heath would beat Wilson'.
11. Letter to Kate Gavron, 17 November 1998.
12. An early draft of the study began generally: 'This is about the changing relationship between white skins and those with brown and black, and the cultures which go with the colours.' *Family and Race* was a very different kind of title from *Kinship and Community*. In itself it registered change.
13. See below, note 29.
14. G. K. Chesterton, 'On Certain Modern Writers and the Institution of the Family' in W. Sheed (ed.), *Essays and Poems* (Penguin edn.), pp. 168–9. Chesterton was focusing on the family and the small community, one of Michael's continuous preoccupations.
15. Letter to Postgate, 16 December 1970. He was using the word 'universe' literally and metaphorically.
16. He had been urged to write on these lines by D. W. B. Baron, then Executive Director of the National Extension College. (Letter to Michael of 10 December 1970.) It would be a 'good idea', Baron stated, 'to increase the BBC publicity for the courses which indeed they are doing and also putting articles in the *Radio Times* on the 9th January'. Enrolments since the beginning of September had been well below half of the previous year's.
17. See J. Tunstall (ed.), *The Open University Opens* (1974). It is interesting to compare what is said in it about students, some of whom provided their own autobiographies, with what was said by National Extension College students in *The National Extension College, A Catalyst for Educational Change*. There were links. One 'older student', 'a sprightly octogenarian', remarked that he was fortunate to have taken the 'Gateway' course of the NEC: 'I cannot praise it too highly as a preparatory measure'. Cf. Jenkins and Perraton, *The Invisible College, NEC*, Ch. 4 'The Students'.
18. The story has not been fully told, but see R. Mason, *Globalising Education: Trends and Applications* (1998); R. I. Roman (with L. Armstrong), *Review of*

World Bank Operations in Non-formal Education and Training (1987); UNESCO, World Education Report (1988); Commission of the European Community, Memorandum on Distance Learning in the European Community (1991); and OECD, Internationalisation of Higher Education (1996).
19. S. K. Bailey (ed.), *Higher Education in the World Community* (1977). See also my essay in it: 'The Role of the International Intellectual Community'.
20. This was the sub-title of Tony Dodds's chapter in *Young at Eighty*. Its main title was 'A Vision of Development'.
21. For Dodds's Tanzanian experience, see his 'Adult Education and Radio Study Groups' in the *Journal of Kicukoni College* (1969).
22. Letter to Elmhirst, 1 January 1971.
23. In 1968 inter-university cooperation in communications technology in Britain was felt 'to rest firstly with the universities themselves'. *University Intercommunications*, first published in 1966, was the medium. For later developments see the Report published by NEC in 1969, 'Linking universities by technology'.
24. An Advisory Group was set up which included Dr. Leslie Farrer-Brown of the Nuffield Foundation, who had invested Foundation resources in the Caribbean area, and Dr. James Maraj, a Trinidadian, who was then Director of the Education Division of the Commonwealth Secretariat. In 1989 he was to become first President of the newly established Commonwealth of Learning. Other members of the Group were Laslett, Jackson, John Scupham, and Professor George Wedell, Professor of Adult Education at Manchester University – and a future senior Brussels civil servant in the European Commission.
25. In a letter to Michael, 29 June 1970, Jackson referred to Mauritius as one possible place to start.
26. Letter to Brian MacArthur, 11 December 1970.
27. Letter to Anthony Greenwood, 21 December 1970.
28. S. Manjulika and V. V. Reddy, *Distance Education in India: a Model for Developing Countries* (1996). Indira Gandhi was a close friend of Jennie Lee, and, despite her fall from power, the national Indian Open University, was to be named after her in 1989. In Pakistan, where Bhutto launched a People's Open University in 1974 – the name had echoes of his 'People's Party' – there were other echoes when the new University was renamed Allam Iqbal after Pakistan's national poet. R. Reddy, Vice Chancellor of India's first open university, Andhra Pradesh and later of IGNOU, gave advice to Pakistan. He was later to be a Vice-President of the Commonwealth of Learning, Perraton served as secretary to the Commonwealth Committee which I chaired and which produced the report on *The Commonwealth of Learning* (1987).
29. Michael even suggested that the Dartington Trustees might visit Mauritius *en bloc*. In December 1970 he sent £100 to Vakjee to pass on to Mrs. Adelette Toolsy at the Training College for the purpose of buying recorders, which she required for children in schools. This, he told Vakjee, was 'one of the most appealing very small pleas' he had heard on the island.
30. Michael also wrote to Vakjee, 3 December 1970, asking what progress had been made on the 'College of the Air project'.
31. Day-to-Day Notes on a Trip by Michael Young, 28 September 1970 onwards.

32. *Ibid.* There was already in existence a UNESCO Swedish-financed correspondence college at Francistown, training uncertificated teachers by a mixture of correspondence, radio and short courses. The students then went on to the Training College. There had also been a Report proposing a University of the Air.
33. The Botswana flag, Michael noted, was black, white and blue, but at Francistown the white was most prominent. On his trip to Botswana Michael reflected on the row in 1950 inside the Labour government over Chief Seretse Khama's marriage to a white woman. Morrison, Michael believed, had come out of the affair badly: he had asked Michael the classic question about how he would feel if his daughter married a black man. Michael did not enjoy a 'black tie ball' on Independence Day during his brief visit. 'Half black, half white', it drew half 'the country's *élite'*.
34. There were known to be 1,500 students in 'continuing schools' run commercially 'with dismally low standards'. There were more 'private students' studying for the UBLS Junior Certificate than there were students in secondary schools.
35. See above, pp. 196–7.
36. There were to be 25 bursaries for full-time students, support for educational magazines to promote 'teenage literacy' and, not least, for course materials books and counselling in connection with educational development.
37. Mauritius College of the Air, *Preliminary Report*, Autumn 1972. 'Failure to get very far on this work would provide warnings against any tendency to be too sanguine about what can be done in the next decade.'
38. Report to IEC on Research Priorities at MCA, Easter 1973.
39. D. Hawkridge, *General Operational Review of Distance Education* (1987).
40. Letter to Keith Hinchcliffe, University of East Anglia, 14 January 1974.
41. See C. Yates and J. Bradley (eds), *Basic Education at a Distance* (2000).
42. Letter to Perraton, 11 April 1973, asking for a copy of Christian Aid's *After School What?*, prepared by the Council of Churches in Kenya, and letter to Edna Healey, 11 April 1973.
43. *Diary*, notes, 1979.
44. Letter to Perraton, Dodds, Janet Jenkins and Philip Baker, 9 August 1977.
45. An Ahmadu Bello University MSc thesis was referred to, Imran Yazidule, *The Study of Radio as a Means of Communicating Agricultural Information to Farms in Northern Nigeria.*
46. 'Some Thoughts on Distance Learning for Adults', discussion paper prepared by (and the names were given in alphabetical order) Baker, Dodds, Jenkins, Perraton and Young.
47. *Distance Teaching in the Third World*, p. 233. Appendix 3, more than 70 pages long, consisted of an annotated directory of distance teaching projects.
48. On the eve of taking up his post at Ahmadu Bello, Michael had written to David Adler, who had become a friend, at the Turret Correspondence College (15 January 1974) saying that he hoped to see him in Johannesburg on 19 March (letter of 4 February 1974) and to visit 'some of the beautiful country not far from the city'. He would be flying from Kano for a meeting with his IEC colleagues in Botswana. They were very uneasy about any South African contacts, but Adler attended a conference at Gaborone in

Botswana at Michael's invitation. There was also a representative of the Namibian Council of Churches.
49. T. Dodds, 'A Vision of Development' in *Young at Eighty*, pp. 33–4.
50. Letter to Kate Gavron, 17 November 1998.
51. 'Interim Report from IEC, Potential for Distance Learning in South Africa', n.d.
52. *Ibid.*
53. The *Guardian*, 15 March 1995.
54. N. Mandela, *Long Walk to Freedom* (1994).
55. Quoted by Dodds in a letter to Michael from the University of Namibia, n.d. (1998).

9 Mutual Aid

1. 'The Challenge to Educational Incrementalism'.
2. See G. D. H. Cole, *A Century of Co-operation* (1944), a book part of which was written at Dartington, and S. Pollard and J. Salt, *Robert Owen, Prophet of the Poor: Essays in Honour of the Two-Hundredth Anniversary of His Birth* (1971). For the international setting see also H. M. Kallen, *The Decline and Rise of the Consumer, A Philosophy of Consumer Cooperation* (1936).
3. Interview with Peter Hennessy for the Channel 4 programme *What Has Become of Us?*. See CR (1995).
4. *The Chipped White Cups of Dover* (1960), p. 112. For the international emphasis in the pamphlet, see above, pp. 259, 262.
5. A footnote in the pamphlet referred to the non-implementation of the Hodgson Committee's *Report on Weights and Measures Legislation* (Cmnd. 8219, 1951).
6. Note of 22 September 1964. For Williams, see above p. 266.
7. See above, pp. 92–3.
8. 'Why Where?' In *Where*, No. 1. See also N. Sargent, 'Consumer Power as a Pillar of Democracy' in *Young at Eighty*, p. 194.
9. Consumer Association, *Annual Reports*, March 1960, March 1965.
10. *Observer*, 17 March 1974.
11. For the significance of the replacement of Lynes by Field, see R. Lowe, 'The Rediscovery of Poverty in the 1960s' in *Contemporary Record* (1995).
12. See the article by Michael and Lucy Syson, 'Women – the New Poor' in *The Observer*, 17 January 1974, and Young, J. Munstermann and K. Schacht, 'Poverty in a West German Town' in *NS*, 6 March 1975.
13. Child Poverty Action Group, *Poverty* (1974); *Better Pensions* (Cmnd. 5713, 1974); *Equality for Women* (Cmnd. 5724, 1974).
14. See below, Afterword.
15. Mitchell had left the Consumers' Association in 1965 to join the National Economic Development Council, which Wilson delegated to George (later Lord George) Brown. He stayed in the SSRC until 1974. See J. Mitchell, 'Management and the Consumer Movement', *Journal of General Management* (1976).
16. See above, p. 38.
17. *Hansard*, House of Lords, 5 April 1978. Burton was drawing attention to the Government's response to a report of the National Economic Development

Organisation in 1976 on nationalised industries and a National Consumer Council report on the same subject.
18. *Ibid.*, 14 May 1982.
19. *Ibid.*, ?1 May 1985.
20. J. Rennie and M. Young, 'Major Influences on University of the Third Age Development' in E. Midwinter (ed.), *Mutual Aid Universities* (1984), p. 102.
21. See R. W. Evans, one of Michael's Trustees, 'Our Little Systems' in *Young at Eighty*, p. 113.
22. 'Cooperative Independent Commission – Revisited' a collection of views in the Society for Cooperative Studies (December 1983).
23. M. Young and M. Rigge, 'A Manifesto for Coops' in *NS*, 26 April 1979.
24. For the role of *New Society* at this time see its tenth anniversary special issue (5 October 1972) which included articles by Shirley Williams and Keith Joseph on 'The Next Ten Years'. Williams, who described poverty as not only an economic state, but 'multiple deprivation', defended the idea of educational priority areas, and claimed that it was essential to combine 'financial support for families' and 'centrally financed programmes to improve and enrich deprived communities'.
25. *Manchester Guardian*, 1973.
26. *NS*, 10 December 1970. The first stretch of the M1 had been opened in 1959. Within the next ten years 600 miles were built.
27. See above, p. 3.
28. There is a mass of writing on voluntary action, some of it going back before Beveridge. (See W. Beveridge, *Voluntary Action* (1948) and Lady Morris, President of the National Federation of Community Organisations, *Voluntary Organisations and Social Progress* (1955).) Some of the later writing emanated from PEP and, after its merger in 1977 with CSSP, its successor PSI. Compare R. Clarke and R. Davies, 'A Chance to Share: Voluntary Services in Society' (PEP Broadsheet, 1975), and A. Richardson and M. Goodman, 'Self-Help and Social Care: Mutual Organisations in Practice (PSI, 1983). Deakin's *Voluntary Sector Commission Report* (1996) was supported, like many other pieces of action-oriented research, by the Joseph Rowntree Foundation. See also P. Willmott, *Community Initiatives, Patterns and Prospects* (PSI, 1989).
29. M. Young and M. Rigge, *Mutual Aid in a Selfish Society* (n.d.), p. 7. It was part of the thesis of the pamphlet that 'with the rise in the standards of life ... fraternity has become rarer' (*ibid.*, p. 6).
30. See above, p. 289.
31. M. Young, H. Young, E. Shuttleworth and W. Tucker, *Report from Hackney* (1981); 'Hackney Survey, a Support for Alternatives' *Where?* (1979). The Hackney Survey was carried out by the ICS and had concerned itself both with facts and attitudes.
32. *NS*, 18 January 1981.
33. *NS*, 17 November 1977.
34. Michael to Williams, 7 December 1980; Williams to Michael, 6 January 1981.
35. Michael hoped, however, that he might still remain a member of the Fabian Society.
36. Letter from Donnison to Michael, 11 May 1981, letter from Michael to Donnison, 20 May 1981; *Fabian News*, April 1981, Chairman's Message. The

Chairman of the Society then was David Lipsey (see above, p. 235) and Brian Abel Smith, a past Treasurer, resumed the post which he had held before.
37. *The Chipped White Cups of Steel*, July 1987, p. 2.
38. Letter to Williams, 6 May 1981.
39. 'An Anniversary Message to the SDP from the Gang of Four'.
40. The other committees with their chairmen included Economic Policy (Jenkins), Industrial Strategy (Bill Rodgers), Decentralisation of Government (David Marquand), Industrial Democracy (Michael Shanks) and the Third World and Development. There were also local policy groups, 'tailoring their programmes to the needs of their own localities'.
41. Letter from Charles Hill to Michael, 12 June 1981.
42. Letter from Wayland Young to Williams (copy sent to Michael), 15 April 1981.
43. He wrote to Maureen Philbine in the Party Office on 1 May 1981 asking for 20 copies.
44. *Young at Eighty*, p. 99.
45. See above, p. 287.
46. Tawney Society, Draft (n.d.), 'Tawney Society Research'. Under this heading four categories were mentioned – 'contracting out of local authority services'; 'trade unions and local authorities'; 'geographical equity'; and 'consumer protection'.
47. The Preface was dated September 1982: the pamphlet bore no other date.
48. Letters to Meade, 20 October, 11 November 1981.
49. *The Middle of the Night*, p. 28.
50. See D. Watt, 'Redefining British Socialism: Labour Needs to Listen to the Voices of the Real World' in *The Listener*, 1 March 1984. He was writing in the centenary year of the Fabian Society. In a BBC broadcast on the centenary he had introduced the voices of Tony Benn, Bernard Crick, Martin Jacques, Neil Kinnock, Len Murray and from outside the Labour Party, Shirley Williams.
51. Letter to Roberts, 8 July 1983.
52. 'Major influences on U3A development' in Midwinter, *op. cit.*, pp. 101–4.
53. See above, pp. 258ff.
54. *Samizdat*, No. 1, 1988.
55. Midwinter, *op. cit.*, p. 17. In this interesting volume Michael (p. 102) praised Midwinter for leading the way in promoting bulk-buy groups as a modern form of consumer cooperation in action.
56. See M. Philibert, 'Contemplating the Development of Universities of the Third Age' in *ibid.*, p. 52. Laslett also visited Denmark, Norway, Sweden and West Germany.
57. He gave a broadcast on Radio 4's *You and Yours* programme on 21 July 1981.
58. It was printed in *NS*, 13 March 1980. Among the demands were a fair share of the educational budget for the elderly.
59. See also C. Handy, 'The Future of Work' (1982). As Warden of St. George's House at Windsor, Handy was responsible for planning and organising studies of the future of work in modern society. He also broadcast on the same theme. He is the author *inter alia* of *Understanding Organisations* (1976). *Gods of Management* (1978, revised edn. 1991) and *The Empty*

Raincoat (1994). He also wrote *Understanding Schools as Organisations* (1986) and *Understanding Voluntary Organisations* (1988).
60. The early story is summarised in A. Cloet, *University of the Third Age, A Rank Fellowship Report on Development 1990–92* (1993), pp. 19–23.
61. See F. Watson, 'The Third Age Project in Devon' in Midwinter, *op. cit.*, p. 81.
62. Pressing the European idea involved the organisation of courses to transfer craft skills from one country to another, for example, bookbinding, from England to Portugal, and tile making from Portugal to England. The memorandum also mentioned peripatetic painting tutors for the housebound. Anglo-Caribbean music was one possible international subject.
63. Gabriel Productions, Interview with Jane Gabriel, 22 March 1994.
64. Letter to Ian Tregarthen Jenkin, 7 August 1986.
65. Freeman was succeeded at the NEC by Ros Morpeth, who had 'risen through the ranks' of the NEC, having joined the College as its Courses Editor in 1977. For the history of the NEC after the formation of he Open College see *The National Extension College, A Catalyst for Educational Change*.
66. Quoted in D. Davies, 'Bringing Out the Artist in Everyone' in *Young at Eighty*, p. 49.
67. There were already links between Devonshire and Yorkshire. When Royston Lambert was Headmaster of Dartington School, an educational link had been made with a large comprehensive school at Coningsbrough. The Yorkshire Elmhirsts were familiar with the story of this. They also knew and admired Clegg.
68. In 1992/3 a two-year grant was made by the Clore Trust to create a course in opera in conjunction with Covent Garden.
69. Some of the questions were discussed systematically as early as 1983 in a PSI publication by A. Richardson and M. Goodman, *Self-Help and Social Care, Mutual Aid Organisation in Practice*.

10 Unfinished Business

1. The Stamp Memorial Lecture, 6 November 1984. Rayner, called into public administration from business, described previous Stamp Lectures as marking 'stages along the slow and winding road to the present'.
2. J. Cunningham, *The Guardian*, 23 December 1995.
3. *London Review of Books*, 25 October 1990.
4. *New Society*, 21 June 1985, 'An Invisible Wind', a review of C. Rawlence (ed.), *About Time*.
5. Schuller had previously worked with OECD in Paris and at the University of Glasgow. After 1985 he moved into academic life, becoming a Senior Lecturer in Continuing Education at the University of Warwick.
6. *New Statesman and Society*, 12 July 1991.
7. GP Interviews, Interview with Jane Gabriel, 22 March 1994.
8. Letter of 14 February 1997.
9. Note by Perraton on the history of the International Research Foundation for Open Learning.

10. *Hansard*, House of Lords, 30 June 1999. The question leading to the discussion was asked by Lord Bridges.
11. ESRC Lecture, *A Haven in a Heartless World* (1990), p. 1.
12. *Daily Telegraph*, 12 October 2000.
13. *A Good Death*, p. 204, p. xvi. None the less, the book is heavily footnoted, the first footnote being a reference to *Social Trends*. Chapter 1 begins: 'The greatest triumph of the century is to have added twenty-five years to the average expectation of life or, to put it another way, subtracted twenty-five years from the expectation of death.' 'The number of people in the United Kingdom at 80 and over nearly trebled between 1951 and 1958 and even centenarians have multiplied.'
14. GP Interviews, Interview with Jane Gabriel, 22 March 1994.
15. *NS*, 8 August 1968.
16. For the 'Chelsea Declaration' see *The Rise of the Meritocracy* (1994 edn.), pp. 158–9.
17. See above, Foreword.
18. M. Young and G. Lemos, 'Mutualism in the Undercliffe Declaration' (1997). Michael and Lemos also co-authored *The Communities We Have Lost and Can Regain* (1997). Lemos had spent his entire career working in and with voluntary organisations, particularly housing associations.
19. GP Interviews, Interview with Geoff Dench, 22 March 1994.
20. Brochure, 'OCA Celebrates 10th Anniversary'. The brochure was printed in Barnsley, and the House of Lords celebration took place on 29 September 1998.
21. Open University Jubilee Lecture (1994).
22. See W. W. Walsh, 'Autobiographical Literature and the Study of Education: Inaugural Lecture as Professor of Education in Leeds University' (1972[?]).
23. Speech to Sociology Section, British Association for the Advance of Science, 11 September 2000. Michael changed his mind about the title of this speech which he now called 'Equality and Public Service'.
24. *The Times*, 11 January 2001. Again there were political cross-currents. For Matthew D'Ancona in the *Sunday Telegraph* (14 January 2001) Brown was 'raiding the Tory Charity Box'.
25. See a paper prepared for the Oxford Conference by R. Veerhoven, Eramus University, Rotterdam.
26. Speech at Aylesbury Estate, Southwark, 2 June 1997.
27. unLTD, 'The Foundation for Social Entrepreneurs Investing in Individuals, Changing Communities'.
28. 'Note for Applicants', School for Social Entrepreneurs, p. 10.

Main Writings of Michael Young

(A selective list in chronological order: * denotes typescript only)

1938 *Manpower Policy*, PEP Broadsheet no. 133.
1940 *Paying for the War*, PEP Broadsheet no. 160.
1941 *London under Bombing*, PEP Broadsheet no. 169.
1942 *Part-time Employment*, PEP Broadsheet no. 185.
1943 *Financial Mysticism*, PEP Broadsheet no. 188.
Will the War Make Us Poorer? (with Henry N. Bunbury) (Oxford Pamphlets on Home Affairs, no. H5).
Employment for All, PEP Broadsheet no. 206.
International Air Transport, PEP Broadsheet no. 208.
1944 *Civil Aviation*, Pilot Press.
Demobilisation and Employment, PEP Broadsheet no. 217.
Reconstruction Plans, PEP Broadsheet no. 227.
1945 *Education in the Services*, PEP Broadsheet no. 234.
Let Us Face the Future, Labour Party Election Manifesto (part-author).
1947 *Watling Revisited*, PEP Broadsheet no. 270.
Labour's Plan for Plenty, Gollancz: Left Book Club.
1948 *What is a Socialised Industry?* Fabian Society.
The Social Sciences, LPRD document 118.*
Scientific Policy Committee: The Social Sciences: Proposal for the Establishment of a Social Science Research Council, LPRD, document 172.*
'Industrial Democracy', *Towards Tomorrow* no. 1, Labour Party discussion pamphlet.
'Public Ownership, the Next Step', *Towards Tomorrow*, no. 2.
'Small Man, Big World: A discussion of socialist democracy', *Towards Tomorrow*, no. 4.
1950 *The Future of Industrial Assurance: Labour's Proposals for Mutual Ownership by the Policyholders*, Labour Party Discussion Pamphlet.
1951 *For Richer For Poorer*, Report to LPRD.*
1952 *Fifty Million Unemployed*, Labour Party Discussion Pamphlet.
'Distribution of Income within the Family', *BJS*, vol. III, no. 4.
'The Meaning of the Coronation', with Edward Shils, *SR*, vol. 1, no. 2 (new series).
Draft Proposal for the Establishment of a London Institute of Community Studies.
1954 'Kinship and Family in East London', *Man*, vol. LIV, no. 5.
'The Role of the Extended Family in a Disaster', *Human Relations*, vol. VI, no. 3.
'The Labour Party and the Middle-class Mind', Fabian Society Address.*
'The Planners and the Planned: the Family', *Journal of Town Planning Institute*, vol. XL, no. 6.

1955 *Seven Million Bathrooms*, Interim Report to Labour Party National Executive Council*
Challenge to Labour.*
Family and Kinship, Address to Family Welfare Association.*
1956 'Social Grading by Manual Workers', with Peter Willmott, *BJS*, vol. VII, no. 4.
1957 *Family and Kinship in East London*, with Peter Willmott, Routledge & Kegan Paul. Penguin paperback edn., 1961. Revised Routledge edn., 1986.
1958 *The Rise of the Meritocracy*, Thames & Hudson. Random House, New York, 1959. Penguin paperback edn., 1961. Transaction Publishers, New Brunswick, New Jersey, 1994 (with new introduction). Also translated into French, German, Italian, Dutch, Danish, Norwegian, Swedish, Finnish, Japanese and Spanish.
1960 *The Chipped White Cups of Dover: a Discussion of the Possibility of a New Progressive Party*, Unit 2.
Family and Class in a London Suburb, with Peter Willmott, Routledge & Kegan Paul. Nel Mentor paperback, 1967.
1961 'Old Age in London and San Francisco', with Hildred Gertz, *BJS*, vol. XII, no. 3.
'The Institute of Community Studies, Bethnal Green', with Peter Willmott, *SR*, vol. X, no. 2.
1962 'Is Your Child in the Unlucky Generation?', *Where?* no. 10.
'Education, Regression and Mobility', with Chris Wallis, *Paper to 5th World Congress of Sociology*, Washington DC.*
1963 *Note on a Possible Reform League*, with Edward Shils, Peter Willmott, Peter Marris, sent to Anthony Crosland.*
'Hunger: Seven Years of Self-Denial', *The Observer*, 24 March.
'In Search of an Explanation of Social Mobility', with John Gibson, *The British Journal of Statistical Psychology*, vol. XVI.
'Announcing the National Extension College', *Where?*, no. 14.
'Who Uses Correspondence Colleges?', with Christine Farrell, *Where?*, no. 14.
'The Mortality of Widowers', with Bernard Benjamin and Chris Wallis, *The Lancet*, 31 August.
1964 *The Future of Independent Schools*, for the Fabian Society.
New Look at Comprehensive Schools, with Michael Armstrong, Fabian Society Research Series no. 237.
'The Greatest Task for Education in the Next Century', *Socialist Commentary*, 1 July.
1965 *Innovation and Research in Education*, with McGeeney, Routledge & Kegan Paul.
'The Flexible School: the Next Step for Comprehensives', with Michael Armstrong, *Where?*, Supplement 5.
1967 'Give Us Back the Thames' and 'The Next 17,000 Tides', both with Peter Willmott, *Observer*, 16 July.
'Educational Priority Areas and Family Allowances', press release, London University Institute of Education, 21 January.
1968 *The Story of the National Extension College*, with Brian Jackson, sent to

Open University Planning Committee.*
'Parent Power, Ideas for England', with Patrick McGeeney, NS, 4 July.
'A Visit to an Elementary School in Kenya', NS, 20 July.
Learning Begins at Home: a Study of a Junior School and its Parents, with Patrick McGeeney, Routledge & Kegan Paul.
'The Liberal Approach: Its Weaknesses and its Strengths', *Daedalus*, vol. 97, no. 4.
Forecasting and the Social Sciences (ed.), Heinemann.

1969 'Social Reform in the Centrifugal Society', Michael was a member of 'The Open Group', NS Pamphlet.
'A New Radicalism', The Open Group.*
'Social Mobility and Genetical Variation', with J. Gibson, Draft Paper for British Association, 10 September.*
Why Our Susan? Comprehensive Schools: the Case for Parental Choice, Harringay Parents Group (distributed by ACE).

1970 'Parish Councils for Cities', NS, 29 January.
'Up Schools', NS, 2 April.
'The Future of Consumer Affluence', Address to 6th International Conference of Consumer Associations, July.*
'How Urgent are London's Motorways?', with Peter Willmott, NS, 10 December.

1971 'Cycles in Social Behaviour', with John Ziman, *Nature*, vol. 229.
'The Increasing Obsolescence of Childhood Education', *The Times Saturday Review*, 9 January.
'On the Air: the End of a Phase', with Brian Jackson and Peter Laslett, *Where?*, no. 53.
'Social Class and the Peak Load Traffic Problems in London', with Peter Willmott, *British Association Paper*.*
The Hornsey Plan: a Role for Neighbourhood Councils, with John Baker, Association of Neighbourhood Councils.*
Review of J. Platt, 'On the Green', with Peter Willmott, NS.
The Young–Chesworth Report, with Donald Chesworth, *Mauritius College of the Air*.

1972 *One Year's Work*, with Tony Dodds and Hilary Perraton, IEC.
'Historical Changes in Social Cycles', *Journal of Interdisciplinary Cycle Research*, vol. 3, no. 2.
Lifeline Telephone Services for the Elderly, with Peter Gregory, National Innovations Centre.
'Is Equality a Dream?', *First Rita Hinden Memorial Lecture, at Bedford College*, 18 November.
'What Might Have Been?', NS, 2 November.
Sport in the London Region, with Peter Willmott, Report to Sports Council.
'Dilemmas in a New Europe', in *The Future is Tomorrow: 17 Prospective Studies*, European Cultural Foundation, Martinus Nijhoff, The Hague.

1973 *The Symmetrical Family: A Study of Work and Leisure in the London Region*, with Peter Willmott, Routledge & Kegan Paul, Penguin paperback 1975.

Multi-Media Education in Swaziland, IEC.
The International Extension College, 1972–73, with Hilary Perraton and Tony Dodds, IEC.
'A Day in the Kitchen', *NS*, 15 November.

1974 'Women – the New Poor', with Lucy Syson, *Observer*, 17 January.
'The Unacquisitive Society', with Tony Lynes, *Observer*, 17 March.
'The Shortening of Childhood and the Lengthening of Education', Opening Address at Centenary Seminar, Universities in a Rich and Poor World, University of Adelaide.
Poverty Report 1974, (ed., Intro. and chapters), Maurice Temple Smith.
'Your Friendly Ideas Man', *Observer*, 20 March.

1975 *For Richer For Poorer: Some Problems of Low-income Consumers* (ed.), HMSO (National Consumer Council).

1976 'Education on the Defensive', with S. Duncan, in Peter Willmott (ed.) *Poverty Report 1976*, Maurice Temple Smith.

1977 'Towards a New Concordance', *NS*, 17 November.

1979 *Mutual Aid in a Selfish Society*, with Marianne Rigge, Mutual Aid Press.
'A Manifesto for Co-ops: a Return to an Older Definition of Socialism?', with Marianne Rigge, *NS*, 26 April.
'China's Co-op Shops', *NS*, 1 November.
'Hackney Survey: Support for Alternatives', *Where*? July/ August.

1980 *Distance Teaching for the Third World: the Lion and the Clockwork Mouse*, with Hilary Perraton, Tony Dodds and Janet Jenkins, Routledge & Kegan Paul, revised edn., 1991, IEC.

1981 'Never Go out after Dark', *NS*, 15 January.
Prospects for Workers' Co-operatives in Europe, with Marianne Rigge, Commission of European Community.
Report from Hackney, with H. Young, E. Shuttleworth and Wyn Tucker, PSI.
Mutual Aid in a Selfish Society, Mutual Aid Press, paper 2.

1982 *The Elmhirsts of Dartington – the Creation of a Utopian Community*, Routledge and Kegan Paul.
Inflation, Unemployment and the Remobilisation of Society, Tawney Society Pamphlet no. 2.
The Middle of the Night (ed. with Peter Hall), Tawney Society Pamphlet no. 4.
'Social Work Bolognese', *NS*, 19 August.

1983 *Revolution from Within, Co-operatives and Co-operation in British Industry*, with M. Rigge, Weidenfeld and Nicolson.
'The Round of Time: a Sociologist's View', 7th *Barnett Shine Memorial Lecture*, Queen Mary College, May.
'It's Time to Grasp the Unemployment Nettle', *The Guardian*, 7 December.
Social Scientist as Innovator (collected papers) ABT Books, Cambridge, Mass., with an introduction by Damel Bell.

1984 'Progressive Education at Dartington, 1930s–1980s', Eighth Curry Lecture, University of Exeter, 7 June.
'The Mutual Aid/Self-Help Movement' in *Mutual Aid Universities* (ed. E. Midwinter), Croom Helm.

1985 'How to Cultivate Martians on an old Scottish Island', *The Guardian*, 3 August.
Preface to D. Gribble, *Considering Children*, Dorling Kindersley.
1986 'Coping Strategies Used by Nurses on Night Duty', with Jeffrey Adams and Simon Folkard, *Ergonomics* vol. 29, no. 2.
1987 *The Chipped White Cups of Steel*, Unit 2.
1988 'Education for the New Work' in *Open Learning in Transition* (ed. N. Paine), NEC.
The Metronomic Society, Harvard University Press and Thames & Hudson.
The Rhythms of Society (ed. with Tom Schuller), Routledge.
'My Hero: Michael Young on FDR', *The Independent Magazine*, 15 October.
'Choice from Cradle to Grave', *Samizdat*, no. 1.
'Christmas Day Remembrance', *The Independent*, 27 December.
1989 'Social Democratic Party and Co-ops', *Journal of Comparative Studies*, no. 64.
'New Dawns for Old Oxford', *The Weekend Guardian*, 5 August.
'More at Stake than a General Election', *Samizdat*, no. 5.
'Will Keir Hardie get Wet in the Rainforest?', *Samizdat*, no. 7.
1990 *Death and Modern Culture*, Lecture given at the University of California at Santa Barbara, 25 February.
'What Do They Stand for Now?', *The Guardian*, 16 April.
'Planetary Ethics and Planetary Politics', with Geoffrey Thomas, *Samizdat*, no. 10.
'The Future of Education', First Dartington Annual Lecture, 22 June.
'Liberating the Old and the Young; the Case for an Ageless Society', Presidential Address to British Association for Advancement of Science, August 2/3.*
'25 Years of the ESRC', with others, *Social Sciences*, issue 7, HMSO, October.
'Down with Age', *London Review of Books*, 25 October.
'From Nation-state to World Society', in *The Alternative: Politics for a Change* (eds. Ben Pimlott, Anthony Wright and Tony Flower) W. H. Allen.
1991 'A Haven in a Heartless World: the Future of the Family', 1st ESRC Annual Lecture: delivered 6 December 1990, published 1991.
'Slaves of Time', *New Statesman and Society*, 12 July.
'Beyond the Chatter', *The Guardian*, 24 July.
The Development of Adult Basic and Secondary Adult Education in South Africa, with Tony Dodds and Greville Rumble, IEC.
'Battered but Triumphant', Obituary for Joan Young, *The Guardian*, 22 November.
Life After Work: the Arrival of the Ageless Society, with Tom Schuller, HarperCollins.
1992 *Campaign for Children's After-school Clubs: the Case for Action*, with Matthew Owen, ICS.
'Change, British Society and the Family', Lecture given to the National Commission on Education, and published in their *Insights into Education and Training*, Heinemann, 1994.

'Death', contribution to *Encyclopedia of Time*, ed. Sam Macey, Garland Publishing Inc.

1993 *The Relevance of Community*, Address at Funerals Conference at Mansfield College, Oxford, 18 April.

1994 *Your Head in Mine*, with Sasha Moorsom, Carcanet Press.
'The Dead Citizen's Charter', Speech to launch National Funerals College, 11 June.
'The Prospects for Open Learning', Lecture given on the 25th anniversary of the Open University, and published in *Open Learning*, vol. 10, no. 1.

1995 'Obituary: Edward Shils', *The Guardian*, 8 February.
'Robben Island Calling', *The Guardian*, 15 March.
A Good Death, with Lesley Cullen, Routledge.
'For the Sake of the Kids', *The Guardian*, 31 May.
'Playtime for the Young East Enders', *The Guardian*, 5 July (launch of Tower Hamlets Summer University).
'Why Where?', *ACE Summer Bulletin*.
'Threatened Americanisation of Privatised Crematoria?', *The Guardian*, 18 October.
Education and Training. Contribution to the 20th anniversary Annual Report of King Baudouin Foundation, Belgium.

1996 'Obituary: Charles Madge', *The Guardian*, 12 January.
'Obituary: Alfred Elmhirst', *The Guardian*, 15 April.
European Consumers at the Turn of the Century. Speech at seminar in Berlin on Comparative Testing of Services organised by Consumentenbond, Germany, 18 April.
A Good Death: Conversations with East Londoners by Michael Young and Lesley Cullen, Routledge.
Governing London (with Jerry White), ICS.
'Robben Island and Back', *Guardian Education*, 9 July.
'Obituary: Sir Nevill Mott', *The Guardian*, 5 August.
'Love Thy Neighbour', *The Guardian* (re Bradford Mutual Housing scheme), 18 September.
'Pixels at an Exhibition', *The Guardian*, 2 October (discussing OCA virtual art gallery).
Can Lifelong Learning Prevent the Breakdown of Society?, Speech at Bremen University, Conference of Studies in European Adult Education, 3–5 October.

1997 'School for the Thoughtful', *The Guardian*, 12 March (on the School for Social Entrepreneurs).
'Roots of Revival' (with G. Lemos), *The Guardian*, 19 March (on housing policy).
'High Degree of Concern', *The Guardian*, 19 July (introducing new SSE).
Communities We Have Lost and Can Regain (with G. Lemos), Lemos and Crane.
'What Are Friends For?', *The Guardian*, 8 October (on publication of *The Communities We Have Lost and Can Regain*).
Contribution to a volume in memory of Sir Nevill Mott. *Sir Nevill Mott: Reminiscences and Appreciations*, Taylor & Francis.

'The Three Pillars of the New Family', *Philosophical Transactions of the Royal Society*, Series B. Biological Sciences: Ageing: science, medicine and society.

1998 'Should We Legalise Cannabis?': 'Yes' by Michael Young, 'No' by Toby Young, *Sun*, 6 January.
'Family and Kinship Revisited' (with G. Lemos), *Prospect*, February.
'Words of Love', *The Guardian*, 27 May (on Baby-Naming Society).
From Universities to Universalities, Address to the 25th anniversary conference of DEASA (Distance Education Associations of Southern Africa), University of Swaziland. Also published in *Open Praxis*, Journal of International Council for Open and Distance Education, 23 October.
Grandparents – The Backbone of the Welfare State. Address to the Annual General Meeting of the Grandparents' Federation, 2 November.

1999 'Do-gooding Inc', *The Guardian*, 16 June (on the School for Social Entrepreneurs).

2000 'New Age Travails' (with Jean Stogdon), *The Guardian*, 12 January.
'After the Vows' (with Rosie Styles), *The Guardian*, 22 March (on Baby-Naming Society).
'Obituary: Peter Willmott', *The Guardian*, 19 April.
'Why ACE Was Started', Foreword to *ACE Bulletin*, April.
Equality and Public Service. Address as Chairman of Sociology Section, British Association for the Advancement of Science, 11 September.
'Ghosts in a Manifesto', *The Guardian*, 12 September.

The Young Family Tree

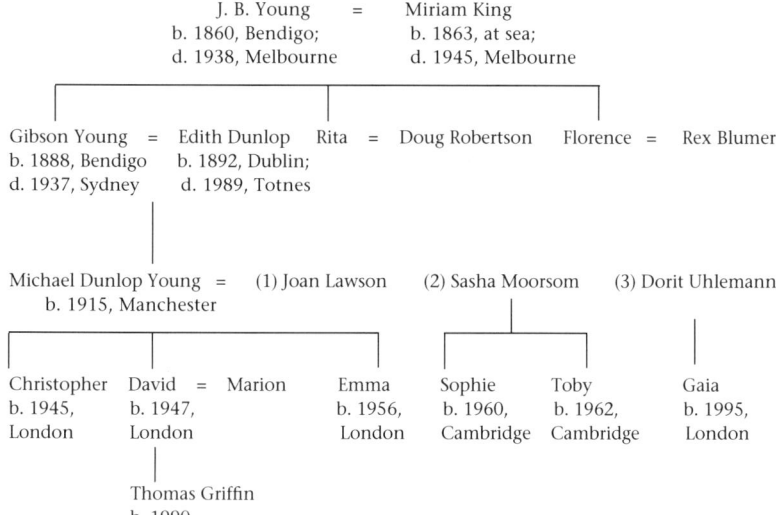

Index

Two place names – and they are far more than this – are left out of this index since they figure so frequently: Bethnal Green and Dartington. So, too, is the name of the subject of the book, Michael Dunlop Young. The names of all other individuals are given in the form that they took when they entered the story. Later changes, including titles, marriages, etc., are not taken account of. The index covers the text of the book only and not the footnotes printed separately.

Abel-Smith, B., 135
Aberdeen, 256
Abrams, M., 284
Achimota, 15, 43
Acland, Sir R., 57, 70, 302
Adamson, W. Campbell, 234, 245
Addison, P., 73
Adelaide, 25
Adler, D., 266
Adrian, Lord, 221
Advisory Centre for Education, 152, 153, 185, 198, 280, 283
Africa, 148, 197, 200, 207, 219, 254, 258, 260, 261, 263, 264, 265, 272, 274, 281, 286, 287, 292
African National Congress, 277
Age, Ageing, 124, 129, 137, 305, 309
'Age Concern', 306
Ahmadu Bello University, 28, 272–3
Ahtik, V., 252
Albu, A., 234
Alexander, Sir W., 214
Allen, D., 41
Allen, Sir R., 240
American Declaration of Independence, 27
Amis, K., 138, 178
Anand, Mulk Raj, 12
Anglia Television, 199, 200
Annan, N., 192, 210, 224, 243
Anthropology, 40, 120, 227, 229
Anthroposophy, 32, 43, 107
Argo Venture, 59
Aristocracy, 157, 170, 172, 178
Army Bureau of Current Affairs, 55
Arnold, M., 179

Aron, R., 7
Arts Council, 78, 306
Ashridge Management College, 256
Asia, 258, 259, 261, 263, 264
Aspirin, 150
Association of Municipal Corporations, 214
Association of Scientific Workers, 183, 220
Association of Teachers in Technical Institutions, 225
Association of University Teachers, 183
Atlantic Charter, 54
Atomic Energy, 169
Attenborough, D., 274
Australia, 9, 11, 25, 27, 30, 31, 44, 99, 100, 112, 157, 261, 272
Aviation, 85, 151
Ayer, A. J., 189, 224

Baden, 285
Bagehot, W., 172, 177
Ball, L.E., 197
Bangladesh, 261, 272, 310
Banks, J.A., 148
Barbour, P., 150
Barker, P., 21, 292
Barlow Committee, 17
Barlow, F., 204
Baron, D., 209
Barry, G., 67
Battersea College of Advanced Technology, 194
Baukema, F., 150
Baumol, W., 252

Baverstock, D., 201
Beaverbrook, Lord, 12, 13, 75
Bell, D., 161
Benney, M., 147
Benton, W., 204
Berlin, Sir I., 250
Bernstein, A., 308
Berrill, Sir K., 195, 310
Bevan, A., 57, 60, 69, 76, 88, 101, 210, 211
Beveridge, W., 45, 46, 51, 58, 59, 67, 69, 218, 234
Bevin, E., 58, 82, 97, 98, 235
Binary Scheme, 223–4
Birkbeck College, 2, 196, 243, 306
Birkett, Sir N., 38
Birmingham, 52, 149, 193, 247, 294
Birnbaum, N., 170
Blackett, Sir P., 250
Blackie, J., 215
Blackstone, T., 181, 188
Blair, T., 288, 303
Bletchley, 9
Blumer, D., 14
Blumer, R.C., 15
Biotechnology, 179
Blunkett, D., 174
Blunt, A., 7
Bondi, H., 209
Booth, C., 20, 115, 136, 143
Boothroyd, B., 311
Botswana, 265, 267
Bowden, V., 199, 209, 215, 250
Bown, L., 272
Boyden, J., 199, 203
Boyle, Sir E., 185, 186, 189, 202
Brady, R.A., 76
Brass Tacks, 293
Bray, Dr. J., 236
Briault, E., 214
Briggs, W., 208
Bristol, 31, 143, 195, 240
Britain Can Make It, 76
British Academy, 232
British Broadcasting Corporation, 19, 35, 132, 198, 199, 201, 202, 215, 236
British Electrical Authority, 81
British Medical Journal, 138

British Overseas Airways, 27
British Society for the Advancement of Science, 221
British Sociological Association, 20
Brixton, 292
Brooke, C., 251
Brunel University, 225
Buddhism, Buddhists, 17, 115, 117
'Bulge', 186, 204
Bullock, A., 209, 234
Bulmer, M., 2, 23
Bunbury, Sir H., 21
Burgess, T., 153, 300, 302
Burns, T., 241
Burton, Lady, 290
Butler, R.A., 79, 102, 151, 175, 176, 184, 225, 299
Butterworth, D., 239

Cairncross, Sir A., 20, 246
California, 286, 287
Callaghan, J., 8, 288, 289, 301
Cambridge, 8, 9, 19, 46, 131, 135, 146, 153, 191, 192, 193, 194, 202, 207, 209, 213, 230, 260, 262, 294, 305
Campaign for Nuclear Disarmament, 74, 169
Campbell, J., 216
Canada, 275
Cardiff, 300
Carnegie Trust, 308
Carron, Sir W., 245
Carr-Saunders, A., 46, 134
Cars, 2, 91, 127–8, 150, 151, 250, 286, 292, 304
Carstairs, M., 134
Carswell, J., 217
Carter, C., 226
Cartwright, A., 22, 137, 152
Carus-Wilson, E.M., 240
Castle, Lady, 287
Catlin, Sir G., 195
Centre for Advanced Study, 8, 192
Centre for Environmental Studies, 245
Chadwick, E., 299
Chamberlain, N., 48
Champernowne, D., 46, 114

Channel 4, 21
Chatto and Windus, 166
Chekhov, M., 215
'Chelsea Manifesto', 179
Cherns, A.B., 227
Chester, D.N., 243
Chesterson, G.K., 261
Chesworth, D., 266, 268
Chicago Television College, 200
Chiffley, B., 99
Child Poverty Action Group, 21, 287, 288
Children, Childhood, 25, 27–8, 137, 140, 141, 178, 185
China, 198, 273, 274
Chipped White Cups of Dover, 259, 262, 282, 298
Chipped White Cups of Steel, 297, 298, 303
Chisholm, S., 21, 22, 134, 240
Chorley, R., 39
Christian Aid, 219
Churchill, W.S., 51, 54, 66, 79, 81, 97, 99, 184
Churchill College, 22, 146, 193, 195, 207, 213
Cinemas, 141
Cirencester, 13
Citrine, Sir W., 81
Civil Servants, Civil Service, 77, 150, 228, 233, 241, 249, 254
Clapham Committee, 227, 230
Clare Foundation, 308
Clark, K., 51
Class, 54, 71, 98, 118, 129, 148, 156, 159, 162, 166, 171, 179, 181, 187, 302
Clay, H., 238
Clegg, A., 190, 247, 257
Clegg, H., 104
Coal, 80, 81
Cockcroft, Sir J., 250
Cole, G.D.H., 20, 39, 58, 64, 82, 104, 294, 304
Cole, M., 58, 104, 261
Colombia, 275
College of Health, 152
Colleges of Advanced Technology, 194,

'Comet', 101, 121, 206
Commonwealth, 259, 262
Communists, Communist Party, 7, 20, 39, 40, 41, 42, 49, 81, 88
'Community', 6, 8, 118, 139, 147
Commuter clubs, 6
Computers, 169, 174, 206, 207, 249
Conservatives, Conservative Party, 40, 73, 97, 130, 161, 175, 179, 181, 186, 218
Consumers Association, 3, 38, 74, 96–7, 103, 142, 148, 206, 239, 281, 283, 284, 288
Cooperatives, Cooperative Movement, 19, 142, 282, 284, 290, 294
Coronation, 5, 84, 119, 170
Correspondence colleges, 203, 262, 272
County Councils Association, 214
Crick, B., 304
Cripps, Sir S., 38, 39, 57, 58, 60, 70, 72, 89, 98, 221
Crosland, A., 21, 98–9, 104, 120, 164, 165, 175, 176, 189, 190, 203, 205, 221–2, 223, 224, 227, 236, 247, 248, 249, 290, 296
Cross, N., 249
Crossman, R.H.S., 50, 98, 101
Crowther, G., 187
Croydon, 300
Curran, C., 201
Curry W.B., 28, 35, 36, 37, 51, 64

D Day, 76
Dalton, H., 68, 72, 80
Dartington Hall Trust, 215
Dartmouth, 32
Data Bank, 256
David Cohen Family Charitable Trust, 308
Davies, D., 308
Davies, E., 29
'Dawn University', 199, 200, 216, 217
Deakin, A., 82, 100
Deakin, N., 256, 294
Dean, M., 293, 302
Debden, 122, 123, 126, 127, 128
Deedes, W.F., 226

Delano, W.A., 35
Dench, G., 21, 270–1
Dent, H.C., 184
Derby, 45
Deng Ziau Ping, 274
Department of Education and Science, 186, 190, 232, 247, 254, 289
Department of Scientific and Industrial Research, 227, 233, 245
Design Council, 34
Detergents, 286
'Development Decade', 260
Dickens, C., 111, 137
Dickinson, H., 207
Dicks, H., 84
Dictionary of Modern Thought, 2
Disasters, 277
Ditchley, 198, 199, 214, 217
Dodds, T., 21, 263, 269, 273, 276, 277, 280
Donnison, D., 223, 248, 297
Donovan, Lord, 243, 254
Dore, R., 301
Drake, M., 216
Drever, J., 235
Drucker, P, 4, 5
Duke, P., 132
Dundee, 247
Dunlop, A., 13
Dunlop, D., 13, 19, 32
Dunne, M., 284
Durkheim, E., 20

East Anglia, University of, 199
Economic and Social Research Council, 9,
Economics, 7, 9, 91, 125, 130, 194, 228, 235, 236, 237, 245, 285, 309
Education, 8, 54, 85, 152, 155, 159ff, 175, 176, 178, 183ff, 224, 230, 235, 246, 270
Educational Priority Areas, 30, 253, 282–3
El Alamein, 76
Elections, 63, 67ff, 87, 88, 94–5, 96, 97, 99, 126, 211, 213, 260, 281, 300, 301, 302, 303
Electric kettles, 150

Eliot, G., 249
Eliot, T.S., 250
Elizabeth II, 5
Ellis, H., 20
Elmgrant Trust, 111, 305, 308
Elmhirst, A. and G., 308
Elmhirst, D., 8, 12, 16, 17, 28, 36, 44, 47, 52, 54, 65, 110, 114, 115, 116, 117, 121, 253
Elmhirst, L., 8, 11, 16, 28, 44, 47, 51, 54, 60, 61, 89, 110, 113, 114, 116, 117, 132, 264
Elmhirst Trust, 206, 308
Elvin, Sir L., 189
Encounter, 164, 221
Engels, F., 88, 89, 93
'Enterprise', 48, 300
'Equality', 157, 158, 173, 174, 178
Essex University, 23, 191, 235, 256, 287
Eugenics, 180
Europe, 306
European Community, 282, 289, 301, 302

Fabians, Fabian Society, 58, 93, 104, 105, 115
'Fair Shares', 81
Falkland Islands, 302
Family, 10, 15, 85, 93, 94, 101, 123, 125, 129, 140, 141, 170, 171, 178, 296
Faringdon, Lord, 120
Farlie, D.J.G., 256
Federal Union, 25, 58
Festival of Britain, 98
Field, F., 148, 287
Fienburg, W, 106, 151, 180
Findlater, R., 160
Firth, R.W., 229, 234, 253
Flanders, A., 104, 245
Fletcher, P., 149
Fleming Report, 176
Florey, Lord, 250
Floud, J., 41, 243
Flower, T., 21, 292, 298, 299, 304, 307
Foot, M., 76, 302
For Richer For Poorer, 83, 87, 89, 101, 115, 155, 290

Ford, B., 167, 180
Ford, H., 11
Ford Foundation, 262, 265
Fordham, P., 149
Forrester, T., 301
Foster, C., 242
Foundation for Sport and the Arts, 308
France, 305
Francis-Williams, Lord, 150
Frankel, M., 122
Frankfurt Institute Statistical Research, 285
'Fraternity', 5
Freedom from Hunger, 260
Freeman, J., 76, 98
Freeman, R., 307
Fremlin, C., 56
Fulton, J., 209, 254, 255
Futures, Futurology, 162, 170, 249

Gabor, D., 249, 250
Gaitskell, D., 152
Gaitskell, H., 71, 81, 97, 98, 101, 104, 204, 282
Galbraith, J.K., 164
Gallup Poll, 22, 96
Galton, F., 180
Gardiner, G., 149
Gavron, K., 22, 260
Gavron, R., 260, 308
Genes, 15, 19, 179
Geography, 127, 229, 240
George V, 45
Germany, 285, 288,
'Gerontocracy', 274
Ginsberg, M., 39
Gittings, A., 310
Glasgow, 203, 204, 210, 227, 297
Glass, D., 122, 165, 250
Glass, R., 122
Glennester, H., 203
'Globalisation', 303
Gluckman, H.M., 243
Goldman, P., 151, 284
Goldthorpe, J.H., 243
Gollancz, V., 76
Good Food Guide, 151
Goodman, Lord, 211, 215, 244

Gorbachev, M., 304
Gorer, G., 134
Grandparents, 125
Grattan, D., 201
Grays Inn, 38, 65
Grebenik, E., 255
Greene, G., 308
Greene, Sir H., 201
Greenwich, 97, 293
Greenwood, A., 59, 265
Griffiths, J., 76, 208
Grimethorp, 81, 85
Grimond, J., 292
Groombridge, B., 284
Gropius, W., 35
Guardian, 293
Gulbenkian Foundation, 206, 308
Gundry, E., 149
Guthrie, D., 284
Guyana, University of, 264

Habakkuk, H.J., 240
Hackney, 287, 292, 293, 295, 298, 300
Hadow Report, 188
Hague, D., 242
Hailsham, Lord, 226
Hale, 11, 14, 30
Halifax, Lord, 50
Hall, P., 21, 108, 240, 241, 292, 301, 302
Halsey, A.H., 21, 25, 247, 248
Hamilton, Major-General, 194, 195
Harrisson, T., 51
Hart, D., 37
Hart, T., 226
Hart, Sir W., 235
Harvard, 195
Harvey, A., 134
Hastings, P., 38
Havering, 300
Healey, D., 8, 78, 83, 288
Healey, E., 273
Health, 6, 9, 22, 152, 211, 263, 282–3, 288, 293
Heard, G., 115
Heath, E., 213, 282, 285, 289, 301
Heller, C., 251
Henderson, P., 43
Henriques, F., 256

Heseltine, M., 299
Hester, J., 262
Heyworth Committee, 225, 226, 233, 251, 254
Highway, 183
Hill, A.B., 227
Hill, Dr. C., 97,
Hill, C., 298
Hill, W.F., 224
Himmelweit, H., 244
Himsworth, Sir H., 238
Hirst, P., 304
History, 3, 9, 10, 15, 119, 160, 162, 167, 174, 175, 178, 229
Hitler/Stalin Pact, 7
Hogben, L., 196
Hoggart, R., 138, 163, 166, 180
Holborn, 150, 152, 236
Holst, I., 18
Home, Sir A.D., 217
Horner, A., 81
Horton, L., 74
House of Lords, 22, 177, 240
Housing, Housing estates, 15, 75, 124, 125, 126, 133, 136, 139, 241, 242, 250, 294, 300
Howard, A., 76
Howe, G., 289
Hoyle, F., 199, 216
Hughes, B., 176
Hull, 195, 201, 202
Hume, D., 2
Hunter, G., 79
Hunter, P., 267
Huxley, A., 166, 169, 249
Huxley, J., 50, 74, 196
Hyndley, Lord, 81

Imperial College, 199, 202
Independent Television Authority, 211
India, 57, 60, 61, 99, 264, 265, 277
'Industrial Democracy', 91, 93, 235
Industrial Revolution, 73, 162
Inflation, 285
Institute of Community Studies, 2, 4, 6, 8, 10, 16, 20, 22, 107, 128, 131, 132, 138, 145, 146, 231, 292, 293, 307–8

International Broadcasting Institute, 244
International Extension College, 3, 21, 260, 262, 264, 277, 281, 310
Interviews, Interviewing, 121, 124, 136, 137, 138, 144
International Organisation of Consumer Unions, 285
Israel, 51

Jackson, B., 147, 148, 153, 202, 206, 207, 214, 216, 218, 224
Jahoda, M., 244
James, E., 174, 175, 191, 235, 240, 246, 253
Jarvis, A., 132
Jefferys, M., 137
Jeffrey, R., 307
Jenkin, I.T., 307
Jenkins, Dame J., 151,
Jenkins, J., 276
Jenkins, R., 104, 151, 205, 289, 296
Jennings, R., 29
Jessup, F., 208
Jones, B., 202, 210
Joseph, Sir K., 130
Joseph Rowntree Memorial Trust, 133
Jouvenel, B. de, 85, 86, 249
Joyce, J., 14
Judge, H., 224

Kahn, H., 261
Kahn, R., 194
Keele, 195, 202, 207, 306
Kent, University of, 251
Kenya, 272, 273
Keynes, J.M., 59, 60, 91, 304
King, A., 242
King, J., 13
Kinnock, N., 296, 302, 304
Klugmann, J., 42
Kogan, M., 189
Kolade, C., 276
Kristol, I., 164
Kropotkin, Prince, 19
Kumar, K., 249

Labour and the Scientific Revolution, 206

Labour Believes in Britain, 77, 87
Labour League of Youth, 80
Labour Party, 3, 7, 40, 50, 63, 64, 66ff, 70, 77, 79, 81, 85, 126, 150, 157, 176, 177, 186, 211, 221, 281, 282, 287, 296
Labour Party Research Department, 3, 8, 39, 63, 64, 77, 79, 83, 85, 89, 90, 108, 203, 205
Labour's Plan for Plenty, 85, 87, 155, 175
Lafitte, F., 20, 51, 52, 243
Lagos, 269, 273, 275
Laine, C., 18
Lancaster University, 226
Landell-Mills, P., 26, 27
Language Line, 6, 293
Lansbury, G., 67
Laski, H., 39, 70, 83, 91, 221
Laski, M., 49
Laslett, P., 10, 20, 21, 83, 193, 194, 198, 199, 200, 202, 207, 210, 215, 216, 218, 246, 305, 306
Law, Lawyers, 41–2, 46, 229–30
Lawson, T., 17
Lawther, W., 81
Leach, B., 18
Leach, E., 243
Lee, D., 209
Lee, D.P., 152
Lee, J., 64, 72, 210, 211, 212, 213
Leeds, 9, 267
Leicester, 179
Lerner, A., 39
Leslie, C., 74
Lesotho, University of, 267
Let Us Face the Future, 4, 69, 72–3, 84, 87, 89
Let Us Win Through Together, 87, 96
Leverhulme Trust, 209, 226, 253
Liberal Party, 13, 40, 297–8, 300, 303
Liddell Hart, B., 53, 64
Life After Work, 1
Lightfoot, M.D., 250
Lilienthal, D., 191
Lilliput, 78
Lindsay, K., 47, 50, 156
Lipsey, R.G., 235, 253
Liverpool, 247

Local, Regional Government, 53–4, 83, 92, 121, 184, 240–1, 298, 301
Lockwood, D., 192
London, 3, 38, 39, 40, 42, 53
London School of Economics, 6, 20, 38, 40, 41, 46, 47, 83–4, 144, 191, 238, 243, 244, 248
London Under Bombing, 53
London University External Degrees, 196, 197, 207, 209, 215, 230, 268
Longman, 161, 166
Lotbinière, S.J. de, 45
Lovell, Sir B., 250
Luce, C., 91
Lyles, Lord, 95
Lynes, T., 287

Macarthur, B., 244, 293
McCall, I., 293
MacColl, D., 3, 79
MacDonald, R., 43
MacIntosh, A., 22, 134
McKenna and Company, 38
Mackenzie, N., 210
Mackenzie, W.J.M., 135, 234
Macmillan, H., 101
Madge, C., 20, 51, 134, 236
Maddox, J., 292
Major, J., 19, 181, 303
Malawi, 267
Malinowski, B., 40
Mallon, J., 45, 122
Malmesbury, 56
Manchester, 135, 175, 177, 184, 249, 298, 300
Manchester Guardian, 81
Mandela, N., 277, 278
Mann, M., 243
Manpower Services Commission, 304, 307
Marcuse, H., 285
Marks and Spencer, 151
Marris, P., 20, 135, 144, 148, 224, 292
Marsden, D., 147, 224
Marshall Plan, 103
Marshall, T.H., 104, 243, 283
Martin, C., 64
Marwick, A., 51
Marx, K., 20, 44, 93, 206

Mass Observation, 20, 56
Matthews, R., 253
Maude, A., 79
Mauritius, 264, 265–6, 268, 269ff, 281
May Day, 44
Mayhew, H., 136
Mayo, E., 82
Meade, J., 30, 31, 71, 301
Medawar, Sir P., 250
Media, 1356, 63, 76, 96, 160, 167, 236, 244, 271
Medical Research Council, 233, 238
Melbourne, 13
'Meritocracy', 2, 3, 274
Michael Prophecy, 63
Midas Trust, 308
Middlesborough, 122
Middleton, J., 1
Middleton, M., 78
Midnight Oil, 200
Midwinter, E., 21, 305
Mikardo, I., 69, 96, 104, 255
Miles, Sir A., 250
Miliband, R., 3, 39
Mills, E., 152
Milne, O., 35
Milton Keynes, 216, 292
Minogue, M., 302
Mitchell, J., 151, 239, 289
'Mobocracy', 167
Moffatt, I., 40, 46
Moir, G., 208
Molefke, P., 267
Morley, J., 159
Morris, Sir C., 209
Morrison, H., 42, 43, 56, 63, 64, 67, 68, 70, 71, 72, 75, 77, 80, 81, 82, 83, 89, 173, 193, 194, 195, 221, 234, 297
Moode, A., 79
Moorsom, S., 17, 18, 192, 198, 272, 273
Morphet, T., 277
Morris, C., 209
Morris, W., 43, 89, 91, 93, 104, 120, 157, 167
Moser, C., 235, 242
Motorcycles, 26, 27
Motorways, 242, 292

Mott, Sir N., 210, 216, 219, 264
Mountford, Sir J., 209
Moyes, A., 252
Multiple Sclerosis Society, 294
Mumford, L., 93
Murdoch, I., 274
Murdoch, R., 168
Murray, Sir K., 238
Murray, L., 234
Music, 12, 13, 18
Mutual Aid, 5, 19, 141, 261, 281, 300, 304, 343
Mutual Aid Centre, 6, 261, 290ff, 304
'Mutualisation', 96, 281, 292

Nash, W., 99
National Coal Board, 81, 89
National Consumer Council, 288, 289, 305
National Economic Development Council, 289
National Economic Review, 231
National Education Acts, 85, 159, 175, 176, 183, 218
National Extension College, 3, 8, 154, 195, 198, 203, 206, 207, 208, 210, 212, 214, 215, 260, 261, 262, 264, 268, 280, 305, 307, 310
National Foundation of Educational Research, 189
National Funeral College, 315
National Institute of Adult Education, 214
National Institute of Economic and Social Research, 231
National Union of Teachers, 185
Nationalisation, 69, 71, 81, 89, 96, 108, 281, 295
Neill, A.S., 29 37
Neuberger, J., 302
Neurath, W., 163
New Deal, 91
New Labour, 161, 175, 181
New Left, 105, 199
New Scientist, 160
New Society, 21, 87, 160, 292, 295, 296
New Statesman, 138, 216
New Towns, 216, 229
New Zealand, 99, 157

News Chronicle, 67
Newsom, J., 153, 187, 209, 222
Newsom Report, 187, 188, 201
Next Thirty Years Committee, 244, 250, 254
Nicholson, M., 47, 48, 49, 51, 64, 80, 81, 221
Nigeria, 28, 218, 265, 268, 269, 272, 273, 275, 276, 277
Norton, D., 21, 306
Nottage, R., 245
Nottingham, 196
Notting Hill, 259
Nuffield College, 146, 226
Nuffield College Reconstruction Survey, 58
Nuffield Foundation, 202, 306
Nuttgens, P., 308
Nyerere, J., 262, 275

Observer, 163, 260
Office of Fair Trading, 294
O'Malley, R., 41
Open College, 307
Open College of the Arts, 305, 306ff
Open University, 3, 4, 8, 9, 21, 28, 195, 196, 199, 202, 206, 207, 210ff, 215, 218, 261, 262, 265, 272, 280, 308
Orwell, G., 168
Owen, D. (later Sir Arthur), 56–7
Owen, D., 296, 297, 303
Owen, R., 19, 93, 149
Oxfam, 269
Oxford, 199, 208
Oxford House, 132, 133

Pahl, R., 241
Painting, Paintings, 12, 18, 33–4, 65
Pakistan, 277
Palmer, V., 11
Paul Hamlyn Foundation, 308
Peace Ballot, 44
Perraton, H., 21, 207, 269, 276, 280, 306
Perry, W., 213, 216, 218, 265
Perth, Lord, 49
Peterson, A.D.C., 153, 199, 210
Peterson, J., 133–4

Phillips, M., 63, 64, 77, 80, 98, 99
Piccinelli, 134
Pickles, W., 75
Picture Post, 62, 160
Pilgrim Trust, 57
Pilkington Committee, 166
Pimlott, B., 304
Pimlott, J.A.R., 45
Plan, Planning, 47, 48, 49, 53, 81
Platt, J., 144, 145
Plowden, B., 188, 247
Plowden Report, 188, 189, 247
'Plutocracy', 157
Poetry, 18, 180
Political and Economic Planning, 3, 21, 22, 47, 49, 50, 51, 52, 58, 59, 77, 79, 128, 131, 137, 227, 231, 260
Porter, G., 251
Post Office, 201
Postgate, Raymond, 151, 261
Postgate, Richmond, 261, 265
Postgraduate students, 237, 244, 251ff
Potter, A.M., 256
Poverty, 248, 287
Powell, E., 31, 295
Power, E., 39
Prager, T., 59
Pre-School Play Groups Association, 294
Price, H., 302
Priestley, J.B., 51, 73ff, 78, 97
Proudhon, P.-J., 20
Provence, 18
Prudential Assurance Company, 58
PSI (Political Studies Institute), 227
Psychoanalysis, 15, 92, 106, 118
Psychology, 25, 82, 92, 98–9, 106, 126, 157, 228, 234, 237, 244
Public Schools, Public Schools Commission, 133, 221, 222
Pye Company, 207

Race relations, 256, 257
Rackham, H.C., 238
Rail, Railways, 1, 2, 22, 27, 242, 275
Rainwater, L., 10
Raison, M., 160
Raison, T., 160

410 *Index*

Rationing, 78, 80
Rayne Trust, 309
Reader Harris, D., 153, 209
Rediffusion, 201
Refrigerators, 286
Refugees, 276, 277
Rents, 38, 289
Research, 4, 34, 87, 132, 135, 137, 145, 221, 246, 260, 267, 268, 270, 283
Research Institute for Consumer Affairs, 284
Riesman, D., 147
Riekke, G., 199
Rigge, M., 22, 116, 293, 294, 296
Robb, J.H., 122
Robben Island, 278
Robbins Report, 187, 189, 191, 217, 218, 235
Roberts, E., 149, 150, 151, 302
Robson, G., 300
Rochdale, 19
Rodrigues, 269
Rodgers, B., 296
Roosevelt, F.D., 11, 37
Ross, V., 41, 42
Rotbarth, L., 48
Routh, D., 79
Rowntree, B.S., 20, 115, 136
Royal Marsden Hospital, 19
Royal Society, 221, 250
Royal Society for the Protection of Birds, 47
Rubinstein, M., 150
Rudinger, E., 150
Rugby, 176
Runciman, W.G., 21, 123
Ruskin College, 108, 157, 158, 176
Russell, B., 29
Russell, K., 29
Russia (Soviet Union), 46, 48, 55, 57, 64, 73, 92, 102, 174, 197, 204, 217, 225

St. Bartholomew's Church, 18
St. Bartholomew's Hospital, 19
St. Pancras Labour Party, 42, 66, 69
Samizdat, 69, 304

Samuel, J., 278
Samuel, R., 10, 147
Santiniketan, 114, 264
Sargent, N., 21, 134, 308
Savage, B.L., 201
School for Social Entrepreneurs, 4, 291
Schools Council, 186, 235
Science and Technology Act, 233
Schuller, T., 1
Schumacher, E.E., 89, 91
Schuster, Sir G., 84
Scotland, 177
Scott, A., 18
Scupham, J., 201, 210
Second World War, 175
Seebohm Report, 254
Service, domestic, national, public, voluntary, 5, 131, 172, 259
Seychelles, 272
Shaw, G.B.S., 165, 167
Sheldon, J.H., 122, 134, 138, 141
Sheppard, Rev. D., 44
Sheppard, G.J., 239
Shils, E., 20, 83, 96, 108–9, 131, 132, 135, 170
Shinwell, E., 81
Shonfield, A., 236ff, 243, 253
Shore, P., 180, 205
Shrewsbury, 294
Sieff, I., 51, 63, 151
Skidelsky, R., 304
Small Man: Big World, 88, 89, 92, 95, 99
Smieton, Dame M., 227
Smith, J., 303
Smith, P., 198
Smoking, 65, 227
Social Democratic Party, 7, 23, 241
Social Science and Government Committee, 255
Social Science Research Council, 3, 21, 22, 55, 92–3, 104, 127, 151, 175, 189, 190, 212, 219, 220ff, 228, 236ff, 283
Social Security, 52, 59, 75–6, 81, 112
Socialist League, 39, 57
'Society', 3, 95

Society for Comparative Studies, 291–2
Sociological Review, 145
Sociology, 7, 10, 20, 39, 40, 83, 85, 107, 126, 135, 137, 144, 146, 162, 192, 193, 194, 227–8, 253
South Africa, 266, 268, 277ff
South African Committee of Higher Education (SACHED), 264, 268, 274, 278
Space, 169
Spectator, 167
Spender, S., 164
Sperrey Gyroscope Company, 55
Sport, 171
SSRC Newsletter, 252
Starr, K., 55
'State', 7, 19, 86, 90, 99, 281, 290, 297, 304, 306, 309
Steel, D., 297, 298
Steiner, R., 14, 17, 32, 115, 154
Stewart, M., 206, 223
Stone, R., 194
Strachey, J., 43, 164
Straight, W., 26–7, 29, 46, 115
Stretton, H., 25
Sudan Open Learning Unit, 277
Summerskill, E., 100
Sun, 19
'Sunrise Semester', 200
Supermarkets, 286, 291
Supple, B., 252
Supply of Goods and Services Bill, 290
Sussex University, 9, 144, 146, 147, 189, 191, 234, 244, 256, 259
Sweden, 148, 150, 258, 292, 293
Swindon, 22, 55, 56, 58, 82,

Tagore, R., 115, 264
Tanzania, 263, 264
Tate and Lyle Ltd, 95
Tavistock Institute of Human Relations, 82, 106, 122, 230, 231, 245
Tawney, R.H., 20, 25, 39, 76, 89, 90, 132, 157, 297
Tawney Newsletter, 300

Tawney Society, 23, 39, 90, 297, 298, 299
Taylor, S., 203
Telephones, 127–8, 203
Television, 139, 140, 166, 198, 199, 200, 201, 202, 204, 208, 217
Television and the Child, 244
Temple, W., 89, 114
Tennessee Valley Authority, 74, 91
Thames and Hudson, 163
Thatcher, M., Thatcherism, 3, 130, 181, 186, 213, 243, 288, 296, 301, 302, 303
The Acquisitive Society, 89
The Economist, 168, 185, 193, 205
The Future of Socialism, 221
The Future of Tomorrow, 261
The Times, 150, 223, 236, 264
'The Two Chairmen', 78
Third Age, 305, 306
Third Age Trust, 306
Third World, 21, 259, 262, 276, 280, 305
Thomas, G., 2
Thompson, E., 105
Thompson, M., 267
Till, B., 308
Time and Tide, 161
Titmuss, R., 20, 40, 83, 104, 120, 134, 138, 146, 234, 235
Tizard, J., 253
Toomey, R., 211
Totnes, 12, 119, 306
Towards Two Thousand, 208, 261
Townsend, P., 20, 25, 133, 135, 141, 146, 148
Tower blocks, 15
Tower Hamlets, 6
Toynbee Hall, 45, 47, 65, 122, 132, 266
Trade Unions, Trade Union Congress, 81, 82, 234, 242, 243, 254, 288, 301
Transport, 242
'Trend', 69, 187
Tribune, 76
Trinder, C., 287
Tucker, W., 21, 34, 307

Turner, P., 29
Turret Correspondence College, 266, 278
TV Times, 200
Twentieth Century, 160

Unesco, 50, 275, 281
Unit 2, 282, 298
United Nations Association, 269
United Nations University, 262
United States, 4, 11, 54, 64, 91, 102, 157, 197, 198, 221, 258, 285
Universities, 183, 185, 225, 262, 271
University Correspondence College, 208
University Grants Committee, 183, 191, 195, 202, 229, 232, 233, 238, 245
University of the Third Age, 21, 305
Utopia, Utopians, 114, 115, 117, 119, 157, 163, 165, 169, 215, 284

Vaizey, J., 152, 203, 209, 222, 223
Vakjee, Sir H., 266
Values, 5, 88, 102, 157, 158, 179, 293
Venables, Sir P., 210

Waddilove, L.J., 133, 240, 242
Wade, D.A.W., 199
Walker, P.G., 247
Wall, W.D., 225
Wallace, W., 134
Walters, A.A., 243
War Aims, 50
War on Want, 269
Ward, C., 304
Warner, S., 308
Warren-Evans, R., 21
Weaver, Sir T., 226, 247
Weber, M., 20, 120
Webb, B. and S., 57, 92, 120, 142, 294
Webb, M., 63
Welch, A., 226
Welfare state, 103, 288, 304
Welford, A.T., 245
Wells, H.G., 20, 28, 165, 225, 249
West Indies, 197
Westerstahl, J., 252

Westinghouse, 14, 82
Where?, 152, 153, 154, 184, 196, 199, 203, 206, 216, 265
Which?, 3, 118, 149, 150, 151, 154, 209
White, J., 267
Whitehead, A.N., 276
Whyte, W.H., 164
Wiener, W.H., 261
Wiggins, D., 2
Wilkinson, E., 120, 196
Wilkinson, G., 68, 70, 120, 196
Will the War Make Us Poorer?, 21
Williams, B., 224
Williams, Sir L., 266, 283
Williams, R., 199
Williams, R.C.G., 196
Williams, S., 195, 224, 289, 298, 299
Willmott, P., 1, 2, 3, 10, 15, 20, 107–8, 110, 111, 112, 117, 132, 135, 137, 138, 140, 141, 142, 145, 151, 176, 191, 207, 241, 290, 292
Willmott, Phyllis, 151
Wilson, A.J.M., 245
Wilson, Sir C., 227, 234
Wilson, H., 96, 150, 196, 203, 205, 206, 210, 213, 216, 225, 233, 243, 287
Wilson, M., 184
Wiltshire, H., 196, 202, 210, 217
Windrush, 55, 259
Winnicott, Dr. D.W., 17, 106
Wolfenden, Lord, 238, 251
Women, 167, 168, 171
Woolf, L., 16, 166
Woolwich, 225
Wootton, B. (Lady), 16, 132, 165, 168
Workers Control, 82
Workers Educational Association, 39, 43, 183, 185, 196, 201, 214
World Power (Energy) Conference, 14
Worswick, D., 234

Yeats, W.B., 14
York University, 134, 191
Young, C., 17

Young, David, 17
Young, David (Lord), 19
Young, Edith, 11, 12, 17, 18, 19, 23–4, 30, 43, 44
Young, Emma, 17
Young, Florence, 14–15, 44, 43
Young, George, 13
Young, Gibson, 11, 12, 32, 43
Young, J.B., 14, 26

Young, Miriam, 13, 18
Young, Sophie, 17, 18
Young, Toby, 19
Young, Wayland, 29, 99

Zambia, 267
Zec cartoon, 76
Zuckerman, S., 187, 209